ORACLE®

Oracle Press™

OCA Oracle Database SQL Certified Expert Exam Guide

(Exam 1Z0-047)

OCA Oracle Database
SQL Certified Expert
Exam Guide

(Exam 1Z0-047)

Steve O'Hearn

New York   Chicago   San Francisco   Lisbon   London   Madrid
Mexico City   Milan   New Delhi   San Juan   Seoul   Singapore   Sydney   Toronto

The McGraw·Hill Companies

Library of Congress Cataloging-in-Publication Data

O'Hearn, Steve.
  OCA Oracle database : SQL certified expert exam guide : (exam 1Z0-047) /
Steve O'Hearn.
    p. cm.
  ISBN 978-0-07-161421-4 (alk. paper)
  1. Electronic data processing personnel—Certification. 2. Database
management—Examinations—Study guides. 3. Oracle (Computer file) 4. SQL
(Computer program language) I. Title.
  QA76.3.O395 2009
  005.75'65—dc22

                                                    2009051641

McGraw-Hill books are available at special quantity discounts to use as premiums and sales promotions, or for use in corporate training programs. To contact a representative, please e-mail us at bulksales@mcgraw-hill.com.

OCA Oracle Database SQL Certified Expert Exam Guide (Exam 1Z0-047)

    4567890 QFR/QFR 1 5 4 3

ISBN: Book p/n 978-0-07-161423-8 and CD p/n 978-0-07-161424-5
of set 978-0-07-161421-4

MHID: Book p/n 0-07-161423-0 and CD p/n 0-07-161424-9
of set 0-07-161421-4

Sponsoring Editor Tim Green	**Copy Editor** Robert Campbell	**Illustration** ContentWorks, Inc.
Editorial Supervisor Janet Walden	**Proofreader** Paul Tyler	**Art Director, Cover** Jeff Weeks
Project Manager ContentWorks, Inc.	**Indexer** Jack Lewis	**Cover Designer** Pattie Lee
Acquisitions Coordinator Meghan Riley	**Production Supervisor** George Anderson	
Technical Editor Alistair Grieve	**Composition** ContentWorks, Inc.	

To my father Don, an outstanding professional and highly accomplished engineer, who always believed in me, and taught me the value of hard work and dedication.

ABOUT THE AUTHOR

Steve O'Hearn is a veteran technology consultant with over 20 years of experience in the design, development, and administration of various Oracle systems for such clients as the U.S. Defense Department, NASA HQ, the FAA, the World Bank, and many others. He first became an Oracle Certified Professional (OCP) in 2001 and is a certified Oracle Database SQL Expert. He has a degree in Business Administration with a specialization in Information Processing from The George Washington University, and his postgraduate work includes the completion of the Future of e-Government Executive Education training at Harvard University's Kennedy School of Government in 2003. He is a member of MENSA.

Mr. O'Hearn has been published in a variety of publications, including the *Harvard Business Review,* and contributed to *Oracle Web Applications 101* from Oracle Press and *Oracle8 Server Unleashed.* He authored the critically acclaimed *OCP Developer: PL/SQL Program Units Exam Guide* from Oracle Press. Mr. O'Hearn is an officially recognized subject matter expert on the topic of database and information technology by the National Press Club, where he is an active member, and where he has chaired or vice-chaired the New Media, High Tech, Publications, and Online Journalism Committees, created the Club's original social network and blog, and won several awards. He has been Vice President and conference coordinator for the Mid-Atlantic Association of Oracle Professionals, where he was also the first webmaster in 1997.

Mr. O'Hearn provides Oracle technology training and tutoring online. He invites any and all inquiries at soh@corbinian.com.

About the Technical Editor

Alistair Grieve started his career as a Tandem NonStop COBOL programmer. Since then he has worked for more than 20 years as a software developer and database administrator, primarily in the financial services sector, in the UK, the U.S.A., and New Zealand. He is also a freelance technical editor.

Mr. Grieve is an Engineering Science graduate of the University of Oxford. He is a Sun Certified Java Programmer (SCJP) and Web Component Developer (SCWCD), as well as an Oracle Certified Professional (OCP) database administrator.

He can be contacted at techedit@gmx.com.

About LearnKey

LearnKey provides self-paced learning content and multimedia delivery solutions to enhance personal skills and business productivity. LearnKey claims the largest library of rich streaming-media training content that engages learners in dynamic media-rich instruction complete with video clips, audio, full motion graphics, and animated illustrations. LearnKey can be found on the Web at www.LearnKey.com.

CONTENTS AT A GLANCE

CONTENTS

ACKNOWLEDGMENTS

s with most large endeavors, this book was the product of many people!

Tim Green, the acquisitions editor, is a man of vision, patience, persistence, and insight. McGraw-Hill is lucky to have him, and I was lucky to get to work with him and his excellent team on this project. Meghan Riley is the perfect combination of professionalism, grace, and delightfulness, and is a joy to work with. Molly Sharp of ContentWorks is focused, thorough, and pleasantly fun to work with as well—the whole team has just been fantastic. Also thanks to fellow Oracle Press author Kevin Loney for a key nugget or two of information along the way.

A huge and very special thank you to my technical editor, Alistair Grieve, who was meticulous, quick, creative, and extremely knowledgeable—I can't think of enough superlatives to use for him here. Let me give you an idea of how detailed-oriented Alistair is: he caught a typo in Chapter 6 in the word "supercalifragilisticexpialidocious." More than that, he was technically brilliant and contributed a great deal to making this book better. Kudos to Tim Green and the other good folks at McGraw-Hill for bringing Alistair on the team.

Thanks to other great members of the team who have supported this effort: Robert Campbell, copy editor, Paul Tyler, proofreader, and Jack Lewis, indexer.

To my very many friends and colleagues whom I've had the pleasure of working and/or serving with over the years at various locations and in various capacities, at such enterprises as Sysorex, ISC, MAOP, EOUG, Boeing, ORI, ARC, the NPC, and elsewhere, including some who are still at those places, and some who have gone on to other adventures—there is no way I could name everyone here who has been instrumental or contributed something important to my life and work. A partial list includes: Jeremy Judson, Salam Qureishi, Nadir Ali, Wendy Loundermon, Athar Javaid, Dan Doherty, Ed Wolfe, Ashley Rubeck, Cindy Shiflett, Phil Hasse, Dave Gagner, Jon Feld, Jay Nielsen, Steve Smith, Edgar Kline, Kathy Gardos, James Perry, Terri Buckler, Mark Tash, Adhil Shaikh, Monique Tribolet, Ed Spinella, Dino Merkezas, Bert Spencer, Steve Vandivier, Karen Owens, Mike Ault, Graham Seibert, Vince Adams, Bob Schnetter, Dave Salmen, Oscar Wood, Josh

Parreco, Craig Kasold, Jennifer Blair, Dave Cooper, Ted Cohen, Steve Cummings, Jimmy Smith, Peter Dube, Ruthie Washburn, Kim Curl, Robin Ruth, Renee Battle, Danny Duong, Hung Nguyen, Drew Daffron, Ken O'Neal, Kim Miller, John Lauder, Mark O'Donnell, Bob Smout, Todd Stottlemeyer, Paul Leslie, David Wise, Dan Rutherford, Laura Taylor, Laura Setliff, Trin Tranh, Wilson Dizard, Lyle Beall, Paul Elliott, John Metelsky, Don Knight, Art Garrison, Marshall Cohen, Mark Wojno, Bill McCarren, Jonathan Salant, Tammy Lytle, Rick Dunham, John Cosgrove, Doug Harbrecht, Audrey Ford, Tim Aquilino, Debbie Beebe, Bill Simpson, Annette Taylor, Fred Wills, Carlesza Harris, Gardner McBride, Cindy McBride, Jim Flyzik, Bob Guerra, John Coffey, Lyle Beall, Bobbie Beall, and to three who are no longer with us: Aaron "Eppie" Epstein, Martin Kuhn, and Gordon Gustin.

To Dan Hinkle, my business associate of many years, who opened up many doors and many opportunities—a special acknowledgment, and of course to Brenda.

Thank you to Bianca Canales for being a great friend, and for providing some key insight at important points in my career; and to Marlene Theriault for special encouragement and very helpful suggestions years ago, which I still benefit from today.

To my very many fantastic Oracle students over the years, too numerous to mention here—each of my classes has had a distinctly wonderful and rewarding personality, and each individual student brings a unique set of experiences and observations to the task of learning, all of which have been fun for me and rewarding to work with, and I've benefited from having met you all—as iron sharpens iron.

A special thank you to my very dear friends Todd and Cindy Bauchspies, and also Mike and Kate Waters, and their gifted and talented sons James and Gavin, and to Phil and Charlotte Jones and Chester and Stephanie and Kenny and Karen, and Harriet Marin and Joe Motz, and of course to Bill Bryant—a huge thanks to all of you for being so patient with my occasional long periods of self-imposed exile while I work on projects such as this book—and still being my friends afterward!

A special thank you to Jim Bauchspies, who is like a second father to me in many ways, both personally and professionally, and to Georgine, who gave me many a home-cooked meal and a warm welcome at just the right time. And to Roy Patterson for making my very first Oracle project a reality back in 1986.

A very special thank you to Lisa, my sweetheart, for being wonderful and especially encouraging!

To my mother, Joan, the best mother anyone could possibly have, and to whom I dedicated my first book. She's always been there for me, through thick and thin, with a song in her voice and a smile in her heart—Mom, you're the best!

Thanks to my father, Don, an accomplished engineer, and a practitioner of project management, who taught me the value of hard work and dedication, both in word and in deed. A published author in his own right, a consummate professional with a great sense of humor, and the person to whom I've dedicated this book.

PREFACE

The most powerful tool in the world today is information. The most powerful information tool in the world is the relational database. The leading relational database in the world is Oracle. And the core language at the foundation of all Oracle products is Oracle's Structured Query Language, or SQL, a language that is common to all major relational databases of all vendors worldwide. This book is designed to prepare you to become a certified expert in that language by preparing you for the Oracle Database SQL Expert exam, 1Z0-047.

The objective of this study guide is to prepare you for the 1Z0-047 exam by familiarizing you with the technology and body of knowledge tested on the exam. Because the primary focus of the book is to help you pass the test, we don't always cover every aspect of the related technology. Some aspects of the technology are only covered to the extent necessary to help you understand what you need to know to pass the exam, but we hope this book will serve you as a valuable professional resource after your exam.

In This Book

This book is organized in such a way as to serve as an in-depth review for the Oracle Database SQL Expert exam for both experienced Oracle professionals and newcomers to SQL technologies. Each chapter covers a major aspect of the exam, with an emphasis on the "why" as well as the "how to" of working with and supporting relational database applications.

On the CD

For more information on the CD-ROM, please see the Appendix "About the CD-ROM" at the back of the book.

Exam Readiness Checklist

At the end of the Introduction you will find an Exam Readiness Checklist. This table has been constructed to allow you to cross-reference the official exam objectives with the objectives as they are presented and covered in this book. The checklist also allows you to gauge your level of expertise on each objective at the outset of your studies. This should allow you to check your progress and make sure you spend the time you need on more difficult or unfamiliar sections. References have been provided for the objective exactly as the vendor presents it, the section of the study guide that covers that objective, and a chapter and page reference.

In Every Chapter

We've created a set of chapter components that call your attention to important items, reinforce important points, and provide helpful exam-taking hints. Take a look at what you'll find in every chapter:

- Every chapter begins with **Certification Objectives**—what you need to know in order to pass the section on the exam dealing with the chapter topic. The Objective headings identify the objectives within the chapter, so you'll always know an objective when you see it!

- **Exam Watch** notes call attention to information about, and potential pitfalls in, the exam. These helpful hints are written by authors who have taken the exams and received their certification—who better to tell you what to worry about? They know what you're about to go through!

- **On the Job** notes describe the issues that come up most often in real-world settings. They provide a valuable perspective on certification- and product-related topics. They point out common mistakes and address questions that have arisen from on-the-job discussions and experience.

- The **Certification Summary** is a succinct review of the chapter and a restatement of salient points regarding the exam.

- ✓ The **Two-Minute Drill** at the end of every chapter is a checklist of the main points of the chapter. It can be used for last-minute review.

- Q&A The **Self Test** offers questions intended to check your knowledge of each chapter. The answers to these questions, as well as explanations of the answers, can be found at the end of each chapter. By taking the Self Test after completing each chapter, you'll reinforce what you've learned from that chapter.

- The **MasterExams** offer questions similar to those found on the certification exam. One MasterExam is on the CD in the back of this book. A second is available online for owners of this book who register. These exams most closely reflect the experience of taking the actual certification exam. As you read each chapter, you'll obtain information about each certification objective topic. However, when you take the real exam, you won't have topic headers to let you know what the question is testing. In addition, the real exam will combine various topics into one question. By taking the MasterExams after completing the book, you'll reinforce what you've learned from the book while becoming familiar with the structure of the exam questions.

Some Pointers

Once you've finished reading this book, set aside some time to do a thorough review. You might want to return to the book several times and make use of all the methods it offers for reviewing the material:

1. *Re-read all the Certification Summaries and Two-Minute Drills*, or have someone quiz you. You also can use the drills as a way to do a quick cram before the exam. You might want to make some flash cards out of 3 × 5 index cards that have the Two-Minute Drill material on them.

2. *Re-read all the Exam Watch notes*. Remember that these notes are written by authors who have taken the exam and passed. They know what you should expect—and what you should be on the lookout for.

3. *Re-take the Self Tests*. Taking the Self Tests right after you've read the chapter is a good idea, because the questions help reinforce what you've just learned. However, it's an even better idea to go back later and do all the questions in the book in one sitting. Pretend that you're taking the live exam. When you go through the questions the first time, you should mark your answers on a separate piece of paper. That way, you can run through the questions as many times as you need to until you feel comfortable with the material.

4. *Take one of the MasterExams*, timed, and without your book, to see how you did. Make notes as you progress to keep a list of topics you think you need to study further before taking the real exam.

INTRODUCTION

Welcome to a book that could change your career, and quite possibly change your life—and all for the better. You're holding in your hands a study guide and roadmap to obtaining the Oracle Database SQL Expert certification. Possession of this book does not guarantee your success. But it increases your odds of success dramatically. You're going to have to work at it. But you can do it—armed with the information contained in this book, you can achieve what few have accomplished: a certification that declares your expertise in the core language at the heart of all major database systems in use in the world today. You live in the Information Age, and SQL is the master language of all serious information that drives the businesses, governments, and organizations that run the world.

Chapter 1 will provide you with some introductory information about the exam and the exam experience. After that, you'll review the topics according to the certification objectives.

These are the officially declared topics, published by Oracle Corporation and stated by the company to be the topics from which the exam draws its questions. This book will not—and cannot—reveal actual exam questions, or their corresponding answers. Those of us who have taken the exam are forbidden to reveal that information. But this book will focus on the topics that the exam addresses, and will teach you the information that, as of this writing, you need to know about the exam.

A good Oracle professional will not limit his or her study to just one book. Oracle Corporation has made a number of manuals available online that describe the full functionality of their products. But those of us who have been in the business a while know that these great resources, valuable and voluminous as they are, can be overwhelming sometimes, cryptic at other times, and generally too difficult to navigate effectively within a person's professional lifetime, without some sort of guide. This book is your guide, but it is much more than that—it is a self-contained study guide, complete with full descriptions, syntax details, sample code, self-tests, and master exams that simulate the real certification exam experience. In other words, you are holding a treasure map to the nuggets of wisdom you need to know to pass the exam and win your certification. It's the product of years of experience, earned through hard work, tested among veteran Oracle professionals from around the world and with many backgrounds and strengths, consolidated into one clearly organized format to empower you to prepare quickly and efficiently to become certified.

The book is designed to serve the following audiences:

- For the veteran who wishes only to zero in on particular topics on an à la carte basis, the book is categorized by certification objective. If you've already seen the published certification objectives and only wish to study up on a few areas, you can do that with this book—find the appropriate section and study those chapters.

- For the reader who wishes a more comprehensive review, the objectives and chapters are sequentially ordered to begin with the fundamentals and work up into the more advanced topics. You can study the book straight through and experience a complete presentation of the knowledge you need to pass the exam.

- For the seasoned practitioner who wants to jump straight to the exam experience—go straight for the back of the book and install the CD, take the exam. Each question is tied back to a section and topic in the book so that any questions you miss will quickly focus your study on the topics you need to brush up on.

The 1Z0-047 exam has been tested against versions 10g and 11g of the Oracle database. For this book, I used Oracle Database 11g, release 1. Some of the screen shots of SQL statements were taken from SQL*Plus, others from SQL Developer. Note that in the SQL Developer's Script Output display, numeric data displays left justified by default, as opposed to SQL*Plus, where numeric data displays right justified by default.

Images of entity-relationship diagrams were taken from the brand new Oracle SQL Data Modeler. The product shipped during the writing of this book, and I took advantage of it on the first day it went live at oracle.com.

Good reading, study well, and the best of luck to you. Your feedback is invited and welcome: soh@corbinian.com.

Exam IZ0-047

Exam Readiness Checklist

Certification Objective	Chapter	Page	Beginner	Intermediate	Expert
Write single-row and multiple-row subqueries	9	349			
Using the Set Operators	12	487			
Describe set operators	12	488			
Use a set operator to combine multiple a single query	12	490			
Control the order of rows returned	12	497			
Manipulating Data	3	93			
Describe each data manipulation language (DML) statement	3	94			
Insert rows into a table	3	98			
Update rows in a table	3	106			
Delete rows from a table	3	111			
Control transactions	3	112			
Using DDL Statements to Create and Manage Tables	2	45			
Categorize the main database objects	2	46			
Review the table structure	2	59			
List the data types that are available for columns	2	60			
Create a simple table	2	50			
Explain how constraints are created at the time of table creation	2	67			
Creating Other Schema Objects	10	381			
Create simple and complex views	10	382			
Retrieve data from views	10	391			
Create, maintain, and use sequences	10	392			
Create and maintain indexes	10	397			
Create private and public synonyms	10	404			
Managing Objects with Data Dictionary Views	14	533			
Use the data dictionary views to research data on your objects	14	534			
Query various data dictionary views	14	542			
Controlling User Access	18	673			

Exam Readiness Checklist

Certification Objective	Chapter	Page	Beginner	Intermediate	Expert
Differentiate system privileges from object privileges	18	674			
Grant privileges on tables	18	686			
View privileges in the data dictionary	18	691			
Grant roles	18	693			
Distinguish between privileges and roles	18	696			
Managing Schema Objects	11	423			
Add constraints	11	436			
Create indexes	11	454			
Create indexes using the CREATE TABLE statement	11	454			
Creating function-based indexes	11	457			
Drop columns and set column UNUSED	11	431			
Perform FLASHBACK operations	11	458			
Create and use external tables	11	468			
Manipulating Large Data Sets	15	559			
Manipulate data using subqueries	15	560			
Describe the features of multitable INSERTs	15	567			
Use the following types of multitable INSERTs (Unconditional, Conditional and Pivot)	15	571			
Merge rows in a table	15	582			
Track the changes to data over a period of time	15	586			
Generating Reports by Grouping Related Data	13	511			
Use the ROLLUP operation to produce subtotal values	13	512			
Use the CUBE operation to produce crosstabulation values	13	515			
Use the GROUPING function to identify the row values created by ROLLUP or CUBE	13	517			
Use GROUPING SETS to produce a single result set	13	519			
Managing Data in Different Time Zones	6	247			
Use various datetime functions	6	247			

Exam Readiness Checklist

Certification Objective	Chapter	Page	Beginner	Intermediate	Expert
Retrieving Data Using Subqueries	9	345			
Write a multiple-column subquery	9	356			
Use scalar subqueries in SQL	9	358			
Solve problems with correlated subqueries	9	360			
Update and delete rows using correlated subqueries	9	362			
Use the EXISTS and NOT EXISTS operators	9	365			
Use the WITH clause	9	366			
Hierarchical Retrieval	16	615			
Interpret the concept of a hierarchical query	16	616			
Create a tree-structured report	16	621			
Format hierarchical data	16	618			
Exclude branches from the tree structure	16	626			
Regular Expression Support	17	639			
Using Meta Characters	17	640			
Regular Expression Functions	17	643			
Replacing Patterns	17	653			
Regular Expressions and Check Constraints	17	659			

Introduction to SQL

Oracle Corporation's implementation of the Structured Query Language, or SQL, is arguably the most powerful and most significant computer language used in the world of government and business today. This chapter begins the process of preparing you to successfully take and pass the Oracle 1Z0-047 exam, titled "Oracle Database SQL Expert". First we'll discuss a few particulars about the exam itself, how it's different from other Oracle certification tests, and what you can expect when you take it. Then we'll begin to address the SQL language; we'll introduce some background information and prepare you to go through a comprehensive analysis and review of the language in order to successfully study for the test. We will explore the background of SQL and its role in the world of computer languages and software development.

If you are a veteran Oracle professional and are taking a bare-bones approach to exam preparation, you might want to read the first section, which provides an overview of the exam, and then perhaps skim through the rest of the chapter, looking for the Exam Watch sections along the way. However, I encourage you to review all of this material, for it will help you to position your thinking with regard to the exam, as well as your career. If you aren't absolutely crystal clear on how prominent SQL is in the marketplace, or how important it is that you have a comprehensive and thorough understanding of all of the capabilities of SQL, then read on. If nothing else, this chapter will help galvanize your career development by informing (or reminding) you of how increasingly crucial it is that you maintain your SQL skills at the highest level, as this is what organizations in the world today require—and this requirement grows with each day, as databases grow, and as the use and potential of the data they contain continue to increase in significance.

CERTIFICATION OBJECTIVE 1.01

The Exam: An Overview

A typical Oracle professional doesn't generally begin his or her career by taking the advanced "1Z0-047 Oracle Database SQL Expert" exam. Since you're reading this book, chances are you've probably taken some of Oracle's other certification tests, such as "1Z0-051 SQL Fundamentals I". The "SQL Expert" exam builds on the "SQL Fundamentals I" exam in terms of both subject matter and complexity. But "SQL Expert" is a very different and unique exam. It is demanding and asks questions that test the full breadth of your knowledge of SQL syntax and processing, and its application to business rules.

A typical question on the SQL Expert exam might go something like this:

- You'll be asked to review an exhibit, which could be a set of data output in a half-dozen columns and perhaps 20 or 30 rows—or it might be an entity-relationship diagram (ERD) containing as many as a half-dozen entities or more.

- Next you'll need to review a set of SQL statements that are intended to operate on the exhibit you were just shown, with a number of SQL statements, in which there might be a series of nested scalar functions, aggregate functions, multitable indices, subqueries of various forms, and/ or the use of different statements and clauses showcasing features such as complex timezone usage, very large datatypes, complex join conditions, etc.

- Some of the code may be correct—some may not, and you'll need to recognize the difference.

- With the sample exhibit and SQL code in front of you, you may be asked to identify the resulting status of the database after the SQL statements execute.

- You may be asked to identify the internal workings of the Oracle database, in order, in accordance with the SQL statements you've been shown.

- The list of possible answers may include more than one correct response, and you must identify each of them.

Does that sound like a lot to do for a single question? Then consider this: for the entire exam, you are allowed 120 minutes to answer 70 questions. That's an average of 1.71 minutes per question.

Think you can handle it? Do you have what it takes to be a formally recognized and officially certified Oracle Database SQL Expert?

Whether you do or not remains to be seen . . . but one thing is for certain. This book will prepare you, strengthen your knowledge, fill in the gaps, and dramatically increase your odds of success.

So get ready for a fun and rewarding challenge and an important milestone in your career. Get ready to enter the world of the technical elite, to join the crème de la crème, to be ranked with the best of the best.

Get ready, for here starts your path to become . . . a certified Oracle Database SQL Expert.

Time's a-wastin' . . . let's get started . . . first, we'll take a detailed look at the official certification objectives of the SQL Expert exam and compare them with the SQL Fundamentals exam.

"SQL Fundamentals I" Versus "SQL Expert"

As I just mentioned, since you're planning on obtaining your SQL Expert certification by taking the "1Z0-047 Oracle Database SQL Expert" exam, then chances are you may have already taken another exam, titled "1Z0-051, SQL Fundamentals I". The two exams share some common objectives, but 047 goes far beyond 051. See Table 1-1 for a comparison of those objectives, and a detailed analysis of where the two exams are similar, and where they are different.

TABLE 1-1	1Z0-051 SQL Fundamentals I	1Z0-047 SQL Expert	Exam Objectives
Comparison: 1Z0-051 and 1Z0-047 Exam Objectives	1.0	1.0	Retrieving Data Using the SQL SELECT Statement
	1.1	1.1	*List the capabilities of SQL SELECT statements*
	1.2	1.2	*Execute a basic SELECT statement*
	—	1.3	*Describe how schema objects work*
	2.0	2.0	Restricting and Sorting Data
	2.1	2.1	*Limit the rows that are retrieved by a query*
	2.2	2.2	*Sort the rows that are retrieved by a query*
	2.3	—	*Use ampersand substitution to restrict and sort output at runtime*
	3.0	3.0	Using Single-Row Functions to Customize Output
	3.1	3.1	*Describe various types of functions that are available in SQL*
	3.2	3.2	*Use character, number, and date functions in SELECT statements*
	(*)	3.3	*Describe the use of conversion functions*

TABLE 1-1	IZ0-051 SQL Fundamentals I	IZ0-047 SQL Expert	Exam Objectives
Comparison: IZ0-051 and IZ0-047 Exam Objectives (Continued)	4.0	(*)	Using Conversion Functions and Conditional Expressions
	4.1	(*)	Describe various types of conversion functions that are available in SQL
	4.2	(*)	Use the TO_CHAR, TO_NUMBER, and TO_DATE conversion functions
	4.3	—	Apply conditional expressions in a SELECT statement
	5.0	4.0	Reporting Aggregated Data Using the Group Functions
	5.1	4.1	Identify the available group functions
	5.2	4.2	Describe the use of group functions
	5.3	4.3	Group data by using the GROUP BY clause
	5.4	4.4	Include or exclude grouped rows by using the HAVING clause
	6.0	5.0	Displaying Data from Multiple Tables
	6.1	5.1	Write SELECT statements to access data from more than one table using equijoins and nonequijoins
	6.2	5.2	Join a table to itself by using a self-join
	6.3	5.3	View data that generally does not meet a join condition by using outer joins
	6.4	5.4	Generate a Cartesian product of all rows from two or more tables
	7.0	6.0	Using Subqueries to Solve Queries
	7.1	6.1	Define subqueries
	7.2	6.2	Describe the types of problems that subqueries can solve
	7.3	6.3	List the types of subqueries
	7.4	6.4	Write single-row and multiple-row subqueries

(Continued)

TABLE 1-1	IZ0-051 SQL Fundamentals I	IZ0-047 SQL Expert	Exam Objectives
Comparison: 1Z0-051 and 1Z0-047 Exam Objectives (Continued)	8.0	7.0	Using the Set Operators
	8.1	7.1	Describe set operators
	8.2	7.2	Use a set operator to combine multiple queries into a single query
	8.3	7.3	Control the order of rows returned
	9.0	8.0	Manipulating Data
	9.1	8.1	Describe each data manipulation language (DML) statement
	9.2	8.2	Insert rows into a table
	9.3	8.3	Update rows in a table
	9.4	8.4	Delete rows from a table
	9.5	8.5	Control transactions
	10.0	9.0	Using DDL Statements to Create and Manage Tables
	10.1	9.1	Categorize the main database objects
	10.2	9.2	Review the table structure
	10.3	9.3	List the data types that are available for columns
	10.4	9.4	Create a simple table
	10.5	9.5	Explain how constraints are created at the time of table creation
	10.6 (**)	1.3 (**)	Describe how schema objects work
	11.0	10.0	Creating Other Schema Objects
	11.1	10.1	Create simple and complex views
	11.2	10.2	Retrieve data from views
	11.3	10.3	Create, maintain, and use sequences
	11.4	10.4	Create and maintain indexes
	11.5	10.5	Create private and public synonyms

	IZ0-051 SQL Fundamentals I	IZ0-047 SQL Expert	Exam Objectives
TABLE 1-1 Comparison: IZ0-051 and IZ0-047 Exam Objectives (Continued)	—	11.0	Managing Objects with Data Dictionary Views
	—	11.1	Use the data dictionary views to research data on your objects
	—	11.2	Query various data dictionary views
	—	12.0	Controlling User Access
	—	12.1	Differentiate system privileges from object privileges
	—	12.2	Grant privileges on tables
	—	12.3	View privileges in the data dictionary
	—	12.4	Grant roles
	—	12.5	Distinguish between privileges and roles
	—	13.0	Managing Schema Objects
	—	13.1	Add constraints
	—	13.2	Create indexes
	—	13.3	Create indexes using the CREATE TABLE statement
	—	13.4	Creating function-based indexes
	—	13.5	Drop columns and set column UNUSED
	—	13.6	Perform FLASHBACK operations
	—	13.7	Create and use external tables
	—	14.0	Manipulating Large Data Sets
	—	14.1	Manipulate data using subqueries
	—	14.2	Describe the features of multitable INSERTs
	—	14.3	Use the following types of multitable INSERTs (Unconditional, Conditional and Pivot)
	—	14.4	Merge rows in a table
	—	14.5	Track the changes to data over a period of time

(Continued)

TABLE 1-1	IZ0-051 SQL Fundamentals I	IZ0-047 SQL Expert	Exam Objectives
Comparison: 1Z0-051 and 1Z0-047 Exam Objectives *(Continued)*	—	15.0	Generating Reports by Grouping Related Data
	—	15.1	*Use the ROLLUP operation to produce subtotal values*
	—	15.2	*Use the CUBE operation to produce crosstabulation values*
	—	15.3	*Use the GROUPING function to identify the row values created by ROLLUP or CUBE*
	—	15.4	*Use GROUPING SETS to produce a single result set*
	—	16.0	Managing Data in Different Time Zones
	—	16.1	*Use various datetime functions*
	—	17.0	Retrieving Data Using Subqueries
	—	17.1	*Write a multiple-column subquery*
	—	17.2	*Use scalar subqueries in SQL*
	—	17.3	*Solve problems with correlated subqueries*
	—	17.4	*Update and delete rows using correlated subqueries*
	—	17.5	*Use the EXISTS and NOT EXISTS operators*
	—	17.6	*Use the WITH clause*
	—	18.0	Hierarchical Retrieval
	—	18.1	*Interpret the concept of a hierarchical query*
	—	18.2	*Create a tree-structured report*
	—	18.3	*Format hierarchical data*
	—	18.4	*Exclude branches from the tree structure*
	—	19.0	Regular Expression Support
	—	19.1	*Using meta characters*
	—	19.2	*Regular expression functions*
	—	19.3	*Replacing patterns*
	—	19.4	*Regular expressions and check constraints*

* Note that conversion functions are addressed by both exams, but with more emphasis in 051 versus 047.
** This is a repeat of item 1.3.

As you can see, both exams look at many of the same features, such as the SELECT statement and its ability to sort rows and convert datatypes, together with its use of functions and expressions; the GROUP BY clause; joining tables; subqueries; the set operators (such as UNION and INTERSECT); the INSERT, UPDATE, and DELETE statements; creating database objects, and more.

All of those topics are on both exams. But SQL Expert goes far beyond this. The SQL Expert exam also addresses topics such as

- The data dictionary
- User access with roles and privileges
- FLASHBACK operations
- External tables
- Function-based indexes
- Constraints
- Multitable INSERTs
- Tracking changes over time
- Conditional INSERTs with pivots
- CUBE
- ROLLUP operations
- GROUPING SETS
- Managing data across multiple time zones
- EXISTS and NOT EXISTS
- The WITH clause
- Multi-column, scalar, and correlated subqueries
- Hierarchical SELECT
- Tree-structured output
- Regular expressions in functions and check constraints
- And more

As you can see, the SQL Expert exam goes much further than the topics addressed by the SQL Fundamentals I exam.

Both exams consist of 70 questions, and two hours are afforded the test taker of either exam. At the time of this writing, the passing scores are published differently at the Oracle.com web site: for "SQL Fundamentals I" it is 60 percent, while "SQL Expert" requires 66 percent. However, note that passing score requirements are subject to change without notice. Oracle Corporation reserves the right to substitute a particular version of the test with another version, and depending on the complexity of the specific questions included in a new version, the passing score may be adjusted accordingly. In fact, Oracle publishes this notice on its web site with regarding to the required passing score for any given exam:

> The passing scores provided on the Oracle Certification Program website are for informational purposes only. Oracle does not recommend an exam preparation strategy targeting the passing score, because passing scores are subject to change without notice.

In other words: study well, and don't plan on trying to achieve the minimal passing score requirement. Instead do the best you possibly can in order to increase your chances of victory.

What to Expect

I've taken the test. Let me share a little with you about what you can expect.

Test Logistics

In my case, I went to the Oracle Corporation web site (oracle.com), clicked the Certification link, and looked for the 1Z0-047 exam page. From there I clicked the link asking me to "register" for the exam. This took me to the Prometric web site (www.prometric.com) where I located a local university that was hosting proctored exams. I found an available time, provided my credit card information for the $125 payment, and a few days later arrived at the testing facility.

When I arrived, I was asked to turn my mobile phone off and give it to the staff, who locked it into a small container. The staff retained the key but handed the container containing my mobile phone to me. I was told I would be able to take the container with me into the testing room, unable to access it inside the locked container. I was told I could recover my phone after the exam.

After providing two forms of ID, I was shown into a large room filled with computers and taken to one that was already logged in to the Prometric automated testing system. I sat down and began. I stepped through a series of disclosures and agreements and finally was presented with the first of what I knew would be 70 questions. The 120-minute timer started with the first question. It clicked off each second in the upper-right corner, and I could monitor it throughout the exam.

All of the questions were multiple-choice. Most of them required me to click a button to display an exhibit, which popped up in a separate window, sized just big enough to show whatever the exhibit was displaying. Generally the exhibit was an entity-relationship diagram, but sometimes it was a listing of data that could've been the contents of a table or the output of a report. The exhibit didn't indicate what it was intended for, but the question would eventually get around to explaining how you were supposed to treat and interpret the exhibit for the question.

Some questions will throw a lot of material at you. You won't necessarily need to analyze every bit of it to answer the question. Be careful with your time—keep an eye on the clock, remember that you have less than two minutes per question on average, and don't get distracted. Remember—your goal is to answer the question, not necessarily to evaluate every line of the code and data element that is presented to you. Some questions will be about one simple concept, and that concept will be shown in the context of a series of several SQL statements or data listings. When you're asked to "look at the exhibit" and "evaluate the following SQL code", you might want to temporarily ignore all of that and glance ahead at the actual question first, so that you know what you'll be looking for in the exhibit and the code. Otherwise, you'll waste time studying some ERD containing over a half-dozen entities with multiple relationships, plus a half-dozen lines of SQL code, when the question might really center on just one or two of those entities and how they should be joined in a multitable query. So don't get distracted—stay focused on the question, and use your time judiciously.

atch *Stay focused on the question. Don't let a large example of SQL text distract you.*

The questions were presented on the screen one at a time. I clicked Next to advance to the next question. I wasn't required to answer each question before advancing.

Each of the questions had an optional check box in the upper-left corner labeled "Mark". I could "mark" any question for future reference, whether I had answered it or not.

When I eventually reached the final question, answered it, and clicked Next, I found myself looking at a summary screen showing the number corresponding to every question of the exam in a singular tabular listing. The questions were identified by number only, and next to each was the letter—or letters—of the answers I had provided. Any question I had "marked" showed a highlighted M next to it. Any question I had not fully answered showed a highlighted *I*—for "incomplete"—next to it. I was easily able to review and complete the answers and review any questions, including those I had marked, before completing the exam.

One factor worth noting regarding questions that require more than one correct answer to be identified: some of these questions will tell you exactly how many correct answers you must choose from the set presented to you. For example, one question may have a total of four possible answers, of which two are correct, and the question will tell you to choose two answers. In this example, if you were to choose a third answer, the automated testing system wouldn't let you do it, but would pop up a small message window telling you to de-select another answer first.

But let's say you don't catch the fact that there were two correct answers, and you only click one, and you move on. Nothing in the system will stop you from moving ahead and leaving the question incomplete with—in this example—only one of the two required answers. In fact you're always allowed to advance and leave any question "incomplete". But the good news is this: once you reach the summary screen at the end, any incomplete questions will be flagged clearly and you'll be able to go back and review.

So in case you think you answered everything, don't be too sure and exit the test prematurely—be sure you take a good look at the summary screen at the end and check for any highlighted "I" markings next to your answers. If you see any and weren't expecting to, it's quite possible that you're dealing with a question that had more correct answers than you thought.

When I was done with my questions and was satisfied that I had answered everything, I clicked Exit on the summary screen, the test score was instantly evaluated, and I was shown my score and passing grade on the screen. In addition, a nearby printer produced a written summary of my performance as well.

I picked up my papers and went to the front desk of the testing center, where a clerk made copies of my papers and kept a set. They unlocked the container containing my mobile phone, which I retrieved, and I left a happy and certified SQL Expert.

Subject Areas

The certification objectives for 1Z0-047 are shown in Table 1-1. They are taken directly from the Oracle Corporation web site as of this writing. They were the same certification objectives at the time that I took the exam.

Warning: the emphasis on the exam is on those objectives not included in the 1Z0-051 exam. That makes sense, of course, but it's not obvious from the published literature—until now. While all topic areas are addressed in some fashion, and

Oracle Corporation reserves the right to change anything and everything about the exam with no warning at any time, be aware that I've taken this exam, and of the 19 stated certification objective categories for 047, my exam provided a greater emphasis on the nine certification objective categories that are not covered by 051. The test does include questions from all categories—including those categories that are included in 051. But the nine unique certification categories not included in 051 are emphasized in 047.

In addition, you'll need to have an ability to read entity-relationship diagrams in order to take this exam, something that's not specifically mentioned in the list of certification objectives. A large number of questions will ask you to look at an "exhibit", and more often than not the exhibit will be some sort of entity-relationship diagram.

Many questions challenge your knowledge of several facts at once. For example, I encountered one question that presented several nested scalar functions in a series of SELECT statements. I had to understand clearly what each individual scalar function did, recognizing syntax issues, understand the data type transformations as one function passed on results to another, confirm whether the parameter positioning was accurate, and identify two facts about the process and end result, all within the concept of a given ERD.

The moral to the story: study this book well, understand everything listed in the certification objectives, pay special attention to those areas that are not included in 051 but are unique to 047, and get all of your facts down cold. And on test day: show up rested and on time, and don't get distracted. Pay attention to the real question and keep track of your time.

You'll be glad you did.

CERTIFICATION OBJECTIVE 1.02

Define and Understand the Basics of the RDBMS

Now that you've taken a look at the exam's certification objectives, let's get started with reviewing the subject of the Structured Query Language (SQL). This section isn't specifically analyzed on the exam, but the information presented here is foundational to an understanding of everything else in the book. If you're a veteran SQL developer, you might want to just skim the rest of this chapter, looking for the

"Exam Watch" sections, and moving on to the next chapter. Otherwise, stay tuned and get your thinking well positioned to focus on the remainder of the book.

We'll start with a cursory review of the reason we have SQL: the relational database management system (RDBMS). This section reviews the history and fundamental principles of the RDBMS.

Relational Databases and Dr. E.F. Codd

Before the advent of the RDBMS, software developers found themselves frequently creating applications that used data. These applications needed features to store, change, and retrieve data in various forms. The data was different in every application, but the required functionality was the same—store it, change it, retrieve it. In spite of this common need for functionality, there was no common approach for getting the job done. There was no standard approach to database design, nor a standard set of logic for the storage, changing, and retrieval—each programmer recreated this logic in every application. The result was a slow development effort and proprietary data structures. Programmers found it difficult at best to share each other's data. Even if they wanted to do it, it was often an arduous, time-consuming effort. Something better was needed.

The concept of a relational database management system was first formally introduced in 1970 in a paper published by an IBM engineer named Dr. E.F. Codd. That paper was titled "A Relational Model of Data for Large Shared Data Banks", and Codd's work revolutionized the software industry.

Codd envisioned a system within which programmers could build their own individual databases, using standard methods and functions, with built-in support for common functions to add, modify, and extract data from the database. In an RDBMS, data is stored in *tables*, each of which consists of one or more *columns* of information.

Consider Figure 1-1, which shows a list of ships with the fictional Codd Cruise Lines. The database table has two columns, which are "Ship ID" and "Ship Name". Each *row* of data includes a bit of information that serves as a unique identifier, which in this example is the "Ship ID" column. For example, the first row has a unique identifier of "1", the second row has a unique identifier of "2", and so on. This unique identifier is a *key* to identifying a particular ship's record. The values found under the "Ship ID" column uniquely identify each ship. This column is considered to be a *primary key* column.

FIGURE 1-1

List of "Codd
Cruise Lines"
ships

Ship ID	Ship Name
1	Codd Crystal
2	Codd Elegance
3	Codd Champion
4	Codd Victorious

Next is Figure 1-2, which is a database table of employees. In this case, we have three columns of data, "Employee ID", "Name", and "Ship ID". The unique identifier here is "Employee ID".

Now, if I were to ask you to identify the ship to which Mike West was assigned, what would you say?

Naturally you would (or should) say it was the "Codd Victorious", and you would determine this by looking in the employees table, finding the record for Mike West, then "relating" that record's Ship ID value to the ship table, and finding that Ship ID 4 "relates" to the ship named "Codd Victorious".

This is an example of the sort of data that an RDBMS might contain, and the sort of processing it does to "relate" data in one table to another table.

A typical database consists of any number of tables, many of which contain key information that is used to *relate* rows of one table to rows of another table. In the example you just saw, each ship record can theoretically relate to multiple records in the "employee" table. In other words, for every *one* ship, there might be *many* employees. These two tables are said to have a *one-to-many* relationship.

A properly structured relational database system will consist of several tables, each of which contains data that uniquely identifies each record, and then "relates" records to each other, using those unique identifiers, according to the needs of the business rules that the database is intended to support.

FIGURE 1-2

List of "Codd
Cruise Lines"
employees

Employee ID	Name	Ship ID
1	Joe Smith	3
2	Mike West	4
3	Alice Lindon	3

Database Normalization

A full analysis of the concept of database normalization is beyond the task of this book, whose intent is to prepare you for the exam. But it's worth noting the *rules of normalization*, which are a set of rules that drive the design of any set of tables that compose a relational database.

The most common levels of normalization are summarized in Table 1-2.

Normalization is a standard method used by database designers intended to reduce the risk of errors in the database. By eliminating, for example, the existence of unnecessary duplication of data and other design weaknesses, the process of normalization can help minimize the occurrence of conflicting data and improve the quality of the data contained within the database.

A database adheres to the first normal form (1NF) when tables are structured in a one-to-many relationship. For example, in our earlier example of "ships" and "employees", we would have been in violation of first normal form if we had instead placed all the ship names in the "employees" table and repeated them and any associated data, such as ship length, with each record of each employee that might happen to be assigned to that ship. By separating "ship" and "employee" data, we established the requirement to be, at a minimum, in first normal form.

TABLE 1-2 Levels of Normalization	Level of Normal Form	Abbreviation	Characterized by
	First Normal Form	1NF	No repeating groups, all tables are two-dimensional.
	Second Normal Form	2NF	1NF plus each data element is identified by one corresponding unique identifier—a *primary key*—that is not a composite and therefore cannot be subdivided into smaller bits of data.
	Third Normal Form	3NF	2NF plus all tables contain no data other than that which describes the intent of the primary key—extraneous data is placed in separate tables.
	Boyce-Codd	BCNF	A slightly modified version of 3NF designed to eliminate structures that might allow some rare logical inconsistencies to appear in the data.
	Fourth Normal Form	4NF	BCNF plus additional logic to ensure that every multivalued dependency is dependent on a superkey.
	Fifth Normal Form	5NF	4NF plus every join dependency for the table is a result of the candidate keys.

Second normal form (2NF) exists when no non-key attribute is dependent upon a part of a composite key.

Third normal form (3NF) is the most commonly used form of normalization for transaction-based database applications. In this form, lookup data is moved to separate tables.

These descriptions are merely a refresher and are not intended to be an exhaustive analysis of database normalization. For that, I refer you to other books in the Oracle Press line that deal with the fundamentals of database design.

Database Design Considerations

Databases may be used for different purposes, and not all purposes require the same sort of design. Furthermore, there are conflicting priorities that any database designer is forced to consider in the design of any database.

For example, the ideal database shouldn't store any data more than once. This way, errors are minimized considerably. After all, when you enter the current phone number for a customer, it should only be located in one place in the database, so you don't end up with a database that requires the end users to update information in more than one location. What if the users forget? Then you'll end up with conflicting information in the database, and that's a bad situation. With only one location for the "customer's current phone number", any changes made to the customer's current phone number will be done easily, and the results will be clear to future users of the database.

Now—as you've already seen, any record in the database should have a unique identifier. So that would imply that the customer's current phone number should have one unique identifier. That's a reasonable requirement. But what happens if the database design becomes complex, and stores a great deal of information in many tables? And what happens if the complexity of the design requires that unique identifier to relate to many tables in order to finally extract the customer's current phone number, buried down inside a set of tables? Depending on your computer hardware, you might experience slow performance if the database grows in size to tens of millions of records, with many interrelated tables.

And now imagine that your database is required to reply instantly to any incoming phone call, in such a way that the office telephone system identifies the incoming phone number via caller ID and sends that phone number to the database. The customer's name must appear immediately on the screen, so that your call center can answer "Hello, Mr. Codd, nice to hear from you again today, your order is on its way".

That means your database has to reply instantly to that particular query. That might require some special consideration, depending on the circumstances. Perhaps you'll choose to copy the set of "customer current phone number" records in a second table to support speedy lookups if the overall system is too slow and cumbersome to handle it.

There are purists out there who would argue this is bad design. But try to explain that to your boss when the hardware budget is tight and your incoming customer phone calls are being passed off anonymously to the call center in violation of corporate policy.

The bottom line is that the database exists to serve the organization, not the other way around, and you'll often find yourself in a situation where your design choices and trade-offs require you to bend the rules of what is considered good design.

on the **Job**

It's important to note that there is not necessarily a single right or wrong way to model every system out there. Some design decisions involve trade-offs of performance (speed of response) versus reduction of duplicate data and complexity of the resulting application. These are the challenges to any data modeler and to any SQL developer.

Now that you have a basic idea of how a database should be structured, how do you actually build it? To accomplish this, you need a tool. This is why the Structured Query Language was created.

CERTIFICATION OBJECTIVE 1.03

Define and Understand the Basics of SQL

The Structured Query Language is often abbreviated with the letters SQL. Some people pronounce it by spelling out the letters, as in "ESS-CUE-ELL".

Others pronounce it as "sequel". Both pronunciations are fine, and both are used by respected professionals in the industry. Whatever you do, just don't call it "squeal".

SQL is a language to

■ Create databases and the objects within them.

■ Store data in those databases.

■ Change and analyze that data.

■ Get that data back out in reports, web pages, or virtually any other use imaginable.

Let's look at a very simple example: consider the ships listed in Figure 1-1. A valid SQL command to create a table in which we could store that information might look like this:

```
CREATE TABLE SHIPS
(SHIP_ID          NUMBER,
 SHIP_NAME        VARCHAR2(20),
 CAPACITY         NUMBER,
 LENGTH           NUMBER );
```

I say "might" look like this because there are a number of options that you might include here, including primary or foreign key declarations, data filtering, storage assignment, and other options that go beyond our simple example. We'll look at many of those options later in the book. But this code definitely works in an Oracle SQL database.

Next, here's a SQL command to add our sample record to this table:

```
INSERT INTO SHIPS (SHIP_ID, SHIP_NAME, CAPACITY, LENGTH)
VALUES (1,'Codd Crystal', 2052, 855);
```

Again, this is a valid command, albeit a simplified version. It inserts one record of information about one ship into our new table SHIPS.

Finally, let's create a SQL command to display the contents of our newly populated SQL table:

```
SELECT   SHIP_NAME, CAPACITY, LENGTH
FROM     SHIPS;
```

FIGURE 1-3

Output of
our sample
SQL SELECT
statement

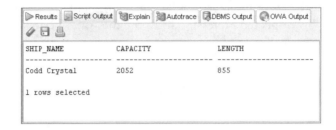

If all has gone correctly, we should get a display that appears something like the display shown in Figure 1-3. (Note: Figure 1-3 shows the output as seen in the Oracle tool known as SQL Developer.)

As you can see, our data is stored in the table, and it is still there—SELECT merely displays the data; it doesn't change the data at all.

At its simplest level, this is what SQL is all about—writing statements to create database objects, and then working with those objects to store and retrieve data.

There are many SQL commands. Some of the more commonly used SQL commands are shown in Table 1-3.

There are more commands than are shown here. For the commands that are shown here, there are many, many clauses, parameters, and other additional features for each one. Later in the book we will look in great detail at each command that is covered by the exam.

TABLE 1-3

Some of the
More Commonly
Used SQL
Commands

SQL Command	Description
SELECT	Retrieves data from a table.
INSERT	Adds new data to a table.
UPDATE	Modifies existing data in a table.
DELETE	Removes existing data from a table.
CREATE object_type	Creates a new database object, such as a table.
ALTER object_type	Modifies the structure of an object, such as a table.
DROP object_type	Removes an existing database object, such as a table.

CERTIFICATION OBJECTIVE 1.04

Understand the Oracle RDBMS and Oracle SQL

So where does Oracle enter the picture? Let's revisit Dr. Codd's story.

After Codd's paper was published in 1970, it eventually created quite a reaction in the software industry and triggered an effort within IBM to create a commercial database product. But as IBM engineers worked on their RDBMS concept and spoke about their efforts at conferences and throughout the industry, they inadvertently inspired a young entrepreneur named Larry Ellison to create an RDBMS product of his own, one that might complement IBM's product and, in the end, actually aligned more closely with Codd's original theories.

That competing product is known today as Oracle, and was officially released first, a few weeks before IBM's product, which today is known as DB2. There are many commercially available RDBMS products on the market. But only one is the dominant and unquestioned leader in the field: Oracle.

Oracle Is the Market Leader

The Oracle relational database management system (RDBMS) is the preeminent data management platform in use throughout the world today. It is the most reliable, comprehensive, robust, scalable, extensible, secure, and dynamic system for managing any amount of information, in any form, on any platform, for any number of end users, in any implementation of business rules available today. Its dominant market share is clear evidence that the marketplace recognizes the established and growing power and significance of Oracle and shows no sign of reversing this trend.

Do we have to elaborate any more on this? Does anyone dare to disagree? I'm very tempted to quote Marvel Comics legend Stan Lee with his signature "'nuff said!" And yet . . . there really is so much more to say here.

I think it's fair to say that a lot of people in the world of technology, finance, and American culture see Microsoft as the number one software maker in the world. Part of the reason is that Bill Gates, the founder of Microsoft, has been the richest man in the world for quite some time now. Not too far behind him, though, is Larry Ellison, the legendary founder of the Oracle Corporation, a company that is often considered the second largest software maker in the world.

None of this is probably new to you, but consider this: Microsoft is behind a wide array of products: the operating system, integrated office software suites, a variety of development tools, games for your PC, the Xbox line, even the MSNBC cable news channel and web site, which is their joint venture with NBC.

Oracle Corporation, on the other hand, is built on the foundation of their flagship database product and the complement of tools that support it. That's really about it. In other words, you could argue that Oracle is the world's number two software company on the strength of what is really just one product, and its associated tools.

It's an amazing testament to the significant position in the world today that's held by the Oracle RDBMS.

on the
Job

Two of the leading competitors to Oracle's RDBMS are Microsoft SQL Server, and IBM's DB2. Both are respectable products. But Microsoft's database only runs on the Microsoft operating systems. It doesn't run on Linux or Unix or other platforms. DB2, on the other hand, does run on multiple platforms and offers some competition to Oracle, but as evidenced by market share, Oracle is still seen as an overall superior product in terms of interoperability, ease of maintenance, integration with other tools, and more.

Since its inception, Oracle Corporation has grown quite dramatically, with no end in sight. Through corporate acquisitions, many of the leading industry commercial application products, such as PeopleSoft, J.D. Edwards, Hyperion, and other products—that started with other companies—are now part of the Oracle family. The annual Oracle Open World conference, once a gathering of a few thousand technical developers, has exploded into a gargantuan event featuring several tens of thousands of attendees from every industry imaginable.

But each of these acquisitions, and all of Oracle's tools, have one feature in common: their dependence on, use of, or relationship to the core product of the company, which to this day is still the Oracle RDBMS. Oracle Corporation used to be fond of reminding Open World attendees that 99 of the top 100 revenue-generating web sites were all built on the Oracle database: Amazon, eBay, Google, Dell, the list goes on and on—all relying on Oracle databases. (One exception: IBM, whose online order processing system uses DB2.)

on the
Job

You may be asking yourself: where is Microsoft Access in relationship to Oracle? The answer is simple: it doesn't have memory management capabilities comparable to Oracle, and is not capable of "scaling up" well, meaning that you cannot easily add large numbers of end users to a given application on an instance of Microsoft Access.

Certification: Oracle SQL Versus ANSI SQL

The certification exam will test you for Oracle SQL. Oracle SQL is close to, but not identical to, the standard established for SQL by the American National Standards Institute, also known as ANSI standard SQL. You will not be required to know the differences between them. There's a lot more I could say here, but it's not relevant to the exam, so let's move on.

Certification: Oracle SQL Versus Oracle SQL*Plus

The certification exam will test you for Oracle SQL, but not for Oracle's enhancements to SQL known as SQL*Plus.

Note, however, that SQL*Plus is a set of commands, and it's also a software tool with an interface into which you can type SQL and SQL*Plus commands and monitor their execution.

You won't be studying SQL*Plus commands in this book, but we will use the SQL*Plus Command Line Interface from time to time to demonstrate Oracle SQL commands.

Oracle's Tools for Working with SQL

Most of Oracle's various products and tools, such as Oracle Financials, Oracle Project, and others, all use SQL. Many development tools, such as Oracle JDeveloper, provide the ability to enter SQL statements and execute them. Two of the most commonly used tools for this purpose are the SQL*Plus Command Line Interface and SQL Developer.

The SQL*Plus Command Line Interface

The SQL*Plus command line interface is a simple way to type SQL commands, execute them, and observe the result. It's a universal system that operates the same way in every operating system.

See Figure 1-4 for an example of what the command line interface looks like.

The advantage to the command line interface is that it functions identically in Windows, Unix, and Linux operating systems. That's one of the many advantages that Oracle has always offered—ease of use in any operating system.

```
SQL*Plus: Release 11.1.0.6.0 - Production on Thu Jun 4 11:14:55 2009

Copyright (c) 1982, 2007, Oracle.  All rights reserved.

Enter user-name: efcodd
Enter password:

Connected to:
Oracle Database 11g Enterprise Edition Release 11.1.0.6.0 - Production
With the Partitioning, OLAP, Data Mining and Real Application Testing options

SQL>
```

SQL Developer

The SQL Developer interface is a GUI-style interactive point-and-click menu-driven interface that's very powerful and gives the developer a quick overview of the entire database. Some commands may be entered by either typing them in or using point-and-click-style interaction with a graphic menu. See Figure 1-5 for an example of what SQL Developer looks like.

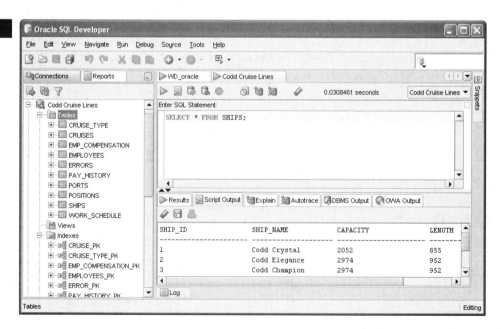

There are other tools that process SQL statements:

- Oracle JDeveloper
- Oracle Application Express
- SQL Workshop
- . . . and others

For purposes of the certification exam, your choice of interface is irrelevant. SQL statements execute correctly in all Oracle interfaces.

e x a m

ⓦ a t c h *The exam will test for your knowledge of the syntax of SQL, not your ability to point and click your way through a GUI. In other words, the fact that you might be able to create a SQL table using a code generator through a point-and-click interface will not help you during the exam. Furthermore, if you are a serious applications architect / programmer, there will eventually come a time—probably frequently—when you need to design and/or program such a feature as part of a larger application, and design and embed SQL code into other programming languages that have no access to the nice GUI tools during application run time. Furthermore, as we'll see in numerous* *instances in this book, there are many types of SQL statements in which you can combine features and clauses in such a way that they appear to be correct, execute without error, and produce lots of output—all of which can be totally erroneous. A trained eye glancing at the SQL code will recognize the mistake; an untrained eye will not even realize there is a problem. In other words: there is no substitution for comprehensive knowledge of the syntax of SQL, neither in the world of the serious software developer, nor on the certification exam. Know your syntax. As you study for this exam, type your commands and make sure they are done correctly.*

Oracle's Documentation for SQL

Oracle Corporation offers a wealth of documentation at its web site, particularly through the Oracle Technology Network, accessible at http://otn.oracle.com. The amount of documentation is almost overwhelming, particularly to a newcomer.

But one volume in particular is of interest to us for the purpose of the certification exam, and that volume is the *SQL Language Reference Manual*. It is a huge book, at close to 1,500 pages long. The size of the PDF version is 22MB. Its syntax charts are complex and go far beyond the needs of the exam. The book contains far more information than what you'll need to pass, all of which is yet another reason why you're brilliant to have obtained this book you now have in your hands. I will refer to the *SQL Language Reference Manual* from time to time, but I will only focus on the parts that are relevant to pass the exam. Other useful references of relevance to this book and the exam include Oracle's *Advanced Application Developer's Guide*, *Concepts*, *Security Guide*, *Globalization Support*, and the *Administrator's Guide*. We will refer to the set of manuals for the Oracle database version 11*g*, Release 1, which is to say version 11.1. The questions for exam 047 have been tested against database versions 10*g* and 11*g*.

CERTIFICATION OBJECTIVE 1.05

Understand the Unique Role of SQL in Modern Software Systems

By becoming a certified expert in Oracle SQL, you're establishing yourself in a very unique position in the world of software systems. Go back and look at the demand for different skills over the past few decades, and you'll see that the demand for many different computer professionals with other skill sets has spiked and fallen. But SQL has always been in steady demand for as long as it has existed.

There's a reason for that. We'll consider two in the next sections.

SQL Is a 4GL

SQL is unusual in the world of computer languages, in that it is arguably the most successful and widely used fourth-generation language, or 4GL. The term "generations" is used in describing computer languages to help to identify where a particular computer language falls on the spectrum of computer languages (see Figure 1-6) between the ones and zeros that a computer speaks versus the plain English or whatever other human language is spoken by the people who use the database. Take a look at Table 1-4.

FIGURE 1-6

Language
spectrum

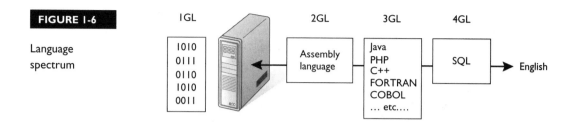

TABLE 1-4

Generations
of Computer
Languages

Generation of Computer Languages	Examples	Code Sample
First	Machine code	`0011011010`
Second	Assembly language	`MV R1 R2`

Third	FORTRAN, COBOL, C, C++, Java, PHP, Perl, etc.	`IF TRUE THEN`
		`. . .`
		`END IF;`

Fourth	SQL, assorted artificial intelligence languages	`SELECT FIRST_NAME` `FROM EMPLOYEES;`

A first-generation language (or 1GL) is really just one single language: machine language, which is made up of the ones and zeros that computers use to communicate. All computers speak in some form of machine language, all the time. You can write a program in machine language, and if you've been around long enough, perhaps you have. But it's tedious.

Second-generation languages (2GLs) include "assembly language", which is still very detailed and tedious, albeit an improvement over machine language. For example, when writing assembly code, you don't just write a command to add two numbers together—instead, you write code that identifies which register in the computer's central processing unit (CPU) contains the first number, and which register contains the second number, then invoke a command to perform the arithmetic and store the result in a third location. In assembly language, the programmer is obligated to deal with very low levels of detail within the computer's hardware to perform relatively common coding tasks. Assembly language is a bit easier to code than machine language, but not much—it's still rather tedious and not much more efficient than machine language.

Third-generation languages (3GLs) are a significant improvement over machine or assembly language, in that their language syntax is much easier to understand for most software developers, relatively speaking. 3GLs include common language features such as variables and constants, "IF THEN ELSE" constructs, loops, error handling, and more. Most of the computer languages in common use today are 3GLs—for example, languages such as Java, C++, and PHP are in this category. The programmer still must code according to the syntax rules of the language, and eventually that code is translated to machine code for the computer to actually execute. But the coding process is far more productive.

The general idea with each generational step away from machine language is to try to get closer to the point where plain spoken human language will be sufficient to program a computer. Whether that goal will ever be fully realized is a subject for another book, but the point here is that the higher the GL number, the closer the language used by the programmer is to human language, and the further away it is from machine language.

So it's interesting to note that all common software languages in general use today are no higher than the third generation, with one exception: SQL.

SQL is unusual in that it is categorized as a fourth generation language, or 4GL. It is the only widely used 4GL in commercial use today. (Other 4GLs include artificial intelligence languages.) As a 4GL, it's theoretically closer to human language than any 3GL. This is good, in that it is more powerful and enables SQL developers to do more work with fewer commands. But it's also tricky, in the sense that this increased power makes it possible to make huge mistakes at a larger degree than a typical 3GL might allow.

In other words, a 4GL carries with it the inherent obligation that its practitioner be well trained, and thoroughly knowledgeable of its power.

SQL: Gateway to the RDBMS for All Other Languages

When an application is said to be compatible with a database like Oracle, then you can be assured of one fact: there's SQL code in that application. The overall application may be written in something else—like Java or C++. But the code that interacts with the Oracle database will be written in SQL.

SQL is the only language that can talk directly to a SQL RDBMS, such as Oracle, from within any other software system, such as a front-end application, or a web service, or even another database. (I'm making the distinction of a "SQL RDBMS" because there are some RDBMS products out there that are not SQL compliant. But the vast majority are SQL compliant.) While any software developer today has a wide variety of tools and languages from which to choose when developing an application, there's only one choice when it comes to database interaction, and that's SQL.

"But," you might say, "I have this friend who wrote a database program in Java." And you probably do. But I guarantee you that embedded somewhere in that application is SQL.

"But," you might say, "I read that Oracle has this other language called PL/SQL for writing applications." And they do. But part of the PL/SQL language syntax is SQL code. Thus the name—"Procedural Language / SQL".

So no matter what language you choose to create an application, if that application is going to converse with an RDBMS—and most serious commercial and government applications will require some sort of RDBMS—then regardless of the language of your application, you'll still end up using SQL to interact with the database. For an illustration, see Figure 1-7.

So how many applications require the use of a database? One might argue that virtually all do.

Given that, here's a question that won't be on the test; this is just between us. Here it is: which of the following answers best describes a typical database? A typical database tends to

- **A.** Shrink in size
- **B.** Stay the same size
- **C.** Grow in size

What do you think the answer is? I'm not sure there's any empirical evidence to back me up on this, but I should think common sense would tell us all that databases tend to grow, and often grow dramatically, all the time, ad infinitum.

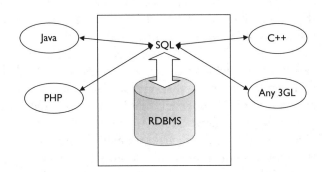

FIGURE 1-7

All 3GLs use SQL to communicate with the RDBMS.

The result: SQL has never gone "out of style" as many other languages have. Demand for other languages ebbs and wanes, but the demand for skilled SQL professionals has been persistently high ever since the early 1980s.

Syntax Isn't Enough

SQL is a deceptively tricky language. It's not a language where a rookie programmer can "try stuff until it works". Sure, that rookie might get some output, but is it the output that the query intended? And if it is correct today, will it be correct tomorrow?

One reason SQL is so tricky is the dynamic nature of the database. It's entirely possible to test a completed SQL script against a given database, testing against every single available record in the database at a given moment in time, and for that script to pass successfully—and yet for the script to suddenly stop working correctly some time later, with no apparent warning. The reason has to do with the nature of databases. Databases aren't static. They change and grow with use over time. It's not enough to test your SQL scripts against existing data or sample data—you must structure your database and write your SQL code with a confident and thorough understanding of all the possible data combinations that might exist now or in the future. This cannot be accomplished with trial and error. You have to have a comprehensive command of all of SQL's capabilities, and apply that thorough understanding to whatever business task you are facing. Anything short of that runs the risk of creating an erroneous program at best, and an unmitigated disaster at worst.

Several years ago I was brought in to clean up a database that was in use at a particular military installation. The problem: a few months before my arrival, someone very high up in the military had demanded to know how much money was being spent on a particular task. The directive went out to whoever could identify the answer. Three different not-quite-as-high-up people took on the task, and eventually all three sent inquiries to this particular installation to get the answer from the one SQL database that existed on the project. The trouble occurred when each of the three incoming requests ended up on the desks of three different SQL programmers at the installation. Each SQL programmer, unaware of the others, created a SELECT statement that he or she thought would produce the answer. Each SQL programmer created a syntactically correct report, but all were logically incorrect—they each produced a totally different number. One number was three times the amount of another. Not one was correct. When all three numbers arrived at the desk of the requesting authority, it created quite an uproar—this was a rather visible project politically. Needless to say, the project was embarrassed, and eventually I was brought in to help clean up the system and prevent such problems from occurring in the future.

But the database system was fine. The problem was a lack of proper understanding on the part of those developers about how the database was structured, and—in this particular case—of how SQL's aggregate functions worked when joining multiple tables in the context of a GROUP BY clause.

e x a m

ⓦ a t c h

One common theme on the exam is to present you with a business case, then a series of SQL statements, and then ask you if the SQL statements will produce the intended result. In other words, the question will not be about syntax. The assumption will be that the code is correct. But does it match the business case? You'll need to recognize the complexities of the SQL language in that situation to determine if the code, which will be syntactically correct, is logically accurate.

So the resulting numbers were all wrong—but hey, the SELECT statement returned an answer, didn't it? So that means it worked, right? Unfortunately, no.

The moral to the story: a successful SQL statement is not one that merely executes without producing an error message. It's one that executes and produces the intended result, both now and—equally important, perhaps dramatically more important—in the future, as new data is added to the system.

There is no way to confidently produce such SQL without having a comprehensive understanding of SQL, the sort of comprehensive understanding for which this certification exam tests. Testing your scripts against sample data won't do the trick by itself. Databases change over time. New records are added, and existing records might be changed or removed. What works today might not produce the same logical result tomorrow. There is no substitute for you, the SQL professional, developing and maintaining a mastery of SQL.

CERTIFICATION OBJECTIVE 1.06

Confirm Appropriate Materials for Study

This section lists some items you may want to gather as you prepare to study for the exam. If you are a seasoned veteran in the Oracle business, you may not need any of it—this book will suffice. But if you'd like to put forth that extra bit of effort, it might be a good idea to get your software and documentation together as listed in this section.

Software

Oracle Corporation states that they have validated the 1Z0-047 exam questions against Oracle database versions 10g and 11g. In other words, you can practice with either version; so either way, you'll be prepared for the exam.

(Note: I used version 11g, Release 1, in preparing the SQL statements for this book.)

If you don't have the software you need, you can download it from the official Oracle Corporation web site, at www.oracle.com.

on the
job
If you haven't joined the Oracle Technology Network, then you should do it right away. There's no charge for it. Visit http://otn.oracle.com and sign up today. From there, you can download a great deal of Oracle software for evaluation and study, including the database itself.

If you install the personal version of Oracle, you'll probably get SQL*Plus and SQL Developer, either of which you can use for entering and executing SQL statements. You'll need one or both of those, or if not them, then some sort of tool for entering and executing SQL commands. Chances are you already have something that you're using anyway, or else you probably wouldn't be considering certification.

Documentation

The book you have in your hands is an outstanding reference and is all you need in the way of documentation. This book is the single best guide you could possibly get to prepare you for taking the exam.

But if you crave more documentation, you can download additional documentation from Oracle's OTN website. Remember that the exam has been tested for versions 10g and 11g of the database. I used 11g, Release 1 for this book. There is a set of documentation for each version. Any one version will do—you may as well get the latest version if you choose to download documentation.

The *SQL Language Reference Manual* is Oracle's "bible" of SQL language syntax. It's good to have on hand as a matter of practice, and to reference from time to time as we cover features about which you may have additional questions. As a study guide for the exam, however, it's overkill: the detail goes far, far beyond the exam requirements and would be extremely difficult to use as a primary study reference. Anyone attempting to use that book alone as a guide for the exam will quickly realize it would be extremely difficult and incredibly time consuming. The manual addresses all aspects of language syntax, whereas the exam does not.

So the best thing you can do is to use this book to guide you through your exam preparation. From time to time in this book, I'll make reference to the *SQL Language Reference Manual*. You won't need it. But some readers may prefer to download a copy to have on hand for further study and exploration of the SQL language.

e x a m

ⓦ a t c h

Like many of Oracle's certification exams, the 1Z0-047 exam includes many multiple-choice questions that have more than one correct answer. In other words, a single question will require you to "select all of the following answers that are correct". The result: you must evaluate each individual answer. Once you find a correct answer, you aren't done— you have to continue checking them all. In other words, on these types of questions you can't rule out any of the answers *based on the process of elimination, since all answers are possible candidates for being correct. One question in this format is really more like several questions rolled into one. The result is a more demanding test that requires you to be more knowledgeable, and requires more of your time to answer. So study well. Review this book thoroughly. This is not a simple exam. But you can do it—equipped with this book, your odds of success increase dramatically.*

Recently, Oracle began publishing an e-magazine called *Oracle Certification E-Magazine*, and it's available at no charge from the Oracle web site. At the time of this writing, you can find it quickly if you take these steps:

- Visit www.oracle.com.
- Use the upper-right corner pair of "search" boxes.
  - Enter the keywords **ORACLE CERTIFICATION EMAGAZINE**.
  - Choose Education in the pop-up list.
  - Click the magnifying glass to activate your search.

This should list the link to the Oracle Certification Magazine's summary page of current and past issues. From there, you can survey the latest and greatest information on any and all of Oracle's certification programs.

CERTIFICATION SUMMARY

The relational database management system, or RDBMS, is a structure within which database programmers can build database objects to store data. Furthermore, the RDBMS comes with built-in support for many types of objects and features that are typically needed by the programmer to perform common steps, such as adding, modifying, and removing data from the database. The tool used by database programmers to communicate with the RDBMS and its objects is the Structured Query Language, which is commonly called SQL. SQL commands such as SELECT and CREATE *object type* are used by SQL programmers to build database objects, store data in them, modify that data, and more.

SQL-based RDBMS products dominate the world of database products in use today. Oracle Corporation's RDBMS has always been, and continues to be, the undisputed industry leader in the field of SQL-based RDBMS products. SQL is the single gateway through which all other languages must go to access any SQL-based RDBMS. Even if an application is written in another computer language, that language will contain embedded SQL statements to interact with any SQL-based RDBMS.

Among all computer languages in use today, SQL is the only widely used fourth-generation language, or 4GL. This means it is a powerful language, but it's also a tricky language to use. You can write commands that are syntactically correct and that execute successfully but are logically incorrect. Furthermore, the database changes over time and SQL code that appears to test correctly now—both syntactically and logically—may fail tomorrow, depending on how the data changes over time. It is imperative that the SQL programmer have a comprehensive command of the SQL language syntax to ensure proper functionality and avoid potential disaster.

TWO-MINUTE DRILL

The Exam: An Overview

❑ This chapter provides introductory material that is important to understand in preparing for the exam.

❑ The 1Z0-047 Oracle Database SQL Expert exam, which is the subject of this exam guide, has 19 certification objective categories, of which ten are common to another exam, 1Z0-051 SQL Fundamentals I. While 1Z0-047 tests for all 19 of its categories, the exam tends to emphasize the nine areas that are unique to 1Z0-047 and not addressed on 1Z0-051.

❑ The exam includes 70 questions and allows 120 minutes to complete them. That's an average of less than two minutes per question.

Define and Understand the Basics of the RDBMS

❑ A relational database consists of collections of data known as tables. A table could be a list of ship names and some statistics about each ship. Another table might be a list of employees who work on different ships. The "relational" aspect to a "relational database" has to do with the common information that "relates" two tables together—for example, the list of employees might include an entry for each employee's ship assignment, which would relate back to the list of ships and each ship's statistics.

❑ A relational database management system, or RDBMS, is a system in which these relational tables and related objects can be created easily, using common functions to add, change, and remove data and database objects from the RDBMS.

Define and Understand the Basics of SQL

❑ The Structured Query Language, or SQL, is the language used by programmers to interact with an RDBMS.

❑ SQL statements can be used to create, alter, and drop database objects, such as tables.

❑ SQL statements can add, change, and remove data from tables and other database objects.

Understand the Oracle RDBMS and Oracle SQL

❏ Oracle Corporation released the first commercial RDBMS product. Today, Oracle is the industry leader in the RDBMS market.

❏ The American National Standards Institute publishes a set of industry-recognized standards for SQL. Oracle's implementation of SQL largely matches the ANSI standard but isn't 100 percent compliant. Oracle's competition is not fully compliant either.

❏ Oracle's SQL*Plus command line interface is a great tool for entering and executing SQL commands from within any operating system platform.

❏ Oracle's SQL Developer tool is a great GUI for entering and executing SQL commands from within the Windows operating system.

❏ The *SQL Language Reference Manual* is Oracle's nearly 1,500-page manual that describes the Oracle implementation of the SQL language.

Understand the Unique Role of SQL in Modern Software Systems

❏ SQL is most widely used fourth-generation language (4GL) in commercial use today.

❏ SQL is the only language for interacting with the RDBMS. Any other programming language must use embedded SQL calls to interact with the RDBMS.

❏ The constantly changing nature of databases makes them a tricky place to test software. If a SQL script is written and tested successfully today, it's entirely possible that it may break down and produce erroneous information later on. The solution is that the script must not only be tested, but must originally be designed and written by a capable SQL developer who understands proper database design and is thoroughly versed in the RDBMS and SQL syntax.

❏ The 1Z0-047 has been validated against Oracle database versions 10g and 11g, so using either to prepare for the exam will be satisfactory.

Confirm Appropriate Materials for Study

❑ This book will prepare you to study and successfully take and pass the exam.

❑ Oracle's *SQL Language Reference Manual* is overkill as an exam study guide, as it contains far more than you'll need for the exam. But it's a good reference companion to this book.

❑ Oracle has recently published an online magazine with the latest news and developments about Oracle's complete line of certification exams covering all of Oracle's products.

SELF TEST

The following questions will help you measure your understanding of the material presented in this chapter. While this particular material is not specifically addressed in the exam, an understanding of this material is assumed on the part of anyone studying for and taking the certification exam. Furthermore, these questions are written in the style and format of the certification exam, so it can be good practice to help you get going. As is the case with the exam, some of these self test questions may have more than one correct answer, so read carefully. Choose all the correct answers for each question.

The Exam: An Overview

1. Which of the following topics are not included in the SQL Fundamentals I exam but are addressed on the SQL Expert exam? (Choose all that apply.)
   A. CUBE
   B. Hierarchical retrieval
   C. FLASHBACK
   D. External tables

2. If you target the specific passing grade requirement of the exam, you can study more efficiently.
   A. True
   B. False

Define and Understand the Basics of the RDBMS

3. A database system is "relational" if it does which of the following? (Choose all that apply.)
   A. Includes "keys" to relate records in one table to records in another table.
   B. Uses SQL.
   C. Stores data.
   D. All databases are "relational".

4. The most commonly used form of database normalization for transaction-based applications is which of the following?
   A. 1NF
   B. 2NF
   C. 3NF
   D. None of the above

5. A table consists of (choose the single best answer):

   A. Names and statements

   B. Rows and columns

   C. Relations

   D. Keywords

Define and Understand the Basics of SQL

6. The language used to create objects in an Oracle database is called:

   A. RDBMS

   B. SQL

   C. Oracle

   D. CREATE

7. Which of the following SQL statements is used to remove a database object, such as a table, from the database?

   A. REMOVE

   B. DROP

   C. KILL

   D. DELETE

Understand the Oracle RDBMS and Oracle SQL

8. Choose all of the following statements that are true:

   A. There's only one right way to design any and every database.

   B. Oracle is the only manufacturer of SQL-compliant databases.

   C. SQL can be used to add data to a table, but not change it.

   D. SQL can be used to add data to a table, and also to change that data.

9. Which of the following tools can be used to execute SQL statements against the database? (Choose all that apply.)

   A. SQL Developer

   B. The *SQL Language Reference Manual*

   C. The SQL*Plus command line interface

   D. None of the above

10. What can be said of the SQL*Plus command line interface? (Choose all that apply.)
    A. It is an ANSI-standard tool for executing SQL commands in the database.
    B. It can be used to format report output in ways that pure SQL cannot do.
    C. It only runs in Windows.
    D. It was created by Microsoft to try to steal market share from Oracle Corporation.

11. Which of the following statements are true? (Choose all that apply.)
    A. Almost all medium- to large-size government agencies, companies, and nonprofits depend on data to stay in business.
    B. Oracle was the first commercial RDBMS product on the market.
    C. Oracle is the leading commercial RDBMS on the market today.
    D. Most revenue-generating web sites depend on the Oracle RDBMS for storing data.

Understand the Unique Role of SQL in Modern Software Systems

12. Which of the following statements about SQL are true? (Choose all that apply.)
    A. A given SQL statement will always produce the same answer, no matter when the statement is executed.
    B. It is not the only choice for communicating with a SQL RDBMS, but it is the best choice.
    C. SQL is a fourth-generation language (4GL).
    D. All commercial implementations of SQL are 100 percent ANSI standard.

13. You can be sure that a SQL SELECT statement is performing as intended if it executes without producing an error message.
    A. True
    B. False

14. You can be sure that a SQL SELECT statement is performing as intended if it executes and returns data from the database.
    A. True
    B. False

15. You can be sure that a SQL statement is performing as intended if it executes and doesn't change any data.
    A. True
    B. False

Confirm Appropriate Materials for Study

16. The 1Z0-047 exam (which is the subject of this book) has been officially validated by Oracle Corporation against which of the following versions of the Oracle database? (Choose all that apply.)

  A. Every version

  B. 9i

  C. 10g

  D. 11g

17. The best exam guide you could possibly get for preparing to take and pass the "1Z0-047 SQL Expert" certification exam is which of the following? (Choose all that apply.)

  A. This book

  B. The book you are holding right now

  C. This here book

  D. Don't make me tell you again

SELF TEST ANSWERS

The Exam: An Overview

1. ☑ **A, B, C,** and **D.** See Table 1-1 for a full listing of all the topics included in either or both of the exams.

2. ☑ **B** is correct. Although, granted, it's a subjective issue, but Oracle Corporation specifically warns against this. The reason: the published minimum requirement for a passing score can be changed without notice.

Define and Understand the Basics of the RDBMS

3. ☑ **A** and **B.** SQL can only be used with an RDBMS. And the "keys" in an RDBMS are the feature that makes a relational database "relational".
   ☒ **C** and **D** are incorrect. It's not true that all databases are "relational"; some are simple flat file databases, and other forms exist as well.

4. ☑ **C.** Third normal form is not the only form that's used, but it's the most common for transactional applications.
   ☒ **A, B,** and **D** are incorrect. First and second normal forms, while not totally unheard of in professional applications, are generally considered poor design and introduce potential problems in many transaction-based database application scenarios.

5. ☑ **B.** Tables consist of rows of data stored in columns. Data is added to a table in rows. Note: technically, if the table happens to be empty, one might argue that there's no data in it. Nevertheless, Oracle documentation often speaks of tables consisting of rows and columns, so we do as well.
   ☒ **A, C,** and **D** are incorrect. Tables have names, it's true, as do a table's columns, but "names" do not singularly form a table's structure. Statements are used to work with tables, not reside in them. Theoretically you could type a statement as text and store it in table, but then the table would see the result as data, and not a statement per se. Tables may optionally relate to other tables, but it's not required. Keywords represent many features throughout the database and in any programming language; they have no unique relationship to a table's structure.

Define and Understand the Basics of SQL

6. ☑ **B.** SQL is the only language that interacts with the database.
   ☒ **A, C,** and **D** are incorrect. The RDBMS is not the language, but the type of system in which the language operates. Oracle is the brand name of the particular RDBMS product from

Oracle Corporation. CREATE is one example of a SQL statement, but not a reference to the language itself.

7. ☑ **B.** The correct SQL statement is DROP, as in DROP TABLE SHIPS.

☒ **A, C,** and **D** are incorrect. REMOVE is not a SQL statement. DELETE is used to remove records from an existing table, but it leaves the table's structure intact, as well as any data not referenced by the DELETE statement. There is no KILL statement in SQL.

Understand the Oracle RDBMS and Oracle SQL

8. ☑ **D.** SQL can be used to create tables, to add data to tables, to modify that data, to remove that data, to remove the table from the database altogether, and more.

☒ **A, B,** and **C** are incorrect. There can be many good ways to design a database; there might be many reasons why a database design would change. Oracle is not the only maker of SQL-compliant databases—other vendors include IBM and Microsoft. And SQL can be used to change data.

9. ☑ **A** and **C.** The SQL Developer tool is a Windows-based interface, and the SQL*Plus command line interface works in any operating system.

☒ **B** and **D** are incorrect. The *SQL Language Reference Manual* is very helpful, but it is just a book, nothing more.

10. ☑ **B.** It provides enhancements to ANSI-standard SQL to support features not provided by the ANSI standard. Among those enhancements is formatting for report output.

☒ **A, C,** and **D** are incorrect. SQL*Plus is not ANSI standard. It runs in any operating system. And it's an Oracle product.

11. ☑ **A, B, C,** and **D.** These are all correct.

Understand the Unique Role of SQL in Modern Software Systems

12. ☑ **C.** SQL is a 4GL.

☒ **A, B,** and **D** are incorrect. SQL statements will not necessarily produce the same answer every time. One reason is that the database is dynamic, and as data is changed in the database, the SQL statement's results will probably change as well. And SQL is the only choice for communicating with a SQL RDBMS. And it's not true that commercial SQL implementations are all completely ANSI compliant—many are not, including Oracle.

13. ☑ **B.** The lack of an error message merely means that the statement's syntax is correct. But the logic may be incorrect. An error message does not result from inaccurate logic in the statement.

14. ☑ **B.** The fact that a query returns data does not mean that the query is performing as intended. The data returned may be different from the desired response.

15. ☑ **B.** Some SQL statements, such as the UPDATE statement, are intended to change data.

Confirm Appropriate Materials for Study

16. ☑ **C** and **D.** The test has been officially validated against these two versions of the database.
    ☒ **A** and **B** are incorrect. The exam tests for functionality that did not exist in earlier versions of the Oracle database.

17. ☑ **A, B, C,** and **D.** Duh.

2

Using DDL Statements to Create and Manage Tables

T his chapter begins to examine the building blocks of a SQL database, which are the objects inside the database that programmers create to store the data that populates the database.

CERTIFICATION OBJECTIVE 2.01

Categorize the Main Database Objects

Database objects are the foundation of any database application. Database objects house and support everything any database application needs in order to form a working application. This section takes a high-level look at the database objects that can be created in an Oracle RDBMS, focusing on those objects that are tested on the exam. Here we will separate database objects into categories and discuss the relationship between objects and schemas. The rest of the book will delve into greater detail on each database object that is included in the exam.

What Are Database Objects?

There are many different types of database objects that can be created in the Oracle RDBMS. The exam looks at eight of those objects in great detail.

The Complete List

A database consists of one or more database objects. The following list shows objects that a database developer can create in the Oracle 11g RDBMS. Those marked with an asterisk are included on the exam. (Source: *SQL Language Reference Manual.*)

Clusters	Index-organized tables
Constraints*	Indextypes
Contexts	Java classes, etc.
Database links	Materialized view logs
Database triggers	Materialized views
Dimensions	Mining models
Directories	Object tables
External procedure libraries	Object types
Indexes*	Object views

Operators
Packages
Profiles
Restore points
Roles*
Rollback segments
Sequences*

Stored functions/procedures
Synonyms*
Tables*
Tablespaces
Users*
Views*

Note that the exam doesn't test for all of these objects. It ignores objects such as PL/SQL program units, Java program units, and objects that are of more interest to database administrators. We will only concern ourselves in this book with those database objects that are included in the exam. The types of database objects on the exam are listed here, in alphabetical order.

Constraints
Indexes
Roles
Sequences

Synonyms
Tables
Users
Views

A Brief Description

Let's take a brief look at the types of objects that are the subject of the exam.

- **TABLE** A structure that can store data. All data is structured in columns and rows. Each column's datatype is explicitly defined.

- **INDEX** An object designed to speed up searches in a table. An INDEX performs much the same way as an index to a book, by copying a relatively small, select amount of information, sorting it for speedy reference, and tying it back to locations in the table for supporting quick lookups of rows in the source table.

- **VIEW** A "filter" through which you can search a table, and interact with a table, but that stores no data itself, and simply serves as a "window" onto one or more tables. VIEW objects can be used to mask portions of the underlying table logic for various reasons—perhaps to simplify business logic, or perhaps to add a layer of security by hiding the real source of information. A VIEW can be used to display certain parts of a table, while hiding other parts of the same table.

- **SEQUENCE** A counter, often used to generate unique numbers as identifiers for new rows as they are added to a table.

- **SYNONYM**   An alias for another object in the database, often used to specify an alternative name for a table or view.
- **CONSTRAINT**   A small bit of logic defined by you, to instruct a particular table about how it will accept, modify, or reject incoming data.
- **USERS**   The "owners" of database objects.
- **ROLES**   A set of one or more privileges that can be granted to a user.

We'll review each of these objects in greater detail throughout the book.

Next: each database object is considered to either be a "schema object", or a "non-schema object". Before we can make sense of that, we must first answer the question: what is a schema?

Schemas

This section describes schemas—what they are, and how they relate to database objects.

What Is a Schema?

A *schema* is a collection of certain database objects, such as tables, indexes, and views, all of which are owned by a user account. You can think of a "schema" as being the same thing as a user account, but there is a slight difference—the user account houses the objects owned by a user, and the schema is that set of objects housed therein. One definition of "schema" that you'll often find in Oracle's documentation—and elsewhere—is that a schema is a "logical collection of database objects". Technically that's true, but it depends on how logical the user chooses to be when building and placing those objects within his or her user account. Ideally there should be some sense to why all those objects are in there, and ideally a "schema" shouldn't be just a random collection of objects, but the fact is that there is nothing built into the Oracle or SQL systems that prevents a user from doing just that—randomly collecting objects into a user account, and thus creating a "schema" of random objects. Ideally, though, a user account should be seen and used as a logical collection of database objects, driven by business rules, collected into one organized entity—the schema.

A schema has the same name as the user account. Keep in mind, though, that it's entirely possible to create a schema (i.e., a user account) whose "owner" isn't a human being at all, but perhaps is an application process, or some other sort of virtual entity—perhaps a particular background process—or whatever makes sense to suit the business rules that are in force. So in other words, one user will often have one user account, and therefore one schema. But the opposite isn't necessarily true. There can be more user accounts than there are actual users.

Now that you understand what a "schema" is, and what a user account is, we can begin to look at different types of database objects, some of which are owned by a user—and are thereby "schema" objects—and some of which are not schema objects but are still database objects nonetheless.

Schema and Non-Schema Objects

All database objects fall into one of two categories, or "types". These "types", as the Oracle documentation calls them, are "schema" and "non-schema". All database objects are said to be either "schema" database objects or "non-schema" database objects.

Table 2-1 shows the list of both "schema" and "non-schema" objects.

"Schema" objects are those objects that can be owned by a user account. "Non-schema" objects cannot be owned by a user account.

For example, the USER object is a non-schema object. Think about it—how can a user account own itself? It cannot, unless you live in a bizarre time warp or want to fracture your brain. Therefore the USER object, which is a user account, is a "non-schema" object, and is a property of the database as a whole. The same is true for ROLE objects. ROLE objects represent one or more privileges that can be granted to one or more USER objects. Therefore a ROLE inherently exists at a level outside of an individual USER account—and it's therefore a "non-schema" object. A PUBLIC SYNONYM is a variation on the SYNONYM object that is owned by the special user account PUBLIC, whose owned objects are automatically available to the entire database by definition, as we'll see later in Chapter 10.

All other objects are "schema" objects—TABLE, INDEX, VIEW, and the others listed in Table 2-1.

TABLE 2-1	Schema Objects	Non-Schema Objects
"Schema" and "Non-Schema" Database Objects	Tables Constraints Indexes Views Sequences Private Synonyms	Users Roles Public Synonyms

CERTIFICATION OBJECTIVE 2.02

Create a Simple Table

The exam expects you to be able to recognize the correct code to create a "simple" table. By "simple", Oracle means that you'll be required to define the table's name, column names, datatypes, and any relevant constraints.

To create a table, we use the SQL command CREATE TABLE. The word CREATE is a SQL reserved word that can be combined with just about any database object (but not all) to form a SQL command. The syntax for the "CREATE *objectType*" statement is shown in this code listing:

```
CREATE objectType objectName attributes;
```

where

- *objectType* is an object listed in Table 2-1 (except for CONSTRAINT).
- *objectName* is a name you specify according to the naming rules and guidelines described later in this chapter.
- *attributes* is anywhere from zero to a series of clauses that are unique to each individual objectType, which we'll review later.

One of the most frequent usages of the SQL command CREATE is to create a TABLE. When we create a table, we'll also create the table's columns and optionally some associated objects.

Let's look at an example of a very basic CREATE TABLE statement.

```
CREATE TABLE work_schedule
   (work_schedule_id  NUMBER,
    start_date        DATE,
    end_date          DATE);
```

If you were to execute this command in a schema that didn't already have a table named "work_schedule" (that's important), then you'd get the result shown in Figure 2-1.

FIGURE 2-1

Results of
CREATE TABLE
work_schedule
statement

Let's analyze the syntax of the preceding example of a CREATE TABLE statement:

- The reserved word CREATE
- The reserved word TABLE
- The name of the table, chosen by you, in accordance with the rules of naming objects, which we review next
- A pair of parentheses, in which are a series of column declarations, each separated by a comma. Column declarations consist of:
  - The name of the column, chosen by you, in accordance with the rules of naming objects
  - The datatype of the column, taken from the list of available datatypes
  - A comma to separate each column definition from the next
  - A semicolon to end the statement, as is the case with all SQL statements

In order to fully understand the syntax as just described, we need to examine two important issues: the rules of naming database objects and the list of available datatypes. Let's look at naming rules next; after that we'll look at datatypes.

Naming a Table or Other Object

Before we move on with the details of creating a table, let's take a look at the rules for naming database objects. These rules apply to tables, views, indexes, and all database objects—including a table's constraints, if any are created. The same naming rules also apply to a table's columns.

All tables have a name. Each table consists of one or more columns, and each column has a name. (For that matter, each database object in the database has its own name—each index, view, constraint, synonym, and object in the database has a name.)

When you use the SQL keyword CREATE to create a database object, you must come up with a name and assign it to the object, and sometimes—as in the case of a table—to individual components within the object, such as the columns of a table.

The rules of naming objects are identical for all of these objects and object components. In other words, these rules apply to names for tables, table columns, views—anything you must name in the database.

Naming Rules—Basics

The rules for naming tables, and any database object, include the following:

- The length of the name must be at least one character, and no more than 30 characters.
- The first character in a name must be a letter.
- After the first letter, names may include letters, numbers, the dollar sign ($), the underscore (_), and the pound sign (#), also known as the hash mark or hash symbol. No other special characters are allowed anywhere in the name.
- Names cannot be reserved words that are set aside for use in SQL statements, such as the reserved words SELECT, CREATE, etc. See the following complete list of reserved words from Oracle's *SQL Language Reference Manual*. These words are off limits when you create names for your database objects.

ACCESS	COMPRESS	FOR
ADD	CONNECT	FROM
ALL	CREATE	GRANT
ALTER	CURRENT	GROUP
AND	DATE	HAVING
ANY	DECIMAL	IDENTIFIED
AS	DEFAULT	IMMEDIATE
ASC	DELETE	IN
AUDIT	DESC	INCREMENT
BETWEEN	DISTINCT	INDEX
BY	DROP	INITIAL
CHAR	ELSE	INSERT
CHECK	EXCLUSIVE	INTEGER
CLUSTER	EXISTS	INTERSECT
COLUMN	FILE	INTO
COMMENT	FLOAT	IS

LEVEL	ORDER	SYNONYM
LIKE	PCTFREE	SYSDATE
LOCK	PRIOR	TABLE
LONG	PRIVILEGES	THEN
MAXEXTENTS	PUBLIC	TO
MINUS	RAW	TRIGGER
MLSLABEL	RENAME	UID
MODE	RESOURCE	UNION
MODIFY	REVOKE	UNIQUE
NOAUDIT	ROW	UPDATE
NOCOMPRESS	ROWID	USER
NOT	ROWNUM	VALIDATE
NOWAIT	ROWS	VALUES
NULL	SELECT	VARCHAR
NUMBER	SESSION	VARCHAR2
OF	SET	VIEW
OFFLINE	SHARE	WHENEVER
ON	SIZE	WHERE
ONLINE	SMALLINT	WITH
OPTION	START	
OR	SUCCESSFUL	

These rules are absolute. If you attempt to create a table or any other database object with a name that violates these rules, the attempt will fail, you'll receive an error code from the database, and your object will not exist.

Case Sensitivity and Double Quotation Marks

The basic rule for case sensitivity with regard to naming database objects is that database objects are case insensitive and will be treated as though they are typed in uppercase letters. This is generally true—but there is an exception, and it depends on whether you use double quotation marks when you create an object. Here are the rules:

- If a name is not enclosed in double quotation marks when it is created, then it will be treated as uppercase regardless of how it is created or referenced.
- If a name is enclosed in double quotation marks, then it is case sensitive and must always be referenced with case sensitivity and with double quotation marks.

For example, consider the following CREATE TABLE statement:

```
CREATE TABLE ports
  (port_id   NUMBER,
   port_name VARCHAR2(20));
```

In this example, you see a valid SQL statement to create a table. The table name is "ports", and in this example, the word "ports" is entered in lowercase letters. The database will automatically convert your lowercase letters into uppercase, and you'll end up with an object called

```
PORTS
```

The object will be stored inside the database using uppercase letters, something we'll be able to confirm once we look at the data dictionary in a future chapter. For now, it's important to note that any future references to this newly created object "ports" in your SQL statements will be acceptable in either upper- or lowercase letters, and the database won't care how you reference it. For example, both

```
SELECT * FROM ports;
```

and

```
SELECT * FROM PORTS;
```

are valid SELECT statements, and both will work just fine, even though the name is stored internally in the database in uppercase letters.

However, the same is not true if you create the object using double quotation marks. Consider this valid CREATE TABLE statement:

```
CREATE TABLE "ports"
  (port_id   NUMBER,
   port_name VARCHAR2(20));
```

The use of double quotation marks here will cause the database to store the object name exactly as you present it within the double quotation marks, which, in this example, is using lowercase letters. The result: the database object name "ports" will be stored inside the database in lowercase letters:

```
ports
```

Furthermore, every future reference will require both double quotation marks and a case-sensitive reference to this database object. For example, this will work:

```
SELECT * FROM "ports";
```

But this will not work:

```
SELECT * FROM "PORTS";
```

This will not work either:

```
SELECT * FROM ports;
```

But wait, there's more! By using double quotation marks, you can also include special characters that are otherwise not allowed—such as spaces. For example, this will work:

```
CREATE TABLE "Company Employees"
   (employee_id  NUMBER,
    name         VARCHAR2(35));
```

But remember that to refer to the table later, you'll still need those double quotation marks, like this:

```
SELECT * FROM "Company Employees";
```

In other words, by using double quotation marks, you can specify database object names that go beyond the standard naming rules of Oracle objects. But if you do this, you will always need to use double quotation marks in every future reference to that object, and you'll have to be specific with regard to the case of your object name. On a practical level, you may not ever require this. Generally, most database objects are created without the use of double quotation marks in the name. But it's important to know the full functionality of this particular feature of the database in case it happens to come up sometime. Just sayin'.

Unique Names and Namespaces

So what happens if you try to create a database object with a name that matches the name of another database object that's already in the database? Can you do it? What happens to the existing database object? Will you be able to use the resulting database object? The answer is that it depends on your object's relationship to that other object that already exists, and also to something called the "namespace".

The *namespace* is a logical boundary within the database that encompasses a particular set of database objects. There are actually several namespaces at work at any given time, depending on the context in which you are working.

Understanding the namespace is necessary in order to understand whether you may or may not specify duplicate names for any particular database object. See Figure 2-2 for a diagram that demonstrates the namespace boundaries. Note

FIGURE 2-2

Diagram of
namespace
boundaries

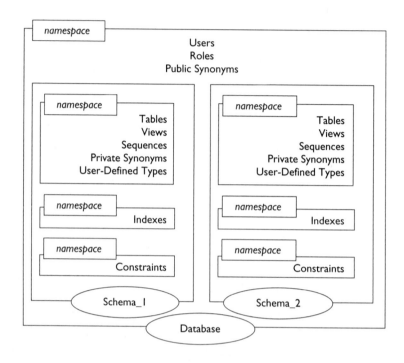

that each square encloses a different namespace. In Figure 2-2, there are several namespaces identified:

- USER, ROLE, and PUBLIC SYNONYM objects are in their own collective namespace.
- TABLE, VIEW, SEQUENCE, PRIVATE SYNONYM, and user-defined TYPE objects have their own unique namespace within a given schema.
- INDEX objects have their own namespace within a given schema.
- CONSTRAINT objects have their own namespace within a given schema.

(Note: we haven't mentioned user-defined types. They aren't on the exam. We include them in this discussion to be complete, but you won't need to understand them for the exam.)

What all of this means is that you must provide unique names for an object within its own namespace. Objects that share a namespace must have unique names within that namespace. Objects in different namespaces are allowed to have identical names. Here are some examples:

- If you create a table in one schema called WORK_SCHEDULE, then you cannot create another table called WORK_SCHEDULE within that same schema. But you can do it in another schema, provided there isn't already a WORK_SCHEDULE in that schema.
- Let's say you have a schema called HR. (As in Human Resources.) In the HR schema, you can create a table called, say, PAYROLL. You cannot create a VIEW in that same schema called PAYROLL. But you could create an INDEX called PAYROLL. You could also create a CONSTRAINT called PAYROLL. But you could not create a SEQUENCE called PAYROLL.
- In the entire database, each USER object must have a unique name. So must each ROLE object.

One thing to note: later we'll see that you can create a TABLE and give it a primary key CONSTRAINT. If you do this, you'll have the option of naming that CONSTRAINT. If you do, the system will automatically create an INDEX for the CONSTRAINT, and it will name the INDEX with the same name as the CONSTRAINT. You can override this and assign your own name with the USING INDEX clause of the CREATE TABLE statement, something we'll see later.

on the
Ü o b   *When naming objects, choose descriptive names that can be pronounced. Be consistent: if your tables of EMPLOYEES, CUSTOMERS, and VENDORS each include a reference to a person's name, make those column names all the same—NAME, LAST_NAME and FIRST_NAME, whatever—just be consistent. Consider using a standard prefix for every database object that's associated with a particular application—for example, for a Human Resources application, prefix each table with "HR_"—but avoid using prefixes that Oracle Corporation uses for its system-defined objects: "SYS_", "ALL_", "DBA_", "GV$", "NLS_", "ROLE_", "USER_", and "V$".*

System-Assigned Names

You'll see a bit later that you may create an object indirectly. This happens, for example, when you create a table, and within the CREATE TABLE statement you optionally define an associated constraint, but without providing a name for the CONSTRAINT. The language syntax of the CREATE TABLE statement allows this to happen, as you'll soon see, and the result is not only your newly created—and named—table, but also a newly created constraint for that table. Some developers refer to these constraints as "anonymous", but they aren't anonymous at all—the system will automatically generate a name for that constraint, a name that adheres to all the rules that we just reviewed.

However, system-defined names probably won't adhere to the naming guidelines we just reviewed. They'll adhere to the rules, yes. But they most assuredly will not adhere to the guidelines. Those guidelines are recommendations that Oracle makes to you, the developer. And as you can probably tell if you reflect on it a little, it won't be possible for the system to automatically generate a name that is, for example, pronounceable and meaningful to your application. Therefore it's good design to avoid the indirect creation of automatically generated names wherever possible. That's a roundabout way of saying: be sure to name all of the database objects you create, including CONSTRAINTS, INDEXES, and others.

However, in order to make sure you name everything, you'll need to know when and how all objects are created, directly and indirectly. We'll review those features throughout the book as we encounter them.

The SQL Statement **CREATE TABLE**

The SQL statement CREATE TABLE is a complex statement with many clauses and parameters. The exam only tests for some of its functionality, including how to create columns, specify data types for those columns, and create constraints.

Here's an example of a relatively simple CREATE TABLE statement.

```
CREATE TABLE cruises
( cruise_id             NUMBER,
  cruise_type_id        NUMBER,
  cruise_name           VARCHAR2(20),
  captain_id            NUMBER NOT NULL,
  start_date            DATE,
  end_date              DATE,
  status                VARCHAR2(5) DEFAULT 'DOCK',
  CONSTRAINT cruise_pk PRIMARY KEY (cruise_id) );
```

In this example, we create a table with seven columns and two constraints. Each of the columns is given a name and a datatype. The datatypes provide some rules and requirements for the data that's entered into the columns. For example, only numbers can be entered into CRUISE_TYPE_ID. Only date values can be entered into START_DATE.

Note that the STATUS column has a default value of 'DOCK'. If a row is added that does not include a value for STATUS, then the value will be automatically assigned as 'DOCK'.

At the end of the CREATE TABLE statement is an additional line that creates a CONSTRAINT. This particular CONSTRAINT defines the CRUISE_ID column as a *primary key*, which means that any row added to the CRUISES table must include a value for CRUISE_ID, and that value must be unique—it cannot duplicate any preexisting value for CRUISE_ID that any other row already present in the table may already have.

There's also a NOT NULL constraint that's applied to the CAPTAIN_ID column. That CONSTRAINT isn't explicitly named, but it's a CONSTRAINT nonetheless, and it will be assigned a system-generated name.

In the remainder of this chapter, we'll look at how you can review the structure of a table. We'll look at the different datatypes you can use to create columns in a table. We'll conclude the chapter by looking at constraints and how they can be created at the time you create a table.

CERTIFICATION OBJECTIVE 2.03

Review the Table Structure

Once you have created a table successfully in the database, you can review the table's structure with the DESCRIBE statement. The DESCRIBE statement, often abbreviated as DESC, isn't a SQL statement; it's a SQL*Plus statement that is unique to Oracle. (Some other product vendors have since implemented DESC in their own unique SQL products.) Even though it isn't SQL, it's important to understand, since DESC is useful for quickly reviewing a table's structure.

Let's take a look at an example. Consider the CREATE TABLE CRUISES statement that we saw earlier, namely:

```
CREATE TABLE cruises
( cruise_id              NUMBER,
  cruise_type_id         NUMBER,
  cruise_name            VARCHAR2(20),
  captain_id             NUMBER NOT NULL,
  start_date             DATE,
  end_date               DATE,
  status                 VARCHAR2(5) DEFAULT 'DOCK',
  CONSTRAINT cruise_pk PRIMARY KEY (cruise_id) );
```

Assuming this SQL statement were executed in the database successfully, resulting in the table CRUISES being stored in the database, then you could issue the following SQL*Plus command:

```
DESC cruises
```

FIGURE 2-3

Result of the command "DESC cruises"

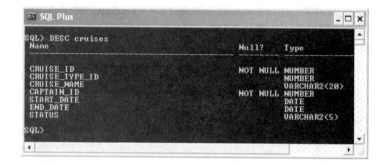

The result is displayed in Figure 2-3. Notice the output list shows a three-column display:

- The first column in the output listing is titled "Name" and shows the table's column names that you specified with the CREATE TABLE statement.
- The second column in the output listing is titled "Null?" It shows if there is a NOT NULL constraint applied to that particular column in the table—in other words, will any row that's added to the database be allowed to omit this particular value, or not?
- The third column in the output listing is titled "Type" and shows the datatype for the particular table's column in question.

For example, the DESC CRUISES output shows us that the CRUISES table has a column titled CAPTAIN_ID, its datatype is NUMBER, and it has a NOT NULL CONSTRAINT applied to it.

CERTIFICATION OBJECTIVE 2.04

List the Data Types That Are Available for Columns

The following section lists and explains data types provided by Oracle that can be assigned to columns in a table. We'll look at examples in later chapters—for now we're interested only in listing and describing them.

Datatypes are assigned to different types of objects in the SQL database and throughout the Oracle system. In a table, each column must be assigned a datatype. A column's datatype defines what sort of information is—and is not—accepted as input

exam

ⓦatch   *Oracle's own
documentation refers to datatypes as
both "datatypes" and "data types". These
two expressions are the same thing.*

into the column. It determines how the values in the column can be used, how they will behave when compared to other values or evaluated in expressions, and how they are sorted.

Most datatypes fall under one of the general categories of numeric, character, or date. There's more to it than this, but most datatypes fall into one of these three general categories. In addition to these three is a category referred to as "Large Database Objects", or LOB datatypes. LOBs can include character data but cannot be included in a primary key, DISTINCT, GROUP BY, ORDER BY, or joins.

Character

Character datatypes are also known as text or string datatypes, and they include the following:

- **CHAR(n)**   The name "char" is short for "character". This is a fixed-length alphanumeric value. Any alphanumeric character is accepted as input. The n indicates how long the value will be. The CHAR(n) datatype pads any remaining unused space with blanks to ensure that the length of your value will always equal the value of n. For example, if you declare a column with datatype of CHAR(5), then a value of, for example, 'A' will be stored—and retrieved—as 'A   ', where A is followed by four blank spaces. Any attempt to enter a value that is longer than n will result in an error, and the value will not be accepted. The inclusion of n is optional; if it's omitted in the declaration, a value of 1 is assumed. The maximum allowed value for n is 2000.

- **VARCHAR2(n)**   The name "varchar" is sort of an abbreviation for "variable character". This is a variable-length alphanumeric value. The n indicates the maximum allowable length of the value stored within, but contrary to CHAR, the VARCHAR2 format will not pad its values with blanks. Its length varies according to the data it contains—hence the name "varchar". Also different from the CHAR datatype is the fact that VARCHAR2 requires n to be specified. The minimum value of n is 1; the maximum allowable length of VARCHAR2 is 4000. (Note: The issue of a maximum value in VARCHAR2 is actually a bit more complex than this— the maximum is technically 4,000 bytes and not really 4,000 characters, and by default most Oracle database implementations are configured so that one character equals one byte. But it's possible to override this, which would theoretically change the maximum number you can use for *n* in a VARCHAR2 declaration. For our purposes here it doesn't really matter—it hasn't been an issue on the exam.)

Numeric

Numeric datatypes include the following:

■ **NUMBER(*n,m*)**   Accepts numeric data, including zero, negative, and positive numbers, where *n* specifies the "precision", which is the maximum number of significant digits (on either side of the decimal point), and *m* is the "scale", meaning the total number of digits to the right of the decimal point. Both *n* and *m* are optional; *n* defaults to the maximum value, *m* defaults to zero. The value for *n* can range from 1 to 38; the value for *m* can range from –84 to 127. Note that these are not the largest *values* you can have, but rather the largest (and smallest) specifications for values you can have—Oracle's *SQL Language Reference Manual* carefully states that the *values* accepted for a NUMBER datatype range from 1.0×10^{-130} up to "but not including" 1.0×10^{126}. If a value entered into a NUMBER column has a precision greater than the specified value, an error message will result and the value will be rejected. On the other hand, if a value is entered that exceeds the declared scale, the entered value will be rounded off (.5 is rounded up) and accepted. Also, a negative value for *m* identifies how many significant digits to the left of the decimal point will be rounded off. See Table 2-2 for an example of how all of this works. It's considered good practice to specify the precision and scale as a part of the overall data integrity check, to place some boundaries around the limits of what the business logic of the intent of the column will accept.

TABLE 2-2	Datatype	Value Entered	Value Stored As
Examples of NUMBER Precision and Scale	NUMBER	4.56	4.56
	NUMBER(2)	4.56	5
	NUMBER(5,2)	4.56	4.56
	NUMBER(5,2)	4.5678	4.57

TABLE 2-2	Datatype	Value Entered	Value Stored As
Examples of NUMBER Precision and Scale *(Continued)*	NUMBER(3,2)	10.56	Nothing is stored. Instead, displays error code ORA-01438: "value larger than specified precision allowed for this column". The reason: the value has a precision of 4 (1,0,5,6—four digits), but NUMBER here is declared with a precision of 3.
	NUMBER(5,-2)	1056.34	1100

Date

Date datatypes are sometimes referred to in Oracle's documentation as "datetimes". Each date datatype consists of "fields", and each field is a component of a date or time, such as hours, or minutes, the month value, etc. See Table 2-3 for a list of the fields that are used in various combinations to form date datatypes. The datatypes that support date and time information include the following:

■ **DATE**   Accepts date and time information. The fields stored include year, month, date, hour, minute, and second. Date values may be stored as literals, or using conversion functions which you'll see later in Chapter 6. Date literals are enclosed in single quotation marks and may be specified in a number of ways. The default Oracle date format for a given calendar day is defined by the parameter NLS_DATE_FORMAT. The value for NLS_DATE_FORMAT for your database implementation can be displayed using the SQL*Plus command SHOW PARAMETER NLS_DATE_FORMAT. (Note that the parameter NLS_TERRITORY can also change the setting for NLS_DATE_FORMAT—its value can be displayed with the SQL*Plus command SHOW PARAMETER NLS_TERRITORY.) The NLS_DATE_FORMAT parameter can be changed with ALTER SESSION or ALTER SYSTEM, which are SQL statements that are not included on the exam. By default, installations in the U.S. and UK use the NLS_DATE_FORMAT of 'DD-MON-RR', where DD is the two-digit day, MON is the three-letter abbreviation for the month, and RR is the two-digit year, where values of RR ranging from 00 to 49 are assumed to be in the 21st century (2000 to 2049), while RR values ranging from 50 to 99 are assumed to be in the 20th century (1950 through 1999). For example, '10-NOV-10' is the first of November, 2010. (Note: The same date in ANSI format is '2010-11-01'. ANSI format is 'YYYY-MM-DD', where YYYY is the four-digit year, MM is the two-digit month, and DD is the two-digit day.) We will have much more to say about dates, formats, and conversions when we discuss functions, in Chapter 6.

- **TIMESTAMP(n)**   An extension of DATE that adds fractional second precision. TIMESTAMP stores year, month, day, hours, minutes, and seconds, and fractional seconds. The value for n specifies the precision for fractional seconds. The range for n is 1–9. If n is omitted, it defaults to a value of 6.

- **TIMESTAMP(n) WITH TIME ZONE**   A variation of TIMESTAMP that adds either a time zone region name, or an offset for time zone. TIMESTAMP WITH TIME ZONE is used in tracking date information across different time zones and geographical areas. The range for n is 1–9. If n is omitted, it defaults to a value of 6.

- **TIMESTAMP(n) WITH LOCAL TIME ZONE**   A variation of TIMESTAMP. The TIMESTAMP WITH LOCAL TIME ZONE differs from TIMESTAMP WITH TIME ZONE in that the time zone offset is not stored with the column's value, and the value retrieved is sent in the user's local session time zone. The offset is calculated automatically. If n is omitted, it defaults to a value of 6.

- **INTERVAL YEAR(n) TO MONTH**   Stores a span of time defined in only year and month values, where n is the number of digits used to define the YEAR value. The range of acceptable values for n is 0–9; the default for n is 2. This datatype is useful for storing the difference between two date values.

- **INTERVAL DAY($n1$) TO SECOND($n2$)**   Stores a span of time defined in days, hours, minutes, and seconds, where $n1$ is the precision for days, and $n2$ is the precision for seconds. The range of values for $n1$ is 0–9, and the default is 2. The value for $n1$ specifies how many digits are accepted in declaring the size of a number for DAY to be specified. The value for $n2$ is the fractional seconds precision for SECOND; acceptable values range from 0 to 9, and the default is 6. Useful for storing the difference between two date values.

TABLE 2-3	Datetime Field	Range of Valid Values
Datetime Fields	YEAR	–4712 to 9999 (excluding the year 0)
	MONTH	01 to 12
	DAY	01 to 31 (Limited as appropriate for months in which there are fewer than 31 days, according to the values in MONTH and YEAR.)
	HOUR	00 to 23
	MINUTE	00 to 59
	SECOND	00 to 59.9(n), where 9(n) is the precision of time in fractional seconds. That portion—9(n)—does not apply to DATE.
	TIMEZONE_HOUR	–12 to 14. Designed to accommodate changes to daylight saving time. Does not apply to DATE or TIMESTAMP.
	TIMEZONE_MINUTE	00 to 59. Does not apply to DATE or TIMESTAMP.
	TIMEZONE_REGION	The list of possible values here is contained in the TZNAME column of the data dictionary view V$TIMEZONE_NAMES. Examples: 'America/Chicago', 'Australia/Queensland'. Does not apply to DATE or TIMESTAMP.
	TIMEZONE_ABBR	The list of possible values here is contained in the TZABBREV column of the data dictionary view V$TIMEZONE_NAMES. Examples: 'CWT', 'LMT'. Does not apply to DATE or TIMESTAMP.

exam

ⓦatch *Heads up: the datatypes that handle time zone differences are very important to the exam—they are specifically referenced in one of the certification objectives. We'll look at functions in Chapter 6 that deal with these datatypes.*

Large Objects (LOBs)

Large object datatypes, also known as LOBs, include the following:

■ **BLOB** The name "BLOB" is an abbreviation for Binary Large OBject. BLOB accepts large binary objects, such as image or video files. Declaration is made without precision or scale. The maximum size is calculated by way of a formula that includes several items, including a starting size of 4GB, something called the CHUNK parameter, and the setting for the database block size, which is a setting that affects all storage in the database. None of this is an issue on the exam. The exam will instead focus on how to use LOB datatypes in SQL language syntax. LOBs can generally be used like other datatypes. Tables may have multiple columns with LOB datatypes. However, LOBs cannot be primary keys, nor used with DISTINCT, GROUP BY, ORDER BY, or joins.

- **CLOB** The name "CLOB" is an abbreviation for Character Large OBject. CLOB accepts large text data elements. Declaration is made without precision or scale. Maximum size is calculated in the same manner that it is for the BLOB datatype.

- **NCLOB** Accepts CLOB data in Unicode. Maximum size is calculated in the same manner that it is for the BLOB datatype. Regarding Unicode—it is a character set that serves as an alternative to ASCII and represents a more universal standard that supports all major languages more easily than the other implementations in use today. Oracle and most other major vendors have adopted Unicode into their products, and common web technologies already support it. Given the increasing role of globalization and multilanguage support, any legacy application deployed without Unicode may inevitably require a conversion effort down the road. Oracle Corporation is officially recommending the use of Unicode as the database national character set for all new system development.

Here's an example of a table that includes a column of the CLOB datatype:

```
CREATE TABLE CRUISE_NOTES
(CRUISE_NOTES_ID NUMBER,
 CRUISE_NOTES    CLOB);
```

The preceding example creates a table with two columns, the second of which is a CLOB. That column can receive extremely large text data as input.

Oracle Corporation discourages the use of the old LONG datatype and encourages you to convert them to LOB datatypes, which have fewer restrictions. For example, you can add more than one LOB column to a table, you can select them, you can insert into tables with LOB columns, and delete rows with LOB values. However, you cannot use LOBs in GROUP BY or ORDER BY.

on the job *All of the datatypes you've seen so far are built in by Oracle and included with SQL. All of these datatypes are known as "built-in" datatypes. However, it's possible for users to create their own unique "user-defined" datatypes. User-defined datatypes are created using the SQL statement CREATE TYPE. They are used in PL/SQL code and are not a subject of the exam.*

Explain How Constraints Are Created at the Time of Table Creation

You can create a CONSTRAINT to support other objects, specifically TABLE objects. As such, there isn't a CREATE CONSTRAINT statement per se. Instead, you create a CONSTRAINT as part of another statement, such as CREATE TABLE or ALTER TABLE. Here's an example of a CREATE TABLE statement that includes the necessary syntax to create a CONSTRAINT:

```
CREATE TABLE positions
( position_id          NUMBER
, position             VARCHAR2(20)
, exempt               CHAR(1)
, CONSTRAINT positions_pk PRIMARY KEY (position_id)
);
```

In the preceding example, we create a TABLE called POSITIONS, which consists of three columns, POSITION_ID, POSITION, and EXEMPT. After the EXEMPT column is defined, this particular example shows an additional line of code to create a CONSTRAINT. That's not the only way to create a constraint, but it's how this example chooses to do it. Also in this example, we are choosing to name the CONSTRAINT, something that we don't necessarily have to do. The CONSTRAINT is named POSITIONS_PK. We're specifying that this CONSTRAINT is of type PRIMARY KEY, and we're applying the CONSTRAINT to the column in this table that's called POSITION_ID, which we defined first.

Let's look at some specifics next.

Creating CONSTRAINTS in the CREATE TABLE Statement

There are two ways in which a CONSTRAINT can be created at the time of TABLE creation: "in line" and "out of line".

CREATE TABLE: "In Line" Constraints

Here is an example of how to create a PRIMARY KEY constraint "in line":

```
CREATE TABLE PORTS
(PORT_ID   NUMBER PRIMARY KEY,
 PORT_NAME VARCHAR2(20));
```

In this example, we create an anonymous PRIMARY KEY constraint on the column PORT_ID. We can optionally give that constraint a name by preceding the reserved words PRIMARY KEY with the reserved word CONSTRAINT, followed by a name we make up according to the rules of naming database objects, like this:

```
CREATE TABLE PORTS
(PORT_ID    NUMBER CONSTRAINT PORT_ID_PK PRIMARY KEY,
 PORT_NAME VARCHAR2(20));
```

These two approaches are referred to as "in line" constraints, since in both examples the declaration of the constraint is included with the column definition.

Here's another "in line" example. This example creates a table with a NOT NULL constraint:

```
CREATE TABLE VENDORS
(VENDOR_ID    NUMBER,
 VENDOR_NAME  VARCHAR2(20),
 STATUS       NUMBER(1) NOT NULL,
 CATEGORY     VARCHAR2(5));
```

The result of this constraint is to ensure that a value for STATUS must be included with each row entered into VENDORS. The value might be zero or any other single digit, but it must be provided—it cannot be left out. It cannot be unknown to the database—in other words, it cannot be NULL.

Here is the same table with a name assigned to the constraint:

```
CREATE TABLE VENDORS
(VENDOR_ID    NUMBER,
 VENDOR_NAME  VARCHAR2(20),
 STATUS       NUMBER(1) CONSTRAINT STATUS_NN NOT NULL,
 CATEGORY     VARCHAR2(5));
```

You may combine multiple constraint declarations in a single CREATE TABLE statement, like this:

```
CREATE TABLE VENDORS
(VENDOR_ID    NUMBER     PRIMARY KEY,
 VENDOR_NAME  VARCHAR2(20),
 STATUS       NUMBER(1) CONSTRAINT STATUS_NN NOT NULL,
 CATEGORY     VARCHAR2(5));
```

Note that if you do not provide a name for a constraint, the system will automatically assign one, and it will be something like this:

```
SYS_C009981
```

You'll see how you'll be able to identify the system-assigned name when you look at the data dictionary, in Chapter 14.

CREATE TABLE: "Out of Line" Constraints

In addition to "in line" constraints, you may optionally define a constraint within a CREATE TABLE statement after the columns have been created. Here's an example of a PRIMARY KEY defined with the "out of line" syntax:

```
CREATE TABLE PORTS
(PORT_ID    NUMBER,
 PORT_NAME  VARCHAR2(20),
 PRIMARY KEY (PORT_ID) );
```

After the final column is defined for the table, there is a comma, followed by the reserved words PRIMARY KEY. Notice that the "out of line" syntax requires that you indicate which column (or columns) are affected by the constraint. Since we're not "in line" with the column, the statement cannot know which column you're intending to constrain, unless you specifically indicate it within the clause.

Here's an "out of line" example that names the constraint:

```
CREATE TABLE PORTS
(PORT_ID    NUMBER,
 PORT_NAME  VARCHAR2(20),
 CONSTRAINT PORT_ID_PK PRIMARY KEY (PORT_ID) );
```

This example gives the constraint a name that we've chosen. As is the case with "in line" constraints, any "out of line" constraints that you do not provide with a name will be named automatically by the system.

Additional Ways to Create Constraints: ALTER TABLE

The CREATE TABLE statement isn't the only way to create a constraint. Constraints may also be created using the ALTER TABLE statement. For example, we can first create the PORTS table like this:

```
CREATE TABLE PORTS
(PORT_ID    NUMBER,
 PORT_NAME  VARCHAR2(20));
```

Afterward, we can ALTER the table to add a constraint by modifying the definition for a column:

```
ALTER TABLE PORTS
  MODIFY PORT_ID PRIMARY KEY;
```

In the preceding code, we're modifying the declaration of the column itself by adding the primary key and letting the system assign a name. That syntax is the ALTER equivalent to this:

```
CREATE TABLE PORTS
(PORT_ID   NUMBER PRIMARY KEY,
 PORT_NAME VARCHAR2(20));
```

In addition, we can use ALTER to do the same with a constraint name we assign, like this:

```
ALTER TABLE PORTS
   MODIFY PORT_ID CONSTRAINT PORT_ID_PK PRIMARY KEY;
```

Those are the "in line" equivalents of ALTER TABLE. Here are the "out of line" equivalents. First, depending on a system-defined name:

```
ALTER TABLE PORTS
   ADD PRIMARY KEY (PORT_ID);
```

Alternatively, we can name the constraint ourselves:

```
ALTER TABLE PORTS
   ADD CONSTRAINT PORT_ID_PK PRIMARY KEY (PORT_ID);
```

We'll explore the methods for using ALTER TABLE to create constraints in more detail in Chapter 11.

Warning: NOT NULL Is Different

We're about to look at the five different types of constraints, but before we do, a word of warning about the syntax variations for one particular constraint: the NOT NULL constraint is a bit different when it comes to syntax. The NOT NULL constraint cannot be created "out of line". In other words, this is invalid:

```
CREATE TABLE PORTS
(PORT_ID    NUMBER,
 PORT_NAME  VARCHAR2(20),
 NOT NULL   (PORT_ID) );
```

This is also invalid:

```
CREATE TABLE PORTS
(PORT_ID    NUMBER,
 PORT_NAME  VARCHAR2(20),
 CONSTRAINT PORT_ID_NN NOT NULL (PORT_ID) );
```

Either of those will produce error messages if you try to execute either one. No table or constraint will be created. And yet, the same syntax is perfectly fine for other types of constraints. For example, here's the UNIQUE constraint:

```
CREATE TABLE PORTS
(PORT_ID    NUMBER,
 PORT_NAME  VARCHAR2(20),
 CONSTRAINT PORT_ID_UN UNIQUE (PORT_ID) );
```

And of course, this is fine, too—this is the PRIMARY KEY constraint:

```
CREATE TABLE PORTS
(PORT_ID    NUMBER,
 PORT_NAME  VARCHAR2(20),
 CONSTRAINT PORT_ID_PK PRIMARY KEY (PORT_ID) );
```

So NOT NULL cannot be declared with the "out of line" format. The others can. But wait, there's more about NOT NULL. This won't work either:

```
ALTER TABLE PORTS
   ADD NOT NULL (PORT_NAME);
```

And this won't either:

```
ALTER TABLE PORTS
   ADD CONSTRAINT PORT_NAME_NN NOT NULL (PORT_NAME);
```

Those won't work because they are the ALTER TABLE equivalents for "out of line" declarations. But the ALTER TABLE "in line" equivalents are fine:

```
ALTER TABLE PORTS
   MODIFY PORT_NAME NOT NULL;
```

And this is also fine:

```
ALTER TABLE PORTS
   MODIFY PORT_NAME CONSTRAINT PORT_NAME_NN NOT NULL;
```

So beware. NOT NULL is a bit unusual. It's a valid constraint and can be created using the other forms of syntax, but not with the "out of line" format.

exam
ⓦatch
The list of certification objectives specifically states in one objective that you will be tested on the topic of creating constraints at the time of table creation, and in a separate certification objective that you will also be tested on how to add constraints to tables after they have already been created.

The Types of CONSTRAINTS

There are several types of constraints that can be applied to a table. They are: PRIMARY KEY, FOREIGN KEY, NOT NULL, CHECK, and UNIQUE. (Note: the REF type is not included on the exam.) Let's explore each of these in detail.

NOT NULL

The NOT NULL constraint is very simple—when applied to a column, it ensures that for any row that is added to the TABLE, the column on which the NOT NULL constraint is applied shall always be provided with a value. Meanwhile, the column's datatype ensures that the data entered into the column is consistent with the datatype's rules.

To fully appreciate this constraint, it helps to understand what the concept of NULL is. So let's take a look.

The Concept of NULL   The reserved word NULL is, in this author's ever-so-humble opinion, one of the most misunderstood aspects of the SQL database. The definition of NULL is the "absence of information". Sometimes it's mischaracterized as "zero" or "blank", but that is incorrect—a "zero", after all, is a known quantity. So is a blank. But NULL is "unknown". It's the way the database acknowledges that it, the database, is merely an imperfect repository of information about some real-life business situation or some other application out there in the world, and the database is ultimately dependent on the data it's been given to mirror that enterprise situation. But ultimately, it's the enterprise—not the database—that is the final authority. So it's entirely possible—and quite likely—that some information hasn't been provided to the database. NULL is a placeholder for where that information goes—where the database has not been given clear instruction about whether a value exists or not, and if it does exist—what value it might be.

For example, consider a table containing the names of customers:

```
CREATE TABLE CUSTOMERS
( FIRST_NAME  VARCHAR2(20),
  MIDDLE_NAME VARCHAR2(20),
  LAST_NAME   VARCHAR2(30));
```

Let's add a row to this table:

```
INSERT INTO CUSTOMERS (FIRST_NAME, LAST_NAME) VALUES ('Angelina', 'Ellison');
```

Notice that no value is provided here for MIDDLE_NAME. When this happens, then in the absence of other information, the database stores a NULL in its place.

Does this mean that somewhere out there in the world is a real-life person named "Angelina Ellison" who has no middle name? Well . . . maybe she does, and maybe she doesn't. The point is that the database doesn't know if she has a middle name or not—the value is unknown to the database.

This becomes very important when it comes to such situations as mathematical expressions. Consider the following expression:

```
CRUISE_PRICE * DISCOUNT
```

Let's say that the value for CRUISE_PRICE is 300, and the value for DISCOUNT is NULL in the database—in other words, maybe there's a discount value out there somewhere, and maybe there isn't. But the database doesn't know either way—it's unknown to the database. The value is NULL. If that's the case, then what is the answer to the equation given in this expression?

The answer for the equation of 300 times NULL is . . . what?

Give up?

The answer is NULL. The reason is simple: "300" multiplied by "I don't know" results in . . . "I don't know".

In other words—perhaps the equation really does have an answer, but if we don't know what the DISCOUNT value is, then we don't have enough information to calculate the answer of the expression. Therefore the answer is unknown—i.e., NULL.

We'll address NULL some more in the section on functions. For now, all that we're concerned with is the NOT NULL constraint. When the NOT NULL constraint is applied to a column, you're requiring that any rows added to the table include a value for that column.

Let's go back to our earlier example. If we had applied a NOT NULL constraint to the MIDDLE_NAME column of the CUSTOMERS table, then we never would have had a row like "Angelina Ellison" with no middle name. The NOT NULL constraint, if applied to the MIDDLE_NAME column, would have required a middle name value for any row being added to the table.

By default, all columns allow NULL values when first created. You must apply a NOT NULL constraint—or an equivalent—to a column to require data for that column.

When we say "or an equivalent", we mean that there are alternative ways to require data in a column—one way is the PRIMARY KEY constraint, which is a NOT NULL rule combined with the UNIQUE constraint, which we'll see next.

If you apply a PRIMARY KEY constraint on a column, you do not need to also apply a NOT NULL constraint. But if there is no PRIMARY KEY constraint for a given column, the NOT NULL constraint will ensure that any rows added to the table will include a value for that particular column.

UNIQUE

The UNIQUE constraint, when applied to a column, ensures that any data added to the column in the future will be unique when compared to data already existing in the column. No other row will possess the same value for that particular column.

A few notes about UNIQUE:

- UNIQUE can be applied to one column or multiple columns.
- UNIQUE, by itself, allows NULL values to be added to the column. It only restricts data that's provided for the column to being one-of-a-kind for the column.

Note that the PRIMARY KEY constraint represents the combination of NOT NULL and UNIQUE. Use the PRIMARY KEY constraint instead of the NOT NULL and UNIQUE constraints if your intent is to create a single unique identifier for each row in the table.

Composite UNIQUE Constraint   You may create a UNIQUE constraint that applies to multiple columns simultaneously. This has the effect of requiring the combination of columns to be unique. In other words, each individual column may repeat data, but collectively the combination of data in all of the columns for any given row will have to be unique.

PRIMARY KEY

The PRIMARY KEY defines one or more columns in a table that will form the unique identifier for each row of data that is added to the table. The PRIMARY KEY constraint is a combination of the NOT NULL and UNIQUE constraints.

A table may have only one PRIMARY KEY constraint.

A single-column PRIMARY KEY is the most common form, and it ensures that for all rows of data added to the table in the future, the column upon which the PRIMARY KEY constraint has been applied will always contain a value, and that value will always be unique when compared to existing values that are already in the table for that particular column.

Here is an example of a CREATE TABLE statement that creates a PRIMARY KEY constraint:

```
CREATE TABLE employees
( employee_id        NUMBER
, ship_id            NUMBER
```

```
, first_name          VARCHAR2(20)
, last_name           VARCHAR2(30)
, position_id         NUMBER
, CONSTRAINT employees_pk PRIMARY KEY (employee_id));
```

In the preceding example, we create a PRIMARY KEY constraint on the EMPLOYEE_ID column. In this example, we've given the constraint a name of EMPLOYEES_PK. (The PK suffix is not required, just one of many good design approaches that clarifies to anyone who might review a long list of database constraints later on that this particular constraint is a primary key.) Now that we've created this table with the PRIMARY KEY constraint, any row that's added to the EMPLOYEES table in the future will require a unique value for each row added.

Composite Primary Keys   A multicolumn PRIMARY KEY is based on two or more columns that collectively serve the same purpose as a single-column PRIMARY KEY. In other words, the combination of column values will collectively have to be unique, and all columns—individually and collectively—will have to contain values.

See Figure 2-4 for some sample data. Notice the three columns CATEGORY, YEAR, and TICKET. Individually each shows data that repeats throughout the data listing. But together each row of combined columns represents unique data. A UNIQUE constraint could be applied to this sort of data in a table.

Here's an example of a CREATE TABLE statement that would create a composite PRIMARY KEY constraint to support Figure 2-4.

```
CREATE TABLE HelpDesk
( HD_Category  NUMBER,
  HD_Year      NUMBER,
  HD_Ticket_No NUMBER,
  HD_Title     VARCHAR2(30),
  CONSTRAINT   HelpDesk_PK PRIMARY KEY (HD_Category, HD_Year,
HD_Ticket_No));
```

The preceding code has the effect of creating NOT NULL and UNIQUE constraints across all three columns. For each row entered in the table "HelpDesk", a value will be required in each of the three columns HD_Category, HD_Year, and HD_Ticket_No, and the combination of those three values will need to be unique for every row. As you saw in the earlier sample data, it's possible to repeat values in the individual columns, but the combination must always be unique in each row.

FIGURE 2-4

Sample data from
HELP_DESK table

Category	Year	Ticket	Title
Order	2009	000001	Inkjet cartridges
Order	2009	000002	Printer paper
Bug Rpt	2009	000001	Screen fails for PDF
Order	2009	000003	Hard drive - external for conference
Bug Rpt	2009	000002	

FOREIGN KEY

A FOREIGN KEY constraint applies to one or more columns in a particular table, and works in conjunction with a second table's PRIMARY KEY constraint. A FOREIGN KEY is the feature that helps ensure that two tables can "relate" to each other, and in many ways really represents the "heart and soul", so to speak, of what a relational database is all about.

The FOREIGN KEY constraint does the following:

- It identifies one or more columns in the current table.
- For each of those columns, it also identifies one or more corresponding columns in a second table.
- It ensures that the other table already has a PRIMARY KEY (or UNIQUE) constraint on the corresponding columns in that second table.
- It then ensures that any future values added to the FOREIGN KEY–constrained columns of the current table are already stored in the corresponding columns of the second table.

In other words, a FOREIGN KEY constraint, along with the PRIMARY KEY constraint on the second referenced table, enforces "referential integrity" between the two tables. This means that the constraints work to ensure that any future data that is added to one or both of the tables continues to support the ability to relate data from one table to another.

Note: the referenced table is not actually required to have a PRIMARY KEY constraint on the referenced columns, but only a UNIQUE constraint on the referenced columns. But you'll recall that a PRIMARY KEY constraint is a combination of the UNIQUE and NOT NULL constraints, so the PRIMARY KEY satisfies the requirement for a UNIQUE constraint.

Let's look at a sample scenario. First, a listing of data in the PORTS table:

```
PORT_ID    PORT_NAME    COUNTRY    CAPACITY
-------    ---------    -------    --------
1          Baltimore    USA        2
2          Charleston   USA        2
3          Tampa        USA        8
4          Miami        USA        6
5          Galveston    USA        4
```

Next, a listing of information in the SHIPS table:

```
SHIP_ID    SHIP_NAME        HOME_PORT_ID
-------    ----------       ------------
1          Codd Crystal     1
2          Codd Elegance    3
3          Codd Champion    4
4          Codd Victorious  4
```

As you might have already surmised, the value for each ship's HOME_PORT_ID should correspond to a PORT_ID value in the PORTS table.

In order to ensure that the two tables only accept incoming rows of data that support this business rule that requires all HOME_PORT_ID values to be valid PORT_ID values, we can create a PRIMARY KEY constraint on the PORTS table (or a UNIQUE constraint), and then a FOREIGN KEY constraint on the SHIPS table that correlates back to the PRIMARY KEY constraint on the PORTS table.

First, the PORTS table:

```
01   CREATE TABLE PORTS
02   (PORT_ID       NUMBER,
03    PORT_NAME     VARCHAR2(20),
04    COUNTRY       VARCHAR2(40),
05    CAPACITY      NUMBER,
06    CONSTRAINT    PORT_PK PRIMARY KEY (PORT_ID));
```

Next, the SHIPS table:

```
07   CREATE TABLE SHIPS
08   (SHIP_ID       NUMBER,
09    SHIP_NAME     VARCHAR2(20),
10    HOME_PORT_ID NUMBER,
11    CONSTRAINT    SHIPS_PORTS_FK FOREIGN KEY (HOME_PORT_ID)
12                                 REFERENCES PORTS (PORT_ID));
```

Note that the foreign key constraint clause in the CREATE TABLE SHIPS statement starts on line 11 and continues through line 12. It references the PORTS table and the PORTS table's PORT_ID column, which already has a PRIMARY KEY constraint applied to it. If it did not already have either a PRIMARY KEY constraint or a UNIQUE constraint on it, then the CREATE TABLE SHIPS statement would result in an error and let you know that the PORTS table already must exist and must have a PRIMARY KEY or UNIQUE constraint on the PORT_ ID column.

The FOREIGN KEY on SHIPS makes sure that any row added to the SHIPS table will only accept values for HOME_PORT_ID if that value already exists in the PORTS table. Note that the HOME_PORT_ID value is not required—if your goal is to ensure that the HOME_PORT_ID value is always provided, you'll have to also add a NOT NULL constraint on HOME_PORT_ID as well as FOREIGN KEY. This is one way to do that:

```
07   CREATE TABLE SHIPS
08   (SHIP_ID      NUMBER,
09    SHIP_NAME    VARCHAR2(20),
10    HOME_PORT_ID NUMBER NOT NULL,
11    CONSTRAINT   SHIPS_PORTS_FK FOREIGN KEY (HOME_PORT_ID)
12                             REFERENCES PORTS (PORT_ID));
```

In the preceding example, we create two separate constraints. Of those two constraints, one of them is on lines 11 through 12, and exists to make the HOME_ PORT_ID column a foreign key, and another constraint—at the end of line 10—to ensure that there is always a value entered for HOME_PORT_ID.

In my professional experience, I find it much easier to create foreign keys with ALTER TABLE statements instead of with CREATE TABLE statements. One reason is that the resulting code is more modular. Note that you cannot create a foreign key constraint that refers to a table that doesn't exist. If your goal is to build a script for creating (and if necessary, re-creating) your entire database, then trying to create all of your foreign key constraints within your CREATE TABLE statements so that they occur after the creation of their respective primary key tables—all of that can suddenly turn into quite a puzzle of trying to ensure your CREATE TABLE statements all run in the correct order so that your referred tables already exist before you create foreign key constraints against them. Not only is such an effort difficult, it may prove to be impossible in a data model where the relationships run in both directions. All of this is an unnecessary effort when you can easily build all of your foreign keys within a series of ALTER TABLE statements, and place them all after your CREATE TABLE statements as a whole. The complexity is completely eliminated with that approach. Other complications you might avoid include the fact that you cannot create a foreign key within a CREATE TABLE statement that uses the "as query" approach—that approach creates the table and populates it with data using a subquery's SELECT statement all at once, which we'll examine in Chapter 15. In that sort of situation, the clause to create a foreign key constraint isn't allowed. Given such restrictions, I find no benefit to struggling to build a foreign key from within the CREATE TABLE statement, and would just as soon use an ALTER TABLE statement where these restrictions don't exist. But . . . that's just me.

CHECK

A CHECK constraint attaches an expression to a constraint. In other words, it applies a small bit of code to define a particular business rule on incoming rows of data. A CHECK constraint may, for example, restrict incoming data so that all incoming values are required to be greater than some minimum value, or fall within a set of predetermined options. A CHECK constraint can ensure that a two-character column only accepts valid abbreviations for American states, for example, or that the date entered in one column is always greater than the date entered in another column.

Here's an example of a CHECK constraint that only allows rows in the VENDORS table with a STATUS value of either 4 or 5.

```
CREATE TABLE VENDORS
(VENDOR_ID    NUMBER,
 VENDOR_NAME  VARCHAR2(20),
 STATUS       NUMBER(1) CHECK (STATUS IN (4,5)),
 CATEGORY     VARCHAR2(5));
```

While rows may be added to VENDORS with no STATUS value, they can only be given a STATUS value if it is either 4 or 5.

Any valid SQL expression may be used in a CHECK constraint.

Multiple Constraints

A table may be declared with multiple constraints. Here's an example:

```
CREATE TABLE VENDORS
(VENDOR_ID    NUMBER CONSTRAINT VENDOR_ID_PK PRIMARY KEY,
 VENDOR_NAME  VARCHAR2(20) NOT NULL,
```

```
STATUS        NUMBER(1) CONSTRAINT STATUS_NN NOT NULL,
CATEGORY      VARCHAR2(20),
CONSTRAINT    STATUS_CK CHECK (STATUS IN (4, 5)),
CONSTRAINT    CATEGORY_CK CHECK
              (CATEGORY IN ('Active','Suspended','Inactive')));
```

In the preceding example, we have a single CREATE TABLE statement that creates a table along with five constraints:

■ A user-named PRIMARY KEY on VENDOR_ID

■ A system-named NOT NULL constraint on VENDOR_NAME

■ A user-named NOT NULL constraint on STATUS

■ Two CHECK constraints: one on STATUS and another on CATEGORY

Any single table may have only one PRIMARY KEY constraint. It can have any other combination of any other constraints.

Datatype Restrictions

There are some restrictions on some constraints. See Table 2-3 for a summary of datatype restrictions on constraints. These restrictions mean that the datatypes identified cannot and will not receive a constraint applied against them if they are of the types indicated in the table with a "NO" in the appropriate field. For example, the PRIMARY KEY constraint cannot include any columns with a datatype of BLOB, CLOB, or TIMESTAMP WITH TIME ZONE. (Note, however, that constraints may be applied to columns that have the datatype of TIMESTAMP WITH LOCAL TIME ZONE.)

TABLE 2-3	Datatype	NOT NULL	UNIQUE	PRIMARY KEY	FOREIGN KEY	CHECK
Datatypes and Constraint Restrictions. NO = Not Allowed	TIMESTAMP WITH TIME ZONE	—	NO	NO	NO	—
	BLOB	—	NO	NO	NO	—
	CLOB	—	NO	NO	NO	—

CERTIFICATION SUMMARY

The main database objects that are subjects of the exam include tables, views, sequences, synonyms, indexes, users, and roles. Constraints, which are not objects, are created to support tables. A table stores data. A constraint is a rule on a table that controls what sort of data can be stored in the table. A view is something that looks and acts like a table but serves as a filter onto one or more tables. A sequence is a counter, and it's often used to generate unique numbers for storing identifiers with new rows that are added to a table. A synonym is an alias for another object. An index is an object that provides lookup support to a table, in order to speed up queries on the table. A user is an object that defines a user account. A role represents a set of one or more privileges that are granted to a user in order for that user to have access rights to other objects.

All database objects are either "schema" or "non-schema" objects. Schema objects are owned by a user and exist within a user account. Non-schema objects exist to support the database at large. Of the main database objects we are looking at for the exam, the schema objects are table, view, sequence, private synonym, index. The non-schema objects are user, role, and public synonym.

We use the CREATE TABLE statement to create a table, name the table, name the columns, assign datatypes to the columns, and optionally create various constraints to the table as well.

Objects that exist in the same namespace must have unique names. Objects that exist in different namespaces may have duplicate names. Indexes have their own namespace within a schema; so do constraints. Beyond that, a schema has one namespace for the collective set of tables, views, sequences, and private synonyms. Outside of the schema, user and role objects, along with public synonyms, share one namespace for the entire database.

Columns must be assigned a datatype when they are created. Datatypes include character, numeric, and date datatypes. Character datatypes include CHAR and VARCHAR2; numeric datatypes include NUMBER and FLOAT; date datatypes include DATE, TIMESTAMP, TIMESTAMP WITH TIME ZONE, TIMESTAMP WITH LOCAL TIME ZONE, INTERVAL YEAR TO MONTH, and INTERVAL DAY TO SECOND. There are also LOB, or Large OBject, datatypes, such as BLOB, CLOB, and NCLOB.

Constraints can be created within the CREATE TABLE statement or afterward, in the ALTER TABLE statement. They can be created "in line", meaning as part of a column's definition, or "out of line", meaning afterward as a separate line item within the CREATE TABLE or ALTER TABLE statement. An exception is NOT NULL, which cannot be created "out of line".

The five types of constraints are NOT NULL, UNIQUE, PRIMARY KEY, FOREIGN KEY, and CHECK.

✓ TWO-MINUTE DRILL

Categorize the Main Database Objects

❑ Tables store data.

❑ Constraints are rules on tables.

❑ Views serve as a sort of "window" onto tables.

❑ Indexes provide lookup support to speed queries on a table, like an index to a book.

❑ Sequences are simple counter objects.

❑ Synonyms are alternative names for existing objects.

❑ Users are objects that own other objects.

❑ Roles are sets of rights, or privileges, that can be granted to a user to give that user access to other objects.

❑ Objects are either "schema" or "non-schema" objects.

❑ Tables, views, indexes, sequences, and private synonyms are "schema" objects.

❑ Users and roles, along with public synonyms, are "non-schema" objects.

Create a Simple Table

❑ The CREATE TABLE statement is used to create a table.

❑ You assign a name to a table by using the rules of naming database objects.

❑ You also assign names to the table's columns using the same rules.

❑ All tables have at least one column.

Review the Table Structure

❑ The DESC command can be used to display a table's structure.

❑ The structure includes the table name, table columns, datatypes, and optional constraints.

List the Data Types That Are Available for Columns

❑ Each column must be assigned a datatype.

❑ Datatypes include numeric, character, and date types, such as VARCHAR2, NUMBER, and DATE.

❑ Datatypes also include large object types, including BLOB.

Explain How Constraints Are Created at the Time of Table Creation

❏ The types of constraints are NOT NULL, UNIQUE, PRIMARY KEY, FOREIGN KEY, and CHECK.

❏ A column with a NOT NULL constraint must be assigned a value for each row that is added to the table.

❏ A UNIQUE constraint requires that if data is added to a column for a given row, that data must be unique for any existing value already in the column.

❏ A PRIMARY KEY constraint is the combination of NOT NULL and UNIQUE.

❏ A PRIMARY KEY may be assigned to one or more columns.

❏ A PRIMARY KEY assigned to multiple columns is called a composite key.

❏ A single table may only have one PRIMARY KEY.

❏ A FOREIGN KEY correlates one or more columns in one table with a set of similar columns in a second table.

❏ A FOREIGN KEY requires that the second table already have a PRIMARY KEY assigned to the correlated columns before the FOREIGN KEY can be created.

❏ Once created, the FOREIGN KEY ensures that any values added to the table will match existing values in the PRIMARY KEY columns of the second table.

❏ Constraints can be created with the CREATE TABLE statement or within the ALTER TABLE statement.

❏ Constraints can be defined as part of the column definitions—"in line"—or after—"out of line".

SELF TEST

The following questions will help you measure your understanding of the material presented in this chapter. Choose one correct answer for each question unless otherwise directed.

Categorize the Main Database Objects

1. A table is which of the following? (Choose all that apply.)
   A. A schema object
   B. A non-schema object
   C. A role
   D. All of the above

2. Which of the following are schema objects? (Choose all that apply.)
   A. SEQUENCE
   B. PASSWORD
   C. INDEX
   D. ROLE

3. A CONSTRAINT is assigned to which of the following? (Choose all that apply.)
   A. TABLE
   B. SYNONYM
   C. SEQUENCE
   D. INDEX

Create a Simple Table

4. Which of the following are valid CREATE TABLE statements? (Choose three.)
   A. ```
CREATE TABLE $ORDERS
(ID NUMBER,
NAME VARCHAR2(30));
```
   B. ```
CREATE TABLE CUSTOMER_HISTORY
(ID NUMBER,
 NAME VARCHAR2(30));
```
   C. ```
CREATE TABLE "Boat Inventory"
(ID NUMBER,
NAME VARCHAR2(30));
```
```

D. `CREATE TABLE workSchedule`
   `(ID NUMBER,`
   `NAME VARCHAR2(30));`

5. Which of the following may follow the reserved word CREATE to form a complete SQL statement? (Choose three.)

   A. TABLE
   B. VIEW
   C. CONSTRAINT
   D. SEQUENCE

6. You are logged in to user FINANCE. It is currently the only schema in the entire database. The following exist in the database:
   – A VIEW named VENDORS
   – A CONSTRAINT named VENDORS
   – An INDEX named CUSTOMER#ADDRESS

   You attempt to execute the following SQL statement:

   ```
   CREATE TABLE CUSTOMER#ADDRESS
      (ID  NUMBER,
       NAME VARCHAR2(30));
   ```

   Which one of the following is true?

   A. The question is flawed because you cannot have an INDEX named CUSTOMER#ADDRESS.
   B. The question is flawed because you cannot have a VIEW and a CONSTRAINT with identical names in the same schema.
   C. The SQL statement will fail to execute and result in an error message because you cannot create a TABLE name with the "#" character.
   D. The SQL statement will fail to execute and result in an error message because you cannot create a TABLE that has the same name as an INDEX in the same schema.
   E. The SQL statement will execute and the TABLE will be created.

7. You have a single database, with only one schema. The following four objects exist in the database:
   – A TABLE named PRODUCT_CATALOG
   – A TABLE named ADS
   – A USER named PRODUCT_CATALOG
   – A VIEW named CONFERENCE_SCHEDULE

How many of the four objects are owned by the schema?

A. 0

B. 2

C. 3

D. 4

8. ROLES:

A. Are schema objects, but only when created from within a user account.

B. Are in the same namespace as CONSTRAINTS.

C. Are in the same namespace as TABLES.

D. Are in the same namespace as USERS.

Review the Table Structure

9. The DESCRIBE, or DESC, command, can be used to do which of the following?

A. Show a table's columns and the datatypes of those columns.

B. Show a brief paragraph describing what the table does.

C. Show a table's name and who created it.

D. Show the data that is contained within a table.

List the Data Types That Are Available for Columns

10. You attempt to execute the following SQL statement:

```
CREATE TABLE VENDORS
(VENDOR_ID    NUMBER,
 VENDOR_NAME VARCHAR2,
 CATEGORY    CHAR);
```

Which one of the following is true?

A. The execution fails because there is no precision indicated for NUMBER.

B. The execution fails because there is no precision indicated for VARCHAR2.

C. The execution fails because there is no precision indicated for CHAR.

D. The execution succeeds and the table is created.

11. The following SQL statements create a table with a column named A, and then add a row to that table.

```
CREATE TABLE NUMBER_TEST (A NUMBER(5,3));
INSERT INTO NUMBER_TEST (A) VALUES (3.1415);
SELECT A FROM NUMBER_TEST;
```

What is the displayed output of the SELECT statement?

A. 3.1415

B. 3.142

C. 3.141

D. None of the above

Explain How Constraints Are Created at the Time of Table Creation

12. Which of the following SQL statements creates a table that will reject attempts to INSERT a row with NULL values entered into the POSITION_ID column?

A.
```
CREATE TABLE POSITIONS
(POSITION_ID NUMBER(3),
 CONSTRAINT POSITION_CON UNIQUE (POSITION_ID));
```

B.
```
CREATE TABLE POSITIONS
(POSITION_ID NUMBER(3),
 CONSTRAINT POSITION_CON PRIMARY KEY (POSITION_ID));
```

C.
```
CREATE TABLE POSITIONS
(POSITION_ID NUMBER(3),
 CONSTRAINT POSITION_CON REQUIRED (POSITION_ID));
```

D. None of the above

13. Review the following SQL statement.

```
CREATE TABLE shipping_Order
( order_ID     NUMBER,
  order_Year   CHAR(2),
  customer_ID NUMBER,
 CONSTRAINT shipping_Order PRIMARY KEY (order_ID, order_Year));
```

Assume there is no table already called SHIPPING_ORDER in the database. What will be the result of an attempt to execute the preceding SQL statement?

A. The statement will fail because the datatype for ORDER_YEAR is a CHAR, and CHAR datatypes aren't allowed in a PRIMARY KEY constraint.

B. The statement will fail because there is no precision for the ORDER_ID column's datatype.

C. The table will be created, but the primary key constraint will not be created because the name does not include the "_PK" suffix.

D. The statement will succeed: the table will be created and the primary key will also be created.

14. Review the following SQL statement.

```
CREATE TABLE personnel
( personnel_ID     NUMBER(6),
  division_ID      NUMBER(6),
  CONSTRAINT personnel_ID_PK PRIMARY KEY (personnel_ID),
  CONSTRAINT division_ID_PK PRIMARY KEY (division_ID));
```

Assume there is no table already called PERSONNEL in the database. What will be the result of an attempt to execute the preceding SQL statement?

A. The statement will fail because you cannot create two primary key constraints on the table.

B. The statement will successfully create the table and the first primary key, but not the second.

C. The statement will successfully create a single table and one composite primary key consisting of two columns.

D. The statement will successfully create the table and two primary keys.

SELF TEST ANSWERS

Categorize the Main Database Objects

1. ☑ **A.** All database objects are either schema or non-schema objects, and a table falls under the category of schema objects.
   ☒ **B, C,** and **D** are incorrect. A table, which is a schema object, is not a non-schema object. A role is another form of a database object.

2. ☑ **A** and **C.** A sequence and an index are both schema objects, and are owned by a schema.
   ☒ **B** and **D** are incorrect. A password is not a database object. A role consists of one or more privileges that are assigned to a user object, and both the user and role objects are non-schema objects.

3. ☑ **A.** A CONSTRAINT is a rule that restricts what sort of data can be added to a table.
   ☒ **B, C,** and **D** are incorrect. You cannot attach a constraint to a synonym, sequence, or index object.

Create a Simple Table

4. ☑ **B, C,** and **D.** Underscores are acceptable characters in any database table name, provided the first character is not an underscore. Quotation marks, when used, enable any character to be used throughout the name, including spaces, although all future references to the name will be case sensitive and require quotation marks. Finally, mixed case can be used to create a table name, although when created, the table name will be stored and treated as uppercase. All future references to the name may continue to be in any case—SQL will perform the necessary case conversion so that the table name, on a practical level, is treated as though it is case insensitive, even though it is stored internally in uppercase.
   ☒ **A** is incorrect. The first character in any database object name must be a letter; it cannot be a number or special character—unless the name is enclosed in double quotation marks, which this was not.

5. ☑ **A, B,** and **D.** The database objects TABLE, VIEW, and SEQUENCE can each be created directly with a CREATE reserved word to form a complete SQL statement.
   ☒ **C** is incorrect. A CONSTRAINT is not created directly with a CREATE CONSTRAINT statement, but instead is created indirectly as a clause within the CREATE TABLE and ALTER TABLE statements.

6. ☑ **E.** The table name may include the "#" character, as long as it isn't the first character in the table name. An INDEX in the same schema is allowed to have the same name since the INDEX is inside its own namespace within the schema, separate from the namespace in which the TABLE will be created.

☒ **A, B, C,** and **D** are incorrect. The question is not flawed—the hash mark (#) is an acceptable character in an object name anywhere from the second character position through to the final character. You are allowed to have a VIEW and a CONSTRAINT with the same names within a single schema, since CONSTRAINTS are contained within their own unique namespace in each schema.

7. ☑ **C.** TABLE and VIEW objects are schema objects, and since we only have one schema in the database, then both have to be owned by the only schema in the database. But the USER object is a non-schema object—in fact, it's the definition of the schema itself. It does not own itself, and it exists at the database level.

☒ **A, B,** and **D** are incorrect.

8. ☑ **D.** Both ROLES and USERS exist at the database level and share the same namespace.

☒ **A, B,** and **C** are incorrect. It doesn't matter that a ROLE is created from within a schema's user account, it's still a non-schema object and exists in the same namespace. CONSTRAINTS and TABLES both have their namespaces within a schema.

Review the Table Structure

9. ☑ **A.** DESC, or DESCRIBE, presents a display showing a table's columns, and the datatypes of those columns.

☒ **B, C,** and **D** are incorrect. The DESC command doesn't show data, the creator, or a text description of the table. All of that information is available through other means, but not the DESC command.

List the Data Types That Are Available for Columns

10. ☑ **B.** The VARCHAR2 datatype requires precision, for example: VARCHAR2(30).

☒ **A, C,** and **D** are incorrect. NUMBER and CHAR can be declared without precision. But VARCHAR2 cannot and the statement will fail.

11. ☑ **B.** The NUMBER datatype has a precision of 5 and a scale of 3. The scale indicates that three digits—but no more than three digits—to the right of the decimal point are allowed. The number is rounded off, and 5 is always rounded up.

☒ **A, C,** and **D** are incorrect.

Explain How Constraints Are Created at the Time of Table Creation

12. ☑ **B.** The primary key constraint performs two main jobs, one of which is to ensure that the column upon which it is applied is never allowed to be NULL. The other job is to ensure that any value added to that column is UNIQUE.

☒ **A, C,** and **D** are incorrect. The UNIQUE constraint allows for NULL values. There is no such thing as a REQUIRED constraint. There is a NOT NULL constraint that essentially does what a REQUIRED constraint might do, if one existed.

13. ☑ **D.** The syntax of the statement is fine. Both the table and the primary key constraint will be successfully created.

☒ **A, B,** and **C** are incorrect. It is perfectly acceptable to create a primary key in any form—single-column or composite—with the CHAR datatype. NUMBER is also fine with or without precision and/or scale. The "_PK" suffix is not required.

14. ☑ **A.** A statement is attempting to create two different primary key constraints, but a table may only have one primary key and no more.

☒ **B, C,** and **D** are incorrect. The syntax is not attempting a composite primary key, but rather two separate primary key constraints, and that is not allowed on any table. The entire statement will fail to execute.

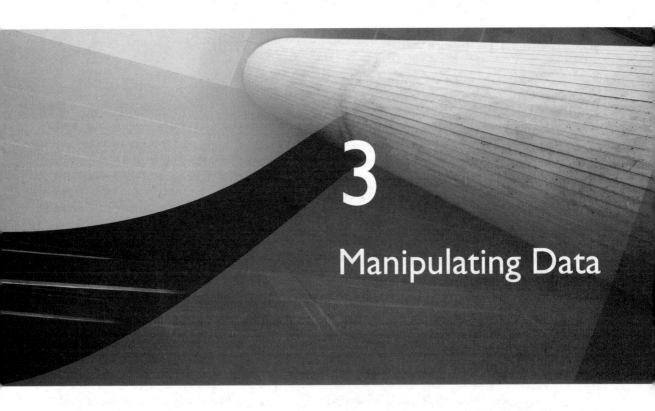

3

Manipulating Data

This chapter begins to look at that part of SQL known as Data Manipulation Language, or DML. We'll get some perspective by looking at DML and where it fits into the larger context of SQL as a whole. Then we'll review DML statements and look at some specific examples and usages of DML statements, and review some supplemental statements that are used to control transactions involving DML.

CERTIFICATION OBJECTIVE 3.01

Describe Each Data Manipulation Language (DML) Statement

In the last chapter, we looked at some DDL statements. Before we look at DML statements in detail, let's put both DDL and DML in context with the rest of the set of the types of SQL statements. Then we'll introduce the DML statements of interest to the exam.

SQL Statement Overview

All SQL statements are categorized into one of six different types of statements. The two largest and most significant "types" are *Data Definition Language (DDL)* and *Data Manipulation Language (DML)*.

The six types of SQL statements in Oracle SQL are shown in Table 3-1. As you can see in the table, many SQL statements are ignored by the exam. Naturally we will only concern ourselves with the exam, so in this book we'll only look at three types of SQL statements: DDL, DML, and TCL.

TABLE 3-1		Six Types of SQL Statements in Oracle SQL		

#	Abbrev.	Type of SQL Statement	SQL Statements and Reserved Words	
			Covered by the Exam	**Ignored by the Exam**
1	DDL	Data Definition Language	CREATE ALTER (1) DROP RENAME TRUNCATE GRANT REVOKE FLASHBACK PURGE COMMENT	ANALYZE AUDIT ASSOCIATE STATISTICS DISASSOCIATE NOAUDIT
2	DML	Data Manipulation Language	SELECT INSERT UPDATE DELETE MERGE	CALL LOCK TABLE EXPLAIN PLAN
3	TCL	Transaction Control Language	COMMIT ROLLBACK SAVEPOINT	SET TRANSACTION SET CONSTRAINT
4		Session Control Statements		ALTER SESSION SET ROLE
5		System Control Statements		ALTER SYSTEM
6		Embedded SQL Statements		Any DML, DDL, or TCL that is integrated into a 3GL.

(1) Except ALTER SYSTEM and ALTER SESSION, which are categorized under "System Control Statements" and "Session Control Statements", respectively.

Data Definition Language (DDL)

DDL refers to those SQL statements that are used to build database objects. Specifically, DDL statements are used to

- Create, alter, and drop tables and other database objects.
- Add comments on a particular object to be stored in the database and associated with that object.

- Issue privileges to users to perform various tasks in the database.
- Initiate performance analysis on objects using built-in tools.

The following section briefly describes DDL statements that are tested by the exam.

- **CREATE** Used to create tables, views, indexes, synonyms, and other objects in the database.
- **ALTER** Used to modify the structure, name, or some other attribute of an already existing object in the database. (Two exceptions are the uses of ALTER with the reserved words SESSION and SYSTEM. ALTER SESSION and ALTER SYSTEM are not technically considered DDL statements but fall under a different category. Neither is included on this exam.)
- **DROP** Used to remove a database object from the database that has already been created with the CREATE statement.
- **RENAME** Changes the name of an existing database object.
- **TRUNCATE** Removes all of the rows—i.e., data—from an existing table in the database. This is a special-purpose way to remove rows that serves as an alternative to the more commonly used DELETE statement.
- **GRANT** Provides "privileges", or rights, to users to perform various tasks in the database.
- **REVOKE** Removes privileges that have been issued with the GRANT statement.
- **FLASHBACK** Restores an earlier version of a table or database.
- **PURGE** Removes database objects from the recycle bin.
- **COMMENT** Adds comments to the data dictionary for database objects you have created.

Each DDL statement is rich with options and clauses. We've already looked at CREATE TABLE; we'll review others as we progress through the book.

Data Manipulation Language (DML)

DML refers to those statements in SQL that are used to work with data in the objects. DML statements are used to add, modify, and delete data in a database object, such as a table.

The following section briefly describes each DML statement that is tested by the exam.

- **SELECT**   Displays data contained within a database table or view.
- **INSERT**   Adds data to a database table.
- **UPDATE**   Modifies existing data in a table.
- **DELETE**   Removes existing data from a table.
- **MERGE**   Performs a combination of INSERT, UPDATE, and/or DELETE statements in one single statement. (MERGE is discussed in Chapter 15.)

The SELECT statement is rather involved and will get several chapters' worth of review. The other DML statements are reviewed in this chapter and in various sections that follow.

Transaction Control Language (TCL)

No discussion of DDL and DML would be complete without a word about *Transaction Control Language*, or *TCL*. TCL statements can be used to save or cancel changes made to a database with DML within a given session.

There are three TCL statements:

- **COMMIT**   Saves data to the database.
- **ROLLBACK**   Restores the database to an earlier state.
- **SAVEPOINT**   Marks a point in a session to which future ROLLBACKS may optionally be issued.

These have been brief summaries; each statement will be thoroughly reviewed in greater detail as we progress through the book.

on the **!** job   *Certain SQL keywords, such as CREATE, are not really a "command" or "statement" by themselves but become a command when combined with other reserved words, as in CREATE TABLE or CREATE SEQUENCE, which are commands or statements. In practice, CREATE may be called a "statement" or "command" by professionals in the field, and even by Oracle Corporation in various forms of documentation. But technically there is a difference. However, this isn't an issue on the exam. Similarly, the terms "command" and "statement" tend to be used interchangeably by Oracle's documentation. If you were to do some searches in the SQL Language Reference Manual, you'll find plenty of examples of SQL statements being referred to as commands. Either is fine. And none of these issues are of concern on the exam.*

DML Statement Descriptions

DML statements are those statements that work with existing database objects to manipulate data.

The DML statements that are of primary importance to the exam are as follows:

- **INSERT**   Add one or more rows of values to a table.
- **UPDATE**   Modify data within one or more existing rows of data in a table.
- **DELETE**   Remove one or more rows of data from a table.
- **SELECT**   Display one or more rows of data from a table.
- **MERGE**   A combination of INSERT, UPDATE, and/or DELETE.

In addition to these DML statements, there are three additional SQL statements that are important for working with DML. These statements are not part of DML but instead are categorized as TCL. These statements are specifically identified by Oracle within the certification objectives for DML, so we'll discuss them in this chapter. These are the statements we need to study:

- **COMMIT**   Save a set of DML modifications performed in the current database session.
- **ROLLBACK**   Undo a set of DML modifications performed during the current database session.
- **SAVEPOINT**   Mark a position within a series of SQL statements in order to reserve the right to perform a selective ROLLBACK of segments of statements later, rather than performing an all-or-nothing ROLLBACK.

CERTIFICATION OBJECTIVE 3.02

Insert Rows into a Table

The SQL statement to add rows to a table is the INSERT statement. The INSERT statement is often used to add one row at a time, but it may also be used to add multiple rows at once by drawing them from elsewhere in the database and adding them to the target table with a single INSERT statement. INSERT may use expressions within its syntax.

INSERT is used to add rows into a TABLE object. It can also be used to add rows to certain VIEW objects, but as we'll see, a VIEW is simply a filter onto one or more tables, so ultimately—INSERT is still adding rows to TABLE objects.

Default Column List

Let's look at an example of an INSERT statement. We're going to add a row to the CRUISES table. First, let's describe the CRUISES table so that we can see the columns—we'll need to know the names and datatypes of those columns so we can build our INSERT statement (see Figure 3-1).

Here's an example of an INSERT statement you could use on this table (line numbers added):

```
01   INSERT INTO CRUISES
02     (CRUISE_ID, CRUISE_TYPE_ID, CRUISE_NAME,
03      CAPTAIN_ID, START_DATE, END_DATE,
04      STATUS)
05   VALUES
06     (1, 1, 'Day At Sea',
07      101, '02-JAN-10', '09-JAN-10',
08      'Sched');
```

FIGURE 3-1

The CRUISES
table

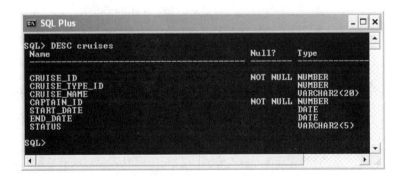

As with all SQL statements, the INSERT statement can be on a single line, or it can span multiple lines. The choice doesn't matter as far as the syntax is concerned. We separated the components of the preceding statement in order to discuss it more easily here. Let's analyze the syntax for this example of INSERT:

- **Line 1**   The reserved words INSERT and INTO, followed by the name of the target table.
- **Lines 2–4**   Within a set of parentheses, a list of the table's columns in no particular order. The order doesn't need to match the order of columns in the table's structure as shown with the DESC command, nor does it need to include all of the table's columns, as long as we provide for all of the "required" columns, i.e., those with a NOT NULL constraint or something comparable (like the PRIMARY KEY constraint).
- **Line 5**   The reserved word VALUES.
- **Lines 6–8**   Within a set of parentheses, a series of expressions, in a very specific order—that is, in the same order as the columns are listed in lines 2–4, for this is how the data will be inserted—the first value in this list will be placed in the first column identified on line 2, and the second value identified in line 6 will be inserted into the second column identified in line 2, etc.

When the INSERT statement is submitted for execution, the following steps will be performed before the statement returns any results:

- The existence and validity of the table in line 1 will be confirmed.
- The existence and validity of the columns in lines 2–4 will be confirmed.
- The expressions in lines 6–8 will be evaluated.
- The datatypes of the expressions in lines 6–8 will be compared against the datatypes of the associated columns and evaluated for compatibility.
- The values of the expressions in lines 6–8 will be applied to any constraints that might exist in the table.

If all requirements for data entry to the target table are satisfied, and the INSERT statement is determined to be valid, then the statement will execute, and the row will be inserted into the table.

In this example, the columns in our INSERT statement (lines 2–4) just happen to line up exactly with the sequence of the columns in the table's structure. In that sort of situation, the column list at the beginning of the INSERT statement is not required. In other words, we could have omitted lines 2–4 in that example. Let's do that—here is a valid alternative to the INSERT statement we just reviewed:

```
01   INSERT INTO CRUISES
02   VALUES
03     (1, 1, 'Day At Sea',
04       101, '02-JAN-10', '09-JAN-10',
05       'Sched');
```

This example will produce the same result, because the expressions in line 3 through line 5 just happen to coincide in number (there are seven) and datatype with the columns in the CRUISES table structure, in order, as we saw in Figure 3-1. If that structure changes, the statement above may fail. For example, if a new column is added to CRUISES, the above example will fail, whereas the prior INSERT example—which names the columns—will probably continue functioning correctly.

As before, all datatypes and constraints must be honored with the INSERT.

If you're following along at home with your own database, note that if you've already entered the earlier version of this particular INSERT statement, this variation will not work because the value for CRUISE_ID is repeated here; since CRUISE_ID is declared as a PRIMARY KEY in the CRUISES table, the duplicate value of "1" will not be accepted in this second INSERT statement, since a "1" already exists from the earlier INSERT. But that aside—the syntax of this INSERT statement is just as valid as the first example we looked at.

So now you're asking yourself—which is better? Identifying the column list by name, or depending on the default approach? The answer is: it depends on the situation. Generally speaking, in my experience, I tend to prefer the method by which I name each column specifically, and not depend on the default. There are several advantages to this approach. One: the table structure might change over time—for example, if the table is dropped and recreated in some sort of future upgrade or maintenance effort, the columns could end up in a different sequence. That could trigger a syntax error with the default INSERT, or it could result in something worse—no syntax error, but a column mismatch where the datatypes happen to line up and the INSERT statement works—technically—but isn't putting the data in the columns you originally intended.

For example, consider the SQL statements shown in Figure 3-2. Here we see a table called TEST_SCORES and an INSERT statement for it. Note that the INSERT uses the default column list. Nothing wrong with that—technically. But now look at Figure 3-3. Notice that the TEST_SCORES columns are in a different order. Yet the same INSERT statement—with the syntax that does not list columns by name—successfully executes. Why? Because SQL sees only the datatypes of the list of values in the INSERT statement. In this case, both values being inserted are numeric literals, and numeric literals are acceptable in either column. So what is the intent here? Is 100 the value for the TEST_SCORE_ID and 85 is the value for the SCORE? Or is it the other way around? The point is that you cannot tell in this particular variation of INSERT statement syntax.

By always enumerating the list of columns, you can avoid any confusion. However, there's one issue to keep in mind: if, in the future, the table into which you are inserting values might be modified in such a way that new columns are added to it, then you'll need to remember to revisit INSERT statements like this and edit them if necessary. If you've enumerated a column list, and the table is later altered with the addition of new columns, your old INSERT statement will continue to function normally; it just won't provide data for the new columns—assuming, of course, that no constraints have been applied to the new columns that would require data. But in all the professional situations I've encountered, these types of issues are less problematic and easier to maintain than the problem of datatype matches that support illogical data entry. The moral of this story: always identify your column names in an INSERT statement.

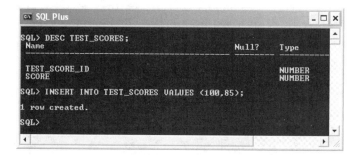

FIGURE 3-2

The TEST_
SCORES table

FIGURE 3-3

The TEST_
SCORES table
with a different
structure

Enumerated Column List

The INSERT syntax we just reviewed assigns values to each column in the table. It accomplishes that feat by first listing, by name, each column in the table, in the same order in which the columns appear in the table's structure. But you are not required to list the columns in order. For example:

```
01   INSERT INTO CRUISES
02     (CRUISE_ID, CRUISE_NAME,
03      STATUS, CAPTAIN_ID, START_DATE, END_DATE)
04   VALUES
05     (2, 'Bermuda and Back',
06      'Done', 101, '07-APR-08', '14-APR-08');
```

This is also a valid INSERT statement. Notice how in lines 2–3 we list the columns in a different order from the table structure. This is fine, so long as the list of expressions to be inserted (lines 5 and 6) are in the order as the column list (lines 2 and 3). And they are:

```
CRUISE_ID   = 2
CRUISE_NAME = 'Bermuda and Back'
STATUS      = 'Done'
CAPTAIN_ID  = 101
START_DATE  = '07-APR-08'
END_DATE    = '14-APR-08'
```

Another change with this INSERT is that we do not include every column in the table. We ignore the column CRUISE_TYPE_ID. That's also fine, provided that all required columns are included, and in this particular table, we have two columns that are NOT NULL, and both are included in this INSERT statement.

Datatype Conversion

When the INSERT statement is evaluated for syntactical correctness, the datatypes of the values listed in lines 6–7 will be compared to the datatypes of the columns identified in lines 2–3. The datatypes must be compatible. But the operative word here is "compatible", not identical. For example, this would actually work:

```
01   INSERT INTO CRUISES   (CRUISE_ID, CAPTAIN_ID)
02   VALUES (2, '101');
```

Notice that the 101 value in line 2 is in quotation marks, identifying that value as a string literal. Normally that is used for text, and in this case the text is being assigned to the column CAPTAIN_ID, which only accepts numeric data. But no error message occurs, and this INSERT will execute. The reason: Oracle SQL is smart enough to figure out that the text contained within the literal value is all numeric data anyway, and will process the INSERT statement correctly. Naturally you don't want to depend on this in serious software application design when you don't have to, but it's an important feature to be aware of.

This feature is known in Oracle documentation as "implicit datatype conversion". Oracle Corporation formally advises that software developers avoid depending on implicit datatype conversion in serious application development, relying instead on explicit datatype conversion, which we'll look at when we review SQL conversion functions such as TO_CHAR, TO_NUMBER, and TO_DATE.

The rule of thumb is that wherever it makes sense, Oracle SQL will perform an implicit datatype conversion if at all possible. Naturally it cannot convert something like 'Montana' to a DATE datatype. But if you try to enter a numeric value such as 2011 into a datatype such as VARCHAR2, an implicit datatype conversion will convert the value of 2011 to '2011' and the statement will succeed.

INSERT and Constraints

If we happen to include data that violates a constraint, then we might get a run-time error. This is important: violation of a constraint is not a syntax error, but a run-time error. For example, let's say we've created a table with the following CREATE TABLE statement:

```
CREATE TABLE CRUISES
(CRUISE_ID NUMBER,
 CRUISE_NAME VARCHAR2(30),
 START_DATE DATE,
 END_DATE   DATE,
 CONSTRAINT CRUISE_ID_PK PRIMARY KEY (CRUISE_ID),
 CONSTRAINT CRUISE_NAME_CK CHECK
            (CRUISE_NAME IN ('Hawaii','Bahamas','Bermuda',
                             'Mexico','Day at Sea')
            )
);
```

This table includes a CHECK constraint that will limit any values for the CRUISE_NAME to one of the listed strings: 'Hawaii', 'Bahamas', 'Bermuda', 'Mexico', or 'Day at Sea'. Anything else will be rejected.

Next, let's peek ahead a little bit and create a SEQUENCE object, like this:

```
CREATE SEQUENCE SEQ_CRUISE_ID;
```

This CREATE SEQUENCE statement creates an object that will dispense individual values, and we'll use it to generate primary key values for our INSERT statements.

Next, let's use that SEQUENCE object and issue the following INSERT statement (line numbers added):

```
01   INSERT INTO CRUISES
02      (CRUISE_ID, CRUISE_NAME)
03   VALUES
04      (SEQ_CRUISE_ID.NEXTVAL, 'Hawaii');
```

This INSERT statement adds a single row to the CRUISES table. The new row consists of two values. In line 4, the first value calls on the newly created SEQUENCE object and asks for the next available value from the sequence, indicated with the reserved word NEXTVAL. Given that our sequence is brand new, and it was created with all the default settings and has never been used before, then the next available value will be 1. The second value we're inserting here is the literal string 'Hawaii', which is syntactically correct, and it also satisfies the constraint object attached to the CRUISE_NAME column in the CREATE TABLE statement.

However, had we violated the constraint, the INSERT could be syntactically correct but logically incorrect. For example, consider this variation on the same INSERT statement:

```
01   INSERT INTO CRUISES
02      (CRUISE_ID, CRUISE_NAME)
03   VALUES
04      (SEQ_CRUISE_ID.NEXTVAL, 'Hawaii and Back');
```

In this example, the string 'Hawaii and Back' violates the CHECK constraint we created for the CRUISES table. Therefore, even though this version of the INSERT statement is syntactically correct, it will fail on execution and the CHECK constraint will reject the attempt to enter this row. See Figure 3-4 for a sample of the execution error resulting from this INSERT statement—and while we're at it, let's show this from the SQL Developer tool instead of the SQL*Plus tool that we've been using up to now.

Note the "ORA-02290" run-time error message. The CHECK constraint is identified, and we see in this display that we're logged in to the "EFCODD_TEST" user account.

We're far from done with INSERT, and we will address more advanced concepts of INSERT in later chapters, when we look at subqueries (Chapter 9) and large data sets (Chapter 15). But first, let's look at the rest of the major DML statements.

FIGURE 3-4

Execution error
for the INSERT
statement

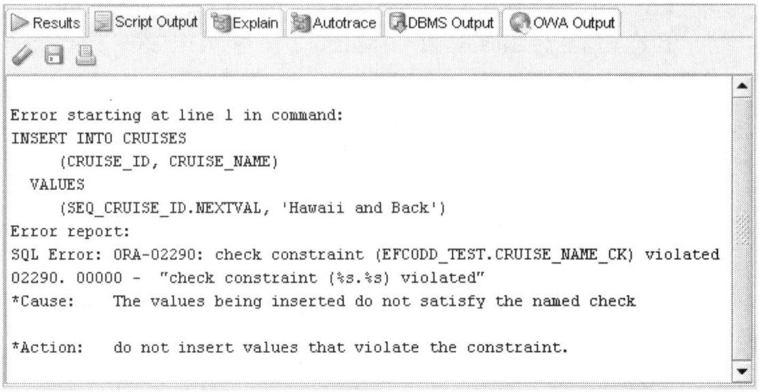

```
Results  Script Output  Explain  Autotrace  DBMS Output  OWA Output

Error starting at line 1 in command:
INSERT INTO CRUISES
      (CRUISE_ID, CRUISE_NAME)
  VALUES
      (SEQ_CRUISE_ID.NEXTVAL, 'Hawaii and Back')
Error report:
SQL Error: ORA-02290: check constraint (EFCODD_TEST.CRUISE_NAME_CK) violated
02290. 00000 -  "check constraint (%s.%s) violated"
*Cause:    The values being inserted do not satisfy the named check

*Action:   do not insert values that violate the constraint.
```

CERTIFICATION OBJECTIVE 3.03

Update Rows in a Table

The UPDATE statement is a DML statement that is used to modify existing data in the database. It operates on one table at a time. It is used to modify one or more columns of data and can be used to change all the rows in a table, or it can be used to change data in only selected rows.

As with INSERT, the UPDATE statement can also work with VIEW objects, and as with INSERT, we'll see later that VIEW objects simply represent one or more TABLE objects, so that any UPDATE that operates on a VIEW is ultimately changing data in TABLE objects.

Let's look at an example of UPDATE.

```
01  UPDATE CRUISES
02    SET  CRUISE_NAME = 'Bahamas',
03         START_DATE  = '01-DEC-11'
04  WHERE  CRUISE_ID = 1;
```

This UPDATE will look for any and all existing rows in the CRUISES table where the value for CRUISE_ID equals 1. For all of those rows, it will change the value for CRUISE_NAME to 'Bahamas', and change the value for START_DATE to '01-DEC-11'.

When we say that it will "change" those values, this example of UPDATE doesn't care if the column in question is already populated with data, or if the existing value is NULL. Either way, UPDATE will overwrite whatever else may or may not already be there, and place the new value in the column.

Also—this particular example is changing all the rows where the CRUISE_ID value is 1, but remember—we specifically created the CRUISES table so that its CRUISE_ID column has a PRIMARY KEY constraint applied to it. In other words—in this example there will only be one row with a CRUISE_ID of 1. But there's nothing inherent in the UPDATE statement itself that makes this restriction; that is solely the result of the constraint. In other words, if all you saw was this UPDATE statement, you would have to say that "all" rows with a value of 1 in the CRUISE_ID column will be updated. This is a major reason why we create PRIMARY KEY constraints—to help UPDATE statements like this identify a single row within a table.

Let's look a little more closely at the syntax of this UPDATE statement.

- **Line 1**   The reserved word UPDATE, followed by the name of the target table
- **Lines 2–3**   One occurrence of the reserved word SET, followed by a series of one or more expressions consisting of four elements:
  - A column name
  - The assignment operator "="
  - An expression resulting in a value appropriate for the column's datatype
  - Either a comma, if additional expressions are to follow—or nothing, if the list of expressions is completed
- **Line 4**   An optional WHERE clause, defining a condition to identify rows in the table

Now that we've reviewed our sample UPDATE in detail, let's observe a few important issues about the UPDATE statement in general:

- The series of columns enumerated in the SET clause does not need to refer to the table's columns in any particular order.
- The SET clause does not need to reference all required columns—i.e., NOT NULL columns. Remember—UPDATE is not adding a row, but modifying existing data. The row is already in the table, so presumably the data within the row already honors all required constraints.
- Any column names that are not included in the UPDATE statement's SET clause will not be changed.

■ Any attempt by UPDATE to change data so that the result would be to cause the row to violate a constraint—will be rejected at execution.

■ The WHERE clause is not required. If it is omitted, the UPDATE will process each row in the table.

Expressions

The UPDATE statement can use expressions to assign values to any given column. Expressions may include literal values, valid column references, mathematical expressions, and SQL functions. Expressions are an involved topic and will be discussed in Chapter 4 when we look at the SELECT statement. For now, let's look at an example to get an idea of what can be done. Here's an UPDATE statement that uses expressions in the SET clause:

```
UPDATE COMPENSATION
   SET  SALARY = SALARY * 1.03,
        LAST_CHANGED_DATE = SYSDATE
 WHERE EMPLOYEE_NUMBER = 83;
```

The preceding statement is an UPDATE statement intended to change data in a table called COMPENSATION. The UPDATE statement will change data in any and all rows with a value of 83 in the EMPLOYEE_NUMBER column. There are two columns whose values are changed:

■ The SALARY column is changed to equal itself times 1.03. This has the effect of increasing its own value by 3 percent.

■ The LAST_CHANGED_DATE column is set to the value of SYSDATE. SYSDATE is a built-in SQL function that contains the current date and time according to the operating system wherever the database is installed.

We'll discuss expressions in full in Chapter 4. The point of this example is to demonstrate how expressions may be used within an UPDATE statement.

Constraints

If the UPDATE statement violates any constraint on a table, the entire UPDATE statement will be rejected, and none of the modifications will be accepted for any of the rows. In other words, if the UPDATE statement attempts to change any data in any column of any row in a table, and any one change results in any one constraint violation, then the entire UPDATE statement is rejected.

For example, review these SQL statements:

```
CREATE TABLE PROJECTS
(   PROJECT_ID    NUMBER PRIMARY KEY
 ,  PROJECT_NAME VARCHAR2(40)
 ,  COST          NUMBER
 ,  CONSTRAINT CK_COST CHECK (COST < 1000000));
INSERT INTO PROJECTS (PROJECT_ID, PROJECT_NAME, COST)
VALUES               (1,'Hull Cleaning', 340000);
INSERT INTO PROJECTS (PROJECT_ID, PROJECT_NAME, COST)
VALUES               (2,'Deck Resurfacing', 964000);
INSERT INTO PROJECTS (PROJECT_ID, PROJECT_NAME, COST)
VALUES               (3,'Lifeboat Inspection', 12000);
```

In this code, we create a table PROJECTS that includes a couple of constraints; one in particular is the CHECK constraint that limits any value in the COST column to numbers that are less than a million.

Now see Figure 3-5. Notice how we issue an UPDATE statement in which we increase the cost of each project by 20 percent. This will cause the row identified by PROJECT_ID 2 to bump up over our limitation on the COST column. The result: the entire UPDATE statement is rejected.

However, see Figure 3-6: here we execute a slight variation of that UPDATE statement where we avoid the problem row, and the UPDATE statement executes.

FIGURE 3-5

UPDATE
statement:
one constraint
violation rejects
the entire
statement.

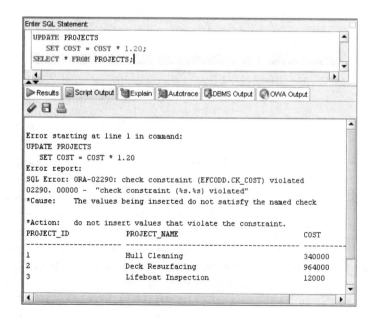

UPDATE
statement: no
constraints
violated

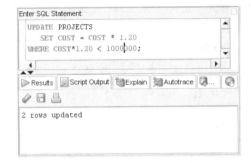

```
Enter SQL Statement:
  UPDATE PROJECTS
     SET COST = COST * 1.20
  WHERE COST*1.20 < 1000000;
```

Results | Script Output | Explain | Autotrace

```
2 rows updated
```

exam

watch

Don't get the UPDATE
statement's SET clause mixed up with the
"set" operators of UNION, INTERSECT,
and MINUS. Those are two completely

separate issues and both are addressed on
the exam. You'll study the "set" operators in
Chapter 12.

The WHERE Clause

The UPDATE statement's WHERE clause is arguably its most powerful and
important feature. WHERE determines which of the existing rows in the table will
be modified by the SET clause. The WHERE clause is not unique to the UPDATE
statement; it's also used for similar purposes with DELETE and SELECT. We'll
review WHERE in more detail in the chapter on the SELECT statement.

on the Job

*A word about terminology: UPDATE can only be used to modify existing rows
in a table. On a practical level, end users may speak in terms of "adding"
data to a table when all they really mean is that they wish to set a value to
a column within an existing row. In other words, when you are speaking with
non-technical users and the subject of "adding" data to a table is discussed,
be aware that this doesn't necessarily mean you'll be using the INSERT
statement—an UPDATE may actually be in order. Similarly, you can use
UPDATE to "remove" values from the table by setting a given row's column
to NULL. But you aren't necessarily removing a row in that situation—just
modifying the contents of it. To remove a row, you need the DELETE statement.*

CERTIFICATION OBJECTIVE 3.04

Delete Rows from a Table

The DELETE statement is used to remove rows from tables in the database. Rows are identified by the WHERE clause of DELETE. If WHERE is omitted, DELETE removes all the rows from the table.

When DELETE identifies a row with the WHERE clause, it removes the entire row from the table, not just an individual data element from within a row. If your goal is to remove a single value from within an existing row, while retaining the row in the table, then you don't use DELETE—you use UPDATE to identify the row and set the desired value to NULL.

The DELETE clause is very simple. Here's an example:

```
01  DELETE FROM PROJECT_LISTING
02  WHERE   CONSTRUCTION_ID = 12;
```

This sample deletes any and all rows in the PROJECT_LISTING table where a column called CONSTRUCTION_ID contains a value of 12. All rows that contain a 12 in the CONSTRUCTION_ID column will be deleted from the table.

Let's look at this sample statement:

- **Line 1** The required reserved word DELETE, followed by the optional reserved word FROM, followed by the required name of the target table
- **Line 2** An optional WHERE clause

As we just said, the reserved word FROM is optional. In other words, this variation of the preceding DELETE statement is also valid:

```
01  DELETE PROJECT_LISTING
02  WHERE   CONSTRUCTION_ID = 12;
```

This DELETE statement performs the same function without the reserved word FROM.

The WHERE clause for DELETE performs the same function as the WHERE clause in the UPDATE statement and in the SELECT statement. It is very powerful, and there's a lot to it. We'll look at it in more detail when we discuss SELECT and throughout other chapters in the book.

One thing to note, however—if you omit the WHERE clause, you'll delete every row in the table.

CERTIFICATION OBJECTIVE 3.05

Control Transactions

So far in this chapter, we've looked at the SQL statements INSERT, UPDATE, and DELETE. Those three statements, along with SELECT, form a set of SQL statements known as Data Manipulation Language, or DML.

There are other types of SQL statement, but one type in particular is of special importance to DML. As mentioned earlier in the chapter, that type is known as Transaction Control Language, or TCL. These statements are important to any SQL session in which you use DML statements, as TCL statements provide the functionality to save or undo the changes made with DML statements.

There are three TCL statements we'll look at in this section: COMMIT, ROLLBACK, and SAVEPOINT.

- **COMMIT**   Saves changes to the database since the session began, or since the most recent commit event in the session, whichever is more recent.
- **ROLLBACK**   Undoes changes to the database back to the last "commit" point in the session.
- **SAVEPOINT**   Provides an optional "commit" marker in a session, in order to empower future "commit" or "rollback" actions by providing one or more optional points at which you may—or may not—undo changes.

Let's look at each statement in more detail.

COMMIT

One reason that women love men who are Oracle professionals: we're not afraid to "commit". The SQL statement COMMIT is used to save changes made to any tables that have been modified by the DML statements INSERT, UPDATE, and DELETE. In other words, COMMIT makes changes to the database permanent, and once committed, those changes can no longer be undone with a ROLLBACK statement. That isn't to say that the data cannot be changed back with additional DML statements; of course it can. But before a COMMIT is executed, changes to the database can be undone with a ROLLBACK statement. After the COMMIT, however, that option no longer exists.

A series of SQL statements is considered a "transaction" by SQL and is treated as one unit. The changes you make within a transaction are not made permanent until they are committed. A commit event completes a transaction.

There are two kinds of commit events:

- An explicit commit, which occurs when the COMMIT statement is executed
- An implicit commit, which occurs automatically when certain database events occur

Until a commit event of either type occurs, no changes that may have been performed to tables in the database are made permanent, and all changes have the potential for being undone.

Explicit commits occur when the COMMIT statement is executed. Implicit commits occur without the COMMIT statement but instead occur when certain types of database events occur. Let's discuss both situations.

Explicit Commit

An explicit commit occurs whenever the COMMIT statement is executed. The syntax of COMMIT is simple:

```
COMMIT;
```

The COMMIT statement has a few parameters that are not required for the exam. One worth noting, however, is the optional keyword WORK, as in

```
COMMIT WORK;
```

The WORK keyword is included for compliance with ANSI standard SQL, but it is not required in Oracle SQL.

To understand how COMMIT works, consider the following series of SQL statements:

```
01   INSERT INTO POSITIONS (POSITION_ID, POSITION_NAME)
02                 VALUES (100, 'Manager');
03   SELECT POSITION_ID, POSITION_NAME
04     FROM POSITIONS;
05   COMMIT;
```

In this series of statements, the change to the table made by the INSERT statement is made permanent by the COMMIT statement. Without it, the INSERT changes could be undone with a ROLLBACK statement.

Implicit Commit

An implicit commit occurs when certain events take place in the database. Those events include

- Immediately before and immediately after an attempt to execute any DDL statement, such as CREATE, ALTER, DROP, GRANT, or REVOKE. Note: even if the DDL statement fails with an execution error (as opposed to a syntax error), the "before" implicit commit is executed and takes effect.

- A normal exit from most of Oracle's utilities and tools, such as SQL*Plus or SQL Developer. (One exception: Oracle's precompilers, which do not perform an implicit commit upon exit but instead perform a rollback.)

When these events take place, an implicit commit is automatically executed—meaning that all uncommitted changes become permanent in the same way as they would if you had executed the COMMIT statement.

Here's an example:

```
UPDATE SHIPS SET HOME_PORT_ID = 12 WHERE SHIP_ID = 31;
ALTER TABLE PORTS ADD AUTHORITY_NOTE VARCHAR2(75);
```

In this example, the change performed with the UPDATE statement has become permanent. Why? Because ALTER TABLE is a DDL statement and carries with it an implicit commit. As far as the SHIPS table is concerned, this would have an equivalent impact:

```
UPDATE SHIPS SET HOME_PORT_ID = 12 WHERE SHIP_ID = 31;
COMMIT;
```

In both examples, the UPDATE statement is committed. The first example results in an implicit commit. The second example—above—results in an explicit commit. From the perspective of the SHIPS table, the ultimate effect is the same—an ALTER TABLE command or a COMMIT command both have the end result of issuing a commit event on the changes involved with the UPDATE statement, and with any previous statements that may have not yet been committed.

COMMIT and Other Users

The COMMIT statement is very important when multiple users are logged in simultaneously. In a typical scenario, a set of database tables will exist and be "owned" by a given user for the benefit of other users throughout the database. Those other users, as we'll see later, must be granted "privileges" to get access to those tables. Those privileges can range from reading, modifying, and deleting data, but for the purpose of our discussion here, we want to look at how COMMIT changes the appearance of the data.

Let's say that one user account owns a schema that includes several tables, and that all users have been granted privileges to see (SELECT) data from these tables, and that only the owning user account retains the privilege of modifying any data in those tables. If that owning user then proceeds to perform a series of DML statements, those changes will be entirely visible to that owning user, but not to any of the other users with read privileges on the tables—until a commit event occurs. Unless the data is committed, the other users will not see the changes. The owning user may perform a large series of INSERT, UPDATE, and DELETE statements, and even print reports and snapshot screen displays showing the results of the modifications, performing SELECT statements to do it—but unless and until a commit event occurs, nobody else in the database, regardless of whatever privileges they may have, will be capable of seeing the changed data. Only after some sort of commit event occurs—either explicit or implicit—do the changes become "permanent", as Oracle likes to say, and therefore visible to the full user population.

Now, let's look at a variation of this scenario. Look at Figure 3-7. In this scenario, USER_1 owns a table SHIPS, and has granted UPDATE privileges to USER_2. This means that USER_2, who does not own the SHIPS table, has the right to issue UPDATE statements and change that data. So USER_2 issues an UPDATE statement on SHIPS—but does not commit the changes. The result: If USER_3 has SELECT privileges and tries to query the SHIPS table owned by USER_1, the changes made by USER_2 are not visible to anyone other than USER_2. USER_3, for example, cannot see the changed data. In this example, the value for CAPTAIN_ID is 0, and USER_2 issues a change to that value and updates it to 7. But USER_3 does not yet see the change, since it hasn't been committed to the database. For that matter, nobody sees the change—other than USER_2. Not even the table owner, USER_1, will see USER_2's change until USER_2 causes a commit event to occur.

FIGURE 3-7

Uncommitted
change

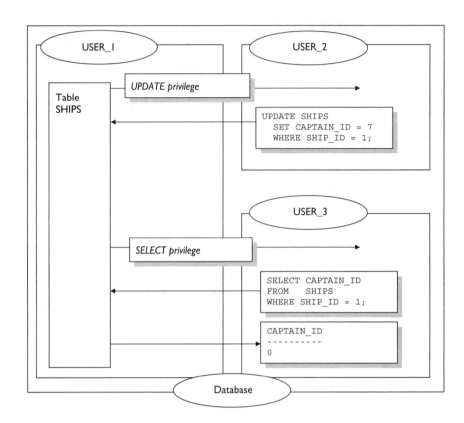

Next, look at Figure 3-8. Here, USER_2 has issued a COMMIT statement to create an explicit commit event. The result: when USER_3 queries the SHIPS table, the change issued by USER_2 is visible.

In this way, changes made prior to any commit event are in a sort of staging area, where the user can work in what is almost a "draft" mode. However, any commit event—explicit or implicit—will make changes permanent and expose the new data to the user population at large.

ROLLBACK

The ROLLBACK statement is somewhat equivalent to the "undo" function common to many software applications. ROLLBACK undoes any changes to the database that have been performed within a given session by the user who issues the ROLLBACK. It does not remove any changes that have already been committed.

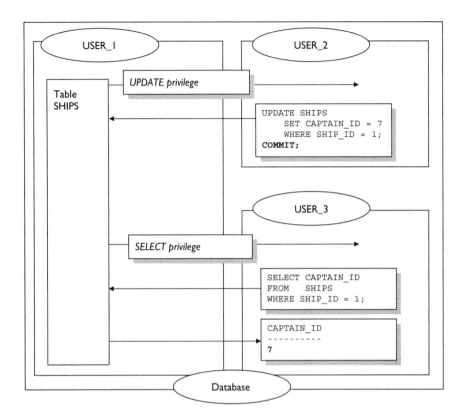

FIGURE 3-8

Committed
change

Also, if other users have committed any changes during their own respective
sessions, those changes are unaffected—the only changes that are rolled back are
those changes issued by the user performing the rollback.

Here's an example:

```
COMMIT;
INSERT INTO PORTS (PORT_ID, PORT_NAME) VALUES (701, 'Chicago');
DELETE FROM SHIPS;
ROLLBACK;
```

In this example, one INSERT statement and one DELETE statement are issued.
The results: we add one row to the PORTS table and delete all of the rows in the
SHIPS table.

But then we issue a ROLLBACK statement, and both changes are eliminated. It
is as if those two DML statements never happened. The PORTS and SHIPS tables
are both restored to their original condition at the time of the last COMMIT event.

Furthermore, since none of the DML statements were ever committed, no users saw the changes—other than, of course, the one who issued the statements.

One aspect that's interesting about this series of statements is that the changes performed by uncommitted DML statements are visible to the issuing user until they are rolled back. For example, see Figure 3-9. The figure shows the following series of steps:

- An explicit COMMIT statement
- A SELECT to demonstrate the data within the SHIPS table
- An UPDATE to change data in the SHIPS table
- The same SELECT statement to demonstrate the changed data
- A ROLLBACK to remove the effects of the UPDATE statement
- The same SELECT statement yet again, showing that the SHIPS table's condition has been restored

At no time during this process did any other user see the effects of the UPDATE statement. The changes were visible only to the user issuing the statements.

FIGURE 3-9

Sample session with ROLLBACK

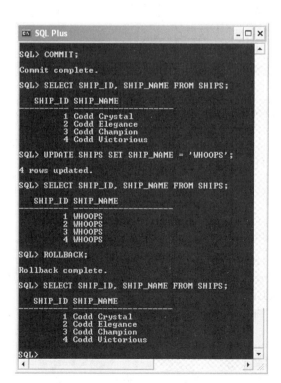

```
SQL> COMMIT;
Commit complete.
SQL> SELECT SHIP_ID, SHIP_NAME FROM SHIPS;

   SHIP_ID SHIP_NAME
---------- ---------------
         1 Codd Crystal
         2 Codd Elegance
         3 Codd Champion
         4 Codd Victorious
SQL> UPDATE SHIPS SET SHIP_NAME = 'WHOOPS';
4 rows updated.
SQL> SELECT SHIP_ID, SHIP_NAME FROM SHIPS;

   SHIP_ID SHIP_NAME
---------- ---------------
         1 WHOOPS
         2 WHOOPS
         3 WHOOPS
         4 WHOOPS
SQL> ROLLBACK;
Rollback complete.
SQL> SELECT SHIP_ID, SHIP_NAME FROM SHIPS;

   SHIP_ID SHIP_NAME
---------- ---------------
         1 Codd Crystal
         2 Codd Elegance
         3 Codd Champion
         4 Codd Victorious
SQL>
```

An implicit rollback occurs when a program abnormally terminates. In other words, uncommitted changes at the time of an abnormal termination of, for example, SQL*Plus or SQL Developer will not be committed to the database.

SAVEPOINT

The SAVEPOINT statement is part of TCL that supports the ROLLBACK and COMMIT statements. The SAVEPOINT statement establishes demarcation points within a transaction in order to empower any following COMMIT and/ or ROLLBACK statements to subdivide the points at which data can be saved or undone.

In other words, without SAVEPOINT, the COMMIT and ROLLBACK statements can only operate on a sort of all-or-nothing basis. Once a series of statements have been executed, the entire series can either be saved or undone in one large group. But if periodic SAVEPOINTs have been issued along the way, then the following COMMIT or ROLLBACK can be designed to save or restore data to those points in time marked by one or more SAVEPOINT statements, thus providing a finer level of detail at which the transaction can be controlled.

Here is an example of SAVEPOINT:

```
01   COMMIT;
02   UPDATE SHIPS SET HOME_PORT_ID = 21 WHERE SHIP_ID = 12;
03   SAVEPOINT SP_1;
04   UPDATE SHIPS SET HOME_PORT_ID = 22 WHERE SHIP_ID = 12;
05   ROLLBACK WORK TO SP_1;
06   COMMIT;
```

In this example, we start with an explicit COMMIT on line 1 and then issue an UPDATE statement. Then on line 3, we issue a SAVEPOINT statement and name it "SP_1". That's followed by a second UPDATE statement. Given that we elected to issue the SAVEPOINT, we have an option on line 5 that we haven't seen yet, and that is to "undo" the previous UPDATE statement, but only that second UPDATE, not the first, and we accomplish this by rolling back to the SAVEPOINT. Then we COMMIT our changes.

End result: the value in the SHIP_ID 12 row for HOME_PORT_ID is 21.

Here's another example; see if you can determine what the resulting value for HOME_PORT_ID will be here:

```
01   COMMIT;
02   UPDATE SHIPS SET HOME_PORT_ID = 21 WHERE SHIP_ID = 12;
03   SAVEPOINT MARK_01;
```

```
04   UPDATE SHIPS SET HOME_PORT_ID = 22 WHERE SHIP_ID = 12;
05   SAVEPOINT MARK_02;
06   UPDATE SHIPS SET HOME_PORT_ID = 23 WHERE SHIP_ID = 12;
07   ROLLBACK TO MARK_02;
08   COMMIT;
```

In this series of SQL statements, what is the resulting value of the SHIPS table's HOME_PORT_ID column where the SHIP_ID is equal to 12? The answer: 22. That is the value that is permanently saved to the database after the final COMMIT statement is executed.

In this example, we created two SAVEPOINTs—one we chose to name "MARK_01", and another we chose to name "MARK_02". We could have chosen any name for these savepoints that we wanted, according to the rules of naming database objects. By naming them, we reserve the right to selectively roll back to one or the other named SAVEPOINT. In this case, we chose to issue a ROLLBACK to the SAVEPOINT named "MARK_02". This statement effectively restores the condition of the entire database to the point where the SAVEPOINT was executed, which, in this example, is prior to the UPDATE statement on line 6. In other words, it's as if the line 6 UPDATE statement had never been executed.

The rules for using SAVEPOINT include the following:

- All SAVEPOINT statements must include a name. Behind the scenes, the SAVEPOINT name you create is associated with a "system change number", or SCN. This is what the SAVEPOINT is marking (you'll read more about SCN in Chapter 11);

- You should not duplicate SAVEPOINT names within a single transaction— and remember that a transaction is a series of one or more SQL statements that ends with a commit event. If you duplicate a name, know that you will not receive a syntax or execution error. Instead, the new SAVEPOINT will simply override the earlier SAVEPOINT, effectively erasing it.

- Once a commit event occurs—either an explicit or implicit commit event— all existing savepoints are erased from memory. Any references to them by future TCL statements will produce an error code.

Regarding that last point, here's an example of what we're talking about:

```
01   COMMIT;
02   UPDATE SHIPS SET HOME_PORT_ID = 21 WHERE SHIP_ID = 12;
03   SAVEPOINT MARK_01;
04   COMMIT;
05   ROLLBACK TO MARK_01;
```

In the preceding example, the ROLLBACK statement on line 5 is wrong for two reasons. One, it's logically irrelevant since there is nothing to roll back—the COMMIT on line 4 permanently saved everything, and no additional SQL statements have been executed by the time the ROLLBACK is executed on line 5. But in addition, the ROLLBACK makes a reference to a SAVEPOINT that does not exist, so it will produce an error. Without the named savepoint reference, the ROLLBACK would execute just fine and simply have no impact on the database. But with the reference to a named SAVEPOINT that no longer exists by the time the ROLLBACK is executed, the result of line 5 is an error code.

SAVEPOINT is particularly useful when managing a large series of transactions in which incremental validation must be required, wherein each individual validation requires a complex series of DML statements that might fail but can be programmatically corrected and validated before moving on to the next increment. A great example of this occurs in the financial world. When reconciling a set of financial books for a given organization, you might find it necessary to validate an account within a larger chart of accounts. During each individual account validation process, there may be a need to roll back some statements before making some changes and attempting validation again. Then, once a given account is validated, you might want to declare that account "temporarily authorized" and then move on to attempt to validate the next account. Furthermore, you may wish to defer a complete COMMIT until all accounts have been validated, and yet not necessarily have to undo everything when a particular account fails, and simply redo that one account before moving on. SAVEPOINT is perfect for this—as each individual account is validated, a SAVEPOINT can be established, so that subsequent account validation attempts that might fail can trigger a ROLLBACK without undoing the earlier accounts that were already successfully validated. Then, when all accounts are validated—and not before—a single COMMIT can declare the full set of validated rows to the database with a permanent save.

ROLLBACK Revisited

Now that we've seen SAVEPOINT, let's take another look at the syntax for ROLLBACK and see how it can be used to roll back to a particular named SAVEPOINT.

So far, we've seen this form of the ROLLBACK statement:

```
ROLLBACK;
```

If the single word ROLLBACK is executed by itself, it will ignore any SAVEPOINT statements that may have been executed since the most recent commit event, and undo any changes made by the user since the time of the last commit event.

However, if ROLLBACK is intended to undo any changes since a named SCN was established by SAVEPOINT, then it can name the SCN specifically. For example, if a SAVEPOINT statement established a demarcation with an SCN named "scn_01", like this:

```
SAVEPOINT scn_01;
```

. . . then a subsequent ROLLBACK can selectively undo changes to this point like this:

```
ROLLBACK WORK TO scn_01;
```

Let's look at the components of this form of the ROLLBACK statement:

- First, the reserved word ROLLBACK
- The optional reserved word WORK
- The required reserved word TO
- The name of an SCN as named by a SAVEPOINT statement that was executed after the most recent commit event

Note that the WORK reserved word is optional. WORK is part of the ANSI standard but is not required in the Oracle implementation.

If a ROLLBACK statement is executed that names a non-existent SAVEPOINT, SQL will display an error code warning that the rollback was attempting to roll back to a save point that was never established. The ROLLBACK will fail, and nothing will change regarding the state of the database. At that point, any outstanding changes will remain in an uncommitted state and could still be committed or rolled back.

CERTIFICATION SUMMARY

There are six types of SQL statements: DDL, DML, TCL, and three others. The exam concerns itself with the first three. DDL, or Data Definition Language, consists of those statements that are used to build objects in the database, change the structure of those objects, or remove those objects from the database. DDL also includes statements to issue or retract privileges for other users to work with database objects. DDL statements include those that start with the reserved words CREATE, ALTER, DROP, GRANT, and REVOKE. We say "start with" because of situations like CREATE, which by itself is only a "reserved word", but when combined with various database object names can become a statement. (A statement is also known as a command.) Examples include CREATE TABLE, CREATE INDEX, and others.

DML is Data Manipulation Language. DML consists of those SQL statements that are used to work with data that is contained within database objects, such as tables. DML statements include INSERT, UPDATE, DELETE, and SELECT.

The INSERT statement adds rows of data to a table. In its simplest form, it adds one row at a time. Its syntax starts with the reserved words INSERT INTO and the name of a single database table, followed by an optional column list, followed by the reserved word VALUES, followed by a list of values to be inserted into the table, enclosed in parentheses. The list of values is presented in the same sequential order as the column list, meaning that for the row that the INSERT statement is adding to the table, the first value in the list will be added to the first column in the column list, then the second value will be added to the second column, and so on. The datatypes of the values should be appropriate for the datatypes of the columns to which the values are being inserted. Any constraints that are not honored will cause the INSERT statement to be rejected at execution time. For example, if a column has a NOT NULL constraint, then the INSERT statement needs to provide a valid value for that particular column or else the entire effort to insert the entire row will fail. If the INSERT statement omits the column list, then the value list is assumed to be in the order of the columns according to the target table's structure, and each column is assumed to be accounted for in the values list.

The UPDATE statement is used to modify rows of data in the table. It includes the optional WHERE clause, which is used to identify which rows the UPDATE is intended to modify. If the WHERE clause is omitted, then the UPDATE statement will attempt to modify all rows in the target table. The UPDATE statement uses the reserved word SET, followed by pairs of column names and values. Each value can be substituted with an expression. Expressions may include literal values, any available table column, mathematical equations, and SQL functions (which we'll review in Chapter 6, among others).

The DELETE statement removes rows from a table. The optional WHERE clause can be used to identify which rows are to be deleted. However, if the WHERE clause is omitted, then every row in the table shall be deleted.

TCL, which is separate from DML, is used extensively within DML transactions in order to control whether data will be committed to the database—i.e., made "permanent" as Oracle documentation (and others) like to say. The TCL commands include COMMIT, ROLLBACK, and SAVEPOINT.

COMMIT makes permanent any outstanding changes to the table since the last commit event. Commits can occur explicitly or implicitly. Explicit commits occur with the simple SQL statement of COMMIT. Implicit commits occur when other events take place in the database, such as any DDL statement. A GRANT, for example, will automatically commit all changes to the database since the last COMMIT.

ROLLBACK can be used to "undo" a series of statements. ROLLBACK used by itself undoes any changes made by the user to the database since the most recent commit event, implicit or explicit, took place. But if a SAVEPOINT has been issued, then the ROLLBACK may optionally roll back to the SAVEPOINT.

SAVEPOINT names a "system change number", or SCN, and empowers future executions of the ROLLBACK statement to go back to earlier versions of the database incrementally.

TWO-MINUTE DRILL

Describe Each Data Manipulation Language (DML) Statement

❑ There are six types of SQL statements; three types are subjects on the exam.

❑ Data Definition Language is DDL.

❑ Data Manipulation Language is DML.

❑ Transaction Control Language is TCL.

❑ There are five DML statements of primary importance to the exam: INSERT, UPDATE, DELETE, SELECT, and MERGE.

❑ INSERT adds rows to a table.

❑ UPDATE modifies existing rows in a table.

❑ DELETE removes existing rows from a table.

❑ SELECT displays data from tables.

❑ MERGE is discussed further in Chapter 15.

Insert Rows into a Table

❑ The INSERT statement adds one or more rows to a table.

❑ The INSERT syntax we reviewed in this chapter consists of the reserved words INSERT INTO, the name of the table, the optional column list, the reserved word VALUES, and the list of values to be entered.

❑ If the INSERT statement is written so that the list of columns in the table is omitted, then the list of values must include one value for each column in the table, and the order of the columns in the table's structure will be how the list of values is expected to be sequenced within the INSERT statement.

❑ The list of values in the INSERT statement may include expressions.

❑ If any values violate any constraints applied to the target table, then an execution error will result—for example, all NOT NULL columns must be provided with some sort of value appropriate to the datatype of the column within the INSERT statement's list of values.

Update Rows in a Table

❑ The UPDATE statement modifies existing data in one or more rows within a database table.

❑ The UPDATE statement syntax starts with the reserved word UPDATE and the name of the target table, the reserved word SET, and then a series of assignment expressions in which the left side element is a table column, then the assignment operator (an equal sign), and then an expression that evaluates to a datatype appropriate for the target table's column identified on the left side of the equal sign, and finally an optional WHERE clause.

❑ If additional assignment expressions are required, each additional assignment expression is preceded by a comma.

❑ If the WHERE clause is omitted, then all the rows in the table are changed according to the series of SET values listed in the UPDATE statement.

Delete Rows from a Table

❑ The DELETE statement is used to remove rows of data from a table.

❑ The syntax starts with the reserved words DELETE and the optional FROM, then the name of the target table, then an optional WHERE clause.

❑ If the WHERE clause is omitted, all of the rows in the table are deleted.

Control Transactions

❑ TCL statements include COMMIT, ROLLBACK, and SAVEPOINT.

❑ There are two types of commit events: explicit commit and implicit commit.

❑ An explicit commit occurs with the COMMIT statement.

❑ An implicit commit occurs immediately before and after certain events that take place in the database, such as the execution of any valid DDL statement, such as CREATE, ALTER, DROP, GRANT, and REVOKE. Each is preceded and followed by an implicit commit.

❑ If a DDL statement fails during execution, the implicit commit that preceded it still is in effect, ensuring that the commit at least occurred, whether the DDL statement was successful or not. The same is not true for syntax errors.

❑ The ROLLBACK statement is used to undo changes to the database.

❑ The SAVEPOINT statement can be used to name a point within a series of SQL statements to which you may optionally roll back changes after additional DML statements are executed.

❑ Once a COMMIT is issued, all existing SAVEPOINTs are erased.

❑ Any ROLLBACK that names non-existing SAVEPOINTs will not execute.

❑ If ROLLBACK is issued without naming a SAVEPOINT, changes made by the user during the current session are rolled back to the most recent commit event.

SELF TEST

The following questions will help you measure your understanding of the material presented in this chapter. Choose the best single answer for each question unless otherwise specified.

Describe Each Data Manipulation Language (DML) Statement

1. Which of the following statements are considered DML? (Choose two.)
   - A. SELECT
   - B. GRANT
   - C. INSERT
   - D. DROP

2. An INSERT statement can be used to:
   - A. Create tables in which to place data.
   - B. Create rows of data in a table.
   - C. Add values to an existing row of data in a table.
   - D. None of the above.

3. By issuing a ROLLBACK statement, a user can choose to undo DML changes he or she has performed on the database during the current session since either (a) the most recent commit event, or (b) any one of a number of demarcation points that may have been established within the session—whichever is more recent. If any such demarcation points exist, they would have been created with the SQL statement whose first keyword is:
   - A. MARK
   - B. SAVEPOINT
   - C. UNDO
   - D. Any DDL statement can do this

Insert Rows into a Table

4. Review the following statement.

```
CREATE TABLE STUDENT_LIST
  (STUDENT_ID  NUMBER,
   NAME        VARCHAR2(30),
   PHONE       VARCHAR2(30));
INSERT INTO STUDENT_LIST
   VALUES (1, 'Joe Wookie', 5551212);
```

The table will create successfully. What will result from the INSERT statement?

A. The INSERT will fail because there is no list of columns after STUDENT_LIST.

B. The INSERT will fail because the literal value for PHONE is numeric and PHONE is a character datatype.

C. The INSERT will execute—the table will contain one row of data.

D. None of the above.

5. Consider the following set of SQL statements:

```
CREATE TABLE INSTRUCTORS
 (INSTRUCTOR_ID  NUMBER,
  NAME           VARCHAR2(20),
  CONSTRAINT     ID_PK   PRIMARY KEY (INSTRUCTOR_ID),
  CONSTRAINT     NAME_UN UNIQUE (NAME));

INSERT INTO INSTRUCTORS (INSTRUCTOR_ID, NAME)
   VALUES (1, 'Howard Jackson');
INSERT INTO INSTRUCTORS (INSTRUCTOR_ID, NAME)
   VALUES (2, 'Trish Mars');
```

The table will create successfully. What will be the result of the two INSERT statements?

A. Neither will execute.

B. The first will execute, but the second will fail.

C. The first will fail, but the second will execute.

D. Both will execute successfully.

6. Consider the following set of SQL statements:

```
CREATE TABLE MAILING_LIST (FIRST_NAME VARCHAR2(20), LAST_NAME VARCHAR2(30));
INSERT INTO MAILING_LIST VALUES ('Smith', 'Mary');
```

What will be the result of the INSERT statement?

A. It will fail because there is no column list in the INSERT statement.

B. It will fail because there is no PRIMARY KEY in the table.

C. It will execute and create a new row in the table.

D. It will fail because the last name and first name values are reversed.

Update Rows in a Table

7. Which of the following reserved words is not required in order to form a syntactically correct UPDATE statement?

A. UPDATE

B. SET

C. WHERE

D. None of the above

8. Which of the following is true about the UPDATE statement? (Choose all that apply.)

   A. It can be used to add rows to a table by setting values to all of the columns.

   B. It can be used to remove a row from a table by setting all of the row's columns to a value of NULL.

   C. For existing rows in a table, UPDATE can add values to any column with a NULL value.

   D. For existing rows in a table, UPDATE can remove values from any column by changing its value to NULL.

9. Review the following SQL statements:

```
CREATE TABLE INSTRUCTORS
   (INSTRUCTOR_ID NUMBER,
    EXEMPT   VARCHAR2(5),
    VACATION NUMBER,
    PAY_RATE NUMBER);
INSERT INTO INSTRUCTORS VALUES (1, 'YES', NULL, 25);
INSERT INTO INSTRUCTORS VALUES (2, NULL,  NULL, NULL);
UPDATE INSTRUCTORS
   SET EXEMPT    = 'YES',
   SET VACATION  = 15
WHERE  PAY_RATE < 50;
```

   What can be said of the statements listed here?

   A. One row will be updated.

   B. Two rows will be updated.

   C. At least one of the statements will not execute.

   D. None of the above.

10. Review the following SQL statements:

```
CREATE TABLE BOUNCERS
  (NIGHTCLUB_CODE NUMBER,
   STRENGTH_INDEX NUMBER);
INSERT INTO BOUNCERS VALUES (1, NULL);
UPDATE BOUNCERS
   SET STRENGTH_INDEX = 10;
```

   What is the end result of the SQL statements listed here?

   A. The BOUNCERS table will contain one row.

   B. The BOUNCERS table will contain two rows.

   C. The UPDATE will fail because there is no WHERE clause.

   D. None of the above.

Delete Rows from a Table

11. Which of the following reserved words is required in a complete DELETE statement? (Choose all that apply.)

A. FROM

B. WHERE

C. DELETE

D. None of the above

12. Consider the following data in a table called PARTS:

```
PNO   PART_TITLE        STATUS
---   ----------------  -------
  1   PROCESSOR V1.0    VALID
  2   ENCASEMENT X770   PENDING
  3   BOARD CPU XER A7  PENDING
```

Which of the following SQL statements will remove the word "VALID" from row 1, resulting in one row with a status of NULL and two rows with a status of 'PENDING'?

A. DELETE FROM PARTS
   WHERE STATUS = 'VALID';

B. DELETE PARTS
   WHERE PNO = 1;

C. DELETE FROM PARTS
   SET STATUS = NULL
   WHERE PNO = 1;

D. None of the above

13. Review the following SQL statements:

```
CREATE TABLE AB_INVOICES (INVOICE_ID NUMBER, VENDOR_ID NUMBER);
ALTER TABLE AB_INVOICES ADD PRIMARY KEY (INVOICE_ID);
INSERT INTO AB_INVOICES VALUES (1,1);
DELETE AB_INVOICES WHERE INVOICE_ID = 2;
```

Which of the following best describes the results of attempting to execute the DELETE statement?

A. The DELETE statement will fail because it is missing a column list between the word DELETE and the name of the table AB_INVOICES.

B. The DELETE statement will execute, but no rows in the table will be removed.

C. The DELETE statement will produce a syntax error because it is referencing a row that does not exist in the database.

D. None of the above.

Control Transactions

14. Review the following SQL statements:

```
01   SELECT PRODUCT_ID FROM PRODUCTS;
02   DROP TABLE SHIP_STAFF;
03   INSERT INTO ENGINEERING (PROJECT_ID, MGR) VALUES (27,21);
04   COMMIT;
05   INSERT INTO ENGINEERING (PROJECT_ID, MGR) VALUES (400,17);
06   ROLLBACK;
```

In this series of SQL statements, which line represents the first commit event?

A. Line 1

B. Line 2

C. Line 4

D. Line 6

15. Review the SQL statements that follow, and assume that there is no table called ADDRESSES already present in the database:

```
CREATE TABLE ADDRESSES (ID NUMBER, ZONE NUMBER, ZIP_CODE VARCHAR2 (5));
INSERT INTO ADDRESSES (ID, ZONE, ZIP_CODE) VALUES (1, 1, '94065');
SAVEPOINT ZONE_CHANGE_01;
UPDATE ADDRESSES SET ZONE = 2 WHERE ZIP_CODE = 94065;
ROLLBACK;
```

What will be the result of the execution of the SQL statements shown here?

A. The ADDRESSES table will have one row with a value of 1 for ZONE.

B. The ADDRESSES table will have one row with a value of 2 for ZONE.

C. The ADDRESSES table will have no rows.

D. None of the above.

SELF TEST ANSWERS

Describe Each Data Manipulation Language (DML) Statement

1. ☑ **A and C.** The DML statements listed are SELECT and INSERT.
   ☒ **B and D** are incorrect. GRANT is DDL. So is DROP.

2. ☑ **B.** It appears a bit tricky to say that the INSERT statement "creates" something, since we've primarily spoken of DDL statements as creating objects, and SQL has already reserved the word CREATE for the statement that creates database objects. But it's important to recognize the purpose of each statement, and with regard to the INSERT, what's important is that you're adding rows of data to a table that weren't there before.
   ☒ **A, C, and D** are incorrect. INSERT creates rows of data that are stored within a table, but it doesn't create the table itself. INSERT may be used to selectively put data in certain columns of a table, but even then, it's creating an entirely new row for the table when it does this, and is incapable of adding data to an existing row—that's the purpose of the UPDATE statement.

3. ☑ **B.** The SAVEPOINT statement will establish a demarcation within a series of transactions so that a subsequent ROLLBACK statement can undo any changes made by the user during the session back to the point of the SAVEPOINT, or to the most recent commit event, whichever is more recent.
   ☒ **A, C, and D** are incorrect. MARK is not a valid SQL statement; neither is UNDO. Any DDL statement will trigger an implicit commit event, but they have no particular and unique correlation to the SAVEPOINT statement and functionality.

Insert Rows into a Table

4. ☑ **C.** The statements are syntactically and logically correct. The INSERT statement omits the column list, requiring the list of values to be provided in the same sequence in which the columns appear in the table's structure, as indicated in the CREATE TABLE statement.
   ☒ **A, B, and D** are incorrect. The PHONE value is fine; character data accepts both numeric and text data. In fact, values like phone numbers and ZIP codes are best treated as character data; otherwise, leading zeros will be truncated, and in the case of a ZIP code, that can be a disaster for a lot of addresses in the Northeastern United States.

5. ☑ **D.** The syntax is fine, and both INSERT statements will execute.
   ☒ **A, B, and C** are incorrect.

6. ☑ **C.** It will create a new row in the table. The fact that the column values are probably reversed may represent a logical error now and create problems down the road, but there's nothing about the statement that will prevent it from executing successfully.

   ☒ **A, B,** and **D** are incorrect. The lack of a column list in the INSERT merely requires there to be a list of values that match the number and datatypes of the columns in the table's structure, and this INSERT statement's list of values satisfies that requirement, albeit in an apparently illogical way, but nevertheless, the requirements for SQL are met. The lack of a PRIMARY KEY on the table probably represents poor design but is not a problem with regard to the successful execution of the SQL statements here.

Update Rows in a Table

7. ☑ **C.** An UPDATE statement does not have to have a WHERE clause. If a WHERE clause is omitted, then every row in the target table is subject to be changed by the UPDATE statement, depending on whether or not any constraints exist on the table and whether they permit or reject the data changes the UPDATE statement is attempting to make.

   ☒ **A, B,** and **D** are incorrect. The reserved word UPDATE is required for a valid UPDATE statement. The same is true for the reserved word SET.

8. ☑ **C and D.** Adding a value to a column in an existing row is the purpose of the UPDATE statement. Setting a value to NULL is as acceptable as setting a value to some other specific value.

   ☒ **A and B** are incorrect. INSERT adds new rows to a table, and DELETE removes them. UPDATE doesn't remove rows from a table. The UPDATE statement can only modify existing rows. If you choose to SET each column's value to NULL—assuming the constraints will allow you to do that—then you'll still have a row in the table; it will simply consist of NULL values. But you'll still have a row. And you cannot create a new row by using SET to set values to each column; all you can do is modify existing rows.

9. ☑ **C.** The UPDATE statement contains an extra occurrence of the reserved word SET. Only the first "SET" belongs; the second should be removed.

   ☒ **A, B,** and **D** are incorrect.

10. ☑ **A.** The INSERT statement enters a single row, and the UPDATE statement modifies that single row, leaving one modified row in the table.

    ☒ **B, C,** and **D** are incorrect. There is only one row in the table—the UPDATE does not add a new row but rather changes the existing row. UPDATE does not require a WHERE clause; without it, the UPDATE statement applies its changes to all the rows in the table, and this table contains one row.

Delete Rows from a Table

11. ☑ **C.** The only required reserved word is DELETE.
    ☒ **A, B,** and **D** are incorrect. FROM is optional. WHERE is also optional.

12. ☑ **D** is correct. DELETE removes entire rows from the database. To remove a single value from a single column requires use of the UPDATE statement.
    ☒ **A, B,** and **C** are incorrect. A and B are valid DELETE statements, either of which will remove the first row from the table, instead of just removing the value for the "status" column. C is an invalid statement that will trigger a syntax error—the SET reserved word has no place in the DELETE statement.

13. ☑ **B.** The syntax is fine, and the statement will execute as intended, which is to remove any rows from the table with an INVOICE_ID value of 2. It just so happens that there aren't any rows that match the stated criteria at the time the DELETE statement is issued—and there's nothing illogical about that.
    ☒ **A, C,** and **D** are incorrect. There is no column list in a DELETE statement before the table name. And the fact that the WHERE clause does not identify any relevant rows is not a syntax problem, nor is it a compilation problem—the statement will simply not delete any rows.

Control Transactions

14. ☑ **B.** Line 2 is a DROP statement, which falls under the type of SQL statements known as Data Definition Language, or DDL. All DDL statements cause an implicit commit to occur.
    ☒ **A, C,** and **D** are incorrect. The SELECT statement has no impact on a commit event at all. Line 4 is an explicit COMMIT, and were it not for line 2, this would be the first commit event in this set of statements. Line 6 undoes the effects of line 5 and undoes the user's changes to the database since the previous commit event, which at this stage is represented by the line 4 commit.

15. ☑ **C.** The ROLLBACK statement does not reference the SAVEPOINT name, so instead it rolls all the way back to the last COMMIT event, which in this case is the implicit commit that occurred with the CREATE TABLE statement.
    ☒ **A, B,** and **D** are incorrect.

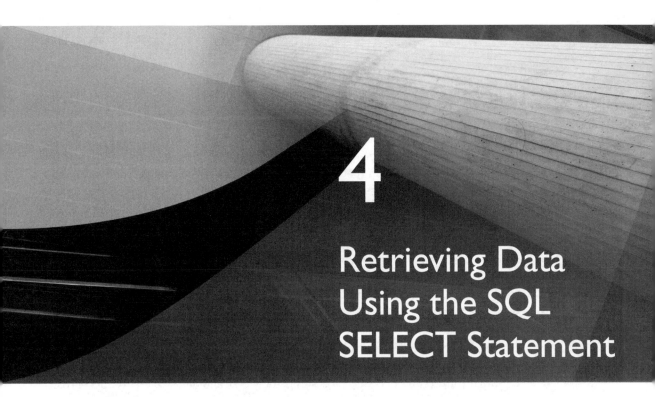

4

Retrieving Data Using the SQL SELECT Statement

This chapter introduces the basic syntax of the most commonly used SQL statement, which is the SELECT statement. The SQL SELECT statement retrieves data from the database. The SELECT statement does not change the data that's stored in the database, but it does have the ability to transform that data as it is pulled out of the database and displayed, and therein lies its power and usefulness. SELECT has the ability to show raw information, but also to edit information before it's displayed. It can perform mathematical analysis on numeric data, and perform string manipulation on text data; it can format raw numbers for financial reports, abbreviate lengthy data, or spell out abbreviations. It can sort rows of data according to date, time, text, and numeric values. It can aggregate multiple rows of information in various ways, showing summary data at various levels, or creating organizational hierarchies. It can join related information from multiple sources and present its findings in a single consolidated form at various levels of detail or aggregation.

In other words, the functionality involved in the SELECT statement is the ultimate reason why most databases exist: to analyze, transform, and present data in virtually any format necessary. It is surprisingly easy and quick to use, yet deceptively tricky in its full implementation in the context of a comprehensive mission-critical application. I'm tempted here to quote the pop singer Billy Joel and say that the SELECT statement is "frequently kind and it's suddenly cruel". But I won't do that. Because in the hands of an Oracle Database SQL Expert, the SELECT statement is a tame and powerful tool that is flexible and infinitely productive.

CERTIFICATION OBJECTIVE 4.01

Execute a Basic SELECT Statement

In this section you'll get a high-level look at the SELECT statement and go through the complete process of creating and executing a simple SELECT statement. We'll discuss some basic rules for forming SELECT statements, including the minimum requirements for formulating a complete executable statement. Then you'll execute a SELECT statement and look at its output.

This section introduces some key concepts that you'll need for the exam, but it's hardly the last word on SELECT that you'll need on the job—nor on the exam.

We'll explore SELECT in greater detail throughout many other sections of this guide. This chapter will get us started.

The SELECT Statement—An Example

Let's take a look at an example of a simple SELECT statement. First, see Figure 4-1 for a sample database table listing of data we'll use for our SELECT statement.

In this figure, our table has three columns and four rows. Let's create a SELECT statement to retrieve this data:

```
01   SELECT    SHIP_ID, SHIP_NAME, CAPACITY
02   FROM      SHIPS
03   ORDER BY SHIP_NAME;
```

If you were to type this SELECT statement into the SQL*Plus interface and execute it, the results might look like Figure 4-2.

FIGURE 4-1

Data in the
SHIPS table

SHIP_ID	SHIP_NAME	CAPACITY
I	Codd Crystal	2052
2	Codd Elegance	2974
3	Codd Champion	2974
4	Codd Victorious	2974

FIGURE 4-2

Output of
SELECT
statement

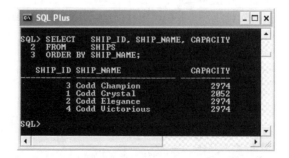

This example demonstrates three clauses in a SELECT statement:

- **On line 1, the expression list**   The expression list, also known as the select list, is a list of one or more expressions. Often the list is merely column names, but it could include expressions consisting of a combination of column names, arithmetic operators, literal values, and SQL functions, as you'll see later. If column names are referenced, they must match the names of existing columns in the table's structure. The select list identifies the data you wish to retrieve. When the results of your statement are displayed, each expression's values are listed in an output column (not to be confused with a database column) in your results. Each expression forms an output column from left to right, horizontally, in the same sequence as you list them in your expression list. In our example, the expression list consists of three columns: SHIP_ID, SHIP_NAME, and CAPACITY; the output will list the SHIP_ID values first, then the SHIP_NAME values to the right of SHIP_ID, and finally the values for CATEGORY.

- **The FROM clause**   This consists of the keyword FROM followed by the name of one or more tables.

- **The ORDER BY clause**   This consists of the keywords ORDER BY, followed by an expression that identifies to the database how you wish the rows to be sorted.

Note that there is no WHERE clause in this SELECT statement example. This means that the results of this particular example will show all of the rows in the table. In order to restrict the output to a certain number of rows, a WHERE clause should be added to define exactly which rows are desired—something you'll look at in detail in the next chapter.

There is more functionality to the SELECT statement than what we're mentioning here. We will review additional features later that may be included in the exam.

SELECT: Minimum Requirements

In order to create a valid SELECT statement that will parse correctly, the following elements are required:

- The SELECT keyword, followed by at least one valid expression in the expression list

- The FROM keyword, followed by at least one valid name of a database table

That is all that is required. Here is an example:

```
SELECT 1
FROM    SHIPS;
```

In this example, we're selecting the literal value of 1 from the table named SHIPS. Obviously we don't need to call on the SHIPS table to understand what the literal value of 1 is—it's just a number 1; there's no trick to it. But the point is that any valid expression can be selected from any valid table, and as long as the SHIPS table is valid, then the preceding SELECT statement is a syntactically correct, if perhaps somewhat useless, SQL statement.

Of course, we can also reference a column name in the table specified in the FROM clause. For example, as long as the SHIPS table has a column called SHIP_NAME, then this is also a valid SELECT statement:

```
SELECT SHIP_NAME
FROM    SHIPS;
```

Any column that may be referenced in the SELECT statement must exist in the table identified in the FROM clause.

Anything less than one item in the SELECT statement's expression list, and one item in the FROM clause, and there is not sufficient information to build a SELECT statement.

SQL statements may be displayed on one line or multiple lines. Any number of line breaks may occur anywhere within a SQL statement, provided that any given line break does not interrupt keywords, literal values, expressions, etc. The semi-colon indicates the termination of the SQL statement.

In the following sections, we'll expand on our knowledge of the SELECT statement.

CERTIFICATION OBJECTIVE 4.02

List the Capabilities of SQL SELECT Statements

You've seen some examples of how the SELECT statement works, and discussed the minimum requirement for a syntactically complete SELECT. Now let's expand our knowledge a bit and look at other clauses that are used in a SELECT, and discuss its capabilities.

The SELECT Statement—An Overview

The SELECT statement is used to retrieve data from one or more tables in the database. It can specifically display a subset of the available data by identifying certain columns and rows, by analyzing data contained within those columns and rows, and/or by performing real-time mathematical calculations or text searches, date or time checking. It can sort the results, format the individual values that are displayed, and more.

Let's look at the individual components that form a SELECT statement. We'll start with the first part, known as the expression list, and sometimes called the select list.

Selecting Columns From Tables

The first part of a SELECT statement is the *select list*, or *expression list*, which generally includes column references. Expressions are listed in the order in which you wish for them to be displayed as output. Each expression is separated from the next by a comma. The last expression is not followed by a comma.

As you might recall from Chapter 1, a table consists of columns and rows. Figure 1-1 showed us a very simple table structure, in which you saw a table called SHIPS, containing two columns—one called SHIP_ID and another called SHIP_NAME. The SHIPS table displayed four rows of data.

Here is an example of a SELECT statement we could create for that SHIPS table in Chapter 1, Figure 1-1.

```
SELECT SHIP_ID, SHIP_NAME
FROM   SHIPS;
```

The columns SHIP_ID and SHIP_NAME are indicated in the column list of this SELECT statement. The results of this SELECT statement are shown in Figure 4-3.

Notice that the output displays the columns in the same sequence in which they are specified in the SELECT statement. The SELECT statement may identify the

FIGURE 4-3

Sample output of a SELECT statement

FIGURE 4-4

Sample output of
the same SELECT
statement with
the column list
reordered

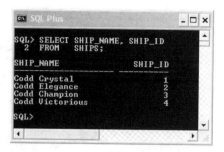

columns in any order, regardless of the order in which the columns appear in the table's structure. For example:

```
SELECT SHIP_NAME, SHIP_ID
FROM    SHIPS;
```

The results of this statement are shown in Figure 4-4.

The select list may include any columns, in any order, and can repeat them as often as is desired.

Pseudocolumns

Pseudocolumns are values that are defined automatically by the Oracle system for every table. Pseudocolumns will not appear in the results of the DESCRIBE statement, and they are not actually stored with the table. But you can SELECT from them as though they were a typical column in the table. Pseudocolumns generally return a different value for each row in the table.

There are many pseudocolumns that can be available within Oracle SQL in different situations, depending on what is transpiring at the time. For example, some are useful only within hierarchical queries, which you'll study in Chapter 16. Two pseudocolumns that are more common and can be useful include the following:

- ■ **ROWNUM**   This is the system-assigned number for a row. If you're looking for some way to number each row of output from a SELECT statement, ROWNUM might do the trick, but beware: ROWNUM is assigned before the ORDER BY clause is processed, not after. See Figure 4-5.

- ■ **ROWID**   This is the system-assigned physical address for a given row. This can change from time to time by the database—for example, if you export a table and then import it, the newly imported version will almost certainly have different ROWID values.

We'll look at other pseudocolumns later as they become relevant.

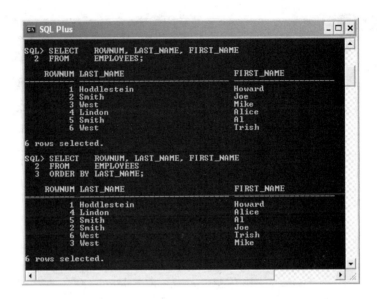

ROWID can be useful for data in tables where a problem might exist. I once was brought in to clean up a database that was in a bit of difficulty. One issue was that of inappropriate duplicate rows in a critical table. I could have used a graphical user interface (GUI) of some sort to selectively delete rows—if one were available, but it wasn't. I was logged in across a command-line interface, and I was able to make use of the DELETE statement by first identifying the duplicate rows and then carefully using the ROWID values of the duplicates I needed to remove.

DISTINCT or UNIQUE

The reserved word DISTINCT can be used with SELECT to identify a unique set of values from a table. UNIQUE performs the same task.

For example, consider the following list of values:

EMPLOYEE_ID	FIRST_NAME	MIDDLE_INITIAL	LAST_NAME
1	Howard	A.	Hoddlestein
2	Joe	R.	Smith
3	Mike	L.	West
4	Alice	W.	Lindon
5	Al	S.	Smith

```
6          Trish     T.          West
7          Joe       M.          Smith
```

If these rows existed in a table called, say, EMPLOYEES, then we might run the following SELECT statement:

```
SELECT DISTINCT LAST_NAME
FROM    EMPLOYEES;
```

Such a query would produce output like Figure 4-6.

DISTINCT analyzes each row returned by the query and returns one unique line of output for each duplicate set of expressions that might be found. DISTINCT operates on the entire set of expressions in the select list. For example, this query looks for distinct combinations of two columns:

```
SELECT DISTINCT LAST_NAME, FIRST_NAME
FROM    EMPLOYEES;
```

This query asks for all distinct combinations of values in LAST_NAME and FIRST_NAME. Given our earlier source data, this query would produce the complete list of names with one exception: there would only be one line with the name "Smith" and "Joe". In other words, DISTINCT takes into consideration all of the column values in the expression list and looks at whether each row is unique or not based on the combination of expressions identified in the SELECT statement's expression list.

The reserved word UNIQUE performs the same task as DISTINCT.

Both DISTINCT and UNIQUE are considered a "clause" of the SELECT statement.

FIGURE 4-6

Output of
SELECT
DISTINCT query

Asterisk: The All-Column Wildcard

The use of a single asterisk in the SELECT list is the equivalent of asking for all the columns in the table, in the order they are defined in the table's structure. For example, consider a table called PORTS with four columns of PORT_ID, PORT_NAME, COUNTRY, and CAPACITY. Given that, the following SELECT statement asks for all of these columns:

```
SELECT *
FROM    PORTS;
```

This statement is a valid SELECT statement that is the equivalent of the following:

```
SELECT PORT_ID, PORT_NAME, COUNTRY, CAPACITY
FROM    PORTS;
```

The output of either query is identical. The asterisk, when used in the column list, tells the database that you simply want to show data from all the columns, whatever they are.

If new columns are added to the table in the future, this "asterisk" query will automatically pick up those new columns in its output, whereas the second example just shown would need to be edited to incorporate the newly added column names.

Expressions

In addition to columns in tables, you may also incorporate expressions into a SELECT statement's select list. Expressions are one way you can "transform" data, as is often said about SELECT statements. Don't be misled by that term of "data transformation"—when you "transform" data using an expression in the select list of a SELECT statement, you're not changing anything in the database, you're simply processing the data after it's retrieved by the SELECT statement, and before it's presented as the final output of your SELECT statement.

Expressions consist of literal values, arithmetic and other operators, and as you'll see later, SQL functions.

Literals

See Table 4-1 for a description of some of the literal values you may use in an expression.

TABLE 4-1	Datatype	Description	Examples
Examples of Literal Values That Can Be Used in an Expression	Number	Any numeral, including decimal points	1 49.12
	Character or String	A set of one or more characters enclosed in single quotation marks (not double quotes)	'Hayden, Doug' 'Acme Internet, Inc.' To include single quotes as part of the string, use two single quotes in succession. For example: 'Isn''t it nice outside?'
	Date	A date that is provided in the format Oracle uses for formatting dates	'10-MAY-09'
	Interval	A period of time, either YEAR TO MONTHS or DAY TO SECONDS. Also valid, when used by themselves, are YEAR, MONTH, DAY, MINUTE, and SECOND.	'INTERVAL '24-3' YEAR(2) TO MONTH' is 24 years and three months, where (2) is the precision for the YEAR component of the value. 'INTERVAL '24' MONTH is 24 months, or, in other words, two years.

The folowing example of a SELECT statement combines column names and expressions:

```
SELECT    EMPLOYEE_ID, SALARY, SALARY*1.05
FROM      PAY_HISTORY
WHERE     END_DATE IS NULL
ORDER BY EMPLOYEE_ID;
```

For each row in the PAY_HISTORY table, this query will produce the EMPLOYEE_ID, SALARY, and a value that represents the SALARY with a 5 percent increase. The first two items in the select list are column names. The third is an arithmetic expression that takes data from the database and performs a multiplication operation on that value for each row in the database. An example of what this output might look like is shown in Figure 4-7.

Output of
PAY_HISTORY
query

 on the job

Expressions can be used in:

- *A SELECT statement's column list, and its WHERE, HAVING, and ORDER BY clauses;*
- *Hierarchical queries with the CONNECT BY, START WITH, and ORDER BY clauses;*
- *An INSERT statement's VALUES clause;*
- *An UPDATE statement's SET clause and WHERE clause;*
- *A DELETE statement's WHERE clause.*

There isn't a specific certification objective about simple expressions. However, expressions are such a common part of the daily life of any SQL developer that you should know them well, be comfortable where they can be used, and not be caught off guard when they appear in the context of a complex exam question that might be focusing on a different topic area. Expressions do appear on the exam, sometimes within a series of SQL statements, along with many other common features of SQL.

Operators and Operator Precedence

Operators are important in expressions. The arithmetic operators you can use in an expression are shown in Table 4-2. These operators may appear in an expression in any order and frequency. For example:

```
SELECT SALARY * (BASE_PAY * (1.03 * YEARS_OF_SERVICE)) / 12
FROM   EMP_COMPENSATION;
```

This example uses a combination of multiplication, division, and parentheses to build a complex expression.

The use of parentheses brings up the important topic of operator precedence. If you're familiar with the basic rules of mathematics, you'll already know the rules of arithmetic operator precedence. SQL adopts the same rules, and they are shown in Table 4-2.

What these rules indicate is the order in which operations are performed within a larger expression that contains multiple operations. Multiplication and division are performed before addition or subtraction, regardless of the sequence in which they are used. For example, consider this arithmetic expression:

```
10 + 15 * 3
```

You might assume that this expression is "10 plus 15", the results of which are multiplied by 3. If so, you would conclude that the result of this equation is 75.

But Oracle will calculate the answer of this expression to be 55. That's because the multiplication is calculated first, like this:

```
15 * 3 = 45
```

This result is placed into the addition operation, which is performed next:

```
10 + 45 = 55
```

TABLE 4-2	Name	Operator	Precedence
Arithmetic Operators in Order of Precedence	Parentheses	( )	1
	Multiplication, Division	*, /	2
	Addition, Subtraction	+, -	3

Now—if we really wanted our original equation to calculate a value of 75 instead of 55, there's a way to make it happen. That method is the placement of parentheses to override any other rules of operator precedence. Any operation enclosed in parentheses will be performed first, before all other operations.

Here's a version of the same expression that uses parentheses to ensure the calculation is performed in sequential order:

```
(10 + 15) * 3
```

The result of this arithmetic expression, as calculated by Oracle, is 75. The reason is the rules of operator precedence.

Parentheses may be nested as many times as is necessary. The deeper the nesting, the higher up in the order of precedence. For example:

```
( 11 - 4 + ((2+3) * .7) / 4)
```

The expression "2+3" will be evaluated first, since it is within the greatest number of parentheses. And incidentally, the answer is 7.875.

Functions

No discussion of expressions would be complete without at least mentioning SQL functions. A function is represented by a descriptive name or abbreviation, such as ADD_MONTHS or SUBSTR. Functions generally:

- Receive one or more bits of incoming data, known as "parameters".
- Perform some task on the data—perhaps to add the parameter values together.
- Produce a single answer representing the results of the function's task.

If you're wondering why I say that functions "generally" do these things, it's because it's technically possible for a function to omit some of these steps. For example, it's theoretically possible in PL/SQL to create a user-defined function that doesn't take any parameters at all and yet produces some form of output. That being said—most functions do all three of the steps listed here.

Parameters may include literal values or table column names.

Here's an example of a SELECT statement that uses a function called UPPER. The UPPER function takes a single character string, changes that string to uppercase characters, and returns the uppercase version of the string.

```
SELECT PORT_NAME, UPPER(PORT_NAME)
FROM   PORTS;
```

FIGURE 4-8

Results of
a SELECT
statement using
the UPPER
function

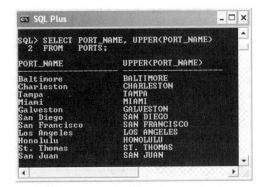

The output is shown in Figure 4-8. As you can see from the listing, the UPPER function changed the data to uppercase.

It's also worth pointing out that in this example, we referenced the same table column twice in a select list. That's perfectly acceptable and potentially useful as it is in this example. Columns may be referenced in a SELECT statement column list as often as you wish in any sequence.

Additional **SELECT** Statement Clauses

In addition to the select list and the FROM clause, there are several additional clauses that can be used in a SELECT statement. Several are briefly described in Table 4-3.

TABLE 4-3

Additional
SELECT
Statement
Clauses

Additional Clauses	Brief Description
WHERE *condition*	Restricts the rows that are returned according to the criteria described in *condition*.
hierarchical_query_clause	Structures the output in a hierarchical order, as you might find in a company organization chart.
ORDER BY *order_by_clause*	Sorts the rows.
GROUP BY *group_by_clause*	Collects rows in groups in order to identify values that are common to the groups, such as aggregate data.
HAVING *condition*	Essentially performs a type of "WHERE" operation for the groups defined in the GROUP BY clause.

Each of these clauses is rich in functionality. For example, one feature that's highlighted on the exam is a feature known as the *subquery*, in which a SELECT statement includes an embedded SELECT statement within it. The subquery is often embedded within the WHERE clause, but may be used elsewhere.

Each of these additional clauses will be explored in detail as we continue.

The Capabilities of SELECT

At the highest level, the SELECT statement can be characterized as having three fundamental capabilities: Projection, Selection, and Joining. These are the three fundamental concepts that drive a relational database.

Let's explore each in a little more detail. To explore these concepts, you'll work with two tables as shown in Figure 4-9.

Projection

Projection refers to the ability of a SELECT statement to choose a subset of the columns in a given table. For example, see Figure 4-10. The SELECT statement is choosing a subset of the columns from the PORTS table that you saw in Figure 4-9.

A query that displays a table's data by choosing a subset of a given table's columns is exhibiting the concept of projection.

Selection

Selection is the ability of a SELECT statement to choose a subset of the rows in a given table. This concept is accomplished by use of the WHERE clause of the SELECT statement. See Figure 4-11 for an example.

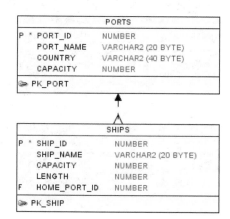

FIGURE 4-9

The PORTS and SHIPS tables

Projection:
a SELECT
statement that
chooses a subset
of columns

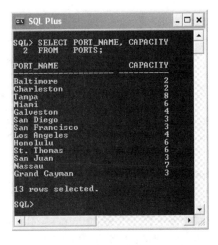

Selection:
a SELECT
statement that
chooses a subset
of rows

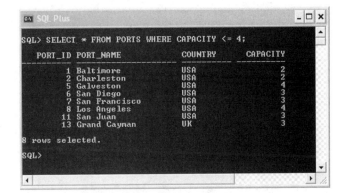

A query that displays a table's data by choosing table rows selectively is exhibiting the concept of selection. In this example, the WHERE clause is limiting our output display to those rows that have a CAPACITY value that's less than or equal to 4. You'll study the WHERE clause in more detail in the next chapter.

Joining

Joining is the reason there's an "R" in RDBMS. Joining is how we "relate" data from one part of the database to another. When we "join" two or more tables, we are specifying to the database that there is common information shared by both tables and we want to link data from those tables together according to the common data the tables share.

FIGURE 4-12

Joining: a SELECT
statement that
relates data from
two tables into
one output listing

A typical database application will consist of many tables that can be joined in a variety of ways. For every additional table you add to a database, you can potentially add a great many additional join possibilities, depending on the structures involved.

An example of a SELECT statement that joins data is displayed in Figure 4-12.

The SELECT in the figure joins the two tables SHIPS and PORTS. The join is accomplished in lines 2 and 3 of the figure, where we see a FROM clause that identifies both tables and then identifies their common link: the PORT_ID column in the PORTS table and the HOME_PORT_ID column in the SHIPS table. This SELECT statement is instructing SQL to find rows in both tables that have a common value in those columns; where rows are found that match, SQL will treat the combination as though they are one row. We'll discuss the mechanics of this later in Chapter 8, but for now, the point is this: any query that displays data from two or more tables by identifying common data in the tables is exhibiting the concept of joining.

CERTIFICATION OBJECTIVE 4.03

Describe How Schema Objects Work

As you've seen, there are several objects in the database. Many are "schema" objects, meaning they are "owned" by a user and exist in a collection within a user account. The schema objects you've looked at include tables, views, indexes, sequences, and synonyms. You've seen how to name them, and how namespaces work. You've also seen a little about privileges, and the fact that a single user can "own" database tables and then grant privileges to other users for performing SELECT, INSERT, UPDATE, and/or DELETE operations on that information.

In this section, we'll look at some of the functionality of database objects and how they work with each other.

Tables

All the data in a database is stored in tables. When you create a new table, the information about that table, such as its name and columns and the datatypes of those columns, is all stored in a set of system-defined tables that are collectively known as the "data dictionary", and which are managed automatically by the Oracle system. (We examine the data dictionary in Chapter 14.) So even data about your data—i.e., "metadata"—is stored in tables.

A table's columns are generally stored in the order in which they are created, but this isn't necessarily true at all times. Also, if you ALTER a table and add a column to its structure, that column will become the last column in the table's structure.

Constraints

A *constraint* is a rule on a table that puts rules and restrictions on the sort of data that is added to a table. Note that it is not a database object, but it is listed in the data dictionary, and can be named with the same naming rules of an object. You've already looked at the different types of constraints: NOT NULL, UNIQUE, PRIMARY KEY, FOREIGN KEY, and CHECK.

If a SQL statement attempts to add, modify, or delete a row to/from a table, and in so doing violates a constraint, the entire SQL statement will fail with an execution error.

Views

A *view* acts like a table. It has a name. You can DESCRIBE the view in the same way you would DESCRIBE a table. You can run a SELECT statement on a view just as you would SELECT from a table. Depending on the kind of view you are working with, you might even be able to execute INSERT, UPDATE, and/or DELETE statements on a view.

But a view is not a table, and it stores no data. A view is nothing more than a SELECT statement that is saved in the database with a name assigned to it. The column structure that the view takes on is formed by the SELECT statement's select list. The datatypes for those columns are picked up automatically from the underlying table, or the expressions used in the SELECT statement used to create the view.

Indexes

An *index* performs the same job that a typical index in a book performs. For example, Oracle Corporation's *SQL Language Reference Manual* for Oracle 11g's 11.1 release is over 1,400 pages long. So what if you were looking for information on the DISTINCT clause of the SELECT statement? You have a few ways to find such information in the book. One way is to sit down and start reading the book at the first page, and keep reading until you find the data you're looking for. A much more efficient way is to flip to the back of the book and find the index, which contains a summary of important topics in alphabetical order. Within a few seconds you can look up the word DISTINCT and note the page number on which it's mentioned (Chapter 19, page 13, in case you were wondering), and flip straight to it. That's a much better approach.

The SQL INDEX object performs in much the same way. When you create an INDEX object, you are identifying one or more columns in a table that you believe will be frequently used to look up data. Then you create the index based on that column—or set of columns—and Oracle literally builds a separate object that takes a unique list of all the data currently in that column, sorts it appropriately according to datatype, and then stores internal addressing information that ties the index back to the source table and the rows contained within.

The result: any future queries on the table that happen to reference any indexed data will cause the following to occur automatically:

- Perform an analysis to determine if the query will benefit by using the index.
- If yes, then redirect the focus temporarily to the index, search the index for any of the desired data identified by the query, and obtain direct locations of the appropriate rows.

The difference in performance is potentially significant. The more data that is stored in a table, the more beneficial an index may be.

Sequences

A *sequence* is a counter, meaning that it issues numbers in a particular series, always keeping track of whatever the next number should be. If you ever watched the classic television sitcom *Seinfeld*, you might recall the episode where Jerry and Elaine go to a bakery to pick up a chocolate bobka, but don't know to take a number from the dispenser when they first arrive, and lose their place in line as the bakery gets crowded. That dispenser—which issues paper tickets identifying the holder as being, say, "number 42" in line—serves the same purpose of a SEQUENCE object in the database.

The primary purpose of a SEQUENCE is to support the process of adding rows to a particular table and providing the next appropriate value for a PRIMARY KEY for the table. That's it. There's nothing inherent in a SEQUENCE object that ties it to a particular table. There's nothing automatic in the SEQUENCE object that necessarily supports a particular table. It's up to the software developer to know how to use the SEQUENCE object correctly, as you've briefly seen already and will explore in detail later when we address the syntax of a SEQUENCE.

Synonyms

A *synonym* is an object that associates an alias with an existing object. If, for example, you already have a table called EMPLOYEE_COMPENSATION_PLANS, you might want to create a SYNONYM for it such as ECP, or something briefer.

There are actually two different SYNONYM objects. There is, simply, the SYNONYM, which is often called a "private synonym", and then there is the PUBLIC SYNONYM.

A private SYNONYM is owned by a user account and can be helpful for a variety of reasons.

A PUBLIC SYNONYM is owned by the system-provided user PUBLIC and when created becomes automatically available to all users in the database.

We'll discuss the SYNONYM and PUBLIC SYNONYM objects in much greater detail in Chapter 10.

CERTIFICATION SUMMARY

The SELECT statement is the most commonly used and most fundamental statement used in SQL. At a minimum, a SELECT statement must include the select list, also known as the expression list, and a FROM clause. The select list can include the names of columns in a table, or expressions. The FROM clause must name a valid table (or view), and any column names referenced in the expression list must be in tables that are identified in the FROM clause. A shorthand way of referencing all columns at once is the asterisk, as in SELECT * FROM PORTS, which is another way of asking for every column name that happens to be in the PORTS table at the time the SELECT statement executes. You can also use the

DISTINCT function to display unique occurrences of data sets from a query. You can substitute DISTINCT with UNIQUE for the same result. Pseudocolumns are defined automatically by the system and are not stored with a table but can be included in the select list of a SELECT statement as though they were columns in a table. Examples include ROWNUM and ROWID.

Expressions may appear in many locations in various SQL statement clauses. Regardless of where an expression may appear, it may include literal values, operators, or SQL functions, as well as column names that are incorporated into the expression. The rules of operator precedence determine the sequence in which operators within an expression are processed.

There are many other clauses in the SELECT statement, including WHERE, GROUP BY, HAVING, ORDER BY, and others. There are three fundamental concepts represented in the SELECT statement: the concepts of projection, selection, and joining. Projection is the ability to retrieve a subset of columns in a table. Selection is the concept of retrieving a subset of rows from a table. Joining refers to the ability to retrieve data from multiple tables and correlate each table's data elements to the other by common identifying information.

Tables store all the data in a database. Views are named SELECT statements. Indexes act just like an index in a book, by providing a separately stored sorted summary of the column data that is being indexed, along with addressing information that points back to the source table. Sequences provide a mechanism to count off primary key values. Synonyms are aliases for other database objects. A private synonym is owned by a user account. A public synonym is owned by the system user PUBLIC. Synonyms can be used to mask more complex object names and simplify table references.

TWO-MINUTE DRILL

Execute a Basic SELECT Statement

- ❏ A SELECT statement must include a select list and a FROM clause.
- ❏ Any columns identified in the select list must be in a table that is identified in the FROM clause.

List the Capabilities of SQL SELECT Statements

- ❏ Pseudocolumns are defined by the system and are not stored with a table.
- ❏ Pseudocolumns may be included in the select list of a SELECT statement.
- ❏ DISTINCT, or UNIQUE, can be used in a SELECT statement to list unique data sets.
- ❏ The asterisk is a shorthand way of referring to all of a table's columns.
- ❏ Expressions can transform data after it is retrieved from the database and before the data is produced as the SELECT statement's output.
- ❏ Expressions may include arithmetic operators, SQL functions, and literal values.
- ❏ Literal values include numbers, characters, dates, and intervals.
- ❏ Arithmetic operators obey the rules of operator precedence.
- ❏ Multiplication and division operators are evaluated before addition and subtraction, regardless of the order in which they appear in an expression.
- ❏ Parentheses have the highest authority in the order of operator precedence, which means that you can place parentheses to override any behavior in the rest of the operations.
- ❏ Functions can be used in expressions along with all of the other elements of expressions.
- ❏ The WHERE clause identifies conditions that individual rows must meet in order to be displayed—in other words, it can be used to "restrict" rows from being displayed.
- ❏ The ORDER BY clause sorts the data set output of a SELECT statement.
- ❏ The GROUP BY clause aggregates sets of records within a SELECT statement.

❑ The HAVING clause can be used with GROUP BY to restrict sets of rows in the same fashion that ORDER BY can be used to restrict individual records.

❑ When a SELECT statement chooses fewer than all of the available columns in a table, it is exhibiting the concept of projection.

❑ Projection is accomplished through the select list, also called the expression list, of the SELECT statement.

❑ When a SELECT statement chooses fewer than all of the available rows in a table, it is exhibiting the concept of selection.

❑ Selection is accomplished with the WHERE clause of the SELECT statement.

❑ When a SELECT statement chooses a combination of rows from more than one table by identifying common data that uniquely identifies rows, it is exhibiting the concept of joining.

❑ Joining can be accomplished in the SELECT statement with the WHERE clause or JOIN clause.

Describe How Schema Objects Work

❑ Tables store all the data in a database.

❑ Views are named SELECT statements.

❑ You can SELECT from a view.

❑ You may be able to INSERT, UPDATE, and DELETE from a view, depending on the view's structure.

❑ An index speeds queries on a table by creating a presorted lookup list for the table's indexed columns, along with an address pointer back to the indexed table.

❑ Sequences keep track of number counters to make the job of adding primary keys and other unique values easier.

❑ Synonyms are alias references to existing database objects, and can be either private or public.

SELF TEST

The following questions will help you measure your understanding of the material presented in this chapter. Choose one correct answer for each question unless otherwise directed.

Execute a Basic SELECT Statement

1. Consider the following table structure:

```
DESC ENGINES
Name           Null? Type
------------ ----- ----------
ENGINE_ID              NUMBER
ENGINE_NAME            VARCHAR2(30)
DISPLACEMENT           NUMBER
```

Now consider the following SELECT statement:

```
SELECT ENGINE_NAME FROM ENGINES;
```

What will be the result of executing the SELECT statement?

A. It will display data from no more than one row of the ENGINES table.

B. It will display data from all of the rows in the ENGINES table, however many there may be.

C. It will fail with a syntax error because it doesn't include the ENGINE_ID column.

D. It will display only the rows in the ENGINES table that contain values for the ENGINE_NAME column.

2. Review the following SELECT statement (Note: line numbers have been added for readability and reference purposes):

```
01    SELECT  1
02    , UPDATE,
03    FROM    EMPLOYEE_REVIEW;
```

Which of the following is incorrect about the SQL statement? (Choose two answers.)

A. There is a number included as the first item in the expression list.

B. The reserved word UPDATE is included as part of the select list.

C. There is a comma at the end of the select list.

D. The comma at the beginning of line 2 should be at the end of line 1.

3. Which of the following is *not* required to form a syntactically correct SELECT statement?
   A. SELECT
   B. A valid name of a column
   C. FROM
   D. A valid name of a table or view

4. Which of the following statements can be said of the SELECT statement's WHERE clause? (Choose two.)
   A. It specifies which columns are to be returned from the table.
   B. It specifies which rows are to be returned from the table.
   C. It is optional.
   D. It does the same thing as ORDER BY.

List the Capabilities of SQL SELECT Statements

5. You are tasked with creating a SELECT statement to retrieve data from a database table named PORTS. The PORTS table has two columns: PORT_ID and PORT_NAME. Which of the following is a valid SELECT statement? (Choose all that apply.)
   A. SELECT * FROM PORTS;
   B. SELECT PORT_NAME, PORT_ID FROM PORTS;
   C. SELECT PORT_ID, PORT_NAME FROM PORTS;
   D. SELECT ALL THE COLUMNS FROM PORTS;

6. Review the exhibit that follows:

```
DESC SHIPS
Name           Null? Type
------------   ----- ----------
SHIP_ID              NUMBER
SHIP_NAME            VARCHAR2(30)
```

   Which of the following SELECT statements will produce a syntax error? (Choose two.)
   A. SELECT FROM SHIPS;
   B. SELECT 1*2, (4+5), SHIP_NAME FROM SHIPS;
   C. SELECT SHIP_ID, SHIP_ID, SHIP_ID FROM SHIPS;
   D. SELECT (SHIP_ID, SHIP_NAME) FROM SHIPS;

7. Consider the following list of rows from a table called CUSTOMERS:

```
CUSTOMER_ID  FIRST_NAME  MIDDLE  LAST_NAME     ZIP_CODE
-----------  ----------  ------  ------------  --------
          1  Bianca      M.      Canales       93053
          2  Hung        A.      Nguyen        92305
          3  Bianca      M.      Jackson       03233
          4  Maya        R.      Canales       10302
          5  Bianca      T.      Canales       90203
```

Now consider the following SQL statement:

```
SELECT DISTINCT LAST_NAME, FIRST_NAME FROM CUSTOMERS;
```

What will be the result of the SELECT statement?

A. It will execute and display 3 rows of data.

B. It will execute and display 4 rows of data.

C. It will execute and display 5 rows of data.

D. It will fail with a syntax error because you cannot use DISTINCT with more than one column in the SELECT statement.

8. Review the SQL statement that follows:

```
SELECT    ROWNUM, *
FROM      PORTS
ORDER BY PORT_NAME;
```

What will be the result of an attempt to execute this statement?

A. It will display each row of the PORTS table, with the first column showing a system-assigned row number in numerical order, starting with 1 and continuing until the last row.

B. It will display each row of the PORTS table, with the first column showing a system-assigned row number in random order, because ORDER BY is processed after the ROWNUM is assigned.

C. It will fail with a syntax error because you cannot use ROWNUM and the asterisk together in a single column list.

D. None of the above.

9. Review the following data listing for a table called ONLINE_ORDERS:

```
UNIT_PRICE  SHIPPING  TAX_MULTIPLIER
----------  --------  --------------
      3.00      4.00            1.10
```

Now consider the following SQL statement:

```
SELECT UNIT_PRICE + SHIPPING * TAX_MULTIPLIER
FROM   ONLINE_ORDERS;
```

What will be the result of this SELECT statement?

A.   12.12

B.   7.70

C.   7.40

D.   .70

10.   Parentheses can be used in an equation to do which of the following?

A.   Avoid the need for using database column names in a select list.

B.   Matrix efficient technologies.

C.   Enclose reserved words.

D.   Override the rules of operator precedence.

11.   A SELECT that draws data from two or more tables by relating common information between them is said to be doing which of the following?

A.   Projecting

B.   Joining

C.   Provisioning

D.   Linking

Describe How Schema Objects Work

12.   The database object that stores lookup information to speed up querying in tables is:

A.   ROWID

B.   INDEX

C.   VIEW

D.   LOOKUP

13.   To create another name for an object, and make that name available to the entire database, you would create which of the following? (Choose the best answer.)

A.   PUBLIC TABLE

B.   SYNONYM

C.   ALIAS

D.   PUBLIC SYNONYM

14. All database data is stored in:

    A. TABLES

    B. TABLES and VIEWS

    C. TABLES, VIEWS, SEQUENCES, and SYNONYMS

    D. None of the above.

15. A database object that is defined by a SELECT statement but contains no data is a:

    A. VIEW

    B. SYNONYM

    C. SEQUENCE

    D. Not possible

SELF TEST ANSWERS

Execute a Basic SELECT Statement

1. ☑ **B.** The lack of the optional WHERE clause indicates that the SELECT will return all of the rows in the table.

   ☒ **A, C,** and **D** are incorrect. The query doesn't require the inclusion of the ENGINE_ID column, nor any particular column. The fact that the ENGINE_NAME column is included has no bearing on the rows that may or may not be returned. If it just so happens that the rows returned have no values for the ENGINE_NAME column, then so be it—the two issues are unrelated as far as the SELECT statement is concerned.

2. ☑ **B** and **C.** The UPDATE reserved word cannot be used in this context. It can only be used in the UPDATE statement. Also, the comma at the end of the expression list on line 2 is incorrect.

   ☒ **A** and **D** are incorrect. The single digit 1 is allowed. It is a numeric literal in this context, not the name of a table column, and besides, no table would let a column be created with a name consisting of the single digit 1 anyway. Also, the comma at the beginning of line 2 is fine; all of the components of the SELECT statement can be included on a single line or spread across multiple consecutive lines; it doesn't matter—the same is true for all SQL statements.

3. ☑ **B.** A column name is not required—you could use a literal value or some other expression, considering that expressions may include column names but are not required to include a column name.

   ☒ **A, C,** and **D** are incorrect. The reserved words SELECT and FROM are required, as is the name of a valid database table or view.

4. ☑ **B** and **C.** WHERE is the clause in which you can spell out the criteria by which data in the table is analyzed. For each row in the table, the WHERE condition is either true or false. If true, the row is displayed; if not true, the row is not included in the SELECT statement's output. The WHERE clause is optional.

   ☒ **A** and **D** are incorrect. WHERE does not determine which columns can be returned in a SELECT statement—the SELECT statement's select list can do that. The ORDER BY performs a very different function—it sorts the rows returned by the WHERE clause according to the criteria spelled out in the ORDER BY clause.

List the Capabilities of SQL SELECT Statements

5. ☑ **A, B,** and **C.** The first example uses the asterisk, which is a shorthand way of referencing every available column in the database table. The second answer is fine—even though the columns are listed in an order that is different from how they are structured in the table, it doesn't matter—you can list the columns in any order you wish.
   ☒ **D** is incorrect. The phrase "ALL THE COLUMNS" is not a valid clause for the SELECT statement.

6. ☑ **A** and **D.** Answer A is missing the select list, also known as the expression list. Answer D uses parentheses incorrectly. Both will produce a syntax error.
   ☒ **B** and **C** are incorrect. In other words, both are valid SELECT statements. Answer B selects two valid expressions and a column name. Answer C selects the same column name several times, which might seem odd, but it's perfectly valid syntactically.

7. ☑ **B.** The DISTINCT clause applies the requirement for unique information across all the columns chosen in the SELECT statement. In this case, the combination of LAST_NAME and FIRST_NAME, together, must be unique across the rows that are returned, and of the five rows of data, two have the same values for LAST_NAME and FIRST_NAME: the rows for CUSTOMER_ID of 1 and 5. Therefore these two rows will be represented by a single row in the output of this particular SELECT statement, and each of the remaining rows will be displayed for LAST_NAME and FIRST_NAME.
   ☒ **A, C,** and **D** are incorrect.

8. ☑ **C.** You cannot use the asterisk together with any other column in the SELECT statement. The asterisk can only be used by itself.
   ☒ **A, B,** and **D** are incorrect. If it weren't for the syntax error that results from the combination of the asterisk and a column reference—or in this particular case, a pseudocolumn reference—then the correct answer might have been B, which is that the ROWNUM would display, but with numbers assigned to the rows before ORDER BY changed the order of the rows, and along with that, the order of the ROWNUM values as well.

9. ☑ **C.** Remember that the orders of operator precedence require that the multiplication be performed first. That means the first action will be to multiply 4 times 1.10, resulting in 4.40. The result of that will be added to 3, thus: 7.40.
   ☒ **A, B,** and **D** are incorrect. You might get 13.2 if you multiply 3 times 4, and then multiply the result times 1.10. But the first two numbers have an operator for addition, not multiplication. And you might get 7.70 if you add 3 plus 4 and then multiply the results by 1.10, but that is not what SQL will do here; instead, SQL will first do the multiplication and then do the addition—see the explanation for the correct answer, C.

10. ☑ **D.** Parentheses are placed at the top of the order of operator precedence, meaning that anything you enclose in parentheses will be evaluated before anything else.

    ☒ **A, B,** and **C** are incorrect. Uh—no. Just—no.

11. ☑ **B.** Joining is the act of relating two tables—or more—and connecting their output by way of identifying common information to produce one combined set of rows. A SELECT statement that performs this feature is often referred to as a "join".

    ☒ **A, C,** and **D** are incorrect. Projecting isn't really the word, but "projection" refers to the act of choosing a subset of columns from the available set of columns in a given table. Provisioning isn't really a concept in Oracle SQL. Linking isn't relevant here, either.

Describe How Schema Objects Work

12. ☑ **B.** The INDEX stores data for speeding up querying.

    ☒ **A, C,** and **D** are incorrect. ROWID is a pseudocolumn, and not a database object. A VIEW names a SELECT statement. LOOKUP is something I made up; it's not a reserved word in Oracle as best as I know.

13. ☑ **D.** The answer is that you would create a PUBLIC SYNONYM.

    ☒ **A, B,** and **C** are incorrect. A public table is not a particular type of object in Oracle SQL, although you could create a table that essentially serves the purpose, as we'll explore when we look at privileges. A SYNONYM is close but not quite the right answer—yes, a SYNONYM is an alias for another database object, but a synonym is not, by default, available to the entire database, although it's possible to make it so, but it's far better to create a PUBLIC SYNONYM for that purpose. And there is no formal object known as ALIAS.

14. ☑ **A.** All data is stored in tables. Even data about the tables you create is stored automatically by Oracle SQL in a set of system-defined and system-maintained tables.

    ☒ **B, C,** and **D** are incorrect.

15. ☑ **A.** A VIEW is created by naming a SELECT statement.

    ☒ **B, C,** and **D** are incorrect. A SYNONYM is created by associating an alias with another database object name. A SEQUENCE is a number counter.

5
Restricting and Sorting Data

This chapter looks at two clauses of the SELECT statement: the WHERE clause and the ORDER BY clause. The WHERE clause specifies the criteria that are required for a row to be included in a SQL statement. Without it, all rows in a given table are retrieved, but with it, a SQL statement can selectively target particular rows for processing. The ORDER BY clause sorts the retrieved rows. It's very flexible: it can sort rows in ascending or descending order, or it can sort by expression lists or take advantage of other powerful features.

A working knowledge of both of these clauses is necessary in order to pass the exam. Let's get started.

CERTIFICATION OBJECTIVE 5.01

Limit the Rows That Are Retrieved by a Query

When building a SELECT statement, your first task is to identify which database table (or tables or views) contains the data you need. You also need to look at the table's structure to choose the columns that will be included in the select list of your SELECT statement. But rarely do you stop there. Most of the time you'll want to limit the rows you'll retrieve to a particular few, based on some sort of business rules. That task is accomplished with the SELECT statement's WHERE clause.

This section will look at the WHERE clause and its usage.

The WHERE Clause

The WHERE clause is one of the more important clauses of three different SQL statements: SELECT, UPDATE, and DELETE.

The purpose of the WHERE clause is to identify rows that you wish to include in your SQL statement. If you're working with a SELECT, then your WHERE clause chooses which rows will be included in your SELECT output. If it's an UPDATE you're working with, the WHERE clause defines which rows will be updated. If a DELETE, the WHERE clause defines which rows will be deleted.

Within any SQL statement, the WHERE clause, if included, always follows the FROM clause. WHERE is optional; it is never required in order to form a complete SQL statement, but if included, it must follow the FROM clause.

The WHERE clause starts with the reserved word WHERE, which is followed by the WHERE condition. The WHERE condition consists of one or more comparisons of expressions. The ultimate goal of the WHERE condition is to determine a value of true or false for each row in the tables (and/or views) identified in the FROM clause. If the WHERE condition returns a true for a given row, that row is included in the SQL statement. If it returns a false for a given row, that row is ignored for the SQL statement.

Let's look at a simple example:

```
01   SELECT EMPLOYEE_ID
02   FROM   WORK_HISTORY
03   WHERE  SHIP_ID = 3;
```

In this example, the WHERE clause on line 3 compares two expressions:

- The first expression is the table column SHIP_ID.
- Next is the comparison operator, which in this case is the equal sign.
- Finally we have the expression consisting of the literal value 3.

The WHERE clause will consider each row in the tables (and/or views) identified in the FROM clause. For this WHERE clause, each row's SHIP_ID value is analyzed to determine if its value equals 3. For each row that contains a value of 3 in the SHIP_ID column, the WHERE condition returns a value of "true" for that row, and that row is included in the SQL statement. All other rows are ignored.

Note that the SELECT statement's select list doesn't include SHIP_ID. The WHERE clause does not need to include any of the columns that are being displayed—any column in the table is available to the WHERE clause. In this particular example, the issue of whether to include a row is based on data that won't be included in the final results of the SELECT statement, and that's fine.

If you leave the WHERE clause out of a SELECT statement, then all rows of the table (or tables) are retrieved.

Here is another example of a WHERE clause:

```
01   SELECT PORT_NAME, CAPACITY
02   FROM   PORTS
03   WHERE  CAPACITY >= 5;
```

This example shows a complete WHERE clause on line 3. In this example, the SELECT statement will show the values for PORT_NAME and CAPACITY for all rows with a value in the CAPACITY column that is greater than or equal to 5.

In the next section we'll examine expressions in WHERE clauses.

Comparing Expressions

The WHERE clause uses a series of comparisons, each of which evaluates for each row to either true or false. Each comparison involves two expressions evaluated by a comparison operator. The expressions are first evaluated, then compared. Here is an example: on the left is an expression that consists solely of the column named SALARY. On the right is an expression that multiplies two numbers together:

```
SALARY >= 50899 * 1.12
```

In this example, if the value in SALARY is greater than or equal to the result of the math equation 50899 times 1.12, the result is true. Otherwise, it's false.

The examples you've seen so far have shown column names on the left, but that's not required—any valid expression may be placed on either side—or both sides—of the comparison operator. Ideally one of the expressions should include data from the table; otherwise, what's the point? But in terms of syntax, that is not required—all that is required is a valid expression on both sides of the comparison operator.

Let's look at another example:

```
START_DATE < END_DATE
```

If the value in the column titled START_DATE is less than the value in the column titled END_DATE, the expression is true; otherwise, it's false. (Note that when SQL compares dates, "less than" means "earlier than". For example, January 1 is less than January 2 of the same year. More on this issue in a bit.)

You've already seen expressions in Chapter 4. The WHERE clause uses "comparison operators" to compare two expressions to each other. See Table 5-1 for a full list of the comparison operators. The operators are relatively self-explanatory, except for IN, LIKE, and IS, all of which we'll discuss in upcoming sections.

TABLE 5-1	Operator	Description
Comparison Operators	=	Equal
	>=	Greater than or equal to
	>	Greater than
	<=	Less than or equal to
	<	Less than
	!=	Not equal

Operator	Description
<>	Not equal
∧=	Not equal
IN	Compares one value on the left side of the operator to a set of one or more values on the right side of the operator. The set of values must be enclosed in parentheses. If the values are presented as constants, they are separated by commas, as in ('Maple', 'Elm', 'Main') or (2009, 2010, 2011). A query may also be used, as in (SELECT PORT_NAME FROM PORTS)—this is called a "subquery" and we'll discuss much more on that topic in Chapter 9.
LIKE	Enables wildcard characters. There are two wildcard characters: _ The underscore is a wildcard character representing a single character. % The percent sign is a wildcard character representing zero or more characters. IS Used with NULL or NOT NULL

TABLE 5-1   Comparison Operators *(Continued)*

Comparing Datatypes

Within a single comparison, both expressions should be the same datatype in order for the comparison to work. There are essentially three general categories of datatypes to consider when performing comparisons—numeric, character string, and date. The rules for comparing datatypes are listed in Table 5-2.

Datatype	Comparison Rules
Numeric	Smaller numbers are less than larger numbers. 1 is less than 10. –3 is less than –1. The number 0 is greater than any negative number.
Character	'A' is less than 'Z'. 'Z' is less than 'a', meaning that uppercase letters are less than lowercase letters. Be careful of situations where numbers are treated as characters. For example, the string '2' is considered to be greater than the string '10', because character strings are treated as text, not numbers, unless SQL is given explicit instructions otherwise—something we'll address later, when we discuss functions that perform datatype conversions. Comparisons are case sensitive by default.
Dates	Yesterday is less than tomorrow. Earlier dates are less than later dates.

TABLE 5-2   Rules for Datatype Comparisons

You may have noticed that I said datatypes "should" be the same for two expressions that are compared to each other. I say "should" because this isn't an absolute rule. Sometimes you can get away with comparing expressions of different datatypes provided that SQL has enough information to perform an automatic datatype conversion and therefore treat both sides of the comparison as though they were the same datatype, even though they are not. While this can work, it's not recommended. The results of such automatic datatype conversions can be a bit tricky and relatively unpredictable, so it's best to avoid such situations. When we discuss SQL functions later, you'll see some functions that can be used to perform explicit datatype conversions, which is the better choice for the SQL professional. In the meantime, don't depend on Oracle SQL's automatic datatype conversion capabilities unless you love to live dangerously and don't mind if the rest of us laugh at you.

Here's an example that compares string values:

```
SELECT *
FROM    EMPLOYEES
WHERE   LAST_NAME = 'Smith';
```

This sample will show all columns in all the rows in the EMPLOYEES table where the value for the LAST_NAME column is the character string 'Smith'.

Note that text searches are case sensitive by default. In other words, this is a different query:

```
SELECT *
FROM    EMPLOYEES
WHERE   LAST_NAME = 'SMITH';
```

The search for employees with a value in the LAST_NAME column of 'SMITH' will not find the same rows that have a LAST_NAME value of 'Smith'. If you wish to do a search on both possibilities, see Chapter 6, where we'll discuss how to handle such situations using SQL functions.

on the **Job** *When comparing dates, I always like to remember the rhyme: "later" dates are "greater" dates. That's my trick for remembering how the rules of date comparison work.*

LIKE

The LIKE comparison operator is useful for performing wildcard searches on character data. It uses wildcard characters that you can embed within a text string.

LIKE works with columns of datatype CHAR and VARCHAR2. Technically it doesn't really work on DATE, but on a practical level it does—it performs an automatic datatype conversion of the DATE values involved before performing the comparison.

The two wildcard symbols are

- The underscore (_), representing a single character
- The percent sign (%), representing zero or more characters

The underscore is used when you are looking for a query in which you are allowing a fixed number of characters. Underscores can be repeated as required. For example, this query is looking for values in the PORT_NAME column that start with the string 'San', followed by a blank space, followed by any four characters:

```
01   SELECT PORT_NAME
02   FROM   PORTS
03   WHERE  PORT_NAME LIKE 'San ____';
```

In case you can't tell, that's four underscores after 'San ' in the preceding query. If you were to run this query against rows with these values:

```
San Diego
San Francisco
San Juan
```

the query will only return this value:

```
San Juan
```

That's because of the four underscores in the query (line 3), which specifically ask for four unknown characters after 'San '. No more, no less.

If you wish to indicate any number of unknown characters, ranging from zero to infinity, then use the percent sign. This query,

```
SELECT PORT_NAME
FROM   PORTS
WHERE  PORT_NAME LIKE 'San%';
```

will find all three rows in the previous example:

```
San Diego
San Francisco
San Juan
```

The percent sign, combined with LIKE, indicates that any number of characters are sought.

Underscores and percent signs may be used in any combination, in any order, in any location within the pattern. For example:

```
SELECT PORT_NAME
FROM   PORTS
WHERE  PORT_NAME LIKE '_o%';
```

This query is looking for values in PORT_NAME with any one random character in the first position, followed by the lower case letter 'o' in the second position, followed by anywhere from zero to an infinite number of characters after the letter 'o'. The following rows match the request:

```
Los Angeles
Honolulu
```

When working with LIKE, you put the wildcard character (or characters) within a string enclosed in single quotes. The string must occur after the reserved word LIKE, not before. In other words, the following is syntactically correct but doesn't perform as you might think it should:

```
SELECT PORT_NAME
FROM   PORTS
WHERE  'G_and%' LIKE PORT_NAME;
```

This query is asking if the string literal 'G_and%' happens to match the value contained within PORT_NAME. This probably isn't what was intended. The point here is that the wildcard characters are only "activated" if the pattern containing them is on the right side of the LIKE reserved word. This is the query that was probably intended:

```
SELECT PORT_NAME
FROM   PORTS
WHERE  PORT_NAME LIKE 'G_and%';
```

This query would find a row containing a PORT_NAME value such as this:

```
Grand Cayman
```

So remember: place the pattern after LIKE, not before. Oracle won't complain if you screw it up. But your output probably won't be what you're intending.

Boolean Logic

The WHERE clause includes support for Boolean logic, whereby multiple expressions can be connected together with a series of Boolean operators. This section looks at those operators, what they are, how they are used, and their order of precedence.

AND, OR

Most WHERE conditions involve more than just one comparison of two expressions. Most WHERE clauses contain several such comparisons. This is where the Boolean operators come in. Two or more comparisons of expressions can be connected together by using various combinations of the Boolean operators AND and OR. There's also a third operator—NOT—and it can be used to invert an AND or OR condition. Boolean operators evaluate multiple comparison expressions and produce a single true or false conclusion from the series of comparisons. For example:

```
01    SELECT  EMPLOYEE_ID
02    FROM    WORK_HISTORY
03    WHERE   SHIP_ID = 3
04            AND
05            STATUS = 'Pending';
```

Let's break this down the way Oracle SQL does. Consider the following data listing:

```
WORK_HISTORY_ID   EMPLOYEE_ID   SHIP_ID   STATUS
---------------   -----------   -------   ------
             10             3         1   Pending
             11             4         4   Active
             12             7         3   Pending
```

For each row, the WHERE condition will do the following:

- Determine if the SHIP_ID value equals 3
- Determine if the STATUS value is equal to the string 'Pending'

The results for each row are as follows:

```
WORK_HISTORY_ID   EMPLOYEE_ID   SHIP_ID   STATUS    SHIP_ID=3?   STATUS='Pending'?
---------------   -----------   -------   -------   ----------   -----------------
             10             3         1   Pending   FALSE        TRUE
             11             4         4   Active    FALSE        FALSE
             12             7         3   Pending   TRUE         TRUE
```

Now let's apply the AND operator to each row:

```
WORK_HISTORY_ID    SHIP_ID=3?              STATUS='Pending'?  RESULT
---------------    ----------              -----------------  --------
             10    FALSE        AND    TRUE                   FALSE
             11    FALSE        AND    FALSE                  FALSE
             12    TRUE         AND    TRUE                   TRUE
```

The rules of Boolean operator evaluation are the same as they are in conventional mathematics. See Table 5-3 for a listing of all the possible results of Boolean operator expressions.

The rules for Booleans are:

■ For AND, both expressions must be true for the combination to be true. Otherwise, the answer is false.

■ For OR, at least one expression needs to be true for the combination to evaluate to true. Otherwise, the answer is false.

The basic syntax for a SELECT statement with a WHERE clause that includes Booleans is as follows:

```
01    SELECT  select_list
02    FROM    from_table
03    WHERE
04            expression comparison_operator expression
05            Boolean_operator
06            expression comparison_operator expression
07            termination_character
```

Lines 4 and 6 represent the same thing—a comparison of two expressions.

TABLE 5-3	**Boolean Expression**	**Result**
Boolean Expression Combinations and Results	TRUE AND TRUE	TRUE
	TRUE AND FALSE	FALSE
	FALSE AND TRUE	FALSE
	FALSE AND FALSE	FALSE
	TRUE OR TRUE	TRUE
	TRUE OR FALSE	TRUE
	FALSE OR TRUE	TRUE
	FALSE OR FALSE	FALSE

A single WHERE clause may include as many of these comparisons as are required, indicated on line 4, and also on line 6—provided they are each separated by a Boolean operator.

NOT

The reserved word NOT is part of the set of Boolean operators. It can be placed in front of an expression to reverse its conclusion from true to false, or vice versa.

For example, let's modify a SELECT statement you saw earlier:

```
01    SELECT EMPLOYEE_ID
02    FROM   WORK_HISTORY
03    WHERE  SHIP_ID = 3
04           AND
05           NOT STATUS = 'Pending';
```

In this SELECT, we've added the reserved word NOT on line 5 to reverse the findings of the comparison of the string 'Pending' to the values in the column STATUS. If you were to run this version of the SELECT against the same three rows you used earlier, you'd get a very different result:

WORK_HISTORY_ID	EMPLOYEE_ID	SHIP_ID	STATUS	*SHIP_ID=3?*	*NOT STATUS='Pending'?*
10	3	1	Pending	FALSE	FALSE
11	4	4	Active	FALSE	TRUE
12	7	3	Pending	TRUE	FALSE

With an AND operator still in use here, now our SELECT statement will return no rows, since AND requires both sides to be true, and in this case none are.

Let's look at another example:

```
01    SELECT EMPLOYEE_ID
02    FROM   WORK_HISTORY
03    WHERE  NOT SHIP_ID = 3;
```

As you can see from this example, NOT can be used without any other Boolean operators.

**o n   t h e
j o b**

If you're an experienced 3GL programmer and have used languages such as Oracle's PL/SQL, this section may have you wondering where the BOOLEAN datatype fits in to SQL. It doesn't. There is no BOOLEAN datatype in SQL. There is in PL/SQL, but not in SQL. Instead, expressions are compared to each other in order to determine a Boolean condition of TRUE or FALSE, and the Boolean operators compare them to determine an answer. The concepts of TRUE and FALSE are significant throughout SQL, as we see with the WHERE condition. But there are no specific datatypes that represent Boolean values.

Operator Precedence

Just as there is a set of rules regarding the order of evaluating arithmetic operators within expressions, so too are there rules for evaluating Boolean operators. It's very important that you remember the order in which SQL evaluates Boolean operators.

The bottom line: NOT is evaluated first. After that, AND is evaluated before OR. For example, consider the following data listing for a table called SHIP_CABINS:

```
ROOM_NUMBER   STYLE       WINDOW
- - - - - - - -   - - - - - - - -   - - - - - - - -
        102   Suite       Ocean
        103   Stateroom   Ocean
        104   Suite       None
        105   Stateroom   Ocean
        106   Suite       None
```

Now consider this SQL statement against the data listing:

```
SELECT  ROOM_NUMBER
FROM    SHIP_CABINS
WHERE   STYLE = 'Suite'
   OR   STYLE = 'Stateroom'
  AND   WINDOW = 'Ocean';
```

How many rows do you think this query will retrieve? Are you thinking . . . three rows, by any chance? If you are, you're not alone; most people tend to. But . . . you'll really get five rows. Why? Because of the rules of Boolean operator precedence. An English-speaking person might read that query as asking for all rows with a STYLE value of either 'Suite' or 'Stateroom' and also with a value for WINDOW of 'Ocean'. But SQL sees this differently—it first evaluates the AND expression. SQL is looking for all the rows where STYLE is 'Stateroom' and WINDOW is 'Ocean' . . . OR . . . . any row with a STYLE value of 'Suite', regardless of its value for WINDOW. In other words, it's doing this:

ROOM_NUMBER	STYLE	WINDOW	Stateroom AND Ocean?		Suite?
102	Suite	Ocean	FALSE	OR	TRUE
103	Stateroom	Ocean	TRUE	OR	FALSE
104	Suite	None	FALSE	OR	TRUE
105	Stateroom	Ocean	TRUE	OR	FALSE
106	Suite	None	FALSE	OR	TRUE

Remember, only one side in an OR must be TRUE. And given this criterion, all five rows will evaluate to true.

You can use parentheses to override the rules of Boolean operator precedence, like this:

```
SELECT ROOM_NUMBER
FROM   SHIP_CABINS
WHERE  (STYLE = 'Suite'
   OR  STYLE = 'Stateroom')
   AND WINDOW = 'Ocean';
```

That query will retrieve three rows.

Additional WHERE Clause Features

The WHERE clause offers some options to streamline the readability of your code. This section describes features that are important to advanced WHERE clause usage.

IN

Sometimes you'll find yourself comparing a single column to a series of various values. For example:

```
SELECT PORT_NAME
FROM   PORTS
WHERE  COUNTRY = 'UK' OR COUNTRY = 'USA' OR COUNTRY = 'Bahamas';
```

That query is correct, but in such situations, you have the option of choosing a different style. You may choose to use the reserved word IN as an alternative. For example:

```
SELECT PORT_NAME
FROM   PORTS
WHERE  COUNTRY IN ('UK', 'USA', 'Bahamas');
```

The rules that govern the use of the IN operator include the following:

- IN can be used with dates, numbers, or text expressions.
- The list of expressions must be enclosed in a set of parentheses.
- The list of expressions must be of the same datatype—or be similar enough that Oracle can perform automatic datatype conversion to make them all the same.
- The list can include anywhere from one expression to several, each separated by commas.

In addition, the Boolean operator NOT may precede the IN operator, as follows:

```
SELECT  PORT_NAME
FROM    PORTS
WHERE   COUNTRY NOT IN ('UK', 'USA', 'Bahamas');
```

The use of NOT will identify rows as true if they do not contain a value from the list.

You'll see later that the reserved word IN is particularly important in the WHERE clause when we're using subqueries, which we'll discuss in Chapter 9.

BETWEEN

In addition to the formats we've seen so far, the WHERE clause also supports a feature that can compare a single expression to a range of values. This technique involves the reserved word BETWEEN. Here's an example:

```
SELECT  PORT_NAME
FROM    PORTS
WHERE   CAPACITY BETWEEN 3 AND 4;
```

This is the equivalent of the following statement:

```
SELECT  PORT_NAME
FROM    PORTS
WHERE   CAPACITY >= 3
  AND   CAPACITY <= 4;
```

Notice that BETWEEN is inclusive. In other words, it doesn't simply look for values "between" the two comparison expressions but also includes values that are equal to the comparison expressions.

The range can be specified using any valid expression.

The range should be from lowest to highest. If you specify the higher value first, and the lower value second, your code will be accepted syntactically but will always return zero rows.

The NOT keyword may also be combined with BETWEEN. The following are valid statements:

```
SELECT  PORT_NAME
FROM    PORTS
WHERE   CAPACITY NOT BETWEEN 3 AND 4;


SELECT  PORT_NAME
FROM    PORTS
WHERE   NOT CAPACITY BETWEEN 3 AND 4;
```

These two examples are equivalent to each other.

IS NULL, IS NOT NULL

Remember that the NULL value represents an unknown value. NULL is the equivalent of "I don't know". Any value that's compared to "I don't know" is going to produce an unknown result—i.e., NULL. For example:

```
SELECT PORT_NAME
FROM    PORTS
WHERE   CAPACITY = NULL;
```

This SQL statement will never retrieve any rows, never ever, never ever ever. Don't believe me? Try it, I'll wait.

Told you. It will not ever retrieve any rows, not even if the value for CAPACITY is NULL within a given row. The reason is that this is asking SQL to compare CAPACITY to a value of "I don't know". But what if the value of CAPACITY in the database table is actually NULL? Shouldn't this work then? Shouldn't you be able to ask if CAPACITY = NULL? Why isn't the expression "NULL = NULL" true?

Well—let me ask you this: I'm thinking of two numbers, and I'm not going to tell you what either one of them are. Instead I'm just going to ask you this: are these two numbers equal to each other? Well? Are they?

Of course you can't possibly know. I think you'd have to say the answer is "I don't know", or NULL. And NULL, in terms of Boolean logic, is always assumed to be FALSE. So any time you create a WHERE condition that ends up as "anything = NULL", the answer will always be FALSE, and you'll never get a row—even if the "anything" is NULL itself.

But what do you do when you really need to test the value of something like CAPACITY to determine if it is NULL or not? There is an answer, and it's the SQL comparison condition IS NULL, and its companion IS NOT NULL.

Let's redo our SELECT statement:

```
SELECT PORT_NAME
FROM    PORTS
WHERE   CAPACITY IS NULL;
```

Now you're asking for rows from the PORTS table where the value for CAPACITY is unknown in the database—which is what IS NULL asks for. That's a very different query than asking if CAPACITY happens to be identical to some number that we haven't identified yet—which is what "= NULL" asks.

The opposite of the IS NULL comparison operator is IS NOT NULL, like this:

```
SELECT PORT_NAME
FROM    PORTS
WHERE   CAPACITY IS NOT NULL;
```

In this query, you're asking for all rows in which the CAPACITY value is identified in the database, i.e., wherever it is not NULL.

These concepts are very important. This is yet another example of one of the many ways in which SQL code might appear to be correct, might execute without any syntax or execution errors, and yet can be totally wrong.

Be sure you get this right. Don't screw it up. If you do, the problems will be subtle and potentially disastrous, and might only become apparent months later after bad data and incorrect reports have been circulated. So remember: Never use this:

```
= NULL
```

There is never a good reason to use that, ever. Always use this instead:

```
IS NULL
```

Got it?

Additional Concepts

There are more ways to customize a WHERE clause than what has been presented here. Upcoming topics that will be addressed in this book—and tested on the exam—include the following:

- Subqueries
- Set operators

These and other issues are important to the WHERE clause and important to the exam. They will be covered on their own in upcoming chapters.

CERTIFICATION OBJECTIVE 5.02

Sort the Rows That Are Retrieved by a Query

This section looks at another clause in the SELECT statement, the ORDER BY clause. ORDER BY is used to sort the rows that are retrieved by a SELECT statement. It sorts by specifying expressions for each row in the table. Sorting can be performed in either ascending or descending order. SQL will sort according to the datatype of the expression that is identified in the ORDER BY. You can include more than one expression. The first expression is given sorting priority, the second is given second-position priority, and so on.

ORDER BY is always the final clause in a SELECT statement. It is only used in SELECT; contrary to the WHERE clause, which can also be used in UPDATE and DELETE, the ORDER BY clause is unique to the SELECT statement and is not used in the other SQL statements.

(Note: in Chapter 9 we'll examine how you may embed a SELECT statement as a subquery within an INSERT, UPDATE, or DELETE statement—so in that regard, it is theoretically possible that an ORDER BY clause might be included in a SELECT statement that is embedded within, for example, an INSERT statement. But that is a separate issue.)

ORDER BY does not change data as it is stored in the table. Data in a table remains unchanged as a result of the ORDER BY. ORDER BY is part of the SELECT statement, and the SELECT statement is incapable of changing data in the database. Note, however, that when SELECT is embedded within other SQL statements like INSERT or UPDATE, changes to the database can result, but not because of SELECT alone. You'll see how that works in Chapter 9.

ORDER BY sorts the output of a SELECT statement for display purposes only. It is always the last step in a SELECT statement, and performs its sort after all the data has been retrieved and processed by the SELECT statement.

Reference by Name

Let's look at an example of ORDER BY in action. Consider the following data listing from a table ADDRESSES.

```
ADDRESS_ID   STREET_ADDRESS             CITY            ST   COUNTRY
----------   -------------------        -------------   --   ------
         1   350 Oracle Parkway         Redwood City    CA   USA
         2   1600 Amphitheatre Parkway  Mountain View   CA   USA
         3   1 Dell Way                 Round Rock      TX   USA
         4   29 E Ohio St               Chicago         IL   USA
         5   5788 Roswell Rd NE         Atlanta         GA   USA
         6   10103 100 St NW            Edmonton        AB   Canada
         7   1221 Avenue of the Americas New York       NY   USA
         8   239 Baker Street           London               UK
         9   1 rue des Carrieres        Quebec City     QC   Canada
        10   2041 S Harbor Blvd         Anaheim         CA   USA
        11   600 N Michigan Ave         Chicago         IL   USA
        12   1515 Sheridan Rd           Wilmette        IL   USA
```

We can select this data and sort it by specifying the column name (or names) in the ORDER BY clause of the SQL statement, as follows:

```
SELECT    ADDRESS_ID, STREET_ADDRESS, CITY, STATE, COUNTRY
FROM      ADDRESSES
ORDER BY STATE;
```

The results are shown in Figure 5-1. Notice in the figure that the rows are sorted in alphabetical order according to the value in the STATE column.

Note that the row with a NULL value for STATE is last. The NULL value is considered the "highest" value.

As we review the output, it becomes clear that we might also wish to alphabetize our information by city for each state. We can do that by modifying our ORDER BY clause ever so slightly:

```
SELECT    ADDRESS_ID, STREET_ADDRESS, CITY, STATE, COUNTRY
FROM      ADDRESSES
ORDER BY STATE, CITY;
```

In the modified version of our ORDER BY, we add a second column to the ORDER BY clause by which we wish to sort. The results of this SELECT statement are displayed in Figure 5-2. The rows have been sorted first by STATE, and then by the CITY value for each STATE.

Note that the choice of columns we include in the ORDER BY clause does not influence which columns we choose to display in the SELECT expression list. It would probably be easier to read if we put the same columns used in the ORDER BY in the same positions as the SELECT expression list. In other words, this query would probably produce a more readable output:

```
SELECT    STATE, CITY, ADDRESS_ID, STREET_ADDRESS, COUNTRY
FROM      ADDRESSES
ORDER BY STATE, CITY;
```

The output of this SELECT would draw attention to our intent, which is to sort data by STATE first, then CITY. But while this might be considered preferential design in certain circumstances, it is by no means required within the syntax of the SQL statement. We're not even required to include the ORDER BY columns in the SELECT statement's expression list at all. This is another perfectly valid SELECT statement:

```
SELECT    ADDRESS_ID, STREET_ADDRESS, COUNTRY
FROM      ADDRESSES
ORDER BY STATE, CITY;
```

FIGURE 5-1

Results of
SELECT with
ORDER BY
STATE

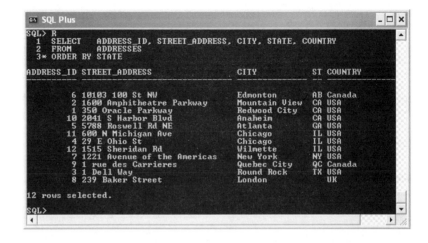

```
SQL> R
  1   SELECT    ADDRESS_ID, STREET_ADDRESS, CITY, STATE, COUNTRY
  2   FROM      ADDRESSES
  3* ORDER BY STATE

ADDRESS_ID STREET_ADDRESS                           CITY         ST COUNTRY
---------- --------------------------------------- ------------ -- -------

         6 10103 100 St NW                          Edmonton     AB Canada
         2 1600 Amphitheatre Parkway                Mountain View CA USA
         1 350 Oracle Parkway                       Redwood City CA USA
        10 2041 S Harbor Blvd                       Anaheim      CA USA
         5 5788 Roswell Rd NE                       Atlanta      GA USA
        11 600 N Michigan Ave                       Chicago      IL USA
         4 29 E Ohio St                             Chicago      IL USA
        12 1515 Sheridan Rd                         Wilmette     IL USA
         7 1221 Avenue of the Americas              New York     NY USA
         9 1 rue des Carrieres                      Quebec City  QC Canada
         3 1 Dell Way                               Round Rock   TX USA
         8 239 Baker Street                         London          UK

12 rows selected.

SQL>
```

FIGURE 5-2

Results of
SELECT with
ORDER BY
STATE, CITY

```
SQL> R
  1   SELECT    ADDRESS_ID, STREET_ADDRESS, CITY, STATE, COUNTRY
  2   FROM      ADDRESSES
  3* ORDER BY STATE, CITY

ADDRESS_ID STREET_ADDRESS                           CITY         ST COUNTRY
---------- --------------------------------------- ------------ -- -------

         6 10103 100 St NW                          Edmonton     AB Canada
        10 2041 S Harbor Blvd                       Anaheim      CA USA
         2 1600 Amphitheatre Parkway                Mountain View CA USA
         1 350 Oracle Parkway                       Redwood City CA USA
         5 5788 Roswell Rd NE                       Atlanta      GA USA
        11 600 N Michigan Ave                       Chicago      IL USA
         4 29 E Ohio St                             Chicago      IL USA
        12 1515 Sheridan Rd                         Wilmette     IL USA
         7 1221 Avenue of the Americas              New York     NY USA
         9 1 rue des Carrieres                      Quebec City  QC Canada
         3 1 Dell Way                               Round Rock   TX USA
         8 239 Baker Street                         London          UK

12 rows selected.

SQL>
```

Notice that we're sorting by columns that aren't included in the SELECT statement's expression list.

Without an ORDER BY clause, there is no guarantee regarding the sequence in which rows will be displayed in a SELECT statement's output. The rows may be produced in a different order from one query to another. The only way to ensure consistency to the output is to include an ORDER BY clause.

ASC and DESC

There are two reserved words that specify the direction of sorting on a given column of the ORDER BY clause. Those reserved words are ASC and DESC.

- ASC is short for "ascending" and indicates that values will be sorted in ascending order. In other words, the lowest, or least, value will be listed first, followed by values of higher, or greater, value. ASC is the default choice and as such does not need to be specified when desired but may be specified for clarity.
- DESC is short for "descending" and indicates that values will be sorted in descending order. In other words, the highest, or greatest, value will be listed first, and values will continue to be listed in decreasing, or lesser, value.

As just stated, the default is ASC. You don't need to specify ASC. The ORDER BY examples you've seen so far have defaulted to ASC without our having to specify it. But you can specify ASC if you wish:

```
SELECT    SHIP_ID, PROJECT_COST, PROJECT_NAME, DAYS
FROM      PROJECTS
ORDER BY SHIP_ID ASC;
```

Here's a variation on the preceding SELECT statement that uses a combination of ASC and DESC:

```
SELECT    SHIP_ID, PROJECT_COST, PROJECT_NAME, DAYS
FROM      PROJECTS
ORDER BY SHIP_ID ASC, PROJECT_COST DESC;
```

The results of this SELECT are displayed in Figure 5-3. Notice that the SHIP_ID values are listed in ascending order, but that for each ship, the PROJECT_COST values are shown from the highest to the lowest values.

ASC and DESC each operate on the individual ORDER BY expressions. There is no way to assign the ASC or DESC to all the ORDER BY expressions collectively; instead, you must place your choice after each individual ORDER BY expression, remembering that ASC is the default and therefore does not need to be specified.

FIGURE 5-3

PROJECTS table
with ORDER BY
ASC and DESC

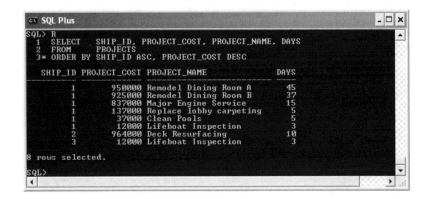

Expressions

Note that the expressions you can include in an ORDER BY clause are not limited to columns in a table. Any expression may be used. In order to be useful, the expression should include a value in the table; otherwise, the value may not change and there won't be any meaningful effect on the rows in the table.

For example, here's a data listing for the PROJECTS table:

PROJECT_ID	SHIP_ID	PROJECT_NAME	PROJECT_COST	DAYS
1	2	Hull Cleaning	340000	20
2	2	Deck Resurfacing	964000	10
3	3	Lifeboat Inspection	12000	3
4	1	Clean Pools	37000	5
5	1	Replace Lobby Carpeting	137000	5
6	1	Major Engine Service	837000	15

This data listing shows a series of projects. For each project, we see the SHIP_ID for which the project is intended, the project's total cost, and the estimated number of days it will take to complete each project.

Looking at the values for PROJECT_COST and DAYS, we see enough information to compute the average cost per day for each project. In other words:

```
PROJECT_COST / DAYS
```

For example, the per-day cost for the three-day "Lifeboat Inspection" will turn out to be 4000, or 12000 divided by 3.

What if we want to sort these rows according to the computed value of the PROJECT_COST / DAYS? No problem:

```
SELECT   *
FROM     PROJECTS
ORDER BY PROJECT_COST / DAYS;
```

That query will achieve the result we're after. Let's vary it a bit in order to see more of what it is we're calculating and sorting:

```
SELECT   PROJECT_ID, PROJECT_NAME, PROJECT_COST, DAYS, PROJECT_
COST/DAYS
FROM     PROJECTS
ORDER BY PROJECT_COST/DAYS;
```

The results of this query are shown in Figure 5-4. Note that the rows are ordered by a value that doesn't exist in the table, but rather a value that is the result of an expression that draws values from the table.

The Column Alias

As you've already seen, a SELECT statement can include expressions in the select list. For example:

```
SELECT   PROJECT_ID, PROJECT_NAME, PROJECT_COST, DAYS, PROJECT_COST/DAYS
FROM     PROJECTS
ORDER BY PROJECT_COST/DAYS;
```

Notice the output in Figure 5-4, and the default title of the fifth column. SQL has used the expression as the title of the column.

FIGURE 5-4

PROJECTS sorted by PROJECT_ COST / DAYS

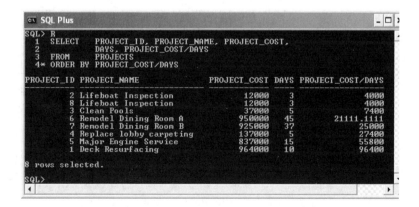

We could have used a SQL feature called the "column alias". Here is the same query with a column alias:

```
01    SELECT    PROJECT_ID, PROJECT_NAME, PROJECT_COST,
02              DAYS, PROJECT_COST/DAYS AS PER_DAY_COST
03    FROM      PROJECTS
04    ORDER BY PER_DAY_COST;
```

Notice the PER_DAY_COST column alias at the end of line 2. The column alias is a name you make up and place just after the column you wish to alias, separated by the optional keyword AS. In this example, the column with the column alias is the final column in the select list. Once the column alias is used, you can reference it from within the ORDER BY clause, as we do on line 4.

The rules for using a column alias include the following:

- Each expression in the SELECT list may optionally be followed by a column alias.
- A column alias is placed after the expression in the select list, separated by the optional keyword AS and a required space.
- If the column alias is enclosed in double quotes, it can include spaces and other special characters.
- If the column alias is not enclosed in double quotes, it is named according to the standard rules for naming database objects.
- The column alias exists within the SQL statement and does not exist outside of the SQL statement.
- The column alias will become the new header in the output of the SQL statement.
- The column alias can be referenced within the ORDER BY clause, but nowhere else—such as WHERE, GROUP BY, or HAVING.

Here's an example of a column alias that uses the double quotation marks. Notice the inclusion of a space in the alias.

```
01    SELECT    PROJECT_ID, PROJECT_NAME, PROJECT_COST,
02              DAYS, PROJECT_COST/DAYS "Cost Per Day"
03    FROM      PROJECTS
04    ORDER BY "Cost Per Day";
```

See the output of this query in Figure 5-5. Notice the column heading for the aliased column—the alias becomes the new heading in the SQL output.

FIGURE 5-5

SELECT output
with column alias

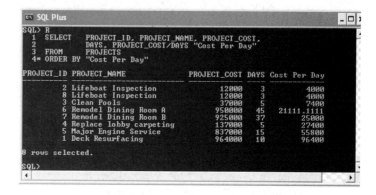

The point of bringing up the alias here, in this discussion about ORDER BY, is this: you can use the column alias when referencing any column with ORDER BY, and it's particularly useful when trying to use ORDER BY with an expression from within the SELECT statement's expression list.

Reference by Position

Another way the ORDER BY clause can identify columns to be sorted is via the "reference by position" method. This only works if the intent of the ORDER BY is to sort rows according to information that is included in the SELECT list. For example:

```
SELECT    PROJECT_ID, PROJECT_NAME, PROJECT_COST,
          DAYS, PROJECT_COST/DAYS FROM    PROJECTS
ORDER BY 5;
```

Notice that we choose to ORDER BY 5 in this SQL statement. The number 5 in this context is referencing the fifth item in the SELECT statement's select list, which is the expression "PROJECT_COST/DAYS".

Any expression in the SELECT list can be referenced using its numeric position. The first expression is considered number 1, the second is number 2, and so on.

Any attempt to reference a position that doesn't exist will produce a SQL error; for example, this is invalid:

```
SELECT    PROJECT_ID, PROJECT_COST/DAYS
FROM      PROJECTS
ORDER BY 5;
```

This statement will not execute. The ORDER BY clause must identify a number that corresponds to an item that is in the SELECT list.

Combinations

ORDER BY can combine the various techniques of reference by name, reference by column alias, and reference by position, for example:

```
SELECT SHIP_ID, PROJECT_COST, PROJECT_NAME "The Project", DAYS
FROM PROJECTS
ORDER BY SHIP_ID DESC, "The Project", 2;
```

This example is a valid statement. It sorts rows by

■ The value of SHIP_ID, in descending order

■ The value in the PROJECT_NAME column, which has a column alias in this SQL statement of "The Project"

■ The value in the PROJECT_COST column, which is the second item in the SELECT list

The output of this query is shown in Figure 5-6.

Remember that ordering a SELECT statement by position is extremely useful in many situations that involve complex SELECT statements. Later you'll see some interesting combinations of multiple SELECT statements—such as the section that looks at using set operators that combine multiple SELECT statements into one—and in those situations, you can always reference an ORDER BY column by position.

FIGURE 5-6

PROJECTS sorted by multiple techniques

```
SQL> R
  1   SELECT SHIP_ID, PROJECT_COST, PROJECT_NAME "The Project", DAYS
  2   FROM PROJECTS
  3*  ORDER BY SHIP_ID DESC, "The Project", 2

  SHIP_ID PROJECT_COST The Project                          DAYS
  ------- ------------ ----------------------------------   ----
        3        12000 Lifeboat Inspection                     3
        2       964000 Deck Resurfacing                       10
        1        37000 Clean Pools                             5
        1        12000 Lifeboat Inspection                     3
        1       837000 Major Engine Service                   15
        1       950000 Remodel Dining Room A                  45
        1       925000 Remodel Dining Room B                  37
        1       137000 Replace lobby carpeting                 5

8 rows selected.

SQL>
```

ORDER BY and NULL

When SELECT performs a sort using ORDER BY, it treats any values that it might find to be NULL as "greater than" any other value. In other words, when you sort by a numeric datatype column, and that column contains NULL values, the NULL values will sort as being greater than all NOT NULL values in the list. The same is true for character datatypes and date datatypes.

CERTIFICATION SUMMARY

The WHERE clause is part of the SQL statements SELECT, UPDATE, and DELETE. It is used to identify the rows that will be affected by the SQL statement. For the SELECT statement, WHERE determines which rows are retrieved. For the UPDATE statement, it determines which rows will be updated. For the DELETE statement, it determines which rows will be deleted. The WHERE clause concerns itself with entire rows, not just the columns that are the subject of the particular SQL statement of which it is a part. The WHERE clause can reference columns that are not in the SELECT list.

The WHERE clause is optional. If included in a SELECT statement, it must follow the FROM clause.

The WHERE clause compares two expressions and determines if the result of the comparison is true or false. At least one of the two expressions should include a column from whatever table the SQL statement is intended to address, so that the WHERE clause is relevant to the SQL statement. The expressions are compared using comparison operators. Examples include the equal sign, the not-equal sign, and the greater-than and less-than signs.

A series of comparisons can be connected together using the Boolean operators AND and OR. The NOT operator can also be included. Together, these expressions can form complex WHERE clauses.

The LIKE operator can activate the wildcard characters. The two wildcard characters are the underscore (_) and the percent sign (%).

The IN operator can compare a single value to a set of values. An expression using the IN operator will evaluate to true if that single value matches any of the values in the expression list.

When using the WHERE clause to locate rows that have a NULL value, never use the "= NULL" comparison, instead always use the IS NULL or IS NOT NULL comparison operators.

The ORDER BY clause of the SELECT statement is the method for sorting the rows of output returned by the SELECT statement. The ORDER BY clause is optional, but if included in a SELECT statement, it is always the final clause of the SELECT statement.

ORDER BY specifies one or more expressions. Each expression is used by ORDER BY to sort each row in the result set. Output rows are sorted first by the first expression, and for any rows that share the same value for the first expression, those rows will be sub-sorted for expression two, and so on.

Expressions for ORDER BY follow the same rules as expressions in the SELECT statement's select list and the WHERE clause. Each expression should ideally reference a column in the table, but this isn't required.

The ASC and DESC reserved words can be used in an ORDER BY clause to determine the direction of sorting for each individual expression. ASC will sort values in ascending order, and DESC will sort in descending order. ASC is the default and need not be specified. The specification of ASC or DESC should follow each expression with a space separating them.

ORDER BY sorts values according to datatypes. With numeric datatypes, low numbers are low, and high numbers are high; with dates, yesterday is lower than tomorrow, and next week is higher than last month; with characters, 'Z' is less than 'a', and the character string '10' is less than the character string '3'.

ORDER BY can specify expressions in the SELECT statement's select list by referencing the column alias, if one was created within the SELECT list. ORDER BY can also identify expressions in the SELECT list by the number corresponding to the position of the item in the SELECT list; for instance, "ORDER BY 1" will sort by the first item in the SELECT list.

ORDER BY can combine all of these features into one series of order items.

A column alias, if specified in the select list, is not recognized in the WHERE, GROUP BY, or HAVING clause.

TWO-MINUTE DRILL

Limit the Rows That Are Retrieved by a Query

❑ The WHERE clause comes after the FROM clause.

❑ WHERE identifies which rows are to be included in the SQL statement.

❑ WHERE is used by SELECT, UPDATE, and DELETE.

❑ WHERE is an optional clause.

❑ Expressions form the building blocks of the WHERE clause.

❑ Expressions may include column names, literal values, and as you'll see in Chapter 6. The WHERE clause compares expressions to each other using comparison operators and determines if the comparisons are true or false.

❑ Boolean operators may separate each comparison to create a complex series of evaluations. Collectively, the final result for each row in the table will either be true or false; if true, the row is returned; if false, it is ignored.

❑ The Boolean operators are AND, OR, and NOT.

❑ The rules of Boolean operator precedence require that NOT be evaluated first, then AND, and then OR.

❑ Parentheses can override any Boolean operator precedence.

❑ When comparing date datatypes: earlier date values are considered "less" than later dates, so anything in January will be "less than" anything in December of the same year.

❑ When comparing character datatypes, the letter 'a' is less than the letter 'z', upper case letters are "lower than" lower case letters, and the character representation of '3' is greater than the character representation of '22', even though the results would be different if they were numeric datatypes.

❑ LIKE can be used to activate wildcard searches.

❑ IN can be used to compare a single expression to a set of one or more expressions.

❑ BETWEEN can be used to see if a particular expression's value is within a range of values. BETWEEN is inclusive, not exclusive, so that BETWEEN 2 and 3 includes the numbers 2 and 3 as part of the range.

❑ Use IS NULL or IS NOT NULL when testing a column to see if its value is NULL.

Sort the Rows That Are Retrieved by a Query

❏ ORDER BY is an optional clause used to sort the rows retrieved in a SELECT statement.

❏ If used, ORDER BY is always the last clause in the SELECT statement.

❏ ORDER BY uses expressions to direct the sorting order of the result set of the SELECT statement.

❏ Each expression is evaluated in order, so that the first item in the ORDER BY will do the initial sort of output rows, the second item listed will sort any rows that share identical data for the first ORDER BY element, and so on.

❏ ORDER BY can sort by columns in the table, regardless of whether the columns appear in the SELECT statement's select list or not.

❏ ORDER BY can also sort by expressions of any kind, following the same rules of expressions that you've seen with the WHERE clause and the select list.

❏ Numeric data is sorted by default in ascending order, from lower numbers to higher.

❏ Character data is sorted by default in ascending order, from 'A' to 'Z'.

❏ Date data is sorted by default in ascending order, from prior dates to later dates.

❏ All sorts default to ascending order, which can be specified with the optional keyword ASC.

❏ Sort order can be changed to descending order with the keyword DESC.

❏ ORDER BY can identify columns by column alias, or by position within the SELECT list.

SELF TEST

The following questions will help you measure your understanding of the material presented in this chapter. Choose one correct answer for each question unless otherwise directed.

Limit the Rows That Are Retrieved by a Query

1. Consider the following SELECT statement:

```
SELECT  PORT_ID
FROM    PORTS
WHERE   1=2;
```

Which of the following is true of the SELECT statement?

A. It will produce a syntax error because the WHERE condition does not refer to any columns in the table.

B. It will produce a syntax error because the WHERE condition returns a FALSE value.

C. It will execute and return all of the rows in the table.

D. It will execute and return none of the rows in the table.

2. Review the information in this exhibit:

```
PORT_ID PORT_NAME                COUNTRY  CAPACITY
------- -------------------- --------  --------
1       Galveston                USA      4
2       San Diego                USA      4
3       San Francisco            USA      3
4       Los Angeles              USA      4
5       San Juan                 USA      3
6       Grand Cayman             UK       3
```

Now consider the following SELECT statement:

```
SELECT  *
FROM    PORTS
WHERE   PORT_NAME LIKE 'San%'
   OR   PORT_NAME LIKE 'Grand%'
  AND   CAPACITY  = 4;
```

How many rows from the data in the exhibit will be returned by the preceding query?

A. None

B. 1

C. 3

D. 6

3. Review the table listing from this PROJECTS table:

```
PROJECT_NAME                  COST
--------------------------    ------
Repair Hallway on Lido Deck   500.00
Fix broken window cabin 12    129.45
```

Next, review this SQL statement:

```
SELECT PROJECT_NAME FROM PROJECTS WHERE COST ^= 500;
```

How many rows will the SELECT statement return?

A. None, because the WHERE condition only wants rows with a cost greater than 500.

B. None, because of the syntax error in the expression "COST ^= 500".

C. 1

D. 2

4. Which of the following statements is true of Boolean operators? For this question, ignore the role of parentheses. (Choose two.)

A. AND is evaluated before NOT.

B. NOT is evaluated last.

C. OR is evaluated after AND.

D. NOT is evaluated first.

5. Review the following data listing for a table VENDORS:

```
VENDOR_ID   CATEGORY
---------   ---------------
        1   Supplier
        2   Teaming Partner
```

Now review the following SQL statement:

```
SELECT VENDOR_ID
FROM    VENDORS
WHERE   CATEGORY IN ('Supplier','Subcontractor','%Partner');
```

How many rows will the SELECT statement return?

A. 2

B. 1

C. 0

D. None—it will fail due to a syntax error

6. Review the following data listing for a table called SHIP_CABINS:

```
ROOM_NUMBER   STYLE      WINDOW
-----------   --------   --------
        102   Suite      Ocean
        103              Ocean
        104
```

The blank values are NULL. Now review the following SQL statement (line numbers are added for readability):

```
01   SELECT ROOM_NUMBER
02   FROM   SHIP_CABINS
03   WHERE  (STYLE = NULL) OR (WINDOW = NULL);
```

How many rows will the SQL statement retrieve?

 A. 0

B. 1

C. 2

D. None because you cannot use parentheses in line 3 to surround the expressions

7. Review the following data listing for a table SHIPS:

```
SHIP_ID   SHIP_NAME        CAPACITY   LENGTH   LIFEBOATS
-------   --------------   --------   ------   ---------
      1   Codd Crystal       2052      855         80
      2   Codd Elegance      2974      952         95
```

In the SHIPS table, SHIP_NAME has a datatype of VARCHAR2(20). All other columns are NUMBER. Now consider the following query (note—line numbers added for readability):

```
01   SELECT SHIP_ID
02   FROM   SHIPS
03   WHERE  CAPACITY BETWEEN 2052 AND 3000
04     AND  LENGTH IN ('100','855')
05     AND  SHIP_NAME LIKE 'Codd_%';
```

How many rows will the SELECT statement return?

A. None, because of a syntax error resulting from a datatype conflict in line 4

B. None, because line 5 is asking for SHIP names that contain an underscore after the string 'Codd', and none do

C. 2

D. 1

8. Assume all table name and column name references in the SQL statement that follows are valid. That being said—what is wrong with the syntax of the following SQL statement?

```
SELECT SHIP_ID
FROM    SHIPS
WHERE    ((2*LIFEBOATS)+57) - CAPACITY IN (LIFEBOATS*20, LIFEBOATS+LENGTH);
```

A. In the WHERE clause there is a syntax error before the word CAPACITY.

B. It needs to have either an equal sign or a not-equal sign.

C. In the WHERE clause there is a syntax error after the word IN.

D. There is nothing wrong with the syntax.

9. Review the following data listing for the SHIPS table:

```
SHIP_ID   SHIP_NAME       CAPACITY   LENGTH   LIFEBOATS
-------   -------------   --------   ------   ---------
      1   Codd Crystal       2052      855          80
      2   Codd Elegance      2974      952          95
```

Now review the following SQL statement (line numbers are added for readability):

```
01    SELECT SHIP_ID FROM    SHIPS
02    WHERE   SHIP_NAME IN ('Codd Elegance','Codd Victorious')
03       OR  (LIFEBOATS >= 80
04       OR   LIFEBOATS <= 100)
05      AND  CAPACITY / LIFEBOATS > 25;
```

Which of the following statements is true about this SELECT statement?

A. The syntax is correct.

B. The syntax on lines 3 and 4 is incorrect.

C. Lines 3 and 4 have correct syntax but could be replaced with OR LIFEBOATS BETWEEN 80 AND 100.

D. Line 5 is missing parentheses.

Sort the Rows That Are Retrieved by a Query

10. Review this SELECT statement:

```
SELECT    SHIP_NAME
FROM      SHIPS
ORDER BY SHIP_ID, CAPACITY DESC;
```

Assume that all table and column references exist within the database. What can be said of this SELECT statement?

   A. The rows will sort in order by SHIP_ID and then by CAPACITY. All rows will sort in descending order.

   B. The rows will sort in order by SHIP_ID in ascending order, and then by CAPACITY in descending order.

   C. The statement will fail to execute because the ORDER BY list includes a column that is not in the select list.

   D. The statement will fail to execute because there is no WHERE clause.

11. Review this SELECT statement:

```
SELECT    PRODUCT_ID, PRODUCT_NAME, UNIT_PRICE, SHIPPING
FROM      PRODUCTS
WHERE     (UNIT_PRICE + SHIPPING) * TAX_RATE > 5
ORDER BY LIKE PRODUCT_NAME;
```

Assume all table and column references exist in the database. What can be said of this SELECT statement?

   A. The statement will execute successfully and as intended.

   B. The statement will execute but not sort because the ORDER BY clause is wrong.

   C. The statement will fail to execute because the ORDER BY clause includes the word LIKE.

   D. None of the above.

12. Which if the following is true of the ORDER BY clause? (Choose two.)

   A. It is optional.

   B. It can be used in the UPDATE statement as well as SELECT and DELETE.

   C. It can sort rows based on data that isn't displayed as part of the SELECT statement.

   D. If the list of ORDER BY expressions uses the "by position" form, then all expressions in the ORDER BY must use the "by position" form.

13. If you are using an ORDER BY to sort values in descending order, in which order will they appear?

   A. If the datatype is numeric, the value 400 will appear first before the value 800.

   B. If the datatype is character, the value 'Michael' will appear first before the value 'Jackson'.

   C. If the datatype is date, the value for June 25, 2010 will appear before the value for August 29, 2010.

   D. If the datatype is character, the value '130' will appear first before '75'.

14. Consider the following data listing for a table called BRANCH_OFFICE_ACCOUNTS:

```
ACCOUNT_ID   CRUISE_NAME   START_DATE   END_DATE
----------   -----------   ----------   --------
         1   Hawaii        11-JUL-11    24-JUL-11
         2   Hawaii        10-OCT-11    23-OCT-11
         3   Mexico        04-OCT-11    17-OCT-11
         4   Mexico        06-DEC-11    19-DEC-11
```

The CRUISE_NAME column is a VARCHAR2 column, and the START_DATE column is of the DATE datatype. Now review the following SELECT statement:

```
SELECT    ACCOUNT_ID, CRUISE_NAME, START_DATE, END_DATE
FROM      BRANCH_OFFICE_ACCOUNTS
ORDER BY CRUISE_NAME DESC, START_DATE ASC;
```

What will be the value in the ACCOUNT_ID column for the first row displayed as a result of this query?

A. 1
B. 2
C. 3
D. 4

15. Consider the following data listing for a table called PAY_HISTORY:

```
PAY_HISTORY_ID    SALARY   START_DATE   END_DATE
--------------    ------   ----------   --------
            1     73922    04-JUN-11
            2     47000    04-JUN-11
            3     37450    04-JUN-11    08-APR-15
            4     91379    05-FEB-12
```

The START_DATE and END_DATE columns are of the DATE datatype. Assume that blank values are NULL. Now review the following SELECT statement:

```
SELECT    PAY_HISTORY_ID, SALARY, START_DATE, END_DATE
FROM      PAY_HISTORY
ORDER BY END_DATE DESC, START_DATE, SALARY;
```

What will be the value in the PAY_HISTORY_ID column for the first row displayed as a result of this query?

A. 1
B. 2
C. 3
D. 4

SELF TEST ANSWERS

Limit the Rows That Are Retrieved by a Query

1. ☑ **D.** Syntactically the expression in the WHERE clause is correct. But since 1 is not equal to 2, the result will be FALSE for every row in the table, no matter how many rows may exist in the table.
☒ **A, B,** and **C** are incorrect. There's nothing wrong with the syntax; the expression will evaluate. If the expression were, say, 1=1, then it would be TRUE for all rows and return every row in the table. But it's FALSE, so nothing is returned.

2. ☑ **C.** The only rows returned will be those that start with the 'San' string. The issue here is comparison operator precedence. AND is evaluated before OR. The latter portion of the WHERE clause is "PORT_NAME LIKE 'Grand%' AND CAPACITY = 4", and this is evaluated first, and it finds no rows at all. Then the results of that portion of the WHERE are compared to "PORT_NAME LIKE 'San%'", which returns three rows, leaving the final result as three rows.
☒ **A, B,** and **D** are incorrect.

3. ☑ **C.** The operator in the expression is a valid operator for the "not equals" comparison. One row has a COST value that is not equal to 500.
☒ **A, B,** and **D** are incorrect. The symbol "^=" does not indicate greater than; that is the operator ">". It is not a syntax error, but rather a valid symbol for the "not equals" comparison.

4. ☑ **C** and **D.** NOT is evaluated first, then AND, and then OR.
☒ **A** and **B** are incorrect.

5. ☑ **B.** The SELECT will return one row, for VENDOR_ID 1 where the CATEGORY equals 'Supplier'.
☒ **A, C,** and **D** are incorrect. The second row will be ignored because even though the set of expressions within the IN clause includes a value for '%Partner' and uses the "percent sign" wildcard character at the beginning, the wildcard isn't activated, because LIKE isn't present in the expression. Therefore, the string is treated as a literal. Had there been a value in CATEGORY of '%Partner', the row would have been returned. The failure to include LIKE is not a syntax error per se; it's just incorrect design of the SELECT statement. One way to change this query into something that is more likely the intended form would be this: *SELECT VENDOR_ID FROM VENDORS WHERE CATEGORY IN ('Supplier', 'Subcontractor') OR CATEGORY LIKE '%Partner'*; That approach would produce two rows and perform the query that was probably intended.

6. ☑ **A.** This query will always retrieve zero rows, no matter what they look like. The use of the "= NULL" expression within the WHERE clause guarantees that fact. Nothing will ever be retrieved, because no SQL engine is capable of confirming that any value is equal to "I don't know".

☒ **B, C,** and **D** are incorrect. If line three had used "IS NULL", as in "WHERE STYLE IS NULL OR WINDOW IS NULL", then the answer would have been C, or two rows. Also if the IS NULL were used and the OR had been AND instead, then one row would have been returned. Regardless, the parentheses are correct here; you are allowed to enclose complete expressions within parentheses within a WHERE clause.

7. ☑ **D.** The query returns the row with a value of SHIP_ID = 1, and no more. The BETWEEN range is inclusive, so the number 2052 is part of the range.

☒ **A, B,** and **C** are incorrect. The LENGTH value is numeric, and the set of expressions inside of IN are strings. However, Oracle SQL will perform an automatic datatype conversion, since the strings all contain numeric data within them anyway, and the operation will succeed. It's not the best design, but it works, and you'll need to be aware of this for the exam. Also, line 5 uses the LIKE operator to activate wildcard characters within the string, and both of the available wildcards are used—the single-character underscore and the multicharacter percent sign. These combine to indicate that any row with a SHIP_NAME that starts with the string 'Codd', followed by at least one character, followed by anywhere from zero to an infinite number of additional characters, will be accepted.

8. ☑ **D.** There is nothing wrong with the syntax.

☒ **A, B,** and **C** are incorrect. The pair of nested parentheses before the word CAPACITY is a valid expression that multiplies the value of the LIFEBOATS column and adds the number 57 to the end of it. Then the entire result is subtracted by whatever the value for CAPACITY might be. The result of that expression will then be compared to whatever is contained in the series of expressions after the IN clause. There are two expressions there: one multiplies the LIFEBOATS value times 20; the second adds the values of the columns named LIFEBOAT and LENGTH. All of these expressions are syntactically valid.

9. ☑ **A.** The syntax is correct. However, there are some issues involving the logic—such as the expression on lines 3 and 4, which don't really do anything—any non-NULL value for LIFEBOATS will be found with these expressions, because of the OR operator on line 4. It would make more sense for that operator to be AND, but regardless, it is syntactically correct.

☒ **B, C,** and **D** are incorrect. Lines 3 and 4 have accurate syntax, but the OR at the beginning of line 4 should probably be an AND. Since it is not, then BETWEEN would not be an equivalent substitute here, since BETWEEN can only test for a range and essentially serves as a replacement of the AND combination, as in "LIFEBOATS >= 80 AND LIFEBOATS <= 100". Line 5 doesn't need any parentheses. They wouldn't hurt anything, necessarily; they just aren't required.

Sort the Rows That Are Retrieved by a Query

10. ☑ **B.** The ORDER BY clause will default to ascending order for SHIP_ID, but CAPACITY is explicitly directed to sort in descending order.

    ☒ **A, C,** and **D** are incorrect. The DESC directive only applies to the CAPACITY column in the ORDER BY clause, not both items. The fact that the ORDER BY clause references columns that are not in the select list is irrelevant; it's okay to do that. The WHERE clause is not required; it's an optional clause, as is the ORDER BY clause.

11. ☑ **C.** The LIKE operator is meaningless in ORDER BY.

    ☒ **A, B,** and **D** are incorrect. The statement will certainly not execute; it will fail to parse due to the syntax error of the LIKE operator in the wrong place. Given that it won't even parse due to syntax errors, it certainly won't execute.

12. ☑ **A** and **C.** ORDER BY is optional; it is not required. It is able to sort rows in the table based on any criteria that are meaningful to the row, and when sorted, any columns may be displayed from those rows in the select list, regardless of the ORDER BY criteria.

    ☒ **B** and **D** are incorrect. It is unique to the SELECT statement and does not appear as an option or otherwise in any other SQL statement. Ordering by position is available to each individual ORDER BY expression and does not depend nor require the same format from other ORDER BY expressions.

13. ☑ **B.** If the values are character, then 'A' is less than 'Z', and if we're listing rows in descending order, then the greater value is shown first. That means the values later in the alphabet are shown first. In comparing the character strings 'Michael' and 'Jackson', the string 'Michael' is greater and will show first in the listing before 'Jackson'.

    ☒ **A, C,** and **D** are incorrect. If the values are numeric, then 400 is less than 800. That means in a descending order listing, where the higher value is listed first, 800 would be listed before 400. With regard to date datatypes, later dates are greater, and August 29, 2010 should list before June 25, 2010. Finally, with regard to numeric values treated as strings, you have to think about how they would appear in the dictionary—the first character is the most important, and in this case, the '7' in '75' indicates that character string is higher than '130', so in a descending pattern, the '75' would be listed before '130'. If those values were treated as numeric values, it might be a different situation. But we're explicitly directed to treat them as character strings.

14. ☑ **C.** The row with an ACCOUNT_ID value of 3 will appear first. The ORDER BY clause sorts by CRUISE_NAME first, in descending order, which places values for Mexico before values for Hawaii, since CRUISE_NAME is a character string, and M is "greater than" H, and descending order places values that are "greater than" the others in the first position. Now, we have two rows with a CRUISE_NAME value of 'Mexico', so the next ORDER BY expression becomes important. That second expression looks at the START_DATE value and sorts in

ascending order, which is the default for all ORDER BY expressions. For dates, this means that "earlier" dates will precede "later" dates. For the two rows with a CRUISE_NAME of 'Mexico', the START_DATE values are '04-OCT-11' and '06-DEC-11'. The October date is "earlier", so that row will appear first—and its value for ACCOUNT_ID is 3.

☒ **A, B,** and **D** are incorrect.

15. ☑ **B.** In the first expression of the ORDER BY, we sort by END_DATE in descending order. Of the four rows, only one has a value for END_DATE; the other rows have NULL values. NULLs are treated as "greater than" the defined values, and since we're sorting in descending order, that places the three rows with NULL values for END_DATE at the top. So we turn our attention to the second item in the ORDER BY clause, which is the START_DATE. This is sorted in ascending order, and that places the two rows with a START_DATE of '04-JUN-11' and a NULL value for END_DATE up at the top of our list. To resolve the conflict about which will be our first row, we turn to the third expression in the ORDER BY, which calls for sorting by SALARY, and in the default ascending order. The two remaining salaries are 73922 and 47000. Of these, the second one is the lowest, and that pushes this row to the top. This row has a PAY_HISTORY_ID value of 2.

☒ **A, C,** and **D** are incorrect.

6

Using Single-Row Functions to Customize Output

Thihis chapter looks at the topic of SQL functions. *Functions* perform unique tasks that boost the capabilities of SQL. There are many SQL functions, and it is important that the certified Oracle Database SQL Expert be familiar with them all, and understand when they will be relevant for use in a particular professional setting.

This chapter looks exclusively at *single-row* functions, which are also known as *scalar* functions. You'll study the topic of *aggregate* functions later in Chapter 7, when you study the GROUP BY clause of the SELECT statement.

CERTIFICATION OBJECTIVE 6.01

Describe Various Types of Functions That Are Available in SQL

Functions have the following three characteristics:

- They accept incoming values, or *parameters* (Note: a few functions take no parameters).
- They incorporate data from the parameters into some sort of process; in other words, they perform some sort of task on the incoming data, such as a calculation or some other activity.
- They return one single answer as a result.

For example, here is a SQL statement that uses a function called INITCAP, which takes a single parameter:

```
SELECT LASTNAME, INITCAP(LASTNAME) FROM ONLINE_SUBSCRIBERS;
```

In this example, for each row that the SELECT statement processes, the SQL built-in function INITCAP takes the column LASTNAME and transforms the text contained within so that the first letter is displayed as a capital letter (initial capital, INITCAP, get it?), and the rest of the text is in lowercase letters. The result of the function is displayed in place of the value for the LASTNAME column. See Figure 6-1 for an example of its output.

Output of
SELECT with
INITCAP

As you can see, a function like INITCAP isn't foolproof—notice how it does a nice transformation on the first two rows but doesn't necessarily produce a desirable result in the third row, where the third letter *L* should still be capitalized. But INITCAP performs its task; it's up to us as developers to know where best to apply it.

When a function is used in a SQL statement, it's often said that it's *called* or *invoked* from the statement.

Functions can be called from anyplace that an expression can be called. In other words, you can invoke a function from:

- A SELECT statement's select list and WHERE clause
- An INSERT statement's list of values
- An UPDATE statement's SET clause and WHERE clause
- A DELETE statement's WHERE clause

. . . and more.

There are a variety of functions available in SQL. The two major types are "built-in" and "user-defined".

Built-in functions are those that are part of the SQL language itself. They are available with every standard implementation of SQL.

User-defined functions are those that are created by users, much the same way a user would create a software application. They are written with features that go beyond the capabilities of SQL, using languages such as PL/SQL. Their construction is beyond the scope of the exam, and therefore this book. This book—and exam—will only deal with built-in functions.

There are a great many built-in functions, and they fall into several categories. It's not important for the exam that you know which category a function is in.

Categories merely serve to make a discussion about functions a little easier to manage. The categories included here are character, number, date, conversion, and other.

Character Functions

Character functions are used to manipulate text. They can be used to perform many jobs on a given string: analyze its length (LENGTH), pad it with extra characters (RPAD, LPAD), trim off unwanted characters (RTRIM, LTRIM, TRIM), locate a given string within a larger string (INSTR), extract a smaller string from a larger string (SUBSTR), and replace text within a string (REPLACE). It's even possible to search for strings that aren't necessarily spelled the same but that sound alike (SOUNDEX), and more. When these are combined together, the possibilities are theoretically endless.

Number Functions

Number functions can perform mathematical analysis. SQL comes with many functions for determining sin (SIN, ASIN, SINH), cosine (COS, ACOS, COSH), and tangent (TAN, ATAN, ATAN2, TANH). You can determine absolute value (ABS), or determine if a given number is positive or negative (SIGN).

A function can round off values (ROUND) and otherwise abbreviate numbers (TRUNC).

Number functions can be incorporated into expressions, and as you've already seen, expressions provide support for standard arithmetic operations of addition (+), subtraction (–), multiplication (*), and division (/). These operators are not functions but are, well, operators. The point here is that you can combine the operators with number functions to produce powerful SQL statements.

Date Functions

The set of available SQL functions includes powerful features for DATE manipulation. You can obtain the current date and time (SYSDATE, SYSTIMESTAMP), "round" off dates to varying degrees of detail (ROUND), and otherwise abbreviate them (TRUNC). You can calculate the differences between two or more dates in many ways.

Simple arithmetic operators will help determine the differences between two dates in terms of days, meaning that if you subtract one date from another, the resulting answer will be a number representing the difference in terms of days. But what if you want something else, like—the difference in terms of months? (The answer is MONTHS_BETWEEN.) There are functions that will assist in managing such tasks. You can add or subtract an entire month and account for spans of time that encompass years (ADD_MONTHS).

What if you have a particular date and wish to know if that date falls on, say, a Saturday or not? This sort of feature can be accomplished with "conversion" functions, which we discuss in the next section.

Conversion Functions

Conversion functions perform many tasks on data of all datatypes. Conversion functions are used primarily to convert values from one datatype to another. They can, for example, convert any numeric value to a text string. They can convert a text string that contains numeric data into a proper numeric datatype. They can take text representations of dates and convert them to a formal DATE datatype.

But conversion functions can do more than this. They are often used to convert data of any datatype into a text string that includes formatting information. For example, if you have a DATE datatype that contains raw information about hours, minutes, seconds, and the date on the calendar, you can transform that into a text string that spells out the entire date in detail, such as "Thursday, July the Fourth, Seventeen Seventy-Six".

Conversion functions can transform raw numeric data into financial formats that include dollar signs and symbols for other international currency, proper placement for commas and periods according to various international formats, and more.

Other Functions

There are some functions that don't quite fit into the categories listed here. USER is a great example—that's a standard function that takes no parameters and simply returns the value showing the name of the current user account. Other functions support advanced features, such as hierarchical queries. We'll look at those functions as we discuss various advanced features throughout the book.

CERTIFICATION OBJECTIVE 6.02

Use Character, Number, and Date Functions in SELECT Statements

This section looks in detail at many of the SQL functions. You'll learn how they work, and you'll see examples of how many of them can be used. For each function discussed here, we address

- The function's list of parameters
- Whether each parameter is required or optional
- What task the function performs
- The output from the function

Rather than present an alphabetical listing of them, the SQL functions presented in this section are listed logically, and related functions are described together. This is not an exhaustive analysis of all the functions available in SQL, but is nevertheless rather comprehensive, focusing primarily on the functions that are most commonly used. Remember: functions are an exam objective. It's important to be familiar with how the major functions work. This section describes the most commonly used functions that are likely to be on the exam.

The DUAL Table

Before we get started, I need to mention the DUAL table, which is something that isn't a function issue per se but is helpful to our purposes here. It is not a "SQL" thing, nor is it necessarily a "function" thing, but it's an "Oracle" thing you should know before we continue. The DUAL table is present in every Oracle database. This special table contains just one column. The column is named DUMMY, and it has a datatype of VARCHAR2(1). The DUAL table contains only one row. That row has a value in DUMMY of 'X'.

The purpose of DUAL is simple—to have something to run a SELECT statement against when you don't wish to retrieve any data in particular but instead simply wish to run a SELECT statement to get some other task accomplished. For example, you'll soon see in this section that there's an Oracle SQL function called SYSDATE that displays the current date according to the operating system of the server on which the Oracle database is installed. If you wish to get the value of SYSDATE without wading through a bunch of table data from your application, you can simply execute the following SQL statement:

```
SELECT SYSDATE FROM DUAL;
```

The result: you'll get one response for the current value of SYSDATE, since you know the DUAL table only has one row.

We'll use the DUAL table from time to time throughout the rest of this chapter as we go through examples of the various SQL functions.

Character Manipulation

This section looks in detail at the more commonly used character functions. Character functions do not necessarily deal exclusively with character data—some of these functions have numeric parameters and even numeric output, like INSTR. But the overall spirit and intent of these functions is to perform the sort of data processing typically associated with text manipulation.

UPPER, LOWER

Syntax: UPPER($s1$), LOWER($s1$)

Parameters: $s1$, a required character string.

Process: Transforms $s1$ into uppercase letters (UPPER) or lowercase letters (LOWER).

Output: Character string.

Example: UPPER can be useful when you are doing a text search and aren't sure whether the data in the table is in uppercase, lowercase, or both. You can use UPPER to force a conversion of all data in the table, then compare that result to an uppercase literal value, thus eliminating any chance of missing mixed case text in the table. For example:

```
SELECT EMPLOYEE_ID
FROM    EMPLOYEES
WHERE   UPPER(LAST_NAME) = 'MCGILLICUTTY';
```

The previous query will return rows from the EMPLOYEES table where the LAST_NAME is 'McGillicutty', 'mcgillicutty', or any other combination of upper- and lowercase letters that equals the letters in the string.

INITCAP

Syntax: INITCAP(*s1*)

Parameters: *s1*, a required character string.

Process: Transforms *s1* into a mixed-case string, where the first letter of each word is capitalized, and each following character is in lowercase letters.

Output: Character string.

Example: Below is a SQL statement that invokes INITCAP three times. The first example passes in the string "napoleon", which is translated into mixed-case letters. The second example takes the string "Red O'Brien" as input. Notice that we need to include the single quote escape character within the string in order for a single quote character to be recognized—since the single quote mark is also the string delimiter, we need to type two single quotes in succession, which is how you instruct SQL to treat a single quote as an actual character within the string, and not the string delimiter. Finally, the third example does the same thing with the string "McDonald's", but notice the result—the results of INITCAP are less than desirable—the first "d" in "McDonald's" is converted to lowercase, and the "s" at the end of "McDonald's" is converted to uppercase—INITCAP interprets the "s" as the start of a new word.

The escape character that activates, or enables, a single quote character to be displayed is a single quote.

```
SELECT INITCAP('napoleon'), INITCAP('RED O''BRIEN'), INITCAP('McDonald''s')
FROM   DUAL;

INITCAP('NAPOLEON') INITCAP('REDO''BRIEN') INITCAP('MCDONALD''S')
------------------- ---------------------- ----------------------
Napoleon            Red O'Brien            Mcdonald'S
```

CONCAT, ||

Syntax: CONCAT(*s1*, *s2*), *s1* || *s2*

Parameters: *s1*, *s2*. Both are character strings; both are required.

Process: Concatenates *s1* and *s2* together into one string.

Output: Character string.

Example:

```
SELECT CONCAT('Hello, ', 'world!')
FROM   DUAL;
```

The equivalent using the double vertical bars:

```
SELECT 'Hello, ' || 'world!'
FROM   DUAL;
```

While CONCAT takes only two parameters, the double vertical bar syntax can be repeated as often as is necessary. For example, this approach creates one string:

```
SELECT 'Hello, ' || 'world!' || ' Great to ' || 'see you.'
FROM   DUAL;

'HELLO,'||'WORLD!'||'GREATTO'||'SEEYOU.'
----------------------------------------
Hello, world! Great to see you.
```

Note that the result here is one single string. Another example:

```
SELECT FIRST_NAME || ' ' || LAST_NAME || ' of ship number ' || SHIP_ID || '.'
FROM    EMPLOYEES
WHERE   LAST_NAME = 'West';

FIRST_NAME||''||LAST_NAME||'OFSHIPNUMBER'||SHIP_ID||'.'
--------------------------------------------------------
Mike West of ship number 4.
Trish West of ship number 2.
```

LPAD, RPAD

Syntax: LPAD(*s1*, *n*, *s2*), RPAD(*s1*, *n*, *s2*).

Parameters: *s1* (character string—required); *n* (number—required); *s2* (character string—optional—*s2* defaults to a single blank space if omitted).

Process: Pad the left of character string *s1* (LPAD) or right of character string *s1* (RPAD) with character string *s2*, so that *s1* is *n* characters long.

Output: Character string.

Example: Take a string literal 'Chapter One—I Am Born' and pad it to the right with 40 occurrences of a single period.

```
SELECT RPAD('Chapter One - I Am Born',40,'.')
FROM    DUAL;

RPAD('CHAPTERONE-IAMBORN',40,'.')
-----------------------------------------
Chapter One - I Am Born................
```

on the
Job
Many SQL functions are useful in and of themselves, but many become more useful when combined with each other. For example, here's a combination of RPAD and LPAD with the concatenation operators, executed against a table called BOOK_CONTENTS:

```
SELECT    RPAD(CHAPTER_TITLE || ' ',30,'.')
          ||
          LPAD(' ' || PAGE_NUMBER,30,'.') "Table of Contents"
FROM      BOOK_CONTENTS
ORDER BY PAGE_NUMBER;

Table of Contents
-----------------------------------------------------------
Introduction ............................................. 1
Chapter 1 ................................................ 5
Chapter 2 ................................................ 23
Chapter 3 ................................................ 57
Index .................................................... 79
```

Notice this example also includes three uses of the concatenation operator:

- *Once to append a single blank after the CHAPTER_TITLE value*
- *Once to put a single blank in front of the PAGE_NUMBER value*
- *Once to combine the output of RPAD and LPAD*

Also note the use of the column alias "Table of Contents", and the ORDER BY to ensure that the rows sort according to PAGE_NUMBER.

e**x**a**m**
ⓦatch
If the "On the Job" code sample showing LPAD and RPAD combined with string concatenation is a mystery to you, then stop and study it. The exam may include questions about several functions combined and nested within each other, like the BOOK_CONTENTS sample shown in the sample.

LTRIM, RTRIM

Syntax: LTRIM(*s1, s2*), RTRIM(*s1, s2*)

Parameters: *s1, s2*—both are character strings. *s1* is required, *s2* is optional—if omitted, it defaults to a single blank space.

Process: Removes occurrences of the *s2* characters from the *s1* string, from either the left side of *s1* (LTRIM) or the right side of *s1* (RTRIM) exclusively.

Output: Character string.

Notes: Ideal for stripping out unnecessary blanks or periods or ellipses, etc.

Example:

```
SELECT RTRIM('Seven thousand-------','-')
FROM   DUAL;

RTRIM('SEVENTHOUSAND--------','-')
----------------------------------
Seven thousand
```

TRIM

Syntax: TRIM(*trim_info trim_char* FROM *trim_source*)

Parameters:

trim_info is one of these keywords: LEADING, TRAILING, BOTH—if omitted, defaults to BOTH.

trim_char is a single character to be trimmed—if omitted, assumed to be a blank.

trim_source is the source string—if omitted, the TRIM function will return a NULL.

Process: Same as LTRIM and RTRIM, with a slightly different syntax.

Output: Character string.

Example: Trim off the dashes at the end of the string 'Seven thousand--------'.

```
SELECT TRIM(TRAILING '-' FROM 'Seven thousand-------')
FROM   DUAL;

TRIM(TRAILING'-'FROM'SEVENTHOUSAND--------')
--------------------------------------------
Seven thousand
```

LENGTH

Syntax: LENGTH(*s*)

Parameters: *s* is the source string (required).

Process: Identifies the length of a given string.

Output: Numeric.

Example: Determine the length of a really long and famous word:

```
SELECT LENGTH('Supercalifragilisticexpialidocious')
FROM    DUAL;

LENGTH('SUPERCALIFRAGILISTICEXPIALIDOCIOUS')
---------------------------------------------
34
```

INSTR

Syntax: INSTR($s1$, $s2$, pos, n)

Parameters: $s1$ is the source string (required); $s2$ is the substring (required); pos is the starting position in $s1$ to start looking for occurrences of $s2$ (optional, default is 1); n is the occurrence of $s2$ to locate (optional, default is 1). If pos is negative, the search in $s1$ for occurrences of $s2$ starts at the end of the string and moves backward.

Process: Locates a string within another string (e.g., IN STRing).

Output: Numeric.

Example: Look for the string 'is' within 'Mississippi', starting at the first character position but looking for the second occurrence of 'is'.

```
SELECT INSTR('Mississippi','is',1,2)
FROM    DUAL;

INSTR('MISSISSIPPI','IS',1,2)
-----------------------------
5
```

The INSTR function is telling us that the second occurrence of 'is' starts at the fifth character in 'Mississippi'.

SUBSTR

Syntax: SUBSTR(s, pos, len)

Parameters: s = a character string, required; pos = a number, required; len = a number, optional.

Process: Extracts a substring from s, starting at the pos character of s, and continuing for len number of characters. If len is omitted, then the substring starts as *pos* and runs through the end of *s*. If *pos* is negative, then the function starts at the end of the string and moves backward.

Output: Character string.

Example: Starting with a source string of 'Name: MARK KENNEDY', extract a substring out of it, beginning at the seventh position and running to the end of the string.

```
SELECT SUBSTR('Name: MARK KENNEDY', 7)
FROM   DUAL;

SUBSTR('NAME:MARKKENNEDY',7)
----------------------------
MARK KENNEDY
```

SOUNDEX

Syntax: SOUNDEX(*s*)

Parameters: *s* = the source string, required.

Process: Translates a source string into its SOUNDEX code.

Output: Character string.

Notes: SOUNDEX is a coding scheme for translating English words into sound-alike patterns. A single SOUNDEX value is relatively worthless. But two combined together can be surprisingly helpful. The reason is that similar-sounding words tend to generate the same SOUNDEX pattern.

To generate a SOUNDEX translation for any word, the first letter remains unchanged. The next series of letters are translated into a numeric code according to the rules shown in Table 6-1. Translation is performed for each letter until three digits are generated. If any letters exist beyond that, they are ignored. For example: The last name "Worthington" has a SOUNDEX pattern of W635: the first letter 'W' remains unchanged; the second letter "o" is ignored per the bottom row of the Table 6-1; the third letter "r" translates into 6 according to Table 6-1; the fourth letter "t" translates into a 3; the fifth letter "h" is ignored—again, according to Table 6-1, which also tells us to ignore the letter "i"; the letter "n" translates into 5, and now that we have one letter "W" and three numbers "635", we are done, and the remaining letters in "Worthington" are ignored. Thus, the SOUNDEX code is W635.

TABLE 6-1	Letter	SOUNDEX Code
	B, F, P, V	1
SOUNDEX Translation Table	C, G, J, K, Q, S, X, Z	2
	D, T	3
	L	4
	M, N	5
	R	6
	All other letters (A, E, H, I, O, U, W, Y)	Ignored

So two words that sound alike, for example, "Worthington" and "Wurthinden", while spelled differently, will nevertheless generate the same SOUNDEX pattern. Here's an example:

```
SELECT  SOUNDEX('Worthington'), SOUNDEX('Worthen')
FROM    DUAL;

SOUNDEX('WORTHINGTON')  SOUNDEX('WORTHEN')
----------------------  ------------------
W635                    W635
```

Notice how the two different words produce the same SOUNDEX pattern. That means we can do queries like this:

```
SELECT  EMPLOYEE_ID, FIRST_NAME, LAST_NAME
FROM    EMPLOYEES
WHERE   SOUNDEX(LAST_NAME) = SOUNDEX('Worthen');

EMPLOYEE_ID            FIRST_NAME            LAST_NAME
---------------------  --------------------  ------------------
7                      Buffy                 Worthington
```

Notice that SOUNDEX is used twice in the WHERE clause. Using it once would probably be useless. This query will find customers with the last name of 'Worthington', 'Wurthinden', 'Worthan', and even 'Wirthen'.

SOUNDEX has something of a bias toward English. For example, the popular Vietnamese name "Nguyen" is pronounced "Nwen", but the SOUNDEX patterns for those two words—"Nguyen" and "Nwen"—are rather different. So SOUNDEX is not perfect, but rather useful nonetheless.

Mathematical Processing

This section describes functions that deal with numeric values. Some numeric functions are pretty simple—such as ABS, which takes a single numeric value and returns its absolute value. There's also SQRT, which takes a single numeric value and returns its square root.

Not all of the input parameters to numeric functions are necessarily numeric, but the overall intent of these functions is to perform numeric analysis and perform the sort of tasks typically associated with numeric data processing.

ROUND—Number

Syntax: ROUND(n, i)

Parameters: n is required, is any number, and can include decimal points. i is an integer, and is optional—if omitted, it will default to 0.

Process: n is rounded depending on the value of i. If i is zero, n is rounded off to the nearest whole number, i.e., zero decimal points. If i is a positive number, n is rounded to i places to the right of the decimal point. If i is a negative number, n is rounded to i places to the left of the decimal point. The number 5 is rounded away from zero.

Output: If i is omitted, ROUND returns a value in the same numeric datatype as n. If i is specified, ROUND returns a datatype of NUMBER.

Example: Round off 12.355143 to two significant digits to the right of the decimal, and also round off 259.99 to the nearest "tens"—i.e., one digit to the left of the decimal:

```
SELECT ROUND(12.355143, 2), ROUND(259.99,-1)
FROM DUAL;

ROUND(12.355143,2)      ROUND(259.99,-1)
--------------------    --------------------
12.36                   260
```

TRUNC—Number

Syntax: TRUNC(n, i)

Parameters: n is required, is any number, and can include decimal points. i is an integer and is optional—if omitted, it will default to 0.

Process: TRUNC "rounds" toward zero—i.e., it truncates the numbers.

Output: If i is omitted, TRUNC returns a value in the same numeric datatype as n. If i is specified, TRUNC returns a datatype of NUMBER.

Example: Using the same numbers we just used with the ROUND example, truncate them instead:

```
SELECT TRUNC(12.355143, 2), TRUNC(259.99,-1)
FROM DUAL;

TRUNC(12.355143,2)      TRUNC(259.99,-1)
--------------------    --------------------
12.35                   250
```

REMAINDER

Syntax: REMAINDER(*n1*, *n2*)

Parameters: *n1* and *n2* are numbers. Both are required.

Process: Identifies the multiple of *n2* that is nearest to *n1*, and returns the difference between those two values.

Output: Numeric.

Example: Test REMAINDER using three sequential numbers: 9, 10, and 11, and compare each against the number 3. Since the first number (9) is a multiple of 3, there is no remainder, so the answer will be 0. The second number (10) represents one more number than the multiple, so the remainder is 1. Notice what happens with the third number (11)—the function doesn't return a 2 as you might expect. Instead, it returns a negative 1, because the nearest integer that's divisible by 3 is 12, which is closer to the 11 than the 9. In other words, REMAINDER identifies the closest multiple of *n2*. If the multiple is higher, REMAINDER returns a negative number to indicate that the closest multiple of *n2* is higher than *n1*.

```
SELECT REMAINDER(9,3), REMAINDER(10,3), REMAINDER(11,3)
FROM    DUAL;

REMAINDER(9,3)        REMAINDER(10,3)       REMAINDER(11,3)
--------------------  --------------------  --------------------
0                     1                     -1
```

MOD

Syntax: MOD(*n1*, *n2*)

Parameters: *n1* and *n2* are numbers. Both are required.

Process: Performs the same task as REMAINDER, except MOD uses FLOOR instead of ROUND in its equation.

Output: Numeric.

Example: Get the MOD of the same three number pairs we tested with REMAINDER. Note the results in the third example—this might be what you would've expected with REMAINDER, and didn't get—but you do get it with MOD.

```
SELECT MOD(9,3), MOD(10,3), MOD(11,3)
FROM   DUAL;

MOD(9,3)              MOD(10,3)             MOD(11,3)
-------------------- --------------------- ---------------------
0                    1                     2
```

Working with Dates

The following section looks at functions that work primarily with DATE datatypes.

SYSDATE

Parameters: None

Process: Returns the current date and time according to the operating system on which the Oracle database server is installed. In other words, if your SQL statement is running on an Oracle server instance from a remote location, then regardless of the location of you or your client, SYSDATE will return the date and time of the operating system on which the server resides. Time information is contained within SYSDATE but doesn't display by default; however, it can be extracted by way of the TO_CHAR conversion function. (Note: it can also be altered by changing the NLS_DATE_FORMAT session parameter.)

Output: Date.

Example: Show the current date according to the operating system where the Oracle server is installed:

```
SELECT SYSDATE FROM DUAL;

SYSDATE
-------------------------
06-JUL-09
```

ROUND—Date

Syntax: ROUND(*d*, *i*)

Parameters: *d* is a date (required); *i* is a format model (optional).

Process: d is rounded off to the nearest date value, at a level of detail specified by i. d is required and specifies a value of the DATE datatype. i is a format model, and specifies the level of detail to which the DATE value will be rounded—i.e., to the nearest day, nearest hour, nearest year, etc. i is optional. Values are biased toward rounding up—for example, when rounding off time, twelve noon rounds up to the next day. Format models are covered in the upcoming section about the TO_CHAR conversion function. But we'll include one in the example that follows to give you an idea of what a format model is.

Output: Date.

Example: This example shows a SELECT statement with three expressions in the select list. The first is SYSDATE, which returns the current date. The second is the same date, rounded to the nearest month, as specified by the 'MM' format model. The third is the same date rounded to the nearest year, as specified by the 'RR' format model.

```
SELECT SYSDATE TODAY,
       ROUND(SYSDATE,'MM') ROUNDED_MONTH,
       ROUND(SYSDATE,'RR') ROUNDED_YEAR
FROM   DUAL;


TODAY                  ROUNDED_MONTH          ROUNDED_YEAR
-------------------    -------------------    -------------------
27-JUL-09              01-AUG-09              01-JAN-10
```

If the optional second parameter is omitted, the DATE value will be rounded to the nearest hour.

(Note: we'll explore more about how DATE values and format models work when we discuss the TO_CHAR conversion function. That's where you'll see how to display the hours for a given DATE value.)

TRUNC—Date

Syntax: TRUNC(d, i)

Parameters: d is a date (required); i is a format model (required).

Process: Performs the same task as ROUND for dates, except TRUNC always rounds down.

Output: Date.

Example:

```
SELECT SYSDATE TODAY,
       TRUNC(SYSDATE,'MM') TRUNCATED_MONTH,
       TRUNC(SYSDATE,'RR') TRUNCATED_YEAR
FROM   DUAL;

TODAY                 TRUNCATED_MONTH       TRUNCATED_YEAR
-------------------   -------------------   -------------------
27-JUL-09             01-JUL-09             01-JAN-09
```

NEXT_DAY

Syntax: NEXT_DAY(*d*, *c*)

Parameters: *d* is a date, required; *c* is a text reference to a day of the week, required.

Process: Returns a valid date representing the first occurrence of the *c* day following the date represented in *d*.

Output: Date.

Example: Show the first occurrence of a Saturday following the 31st of May, 2011.

```
SELECT NEXT_DAY('31-MAY-11','Saturday')
FROM   DUAL;

NEXT_DAY('31-MAY-11','SATURDAY')
-------------------------
04-JUN-11
```

LAST_DAY

Syntax: LAST_DAY(*d*)

Parameters: *d* is a date, required.

Process: Returns the last day of the month in which *d* falls.

Output: Date.

Example: Show the last days of February in 2011 and 2012.

```
SELECT LAST_DAY('14-FEB-11'), LAST_DAY('20-FEB-12')
FROM   DUAL;

LAST_DAY('14-FEB-11')     LAST_DAY('20-FEB-12')
-------------------------  -------------------------
28-FEB-11                 29-FEB-12
```

ADD_MONTHS

Syntax: ADD_MONTHS(*d*, *n*)

Parameters: *d* is a date, required; *n* is a whole number, required.

Process: Adds *n* months to *d*, and returns a valid date value for the result.

Output: Date.

Example: Add four months to November 1, 2011.

```
SELECT  ADD_MONTHS('31-JAN-11',1),
        ADD_MONTHS('01-NOV-11',4)
FROM    DUAL;

ADD_MONTHS('31-JAN-11',1) ADD_MONTHS('01-NOV-11',4)
------------------------- -------------------------
28-FEB-11                 01-MAR-12
```

on the **Job**

There is no "SUBTRACT_MONTHS" function. Instead—use ADD_MONTHS to add a negative number of months, and you'll subtract them instead.

MONTHS_BETWEEN

Syntax: MONTHS_BETWEEN(*d1*, *d2*)

Parameters: *d1* and *d2* are dates, required.

Process: Determines the number of months between the two dates. The result does not round off automatically—if the result is a partial month, MONTHS_BETWEEN shows a real number result. Whole months are counted according to the calendar months involved—if the time spans, say, a February that has 29 days, then the one month time span for that time period will be 29 days. In other words:

```
MONTHS_BETWEEN('01-JAN-12', '01-FEB-12') = -1=

MONTHS_BETWEEN('01-JAN-12', '01-MAR-12') = -2=

MONTHS_BETWEEN('10-AUG-14', '10-JUL-14') = 1=
```

Note that the answer may be opposite of what you would expect. The first parameter is expected to be the greater value; the second is expected to be the lesser. But that's not required, and as you can see from these examples, either approach works, but notice the sign of the result—if the second parameter is the greater value, the result is a negative number.

Output: Number.

Example: Display the number of months between June 12, 2014, and October 3, 2013.

```
SELECT MONTHS_BETWEEN('12-JUN-14','03-OCT-13')
FROM    DUAL;

MONTHS_BETWEEN('12-JUN-14','03-OCT-13')
---------------------------------------
8.29032258064516129032258064516129032258
```

NUMTOYMINTERVAL

Syntax: NUMTOYMINTERVAL (n, *interval_unit*)

Parameters: *n* = number (required). *interval_unit* = one of the following values: 'YEAR' or 'MONTH'.

Process: Transform the number *n* into a value that represents the *interval_unit* amount of time.

Output: A value in the INTERVAL YEAR TO MONTH datatype.

Example: The following example takes the number 27 and transforms it into a value representing a time interval of 27 months, which equates to 2 years and 3 months, in the INTERVAL YEAR TO MONTH datatype. The "2-3" value shows 2 years, 3 months is the amount of time that results.

```
SELECT NUMTOYMINTERVAL(27,'MONTH')
FROM    DUAL;

NUMTOYMINTERVAL(27,'MONTH')
---------------------------
2-3
```

NUMTODSINTERVAL

Syntax: NUMTODSINTERVAL (n, *interval_unit*)

Parameters: *n* = number (required). *interval_unit* = one of the following: 'DAY', 'HOUR', 'MINUTE', or 'SECOND'.

Process: Converts the numeric value into an interval of time according to the value of *interval_unit*.

Output: A value of the datatype INTERVAL DAY TO SECOND.

Example: The following example translates 36 hours into its formal representation of 1 day, 12 hours in the datatype INTERVAL DAY TO SECOND, which displays a single number for day, followed by hours, minutes, seconds, and fractional seconds.

```
SELECT NUMTODSINTERVAL(36, 'HOUR')
FROM    DUAL;

NUMTODSINTERVAL(36, 'HOUR')
---------------------------
1 12:0:0.0
```

Other Functions

This section looks at some additional commonly used functions.

NVL

Syntax: NVL(*e1*, *e2*)

Parameters: *e1* and *e2* are expressions, both are required, and both should be of the same datatype, but automatic datatype conversion applies here, so values may be different as long as they are capable of being converted to the same datatype automatically.

Process: If *e1* has a value of NULL, then NVL returns the value for *e2*. Otherwise it returns *e1*. The intent of NVL is to use it in a query where multiple rows are being returned, and you expect that perhaps some of the rows might be NULL. There's nothing wrong with that in and of itself, but what if you are performing some sort of processing that can't take a value of NULL? For example, a single NULL value within a mathematical calculation will automatically make the answer NULL. You can use NVL to substitute something meaningful in the place of NULL—such as a zero—in order to satisfy the outer function.

Output: If *e1* has a character datatype, the output will be VARCHAR2. If *e1* is numeric, the output will be numeric. If the output is NULL, then it's NULL.

Example: Note that we have three expressions in the SELECT list that follows. The first simply shows that we're using NVL to replace the literal value for NULL with a zero. Useless by itself but it proves the point of what the NVL function does. The second expression shows an equation in which we add 14 to NULL and subtract 4 from the result. But what is 14 plus NULL? It's NULL. So is NULL minus 4. So in the third expression, we use NVL to replace NULL with a 0, and we get an answer of 10.

```
SELECT NVL(NULL,0) FIRST_ANSWER,
       14+NULL-4 SECOND_ANSWER,
       14+NVL(NULL,0)-4 THIRD_ANSWER
FROM   DUAL;

FIRST_ANSWER            SECOND_ANSWER          THIRD_ANSWER
--------------------    --------------------   --------------------
0                                              10
```

The purpose of the preceding example is to show what you can do with NVL. A more likely scenario would be something like this:

```
SELECT SQ_FT + NVL(BALCONY_SQ_FT,0)
FROM   SHIP_CABINS;
```

This SQL code adds the square feet of a ship's cabin with the square feet of its balcony. But what if there isn't a balcony, and a NULL value is returned for BALCONY_SQ_FT? The entire result would be NULL, unless we use the NVL function as we do in the preceding example.

DECODE

Syntax: DECODE(*e*, *search_expression*, *d*)

Parameters: *e*, *search_expression*, and *d* are all expressions. The first two are required; the third is optional.

Process: *e* is a required expression; *search_expression* is a series of pairs of expressions, *se1* and *se2*, each separated by commas; if *e* equals *se1*, then DECODE should return *se2*. Otherwise, it should return *d*. If *d* is omitted, DECODE will return NULL.

In DECODE, two NULL values are considered to be equivalent. NULL compared to NULL will produce a TRUE result and send the corresponding value back if required.

Output: If the datatypes of *e* and the first occurrence of *se1* are character, DECODE will return a value of datatype VARCHAR2. If the datatypes of *e* and the first occurrence of *se1* are numeric, DECODE will return a value of numeric datatype.

Example: In the example that follows, we select rows from ADDRESSES by looking at the STATE column value as is, and then also using DECODE to translate the values in STATE according to the *search_expression* in DECODE, which in this case only looks at two state values but could have easily been expanded to translate, or decode, all of the state values. The final item in

DECODE is 'Other', which is assigned to all values of STATE that aren't found in our *search_expression* list—including the NULL value for STATE.

```
SELECT STATE, DECODE(STATE,'CA', 'California',
                           'IL','Illinois',
                           'Other') AS DECODED_STATE
FROM    ADDRESSES;

STATE DECODED_STATE
----- -------------
CA    California
TX    Other
IL    Illinois
AB    Other
NY    Other
      Other
QC    Other
```

The DECODE function is often referred to as the "IF-THEN-ELSE" of Oracle SQL.

CASE

Syntax: CASE *expression1* WHEN *condition1* THEN *result1* WHEN *condition2* THEN *result2* . . . ELSE *resultfinal* END

Parameters: *expression1* can be a column in a SELECT statement's select list, or any other valid expression; required. If *expression1* evaluates to a value that is equal to *condition1*, then the function returns result1. Additional WHEN/THEN comparison pairs may be included. The first pair is required; additional pairs are optional. An optional ELSE at the end will return the value of *resultfinal* if no WHEN/THEN comparison pair matched.

Process: Compare all the pairs to determine which value will be returned. If no values match, *resultfinal* is returned. If no values match and no ELSE clause is included, NULL is returned.

Example:

```
SELECT CASE 'option1'
        WHEN 'option1' THEN 'found it'
        WHEN 'option2' THEN 'did not find it'
        END AS "Answer"
FROM    DUAL;

Answer
----------------
found it
```

The function starts with the keyword CASE and ends with the keyword END. The CASE expression may include a column name, like this:

```
SELECT SHIP_NAME,
       CAPACITY,
       CASE CAPACITY WHEN 2052 THEN 'MEDIUM' WHEN 2974 THEN
'LARGE' END AS "SIZE"
FROM   SHIPS
WHERE  SHIP_ID <= 4;

SHIP_NAME              CAPACITY                SIZE
--------------------   ----------------------  ------
Codd Crystal           2052                    MEDIUM
Codd Elegance          2974                    LARGE
Codd Champion          2974                    LARGE
Codd Victorious        2974                    LARGE
```

Note that in this example, the CASE function takes in a numeric value and returns a text string.

NULLIF

Syntax: NULLIF(*e1*, *e2*)

Parameters: *e1* and *e2* are both expressions; required. Must be the same datatype.

Process: If *e1* and *e2* are the same, NULLIF returns NULL. Otherwise, it returns *e1*.

Output: An expression matching the datatypes of the input parameters.

Example: NULLIF is good for comparing multiple rows wherein an older and newer version of a particular value lies, and you wish to cull out those that are either still not updated, or have been already. For example:

```
SELECT TEST_SCORE,
       UPDATED_TEST_SCORE,
       NULLIF(UPDATED_TEST_SCORE,TEST_SCORE) REVISION_ONLY
FROM   SCORES;

TEST_SCORE UPDATED_TEST_SCORE REVISION_ONLY
---------- ------------------ -------------
95         95
55         75                 75
83         83
```

In the preceding example, the column UPDATED_TEST_SCORE represents a set of values that includes older TEST_SCORE values and those that have been revised for some reason. The NULLIF function helps filter out only those values that represent changes to the older original values, as evidenced in the third SELECT column with the column alias of REVISION_ONLY.

Nesting Functions

When a function is placed within an expression in such a way that its output becomes the parameter for another function, it is said to be "nested". When one function is "nested" within another, the nested function executes first. The nested function is also considered the "inner" function, as opposed to the "outer" function, which receives the output of the inner function as an input parameter.

Here's an example that nests one function within another. The combination of SUBSTR and INSTR can be very helpful in locating strings whose position varies within a string but varies relative to a fixed distance to another string. The classic example is common in address information, when you are looking for the two-letter state abbreviation that is often found after the comma plus one blank space. See Figure 6-2 for an example. The first column shows the column ADDRESS2 unchanged. Notice, however, that each string contains a two-letter state abbreviation, and that each state is after a comma plus one blank space. We can use that consistent pattern to our advantage. The second column shows how we can use the INSTR function to find the exact location of that comma in each individual row of ADDRESS2. Finally, the third column shows how we can nest the output of each row's INSTR result within a SUBSTR function. By adding 2 to the results of INSTR (one for the comma, one for the space), we locate the precise start of the two-letter state abbreviation within each occurrence of ADDRESS2 and thus are able to extract the value for the third column, STATE.

Finally, note that we order the output by the findings of the third column. Pretty interesting that we can sort rows of data by a substring of a column whose position changes within each row of the table—but it's entirely possible through the use of nested functions.

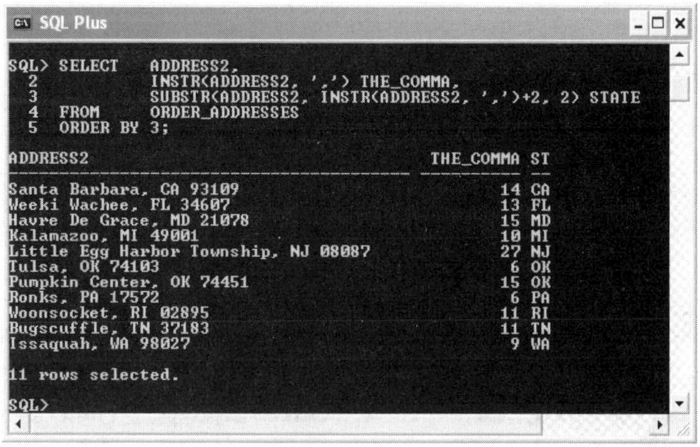

FIGURE 6-2

SUBSTR and
INSTR combined
together

```
SQL Plus                                                        _ □ ×

SQL> SELECT      ADDRESS2,
  2              INSTR(ADDRESS2, ',') THE_COMMA,
  3              SUBSTR(ADDRESS2, INSTR(ADDRESS2, ',')+2, 2) STATE
  4   FROM     ORDER_ADDRESSES
  5   ORDER BY 3;

ADDRESS2                                          THE_COMMA ST
--------------------------------------------------------------
Santa Barbara, CA 93109                                  14 CA
Weeki Wachee, FL 34607                                   13 FL
Havre De Grace, MD 21078                                 15 MD
Kalamazoo, MI 49001                                      10 MI
Little Egg Harbor Township, NJ 08087                     27 NJ
Tulsa, OK 74103                                           6 OK
Pumpkin Center, OK 74451                                 15 OK
Ronks, PA 17572                                           6 PA
Woonsocket, RI 02895                                     11 RI
Bugscuffle, TN 37183                                     11 TN
Issaquah, WA 98027                                        9 WA

11 rows selected.

SQL>
```

CERTIFICATION OBJECTIVE 6.03

Describe the Use of Conversion Functions

Conversion functions convert the datatype of an expression from one datatype
to another. Some will also transform the format of the data at the same time.
Conversion functions are not necessarily required in all situations—many automatic
datatype conversions are performed by SQL without prompting. However, automatic
conversions are not always performed, and explicit datatype conversions are always
considered to be good design.

Here is an example—this is an INSERT statement that attempts to store data
into two columns. The CALL_ID column is of the NUMBER datatype. The
CALL_DATE_TZ column is of the datatype TIMESTAMP WITH TIME ZONE.
Here's an attempt to INSERT data into that table:

```
INSERT INTO CALLS (CALL_ID, CALL_DATE_TZ)
VALUES            (1, '24-MAY-12 10:15:30');

Error starting at line 1 in command:
INSERT INTO CALLS (CALL_ID, CALL_DATE_TZ)
VALUES            (1, '24-MAY-12 10:15:30')
Error report:
SQL Error: ORA-01840: input value not long enough for date format
01840. 00000 -  "input value not long enough for date format"
```

Now let's try that same INSERT statement with a conversion function:

```
INSERT INTO CALLS (CALL_ID, CALL_DATE_TZ)
VALUES             (1, TO_TIMESTAMP_TZ('24-MAY-12 10:15:30',
                                       'DD-MON-RR HH24:MI:SS')  );
```

```
1 rows inserted
```

In this example, the TO_TIMESTAMP_TZ conversion function is used to send the same data we used in our previous INSERT. This particular conversion function uses a "format model" that describes the format of the data to the database. The format model in this instance is 'DD-MON-RR HH24:MI:SS'. This helps to ensure that the input data is recognized correctly.

The next section describes many conversion functions with examples of their use.

Conversion Functions

There are a number of functions intended to convert values of one datatype to another datatype. They are discussed in this section. Some of the most commonly used are TO_NUMBER, TO_CHAR, and TO_DATE. In addition, TO_TIMESTAMP is useful for situations involving the use of fractional seconds, and TO_DSINTERVAL and TO_YMINTERVAL deal with the datatypes of time intervals.

TO_NUMBER

Syntax: TO_NUMBER(*e1*, *format_model*, *nls_parms*)

Parameters: *e1* is an expression (required). *format_model* is the optional format model. See Table 6-2 for a complete list of elements that make up the format model.

There is an optional third parameter representing NLS settings. It allows you to identify any of the three NLS parameters defined in Table 6-3. If included, the third parameter for TO_NUMBER consists of a single string that encompasses any one or more of those three NLS parameters. For example, the following is one example of the *nls_parms* parameter that provides a specification of two of the NLS parameters:

```
' nls_currency = ''USD'' nls_numeric_characters = '',.'' '
```

Note that since the values are enclosed in single quotes, yet include single quotes themselves, then each occurrence of the single quotes within the string must be preceded by the escape character—which is a single quote—in order to clarify that the value is in fact a single quote as part of the string, rather than the end of the overall string literal value.

These values can be used to declare non-standard NLS parameter values within the incoming *e1* parameter.

Process: Transform *e1* from an expression, perhaps a character string, into a numeric value, using *format_model* to determine what format *e1* may take, and where to extract the numeric values from among the formatting information.

Output: Numeric.

Example: In the example that follows, our starting value is a string, '$17,000.23'. This isn't a numeric datatype but a character string containing a dollar sign and a comma. The format model here explains that the dollar sign is a symbol, and the format model makes it clear where the significant numeric data can be found in the source column. The "9" element below is not a literal number 9, but rather an element of the format model that indicates the presence of any digit. It is repeated to indicate the upper bound of acceptable values. Finally the output is displayed—a raw numeric value extracted from the character string '$17,000.23'.

```
SELECT  TO_NUMBER('$17,000.23','$999,999.99')
FROM    DUAL;

TO_NUMBER('$17,000.23','$999,999.99')
-------------------------------------
17000.23
```

Here is a similar example showing the use of the *nls_parms* parameter.

```
SELECT  TO_NUMBER('17.000,23',
                  '999G999D99',
                  'nls_numeric_characters='',.'' ')
                  REFORMATTED_NUMBER
FROM    DUAL;

REFORMATTED_NUMBER
----------------------
17000.23
```

In this example, the incoming value shows a decimal point to mark "thousands" and the comma to mark the decimal point. The *nls_parms* value clarifies this to the TO_NUMBER function, along with the format mask, and the incoming value is interpreted and translated, as shown in the displayed output.

See Table 6-2 for a complete list of the elements that can be included in a numeric format model.

	Element	Example	Description
TABLE 6-2 Number Format Elements	, .	9,999.99	Commas and decimal points will pass through wherever they are included. Warning: only one period allowed per format mask.
	$	$999.99	Leading dollar sign.
	0	0099.99	Leading or trailing 0.
	9	999	Any digit.
	B	B999	Leading blank for integers.
	C	C999	The ISO currency symbol as defined in the NLS_ISO_ CURRENCY parameter.
	D	999D99	Returns the current decimal character as defined by the NLS_NUMERIC_CHARACTERS parameter. The default value is a period.
	EEEE	9.9EEE	Returns a value in scientific notation.
	G	9G999	Returns the group separator (e.g., a comma).
	L	L999	Returns the local currency symbol.
	MI	999MI	Returns negative value with trailing minus sign; returns positive value with a trailing blank.
	PR	999PR	Returns negative values in angle brackets.
	RN rn	RN	Returns values in Roman numerals, uppercase. Put RN in lowercase, as "rn", for Roman numerals in lowercase.
	S (prefix)	S9999	Returns negative values with a leading minus sign, positive values with a leading positive sign. Note: Can only appear in the first or last position of a format mask.
	S (suffix)	9999S	Returns negative values with a trailing minus sign, positive values with a trailing positive sign. Note: Can only appear in the first or last position of a format mask.
	TM	TM	The text minimum number format model returns the smallest number of characters possible.
	U	U999	Returns the Euro currency symbol or whatever is indicated by the NLS_DUAL_CURRENCY parameter.
	V	999V99	Returns a value multiplied by 10^n, where n is the number of 9s after the V.
	X	XXXX	Returns the hexadecimal value.

TABLE 6-3	NLS Parameter	Description
The NLS Parameters	NLS_NUMERIC_CHARACTERS = 'dg'	d = decimal character—see D in Table 6-2. g = group separator—see G in Table 6-2.
	NLS_CURRENCY = 'text'	text = local currency symbol—see L in Table 6-2.
	NLS_ISO_CURRENCY = 'currency'	currency = international currency symbol—see C in Table 6-2.

TO_CHAR

The TO_CHAR function converts data from various datatypes to character data. There are actually three different TO_CHAR functions. They are, in the most technical of terms, three "overloaded" functions. An "overloaded" function is one that shares a name with another function, but where each is differentiated by their respective parameter lists. Each parameter list represents a different function. There are three versions of TO_CHAR: one whose first parameter is a character string, another whose first parameter is a date, and another whose first parameter is numeric.

The following sections describe each of the three TO_CHAR functions.

TO_CHAR—CHARACTER   Syntax: TO_CHAR(c)

Parameters: c is either an NCHAR, an NVARCHAR2, a CLOB, or an NCLOB.

Process: Transforms the incoming parameter into a VARCHAR2.

Output: VARCHAR2.

Example:

```
SELECT TO_CHAR('Hello') FROM DUAL;

TO_CHAR('HELLO')
----------------
Hello
```

There are situations where you'll work with datatypes that cannot accept, for example, CLOB data, but can accept the output of TO_CHAR—such as a VARCHAR2 datatype.

TO_CHAR—NUMBER Syntax: TO_CHAR(*n*, *format_model*, *nls_parms*)

Parameters: *n* is a number (required). Format_model is optional. A format model consists of one or more format elements, which we saw earlier listed in Table 6-2. The *nls_parms* value is the same parameter we saw earlier with the TO_NUMBER function.

Process: Transforms *n* into a character string, using the optional format model for guidance as to how to format the output with any special characters that may be desired, such as dollar signs or other financial symbols, special handling of negative numbers, etc.

Output: Character.

Example: Format the number 198 with a dollar sign and penny specification.

```
SELECT TO_CHAR(198,'$999.99') FROM DUAL;

TO_CHAR(198,'$999.99')
----------------------
 $198.00
```

TO_CHAR—DATE Syntax: TO_CHAR(*d*, *format_model*, *nls_parms*)

Parameters: *d* is a date or a date interval (required). *Format_model* is optional and can be used to format data in a variety of ways. See Table 6-4 for details on format models for date datatypes. The *nls_parms* parameter is the same we saw earlier, for the TO_NUMBER function.

Output: Character.

Example: Here's an example of the use of a date format model as described in Table 6-4:

```
SELECT TO_CHAR(SYSDATE, 'DAY, "THE" DD "OF" MONTH, RRRR')
FROM DUAL;

TO_CHAR(SYSDATE,'DAY,"THE"DD"OF"MONTH,RRRR')
--------------------------------------------
THURSDAY , THE 02 OF JULY      , 2009
```

The "FM" code is a format mask that cleans up all of the trailing blanks, as follows:

```
SELECT TO_CHAR(SYSDATE, 'FMDAY, "THE" DD "OF" MONTH, RRRR')
FROM DUAL;
```

```
TO_CHAR(SYSDATE,'FMDAY,"THE"DD"OF"MONTH,RRRR')
----------------------------------------------
THURSDAY, THE 2 OF JULY, 2009
```

Changing the format masks to mixed case sends an implied message to mix-case the output as well:

```
SELECT TO_CHAR(SYSDATE,'FMDay, "the" Dd "of" Month, RRRR')
FROM DUAL;

TO_CHAR(SYSDATE,'FMDAY,"THE"DD"OF"MONTH,RRRR')

----------------------------------------------
Thursday, the 2 of July, 2009
```

Adding the "th" indicator introduces an additional improvement. The inclusion of "th" will append whatever is appropriate after the date—for 1, you'll get "1st", for 2, you'll get "2nd", etc. For example,

```
SELECT TO_CHAR(SYSDATE,'FMDay, "the" Ddth "of" Month, RRRR')
FROM DUAL;

TO_CHAR(SYSDATE,'FMDAY,"THE"DDTH"OF"MONTH,RRRR')
------------------------------------------------
Thursday, the 2nd of July, 2009
```

The format model is the secret to extracting the time values from SYSDATE. For example,

```
SELECT TO_CHAR(SYSDATE,'HH24:MI:SS AM') FROM DUAL;

TO_CHAR(SYSDATE,'HH24:MI:SSAM')
-------------------------------
17:48:16 PM
```

Notice in this example we can use either AM or PM to indicate where we want the morning/afternoon indicator to be located, and whether we want it to include periods or not. Whether we use AM or PM makes no difference; the appropriate indicator will appear wherever the format model directs, as shown in the preceding example.

The SYSDATE function displays the date by default. But buried inside of it is also the time of day, in hours, minutes, and seconds. The full set of data can be extracted from SYSDATE with the format model parameters of the TO_CHAR function, as shown in Table 6-4. But beware, there is danger here . . . and it's yet another example of how tricky SQL can be. Take a look at this SQL statement:

```
SELECT TO_CHAR(SYSDATE, 'DD-MON-RRRR HH:MM:SS') "Today's Date
And Time"
FROM    DUAL;
```

See anything wrong with it? Perhaps not. Most developers don't; this can trip up even the most experienced and seasoned of SQL professionals. Try it on any database instance, and it will work, and the output will probably appear to be correct. But look closely at the value displayed for that portion of the format model represented by the MM. Then look at Table 6-4. MM is not "minutes"; it is "months". If you want minutes, you need to use "MI", as in "HH:MI:SS". Watch this one, folks; it's very tricky—the syntax is technically correct, the execution will be successful, and the test data looks correct at a glance. But it's still wrong. The sharp eye of a certified Oracle Database SQL Expert should flag this.

TABLE 6-4	Element	Description
Date Format Elements	AD / A.D. BC / B.C.	Anno Domini or Before Christ indicator, with or without periods
	AM / A.M. PM / P.M.	Morning or afternoon hours, with or without periods
	CC / SCC	Century
	D	Day of the week, 1 through 7
	DAY	The name of the day spelled out
	DD	Day of the month, 1 through 31
	DDD	Day of the year, 1 through 366
	DL	Long date format, as determined by the NLS_DATE_FORMAT parameter. Appearance is determined by NLS_TERRITORY and NLS_LANGUAGE parameters. Sample AMERICAN_AMERICA output is 'Monday, July 27, 2009'
	DS	Short date format. Appearance is determined by NLS_TERRITORY and NLS_LANGUAGE parameters. Sample AMERICAN_AMERICA output is '7/27/2009'
	DY	Abbreviated name of day. SUN, MON, TUE, etc.
	E	Abbreviated era name
	EE	Full era name

TABLE 6-4	Element	Description
Date Format Elements (*Continued*)	FF	Fractional seconds
	FM	Used in combination with other elements to direct the suppression of leading or trailing blanks
	FX	Exact matching between the character data and the format model
	HH, HH12	Hour of the day, 1 through 12 (both are identical)
	HH24	Hour of day, 1 through 24
	IW	Week of the year, 1 through 53
	I IY IYY	Last 1, 2, or 3 digits of the ISO year
	J	Julian day, counted as the number of days since January 1, 4712 B.C.
	MI	Minute. 0 through 59
	MM	Month in double digits, 01 through 12
	MON	Abbreviated name of month, e.g., JAN, FEB, MAR
	MONTH	Name of month spelled out
	PR	If negative, numbers are enclosed within angle brackets (<>). If positive, returned with leading and trailing spaces. PR follows specification, for example: 9999PR
	Q	Quarter of year
	RM	Roman numeral month
	RR	Accepts twentieth-century dates in the twenty-first century using only two digits. 00 through 49 is interpreted as 2000 through 2049. 50 through 99 is interpreted as 1950 through 1999
	RRRR	The four-digit year. If provided a two-digit year, it returns the same value as RR
	SS	Seconds, 0 through 59
	SSSS	Seconds past midnight, 0 through 86399
	TS	The short time format. Only allowable when specified with the DL or DS format model element, separated by white space
	TZD	Abbreviated time zone with Daylight Saving Time. Only valid in timestamp and interval formats. Examples: 'EST', 'CMT'
	TZH	Time zone hour. Not valid in DATE datatypes; only valid in timestamp and interval formats. '00' through '12'

(*Continued*)

TABLE 6-4	Element	Description
Date Format Elements (*Continued*)	TZM	Time zone minute. Only valid in timestamp and interval formats. '00' through '59'
	TZR	Time zone region information. Not valid in DATE datatypes; only valid in timestamp and interval formats. Example: 'America/Los_Angeles'
	WW	The week of the year, 1 through 53. Week 1 starts on the first day of the year and ends on the seventh day of the year
	W	The week of the month, 1 through 5. Week 1 starts on the first day of the month and ends on the seventh day of the month
	X	Local radix character
	Y,YYY	The year with the comma in position
	YEAR, SYEAR	The year spelled out in English. The S version causes BC dates to display with a minus sign prefix
	YYYY, SYYYY	The four-digit year. The S version causes BC dates to display with a minus sign prefix
	YYY, YY, Y	The last 3, 2, or 1 digits of the year
	- / , . ; :	Punctuation that is accepted in place and passed through as is
	"text"	Literal value. Display as is.

TO_DATE

Syntax: TO_DATE(*c*, *format_model*, *nls_parms*)

Parameters: *c* = a character string (required); *format_model* is a format model according to Table 6-4. The *nls_parms* value is the same parameter you saw earlier with the TO_NUMBER function.

Process: Transform the value contained within *c* into a valid DATE datatype by structuring *format_model* to describe how the character string is formed, identifying the date information accordingly.

Output: Date.

Example: Convert a non-standard date representation to the default format.

```
SELECT TO_DATE('2009-01-31','RRRR-MM-DD')
FROM   DUAL;

TO_DATE('2009-01-31','RRRR-MM-DD')
----------------------
31-JAN-09
```

TO_TIMESTAMP

Syntax: TO_TIMESTAMP (*c, format_model, nls_parms*)

Parameters: *c* is a character datatype (required); *format_model* must define the format of *c* corresponding to TIMESTAMP format model elements—optional, the default requirement is that *c* must be in the TIMESTAMP format. The *nls_parms* value is the same parameter you saw earlier with the TO_NUMBER function.

Process: Converts *c* data to the TIMESTAMP datatype, which differs from DATE in that it includes fractional seconds. The *format_model* defines the pattern of *c*'s date information to the function so the various elements of TIMESTAMP are identified—information for year, month, day, hours, minutes, seconds, and fractional seconds.

Output: A value in the TIMESTAMP datatype.

Example: Here is a character representation of a date. The format model is included to define the pattern and inform the TIMESTAMP function where the DD information is, where the MON information is, etc.

```
SELECT TO_TIMESTAMP('2020-JAN-01 13:34:00:093423',
                    'RRRR-MON-DD HH24:MI:SS:FF') EVENT_TIME
FROM   DUAL;

EVENT_TIME
------------------------
01-JAN-20 01.34.00.093423000 PM
```

TO_DSINTERVAL

Syntax: TO_DSINTERVAL (*sql_format, nls_parms*)

Parameters: *sql_format* is a character string in the format required for a INTERVAL DAY TO SECOND datatype, which is 'DAYS HH24:MI:SS.FF'. For example, '15 14:05:10.001' is the INTERVAL DAY TO SECOND representation for 15 days, 14 hours, 5 minutes, and 10.001 seconds. The *nls_parms* value is the same parameter you saw earlier with the TO_NUMBER function.

Process: Transforms the incoming value represented in *sql_format* to a value of INTERVAL DAY TO SECOND datatype.

Output: A value in the INTERVAL DAY TO SECOND datatype.

Example: The following converts a value representing 40 days, 8 hours, 30 minutes, and 0.03225 seconds into the INTERVAL DAY TO SECOND datatype.

```
SELECT TO_DSINTERVAL('40 08:30:00.03225') EVENT_TIME
FROM   DUAL;

EVENT_TIME
-----------
40 8:30:0.032250000
```

TO_YMINTERVAL

Syntax: TO_YMINTERVAL ('y-m')

Parameters: y and m are numbers contained within a string, required.

Process: Tranforms y and m into the years and months in a format of the datatype INTERVAL YEAR TO MONTHS.

Output: A value in the INTERVAL YEAR TO MONTHS datatype.

Example: Convert the character expression showing 4 years and 6 months into the datatype INTERVAL YEAR TO MONTHS.

```
SELECT TO_YMINTERVAL('04-06') EVENT_TIME
FROM   DUAL;

EVENT_TIME
-----------
4-6
```

Automatic Datatype Conversions

This section would be remiss if we didn't at least mention the concept of automatic datatype conversions. We've mentioned them before, but it's worth pointing out here that some datatype conversions occur automatically in the database. For example:

```
SELECT 'Chapter ' || 1 || ' . . . I am born.'
FROM   DUAL;

'CHAPTER'||1||'...IAMBORN.'
--------------------------
Chapter 1 . . . I am born.
```

In this sample, we concatenate three expressions into one. The center expression is a numeric literal—and yet, the concatenation operators are only intended to connect string values together. But SQL is smart enough to recognize what is happening, and it performs an automatic datatype conversion of the numeric 1 into a character '1' and then completes the concatenation.

Another example (line numbers added):

```
01    SELECT SYSDATE,
02           ADD_MONTHS(SYSDATE,
03                      SUBSTR('plus 3 months',6,1)) PLUS_THREE
04    FROM   DUAL;
05
06    SYSDATE                    PLUS_THREE
07    ------------------------   ------------------------
08    28-JUL-09                  28-OCT-09
```

In this example, the SUBSTR function in line 3 returns a string value of '3', which is automatically converted to a numeric datatype, since a numeric is what is required for the ADD_MONTHS function in lines 2 and 3.

As I've stated before, the general rule of thumb is this: automatic datatype conversions can and do happen wherever they can be done without losing data precision. However, good software does not depend on them but instead is written with explicit datatype conversions—using the conversion functions discussed here—wherever required.

CERTIFICATION OBJECTIVE 6.04

Manage Data in Different Time Zones—Use Various Datetime Functions

Oracle SQL contains a number of features to support the management of local and remote time zones. For example, a help desk that is located in one time zone that takes phone calls from one or more additional time zones must be able to track the times of incoming phone calls and associated responses, and be able to do so in such a way that all the different time zones will fully understand the information.

For any given transaction, there are three time zones to be concerned with:

■ The UTC time, which is the absolute universal standard against which all other times are based

■ The database time zone, which is the time zone of the location where the database is installed (accessible by the function DBTIMEZONE)

■ The session time zone, which is the time zone of the user (accessible by the function SESSIONTIMEZONE)

Oracle recommends setting the database time to UTC time. That way you simplify the overall process, as well as speed performance by eliminating an extra time offset. However, such a configuration step is not required, nor necessarily desired, depending on your particular business rule requirements.

Note that the DATE and TIMESTAMP datatypes do not support time zone differences. However, there are two datatypes that do work with time zones. They are called TIMESTAMP WITH TIME ZONE and TIMESTAMP WITH LOCAL TIME ZONE. See Table 6-5 for a comparison of these datatypes with DATE and TIMESTAMP and their different features.

The TIMESTAMP WITH TIME ZONE and TIMESTAMP WITH LOCAL TIME ZONE datatypes differ in the way they handle time zones. Both datatypes store the source data's date and time. The former—TIMESTAMP WITH TIME ZONE—also stores the time zone. The latter—TIMESTAMP WITH LOCAL TIME ZONE—does not store the time zone but stores the time normalized to UTC time. When queried, it presents its data in the user's local time zone. It uses an offset from UTC time.

In the next few sections, we'll look into the details of how this works.

on the
Job

If you are working with an application in which the time zone for a given event is important, use TIMESTAMP WITH TIME ZONE. But if you require a system in which that isn't necessary—a system that is more concerned with multiple users across multiple time zones who should be able to each see data displayed in terms of their own local time as defined by their own local client machine—use TIMESTAMP WITH LOCAL TIME ZONE. However, note that web-based applications often show time according to the time on the web server, rather than the local client, so unless special steps are taken with regard to web browser interfaces, the TIMESTAMP WITH LOCAL TIME ZONE may provide no benefit to such an application.

	Datatype	Fractional Seconds	Time Zone
TABLE 6-5	DATE	No	No
Datetime	TIMESTAMP	Yes	No
Datatypes and	TIMESTAMP WITH TIME ZONE	Yes	Explicit
Time Zones	TIMESTAMP WITH LOCAL TIME ZONE	Yes	Relative

Database Time vs. Session Time

Two system variables that track times are important for our purposes here:

- The database time zone, as defined by the function DBTIMEZONE
- The session time zone, as defined by the function SESSIONTIMEZONE

```
SELECT DBTIMEZONE, SESSIONTIMEZONE
FROM    DUAL;

DBTIMEZONE SESSIONTIMEZONE
---------- ----------------
+00:00     America/New_York
```

According to this example, the database time zone is UTC+0, which is to say that it's set to UTC. The session time zone is 'America/New_York'.

To change the database time zone:

```
ALTER DATABASE SET TIME_ZONE = 'Europe/Zurich';
```

Note: you cannot change the database time zone if the database already contains any tables with columns of the TIMESTAMP WITH LOCAL TIME ZONE datatype.

To change the session time zone:

```
ALTER SESSION SET TIME_ZONE = 'America/Los_Angeles';
```

If you are trying to change the database time zone and find that you cannot because you already have tables with the TIMESTAMP WITH LOCAL TIME ZONE datatype, you can easily locate those tables by querying the data

dictionary, which I discuss in Chapter 14. For now, know that this query will locate those table names for you, along with their owners:

```
SELECT    OWNER, TABLE_NAME, COLUMN_NAME, DATA_TYPE
FROM      DBA_TAB_COLUMNS
WHERE     DATA_TYPE LIKE '%LOCAL TIME ZONE%'
ORDER BY OWNER, TABLE_NAME, COLUMN_NAME;
```

Coordinated Universal Time (UTC)

The Coordinated Universal Time, or UTC, is the new name for Greenwich Mean Time (GMT). It is the universal standard for measuring time internationally. Technically there are differences between UTC and GMT, but for our purposes those differences are irrelevant. The primary issue for us to be aware of is that UTC measures time as it exists at the Royal Observatory in Greenwich, London. (Generally that's true. There are exceptions, but they go beyond the scope of our discussion here.) All other time around the world is measured as an offset of time relative to that location. In other words, the American east coast is 5 hours "behind" the time in Greenwich, London, so New York, for example, is considered –5:00 UTC. (This is with Standard Time in force.) This and all other times are defined in terms of their difference from Greenwich, i.e., plus or minus UTC.

In the world of SQL, the UTC time is the top authority. The second-level authority is the database server. The third authority is the client system.

Time on the database server is measured relative to UTC. In an application that deals with multiple time zones and the associated datatypes, it's not uncommon to set the time zone for the database server to be identical to UTC, regardless of its actual location.

Time Zone Datatypes

There are two special datatypes for managing time across multiple time zones, described here. They are:

- TIMESTAMP WITH TIME ZONE
- TIMESTAMP WITH LOCAL TIME ZONE

To understand them, you must first understand the concepts of the time zone region name and time zone offset. Let's discuss time zone region names and then review the TIMESTAMP datatype (which does not store time zone data), after which we'll discuss the two time zone datatypes.

Time Zone Region Name

Time Zone Region Names are text descriptions of the various time zones available as part of the UTC system. Each text description has a name and an abbreviation. Examples include those listed in Table 6-6.

Notice in the table that time zone names have more than one associated abbreviation. That's because the abbreviations refer to something other than the particular geographical location for the time zone. For example, 'America/Chicago' includes the abbreviations CDT, CST, and others. These refer to

- Central Daylight Time (UTC-5)
- Central Standard Time (UTC-6)
- Eastern Standard Time (UTC-5)
- Local Mean Time (UTC-6)

The list of available time zone region names in any given database is available in the data dictionary. The data dictionary is a topic we'll cover in some detail later in the book. For now, it's worth noting simply that you can issue the

TABLE 6-6	Name	Abbreviation
Examples of Time Zone Names and Abbreviations	America/Chicago	CDT
	America/Chicago	CST
	America/Chicago	EST
	America/Chicago	LMT
	Asia/Macau	CST
	Asia/Macau	LMT
	Asia/Macau	MOST
	Asia/Macau	MOT
	Australia/Brisbane	EST
	Australia/Brisbane	LMT
	Europe/Vienna	CEST
	Europe/Vienna	CET
	Europe/Vienna	LMT

following query from any user account and obtain a list of the available time zones in your database:

```
SELECT    TZABBREV, TZNAME
FROM      V$TIMEZONE_NAMES
ORDER BY TZABBREV, TZNAME;
```

This query lists the time zone abbreviations, along with the many time zone names that exist within each one, alphabetized.

The advantage to using time zone region names in the database is that any changes affecting Daylight Saving Time are automatically managed, which is not true when time zone information is stored according to time zone offset.

Time Zone Offset

A time zone offset takes the following format:

```
+/- TZH:TZM
```

The TZH and TZM format models were listed in Table 6-4. An example of a time zone offset is

```
-05:00
```

This example represents a time zone offset of "minus five hours". The New York time zone has an offset of "-05:00" from UTC when Daylight Standard Time (also known as Standard Time) is in effect, and "-4:00" when Daylight Saving Time is in effect.

Note, however, than if you store time zone information in the "time zone offset" format, your data won't be adjusted for changes between Standard Time and Daylight Saving Time. Time zone information stored in the "time zone region name" format will reflect such changes.

As a reminder, the TIMESTAMP datatype is the same as DATE, but with fractional seconds included. The time zone datatypes build on the TIMESTAMP datatype, as described next.

TIMESTAMP WITH TIME ZONE Datatype

The TIMESTAMP WITH TIME ZONE datatype is an Oracle SQL datatype that is similar to the TIMESTAMP datatype, but it adds the following fields: TIMEZONE_HOUR, TIMEZONE_MINUTE, TIMEZONE_REGION, TIMEZONE_ABBR. The time zone is stored in one of two ways:

- A time zone region name, or
- A time zone offset from UTC

The time zone region name is a text representation describing one of the many approved time zone regions.

The time zone offset is the interval between the local time and the UTC.

As we've stated, Oracle officially recommends that you store time zone information using the time zone region name rather than the time zone offset from the UTC, so that adjustments involving Daylight Saving Time (DST) will be automatically taken into account by the system when you use the time zone region name.

TIMESTAMP WITH LOCAL TIME ZONE Datatype

TIMESTAMP WITH LOCAL TIME ZONE is a datatype that is also similar to the TIMESTAMP datatype, but it stores the time normalized to the database time zone. In other words, no information is stored about the time zone of the data. However, when a user queries data of the TIMESTAMP WITH LOCAL TIME ZONE type, the data is presented in terms of the user's local time zone.

Time Zone Functions

Time zone functions are those functions that work with the datatypes and data objects that support the management of time within a database whose user base spans multiple time zones.

DBTIMEZONE

Syntax: DBTIMEZONE

Parameters: None.

Process: Returns the time zone for the database.

Output: Character.

Example: Here's a database whose time is set to UTC exactly, no offset.

```
SELECT DBTIMEZONE FROM DUAL;

DBTIMEZONE
----------
+00:00
```

Oracle officially recommends that the database time zone be set to UTC, in order to speed performance by avoiding unnecessary time zone calculations.

SESSIONTIMEZONE

Syntax: SESSIONTIMEZONE

Parameters: None.

Process: Returns the time zone for the current session. The format of the output is dependent on the most recent execution of the ALTER SESSION statement. The options are: (a) time zone offset, (b) time zone regional name. The better choice is (b), time zone regional name, if you want the database to perform adjustments to support Standard Time and Daylight Saving Time changes automatically.

Output: Character.

Example: Obtain the session time:

```
SELECT SESSIONTIMEZONE FROM DUAL;

SESSIONTIMEZONE
----------------
America/New_York
```

CURRENT_DATE, CURRENT_TIMESTAMP

Syntax: CURRENT_DATE, CURRENT_TIMESTAMP(t)

Parameters: None for CURRENT_DATE. For CURRENT_TIMESTAMP, t = local time zone's fractional second precision. Ranges between 0 and 9. Optional; defaults to 6.

Process: Returns the current date and current timestamp within the session time zone.

Output: CURRENT_DATE returns a value of the DATE datatype; CURRENT_TIMESTAMP returns a value of the TIMESTAMP WITH TIME ZONE datatype.

Example: Here is an example:

```
SELECT CURRENT_DATE, CURRENT_TIMESTAMP
FROM   DUAL;
```

```
CURRENT_DATE             CURRENT_TIMESTAMP
-------------------------- ------------------
08-JUL-09                08-JUL-09 03.03.50.843000000 PM AMERICA/NEW_YORK
```

Note the first part of the value returned by CURRENT_TIMESTAMP. It's the same as the CURRENT_DATE function, plus additional information showing time. DATE datatype values actually store information for hours, minutes, and seconds; the TO_CHAR conversion function is capable of displaying that detail. But DATE datatypes do not store fractional seconds; TIMESTAMP does. The local time zone information shown with the TIMESTAMP output is not stored within the TIMESTAMP but reflects the local time zone defined by SESSIONTIMEZONE.

LOCALTIMESTAMP

Syntax: LOCALTIMESTAMP(*t*)

Parameters: *t* = local time zone's fractional second precision. Ranges between 0 and 9. Optional; defaults to 6.

Process: Displays the user session's local time, as opposed to the database time zone, which may be different. The value is displayed including year, month, day, hours, minutes, and seconds, including fractional seconds.

Output: A value of datatype TIMESTAMP.

Example: Show the local time to a fractional-second precision of four digits to the right of the decimal point.

```
SELECT LOCALTIMESTAMP(4) FROM   DUAL;

LOCALTIMESTAMP(4)
-------------------------
09-JUL-09 12.18.20.031300000 AM
```

SYSTIMESTAMP

Syntax: SYSTIMESTAMP

Parameters: None.

Process: Returns the system date, including fractional seconds, of the operating system on which the database is installed. This is the TIMESTAMP equivalent to the SYSDATE function.

Output: The system date in the TIMESTAMP WITH TIME ZONE datatype.

Example: Show the database's operating system date and time with fractional seconds included.

```
SELECT SYSTIMESTAMP FROM DUAL;

SYSTIMESTAMP
-------------
09-JUL-09 12.21.27.437000000 AM -04:00
```

NEW_TIME

Syntax: NEW_TIME(*d*, *t1*, *t2*)

Parameters: *d* is a DATE datatype and is required. *t1* and *t2* are time zone indications taken from Table 6-7.

Process: For a given value of *d*, NEW_TIME translates the time *d* according to the offset specified between *t1* and *t2*. In other words, *t1* is assumed to be the time zone in which *d* is recorded, so NEW_TIME will convert that time into the *t2* time zone.

Output: A value in DATE datatype.

Example:

```
SELECT TO_CHAR(
        NEW_TIME(
          TO_DATE('1983-JAN-03 14:30:56','RRRR-MON-DD HH24:MI:SS'),
          'AST',
          'HST')
        ,'DD-MON-RR HH:MI:SS') NEW_DATE
FROM    DUAL;

NEW_DATE
------------------
03-JAN-83 08:30:56
```

TABLE 6-7	Time Zones	Standard Time	Daylight Saving Time
Time Zone Values for the NEW_TIME Function	Atlantic	AST	ADT
	Bering	BST	BDT
	Central	CST	CDT
	Eastern	EST	EDT
	Greenwich	UTC	
	Alaska-Hawaii	HST	HDT
	Mountain	MST	MDT
	Newfoundland	NST	
	Pacific	PST	PDT
	Yukon	YST	YDT

Time Zone Conversion Functions

The following section describes functions that convert time zone datatypes.

FROM_TZ

Syntax: FROM_TZ(*ts*, *tz*)

Parameters: *ts* is a TIMESTAMP value (required); *tz* is a time zone reference (required).

Process: Transforms *ts*, a TIMESTAMP value, and *tz*, a character value representing the time zone, into a value of the datatype TIMESTAMP WITH TIME ZONE.

The second parameter, *tz*, can be in one of two formats: either the format of 'TZH:TZM', where TZH and TZM are time zone hours and time zone minutes, as described in Table 6-4; or the format of a character expression that results in a string in the TZR with optional TZD format, also as described in Table 6-4.

Output: A value of the TIMESTAMP WITH TIME ZONE datatype.

Example: Starting with the character string '2012-10-12 07:45:30', convert it to the TIMESTAMP datatype, and then convert it to the TIMESTAMP WITH TIME ZONE by included a corresponding time zone offset value of '7:30'.

```
SELECT FROM_TZ( TIMESTAMP '2012-10-12 07:45:30', '+07:30')
FROM   DUAL;

FROM_TZ(TIMESTAMP'2012-10-1207:45:30','+07:30')
----------------------------------------------
12-OCT-12 07.45.30.000000000 AM +07:30
```

TO_TIMESTAMP_TZ

Syntax: TO_TIMESTAMP_TZ(*c*, *format_model*, *nls_parms*)

Parameters: *c* is a character string (required). The *format_model* must define the format of *c* corresponding to TIMESTAMP WITH TIME ZONE format model elements—optional, the default requirement is that *c* must be in the TIMESTAMP format. The optional *nls_parms* value is the same parameter you saw earlier with the TO_NUMBER function.

Process: Transforms *c* into a value of TIMESTAMP WITH TIME ZONE, where *format_model* defines the format in which *c* stores the TIMESTAMP WITH TIME ZONE information. The time zone will default to that defined by the SESSION parameter.

Output: A value in the TIMESTAMP WITH TIME ZONE datatype.

Example: Convert the character string '17-04-2013 16:45:30' to a datatype of TIMESTAMP WITH TIME ZONE by providing a format mask.

```
SELECT TO_TIMESTAMP_TZ('17-04-2013 16:45:30','DD-MM-RRRR
HH24:MI:SS') "Time"
FROM   DUAL;


Time
-------------
17-APR-13 04.45.30.000000000 PM AMERICA/NEW_YORK
```

on the **job** *Note that there isn't a conversion function that specifically converts values into the TIMESTAMP WITH LOCAL TIME ZONE datatype. For that, use CAST—see the next description.*

CAST

Syntax: CAST(*e* AS *d*)

Parameters: *e* is an expression; *d* is a datatype.

Process: Converts *e* to *d*. Particularly useful for converting text representations of datetime information into datetime formats, particularly TIMESTAMP WITH LOCAL TIME ZONE.

Output: A value in the *d* datatype.

Example: In the following, we convert a value in the default timestamp format, presented as a literal value:

```
SELECT CAST('19-JAN-10 11:35:30'
            AS TIMESTAMP WITH LOCAL TIME ZONE) "Converted LTZ"
FROM   DUAL;
```

```
Converted LTZ
-------------
19-JAN-10 11.35.30.000000000 AM
```

If we wish to use a format mask for any reason, we can nest a call to, for example, the TO_TIMESTAMP conversion function, as follows:

```
SELECT CAST(TO_TIMESTAMP('19-JAN-10 14:35:30','DD-MON-RR
HH24:MI:SS')
           AS TIMESTAMP WITH LOCAL TIME ZONE) "Converted LTZ"
FROM    DUAL;

Converted LTZ
-------------
19-JAN-10 02.35.30.000000000 PM
```

EXTRACT

Syntax: EXTRACT(*fm* FROM *e*)

Parameters: *fm* is a format model element from Table 6-8 (required); *e* is a timestamp expression.

Process: Extracts the value indicated by *fm* from *e*, where *fm* is one of the following keywords: YEAR, MONTH, DAY, HOUR, MINUTE, SECOND, TIMEZONE_HOUR, TIMEZONE_MINUTE, TIMEZONE_REGION, TIMEZONE_ABBR; and *e* is an expression representing a datetime datatype.

Output: Character if you extract TIMEZONE_REGION or TIMEZONE_ABBR data; numeric for all other extractions.

Example:

```
SELECT EXTRACT(MINUTE FROM TO_TIMESTAMP('2009-10-11 12:13:14',
               'RRRR-MM-DD HH24:MI:SS')) "Minute"
FROM    DUAL;

Minute
--------------------
13
```

| TABLE 6-8 | | Format Elements and the EXTRACT Function | | | | |

Keyword	DATE	TIME STAMP	TIME STAMP WITH TIME ZONE	TIME STAMP WITH LOCAL TIME ZONE	INTERVAL YEAR TO MONTH	INTERVAL DAY TO SECOND
YEAR	X	X	X	X	X	—
MONTH	X	X	X	X	X	—
DAY	X	X	X	X	—	X
HOUR	—	X	X	X	—	X
MINUTE	—	X	X	X	—	X
SECOND	—	X	X	X	—	X
TIMEZONE_HOUR	—	—	X	X*	—	—
TIMEZONE_MINUTE	—	—	X	X*	—	—
TIMEZONE_REGION	—	—	X	X*	—	—
TIMEZONE_ABBR	—	—	X	X*	—	—

* Note that the TIMESTAMP WITH LOCAL TIME ZONE only stores—and therefore only returns—local session time zone data.

SYS_EXTRACT_UTC

Syntax: SYS_EXTRACT_UTC(*dtz*)

Parameters: *dtz* is any datetime value with a time zone included.

Process: Extracts the UTC from a datetime value.

Output: A value of datatype TIMESTAMP.

Example: The sample that follows passes in a date of March 25, 2012, 9:55 A.M., as a TIMESTAMP converted value with an offset of –4 hours. The datetime value is normalized for UTC and the UTC time is displayed as output.

```
SELECT SYS_EXTRACT_UTC(TIMESTAMP '2012-03-25 09:55:00 -04:00') "HQ"
FROM   DUAL;
```

```
HQ
------------------------
25-MAR-12 01.55.00.000000000 PM
```

AT TIME ZONE, AT LOCAL

The datetime datatypes have some additional support for converting among datatypes that we'll list here.

Expression AT TIME ZONE

The best way to understand the concept of the AT TIME ZONE conversion expression is with an example. First, let's look at our system value for DBTIMEZONE and SESSIONTIMEZONE:

```
SELECT DBTIMEZONE, SESSIONTIMEZONE FROM DUAL;

DBTIMEZONE SESSIONTIMEZONE
---------- ----------------------------
+00:00     America/New_York
```

So you can see that our DBTIMEZONE is set to UTC, since its UTC offset is zero. Meanwhile, our local session is in the New York time zone.

Now, armed with that information, let's take a character string that defines a particular datetime value in the TIMESTAMP datatype. We'll use the TO_TIMESTAMP conversion function to do this, and then we'll transform it to be AT TIME ZONE DBTIMEZONE, giving the output a column alias of "DB Time". This code shows how (line numbers added):

```
01    SELECT TO_TIMESTAMP('2012-MAY-24 02:00:00','RRRR-MON-DD HH24:MI:SS')
02          AT TIME ZONE DBTIMEZONE "DB Time"
03    FROM    DUAL;
04
05    DB Time
06    ------------
07    24-MAY-12 06.00.00.000000000 AM +00:00
```

Note that the end of line 2 is an optional column alias, specified after the AT TIME ZONE expression.

The SQL statement includes the TO_TIMESTAMP function to define a value in the TIMESTAMP datatype, which is then followed by the "AT TIME ZONE" keywords, which are setting up the value to be transformed into its equivalent in another time zone. In this example, the target time zone is the value for DBTIMEZONE, but in its place we could use any of the following:

- SESSIONTIMEZONE
- A valid time zone name, such as 'America/Chicago'
- A time zone offset in the 'hh:mm' format, such as '+04:00' (since Daylight Saving Time is in effect at this time, the UTF offset to New York is only 4 hours)
- An expression that produces any of the preceding values

The AT TIME ZONE keywords can be preceded by the datatypes:

- TIMESTAMP
- TIMESTAMP WITH TIME ZONE
- TIMESTAMP WITH LOCAL TIME ZONE

. . . but not the DATE datatype.

The returned value represents the original time translated into the time zone as specified in the AT TIME ZONE expression.

Expression AT LOCAL

The AT LOCAL expression converts the source data into the local time equivalent, as shown in this code (line numbers added):

```
01   SELECT FROM_TZ(
02          CAST(
03            TO_DATE('1999-12-01 11:00:00',
04                  'RRRR-MM-DD HH:MI:SS') AS TIMESTAMP
05            ), 'America/Los_Angeles'
06              ) AT LOCAL "East Coast Time"
07   FROM DUAL;
08
09   East Coast Time
10   --------------
11   01-DEC-99 02.00.00.000000000 PM AMERICA/NEW_YORK
```

Note the column alias at the end of line 6, specified after the AT LOCAL expression.

The AT LOCAL expression takes no value but simply converts the source value to whatever the session time zone indicates, which in this example is America/ New_York time, as indicated by the translated value shown in line 11, the output of the query.

CERTIFICATION SUMMARY

SQL functions perform a wide variety of tasks, ranging from mathematical calculations to text analysis and date conversions. Functions can be called from almost any SQL statement, and from a variety of locations within various SQL statements. SQL functions can be called from the SELECT statement's select list and WHERE clause; from the INSERT statement's value list; from the UPDATE statement's SET clause and WHERE clause; and from the DELETE statement's WHERE clause.

Function takes anywhere from zero to multiple input parameter values. Each function does some sort of processing that incorporates the input parameters, and perhaps some other data as well. Each function sends back exactly one result.

Character functions perform tasks associated with string manipulation and text analysis. Character functions include UPPER, LOWER, INITCAP, CONCAT, LPAD, RPAD, LENGTH, INSTR, SUBSTR, and others. Character functions accept input parameters that may be character data and may include other datatypes, such as numeric parameters. And while each character function returns exactly one value, as do all functions, the character functions do not necessarily return character data as their return value. For example, LENGTH returns a number indicating the length of a given character string. But each performs a task associated with character strings.

Number functions, also referred to as numeric functions, perform analysis on numbers. They include ROUND, REMAINDER, MOD, and others.

Date functions work with date and datetime information. Date functions include SYSDATE, ROUND (for dates), TRUNC (for dates), NEXT_DAY, LAST_DAY, ADD_MONTHS, MONTHS_BETWEEN, NUMTOYMINTERVAL, NUMTODSINTERVAL, and others.

Other functions perform tasks that may or may not perform processing on one or more datatype. Other functions include NVL, DECODE, and NULLIF.

Functions may be nested within each other, so that the output of one function serves as the input parameter of another.

Conversion functions include TO_NUMBER, TO_CHAR, TO_DATE, TO_ TIMESTAMP, TO_DSINTERVAL, TO_YMINTERVAL, and others.

Multiple time zones can be handled in a variety of ways. There is a central system-wide value that stores the time zone for the database, called DBTIMEZONE. This can be set to the UTC time or to an offset of it. Local sessions, in turn, can be in different time zones. Each session's time zone can be analyzed individually by way of the SESSIONTIMEZONE function. The time zone data can be stored in the TIMESTAMP and TIMESTAMP WITH TIME ZONE datatypes. TIMESTAMP WITH LOCAL TIME ZONE stores data in the time zone of the database server, yet displays the date data in the local session time zone of the end user. Functions that can support time zone management include DBTIMEZONE, SESSIONTIMEZONE, CURRENT_DATE, CURRENT_TIMESTAMP, LOCALTIMESTAMP, SYSTIMESTAMP, NEW_TIME, and others.

Time zone conversion functions include FROM_TZ, TO_TIMESTAMP_TZ, CAST, EXTRACT, and SYS_EXTRACT_UTC.

TWO-MINUTE DRILL

Describe Various Types of Functions That Are Available in SQL

- ❑ SQL functions accept one or more input parameters. A few take no parameters.
- ❑ Each function returns one value; no more, no less.
- ❑ SQL functions perform tasks of various kinds.
- ❑ Functions can be included anywhere a SQL expression can be included, provided that the rules of datatypes are respected.
- ❑ Functions can be included in the WHERE clause of the SELECT, UPDATE, and DELETE statements.
- ❑ Functions can be included in the SELECT expression list, INSERT value list, and UPDATE SET clause.

Use Character, Number, and Date Functions in SELECT Statements

- ❑ Character functions include text cleanup and conversion functions.
- ❑ UPPER, LOWER, and INITCAP can manage the case of a string.
- ❑ LPAD and RPAD can pad a string with specified characters.
- ❑ INSTR, SUBSTR, CONCAT, and LENGTH can be used to divide up and put together different strings.
- ❑ Numeric functions perform analysis and calculations.
- ❑ TRUNC always rounds toward zero.
- ❑ REMAINDER and MOD are variations on division and leftover values.
- ❑ Date functions offer a variety of features to support the tracking of centuries, decades, years, quarters, months, weeks, days, hours, minutes, seconds, and fractions of seconds, as well as times across different time zones.
- ❑ Other functions include LEAST, GREATEST, NVL, NVL2, DECODE, and NULLIF.

Describe the Use of Conversion Functions

❑ Conversion functions include TO_NUMBER, TO_CHAR, and TO_DATE.

❑ TO_CHAR can convert from character, date, or numeric data, and into character data.

❑ The conversion function TO_TIMESTAMP can convert to the TIMESTAMP datatype, which is the same as DATE but adds fractional seconds.

❑ The functions TO_DSINTERVAL and TO_YMINTERVAL convert to interval datatypes INTERVAL DAY TO SECOND and INTERVAL YEAR TO MONTH.

Manage Data in Different Time Zones—Use Various Datetime Functions

❑ Time zone management can be performed with datatypes like TIMESTAMP, TIMESTAMP WITH TIME ZONE, and TIMESTAMP WITH LOCAL TIME ZONE.

❑ The DBTIMEZONE returns the value of the database server's time zone as an offset to UTC.

❑ The SESSIONTIMEZONE returns the value of the particular user session's local time zone.

❑ The conversion function TO_TIMESTAMP_TZ converts to TIMESTAMP WITH TIME ZONE, which is the same as TIMESTAMP but with time zone information.

SELF TEST

The following questions will help you measure your understanding of the material presented in this chapter. Choose one correct answer for each question unless otherwise directed.

Describe Various Types of Functions That Are Available in SQL

1. Which of the following is true of functions?
   A. They never return a value.
   B. They often return a value.
   C. They always return a value.
   D. There is no consistent answer to whether they return a value or not.

2. Which of the following is true of character functions?
   A. They always accept characters as parameters and nothing else.
   B. They always return a character value.
   C. They are generally used to process text data.
   D. They generally have the letters CHAR somewhere in the function name.

3. Built-in SQL functions: (Choose three.)
   A. Can be invoked from a DELETE statement's WHERE clause.
   B. Are written by SQL developers and also known as "user-defined" functions.
   C. Are available for use from the UPDATE statement.
   D. Are available for use within a SELECT statement's WHERE clause, as well as the SELECT statement's expression list.

Use Character, Number, and Date Functions in SELECT Statements

4. Review this SQL statement:

```
SELECT SUBSTR('2009',1,2) || LTRIM('1124','1') FROM DUAL;
```

What will be the result of the SQL statement?
   A. 2024
   B. 221
   C. 20124
   D. A syntax error

5. Review this SQL statement:

```
SELECT TRUNC(ROUND(ABS(-1.7),2)) FROM DUAL;
```

What will be the result of the SQL statement?

 A. 1
B. 2
C. 3
D. 4

6. Review this SQL statement:

```
SELECT LASTNAME FROM CUSTOMERS WHERE LASTNAME = SOUNDEX('Franklin');
```

What are some possible results for the query?

A. Franklyn
B. Phrankline
C. None of the above
D. There's not enough information present to know the answer

7. Review this SQL statement:

```
SELECT MONTHS_BETWEEN(LAST_DAY('15-JAN-12')+1,'01-APR-12')FROM DUAL;
```

What will result from the query above?

A. 2
B. 3
C. −2
D. −3

Describe the Use of Conversion Functions

8. If you wish to display a numeric value with dollar signs and commas, which of the following is the best approach to take?

A. The TO_NUMBER function with a format model
B. The TO_CHAR function with a format model
C. A combination of string literals that contain commas and dollar signs, along with the CONCAT function
D. The MONEY datatype

9. Which of the following SQL statements will display the current time, in hours, minutes, and seconds, as determined by the operating system on which the database server resides?

   A. SELECT TO_CHAR(SYSDATE) FROM DUAL;

   B. SELECT TO_CHAR(SYSDATE, 'HR:MI:SE') FROM DUAL;

   C. SELECT TO_CHAR(SYSDATE, 'HH:MI:SS') FROM DUAL;

   D. SELECT TO_CHAR(SYSDATE, 'HH:MM:SS') FROM DUAL;

10. Which query returns an expression of the datatype INTERVAL YEAR TO MONTHS representing an interval of 1 year and 3 months?

    A. SELECT TO_YMINTERVAL('01:03') FROM DUAL;

    B. SELECT TO_YMINTERVAL('01-03') FROM DUAL;

    C. SELECT TO_INTERVALYM('01:03') FROM DUAL;

    D. SELECT TO_INTERVALYM('01-03') FROM DUAL;

Manage Data in Different Time Zones—Use Various Datetime Functions

11. Which of the following SQL datatypes cannot store fractional seconds?

    A. DATE

    B. TIMESTAMP WITH LOCAL TIME ZONE

    C. TIMESTAMP

    D. INTERVAL DAY TO SECOND

12. Your database server is in Beijing, China. You are supporting an application with user sessions originating out of Beijing and Atlanta. You wish to ensure that your application stores dates in such a way that if your Beijing team stores datetime data, such as "9 PM Beijing", your Atlanta users will see "9 PM Beijing" instead of the equivalent time in Atlanta. Which datatype is the best choice?

    A. TIMESTAMP

    B. TIMESTAMP WITH TIME ZONE

    C. TIMESTAMP WITH LOCAL TIME ZONE

    D. It cannot be done

13. Pacific Standard Time is abbreviated PST. PST is an example of which format model element?

    A. TZD

    B. TZH

    C. TZM

    D. TZR

14. Review the following code:

```
CREATE TABLE EMAIL_RESPONSE
(  EMAIL_RESPONSE_ID    NUMBER,
   EMAIL_SENT           TIMESTAMP WITH LOCAL TIME ZONE,
   EMAIL_RECEIVED       TIMESTAMP WITH TIME ZONE);
ALTER SESSION SET TIME_ZONE = 'America/Los_Angeles';
INSERT INTO EMAIL_RESPONSE VALUES (1,SYSDATE,SYSDATE);
ALTER SESSION SET TIME_ZONE = 'America/Chicago';
SELECT EMAIL_SENT FROM EMAIL_RESPONSE;
```

If this code is executed at '01-DEC-11 02:00:00.000000000' in the 'America/Los_Angeles' time zone, and the offset between Los Angeles and Chicago is +02:00, then what time value is displayed as a result of the SELECT statement?

A. '01-DEC-11 02:00:00.000000000'

B. '01-DEC-11 04:00:00.000000000'

C. '01-DEC-11 02:02:00.000000000'

D. None of the above

15. Examine the code displayed in 14, and consider the result of this SQL statement if it were executed after that code:

```
SELECT EXTRACT(TIMEZONE_REGION FROM EMAIL_RECEIVED) "Region"
FROM EMAIL_RESPONSE;
```

Which of the following is the most likely response to the preceding SQL statement? (Choose the one best answer.)

A. 'America/Los_Angeles'

B. 'America/Chicago'

C. +02:00

D. '01-DEC-11'

SELF TEST ANSWERS

Describe Various Types of Functions That Are Available in SQL

1. ☑   **C.** They always return a single value.
     ☒   **A, B,** and **D** are incorrect.

2. ☑   **C.** They are generally used to process text data.
     ☒   **A, B,** and **D** are incorrect. They do not all accept characters as input parameters—some, such as SUBSTR, take numeric input parameters. They do not always return a character value—LENGTH does not. And they do not all have CHAR in their function name.

3. ☑   **A, C,** and **D.** The functions that are reviewed in this chapter are known as built-in functions and are available to be used anywhere in SQL where an expression can be used. That includes a SELECT statement's expression list, an UPDATE statement's SET clauses, an INSERT statement's list of input values, and the WHERE clause of any SQL statement—SELECT, UPDATE, and DELETE.
     ☒   **B** is incorrect. Built-in functions and user-defined functions are separate categories. Both can be invoked from the same places—such as a SELECT statement's WHERE clause—but user-defined functions are written in languages such as PL/SQL. This chapter only looked at built-in functions.

Use Character, Number, and Date Functions in SELECT Statements

4. ☑   **A.** The SUBSTR function will extract data from the string ('2009') starting at the first position (1), and lasting for 2 characters (2), resulting in an answer of '20'. The LTRIM function will trim off all occurrences of the '1' from the left side of '1124', resulting in '24'. The two results are concatenated together for a final result of '2024'.
     ☒   **B, C,** and **D** are incorrect. There is no syntax error present in the code. Even though the values evaluated by both functions include data that consists of numerals, both are enclosed in single quotes and therefore are treated as character data. Even if they were not enclosed in single quotes, SQL would perform an automatic datatype conversion anyway.

5. ☑   **A.** The result will be 1. The ABS function determines absolute value. As the innermost function, it will be evaluated first, resulting in an answer of 1.7. The ROUND function will process the value of 1.7 and round it to the nearest two digits to the right of the decimal point, and the result will still be 1.7. Finally, TRUNC will truncate the value down to a one.
     ☒   **B, C,** and **D** are incorrect.

6. ☑ C. None of the above is correct.

☒ A, B, and D are incorrect. SOUNDEX is only used on the right side of the WHERE clause comparison, and that means the value for FRANKLIN will be converted to its SOUNDEX code and then compared to the actual last names in the table. Without looking at the SOUNDEX lookup table, we can tell that the SOUNDEX code will be a single letter *F* followed by some three numbers. Therefore it cannot possibly be either *A* or *B*. And there's certainly enough information presented in the scenario to recognize that the answer cannot be either *A* nor *B*.

7. ☑ C. The answer will be –2. First, the LAST_DAY function will transform the value of '15-JAN-12' to '31-JAN-12', and then the result of that will be added to 1, so that the first of February will result: '01-FEB-12'. The difference between that date and '01-APR-12' will be a negative 2.

☒ A, B, and D are incorrect.

Describe the Use of Conversion Functions

8. ☑ B. The TO_CHAR function would work, along with a format model, such as TO_CHAR(rawNumber, '$999,999.99').

☒ A, C, and D are incorrect. The TO_NUMBER function works with format masks, but it converts from characters to numeric values, not the other way around. You may be able to use a combination of concatenation and string literals, but it would be painstakingly difficult, particularly in a dynamic environment where the significant numbers involved could fluctuate. There is no MONEY datatype in Oracle SQL.

9. ☑ C. The correct format mask is 'HH:MI:SS'.

☒ A, B, and D are incorrect. TO_CHAR with no format mask executes successfully but does nothing and shows the date alone. There is no 'SE' format mask. Answer D is tricky—it works, and it produces output, but the 'MM' format mask indicates months, not minutes, and is logically incorrect.

10. ☑ B. The TO_YMINTERVAL function is correct, with the single parameter of a string containing two numbers, separated by a dash, where the first represents years in the interval, and the second represents the number of months in the interval.

☒ A, C, and D are incorrect. There is no TO_INTERVALYM function. And the use of a colon is inappropriate in the TO_YMINTERVAL function.

Manage Data in Different Time Zones—Use Various Datetime Functions

11. ☑ A. DATE cannot store fractional seconds. It can store year, month, day, hours, minutes, and seconds. But not fractional seconds.

☒ **B, C,** and **D** are incorrect. Both the TIMESTAMP WITH LOCAL TIME ZONE and TIMESTAMP datatypes have the ability to store fractional seconds. So can TIMESTAMP WITH TIME ZONE. INTERVAL DAY TO SECOND also can store fractional seconds.

12. ☑ **B.** TIMESTAMP WITH TIME ZONE will record the time as is, and any future query will retrieve it as is, regardless of the origination of the query.
☒ **A, C,** and **D** are incorrect. TIMESTAMP cannot store time zone information. TIMESTAMP WITH LOCAL TIME ZONE will translate time data into the user session's time zone.

13. ☑ **A.** TZD means a time zone with Daylight Saving Time built in. Other examples include EDT, EST, CST, and PDT.
☒ **B, C,** and **D** are incorrect. TZH is time zone hours. TZM is time zone minutes. TZR is time zone region.

14. ☑ **B.** The TIMESTAMP WITH LOCAL TIME ZONE datatype ensures that datetime data stored at a particular time will adjust when the session time zone changes. In this case, we moved our session time zone to an alternative with a plus two hour time difference. That means that if we stored our data at 2 A.M. local time in Los Angeles, then at the same time it's 4 A.M. in Chicago.
☒ **A, C,** and **D** are incorrect.

15. ☑ **A.** 'America/Los_Angeles' is the time zone region for the EMAIL_RECEIVED column, and since the datatype is TIMESTAMP WITH TIME ZONE, the time zone is stored within the value and extracted, regardless of the location of the end user executing the query—who, in this instance, is executing the query from a local session that's been set to 'America/Chicago'.
☒ **B, C,** and **D** are incorrect. The TIMESTAMP WITH TIME ZONE retains the time zone of the value, as opposed to 'America/Chicago', which is the time zone of the local session. +02:00 is the offset, not a value for TIMEZONE_REGION. '01-DEC-11' is a date literal.

7

Reporting Aggregated Data Using the Group Functions

T his chapter reviews the features in SQL that identify individual rows in a given table and aggregate summary information about them. We'll look at aggregate functions, and also at two new clauses in the SELECT statement: the GROUP BY clause and its companion, the HAVING clause. You will need to fully understand these capabilities in order to pass the exam.

CERTIFICATION OBJECTIVE 7.01

Identify the Available Group Functions

The functions we reviewed in the last chapter are referred to as *single-row* functions. The term "single-row" means that each function returns one value for each one row it encounters. Another term for "single-row" function is *scalar* function.

There is a second category of functions that is referred to as *group* functions. A group function returns one value for each set of zero or more rows it encounters. Another term for group function is *multirow or aggregate* function. Aggregate functions are typically used with a SELECT statement that selects many rows, where the aggregate function scans a set of rows and returns a single answer for all of them.

Table 7-1 shows a summary list of some of the more commonly used aggregate functions available in SQL.

TABLE 7-1	Function(s)	Description
Commonly Used Aggregate Functions— Overview	COUNT, SUM, MIN, MAX, AVG, MEDIAN	The more commonly used aggregate functions
	VARIANCE, VAR_POP, VAR_SAMP, COVAR_POP, COVAR_SAMP, STDDEV, STDDEV_POP, STDDEV_SAMP	Variance and standard deviation, with options for population standard deviation and cumulative standard deviation
	RANK, DENSE_RANK, PERCENT_RANK PERCENTILE_CONT, PERCENTILE_DISC, CUME_DIST, FIRST, LAST	Ranking functions and associated keywords
	GROUP_ID, GROUPING, GROUPING_ID	Grouping features for use with GROUP BY . . . ROLLUP and CUBE

The first thing to recognize about aggregate functions is that they

- Process data from zero or more rows.
- Return one—and only one—row's worth of data as their result.

Aggregate functions can work with different datatypes. While numeric aggregate functions are the most common, some aggregates process data with character and date datatypes.

Aggregate functions must be treated separately from scalar functions because they behave differently and impose a variety of requirements on any SELECT statement that might invoke them. For example, since only one value is returned for any set of zero or more rows, then a typical single SELECT statement cannot mix aggregate and scalar functions in the same select list—after all, if single-row expressions return one value per row, but multirow functions return only one value, then how can tabular output be structured? There are limited exceptions to this, which we'll study in this chapter. But for now, note that you cannot mix scalar and aggregate functions using what we've reviewed so far in this book.

We'll review the detailed functionality of some of the more commonly used aggregate functions in the next section.

CERTIFICATION OBJECTIVE 7.02

Describe the Use of Group Functions

Aggregate functions can be called from four places in a SELECT statement: the select list, the ORDER BY clause, and either of two new clauses we'll look at in this chapter: the GROUP BY clause and the HAVING clause. Both the GROUP BY and HAVING clauses are unique to the SELECT statement; they do not exist in other SQL statements.

The major aggregate functions are described in detail in the following sections.

COUNT

Syntax: COUNT(*e1*)

Parameters: *e1* is an expression. *e1* can be any datatype.

The COUNT function determines the number of occurrences of non-NULL values. It considers the value of an expression and determines if that value is NOT NULL for each row it encounters.

The VENDORS
table

VENDORS	
P * VENDOR_ID	NUMBER
VENDOR_NAME	VARCHAR2 (20 BYTE)
STATUS	NUMBER (3)
CATEGORY	VARCHAR2 (10 BYTE)
⮜ PK_VENDOR_ID	

For example, let's work with the VENDORS table, shown in Figure 7-1.
Let's look at all the rows in the VENDORS table:

```
SELECT VENDOR_NAME, STATUS, CATEGORY
FROM   VENDORS;
```

Here's the output, showing that we have two rows in the table:

```
VENDOR_NAME            STATUS                  CATEGORY
-------------------    --------------------    ----------
Acme Steaks            17
Acme Poker Chips
```

We haven't selected every column here, and we don't need to for our purposes.
But assume that the blank entries in the output are NULL values, and not blank
spaces—so that the STATUS column contains only one value, and CATEGORY
has none.

Now let's look at the following SELECT statement that tries to count occurrences
of data in each of these columns:

```
SELECT COUNT(VENDOR_NAME), COUNT(STATUS), COUNT(CATEGORY)
FROM   VENDORS;

COUNT(VENDOR_NAME)     COUNT(STATUS)           COUNT(CATEGORY)
--------------------   --------------------    --------------------
2                      1                       0
```

Notice that COUNT ignores any and all values that are NULL. Finally, we can
simply count the number of rows in the entire table:

```
SELECT COUNT(*)
FROM   VENDORS;

COUNT(*)
--------------------
2
```

COUNT will only return the value of non-NULL values in columns.

Recall that "SELECT * FROM table" is the shorthand way of asking to SELECT all the columns in a given table. The COUNT function is often used with the asterisk in this fashion to get a quick count on all the rows in a given table using COUNT(*).

We could have mixed these functions in various combinations:

```
SELECT COUNT(*), COUNT(VENDOR_NAME)
FROM    VENDORS;

COUNT(*)                    COUNT(VENDOR_NAME)
--------------------        --------------------
2                           2
```

Note that a COUNT of the asterisk is asking for a count of all rows. In the rare situation where a row contains nothing but NULL values, COUNT(*) will still count that row.

It's worth noting that COUNT will never return a NULL value. If it encounters no values at all, it will at least return a value of 0 (zero). This is not the case with all of the aggregates, but it's true with COUNT. This becomes important when working with subqueries, which we'll study in Chapter 9.

The DISTINCT and ALL operators can be used with aggregate functions. For example, here is an example showing DISTINCT and ALL used within a COUNT function:

```
SELECT COUNT(DISTINCT LAST_NAME), COUNT(ALL LAST_NAME)
FROM EMPLOYEES;

COUNT(DISTINCTLAST_NAME)  COUNT(ALLLAST_NAME)
--------------------      --------------------
5                         7
```

This example tells us that the table called EMPLOYEES has seven rows with values for LAST_NAME, of which five are unique values for LAST_NAME, so two are duplicates. Also remember that DISTINCT and/or ALL cannot be used with the asterisk.

The COUNT function counts occurrences of data, not NULL values. But when combined with the asterisk, as in "SELECT COUNT(*) FROM VENDORS", it counts occurrences of rows—and will include rows with all NULL values in the results.

SUM

Syntax: SUM(*e1*)

Parameters: *e1* is an expression whose datatype is numeric.

The SUM function adds numeric values in a given column. It only takes numeric data as input. SUM adds all the values in all the rows and returns a single answer. For example:

```
SELECT  SUM(SUBTOTAL)
FROM    ORDERS;
```

Such a query will add up all of the values for SUBTOTAL in the ORDERS table and produce a single result. Another example:

```
SELECT  SUM(SUBTOTAL)
FROM    ORDERS
WHERE   ORDER_DATE = SYSDATE;
```

This query will find any and all rows for which ORDER_DATE is equal to the system's date for today, and then add up all of the values in the SUBTOTAL column and produce a single answer.

MIN, MAX

Syntax: MIN(*e1*); MAX(*e1*)

Parameters: *e1* is an expression with a datatype of character, date, or number.

For a given set of rows identified by a SELECT statement, MIN returns the single minimum value, and MAX returns the single maximum value. MIN and MAX can work with numeric, date, and character data, and they use the same basic logic that ORDER BY uses for the different datatypes:

- **Numeric**   Low numbers are MIN; high numbers are MAX.
- **Data**   Earlier dates are MIN; later dates are MAX.
- **Character**   'A' is less than 'Z'; 'Z' is less than 'a'. The string value '2' is greater than the string value '100'. The character '1' is less than the characters '10'. Earlier dates are less than later dates.

For example, consider the following list of data from the table EMPLOYEES:

```
LAST_NAME
------------------------------
Hoddlestein
Smith
```

```
Lindon
West
Worthington
```

Now let's identify MIN and MAX values:

```
SELECT MIN(LAST_NAME), MAX(LAST_NAME) FROM EMPLOYEES;

MIN(LAST_NAME)                      MAX(LAST_NAME)
----------------------------        ----------------------------
Hoddlestein                         Worthington
```

Note that "Hoddlestein" is alphabetically the first value from the list of LAST_NAME values.

Even though the data returned by MIN and MAX represents the data found within a single row in the list, do not be tricked into thinking that this represents a "single-row" answer—it does not. SQL sees each response of MIN and MAX as an "aggregate" answer, meaning that the individual value is the answer representing the full set of rows.

AVG

Syntax: AVG(*e1*)

Parameters: *e1* is an expression with a numeric datatype.

The AVG function computes the average value for a set of rows. AVG only works with numeric data. It ignores NULL values. For example, let's look at the PAY_HISTORY table; after that, we'll ask for the average value of all the values within the SALARY column.

```
SELECT PAY_HISTORY_ID, SALARY FROM PAY_HISTORY;

PAY_HISTORY_ID            SALARY
--------------------      ----------------------
1                         73922
2                         47000
3                         58000
4                         37450
5                         91379
6                         45500

SELECT AVG(SALARY) FROM PAY_HISTORY;

AVG(SALARY)
----------------------
58875.16666666666666666666666666666667
```

While we're at it, we can nest the results of this query within the scalar function ROUND, like so:

```
SELECT ROUND(AVG(SALARY),2) FROM PAY_HISTORY;

ROUND(AVG(SALARY),2)
--------------------
58875.17
```

We can get really fancy and format the data using the TO_CHAR function and a format model:

```
SELECT TO_CHAR(ROUND(AVG(SALARY),2),'$999,999.99') FROM PAY_HISTORY;

TO_CHAR(ROUND(AVG(SALARY),2),'$999,999.99')
-------------------------------------------
 $58,875.17
```

In these last few examples of SELECT statements, we've nested a single aggregate function within two scalar, or single-row, functions. You can incorporate a single aggregate function within as many nested scalar functions as you wish. The aggregate function need not be the innermost function—you can include one aggregate function with any number of scalar functions in a nested combination, provided that all of the parameter datatypes are respected. But if you wish to include two aggregate functions within a nested combination, hold off—we'll address that issue later in this chapter. It's more complex than it might appear.

DISTINCT and ALL are available for use with AVG. In the event that a table's data listing includes some repeated values, the use of DISTINCT will transform the results so that the average is computed only on unique occurrences of each value.

MEDIAN

Syntax: MEDIAN(*e1*)

Parameters: *e1* is an expression with a numeric or date datatype.

MEDIAN can operate on numeric or data datatypes. It ignores NULL values. The MEDIAN function is somewhat related to AVG. MEDIAN performs as you might expect: from a set of data, MEDIAN returns either the middle value or, if that isn't easily identified, then an interpolated value from within the middle. In other words, MEDIAN will sort the values, and if there is an odd number of values, it will identify the value in the middle of the list; otherwise, if there an even number of values, it will locate the two values in the middle of the list and perform linear interpolation between them to locate a result.

Here's an example—if you were to execute the following SQL statements:

```
CREATE TABLE TEST_MEDIAN (A NUMBER(3));
INSERT INTO TEST_MEDIAN VALUES (1);
INSERT INTO TEST_MEDIAN VALUES (10);
INSERT INTO TEST_MEDIAN VALUES (3);
SELECT MEDIAN(A) FROM TEST_MEDIAN;
```

The value returned by the SELECT statement would be 3.

RANK

Syntax: RANK($c1$) WITHIN GROUP (ORDER BY $e1$)

Parameters: $c1$ is a constant; $e1$ is an expression with a datatype matching the corresponding $c1$ datatype. Numeric and character pairs are allowed.

In this format, the parameters can be repeated in such a way that for each $c1$, you can have a corresponding $e1$, for each $c2$ (if included), there must be a corresponding $e2$, etc. Each successive parameter is separated from the previous parameter by a comma, as in

```
RANK(c1, c2, c3) WITHIN GROUP (ORDER BY e1, e2, e3)
```

Also, the datatype of $c1$ must match the datatype of $e1$, and the datatype of $c2$ (if included) must match the datatype of $e2$, etc.

The RANK function calculates the rank of a value within a group of values. Ranks may not be consecutive numbers, since SQL counts tied rows individually, so if three rows are tied for first, they will each be ranked 1, 1, and 1, and the next row will be ranked 4.

For example:

```
SELECT    RANK(300) WITHIN GROUP (ORDER BY SQ_FT)
FROM      SHIP_CABINS;

RANK(300)WITHINGROUP(ORDERBYSQ_FT)
------------------------------------
6
```

This answer of 6 is telling us when we sort the rows of the SHIP_CABINS table, and then consider the literal value 300 and compare it to the values in the SQ_FT column, that the value 300, if inserted into the table, and if sorted with the existing rows, would be the sixth row in the listing. In other words, there are five rows with a SQ_FT value less than 300.

FIRST, LAST

Syntax: *aggregate_function* KEEP (DENSE_RANK FIRST ORDER BY *e1*)
aggregate_function KEEP (DENSE_RANK LAST ORDER BY *e1*)

Parameters: *e1* is an expression with a numeric or character datatype.

The aggregate functions FIRST and LAST are similar. For a given range of sorted values, they return either the first value (FIRST) or the last value (LAST) of the population of rows defining *e1*, in the sorted order. For example:

```
SELECT    MAX(SQ_FT) KEEP (DENSE_RANK FIRST ORDER BY GUESTS)
          "Largest"
FROM      SHIP_CABINS;

Largest
---------------------
225
```

In this example, we are doing the following:

- First, we're sorting all the rows in the SHIP_CABINS table according to the value in the GUESTS column, and identifying the FIRST value in that sort order, which is a complex way of saying that we're identifying the lowest value for the GUESTS column.

- For all rows with a GUEST value that matches the lowest value we just found, determine the MAX value for SQ_FT.

In others, display the highest number of square feet for any and all cabins that accommodate the lowest number of guests according to the GUESTS column.

on the
Job

Experienced professionals might recognize that FIRST and LAST perform tasks that can also be done with certain usages of self-joins or views, which we examine in later chapters. While self-joins and views are beneficial for a variety of reasons, the use of FIRST or LAST as shown above will achieve performance improvements over the alternative approaches.

GROUPING

The aggregate function GROUPING is discussed in detail in its own section in Chapter 13.

Others

There are more aggregate functions than are described in this section. They include functions to work with nested tables, functions to perform linear regression analysis, and various forms of statistical analysis. These functions aren't specifically referenced in the certification exam guide objectives, so we won't review them all here. But you can find full descriptions of them in Oracle Corporation's *SQL Language Reference Manual*.

CERTIFICATION OBJECTIVE 7.03

Group Data by Using the GROUP BY Clause

The GROUP BY clause is an optional clause within the SELECT statement. Its purpose is to group sets of rows together and treat each individual set as a whole. In other words, GROUP BY identifies subsets of rows within the larger set of rows being considered by the SELECT statement. In this way, it's sort of like creating a series of "mini-select" statements within the larger SELECT statement.

Let's take another look at the SHIP_CABINS table, which now has some new columns since the last time we worked with it (see Figure 7-2).

FIGURE 7-2

The
SHIP_CABINS
table

SHIP_CABINS	
P * SHIP_CABIN_ID	NUMBER
SHIP_ID	NUMBER (7)
ROOM_NUMBER	VARCHAR2 (5 BYTE)
ROOM_STYLE	VARCHAR2 (10 BYTE)
ROOM_TYPE	VARCHAR2 (20 BYTE)
WINDOW	VARCHAR2 (10 BYTE)
GUESTS	NUMBER (3)
SQ_FT	NUMBER (6)
BALCONY_SQ_FT	NUMBER (6)
⌐ PK_SHIP_CABIN_ID	

Let's run this SELECT statement against the table, looking only at rows where SHIP_ID = 1:

```
SELECT    SHIP_CABIN_ID, ROOM_NUMBER, ROOM_STYLE,
          ROOM_TYPE,     WINDOW,      GUESTS,     SQ_FT
FROM      SHIP_CABINS
WHERE     SHIP_ID = 1;
```

The results are shown here:

SHIP_CABIN_ID	ROOM_NUMBER	ROOM_STYLE	ROOM_TYPE	WINDOW	GUESTS	SQ_FT
1	102	Suite	Standard	Ocean	4	533
2	103	Stateroom	Standard	Ocean	2	160
3	104	Suite	Standard	None	4	533
4	105	Stateroom	Standard	Ocean	3	205
5	106	Suite	Standard	None	6	586
6	107	Suite	Royal	Ocean	5	1524
7	108	Stateroom	Large	None	2	211
8	109	Stateroom	Standard	None	2	180
9	110	Stateroom	Large	None	2	225
10	702	Suite	Presidential	None	5	1142
11	703	Suite	Royal	Ocean	5	1745
12	704	Suite	Skyloft	Ocean	8	722

This data listing shows several rows of data. Take a look at the column called SQ_FT, showing the number of square feet of each room on the ship. Let's compute the average square feet for rooms and round off the answer:

```
SELECT    ROUND(AVG(SQ_FT),2)
FROM      SHIP_CABINS
WHERE     SHIP_ID = 1;
```

The result:

```
ROUND(AVG(SQ_FT),2)
---------------------
647.17
```

That's the average for all of the cabins on the ship. But look at the data listing, and you'll see that each of the ship's cabins seems to fall into one of two different categories according to the data in the ROOM_STYLE column. Each room is either a 'Suite' or a 'Stateroom'.

If we wanted to look at the average for the two individual values for ROOM_ STYLE, we could run two individual queries, like this:

```
SELECT    ROUND(AVG(SQ_FT),2)
FROM      SHIP_CABINS
WHERE     SHIP_ID = 1  AND  ROOM_STYLE = 'Stateroom';

ROUND(AVG(SQ_FT),2)
--------------------
196.2

SELECT    ROUND(AVG(SQ_FT),2)
FROM      SHIP_CABINS
WHERE     SHIP_ID = 1  AND  ROOM_STYLE = 'Suite';

ROUND(AVG(SQ_FT),2)
--------------------
969.29
```

That is useful information, but a relatively cumbersome way to get it. Using this approach, we have to (a) identify the individual values for ROOM_STYLE and type them carefully into our queries, (b) run multiple queries, and (c) obtain our output via multiple queries.

The better way to get this done is with the GROUP BY clause. We can get the same information by telling SQL to "group" the rows according to their values for ROOM_STYLE, whatever they may be. Here's the query:

```
SELECT    ROOM_STYLE, ROUND(AVG(SQ_FT),2)
FROM      SHIP_CABINS
WHERE     SHIP_ID = 1
GROUP BY ROOM_STYLE;

ROOM_STYLE ROUND(AVG(SQ_FT),2)
---------- --------------------
Suite      969.29
Stateroom  196.2
```

In this particular example, we add the GROUP BY clause to tell SQL to "group" the rows that have the same value for ROOM_STYLE, and then compute the AVG function for each group, rather than for all of the rows in the table. Note that we're still using the WHERE clause, so we only address rows with a SHIP_ID value of 1.

To get an idea of what SQL does with this query, let's first sort the rows according to ROOM_STYLE and highlight the two different groups of rows.

SHIP_CABIN_ID	ROOM_NUMBER	ROOM_STYLE	ROOM_TYPE	WINDOW	GUESTS	SQ_FT
1	102	*Suite*	*Standard*	*Ocean*	*4*	*533*
3	104	*Suite*	*Standard*	*None*	*4*	*533*
5	106	*Suite*	*Standard*	*None*	*6*	*586*
6	107	*Suite*	*Royal*	*Ocean*	*5*	*1524*
10	702	*Suite*	*Presidential*	*None*	*5*	*1142*
11	703	*Suite*	*Royal*	*Ocean*	*5*	*1745*
12	704	*Suite*	*Skyloft*	*Ocean*	*8*	*722*
2	103	**Stateroom**	**Standard**	**Ocean**	**2**	**160**
4	105	**Stateroom**	**Standard**	**Ocean**	**3**	**205**
7	108	**Stateroom**	**Large**	**None**	**2**	**211**
8	109	**Stateroom**	**Standard**	**None**	**2**	**180**
9	110	**Stateroom**	**Large**	**None**	**2**	**225**

Our GROUP BY query didn't include an ORDER BY clause, but we chose to sort these rows to highlight the fact that there are two groups of rows.

Note the values in the column ROOM_STYLE. Note that the rows with a ROOM_STYLE of 'Suite' are italicized and those with a ROOM_STYLE of 'Stateroom' are in bold.

Now go back and look at our SELECT statement. Did we specify anything about 'Suite' or 'Stateroom'? Not specifically. We didn't have to. The directive to GROUP BY ROOM_STYLE tells SQL to "group" each set of rows that share the same value for ROOM_STYLE, whatever that may be.

We could have included multiple aggregate functions in this query's select list if we wanted to, for example:

```
SELECT    ROOM_STYLE,
          ROUND(AVG(SQ_FT),2) "Average SQ FT",
          MIN(GUESTS) "Minimum # of Guests",
          COUNT(SHIP_CABIN_ID) "Total # of cabins"
FROM      SHIP_CABINS
WHERE     SHIP_ID = 1
GROUP BY ROOM_STYLE;
```

ROOM_STYLE	Average SQ FT	Minimum # of Guests	Total # of cabins
Suite	969.29	4	7
Stateroom	196.2	2	5

The rules for forming a GROUP BY clause are as follows:

- The GROUP BY can specify any number of valid expressions, including columns of the table.
- Generally the GROUP BY is used to specify columns in the table that will contain common data, in order to "group" rows together for performing some sort of aggregate function on the set of rows.
- The only items allowed in the select list of a SELECT that includes a GROUP BY clause are
    - Expressions that are specified in the GROUP BY
    - Aggregate functions
- Expressions that are specified in the GROUP BY do not have to be included in the SELECT statement's select list.

Let's try grouping this same set of rows by something else. In this query, we'll group by the ROOM_TYPE column instead. We'll add a few other features as well:

```
SELECT    ROOM_TYPE,
          TO_CHAR(ROUND(AVG(SQ_FT),2),'999,999.99') "Average SQ FT",
          MAX(GUESTS) "Maximum # of Guests",
          COUNT(SHIP_CABIN_ID) "Total # of cabins"
FROM      SHIP_CABINS
WHERE     SHIP_ID = 1
GROUP BY ROOM_TYPE
ORDER BY 2 DESC;
```

ROOM_TYPE	Average SQ FT	Maximum # of Guests	Total # of cabins
Royal	1,634.50	5	2
Presidential	1,142.00	5	1
Skyloft	722.00	8	1
Standard	366.17	6	6
Large	218.00	2	2

Notice the following changes to our query:

- As we stated, we chose to GROUP BY the ROOM_TYPE column. We also put ROOM_TYPE in the select list.
- We added an ORDER BY clause that is sorting on the second column from the select list, which in this case is the AVG of the SQ_FT column.

■ We replaced the MIN function with the MAX function, just for fun.

■ Unrelated to the GROUP BY functionality, we chose to put a format model with the AVG output to clean it up a little.

■ We also added a column alias for each of the last three expressions, omitting the optional keyword AS for each alias.

Notice the results of our modified SELECT with GROUP BY clause:

■ The values for ROOM_TYPE are automatically listed, and in this case, five values were found—so we have five rows in our output, each representing a set of rows in the source table.

■ The aggregate functions of AVG, MIN, and COUNT are all calculated for each individual group.

That last point is important. It's the entire purpose of the GROUP BY function. If you don't understand it, then try this—look at the output of the first row, which is for the ROOM_TYPE value of 'Royal', and consider that the individual row you are seeing in the output is the same data you would get if you ran this query alone, without the GROUP BY clause:

```
SELECT    TO_CHAR(ROUND(AVG(SQ_FT),2),'999,999.99') "Average SQ FT",
          MAX(GUESTS) "Maximum # of Guests",
          COUNT(SHIP_CABIN_ID) "Total # of cabins"
FROM      SHIP_CABINS
WHERE     SHIP_ID = 1 AND ROOM_TYPE = 'Royal'
ORDER BY 1 DESC;

Average SQ FT Maximum # of Guests    Total # of cabins
------------- ---------------------- ----------------------
   1,634.50   5                      2
```

In the preceding query, we've eliminated the GROUP BY clause and introduced a WHERE clause to only look at ROOM_TYPE = 'Royal'. The result is the same data we find in the first row of the GROUP BY we ran earlier, except for the text value of 'Royal', which we can't include in this SELECT. The reason we can't include it: a SELECT can only include expressions in the select list that are defined at the same level of detail as each other. The aggregate functions AVG, MAX, and COUNT—and all other aggregate functions—have the effect of defining a single value representing all of the rows in the SELECT statement. This is why they are called "aggregate" functions: they represent the "aggregate" of all the rows. A single column value cannot do that—ah, that is, unless we specify that column within a GROUP BY clause. Putting a scalar (single-row) value in a GROUP BY clause has the effect of transforming the reference to that column into an aggregate value, thus transforming it to the level where its value represents the aggregate of rows, just like an aggregate function.

Grouping by a particular column essentially transforms that column into an aggregate value—if only temporarily for the purpose of the query.

Multiple Columns

You can use GROUP BY with multiple columns:

```
SELECT    ROOM_STYLE,
          ROOM_TYPE,
          TO_CHAR(MIN(SQ_FT),'9,999') "Min",
          TO_CHAR(MAX(SQ_FT),'9,999') "Max",
          TO_CHAR(MIN(SQ_FT)-MAX(SQ_FT),'9,999') "Diff"
FROM      SHIP_CABINS
WHERE     SHIP_ID = 1
GROUP BY ROOM_STYLE, ROOM_TYPE
ORDER BY 3;


ROOM_STYLE ROOM_TYPE                 Min    Max    Diff
---------- --------------------    ------ ------ ------
Stateroom  Standard                   160    205    -45
Stateroom  Large                      211    225    -14
Suite      Standard                   533    586    -53
Suite      Skyloft                    722    722      0
Suite      Presidential             1,142  1,142      0
Suite      Royal                    1,524  1,745   -221
```

In the preceding example, note the following:

- The GROUP BY clause includes two columns from the table: ROOM_STYLE and ROOM_TYPE. This tells SQL to group all rows that share the same value for both the ROOM_STYLE and the ROOM_TYPE columns, and apparently there are six such groups, according to the output.
- The SELECT statement's select list happens to include the ROOM_STYLE and ROOM_TYPE columns in the same positions as they are in the GROUP BY clause; this is not required, but it makes the output listing easy to read.
- The ORDER BY clause tells SQL to sort the rows based on the value in the third item in the select list, which is the MIN aggregate function.
- Each of the aggregate functions is formatted with the TO_CHAR format model, to include commas where appropriate and narrow the columns to a reasonable width.

■ The final column in our select list is an expression that calculates the MIN and MAX values and determines the difference between them, and formats the results.

Clearly there's a lot going on in this SELECT statement, but it's a great example of a GROUP BY in action.

ORDER BY Revisited

When a GROUP BY is used in a SELECT statement, then if there is an ORDER BY clause included as well, its use will be somewhat restricted. The list of columns and/or expressions in an ORDER BY that is part of a SELECT statement that uses GROUP BY is limited to the following:

■ Expressions specified in the GROUP BY clause

■ Expressions specified in the select list, referenced by position, name, or alias

■ Aggregate functions, regardless of whether the aggregate function is specified elsewhere in the SELECT statement

■ The functions USER, SYSDATE, and UID

ⓦatch
A single SELECT statement can produce output at just one level of aggregation. This is why a SELECT statement cannot mix scalar and aggregate values in a select list.

One thing you cannot include in the ORDER BY is this: columns in the table that aren't specified in the GROUP BY clause. That's not the case for SELECT statements in general—in a scalar SELECT you can ORDER BY columns in the table whether they are included in the SELECT or not. But that's not true when a GROUP BY is involved. ORDER BY is more limited.

Nesting Functions

You might recall from our examples that we've nested functions in some of our SQL statements. The concept of nesting functions refers to the practice of positioning a function in such a way that the value it returns becomes the input parameter for another function. For example:

```
SELECT TO_CHAR(MEDIAN(SQ_FT),'999.99') FROM SHIP_CABINS;
```

In this example, the MEDIAN aggregate function is "nested" within the TO_CHAR function. Thus the MEDIAN function, in this example, is the "inner" function, and it returns a value that becomes an input parameter to the TO_CHAR conversion function, which is the "outer" function. As long as the datatypes match up, nesting is allowed. In this instance, MEDIAN can only be used like this if it is returning a value of the datatype that TO_CHAR can accept.

Now, remember that there are two general types of functions: single-row, or scalar, functions; and multirow, or aggregate, functions. Scalar functions return one value for each row encountered by the SQL statement in which the scalar function is applied. Aggregate functions return one value for every zero or more rows encountered by the SQL statement.

The rules for nesting functions differ, depending on whether you are nesting aggregate or scalar functions.

Scalar functions can be nested multiple times, as long as the datatypes match. The reason is that scalar functions all operate on the same level of detail within the rows—for every one row, a scalar function returns one value.

Aggregate functions, on the other hand, behave differently than scalar functions when it comes to nesting. The reason is that aggregates combine data from multiple rows into a single row. Once that has been accomplished, your resulting value no longer represents the same level of detail you were originally dealing with.

For example, let's look again at the SHIP_CABINS table and consider a simple SELECT statement with a GROUP BY clause:

```
SELECT    ROOM_STYLE, ROOM_TYPE, MAX(SQ_FT)
FROM      SHIP_CABINS
WHERE     SHIP_ID = 1
GROUP BY ROOM_STYLE, ROOM_TYPE;


ROOM_STYLE ROOM_TYPE            MAX(SQ_FT)
---------- -------------------- ---------------------
Stateroom  Standard             205
Suite      Standard             586
Stateroom  Large                225
Suite      Skyloft              722
Suite      Royal                1745
Suite      Presidential         1142
```

This SELECT groups rows according to ROOM_STYLE and ROOM_TYPE, as we've seen, and displays the MAX value for SQ_FT within each group. The result is six rows, which tells us that we have six unique groups for ROOM_STYLE and ROOM_TYPE. It tells us nothing about the number of rows that might be found within the source data—but just so you know, it's the same data list we saw earlier in this chapter, which consisted of twelve rows.

Now let's try to compute the AVG value of these six MAX values:

```
SELECT    ROOM_STYLE, ROOM_TYPE, AVG(MAX(SQ_FT))
FROM      SHIP_CABINS
WHERE     SHIP_ID = 1
GROUP BY ROOM_STYLE, ROOM_TYPE;
```

If we try to execute this SELECT statement, this will be the result:

```
Error starting at line 1 in command:
SELECT    ROOM_STYLE, ROOM_TYPE, AVG(MAX(SQ_FT))
FROM      SHIP_CABINS
WHERE     SHIP_ID = 1
GROUP BY ROOM_STYLE, ROOM_TYPE
Error at Command Line:1 Column:9
Error report:
SQL Error: ORA-00937: not a single-group group function
00937. 00000 -  "not a single-group group function"
```

Why are we getting this error? The reason is simple: by introducing AVG into the SELECT statement's expression list, we are moving up the level of aggregation a higher degree, and we are informing SQL that we simply want one answer for all of those grouped rows. The problem: our GROUP BY is trying to display only one answer for all the rows, but there are six different ROOM_STYLE and ROOM_ TYPE values for those rows—there is no single answer that can represent all six of those rows.

One solution is to modify our SELECT statement by removing items from the select list that are at inconsistent levels of detail, like this:

```
SELECT    AVG(MAX(SQ_FT))
FROM      SHIP_CABINS
WHERE     SHIP_ID = 1
GROUP BY ROOM_STYLE, ROOM_TYPE;

AVG(MAX(SQ_FT))
--------------------
770.833333333333333333333333333333333333
```

Now we get an answer, and we can see the result displays in just one row, which in turn represents the six rows from the previous query, which itself represented twelve rows. So we have aggregated 12 rows into 6, and then 6 into 1—all with one query. In other words, this latest SELECT statement and its AVG result represents an aggregation of an aggregation.

Let's try a third level of nested aggregate:

```
SELECT    COUNT(AVG(MAX(SQ_FT)))
FROM      SHIP_CABINS
WHERE     SHIP_ID = 1
GROUP BY ROOM_STYLE, ROOM_TYPE;

Error starting at line 1 in command:
SELECT    COUNT(AVG(MAX(SQ_FT)))
FROM      SHIP_CABINS
WHERE     SHIP_ID = 1
GROUP BY ROOM_STYLE, ROOM_TYPE
Error at Command Line:1 Column:19
Error report:
SQL Error: ORA-00935: group function is nested too deeply
00935. 00000 -  "group function is nested too deeply"
```

It can't be done. Two levels deep is the furthest you can go with nested aggregate functions.

However—we are allowed to introduce nested scalar functions at any time. For example:

```
SELECT    ROUND(AVG(MAX(SQ_FT)))
FROM      SHIP_CABINS
WHERE     SHIP_ID = 1
GROUP BY ROOM_STYLE, ROOM_TYPE;

ROUND(AVG(MAX(SQ_FT)))
----------------------
771
```

To sum up:

- You are allowed to nest aggregate functions up to two levels deep.
- Each time you introduce an aggregate function, you are "rolling up" lower-level data into higher-level summary data.
- Your SELECT statement's select list must always respect the level of aggregation and can only include expressions that are all at the same level of aggregation.

And finally—remember that scalar functions can be nested at any time and have no effect on modifying the levels of row aggregation.

CERTIFICATION OBJECTIVE 7.04

Include or Exclude Grouped Rows by Using the HAVING Clause

The HAVING clause can exclude specific groups of rows defined in the GROUP BY clause. In other words, it performs the same task as the WHERE clause does for the rest of the SELECT statement. The difference is that WHERE deals with individual rows, while HAVING deals with groups of rows as defined in the GROUP BY clause.

The HAVING clause does not define the groups of rows themselves; those groups must already be defined by the GROUP BY clause. HAVING defines the criteria upon which each of the GROUP BY groups will either be included or excluded.

The HAVING clause can only be invoked in a SELECT statement where the GROUP BY clause is present.

If it is included, GROUP BY and HAVING must follow WHERE (if included) and precede ORDER BY (if included). Table 7-2 shows these relationships.

The HAVING function can be used like the WHERE clause to determine which rows will be included—or excluded—from your query. HAVING deals with the groups of rows identified in the GROUP BY clause. Any group that is identified in GROUP BY can be referenced by HAVING to be included in or excluded from the SQL statement.

TABLE 7-2	Sequence	Clause	Required / Optional?	Note
Clauses in a SELECT Statement	1	SELECT	Required	
	2	FROM	Required	
	3	WHERE	Optional	
	4	GROUP BY	Optional	HAVING is only allowed with a GROUP BY clause. HAVING and GROUP BY may occur in either order.
	4	HAVING	Optional	
	6	ORDER BY	Optional	

For example:

```
01    SELECT    ROOM_STYLE,
02              ROOM_TYPE,
03              TO_CHAR(MIN(SQ_FT),'9,999') "Min"
04    FROM      SHIP_CABINS
05    WHERE     SHIP_ID = 1
06    GROUP BY ROOM_STYLE, ROOM_TYPE
07    HAVING    ROOM_TYPE IN ('Standard', 'Large')
08       OR     MIN(SQ_FT) > 1200
09    ORDER BY 3;
10
11    ROOM_STYLE ROOM_TYPE              Min
12    ---------- -------------------- ------
13    Stateroom  Standard                160
14    Stateroom  Large                   211
15    Suite      Standard                533
16    Suite      Royal                 1,524
```

In this example, we've added the HAVING clause, which is on lines 7 and 8. The output starts on line 11. In this example, the HAVING clause consists of

```
07    HAVING    ROOM_TYPE IN ('Standard', 'Large')
08       OR     MIN(SQ_FT) > 1200
```

This HAVING restricts the groups identified in the GROUP BY clause to only those rows where ROOM_TYPE = 'Standard' or ROOM_TYPE = 'Large', OR the value for MIN(SQ_FT) is greater than 1200.

As the preceding example shows, HAVING can use the same Boolean operators that WHERE does—AND, OR, and NOT. The only restrictions on HAVING:

- It can only be used in SELECT statements that have a GROUP BY clause.
- It can only compare expressions that reference groups as defined in the GROUP BY clause, and aggregate functions.

HAVING can include scalar functions as long as these restrictions are respected. In other words, a scalar function can be incorporated into a larger expression that references a GROUP BY group or an aggregate function. Just remember that HAVING deals with groups of rows, not individual rows.

CERTIFICATION SUMMARY

Multirow functions differ from single-row functions in that they return one value for a group of rows, whereas single-row functions return one answer for each individual row. Single-row functions are also referred to as "scalar" functions; multirow functions are also referred to as "aggregate" functions. The available aggregate functions in SQL include the commonly used functions COUNT, SUM, MIN, MAX, AVG, and MEDIAN. There are functions to support standard deviation and variance, ranking, linear regression analysis, grouping with ROLLUP and CUBE, XML support, and working with nested tables.

Aggregate functions can be called from four places in a SELECT statement: the select list, the GROUP BY clause, the HAVING clause, and the ORDER BY clause.

If an aggregate function appears in the select list of the SELECT statement, then all other expressions must be at the same level of aggregation. You cannot mix scalar and aggregate values together in the select list.

The GROUP BY clause specifies one or more expressions that SQL is to use to group rows together. Any values displayed in the SELECT output must be displayed once for each group. In this fashion, the GROUP BY can transform a single column reference into an "aggregate" reference by specifying that column as a GROUP BY item.

Any column or expression specified in the GROUP BY clause can also be included in the SELECT statement's select list. However, this is not required.

The HAVING clause can be used to filter out groups that have been specified with the GROUP BY clause. HAVING works much like the WHERE clause does: while the WHERE clause filters out individual rows, HAVING does the same thing for groups of rows. HAVING is only allowed if the GROUP BY clause is also present.

If HAVING and GROUP BY are included in a SELECT statement, they must follow the WHERE clause (if used) and precede the ORDER BY clause (if used). GROUP BY often precedes HAVING, but the two can occur in either order in the SELECT statement's syntax.

TWO-MINUTE DRILL

Identify the Available Group Functions

❑ Group functions are also known as aggregate, or multirow, functions.

❑ Multirow functions return one value for every set of zero or more rows considered within a SELECT statement.

❑ There are group functions to determine minimum and maximum values, calculate averages, and more.

❑ Group functions can be used to determine rank within a group of rows.

Describe the Use of Group Functions

❑ Aggregate and scalar data cannot be included in the same SELECT statement's select list.

❑ The COUNT function counts occurrences of data, as opposed to the SUM function, which adds up numeric values.

❑ The MIN and MAX functions can operate on date, character, or numeric data.

❑ The AVG and MEDIAN functions can perform average and median calculations, and they can ignore NULL values in their computations.

❑ Some functions such as RANK use the keywords 'WITHIN GROUP (ORDER BY)' to process a value and identify its ranking within the overall set of rows in the data set.

Group Data by Using the GROUP BY Clause

❑ The GROUP BY clause is an optional clause in the SELECT statement in which you can specify how to group rows together in order to process them as a group.

❑ The row groups identified by GROUP BY can have aggregate functions applied to them, so that the final result of the SELECT is not a single aggregate value, but a series of aggregate function results, one per group.

❑ GROUP BY can specify columns in a table, which will have the effect of grouping rows in the SELECT that share the same values in those columns.

❑ Whatever you specify in the GROUP BY may also be included in the SELECT statement's select list—but this is not required.

❑ The effect of GROUP BY on a column is to change that column into an "aggregate" value; in other words, by grouping rows that have common data for a given column, and by specifying the column in the GROUP BY, you elevate the information in the column from "scalar" to "aggregate" for the purposes of that SELECT statement.

❑ GROUP BY can specify one or more expressions.

Include or Exclude Grouped Rows by Using the HAVING Clause

❑ The HAVING clause is an optional clause for the SELECT statement that works in coordination with GROUP BY.

❑ You cannot use HAVING unless GROUP BY is present.

❑ HAVING specifies groups of rows that will be included in the output of the SELECT statement.

❑ HAVING performs the same function for GROUP BY that WHERE performs for the rest of the SELECT statement.

❑ HAVING specifies groups using the same expression logic and syntax that WHERE would use.

❑ The GROUP BY and HAVING clauses are not required, but if used, they must follow the WHERE clause and precede the ORDER BY clause.

❑ While GROUP BY typically precedes HAVING in common practice, this is not required, and they can appear in either order.

SELF TEST

The following questions will help you measure your understanding of the material presented in this chapter. Choose one correct answer for each question unless otherwise directed.

Identify the Available Group Functions

1. Aggregate functions: (Choose two.)
   A. Return one value for each group of rows specified in a SELECT statement.
   B. Are also called group functions.
   C. Must be used in SELECT statements that select multiple rows.
   D. Can only operate with numeric data.

2. Review the following illustration:

```
        CRUISE_ORDERS
P * CRUISE_ORDER_ID    NUMBER
P * ORDER_DATE         DATE
PK_CO
```

   Now review this SQL statement:

   ```
   SELECT CRUISE_ORDER_ID, COUNT(ORDER_DATE)
   FROM   CRUISE_ORDERS;
   ```

   What can be said of this statement?
   A. It will fail to execute because ORDER_DATE is a date datatype, and no aggregate function can work with a date datatype.
   B. It will fail to execute because it mixes scalar and aggregate data in the select list.
   C. It will execute successfully but not produce any meaningful output.
   D. There is nothing wrong with the SQL statement.

Describe the Use of Group Functions

3. Which of the following aggregate functions can be used on character data? (Choose two.)
   A. COUNT
   B. MIN
   C. AVG
   D. MEDIAN

4. Examine the following data listing of a table called PERMITS:

```
PERMIT_ID    FILED_DATE    VENDOR_ID
---------    ----------    ---------
1            05-DEC-09     101
2            12-DEC-09     310903
3            14-DEC-09     101
```

Which one of the following aggregate functions could be used to determine how many permits have been filed by VENDOR_ID 101?

A. SUM

B. COUNT

C. MEDIAN

D. HAVING

5. Review the illustration from question 2, and then review the following SQL statement:

```
SELECT AVG(CRUISE_ORDER_ID), MIN(ORDER_DATE)
FROM    CRUISE_ORDERS;
```

What will result from an attempt to execute this SQL statement on the CRUISE_ORDERS table?

A. It will fail with an execution error, because you cannot use the AVG function on a PRIMARY KEY column.

B. It will fail with an execution error, because you cannot use the MIN function on a DATE datatype.

C. It will fail with an execution error if the table contains only one row.

D. It will execute and perform as intended.

6. Review the following data listing from a table SCORES:

```
SCORE_ID    TEST_SCORE
--------    ----------
1           95
2
3           85
```

Now consider the following query:

```
SELECT   TO_CHAR(AVG(TEST_SCORE),'999,999.99') FROM SCORES;
```

What will be the result of this query?

A. It will result in a syntax error because of the TO_CHAR function.

B. It will result in an execution error.

C. 90.00.

D. 60.00.

7. Review the following illustration:

PROJECTS	
P * PROJECT_ID	NUMBER
SHIP_ID	NUMBER
PURPOSE	VARCHAR2 (30 BYTE)
PROJECT_NAME	VARCHAR2 (40 BYTE)
PROJECT_COST	NUMBER
DAYS	NUMBER
⊫ PK_PROJECT_ID	

Which of the following SQL statements will execute correctly?

A. `SELECT RANK(100000) WITHIN GROUP (ORDER BY PROJECT_COST) FROM PROJECTS;`

B. `SELECT RANK(100,000) WITHIN GROUP (ORDER BY PROJECT_COST) FROM PROJECTS;`

C. `SELECT RANK(7500000) GROUP BY (ORDER BY PROJECT_COST) FROM PROJECTS;`

D. `SELECT RANK('Upgrade') WITHIN GROUP (ORDER BY PROJECT_COST) FROM PROJECTS;`

8. Which of the following aggregate functions ignores NULL values in its calculations? (Choose all that apply.)

A. MEDIAN

B. AVG

C. SUM

D. MAX

9. An aggregate function can be called from: (Choose two.)

A. The HAVING clause of an INSERT statement

B. The ORDER BY clause of a SELECT statement

C. The expression list of a DELETE statement

D. The select list of a SELECT statement

Group Data by Using the GROUP BY Clause

10. Review the illustration from question 7. Your task is to define a SELECT statement that groups rows according to their value for PURPOSE, and for each purpose, computes the total number of DAYS. Which one of the following queries will perform this task?

A. ```
   SELECT SUM(DAYS), PURPOSE
   FROM PROJECTS
   GROUP BY PURPOSE;
   ```

B. ```
   SELECT SUM(DAYS), PURPOSE
   FROM PROJECTS
   GROUP BY PURPOSE, SUM(DAYS);
   ```

C. ```
   SELECT PURPOSE, COUNT(DAYS)
   FROM PROJECTS
   GROUP BY PURPOSE;
   ```

D. ```
   SELECT PURPOSE, RANK(DAYS) ON (ORDER BY)
   FROM PROJECTS
   GROUP BY PURPOSE;
   ```

11. Review the illustration from question 2, and then look at the SQL code that follows (line numbers are added):

```
01  SELECT   TO_CHAR(ORDER_DATE,'Q') "Quarter", COUNT(*)
02  FROM     CRUISE_ORDERS
03  WHERE    TO_CHAR(ORDER_DATE,'YYYY') = '2009'
04  GROUP BY TO_CHAR(ORDER_DATE,'Q');
```

Recall that the 'Q' format model is for quarter, so that TO_CHAR using a DATE datatype with the 'Q' format mask is translating the date into the quarter in which it falls—1, 2, 3, or 4. Given that, which of the following statements is true of the SQL statement?

A. It will fail because of a syntax error in line 4, since you cannot use the TO_CHAR function in the GROUP BY clause.

B. It will fail because of a syntax error in line 1, since you cannot use the TO_CHAR function with the COUNT aggregate function.

C. It will execute and show the number of orders in the CRUISE_ORDERS table for each quarter in the year 2009.

D. None of the above.

12. Review the illustration from question 7, and then look at the SQL code that follows (line numbers are added):

```
01    SELECT    COUNT(COUNT(PROJECT_COST))
02    FROM      PROJECTS
03    GROUP BY PURPOSE;
```

What will happen if you try to execute this query on the PROJECTS table?

A. It will fail with a syntax error because line 1 is not correct.

B. It will fail with an execution error because you cannot use a VARCHAR2 column in a GROUP BY clause.

C. It will succeed and display one row for each different value in the PURPOSE column.

D. It will succeed and display one row.

Include or Exclude Grouped Rows by Using the HAVING Clause

13. Which of the following statements is true about HAVING? (Choose two.)

A. It can be used only in the SELECT statement.

B. It must occur after the GROUP BY clause.

C. It must occur after the WHERE clause.

D. It cannot reference an expression unless that expression is first referenced in the GROUP BY clause.

14. Review the illustration from question 7, and review the SQL statement that follows (line numbers added):

```
01    SELECT    SHIP_ID, MAX(DAYS)
02    FROM      PROJECTS
03    GROUP BY SHIP_ID
04    HAVING    AVG(PROJECT_COST) < 500000;
```

Which of the following statements is true for this SQL statement?

A. It will fail to execute due to a syntax error on line 4.

B. It will include only those rows with a PROJECT_COST value of less than 500000.

C. It will include only those groups of rows for a given SHIP_ID with an average value of PROJECT_COST less than 500000.

D. It will fail to execute because of a syntax error on line 1.

15. Review the illustration from question 7. Your assignment: create a SELECT statement that queries the PROJECTS table, to show the average project cost for each PURPOSE. You know there are only two values for PURPOSE in the table: 'Upgrade' or 'Maintenance'. You want to restrict output to those rows where the DAYS are greater than 3. Which of the following SELECT statements will perform this task?

A.
```
SELECT PURPOSE, AVG(PROJECT_COST)
FROM PROJECTS
WHERE DAYS > 3
GROUP BY PURPOSE;
```

B.
```
SELECT PURPOSE, AVG(PROJECT_COST)
FROM PROJECTS
GROUP BY PURPOSE
HAVING DAYS > 3;
```

C.
```
SELECT PURPOSE, AVG(PROJECT_COST)
FROM PROJECTS
GROUP BY PURPOSE, (DAYS > 3);
```

D.
```
SELECT PURPOSE, AVG(PROJECT_COST)
FROM PROJECTS
WHERE DAYS > 3
GROUP BY PURPOSE, DAYS
HAVING DAYS > 3;
```

SELF TEST ANSWERS

Identify the Available Group Functions

1. ☑ **A** and **B.** Aggregate functions return one value for each group of rows in the SELECT
statement. They are also referred to as "group" functions, or "multirow" functions.

   ☒ **C** and **D** are incorrect. A SELECT statement may return zero rows, or one row, or multiple
   rows, without being required to use an aggregate function. Some aggregate functions operate on
   character and date datatypes; they are not restricted to numeric data.

2. ☑ **B.** It mixes scalar data—the CRUISE_ORDER_ID column—and aggregate data—the
COUNT function applied to the ORDER_DATE column. This is not possible without a
GROUP BY clause. The GROUP BY clause could be used to transform the CRUISE_ORDER_
ID column into an aggregate value by specifying "GROUP BY CRUISE_ORDER_ID" at the
end of the statement before the semicolon termination character.

   ☒ **A, C,** and **D** are incorrect. Some aggregate functions can work with the date datatype, and
   COUNT is one of them.

Describe the Use of Group Functions

3. ☑ **A** and **B.** COUNT numbers occurrences of data. That data can include character, date, or
numeric datatypes. MIN determines the minimum value but will work with character data to
determine the value representing the value that would appear first in an alphabetic sorting of
the candidate values.

   ☒ **C** and **D** are incorrect. AVG and MEDIAN work with numeric data only.

4. ☑ **B.** COUNT will determine the occurrences of VENDOR_ID in the data listing.

   ☒ **A, C,** and **D** are incorrect. SUM adds numbers, which is not desired here. MEDIAN
   determines an average value. HAVING is not an aggregate function, it is a clause of the
   SELECT statement.

5. ☑ **D.** It will execute. The statement is syntactically correct.

   ☒ **A, B,** and **C** are incorrect. You can use AVG with a PRIMARY KEY column. It might not
   produce any useful information, but it's allowed. You can also use MIN with DATE datatypes, as
   well as character strings. It doesn't matter if the table has only one row; the statement will still
   work. You are allowed to use an aggregate function on zero, one, or more rows.

6. ☑ **C.** The AVG will compute by ignoring the NULL value and averaging the remaining
values, resulting in an answer of 90.00.

   ☒ **A, B,** and **D** are incorrect. There is no syntax error here; the TO_CHAR function
   correctly formats the output to include commas if necessary. There will be no execution

error, either. If the AVG function included NULL values, and, say, treated them as zeros, then the answer would be 60.00. That could be accomplished with the NVL function, as in AVG(NVL(TEST_SCORE,0)). But that's not included as an option here.

7. ☑ **A.** The request to RANK the literal numeric value of 100000 within the set of values for PROJECT_COST asks SQL to establish a numeric ranking for the value 100000 within the set of rows, and indicate where a row containing a value of 100000 for PROJECT_COST would fall within the sorted list, if there were such a row.

☒ **B, C,** and **D** are incorrect. The numeric literal value cannot include a comma—in other words, within the arguments for RANK, the value of "100,000" (without quotes) is not seen as one hundred thousand, but instead is seen as one hundred, followed by a second parameter of three zeros. Two parameters cannot be accepted by RANK unless there are two corresponding WITHIN GROUP expressions; there is only one in the answer provided. In answer C, the GROUP BY is misplaced. In answer D, 'Upgrade' represents an invalid datatype because the datatypes of both RANK and ORDER BY must match, and in this example, PROJECT_COST is a numeric datatype, as we see in the accompanying exhibit.

8. ☑ **A, B, C,** and **D.** All of the functions mentioned ignore null values. MAX in particular is worth emphasizing—remember that NULL values sort higher than NOT NULL values when ORDER BY sorts on a column containing NULL values. However, while that is true, only NOT NULL values are considered by the MAX function. The same is true for the other functions listed in the question.

☒ **None** are incorrect.

9. ☑ **B** and **D.** The SELECT statement allows an aggregate function to be called from the ORDER BY clause and the select list. If you specify an aggregate function from within an ORDER BY clause when a GROUP BY clause is present, the ORDER BY will sort the aggregate rows that each represent a group of rows.

☒ **A** and **C** are incorrect. There is no HAVING clause in an INSERT statement. There is no expression list in a DELETE statement.

Group Data by Using the GROUP BY Clause

10. ☑ **A.** Some might prefer to place the PURPOSE column before the SUM(DAYS) expression in the SELECT expression list, but that is not required.

☒ **B, C,** and **D** are incorrect. Answer B is syntactically incorrect, since you cannot put an aggregate function within a GROUP BY clause. Answer C is incorrect because the COUNT function is used instead of SUM. COUNT would count the occurrences of data, rather than sum up the values. Answer D is just a random combination of reserved words and nonsense.

11. ☑ **C.** The statement is syntactically correct and will execute.

☒ **A, B,** and **D** are incorrect. The TO_CHAR function is a scalar function and, as such, is not subject to the same restrictions that any aggregate function is. For example, the TO_CHAR used in the GROUP BY clause is fine. And by using the TO_CHAR expression in the GROUP BY, it can also be used in the SELECT expression list in line 1, along with the aggregate function COUNT.

12. ☑ **D.** It will succeed and display one row. The reason you know this is because line 1 shows an aggregate of an aggregate with a GROUP BY clause.

☒ **A, B,** and **C** are incorrect. Line 1 is correct; you are allowed to nest one aggregate within one other aggregate function. You can GROUP BY any datatype; there is no restriction on grouping by character data. If you were to use only one aggregate function, the result would display one row for each unique value of PURPOSE. But by nesting COUNT within COUNT, you are adding up all of those rows and displaying one aggregate answer.

Include or Exclude Grouped Rows by Using the HAVING Clause

13. ☑ **A** and **C.** HAVING is only valid in the SELECT statement, not the other SQL statements. HAVING must occur after the WHERE clause.

☒ **B** and **D** are incorrect. HAVING cannot be used without GROUP BY, but it is not required to follow GROUP BY. HAVING is not limited to expressions identified in the GROUP BY clause; instead, it is limited to any valid expression that addresses the groups established within the GROUP BY clause. In other words, aggregate functions can be invoked from within HAVING, whether they are called by GROUP BY or not.

14. ☑ **C.** The statement is syntactically correct and will produce a series of rows of data. Each row will represent all values for each SHIP_ID value in the table. Each row representing each SHIP_ID will have one maximum value for DAYS. Any set of rows for SHIP_ID whose average value of PROJECT_COST is less than 500000 will be included; all others will be excluded.

☒ **A, B,** and **D** are incorrect. There is no syntax error on line 4. The HAVING clause is not required to reference anything in the GROUP BY. HAVING can reference aggregate functions; its only limitation is that it cannot directly reference columns in the table if those columns have not been included in the GROUP BY clause. (Columns omitted from GROUP BY may be incorporated in certain expressions in HAVING but cannot be directly referenced as standalone columns.) Answer B could only be true if the WHERE clause were present and filtering rows as answer B describes—the HAVING clause doesn't include or exclude rows on an individual basis but instead includes or excludes groups of rows as defined by the GROUP BY clause and the HAVING clause.

15. ☑ **A.** One of the most important aspects of understanding HAVING is to know when *not* to use it, and this is a great example of that—nothing in this question says anything about restricting groups of data, and that is the only reason why you would use HAVING. The WHERE clause achieves the task of ensuring that only rows where DAYS are greater than three will be considered.

    ☒ **B, C,** and **D** are incorrect. The task defined by the question doesn't require HAVING. There is no description in the question that asks for anything about the GROUPS to be excluded. Answer B is syntactically incorrect because HAVING can only reference aggregate functions or columns that are identified in the GROUP BY, and this does neither. Answer C is syntactically incorrect because you cannot enclose the final expression in parentheses by itself. Answer D is syntactically correct but does not produce the answer that is described in the question—it will instead group all the rows by both PURPOSE and DAYS, which is not what was asked for—such a query can potentially produce many more rows than just the two expected. In other words, instead of getting one group of rows per value in PURPOSE, you'll get a finer division of detail with each set of rows containing a unique combination of both PURPOSE and DAYS, and that is something different.

8

Displaying Data from Multiple Tables

CERTIFICATION OBJECTIVES

T his chapter reviews various types of joins. A *join* is a SELECT statement that retrieves data from two or more tables and connects that data together to produce a combined set of output. The SELECT statement specifies data in one table that is identical to data in another table. Tables that share common data elements that support joins are said to be "related" to each other. This is why a SQL database is called a "relational database management system"; joining tables is the whole purpose of SQL database systems.

This chapter will look at

- Equijoins, which use the equality operator
- Non-equijoins, which do not use the equality operator
- INNER joins
- OUTER joins
- NATURAL joins
- Cross-joins (also known as Cartesian products)
- Self-joins

We'll discuss the syntax of all of these forms of joins, and look at the use of table aliases, as well as a number of examples.

CERTIFICATION OBJECTIVE 8.01

Write SELECT Statements to Access Data from More Than One Table Using Equijoins and Non-Equijoins/View Data That Generally Does Not Meet a Join Condition by Using Outer Joins

There are several types of joins in SQL. The most common is the *equijoin*. Another is the *non-equijoin*. We'll discuss both in this section. Before that, however, let's discuss some concepts that will help us during our discussion about joining tables— let's revisit PRIMARY KEY and FOREIGN KEY constraints.

KEY Relationships

We've already seen how tables have PRIMARY KEYS and FOREIGN KEYS. Just to review:

- The PRIMARY KEY is a unique identifier in a particular table.
- The FOREIGN KEY is a copy of some (or all) of one table's PRIMARY KEY data in a second table, so that the second table can relate back to the first.

For example, see Figure 8-1. The PORTS and SHIPS tables both have their own primary key columns. For PORTS, it's the PORT_ID column. For SHIPS, it's the SHIP_ID column. And incidentally—we're choosing to name our primary key columns with the "_ID" suffix, but that's not required in SQL.

Notice that the SHIPS table also has something called the HOME_PORT_ID column. The intent of this column is to contain values that are also found in the PORTS table's PORT_ID column. How can you tell this is the case? Well . . . because I'm telling you now, really, there's nothing inherent in the table structures alone that guarantees that this is the intent. The fact that the phrase PORT_ID is found in the HOME_PORT_ID column name is a clue, but not a guarantee.

However, note the diagram in Figure 8-1, and the crow's foot line in the center of the diagram that connects the two tables together. Figure 8-1 is a simple entity relationship diagram (ERD). The crow's foot line shows you the relationship between the two entities, or tables, of SHIPS and PORTS. The line is a clue that there's a FOREIGN KEY on the SHIPS table that relates to the PORTS table. The "F" in the SHIPS entity to the left of the HOME_PORT_ID column name indicates

FIGURE 8-1

The PORTS and SHIPS tables

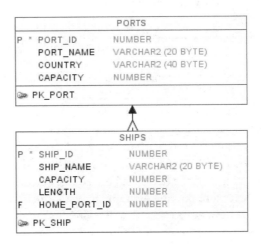

that the FOREIGN KEY in SHIPS is a constraint on the HOME_PORT_ID column. However, nothing in this particular ERD indicates which column in the PORTS table is the referenced column of the FOREIGN KEY constraint. As we'll see later in this chapter, it's the PORT_ID column of SHIPS. This FOREIGN KEY helps to ensure that no data entered into the HOME_PORT_ID column of SHIPS will be accepted unless that data is already present in the PORT_ID column of the PORTS table. We saw earlier how to create foreign key constraints that do precisely this task.

The ERD shows the crow's foot pointing toward the SHIPS entity. This means that for every one row in PORTS, there could theoretically be many rows in SHIPS. This is because you can add as many rows to the SHIPS table as you wish for any one PORT_ID value, by simply repeating that value in each row's HOME_PORT_ID column. But for any given SHIP table row, there can only be one corresponding PORT table row. The relationship between these two tables is said to be "one-to-many", meaning that there can only be one row in PORT for any number of rows in SHIPS.

The crow's foot points one line in the direction of the "one" side of that relationship, and points the "many" lines—three lines to be precise—in the direction of the "many" side of that relationship.

The "one-to-many" relationship does not require there to be many rows in the SHIPS table that correspond to any given row in the PORTS table. It merely allows for the possibility.

The reason for including this paragraph in this chapter is to remind you why those PRIMARY KEY and FOREIGN KEY constraints exist—to support the type of joining we're about to do in this chapter.

But there's an important point to be made here: you can join tables without the presence of PRIMARY KEY and FOREIGN KEY constraints. There is no official connection in the database between key constraints and table joins. Key constraints are helpful to provide data integrity and increase the odds of success and meaningful results from table joins. But they are not required.

So—with that point established—let's start joining tables.

Types of Joins

Joins are characterized in many ways. One way a join is defined is in terms of whether it is an inner join or an outer join. Another issue is that of equijoins and non-equijoins. These descriptions are not mutually exclusive descriptions.

Inner Versus Outer Joins

There are two major categories of syntax for creating joins in Oracle SQL:

- Inner joins connect rows in two or more tables if and only if there are matched rows in all the tables being joined.
- Outer joins connect rows in two or more tables in a way that is more inclusive—if data exists in one table that has no matching values in another, the unmatched row will still be included in the output.

Equijoins Versus Non-Equijoins

Separate from the issue of inner and outer joins is the issue of equijoin versus non-equijoin:

- Equijoins connect data in two or more tables by looking for common data among the tables' columns. In other words, an equijoin looks for an exact match of data.
- Non-equijoins connect data by looking for relationships that don't involve equality, such as "less than" or "greater than" relationships, or situations where data in one table is within a range of values in another.

Most of the joins we'll work with will be equijoins, but we'll look at non-equijoins as well.

Other Joins

There are other joins that we'll review in this chapter, such as self, cross-, and natural joins. These descriptions include joins that fall into the categories we've already seen of "equijoin" and "non-equijoin", or "inner" and "outer" join. We'll review each separately.

Inner Joins

The first type of join we'll review is an *inner* join. An inner join connects rows between two or more tables if and only if there are matched rows in all joined tables. If there isn't a match in all tables, then none of the data for that row is included in the inner join's output.

For example, let's connect two tables with an inner join—look again at Figure 8-1. Every ship in the SHIPS table can be assigned a home port in the PORTS table. This is recorded in the database by assigning a HOME_PORT_ID to each record in the SHIPS table. This is why the SHIPS table includes a column called HOME_PORT_ID, which is designated a FOREIGN KEY. The FOREIGN KEY constraint points to the PORT_ID column in the PORTS table, so that any entry in the SHIPS table's HOME_PORT_ID will represent a value that already exists in the PORTS table's PORT_ID column.

Let's look at our sample data in these tables. First the PORTS table:

PORT_ID	PORT_NAME
1	Baltimore
2	Charleston
3	Tampa
4	Miami

Next, the SHIPS table:

SHIP_ID	SHIP_NAME	HOME_PORT_ID
1	Codd Crystal	1
2	Codd Elegance	3
3	Codd Champion	
4	Codd Victorious	3
5	Codd Grandeur	2
6	Codd Prince	2

As you can see from these data listings, many ships have a HOME_PORT_ID that matches a PORT_ID in the PORTS table. If you were to identify the home port for, say, the 'Codd Elegance', you would see that it's PORT_ID 3, which is Tampa. And what you just saw in making that connection is what you have to spell out to SQL so that SQL can do the same thing. In other words, to join these tables together, we can

- Identify both tables in the FROM clause, separated by the keywords INNER JOIN.
- Define the column from each table that is being used to join the data in the ON condition.

Here's the code for an inner join:

```
01   SELECT    SHIP_ID, SHIP_NAME, PORT_NAME
02   FROM      SHIPS INNER JOIN PORTS
03   ON        HOME_PORT_ID = PORT_ID
04   ORDER BY SHIP_ID;
```

The ORDER BY is something we added; it's not required for the join.

Note that the keyword INNER is not required; we can eliminate it and go with this approach:

```
01   SELECT    SHIP_ID, SHIP_NAME, PORT_NAME
02   FROM      SHIPS JOIN PORTS
03   ON        HOME_PORT_ID = PORT_ID
04   ORDER BY SHIP_ID;
```

This query is the same as the INNER JOIN query with one variation: we removed the optional keyword INNER from line 2. Everything else is the same.

Whichever syntax we use—with or without the keyword INNER—the result is the same:

SHIP_ID	SHIP_NAME	PORT_NAME
1	Codd Crystal	Baltimore
2	Codd Elegance	Tampa
4	Codd Victorious	Tampa
5	Codd Grandeur	Charleston
6	Codd Prince	Charleston

That's the output from our inner join.

Note that we can add additional WHERE clause criteria to our join. Let's say we wanted to restrict our output so that only the 'Charleston' rows were included. Let's modify the INNER JOIN syntax:

```
01   SELECT    SHIP_ID, SHIP_NAME, PORT_NAME
02   FROM      SHIPS INNER JOIN PORTS
03   ON        HOME_PORT_ID = PORT_ID
04   WHERE     PORT_NAME = 'Charleston'
05   ORDER BY SHIP_ID;
```

The result will be to limit our results to only those ships that are ported in Charleston.

Now go back before we added the WHERE clause, and look at our original output from the first inner join. Do you see something missing? Look for the 'Codd Champion'—it isn't in the output. The reason is because the 'Codd Champion', aka SHIP_ID 3, has no assigned value for HOME_PORT_ID. As a result, there is no matching row in the PORTS table, and since we used an "inner join" format, we only produce output if there are matched rows in all joined tables. The result: 'Codd Champion' is omitted. And that's not all—we also don't see any value for the PORT_ID 4, 'Miami'. The reason is the same—there is no ship assigned to Miami as a home port.

This is why our join is an "inner join". It only shows records that have matched rows in both tables. But if you want to show data from rows that aren't necessarily matched in all tables, then you want to use the "outer join" format.

Older Inner Join Syntax

Before we move on to outer joins, let's review an old variation to the syntax we just reviewed for an inner join. Here it is:

```
01   SELECT    S.SHIP_ID, S.SHIP_NAME, P.PORT_NAME
02   FROM      SHIPS S, PORTS P
03   WHERE     S.HOME_PORT_ID = P.PORT_ID
04   ORDER BY S.SHIP_ID;
```

In this form, the join is accomplished in lines 2 and 3, where we list the joined tables in the FROM clause, and also identify the join criterion in line 3 with an equal sign. In this syntax, there is no keyword JOIN or ON. The WHERE clause can include additional criteria as any WHERE clause might, for example:

```
01   SELECT    S.SHIP_ID, S.SHIP_NAME, P.PORT_NAME
02   FROM      SHIPS S, PORTS P
03   WHERE     S.HOME_PORT_ID = P.PORT_ID
04     AND     PORT_NAME = 'Charleston'
05   ORDER BY S.SHIP_ID;
```

This is the older form of an inner join that Oracle has used, and it still works. But the version we reviewed earlier—the version that uses the JOIN and ON keywords—is preferred and is consistent with the ANSI standard for SQL joins.

Outer Joins

An *outer* join is a join that displays data from the same rows an inner join does, but also adds data from rows that don't necessarily have matches in all the tables that are joined together. There are three types of outer joins—LEFT, RIGHT, and FULL. Each is described here.

LEFT OUTER JOIN

To see one type of outer join in action, let's continue with our example and modify our query just a little to make it an outer join:

```
01  SELECT    SHIP_ID, SHIP_NAME, PORT_NAME
02  FROM      SHIPS LEFT OUTER JOIN PORTS
03  ON        HOME_PORT_ID = PORT_ID
04  ORDER BY SHIP_ID;
```

Notice the addition of the keyword LEFT in line 2. The resulting output of this code is

SHIP_ID	SHIP_NAME	PORT_NAME
1	Codd Crystal	Baltimore
2	Codd Elegance	Tampa
3	Codd Champion	
4	Codd Victorious	Tampa
5	Codd Grandeur	Charleston
6	Codd Prince	Charleston

By changing our FROM clause from a JOIN to a LEFT OUTER JOIN, we have changed the query from an inner join to an outer join. (Remember that JOIN defaults to INNER JOIN.) And notice that our output now includes data for SHIP_ID 3. Also notice that the row for SHIP_ID 3 shows no value for PORT_NAME, which is correct—no HOME_PORT_ID value was assigned to it.

Also note: the OUTER keyword is optional. In other words, this is just as good:

```
01  SELECT    SHIP_ID, SHIP_NAME, PORT_NAME
02  FROM      SHIPS LEFT JOIN PORTS
03  ON        HOME_PORT_ID = PORT_ID
04  ORDER BY SHIP_ID;
```

In this example, OUTER is omitted, but the effect is the same.

RIGHT OUTER JOIN

But we still don't see our PORT_NAME of 'Miami'. So let's change our query again:

```
01  SELECT    SHIP_ID, SHIP_NAME, PORT_NAME
02  FROM      SHIPS RIGHT OUTER JOIN PORTS
03  ON        HOME_PORT_ID = PORT_ID
04  ORDER BY SHIP_ID;
```

Note that we've replaced the keyword LEFT with the keyword RIGHT in line 2. The result:

```
SHIP_ID                 SHIP_NAME               PORT_NAME
----------------------  ---------------------   ----------------------
1                       Codd Crystal            Baltimore
2                       Codd Elegance           Tampa
4                       Codd Victorious         Tampa
5                       Codd Grandeur           Charleston
6                       Codd Prince             Charleston
                                                Miami
```

We've now included the row for 'Miami'. But we lost our row with the 'Codd Champion'. That's because this RIGHT OUTER JOIN favors unmatched rows on the right side of the join, which is the PORTS table (see line 2 of the SELECT statement), but we took away our LEFT OUTER JOIN to SHIPS.

As before, OUTER is optional. RIGHT JOIN will do the same thing as RIGHT OUTER JOIN.

FULL OUTER JOIN

If we want to combine the effects of a RIGHT OUTER JOIN and LEFT OUTER JOIN together, we can use the FULL OUTER JOIN:

```
01   SELECT   SHIP_ID, SHIP_NAME, PORT_NAME
02   FROM     SHIPS FULL OUTER JOIN PORTS
03   ON       HOME_PORT_ID = PORT_ID
04   ORDER BY SHIP_ID;
```

Line 2 shows the use of the keywords FULL OUTER JOIN, and the output is:

```
SHIP_ID                 SHIP_NAME               PORT_NAME
----------------------  ---------------------   ----------------------
1                       Codd Crystal            Baltimore
2                       Codd Elegance           Tampa
3                       Codd Champion
4                       Codd Victorious         Tampa
5                       Codd Grandeur           Charleston
6                       Codd Prince             Charleston
                                                Miami
```

And here we have all of our records, matched or not.

And as before—you guessed it—the keyword OUTER is optional.

Deprecated Outer Join Syntax: (+)

And now a word to my fellow longtime veteran Oracle professionals. If you've been looking for the plus sign somewhere in the syntax for our discussion on inner and outer joins, you're out of luck. The famous—or infamous—plus sign, a longtime friend of many veteran Oracle professionals, is on its way out the door. It still works. But Oracle Corporation is in the process of kicking it to the curb. Oracle Corporation has officially declared it deprecated.

This is what I mean: if you were to go back to the LEFT OUTER JOIN example, and translate it back into the old form of Oracle table joins, the SELECT statement would look like this:

```
01   SELECT    SHIP_ID, SHIP_NAME, PORT_NAME
02   FROM      SHIPS, PORTS
03   WHERE     HOME_PORT_ID = PORT_ID(+)
04   ORDER BY SHIP_ID;
```

Note the special characters at the end of line 3. The plus sign in parentheses defines this query as a left outer join. The plus sign is on the right side in order to define a left outer join. This is the old syntax, and it still works.

But it's not on the exam. It was never ANSI standard anyway. Furthermore, Oracle Corporation formally recommends that you avoid using it from now on and stick with the keywords INNER JOIN, OUTER JOIN, and all the other related keywords.

The old format still works. But you won't be tested on it—you'll be tested on the new format.

Using Table Aliases

In our examples so far, we've joined tables using columns that have had different column names. This isn't always the case, however. For example, look at the two tables in Figure 8-2.

The EMPLOYEES table and the ADDRESSES table both have a column called EMPLOYEE_ID. That column is the PRIMARY KEY in EMPLOYEES, and it's the FOREIGN KEY in ADDRESSES. Using what we've seen so far, we might try this syntax:

```
01   SELECT    EMPLOYEE_ID, LAST_NAME, STREET_ADDRESS
02   FROM      EMPLOYEES INNER JOIN ADDRESSES
03   ON        EMPLOYEE_ID = EMPLOYEE_ID;
```

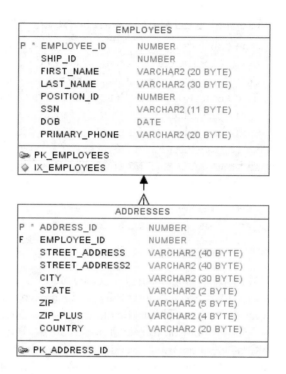

FIGURE 8-2

The EMPLOYEES and ADDRESSES tables

There's a problem with this syntax. Look at line 1. The first item in our SELECT statement's select list is EMPLOYEE_ID, but which table's EMPLOYEE_ID are we intending here? Chances are it won't make that much of a difference with regard to data display, since both columns contain the same data—unless we use a form of OUTER JOIN, in which case there may be a difference. Regardless, that's no help to us here, because SQL will reject this statement anyway due to the ambiguous column reference.

One solution is to use the full table name as a prefix to the column:

```
01  SELECT    EMPLOYEES.EMPLOYEE_ID, LAST_NAME, STREET_ADDRESS
02  FROM      EMPLOYEES INNER JOIN ADDRESSES
03  ON        EMPLOYEES.EMPLOYEE_ID = ADDRESSES.EMPLOYEE_ID;
```

We've added the full table name in front of each reference to EMPLOYEE_ID, separated by a period, to clarify our intent. Note that we needed to make these changes three times—once on line 1, and twice on line 3. This is perfectly acceptable and represents clear and thorough design.

There's an alternative, however, and it's the table alias. Here's an example of the table alias in action:

```
01   SELECT    EM.EMPLOYEE_ID, LAST_NAME, STREET_ADDRESS
02   FROM      EMPLOYEES EM INNER JOIN ADDRESSES AD
03   ON        EM.EMPLOYEE_ID = AD.EMPLOYEE_ID;
```

First look at line 2. After each table referenced in the FROM clause, we left a space, followed by a name we specify. The name needs to match the rules for naming database objects. For EMPLOYEES we chose EM, and for ADDRESSES we chose AD. We could have chosen anything within the rules of naming database objects.

Since we chose to create table aliases, we were also able to use the table alias as prefixes on lines 1 and 3. The result is a more easily readable query.

There's no right or wrong answer as to which approach you should choose—either the full table name prefix or the table alias prefix. Either way, you should consider the following points:

- When writing any query in which a column reference is ambiguous, you must do something to identify the column clearly to the SQL statement. Otherwise, you'll get an error message and the SQL statement won't execute.
- The use of table prefixes and table aliases is on the exam.

The table alias is more commonly used, in my ever-so-humble opinion. But both work.

Also note: table aliases can be used in INSERT, UPDATE, and DELETE statements, as well as SELECT.

NATURAL Joins

So far, many of the examples we've seen have joined tables using columns of different names—such as HOME_PORT_ID and PORT_ID. It's more common, however, for such columns to be named with the same name. In other words, when database designers create two tables and intend to link them together, it's good design to give identical names to any columns that will be linked. That's not to say the opposite is true—it's not necessarily bad design to do otherwise—it all depends on readability and intent. But the point for our discussion here is that you will often work with tables that share identical column names, and it will be these columns upon which your joins will probably be built.

For example, review Figure 8-2 again. As we saw in the last section, the two tables shown both have a column called EMPLOYEE_ID. This column is a FOREIGN KEY in the ADDRESSES table, and the PRIMARY KEY of the EMPLOYEES table.

The natural join approach tells SQL to locate any columns in the two tables with a common name, and use them to join the tables. Here's an example:

```
01  SELECT    EMPLOYEE_ID, LAST_NAME, STREET_ADDRESS
02  FROM      EMPLOYEES NATURAL JOIN ADDRESSES;
```

Notice the use of the keywords NATURAL JOIN in line 2. Also notice that there's no keyword ON anywhere, and nowhere that we establish the join between the two common columns—which in these two tables are EMPLOYEES.EMPLOYEE_ID and ADDRESSES.EMPLOYEE_ID. The NATURAL JOIN doesn't require an explicit declaration of these columns, provided that the column names are identical.

Also notice something else: see the reference to EMPLOYEE_ID in line 1? Remember that there are two EMPLOYEE_ID columns—one in EMPLOYEES and one in ADDRESSES. Normally such a reference in a join would require a table alias. But the natural join forbids such table prefixes on join column names. Their use would result in a syntax error. However, table prefixes are allowed on other columns—but not the join columns in a natural join.

Finally, a natural join is an inner join. This is why the NATURAL JOIN syntax can get away without a table alias in line 1 above—by restricting itself to an inner join, the EMPLOYEE_ID column will always have the same value, regardless of which table's EMPLOYEE_ID is intended. Unmatched rows are omitted in an inner join.

You cannot perform an outer join with the NATURAL keyword. But there's something similar that will support outer joins, and it's the USING keyword—that's next.

USING

The keyword USING is similar to the natural join, in the sense that its use depends on the presence of identically named columns in the JOIN. However, USING can be used with both inner and outer joins. For example:

```
01  SELECT    EMPLOYEE_ID, LAST_NAME, STREET_ADDRESS
02  FROM      EMPLOYEES LEFT JOIN ADDRESSES
03            USING (EMPLOYEE_ID);
```

Note the syntax here—we're using a LEFT JOIN on two tables that share the same column name EMPLOYEE_ID. As we've already seen, this is a variation of an outer join. The keyword OUTER is optional and omitted from this example.

Notice the keyword USING on line 3. USING is followed by a column name enclosed in parentheses. No table name prefix is allowed before the column name, not here, and not elsewhere in the statement—such as line 1.

Since the table name prefix is not allowed in line 1, how do you know which table's EMPLOYEE_ID is intended in the select list in line 1? The answer is that it may be one or the other, depending on the row. In an outer join, which is also an equijoin, the values in both tables for EMPLOYEE_ID will either be identical to each other, or will include one NULL value in one of the two table's columns. The output, therefore, will show a value if any is present in either table; otherwise, a NULL value will display. The reason this works is that the values will never conflict in an outer join —the join condition, by definition, will reject conflicting values and exclude rows with conflicting values for the join condition. The result is this: if you include the join column in the select list—such as the EMPLOYEE_ID column in line 1 of the example—then the output of an outer join's "join column" specified with the USING clause will show a value wherever a value is present in either table's join column; otherwise, it will display a NULL value.

The USING keyword does basically the same thing as the natural join in the sense that the connection between the joined tables is performed automatically. The difference is that USING lets us perform an outer join as well as an inner join.

Multitable Joins

So far we've only looked at joins that connect two tables. But joins can connect two, three, or more tables. For example, see Figure 8-3.

These three tables can be joined together in a SELECT statement like this:

```
01   SELECT   P.PORT_NAME, S.SHIP_NAME, SC.ROOM_NUMBER
02   FROM     PORTS P JOIN SHIPS S ON P.PORT_ID = S.HOME_PORT_ID
03                JOIN SHIP_CABINS SC ON S.SHIP_ID = SC.SHIP_ID;
```

Notice the syntax for this SELECT statement that joins three tables:

- The FROM keyword appears once.
- After line 2, when the original two-table join completes, line 3 opens with the keyword JOIN.
- Line 3 continues with the third table name, followed by a table alias, followed by the explicitly defined join criteria.

Line 3 in the preceding SELECT statement can be repeated and edited as required in order to join additional tables beyond these three.

FIGURE 8-3

PORTS,
SHIPS, and
SHIP_CABINS
tables

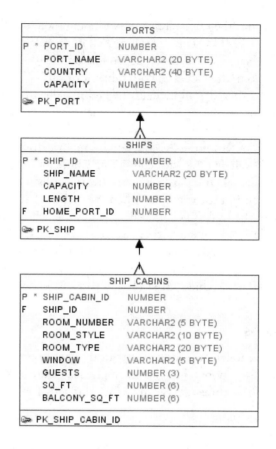

Non-Equijoins

So far, all the joins we've seen have been *equijoins*. In other words, the joins have used columns containing common data values among the join tables, and joined rows in the tables based on finding equal values in the join columns.

Non-equijoins relate one row to another by way of non-equal comparisons, such as comparisons of greater or lesser value, or perhaps comparisons that look for a range of values. Such joins are unusual but important. And they are part of the certification exam criteria.

Let's look at an example. See Figure 8-4.

FIGURE 8-4

The SCORES and
GRADING tables

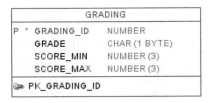

Note that these tables do not have a FOREIGN KEY relationship. As we've already noted, that is not required in order to join tables.

Let's look at some data in these tables. First, SCORES:

```
SCORE_ID                        TEST_SCORE
---------------------           ----------
1                               95
2                               55
3                               83
```

Next, GRADING:

```
GRADING_ID                      GRADE SCORE_MIN                     SCORE_MAX
---------------------           ----- ----------------------       -----------
1                               A     90                            100
2                               B     80                            89
3                               C     70                            79
4                               D     60                            69
5                               E     50                            59
```

The idea here is that the SCORES table lists some actual scores on exams, and the GRADING table contains information about grading criteria.

In the SCORES table, we have a row of data showing that the test identified with a SCORE_ID of 1 received a score of 95. According to the GRADING table, that should be a grade of A.

Let's create a SELECT statement that joins these tables together to determine each test score's grades (line numbers added):

```
01  SELECT S.SCORE_ID, S.TEST_SCORE, G.GRADE
02  FROM   SCORES S JOIN GRADING G
03     ON  S.TEST_SCORE BETWEEN G.SCORE_MIN AND G.SCORE_MAX;
```

Note the syntax of this join. On line 2 we have a typical JOIN syntax, but on line 3, instead of the equijoin, we connect the two tables by comparing the value in the TEST_SCORE column of SCORES and see if it's BETWEEN the values for the GRADING table's SCORE_MIN and SCORE_MAX columns.

Here is the output:

```
SCORE_ID                TEST_SCORE GRADE
----------------------- ---------- -----
1                       95         A
3                       83         B
2                       55         E
```

This is an example of a non-equijoin. The syntax of the ON condition in a non-equijoin is similar to the syntax for the WHERE clause in the SELECT, in that you can use comparison expressions, the 'greater than' or 'less than' operators, SQL functions, and Boolean operators to connect a series of comparisons together.

CERTIFICATION OBJECTIVE 8.02

Join a Table to Itself by Using a Self-Join

A *self-join* is a table that is joined to itself. A self-join connects a column in a table with a column—often a different column—in the same table.

(Note: Syntactically you can join a column to itself in the same table, as opposed to a different column in the same table. It doesn't do much logically, but the syntax will execute.)

Self-joins can use all the same variations on join criteria that any other table join can use. In other words, self-joins can be inner joins or outer joins, equijoins or non-equijoins, etc.

Let's write a self-joining SELECT statement. For starters, see Figure 8-5. The POSITIONS table lists job titles within our Codd Cruises organization.

Here's a listing of some of the columns in the POSITIONS table:

```
POSITION_ID             POSITION             REPORTS_TO
----------------------- -------------------- ----------------
1                       Captain
2                       Director             1
3                       Manager              2
4                       Crew Chief           2
5                       Crew                 4
```

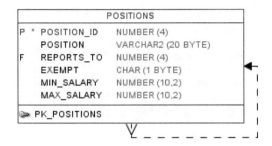

FIGURE 8-5

The POSITIONS table

Note the column REPORTS_TO. It indicates that, for example, the 'Crew Chief' reports to the position of POSITION_ID 2, which is 'Director'.

Self-Referencing Foreign Keys

The POSITIONS table is supported with a foreign key that points to itself, which is created with this SQL statement:

```
ALTER TABLE POSITIONS
ADD CONSTRAINT FK_PO_PO FOREIGN KEY (REPORTS_TO)
    REFERENCES POSITIONS (POSITION_ID);
```

Note that a foreign key is advised, but not required in order to perform the self-join.

Self-Join Syntax

Now that we have our table, our data, and our optional foreign key constraint, let's look at a query that will connect all of this together. To create the self-join, we need to do the following:

- Identify the table twice in the FROM clause.
- Define our join criteria—which in this case will be an OUTER join so that we can include the highest-level position that doesn't have a REPORTS_TO value—and therefore isn't "matched" with anything.
- Apply a table alias to all appropriate references, being careful to join the REPORTS_TO column in the first table reference to the POSITION_ID column in the second table reference.

Here's the query:

```
SELECT    A.POSITION_ID, A.POSITION, B.POSITION BOSS
FROM      POSITIONS A LEFT OUTER JOIN POSITIONS B
ON        A.REPORTS_TO = B.POSITION_ID
ORDER BY A.POSITION_ID;
```

And here's the output:

```
POSITION_ID                    POSITION               BOSS
--------------------           --------------------   --------------------
1                              Captain
2                              Director               Captain
3                              Manager                Director
4                              Crew Chief             Director
5                              Crew                   Crew Chief
```

exam
ⓦatch   *Be sure you have a solid command of the join syntax for all forms of joins. That should include NATURAL, USING, and the various inner joins and outer joins. All forms are fair game on the exam.*

The result: a listing of positions, and the supervisor each reports to. All of this data is found in the one table POSITIONS. You can see that in the SELECT statement's output, both the POSITION column and the BOSS column contain data that is found in the POSITION column of the POSITIONS table. But the self-join produces a meaningful output display.

CERTIFICATION OBJECTIVE 8.03

Generate a Cartesian Product of All Rows from Two or More Tables

A *Cartesian product* occurs when two or more tables are included in a SELECT statement without a join condition. When a SELECT statement references two or more tables in the FROM clause without a JOIN, SQL will still execute the statement, connecting each row in one table with every row in the other.

A Cartesian product is also known as a *cross-join*.

For example, consider the following data listing from table VENDORS:

```
VENDOR_ID   VENDOR_NAME
---------   -----------
1           Acme Steaks
2           Acme Poker Chips
```

Now consider the data listing of a table ONLINE_SUBSCRIBERS:

```
ONLINE_SUBSCRIBER_ID   LASTNAME
--------------------   --------
1                      KLINE
2                      bryant
3                      McLean
```

Finally, let's create a Cartesian product on these two tables:

```
SELECT *
FROM    VENDORS, ONLINE_SUBSCRIBERS;
```

That's it. The output is as follows:

VENDOR_ID	VENDOR_NAME	ONLINE_SUBSCRIBER_ID	LASTNAME
1	Acme Steaks	1	KLINE
1	Acme Steaks	2	bryant
1	Acme Steaks	3	McLean
2	Acme Poker Chips	1	KLINE
2	Acme Poker Chips	2	bryant
2	Acme Poker Chips	3	McLean

Note the result: each row of VENDORS is joined to every row of ONLINE_SUBSCRIBERS.

Another way to perform the same cross join is this:

```
SELECT *
FROM    VENDORS CROSS JOIN ONLINE_SUBSCRIBERS;
```

Note the use of the keywords CROSS and JOIN.

Is this useful? I don't think so. Even the Oracle Corporation's *SQL Language Reference Manual* refers to a Cartesian product as "rarely useful". (See the *SQL Language Reference Manual*, for Oracle Database Release 11.1, pages 9–11—of all things.) The most important take-away on this topic is simple: always be sure to include a join condition in your queries. If you don't, Oracle won't complain; it will just deluge you with exponentially many more rows of output than you probably anticipated. So watch it.

A few things to consider with Cartesian products:

- They are mentioned in the certification exam objectives.
- There are generally considered to be a "mistake" in professional applications.
- If you ever find a reasonable use for one, please let me know at soh@corbinian.com. The first person to notify me of such an application will win $10 in cash from me.

That being said, they are on the exam, so know the term and the functionality.

CERTIFICATION SUMMARY

There are several ways to join tables in SQL. The *inner join* compares common values in rows of two or more tables and returns data from a row only if that row has a match in the joined table. The *outer join* will show a row as output whether that row has a joined row in another table or not.

Some joins are equijoins, which means that they join rows in one table with rows in another table by looking for values in both rows that are equal to each other. Non-equijoins look for values that have some relationship other than equality, such as greater than, less than, or in between a range of values.

Primary key and foreign key relationships help to protect the integrity of data in columns that are intended to join tables, but their presence is not required in order to create a successful join.

When two or more tables are joined, any of their columns may be included in the SELECT statement's select list. However, a syntax error may result if the two tables have columns that share the same name. In such situations, the table name can be placed in front of the column name as a prefix to eliminate any ambiguity. As an alternative, the table can be assigned an alias name that will last only long enough for the SELECT statement to execute. The alias can then be used as a prefix in front of any column name, and it may be required in front of the otherwise ambiguous column names.

A natural join does not specify which columns are being used to connect two or more tables together, relying instead on the assumption that the columns to form the join have the same name as each other. Natural joins are inner joins.

The USING keyword can do something similar to NATURAL, but for other forms of joins, including outer joins. USING can name the common column one time, and the SELECT statement will complete the join based on that column, as well as eliminating the need for a table prefix or alias in front of the key column.

Multi-table joins can be performed with any join.

Non-equijoins use comparison operators, Boolean logic, and anything else to establish comparison logic between two or more tables in a join.

A self-join occurs when a table is joined to itself. Typically one column in the table is joined to a different column in the same table.

A Cartesian product results when two tables are listed in the FROM clause of a SELECT statement, but no join criteria are provided. SQL will accept the statement and execute it, joining each row in one table with every row in the other table. The results are rarely useful.

TWO-MINUTE DRILL

Write SELECT Statements to Access Data from More Than One Table Using Equijoins and Non-Equijoins/View Data That Generally Does Not Meet a Join Condition by Using Outer Joins

❑ A join is any SELECT statement that selects from two or more tables.

❑ A join will connect rows in one table with rows in another table.

❑ The equijoin identifies a particular column in one table's rows, and relates that column to another table's rows, and looks for equal values in order to join pairs of rows together.

❑ The non-equijoin differs from the equijoin in that it doesn't look for exact matches but instead looks for relative matches, such as one table's value that is between two values in the second table.

❑ The inner join compares a row in one table to rows in another table and only produces output from the first row if a matching row in the second table is found.

❑ The outer join compares rows in two tables and produces output whether there is a matching row or not—the left outer join shows all the rows in one table and only the matching rows in the second; the right outer join does the same thing in reverse; the full outer join shows all rows in both tables one way or the other—either as a matched rowset or as a standalone row.

❑ The table alias only exists for the duration of the SQL statement in which it is declared.

❑ Table aliases are necessary to eliminate ambiguity in referring to columns of the same name in a join.

❑ The natural join does not name the connecting column but assumes that two or more tables have columns with identical names, and that these are intended to be the connecting, or joining, columns.

❑ The USING keyword can empower an inner, outer, or other join to connect based on a set of commonly named columns, in much the same fashion as a natural join.

❑ Joins can connect two, three, or more tables.

Join a Table to Itself by Using a Self-Join

- ❑ The self-join connects a table to itself.
- ❑ Self-joins typically connect a column in a table with another column in the same table.
- ❑ Self-joins can also be referred to as recursive joins.
- ❑ Self-joins can otherwise behave as equijoins, non-equijoins, inner joins, and outer joins.

Generate a Cartesian Product of All Rows from Two or More Tables

- ❑ The Cartesian product is also known as a cross-join.
- ❑ The cross-join connects every row in one table with every row in the other table.
- ❑ It is created by selecting from two or more tables without a join condition of any kind.
- ❑ The Cartesian product is rarely useful.

SELF TEST

The following questions will help you measure your understanding of the material presented in this chapter. Choose all the correct answers for each question.

Write SELECT Statements to Access Data from More Than One Table Using Equijoins and Non-Equijoins/View Data That Generally Does Not Meet a Join Condition by Using Outer Joins

I. Review the INVOICES and VENDORS tables:

```
                    VENDORS
P  *  VENDOR_ID         NUMBER
      VENDOR_NAME       VARCHAR2 (20 BYTE)
      STATUS            NUMBER (3)
      CATEGORY          VARCHAR2 (10 BYTE)

   PK_VENDOR_ID
```

```
                    INVOICES
P  *  INVOICE_ID         NUMBER
      INVOICE_DATE       DATE
      ACCOUNT_NUMBER     VARCHAR2 (80 BYTE)
      TERMS_OF_DISCOUNT  VARCHAR2 (20 BYTE)
F     VENDOR_ID          NUMBER
      TOTAL_PRICE        NUMBER (8,2)
      SHIPPING_DATE      DATE

   PK_INVOICE_ID
```

Which of the following is a syntactically correct outer join query? (Choose two.)

A. SELECT VENDOR_NAME, INVOICE_DATE
   FROM   VENDORS LEFT JOIN INVOICES
   ON   VENDORS.VENDOR_ID = INVOICES.VENDOR_ID;

B. SELECT VENDOR_NAME, INVOICE_DATE
   FROM   VENDORS OUTER JOIN INVOICES
   ON   VENDORS.VENDOR_ID = INVOICES.VENDOR_ID;

C. SELECT VENDOR_NAME, INVOICE_DATE
   FROM   VENDORS RIGHT OUTER JOIN INVOICES
   ON   VENDORS.VENDOR_ID = INVOICES.VENDOR_ID;

D. SELECT VENDOR_NAME, INVOICE_DATE
   FROM   VENDORS FULL OUTER INVOICES
   ON   VENDORS.VENDOR_ID = INVOICES.VENDOR_ID;

2. You have two tables. One table is called CUSTOMERS. Another is called PURCHASES, and it records a list of customer transactions. Your goal is to create a SELECT statement that will show all customers by last name in alphabetical order, along with any purchases they may have made in the past two weeks as recorded in the PURCHASES table. It's possible that many customers have made no purchases in the past two weeks, but you still want them included in the output. Both tables contain a column called CUSTOMER_ID. Which of the following will be true of the SELECT statement you'll need to create? (Choose two.)

 A. It will be an inner join.
 B. It will be an outer join.
 C. It will be a cross-join.
 D. It will be an equijoin.

3. Review the SQL statement:

```
SELECT    V.VENDOR_ID, INV.INVOICE_DATE
FROM      VENDORS V INNER JOIN INVOICES INV
ON        V.VENDOR_ID = INV.VENDOR_ID;
```

Which one of the following keywords in this statement is optional?

 A. JOIN
 B. INNER
 C. ON
 D. All are required

4. Review the illustration from question 1 and then review the SQL statement (line numbers added):

```
01  SELECT VENDOR_ID, INVOICE_DATE, TOTAL_PRICE
02  FROM   VENDORS JOIN INVOICES
03  USING (VENDOR_ID);
```

Which of the following statements is true for the SQL statement?

 A. It will execute successfully.
 B. It will fail with a syntax error because there is no ON clause.
 C. It will fail with a syntax error on line 1 because VENDOR_ID is ambiguous.
 D. It will fail with a syntax error on line 3 because of the parentheses around VENDOR_ID.

5. Review the illustration from question 1 and then review the SQL statement (line numbers added):

```
01  SELECT VENDOR_ID, INVOICE_DATE, TOTAL_PRICE
02  FROM   VENDORS JOIN INVOICES
03  USING (VENDOR_ID);
```

What kind of join is this? (Choose two.)

A. INNER
B. OUTER
C. NATURAL
D. Equijoin

6. A table alias: (Choose two.)

A. Renames a table in the database so that future joins can use the new name.

B. Is the same thing as a SYNONYM.

C. Exists only for the SQL statement that declared it.

D. Can be used to clear up ambiguity in the query.

7. Review the POSITIONS, EMPLOYEES, and PAY_HISTORY tables:

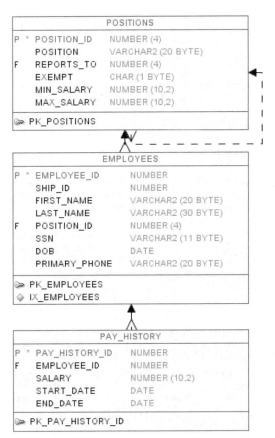

Review the following SQL statement:

```
SELECT LAST_NAME, POSITION, SALARY
FROM   POSITIONS P JOIN EMPLOYEES   E  ON P.POSITION_ID = E.POSITION_ID
                   JOIN PAY_HISTORY PH ON E.EMPLOYEE_ID = PH.EMPLOYEE_ID;
```

Which of the following is true for the SQL statement: (Choose two.)

A. It will fail because there are no table aliases.

B. It will execute successfully.

C. It is an outer join.

D. It connects three tables.

8. Review the illustration from question 7 and then review the following SQL statement (line numbers added):

```
01  SELECT A.EMPLOYEE_ID, B.POSITION
02  FROM   PAY_HISTORY A JOIN POSITIONS B
03     ON  A.SALARY < B.MAX_SALARY AND A.SALARY > B.MIN_SALARY;
```

Which of the following statements accurately describe the SQL statement? (Choose two.)

A. It contains a syntax error on line 3.

B. It is an inner join.

C. It is a non-equijoin.

D. It contains a syntax error on line 2, and should have an additional keyword with the JOIN keyword.

9. How many tables can be included in a JOIN?

A. Only two

B. As many as you like, provided they are all constrained with PRIMARY KEY and FOREIGN KEY constraints to ensure that the join condition will work

C. Two, three, or more

D. No more than seven

10. The difference between an INNER and an OUTER join is:

A. The INNER join relates a table to itself; the OUTER join relates a table to other tables.

B. The INNER join displays rows that match in all joined tables; the OUTER join shows data that doesn't necessarily match.

C. The OUTER join relates a table to tables in other user accounts; the INNER does not.

D. The INNER runs on data inside the table; the OUTER runs on data outside of the table.

Join a Table to Itself by Using a Self-Join

11. A self-join is: (Choose two.)

   A. A SELECT statement that specifies one table once in the FROM clause

   B. A SELECT statement that specifies one table twice in the FROM clause

   C. A SELECT statement that joins a table to itself by connecting a column in the table to a different column in the same table

   D. A SELECT statement that uses the SELF JOIN keywords

12. Review the illustration from question 7. Which of the following is a valid self-join statement? (Choose all that apply.)

   A.
```
SELECT P1.POSITION_ID, P1.MIN_SALARY, P1.MAX_SALARY
FROM    POSITIONS P1 JOIN POSITIONS P2
ON      P1.REPORTS_TO = P2.POSITION_ID;
```

   B.
```
SELECT P1.POSITION_ID, P1.MIN_SALARY, P1.MAX_SALARY
FROM    POSITIONS P1 SELF JOIN POSITIONS P2
ON      P1.REPORTS_TO = P2.POSITION_ID;
```

   C.
```
SELECT P1.POSITION_ID, P1.MIN_SALARY, P1.MAX_SALARY
FROM    POSITIONS P1 INNER JOIN POSITIONS P2
ON      P1.REPORTS_TO = P2.POSITION_ID;
```

   D.
```
SELECT P1.POSITION_ID, P1.MIN_SALARY, P1.MAX_SALARY
FROM    POSITIONS P1 RIGHT OUTER JOIN POSITIONS P2
ON      P1.REPORTS_TO = P2.POSITION_ID;
```

Generate a Cartesian Product of All Rows from Two or More Tables

13. Review the following SQL statement:

```
SELECT *
FROM    INSTRUCTORS CROSS JOIN SCORES;
```

The INSTRUCTORS table contains a total of three rows. The SCORES table contains a total of four rows. How many rows will the SELECT statement return?

   A. 3

   B. 4

   C. 12

   D. There is not enough information to determine the answer

14. Review the illustration from question 1 and the following SELECT statement:

```
SELECT VEN.VENDOR_ID, INV.INVOICE_ID, VEN.VENDOR_NAME
FROM    VENDORS VEN, INVOICES INV;
```

Which of the following best describes the syntax of the SELECT statement?

   A. It is a natural join.

   B. It is rarely useful.

   C. It will not execute due to a syntax error.

   D. It will not execute due to a logic error.

15. What is the defining aspect of a SELECT statement that produces a Cartesian product? (Choose the best answer.)

   A. The lack of any JOIN criteria

   B. The keyword CARTESIAN

   C. A FROM statement that mentions two or more tables, but with no presence elsewhere of the keywords INNER or OUTER

   D. None of the above

SELF TEST ANSWERS

Write SELECT Statements to Access Data from More Than One Table Using Equijoins and Non-Equijoins/View Data That Generally Does Not Meet a Join Condition by Using Outer Joins

1. ☑ **A and C.** The LEFT JOIN . . . ON syntax is correct. So is the RIGHT OUTER JOIN . . . ON syntax. Remember that the keyword OUTER is optional.
   ☒ **B and D** are incorrect. The OUTER . . . ON syntax is incorrect; there is no OUTER by itself. The FULL OUTER . . . ON syntax is also incorrect. In neither of these is the required keyword JOIN present.

2. ☑ **B and D.** The SELECT will have to be an outer join in order to include all records in the CUSTOMERS table whether or not they have a corresponding row in the PURCHASES table in the last two weeks. Also, since both tables contain a CUSTOMER_ID, you'll use an equijoin to locate exact matches between the two tables.
   ☒ **A and C** are incorrect. The query cannot be an inner join, because if it were, it would only show customers who have made purchases in the past two weeks. It cannot be a cross-join, which is a Cartesian product, because all that would do is connect every customer with every purchase without any regard for whether the customer actually made the purchase, or if someone else did.

3. ☑ **B.** INNER is optional. When creating an INNER JOIN, you can just use the term JOIN without the reserved word INNER, and the join will be assumed to be INNER.
   ☒ **A, C, and D** are incorrect. JOIN is required. So is ON.

4. ☑ **A.** It will execute successfully.
   ☒ **B, C, and D** are incorrect. Even though this is a JOIN, the presence of USING eliminates the need for an ON clause. With USING, a table alias is not required, nor is one allowed in the select list. The parentheses around VENDOR_ID on line 3 are fine.

5. ☑ **A and D.** The INNER keyword is optional, but that is what this is by default. It's also an equijoin, in that the two tables are joined by defining values that match equally in the VENDOR_ID column—this is specified by use of the USING clause on line 3, which is equivalent to ON VENDORS.VENDOR_ID = INVOICES.VENDOR_ID.
   ☒ **B and C** are incorrect. It is not an OUTER join; if it were, it would say so. It is not a NATURAL join for the same reason—if it were, it would say so.

6. ☑ **C and D.** The table alias goes away after the query is over. It can be used to clear up confusion in the syntax of a statement by adding it as a prefix at the beginning of any column that shares the same name with another column in a joined table.
   ☒ **A and B** are incorrect. The table alias is not the same as a SYNONYM. The table alias only survives within the SQL statement that calls it; after that, it goes away.

7. ☑ **B and D.** It will execute successfully, and it connects three tables.
☒ **A and C** are incorrect. It does not require table aliases. It is an inner join, not an outer join.

8. ☑ **B and C.** The query is an inner join. The keyword INNER is optional and omitted in this instance. The query is a non-equijoin, wherein the ON condition compares the PAY_HISTORY table's SALARY column of values to the MAX_SALARY and MIN_SALARY of the POSITIONS table.
☒ **A and D** are incorrect. The statement contains no syntax errors.

9. ☑ **C.** You can join as many tables as you wish.
☒ **A, B,** and **D** are incorrect. You are not limited to two tables, nor are you required to only join tables that have constraints on them. You are not limited to seven tables.

10. ☑ **B.** The INNER shows only data when there's a row-to-row match between tables, whereas OUTER can show data for rows in one table that don't match the rows in the joined table.
☒ **A, C,** and **D** are incorrect. Wrong, wrong, wrong.

Join a Table to Itself by Using a Self-Join

11. ☑ **B and C.** In a self-join, the table name is repeated twice in the FROM clause, and perhaps more than twice. A self-join is most commonly used to join a column in a table to a different column within the same table.
☒ **A and D** are incorrect. The self-join syntax names the same name twice—or more—in the FROM clause. There is no syntax in Oracle SQL involving the keywords SELF JOIN.

12. ☑ **A, C,** and **D.** All of these are valid SQL statements. The first is a typical inner join. Answer C spells out the optional word INNER for the same result as Answer A. Answer D defines a valid outer join yet is still a self-join.
☒ **B** is incorrect. There is no keyword SELF, as in SELF JOIN.

Generate a Cartesian Product of All Rows from Two or More Tables

13. ☑ **C.** The SELECT statement is a cross-join, which forms a Cartesian product, since it joins two tables without providing any join criteria. Therefore it will connect each row in the first table with every row in the second table. In other words, the first of the three rows in INSTRUCTORS will be connected with every one of the four rows in SCORES, for a total of four rows. This will be repeated for all three INSTRUCTOR rows, until there are 12 rows of output (3×4).
☒ **A, B,** and **D** are incorrect.

14. ☑ **B.** The SQL statement is a Cartesian product, since no join condition is specified. Oracle's documentation publishes commentary that specifically describes this form of a join as "rarely useful". That being said—Cartesian products are included on the exam.
☒ **A, C,** and **D** are incorrect. The syntax is correct and the statement will execute. It is not a natural join—a natural join uses reserved words such as NATURAL.

15. ☑ **A.** The lack of any JOIN criteria will do it.
☒ **B, C,** and **D** are incorrect. There is no keyword CARTESIAN. The lack of keywords INNER or OUTER has no bearing on whether a query produces a Cartesian product or not.

9
Retrieving Data Using Subqueries

T his chapter looks at subqueries. A *subquery* is a SELECT statement within a larger SQL statement. The subquery concept builds on many of the features we've already looked at, and expands on them in a powerful mechanism that expands the capabilities of SQL. Subqueries introduce some complexities that are important to master. They are an important part of the certification exam.

Define Subqueries

As we've already seen, a query is a SELECT statement. Give that, a subquery is a SELECT statement that exists within another SQL statement—sort of a "sub" SQL statement. SQL statements that accept subqueries include SELECT, INSERT, UPDATE, and DELETE. Subqueries are not limited to DML—they can also be used in a CREATE TABLE or CREATE VIEW statement as well.

Most subqueries are syntactically autonomous, meaning that you could execute the subquery successfully on its own, separate from the parent query. However, some subqueries are not standalone queries but instead are "correlated" to the larger parent query in a way that ties the two queries together.

A subquery is a SELECT statement that may return one or more columns in one or more rows.

A SQL statement that includes a subquery as part of its code is considered the "parent" to the subquery. A parent SQL statement may include one or more subqueries in its syntax. Subqueries may have their own subqueries. In other words, a SQL statement may have a subquery, which in turn may have another subquery within it, and on and on. The starting SQL statement in such a situation is the "top-level" query, and any subsequent subquery that contains a subquery within it is a "parent" to its subquery. A "parent" query may also be referred to as an "outer" query.

Any valid SELECT statement can qualify as a subquery of another statement. The sort of SELECT statements that can be made into a subquery include those that retrieve data from one or more tables or views, those that use complex expressions or scalar or aggregate functions, and those that include the WHERE and GROUP BY clauses, HAVING clauses, joins, or any of the other features available to SELECT statements.

A subquery is not restricted to retrieving data from the same table or tables as the parent query. In fact, subqueries often retrieve data from tables other than those specified in the parent query. The tables of the subquery are not required to have any key relationship or join or other logical relationship to the tables of the parent query. But such a relationship may exist between the parent and the subquery—it's just not required.

Some subqueries can be tied into the parent query. Known as "correlated" subqueries, such statements can achieve single-statement results that cannot otherwise be accomplished by a single statement.

CERTIFICATION OBJECTIVE 9.02

Describe the Types of Problems That Subqueries Can Solve

Subqueries can be used to solve a variety of problems. Some are listed here:

- **Complex multistage queries**   Subqueries can find answers to questions and then use those answers to ask new questions. In other words, in a single SELECT statement's WHERE clause, a subquery can find data based on some criteria, then use that answer to identify a secondary answer, and then pass that answer on to the parent query, all in the same SQL statement. This can be repeated within multiple stages in ways that a standalone parent query cannot do without the use of a subquery.

- **Creating populated tables**   A subquery can be incorporated into a CREATE TABLE statement to quickly create and populate a table from an existing data source at the time the table is created.

- **Large data set manipulation**   Subqueries can be incorporated into an INSERT or UPDATE statement to move large amounts of data and insert or update many rows of information by moving data from one source into another in a single SQL statement.

- **Creating named views**   A subquery is used to create view objects at the time of creation. This topic is explored in Chapter 10 in which we create views.

■ **Dynamic view definition** A subquery can be used to replace a table reference in a FROM clause. This form of subquery, also known as an inline view, is discussed in Chapter 10.

■ **Dynamic expression definition with scalar subqueries** There's a particular form of subquery that will only return one column's worth of data in one row—which is to say, it will return a single value. Such a subquery can be used in almost any place in a SQL statement where an expression can be used.

As you can see, subqueries are powerful, can do a wide variety of tasks, and can occur in almost any SQL statement in almost any clause. This chapter will explore many examples of these usages of subqueries.

CERTIFICATION OBJECTIVE 9.03

List the Types of Subqueries

There are many different types of subqueries. Here are the major types:

■ **Single-row subqueries** A single-row subquery returns a single row's worth of data in its result. Single-row subqueries may include multiple columns' worth of data, or a single column's worth of data.

■ **Multiple-row subqueries** A multiple-row subquery returns zero, one, or more rows in its result. It is not guaranteed to return multiple rows, but it may do so, and thus the parent query should be structured to receive multiple rows just in case. For example, if the parent query uses an equal sign to compare its own value with the returned value of the multiple-row subquery, then the parent query (and therefore the query as a whole) may fail with an execution error—it depends on whether the multiple-row subquery actually returns multiple rows. It might not, but it certainly can at any time. Therefore the parent query to a multirow subquery typically uses a comparison operator that allows for multiple rows of values to be returned.

■ **Multiple-column subqueries** Multiple-column subqueries return more than one column in their result. This requires the parent query to receive multiple columns from the subquery and involves special syntax considerations. A multiple-column subquery can be either a single-row or multiple-row subquery.

■ **Correlated subqueries**   A correlated subquery is a subquery that specifies columns that belong to tables that are also referenced by the parent query. In a multilevel series of subqueries and sub-subqueries, the correlated parent query can be any number of levels higher than the subquery. The correlation involves more than the subquery merely accessing the same tables and columns through its own direct call to the table; rather, the correlated subquery performs row-by-row analysis in cooperation with the parent query, accessing data, and referencing that data in its own expressions, in order to coordinate row processing together with the correlated parent. Correlated subqueries can exist in SELECT, UPDATE, and DELETE statements. A correlated subquery may also be a single-row, multiple-row, or multiple-column subquery.

■ **Scalar subqueries**   If a single-row subquery consists of only one column's worth of output, then it is known as a *scalar subquery*. Scalar subqueries can be used in almost any location that an expression can be used, which is not true for other forms of subquery. A scalar subquery can also be correlated.

Note that the different types of subqueries aren't mutually exclusive. A single type of subquery may fall into multiple categories of subqueries described in this chapter.

As you can see, there are many different types of subqueries. Let's begin looking at them in detail.

CERTIFICATION OBJECTIVE 9.04

Write Single-Row and Multiple-Row Subqueries

In this section, we'll create subqueries that return one expression in either a single-row or multiple-row answer.

Single-Row Subqueries

A single-row subquery is a SELECT statement within another SQL statement. One of its benefits is the ability to perform multiple-step queries in a single SQL statement.

For example, let's say you're tasked with the job of identifying the names of employees of our fictional company, Codd Cruise Lines. You're tasked to look for employees who are assigned to the same ship as an employee named Al Smith. See Figure 9-1 for the ERD of the table we'll work with.

You could perform this task in two steps. Step one: find the SHIP_ID of the ship on which Al Smith is assigned, like this:

```
SELECT  SHIP_ID
FROM    EMPLOYEES
WHERE   LAST_NAME = 'Smith' AND  FIRST_NAME = 'Al';

SHIP_ID
----------------------
1
```

Step two: use the SHIP_ID value to locate other employees on the same ship.

```
SELECT EMPLOYEE_ID, LAST_NAME, FIRST_NAME
FROM    EMPLOYEES
WHERE   SHIP_ID = 1
  AND   NOT (LAST_NAME = 'Smith' AND  FIRST_NAME = 'Al');

EMPLOYEE_ID              LAST_NAME                          FIRST_NAME
--------------------     ------------------------------     --------------------
1                        Hoddlestein                        Howard
7                        Worthington                        Buffy
```

FIGURE 9-1

The EMPLOYEES table

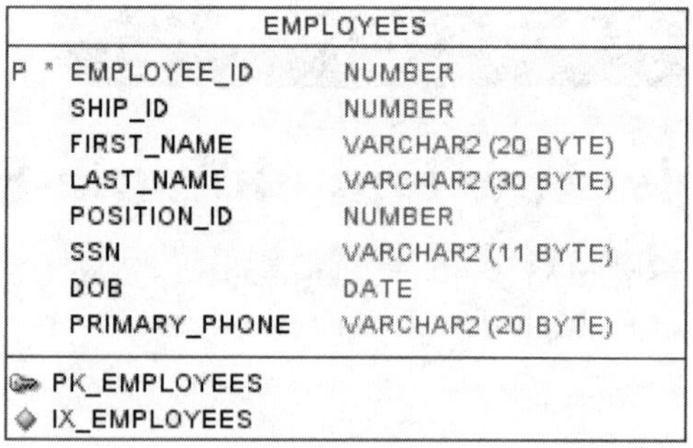

EMPLOYEES		
P * EMPLOYEE_ID	NUMBER	
SHIP_ID	NUMBER	
FIRST_NAME	VARCHAR2 (20 BYTE)	
LAST_NAME	VARCHAR2 (30 BYTE)	
POSITION_ID	NUMBER	
SSN	VARCHAR2 (11 BYTE)	
DOB	DATE	
PRIMARY_PHONE	VARCHAR2 (20 BYTE)	
⬡ PK_EMPLOYEES		
◇ IX_EMPLOYEES		

There's an answer—in two steps. Not bad.

But a subquery could have discovered the answer in one step, like this (line numbers added):

```
01   SELECT EMPLOYEE_ID, LAST_NAME, FIRST_NAME
02   FROM    EMPLOYEES
03   WHERE   SHIP_ID = (SELECT SHIP_ID
04                      FROM    EMPLOYEES
05                      WHERE   LAST_NAME = 'Smith'
06                      AND     FIRST_NAME = 'Al')
07   AND   NOT (LAST_NAME = 'Smith' AND  FIRST_NAME = 'Al');
```

This one query achieves the same thing as the previous two queries. Note what we've done here—we've edited the second of the previous two queries by replacing 'SHIP_ID = 1' with 'SHIP_ID = ' and the subquery on lines 3 through 6. We've literally placed the first of the previous two queries within the second of those two queries.

There is an inherent risk with this particular syntax. Notice the equal sign on line 3. That's the parent query's way of saying that it is expecting one—and only one—row from the subquery. In other words, it is expecting this query to be a single-row subquery.

Here's the problem: what happens if that subquery returns more than one row? What if there is more than one Al Smith in the EMPLOYEES table?

Let's find out—let try searching for employees who work on the same ship as anyone whose last name is 'Smith', regardless of first name:

```
01   SELECT EMPLOYEE_ID, LAST_NAME, FIRST_NAME
02   FROM    EMPLOYEES
03   WHERE   SHIP_ID = (SELECT SHIP_ID
04                      FROM    EMPLOYEES
05                      WHERE   LAST_NAME = 'Smith')
06   AND   NOT (LAST_NAME = 'Smith');

Error starting at line 1 in command:
Error report:
SQL Error: ORA-01427: single-row subquery returns more than one row
01427. 00000 -  "single-row subquery returns more than one row"
```

Notice the text of the error message: "single-row subquery returns more than one row". In other words, we apparently do have more than one person in the EMPLOYEES table with a last name of 'Smith'.

This creates a problem. Our query has an equal sign on line 3, and that's why our subquery is expected to be a "single-row" query.

There are a few alternatives we could take here. If we wish to retain the integrity of the single-row subquery, then we need to edit that subquery to ensure that it will return one, and only one, row.

There are many ways to guarantee a one-row response. For example, a subquery that uses a WHERE criterion based on a primary key or some other unique value will return only one value, like this:

```
SELECT SHIP_ID FROM EMPLOYEES WHERE EMPLOYEE_ID = 5;
```

Of course, that assumes you know the value for the appropriate EMPLOYEE_ID.

Another example would be a subquery that returns an aggregate function without a GROUP BY clause, like this:

```
SELECT MIN(SHIP_ID) FROM EMPLOYEES WHERE LAST_NAME = 'Smith';
```

Aggregate functions always return a single row, as long as no GROUP BY is involved. Logically, though, this isn't always an option to solve the particular business challenge you might be facing.

Still another example would be a subquery that uses the ROWNUM feature to limit the number of rows in the response, like this:

```
SELECT SHIP_ID FROM EMPLOYEES WHERE LAST_NAME = 'Smith' AND ROWNUM < 2;
```

Remember that the ROWNUM pseudocolumn assigns row numbers to the query's output (before processing the ORDER BY clause) and can be effective in limiting output. In this example, it ensures that we only receive a one-row response. But again—this may not logically support the original intent of your query.

These are examples of ways in which you might limit the subquery to one row of output.

The moral of the story: use the single-row subquery when you know the result will be one row. Otherwise, you'd better use something other than the single-row subquery format, or else you'll run the risk of an execution error.

Also—if the subquery returns no rows at all, then no error will result. The query will execute, but the subquery will return a NULL value to the parent query.

on the **Job**

Keep in mind—a failed execution attempt in SQL isn't necessarily a bad thing. Sometimes it's a good idea to create a single-row subquery in situations where you want to deliberately fail the parent query if multiple rows are found in the subquery. This can be a useful feature that can help flag bigger problems elsewhere in the database, such as the failure of a unique identifying mechanism like a primary key, or some other logical error beyond your immediate SQL code. When your SQL statements are embedded within some other programs that have the capabilities of handling failures, or "exceptions" as Oracle PL/SQL calls them, you can program those systems to take evasive or corrective actions and address what might be a much bigger problem.

You can use multiple subqueries within a single WHERE clause. Here's a SQL statement with more than one subquery (line numbers added):

```
01    SELECT EMPLOYEE_ID, LAST_NAME, FIRST_NAME
02    FROM    EMPLOYEES
03    WHERE   SHIP_ID = (SELECT SHIP_ID FROM EMPLOYEES
04                        WHERE LAST_NAME = 'Smith' AND FIRST_NAME = 'Al')
05        AND NOT (LAST_NAME = 'Smith' AND  FIRST_NAME = 'Al')
06        AND SSN    = (SELECT SOCIAL_NUMBER FROM EMP_BENEFITS
07                        WHERE EMP_BENEFITS_ID = 17);
```

Notice in the example what is happening on line 6. In that portion of the query, we are comparing a parent column named SSN to the subquery column called SOCIAL_NUMBER. Subqueries do not have to share the same column name with the parent query. The only thing that is required is that the datatypes for SSN and SOCIAL_NUMBER be the same. If the datatypes match up, the comparison is valid.

The comparison conditions available for use with single-row subqueries are listed in Table 9-1.

TABLE 9-1	Comparison Conditions	Description
Single-Row Subquery Comparison Conditions	=	Equal
	<>	Not equal
	!=	Not equal
	^=	Not equal
	>	Greater than
	>=	Greater than or equal to
	<	Less than

(Continued)

	Comparison Conditions	Description
TABLE 9-1 Single-Row Subquery Comparison Conditions (*Continued*)	<=	Less than or equal to
	LIKE	Enables wildcard characters. There are two wildcard characters: _ The underscore is a wildcard character representing a single character. % The percent sign is a wildcard character representing one or more values.
	IN	Compares one value on the left side of the operator to a set of one or more values on the right side of the operator. The set of values must be enclosed in parentheses. If the values are presented as constants, they are separated by commas, as in ('Maple', 'Elm', 'Main') or (2009, 2010, 2011). A query may also be used, as in (SELECT PORT_NAME FROM PORTS).

The keyword IN deserves special attention. When the keyword IN is used, the parent query sees the subquery as potentially a multiple-row subquery, which we'll discuss in the next section.

So—single-row subqueries are very useful for performing multistep queries when you can guarantee that the subquery will return a single row. But when your subquery returns multiple rows, you need to take a different approach—let's look at that next.

Multiple-Row Subqueries

A multiple-row subquery returns more than one row of answers to the parent query. For example, we saw in our earlier example that there is apparently more than one employee in our EMPLOYEES table with a last name of 'Smith'. Because of that fact, we couldn't use the single-row query format with a subquery that searched for rows with a LAST_NAME value of 'Smith'. But we can use that subquery in the multiple-row format, as shown here (line numbers added):

```
01  SELECT    SHIP_ID, LAST_NAME, FIRST_NAME
02  FROM      EMPLOYEES
03  WHERE     SHIP_ID IN (SELECT SHIP_ID FROM EMPLOYEES WHERE LAST_NAME = 'Smith')
04  ORDER BY  SHIP_ID, LAST_NAME;
```

Now our query is asking to list the employees who work on a ship with anyone named 'Smith', and list the Smiths themselves. But for our purposes, note line 3, where we replaced the equal sign with the reserved word IN. As a result of that one change, we no longer get an error message but instead get this:

```
SHIP_ID                       LAST_NAME                       FIRST_NAME
-----------                   -------------------------       --------------------
1                             Hoddlestein                     Howard
1                             Smith                           Al
1                             Worthington                     Buffy
3                             Lindon                          Alice
3                             Smith                           Joe
```

Remember from our discussion of the WHERE clause and the set of comparison operators that the keyword IN allows the WHERE clause to compare one value to a set of values. The same dynamic is at work here. IN allows the subquery to return multiple rows. The presence of the keyword IN directs the parent query to allow the subquery to be a multiple-row subquery.

Note that the subquery doesn't have to return multiple rows. The presence of IN simply allows for the possibility.

Notice we didn't get an execution error this time. Instead we obtained output and can now see that we have an employee named 'Smith' assigned to SHIP_ID 1, and another on SHIP_ID 3.

The comparison operators that can be used with a multirow subquery are listed in Table 9-2.

TABLE 9-2 Multirow Subquery Comparison Conditions	**Comparison Conditions**	**Description**
	IN	Compares a subject value to a set of values. Returns TRUE if the subject value equals any of the values in the set. Returns FALSE if the subquery returns no rows.
	NOT	Used with IN to reverse the result. Returns TRUE if the subquery returns no rows.
	ANY	Used in combination with single-row comparison conditions (such as = or >) to compare a subject value with a multirow subquery. Returns TRUE if the subject value finds a match consistent with the comparison operator in any of the rows returned by the subquery. Returns FALSE if the subquery returns no rows.
	SOME	Same as ANY.

(Continued)

	Comparison Conditions	Description
TABLE 9-2 Multirow Subquery Comparison Conditions *(Continued)*	ALL	Used in combination with single-row comparison conditions to compare a subject value with a multirow subquery. Returns TRUE if the subject value finds a match consistent with the comparison operator in all of the rows returned by the subquery. Returns TRUE if the subquery returns no rows. Example: Find all products with a price that's greater than all of the products in the 'Luxury' category: SELECT * FROM PRODUCTS WHERE PRICE > ALL (SELECT PRICE FROM PRODUCTS WHERE CATEGORY = 'Luxury');

e x a m

ⓦatch *The use of greater-than or lesser-than comparison conditions does not support multirow subqueries unless combined with ALL, ANY, or SOME. By themselves, they are used with single-row subqueries.*

The keywords shown in Table 9-2 indicate that the parent query is expecting the subquery to be a multirow subquery. A multirow subquery may return anywhere from zero to multiple rows of answers.

CERTIFICATION OBJECTIVE 9.05

Write a Multiple-Column Subquery

The subqueries we've looked at so far compare one value in the parent query with one column's worth of data from a subquery. But it is possible to compare multiple columns at once, as we'll see in this section.

Here's an example of a multiple-column subquery (line numbers added):

```
01   SELECT EMPLOYEE_ID
02   FROM   EMPLOYEES
03   WHERE  (FIRST_NAME, LAST_NAME) IN
04                (SELECT FIRST_NAME, LAST_NAME
05                 FROM CRUISE_CUSTOMERS)
06     AND  SHIP_ID = 1;
```

In this example, we are querying the EMPLOYEES table and looking for the EMPLOYEE_ID of anyone with a first name and last name that matches a customer in the CRUISE_CUSTOMERS table. Notice the syntax:

- The multiple-column list of the parent query is enclosed in parentheses (line 3).
- The columns are separated by commas (line 3).
- The datatypes of the columns must match—meaning that the columns on line 3 must match the datatypes of the columns identified on line 4.

Other than that, everything else is standard. This particular example happens to allow for a multirow subquery (note the IN at the end of line 3) but that is not required for a multiple-column subquery.

The columns in our preceding example share the same name in both the parent query and the subquery. This, however, is not required. All that is required is that the datatypes of the columns match. For example, see the tables in Figure 9-2, and then review this query:

```
01   SELECT  INVOICE_ID
02   FROM    INVOICES
03   WHERE   (INVOICE_DATE, TOTAL_PRICE) =
04                 (SELECT  START_DATE, SALARY
05                    FROM  PAY_HISTORY
06                    WHERE  PAY_HISTORY_ID = 4);
```

FIGURE 9-2

The INVOICES and PAY_ HISTORY tables

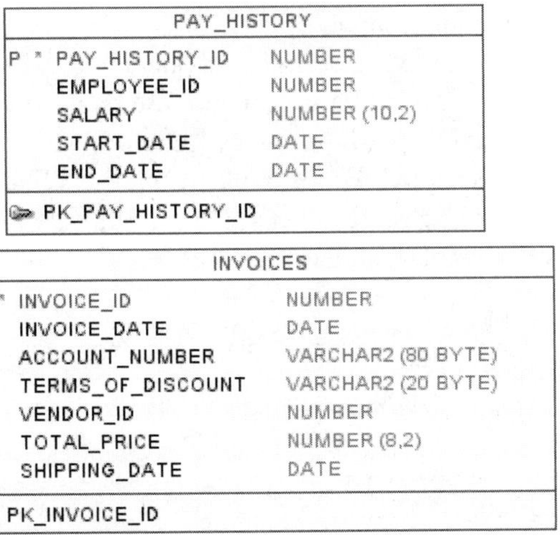

PAY_HISTORY		
P * PAY_HISTORY_ID	NUMBER	
EMPLOYEE_ID	NUMBER	
SALARY	NUMBER (10,2)	
START_DATE	DATE	
END_DATE	DATE	
PK_PAY_HISTORY_ID		

INVOICES		
P * INVOICE_ID	NUMBER	
INVOICE_DATE	DATE	
ACCOUNT_NUMBER	VARCHAR2 (80 BYTE)	
TERMS_OF_DISCOUNT	VARCHAR2 (20 BYTE)	
VENDOR_ID	NUMBER	
TOTAL_PRICE	NUMBER (8,2)	
SHIPPING_DATE	DATE	
PK_INVOICE_ID		

ⓦ**atch** *A correlated subquery can include multiple expressions in the select list, as long as the parent query compares its results to the same number of expressions, each of which must have a matching datatype.*

In this query, we compare the values of the INVOICES table's INVOICE_DATE and TOTAL_PRICE columns with the START_DATE and SALARY columns in the PAY_HISTORY table. The column names don't match, but the datatypes do.

As we've seen, a multiple-column subquery can compare two or more columns at once. The comparisons are subject to the same rules and restrictions involving single-row and multiple-row subqueries. The column names involved don't need to have the same names, but they do need to have the same datatypes, or comparable datatypes such that automatic datatype conversion is capable of making them the same datatypes.

CERTIFICATION OBJECTIVE 9.06

Use Scalar Subqueries in SQL

A scalar subquery returns one row with one column. In other words, it returns one column of data within one row, all the time. The scalar subquery is a single-row, single-column subquery.

We can use this sort of a subquery in a WHERE clause, and we've already seen how that works. But we can also use this particular type of subquery in many other locations. You can use a scalar subquery within most any place that you can use any valid expression. For example, recall the VENDORS and INVOICES tables from Chapter 8's Self Test. Let's create a SELECT statement that demonstrates one of the uses of a scalar subquery:

```
SELECT    VENDOR_NAME,
          (SELECT TERMS_OF_DISCOUNT FROM INVOICES WHERE INVOICE_ID = 1) AS DISCOUNT
FROM      VENDORS
ORDER BY VENDOR_NAME;

VENDOR_NAME             DISCOUNT
-------------------     --------------------
Acme Poker Chips        2 pct on 30
Acme Steaks             2 pct on 30
```

In this example, we've placed the scalar subquery as a second expression within the SELECT statement's select list. We've also chosen to give a column alias to this second item in the select list. Notice the output—the data under the DISCOUNT column heading is the result of our scalar subquery.

Scalar subqueries must always be enclosed in parentheses. If the parent query in which it is being included already has a set of parentheses present, the scalar subquery will still require its own set of parentheses—they are an integral part of the scalar subquery's syntax.

Scalar subquery expressions cannot be used in the following locations:

- In CHECK constraints
- In GROUP BY clauses
- In HAVING clauses
- In a function-based index (which is coming up in Chapter 11)
- As a DEFAULT value for a column
- In the RETURNING clause of any DML statement
- In the WHEN conditions of CASE
- In the START WITH and CONNECT BY clauses, which we discuss in Chapter 16.

Other than that, they can be used anywhere you would use an expression.

exam

ⓦatch

Heads up—the topic of scalar subqueries is featured on the exam. You should be comfortable with all the various places in which the scalar subquery can be used—and cannot be used. Get familiar with the syntax and usage, and you'll improve your odds of success on the exam.

Scalar subqueries are not limited to SELECT statements. Here's an example of a scalar subquery within an INSERT statement (line numbers added):

```
01   INSERT INTO EMPLOYEES
02      (   EMPLOYEE_ID,
03          SHIP_ID)
04   VALUES
05      (   SEQ_EMPLOYEE_ID.NEXTVAL,
06          (SELECT SHIP_ID FROM SHIPS WHERE SHIP_NAME = 'Codd Champion')
07      );
```

In this SQL statement, a scalar subquery is used at line 6 to extract a value from the table SHIPS to include in the INSERT statement for EMPLOYEES. Remember: anywhere a valid SQL expression can be used, a scalar subquery can probably be used as well, subject to the limitations just listed.

Note that if a scalar subquery that returns no value—in other words, NULL—is used in an UPDATE or INSERT to assign value, it will assign NULL.

CERTIFICATION OBJECTIVE 9.07

Solve Problems with Correlated Subqueries

A correlated subquery is a query that is integrated with a parent query. Correlated subqueries include references to elements of a parent query, and thus, they do not exist as standalone queries, as do the examples we've seen so far. Up to now, any of the subqueries we've looked at could be executed on their own. That's not the case with a correlated subquery.

Let's take a look at an example using the SHIP_CABINS table. Back in Chapter 7, we saw the SHIP_CABINS table in Figure 7-2, along with a data listing showing the 12 rows of information in our sample table. Each row in SHIP_CABINS shows that a cabin is of ROOM_STYLE 'Suite' or 'Stateroom'. Each individual room's value for SQ_FT is shown, and they are not all the same.

Our current challenge is to create a single query that lists all the cabins in the ship whose size—as measured by the SQ_FT column—is larger than the average cabin for its ROOM_STYLE.

In other words, we need to

- Identify the average square footage for each ROOM_STYLE in SHIP_CABINS, and then use that value to
- Display each ship cabin whose SQ_FT is greater than the average for its ROOM_STYLE.

Without a correlated subquery, we'd be required to create separate queries to get this information. We would need

- One query to get the averages
- Another query—or queries—to compare the individual averages for each ROOM_STYLE

But with a correlated subquery, we can do it all at once. Here's the SQL:

```
01    SELECT    A.SHIP_CABIN_ID, A.ROOM_STYLE, A.ROOM_NUMBER, A.SQ_FT
02    FROM      SHIP_CABINS A
03    WHERE     A.SQ_FT > (SELECT AVG(SQ_FT)
04                         FROM   SHIP_CABINS
05                         WHERE  ROOM_STYLE = A.ROOM_STYLE)
06    ORDER BY A.ROOM_NUMBER;
```

Note the subquery that starts on line 3 and continues through and including line 5. In particular, note the second ROOM_STYLE at the end of line 5. See the table alias of 'A'? That is a reference to a column of the parent query—not the subquery. See line 2 to confirm that the parent query's table is aliased with the 'A' prefix.

This is the "correlation" in this "correlated subquery". This query is not executing as a standalone query and then passing back its result, as non-correlated subqueries do. Instead, the correlated subquery is executing once for each value that the parent query finds for each row, passing the value for the ROOM_STYLE column into the subquery and determining the average square footage for that particular ROOM_STYLE. Finally, it uses the result of that query in line 3 to determine if the row in the parent query is greater than the average of SQ_FT for the ROOM_TYPE, or not.

Here's the output:

```
SHIP_CABIN_ID          ROOM_STYLE ROOM_NUMBER SQ_FT
---------------------  ---------- ----------- ----------------------
4                      Stateroom  105         205
6                      Suite      107         1524
7                      Stateroom  108         211
9                      Stateroom  110         225
10                     Suite      702         1142
11                     Suite      703         1745
```

One way to validate these results would be to get a list of each ROOM_STYLE and its average value for SQ_FT. Here's a query to calculate that information:

```
SELECT    ROOM_STYLE, AVG(SQ_FT)
FROM      SHIP_CABINS
GROUP BY ROOM_STYLE;

ROOM_STYLE AVG(SQ_FT)
---------- ----------------------
Suite      969.285714285714285714285714285714
Stateroom  196.2
```

This output confirms the average SQ_FT for each ROOM_STYLE, information we could use to go back and confirm that our correlated subquery only displayed room numbers whose individual SQ_FT values are higher than the average for the appropriate ROOM_STYLE. And they are.

Correlated subqueries can exist in SELECT, UPDATE, and DELETE statements. They are "correlated" by way of a column reference from the parent query within the subquery.

A table alias is not necessarily required in the subquery if no column name conflict exists. In our example, there was such a conflict, so we were required to use a table alias. But that's not necessarily required in any correlated subquery. We could have just referenced any column from the parent query, and as long as there isn't an identically named column in the subquery, no table alias is required.

Its important to note that correlated subqueries may introduce performance degradation into a query. The process of correlating rows from one or more subqueries with the outer, or parent, query or queries may consume a significant amount of processing time. However, sometimes a correlated subquery can accomplish tasks that no other form of query may accomplish.

CERTIFICATION OBJECTIVE 9.08

Update and Delete Rows Using Correlated Subqueries

Let's look at the use of correlated subqueries in an UPDATE statement and a DELETE statement.

UPDATE with a Correlated Subquery

An UPDATE statement can have a correlated subquery:

- In the SET clause
- In the WHERE clause

As we saw in the preceding section, the correlated subquery will require some way to identify an expression as being from the parent query. The most common way to do this is to assign a table alias to the table name in the UPDATE and then use that same table alias within the correlated subquery.

Let's look at an example. First, review the INVOICES table that we saw earlier, in Figure 9-2. Our task is to go back to our historical invoices and give a 10 percent discount to whoever placed our single biggest invoice for their respective quarter. So in the first quarter, we need to find the single biggest invoice and determine a 10 percent discount on that invoice, then do the same thing for the second quarter, and so on.

To accomplish this feat, we'll need to modify the invoice so that we change the value in the INVOICES table's TERMS_OF_DISCOUNT column to the string '10 PCT'—and only for the appropriate invoice record. And we'll need to

- Identify the row with the highest value for TOTAL_PRICE for any given quarter, which we can identify using the TO_CHAR format mask 'Q' on the ORDER_DATE column.

- Update an invoice only if it has the highest TOTAL_PRICE for the quarter.

Here's an UPDATE statement that does the trick:

```
01    UPDATE INVOICES INV
02       SET TERMS_OF_DISCOUNT = '10 PCT'
03     WHERE TOTAL_PRICE = (SELECT MAX(TOTAL_PRICE)
04                          FROM   INVOICES
05                          WHERE  TO_CHAR(INVOICE_DATE, 'RRRR-Q') =
06                                 TO_CHAR(INV.INVOICE_DATE, 'RRRR-Q'));
```

Notice the following items in the preceding query:

- We choose to create a table alias "INV" which is declared at the end of line 1 and referenced in line 6.

- The subquery starts in line 3 and runs through line 6.

- The correlation occurs in lines 5 and 6, where the subquery's reference to INVOICE_DATE is compared to the parent query's INV.INVOICE_DATE. The comparison is performed by converting both dates to the 'RRRR-Q' format, which means the year and quarter, so that, for example, the date '31-MAY-11' would convert to '2011-2'.

- On line 3 is the comparison between the parent query and the subquery, which is an equal sign, indicating that the parent query is expecting a single-row subquery. Given that the subquery is returning the aggregate value MAX for TOTAL_PRICE, and no GROUP BY is involved in the subquery, then the subquery will indeed return no more than one row.

Here is an example of a correlated subquery used in the SET clause of an UPDATE statement:

```
01    UPDATE PORTS P
02    SET    CAPACITY = (SELECT COUNT(*)
03                         FROM SHIPS
04                         WHERE HOME_PORT_ID = P.PORT_ID)
05    WHERE  EXISTS (SELECT *
06                     FROM SHIPS
07                     WHERE HOME_PORT_ID = P.PORT_ID);
```

In the preceding code, we do the following:

Lines 5 through 7: We look for records in the PORTS table that any ship calls its home port, by way of the HOME_PORT_ID column. We use the keyword EXISTS, which we'll review in the very next section, but for now—know that EXISTS tells us quite simply if there are any rows returned by the subquery at all. In other words, we're simply asking if there are any rows in SHIPS that contain a value for HOME_PORT_ ID that corresponds to a given row in the parent UPDATE statement's PORTS table. If yes, the subquery returns a TRUE.

Lines 2 through 4: Then, if we find such PORTS, we update their capacity to equal the total number of ships in the SHIPS table currently calling that port home—this is accomplished in the correlated subquery that counts the number of records in SHIPS that share the same HOME_PORT_ID value with the parent UPDATE.

Note that this example of an UPDATE uses two correlated subqueries—both of the subqueries are correlated, because both include the P.PORT_ID reference in their WHERE clauses, on lines 4 and 7.

on the
Ụ o b

Note that a subquery of the form SELECT COUNT(*) FROM TABLE will always be a single-row subquery. If no rows are found, the subquery returns a single row with a value of zero. If multiple rows exist in the table, the subquery returns a single row with a value representing the number of rows found. This is true for queries using the COUNT function, but not for queries using other aggregates, such as AVG, MIN, MAN, or SUM. This is unique to COUNT.

Next we'll look at how we can use correlated subqueries in a DELETE statement.

DELETE with a Correlated Subquery

The DELETE statement can be used with a correlated subquery in the WHERE clause to determine which rows to delete from a given table. The syntax is similar to the correlated subquery syntax for SELECT and UPDATE statements.

Let's take a look at a DELETE statement for the SHIP_CABINS table. This DELETE will remove those cabins with the smallest balcony square footage for each ROOM_TYPE and ROOM_STYLE. In other words, for a given ROOM_TYPE of 'Suite' and a ROOM_STYLE of 'Ocean View', we'll remove the row for the cabin with the smallest balcony, and then we'll move on and do the same for the 'Stateroom' with 'Ocean View' that has the smallest balcony, etc. Here's the query (line numbers added):

Correlated subqueries are not limited to the SELECT statement— they can also be used in UPDATE or DELETE statements.

```
01    DELETE FROM SHIP_CABINS S1
02    WHERE  S1.BALCONY_SQ_FT =
03              (SELECT MIN(BALCONY_SQ_FT)
04              FROM   SHIP_CABINS S2
05              WHERE  S1.ROOM_TYPE  = S2.ROOM_TYPE
06              AND    S1.ROOM_STYLE = S2.ROOM_STYLE);
```

Notice that in this example, the correlation involves two columns, in lines 5 and 6.

CERTIFICATION OBJECTIVE 9.09

Use the **EXISTS** and **NOT EXISTS** Operators

The EXISTS keyword tests for the existence of any rows in a subquery. If no rows are found, the answer is FALSE. Otherwise, the subquery returns TRUE. NOT EXISTS reverses the results.

Let's look at an example—the following query looks for PORTS that have any sort of record at all in the SHIPS table with a HOME_PORT_ID value that matches any of the PORT_ID values. Here's the query:

```
01    SELECT PORT_ID, PORT_NAME
02    FROM   PORTS P1
03    WHERE  EXISTS (SELECT *
04                   FROM   SHIPS S1
05                   WHERE  P1.PORT_ID = S1.HOME_PORT_ID);
```

EXISTS does not compare anything to the subquery. There is no "expression equals expression" format with EXISTS. Its syntax is simple: the keywords WHERE EXISTS and the subquery. Nothing more.

Note the keyword EXISTS on line 3. The entire subquery is executed, even though EXISTS need only know whether or not the subquery returns any rows—so beware using EXISTS with subqueries that return large numbers of rows.

It's worth noting that this sort of query is sometimes referred to as a "semijoin". A *semijoin* is a SELECT statement that uses the EXISTS keyword to compare rows in a table with rows in another table.

CERTIFICATION OBJECTIVE 9.10

Use the WITH Clause

You can use the keyword WITH to assign a name to a subquery block. Once the name is assigned, you can reference the name from elsewhere in the query.

WITH is considered a clause of the SELECT statement.

Let's look at an example—we'll use WITH to declare two different subqueries. We'll name one PORT_BOOKINGS and the other DENSEST_PORT (see the following listing, lines 2 and 8), and then invoke both of them by name in a SELECT statement (lines 12 through 14). Here's the code (line numbers added):

```
01    WITH
02      PORT_BOOKINGS AS (
03        SELECT P.PORT_ID, P.PORT_NAME, COUNT(S.SHIP_ID) CT
04        FROM    PORTS P, SHIPS S
05        WHERE   P.PORT_ID  = S.HOME_PORT_ID
06        GROUP BY P.PORT_ID, P.PORT_NAME
07      ),
08      DENSEST_PORT  AS (
09        SELECT MAX MAX_CT
10        FROM    PORT_BOOKINGS
11      )
12    SELECT PORT_NAME
13    FROM    PORT_BOOKINGS
14    WHERE   CT = (SELECT MAX_CT FROM DENSEST_PORT);
```

Note that neither PORT_BOOKINGS nor DENSEST_PORT is a database object. They are the names of queries that exist solely within this WITH/SELECT statement.

Also note the subqueries on lines 3 through 6, and on lines 9 through 10. Also note that the only semicolon is at the end of the entire statement, not at the end of any individual SQL statement within the overall WITH statement.

Internally, Oracle SQL treats a named query within the WITH clause as a temporary table or as an inline view. (We examine inline views in Chapter 10.)

The WITH clause can be used in the top-level query of a SELECT statement and in many (but not all) subqueries of the SELECT statement, such as shown in line 14. If you use WITH to name a subquery, that name isn't recognized within the subquery itself but is recognized in most every other location in the overall query. In other words, consider line 8, where we name and specify the subquery DENSEST_PORT. We couldn't reference the name DENSEST_PORT in lines 9 through 10, but we can reference the name everywhere else.

CERTIFICATION SUMMARY

A subquery is a SELECT statement that exists within a larger SQL statement. Subqueries may be included in a SELECT, INSERT, UPDATE, or DELETE statement. Subqueries may also be used in a CREATE TABLE statement.

Subqueries can be used in WHERE clauses of SELECT, UPDATE, and DELETE statements. They can be used in the UPDATE . . . SET clause, and the INSERT list of values. Depending on the type of subquery, it may be able to substitute for any expression almost anywhere an expression is accepted, including the select list of a SELECT statement.

Subqueries can perform multiple-step queries in a single SQL statement. They can be used to reference lookup information from a given query. They can populate a table at the time of creation in a CREATE TABLE statement. They are used to create views.

There are many types of subqueries, including single-row, multiple-row, multiple-column, scalar, and correlated.

Single-row subqueries return one row of data to the parent query. Multiple-row subqueries can return anywhere from zero to one to more than one row. Multiple-column subqueries are compared to rows in the parent query using multiple columns at once. Scalar subqueries return one row and one column's worth of data at all times. Correlated subqueries contain conditions in the subquery that connects rows of data with rows in the parent query, much as a join might do.

Single-row subqueries use comparison conditions such as the equal sign or LIKE to compare their results to the parent query. Multiple-row subqueries use comparison conditions such as IN, NOT IN, ANY, and ALL.

The EXISTS keyword can be used to test if a subquery contains any rows whatsoever. NOT EXISTS reverses the results.

The WITH clause can assign names to subqueries temporarily within a given SELECT statement's execution.

TWO-MINUTE DRILL

Define Subqueries

❑ A subquery is a SELECT statement contained within a SQL statement.

❑ The outer SQL statement is called the parent. The outermost level is the top level.

❑ A top-level SQL statement containing a subquery may be a SELECT, INSERT, UPDATE, or DELETE, or else a CREATE TABLE or CREATE VIEW.

❑ Subqueries may be nested within other subqueries.

❑ Many subqueries could function as standalone queries. Some are correlated, meaning that they contain references that tie them into their parent queries.

Describe the Types of Problems That Subqueries Can Solve

❑ A subquery can provide lookup data to assist a parent query in completing a WHERE clause or something comparable.

❑ Subqueries can help combine multiple steps into a single query, reducing what otherwise might be several consecutive SQL statements into a single statement.

❑ Subqueries in a CREATE TABLE or INSERT or UPDATE statement can draw from data from the database to populate database objects quickly.

❑ Subqueries can name queries for subsequent reference.

List the Types of Subqueries

❑ A single-row subquery returns one row of data to the parent query.

❑ A multiple-row subquery may return more than one row of data to the parent query.

❑ Multiple-column subqueries return two or more columns worth of data at once to the parent query, which must test for all of the columns at once.

❑ Correlated subqueries use data from a parent query to determine their own result.

❑ Scalar subqueries always return one value, represented in one column of one row, every time.

❑ The multiple-column subquery may be of the single-row or multiple-row type of subquery.

❑ A correlated subquery might be a single-row, multiple-row, or multiple-column subquery.

Write Single-Row and Multiple-Row Subqueries

❑ The results of a single-row subquery can be compared from within the parent using a scalar comparison operator, such as the equal sign, or the greater-than or less-than sign.

❑ The column names are not required to match in such a comparison, but the datatypes must match, so that the parent query may compare columns of any name to subquery columns of any name, provided the datatypes match.

❑ Multiple-row subqueries are compared differently to the parent query than single-row, using the multiple-row comparison conditions, such as IN, ANY, or ALL, in combination with single-row comparison operators such as >, to avoid getting an execution error message.

Write a Multiple-Column Subquery

❑ Multiple-column subqueries return several columns' worth of data to the parent query all at once.

❑ The parent query must compare all of the columns together; the datatypes of each expression comparison much match between the parent and the subquery.

❑ Multiple-column subqueries may return single-row or multiple-row answers.

Use Scalar Subqueries in SQL

❑ Scalar subqueries return data in the form of one value, in one column's worth of one row.

❑ Scalar subqueries may be used almost anywhere that any expression could be used.

Solve Problems with Correlated Subqueries

❑ Correlated subqueries use data from the parent in subquery predicates to determine what data to return to the parent query.

❑ Correlated subqueries may present some performance degradation; however, they can perform tasks that could not otherwise be accomplished in a single query.

Update and Delete Rows Using Correlated Subqueries

❑ The UPDATE and DELETE statements can use correlated subqueries.

❑ The UPDATE can use correlated subqueries in the SET or the WHERE clause.

❑ The DELETE statement can use correlated subqueries in the WHERE clause.

Use the EXISTS and NOT EXISTS Operators

❑ The EXISTS operator can be used by a parent query to test a subquery and determine if it returns any rows at all.

❑ NOT EXISTS reverses the findings of EXISTS.

Use the WITH Clause

❑ The WITH clause can dynamically name a subquery so that the SELECT statement following the WITH clause can reference that subquery by name, treating it as a dynamic table in real time.

❑ Any subquery names assigned within the WITH clause are only good for that statement; they are not stored in the database.

SELF TEST

The following questions will help you measure your understanding of the material presented in this chapter. Choose one correct answer for each question unless otherwise directed.

Define Subqueries

1. Which of the following forms of subquery never returns more than one row?
   A. Scalar
   B. Correlated
   C. Multiple-column
   D. None of the above

Describe the Types of Problems That Subqueries Can Solve

2. Which of the following can be accomplished with a subquery?
   A. Populate a new table at the time it is created with new data.
   B. Populate a new table at the time it is created with data found elsewhere in the database.
   C. Populate an existing table with new data not curently in the database.
   D. None of the above.

List the Types of Subqueries

3. Which of the following statements is true? (Choose two.)
   A. A single-row subquery can also be a multiple-row subquery.
   B. A single-row subquery can also be a multiple-column subquery.
   C. A scalar subquery can also be a multiple-column subquery.
   D. A correlated subquery can also be a single-row subquery.

4. A subquery that includes references back to the parent query, and thus cannot execute as a standalone query, is: (Choose the best answer.)
   A. A scalar subquery
   B. A correlated subquery
   C. A multiple-column subquery
   D. A referential subquery

Write Single-Row and Multiple-Row Subqueries

5. Which of the following comparison operators may be used with a multiple-row subquery? (Choose two.)

    A. =

    B. >= ALL

    C. LIKE

    D. IN

6. Review the PORTS and SHIPS tables:

PORTS		
P * PORT_ID	NUMBER	
PORT_NAME	VARCHAR2 (20 BYTE)	
COUNTRY	VARCHAR2 (40 BYTE)	
CAPACITY	NUMBER	
PK_PORT		

SHIPS		
P * SHIP_ID	NUMBER	
SHIP_NAME	VARCHAR2 (20 BYTE)	
CAPACITY	NUMBER	
LENGTH	NUMBER	
F HOME_PORT_ID	NUMBER	
PK_SHIP		

Then review the following SQL code (line numbers added):

```
01    SELECT P.COUNTRY, P.CAPACITY
02    FROM   PORTS P
03    WHERE  P.PORT_ID > (SELECT S.HOME_PORT_ID
04                        FROM SHIPS S WHERE S.LENGTH > 900);
```

You know that there are five rows in the SHIPS table with a length greater than 900. What will result from an attempt to execute this SQL statement?

    A. An execution error will result because the subquery will return more than one row and the parent query is expecting only one row from the subquery.

    B. A syntax error will result because PORT_ID and HOME_PORT_ID in line 3 have different column names.

    C. The statement will execute and produce output as intended.

    D. None of the above.

Write a Multiple-Column Subquery

7. Which of the following is true about the multiple-column subquery?

A. Only two columns may be compared between the parent and the subquery.

B. The names of the columns being compared must match.

C. The datatypes of the columns being compared must match.

D. A multiple-column subquery can also be a scalar subquery.

Use Scalar Subqueries in SQL

8. A scalar subquery may *not* be used in which of the following clauses and/or SQL statements?

A. The select list of a SELECT statement

B. The VALUES list of an INSERT statement

C. The SET clause of an UPDATE statement

D. The GROUP BY clause of a SELECT statement

Solve Problems with Correlated Subqueries

9. Review the WORK_HISTORY table:

WORK_HISTORY	
P * WORK_HISTORY_ID	NUMBER
EMPLOYEE_ID	NUMBER
START_DATE	DATE
END_DATE	DATE
SHIP_ID	NUMBER
STATUS	VARCHAR2 (10 BYTE)
⇒ PK_WORK_HISTORY	

Your task is to create a query that will list—for each ship—all of the EMPLOYEE_ID values for all the employees who have the shortest work history for their ship. In other words, if there are two ships, you want to list all of the employees assigned to the first ship who have the shortest work history, and all of the employees assigned to the second ship who have the shortest work history, etc. Which of the following queries will accomplish this task? (Choose two.)

A.
```
SELECT EMPLOYEE_ID FROM WORK_HISTORY W1
WHERE ABS(START_DATE - END_DATE) =
      (SELECT MIN(ABS(START_DATE - END_DATE))
       FROM WORK_HISTORY
       WHERE SHIP_ID = W1.SHIP_ID);
```

B.
```
SELECT EMPLOYEE_ID FROM WORK_HISTORY W1
WHERE ABS(START_DATE - END_DATE) =
      (SELECT MIN(ABS(START_DATE - END_DATE))
       FROM WORK_HISTORY);
```

C.
```
SELECT EMPLOYEE_ID FROM WORK_HISTORY W1
WHERE ABS(START_DATE - END_DATE) <= ALL
      (SELECT ABS(START_DATE - END_DATE)
       FROM WORK_HISTORY
       WHERE SHIP_ID = W1.SHIP_ID);
```

D.
```
SELECT EMPLOYEE_ID FROM WORK_HISTORY W1
WHERE ABS(START_DATE - END_DATE) <
      (SELECT MIN(ABS(START_DATE - END_DATE))
       FROM WORK_HISTORY
       WHERE SHIP_ID = W1.SHIP_ID);
```

10. Review the illustration from question 6. Your team is tasked with the job of creating a list of the ships with the least capacity in each port. In other words, each ship has a home port. For each port that is a home port to ships, which of each port's ships has the least capacity? Your team produces the following query in answer to this task (line numbers added):

```
01    SELECT S1.SHIP_NAME, (SELECT PORT_NAME
02                          FROM    PORTS
03                          WHERE   PORT_ID = S1.HOME_PORT_ID) HOME_PORT
04    FROM    SHIPS S1
05    WHERE   S1.CAPACITY = (SELECT MIN(CAPACITY)
06                          FROM    SHIPS S2
07                          WHERE   S2.HOME_PORT_ID = S1.HOME_PORT_ID);
```

Which of the following statements is true about this SQL statement?

A. The statement will fail with a syntax error because of the subquery on lines 1 through 3.

B. The statement will fail with an execution error because of the subquery on lines 1 through 3.

C. The statement will execute but will return meaningless information.

D. The statement will execute successfully as intended.

Update and Delete Rows Using Correlated Subqueries

11. A correlated subquery may be used in: (Choose three.)
- A. The SET clause of an UPDATE statement
- B. The WHERE clause of an UPDATE statement
- C. The WHERE clause of a DELETE statement
- D. The FROM clause of a DELETE statement

12. Review the illustration from question 6, and the following SQL code:

```
01   UPDATE  PORTS P
02   SET     CAPACITY = CAPACITY + 1
03   WHERE   EXISTS (SELECT *
04                   FROM SHIPS
05                   WHERE HOME_PORT_ID = P.PORT_ID);
```

The PORTS table has 15 rows. The SHIPS table has 20 rows. Each row in PORTS has a unique value for PORT_ID. Each PORT_ID value is represented in the HOME_PORT_ID column of at least one row of the SHIPS table. What can be said of this UPDATE statement?
- A. The value for CAPACITY will increase once for each of the 15 rows in the PORTS table.
- B. The value for CAPACITY will increase by 20 for each of the 15 rows in the PORTS table.
- C. The value for CAPACITY will not increase.
- D. The statement will fail to execute due to an error in the syntax.

Use the EXISTS and NOT EXISTS Operators

13. Another name for an EXISTS query is:
- A. Demijoin
- B. Multiple-column subquery
- C. Cross-join
- D. Semijoin

14. Review the illustration from question 6, and the following SQL code:

```
01   DELETE FROM PORTS P
02   WHERE   PORT_ID NOT EXISTS (SELECT PORT_ID
03                               FROM    SHIPS
04                               WHERE   HOME_PORT_ID = P.PORT_ID);
```

The code is attempting to delete any row in the PORTS table that is not a home port for any ship in the SHIPS table, as indicated by the HOME_PORT_ID column. In other words, only keep the PORTS that are currently the HOME_PORT_ID for a ship in the SHIPS table; get rid of all other PORT rows. That's the intent of the SQL statement. What will result from an attempt to execute the preceding SQL statement?

A. It will fail because of a syntax error on line 2.

B. It will fail because of a syntax error on line 4.

C. It will fail because of an execution error in the subquery.

D. It will execute successfully and perform as intended.

Use the WITH Clause

15. The WITH clause can be used to name a subquery, and: (Choose two.)

A. The name of the subquery can be used in the SELECT statement following the WITH clause.

B. The name of the subquery can be joined to other tables in the SELECT statement following the WITH clause.

C. The name of the subquery is stored in the database by the WITH statement, and can be referenced by other SQL statements in later sessions.

D. The name of the subquery can be invoked from within the subquery that is named.

SELF TEST ANSWERS

Define Subqueries

1. ☑ **A.** Scalar subqueries always return a single value, which is to say it returns one row's worth of data, one column's worth in that one row.
   ☒ **B, C,** and **D** are incorrect. A correlated subquery may or may not return multiple rows. Multiple-column subqueries may or may not return multiple rows.

Describe the Types of Problems That Subqueries Can Solve

2. ☑ **B.** A subquery can be used in a CREATE TABLE statement to populate a new table with data already in existence in the database.
   ☒ **A, C,** and **D** are incorrect. You cannot use a subquery to add new data to the database.

List the Types of Subqueries

3. ☑ **B** and **D.** A single-row subquery may consist of multiple columns in its single row. And it also may be correlated.
   ☒ **A** and **C** are incorrect. A single-row subquery cannot, by definition, also be a multiple-row subquery. Duh. A scalar subquery by definition can only be one column in one row, so it cannot be a multiple-column subquery. Double-duh.

4. ☑ **B.** A correlated subquery is the best answer. The name indicates that the subquery is correlated to the parent query. Technically, "scalar" and "multiple-column" subqueries may also be correlated, but we asked for the "best answer", and clearly that is "correlated subquery".
   ☒ **A, C,** and **D** are incorrect. Technically, a scalar subquery may also be a correlated subquery, which is why the question asked you to pick the "best answer"—the term "correlated" refers specifically to the concept of referring back to the parent query, whereas a scalar subquery refers specifically to a subquery's return value as being a single value. The same is true for a multiple-column subquery—that may also be a correlated subquery, but the term "multiple-column" is intended to emphasize the fact that it returns multiple columns' worth of results at once. Finally, a referential subquery isn't anything; we just made that up.

Write Single-Row and Multiple-Row Subqueries

5. ☑ **B and D.** The ">=ALL" is "greater than all" of the values returned by the subquery, which is ideal for a multiple-row query. The "IN" comparison operator is also useful.
   ☒ **A and C** are incorrect. The "=" sign is restricted only to single-row subqueries. The LIKE operator is also limited to single-row subqueries.

6. ☑ **A.** The query will produce an execution error because the parent query is expecting a single-row answer from the subquery—you know this because of the comparison operator in line 3, the greater-than sign is a single-row comparison operator. The better choice here might be "> ANY" or "> ALL", depending on the situation.
   ☒ **B, C,** and **D** are incorrect. There is nothing wrong with PORT_ID and HOME_PORT_ID having different column names. As long as their datatypes match, all is well, and you know their datatypes match according to the illustration from question 6.

Write a Multiple-Column Subquery

7. ☑ **C.** The datatypes of the columns being compared must match.
   ☒ **A, B,** and **D** are incorrect. Multiple-column subqueries may involve two or more columns. The names of the columns do not have to match, just the datatypes. A multiple-column subquery cannot be a scalar subquery, since, by definition, scalar subqueries return a value of one row and one column, no more.

Use Scalar Subqueries in SQL

8. ☑ **D.** Scalar subqueries may not be used in a GROUP BY clause.
   ☒ **A, B,** and **C** are incorrect. Scalar subqueries are allowed in all of the locations listed in these answers—a SELECT expression list, an INSERT values list, an UPDATE's SET clause. Anywhere an expression can be used, a scalar expression can probably be used—subject to the limitations detailed in the chapter.

Solve Problems with Correlated Subqueries

9. ☑ **A and C.** Answer A is a classic correlated subquery, connecting the subquery to the parent by way of the W1.SHIP_ID value. Answer C also works with the "<= ALL" comparison condition.
   ☒ **B and D** are incorrect. Answer B is missing the join in the subquery that connects the subquery with the parent query. Answer D compares the parent query's WHERE clause value to the subquery with a less-than sign, which won't work—the subquery is already selecting the minimum value from the subquery, so the parent query can't find anything that will be less than the minimum.

10. ☑ **D.** The statement is syntactically fine. The SELECT includes two correlated subqueries. The first, in lines 1 through 3, is an expression in the SELECT statement's select list. This subquery is correlated by way of the reference at the end of line 3. The second correlated subquery is in lines 5 through 7, and it obtains the minimum capacity value for ships belonging to each port.
☒ **A, B,** and **C** are incorrect. The statement will not fail, not with a syntax problem nor with an execution problem. The data it returns is exactly as requested.

Update and Delete Rows Using Correlated Subqueries

11. ☑ **A, B,** and **C.** A correlated subquery may be used in any of these answers.
☒ **D** is incorrect. A correlated subquery cannot be used in the FROM clause of a DELETE statement. Note, however, that the question is asking specifically about correlated subqueries. While you cannot have a correlated subquery in the FROM clause of the DELETE, we'll later see that an "inline view" can be used there, and an "inline view" is essentially a subquery—but not a correlated subquery.

12. ☑ **A.** The CAPACITY will increase once for each row processed by the UPDATE if that row is found in the subquery.
☒ **B, C,** and **D** are incorrect.

Use the EXISTS and NOT EXISTS Operators

13. ☑ **D.** The semijoin is the correct answer.
☒ **A, B,** and **C** are incorrect. There is no such thing as a demijoin. A multiple-column subquery requires several columns on both sides of the comparison condition. A cross-join is a table join with no join criteria.

14. ☑ **A.** It will fail because of a syntax error on line 2—the first reference to PORT_ID should be removed. EXISTS does not compare the subquery to anything. In other words, line 2 should be "WHERE NOT EXISTS (SELECT *", without the first PORT_ID reference. Other than that, everything else about the query is fine.
☒ **B, C,** and **D** are incorrect. Line 4 has no syntax errors. Nor does the subquery contain any execution errors. But neither will the SQL execute, for the reasons we described for the right answer.

Use the WITH Clause

15. ☑ **A and B.** The name can be used in the SELECT following the WITH clause.
☒ **C and D** are incorrect. The name is not stored in the database by the WITH statement. It exists only for the WITH clause itself and is not recognized outside of the WITH clause. The one place within the WITH clause that does not recognize the subquery name is within the named subquery itself.

10
Creating Other Schema Objects

CERTIFICATION OBJECTIVES

T his chapter introduces a number of other schema objects that are necessary to understand in order to create a complete application. These objects include the view, sequence, index, and synonym. Each is uniquely important in a variety of ways.

Create and Use Simple and Complex Views

A *view* is a SELECT statement with a name, stored in the database, and accessible as though it were a table. Earlier you saw the WITH clause that can assign a name to a query within a single SELECT statement. The view object does the same thing in a more permanent manner, meaning that the view object resides in the database alongside tables and other database objects.

Once you've created a view, you can refer to it in SELECT statements as though it were a table. Nothing about the SELECT is different—anyone looking at a given SELECT statement will not be able to determine from the SELECT statement alone if the FROM clause specifies a table or a view.

Views are useful for a variety of reasons. One benefit is security. For example, consider a typical scenario where you have a large table that contains a combination of some sensitive information along with some information that is of a general interest. You might create a view that queries the general interest columns of the large table, then grant privileges on that view to the general population of users. Those users may now query the view, and get direct access to the general information without having access to more sensitive data that exists in the underlying table. Views are a great way to mask certain data while giving access to other data in the same table.

Another benefit to views is their ability to make a complex query easier to work with. For example, you might create a view that is built on a complex join, so that the complexity is built into the view. The result is a view object that appears to be a single table, which you may now query as though it were a table. You can even join the view with other tables and other views. In this situation, a view can be used to simplify the complexity of a commonly used join.

In the next section, we'll create a view object.

Creating Views

Let's look at an example. First, review Figure 10-1. We'll start with just the EMPLOYEES table—notice that it includes columns for employee ID, name, social security number, date of birth, and primary phone number.

So here's a problem: what if you wanted to give access to this table so that other people in the organization can get the phone numbers of employees? Think about that sensitive information, including social security numbers, and you might have second thoughts about having anybody query the EMPLOYEES table.

One solution to this predicament is to use a view. Let's create a view for the EMPLOYEES table:

```
CREATE VIEW VW_EMPLOYEES AS
      SELECT EMPLOYEE_ID, LAST_NAME, FIRST_NAME, PRIMARY_PHONE
      FROM    EMPLOYEES;
```

If we execute this statement in SQL, we'll get the following message:

```
CREATE VIEW succeeded.
```

(Note: this statement is the message displayed by SQL Developer. SQL*Plus will display "View created".)

FIGURE 10-1

Diagrams for the
EMPLOYEES and
PAY_HISTORY
tables

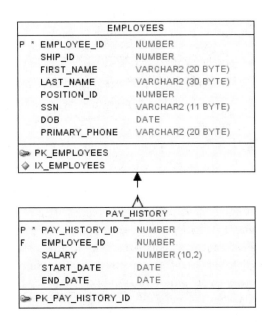

Now that we have this view, we can work with it just as if it were a table. For example, we can DESCRIBE it:

```
DESC VW_EMPLOYEES;
```

```
Name                              Null       Type
------------------------------  --------   -------------
EMPLOYEE_ID                     NOT NULL   NUMBER
LAST_NAME                                  VARCHAR2(30)
FIRST_NAME                                 VARCHAR2(20)
PRIMARY_PHONE                              VARCHAR2(20)
```

Additionally, we can SELECT from it as if it were a table:

```
SELECT * FROM VW_EMPLOYEES;
```

```
SELECT    FIRST_NAME || ' ' || LAST_NAME "Employee"
FROM      VW_EMPLOYEES
ORDER BY PRIMARY_PHONE;
```

The results will display just like any table. Anyone using VW_EMPLOYEES, running SELECT statements on it, describing its structure, doing anything they might wish using SQL commands—may not ever realize it's not a table at all. The fact that it's a view isn't necessarily obvious. We chose to name it with a VW_ prefix for our own purposes, but we could have given it any name we wished.

The syntax rules for creating a view are

- The keywords CREATE VIEW
- The optional keywords OR REPLACE
- A name for the view, specified according to the rules for naming database objects
- The keyword AS
- Finally, a valid SELECT statement, with a few restrictions

One of the requirements of the CREATE VIEW statement is this: the resulting VIEW must have valid column names. This means that if you choose a SELECT statement that incorporates any complex expressions within the select list, each expression must be assigned a column alias, or column names must be assigned by the CREATE VIEW statement itself. For example, let's use the OR REPLACE option to create a new version of our VW_EMPLOYEES view (line numbers added):

```
01  CREATE OR REPLACE VIEW VW_EMPLOYEES AS
02       SELECT EMPLOYEE_ID,
03              LAST_NAME || ', ' || FIRST_NAME,
04              PRIMARY_PHONE
05       FROM   EMPLOYEES;
06
07  Error starting at line 1 in command:
08  CREATE OR REPLACE VIEW VW_EMPLOYEES AS
09       SELECT EMPLOYEE_ID,
10              LAST_NAME || ', ' || FIRST_NAME,
11              PRIMARY_PHONE
12       FROM   EMPLOYEES
13  Error at Command Line:3 Column:33
14  Error report:
15  SQL Error: ORA-00998: must name this expression with a column alias
16  00998. 00000 -  "must name this expression with a column alias"
```

What went wrong? The problem is on line 3, where we specify the expression that forms the second column in our SELECT expression list. Notice that it concatenates the columns LAST_NAME with a comma, a space, and then the FIRST_NAME column. Here's the problem: what is the name of this column? There isn't one assigned, but the CREATE VIEW statement requires one. Therefore—the attempted CREATE VIEW statement fails.

To correct the problem, we can specify column names in the CREATE VIEW statement, like this (line numbers added):

```
01  CREATE OR REPLACE VIEW VW_EMPLOYEES (ID, NAME, PHONE) AS
02       SELECT EMPLOYEE_ID,
03              LAST_NAME || ', ' || FIRST_NAME EMP_NAME,
04              PRIMARY_PHONE
05       FROM   EMPLOYEES;
```

Now we'll have a view consisting of three columns with the names ID, NAME, and PHONE. Alternatively, we could have used a column alias in the SELECT statement.

You can use complex queries to create views. For example, let's go back to Figure 10-1 and build a query that joins data from the PAY_HISTORY table into our view, as follows (line numbers added):

```
01  CREATE VIEW EMP_TREND AS
02    SELECT   EMP.SHIP_ID, MIN(SALARY) MIN_SALARY
03    FROM     EMPLOYEES EMP LEFT JOIN PAY_HISTORY PAY
04    ON       EMP.EMPLOYEE_ID = PAY.EMPLOYEE_ID
05    WHERE    END_DATE IS NULL
06    GROUP BY EMP.SHIP_ID;
```

This statement uses a SELECT statement with a join, a GROUP BY, a WHERE clause, and aggregate functions; it creates a VIEW out of all of it.

VIEW objects can be based on SELECT statements with subqueries, functions, and more.

```
CREATE OR REPLACE VIEW SHIP_ONE_CABINS AS
      SELECT * FROM SHIP_CABINS WHERE SHIP_ID = 1;
```

The view created with this statement will consist only of the rows in the SHIP_ CABINS table where the SHIP_ID value is equal to 1. The SHIP_CABINS table may contain more rows than those with a SHIP_ID of 1, but those rows won't be found by way of any query on the SHIP_ONE_CABINS view.

Also—take note again of the optional keywords OR REPLACE in the CREATE VIEW statement. These words don't work with CREATE TABLE, but they do with CREATE VIEW. Be careful with them—when included, they will give you no warning if you are or are not overwriting some existing view. They will simply overwrite what may have gone before and replace it with the new view. It's a convenient option that is very powerful—so be careful with it. You have been warned.

Views and Constraints

You can create constraints on a view in the same way you can create them on a table. HOWEVER: Oracle doesn't enforce them without special configuration that's available primarily to support certain data warehousing requirements. This subject is worth noting but not specifically addressed on the exam.

Updatable Views

You've seen how we can SELECT from a view. But can we also use INSERT and UPDATE, and DELETE?

The answer is: it depends. If the view contains enough information to satisfy all of the constraints in any underlying tables, then yes, you can use INSERT, UPDATE, or DELETE statements on the view. Otherwise no.

Depending on the nature of the constraints, it may be possible to use some DML statements but not others on the view. For example, if the view fails to include any columns from the underlying table that have NOT NULL constraints, you will not be able to execute an INSERT statement, but you may be able to issue an UPDATE or DELETE statement.

For example, let's revisit the EMPLOYEES table in Figure 10-1. Let's make a new view on that table, like this:

```
CREATE OR REPLACE VIEW EMP_PHONE_BOOK
     AS SELECT LAST_NAME, FIRST_NAME, PRIMARY_PHONE FROM EMPLOYEES;
```

This view contains just enough information to print an employee phone book, including their names and phone numbers. Once we've created this view, we can select from it, like this:

```
SELECT   LAST_NAME, FIRST_NAME, PRIMARY_PHONE
FROM     EMP_PHONE_BOOK
ORDER BY LAST_NAME, FIRST_NAME;
```

Fantastic. But wait—we just hired someone new, her name is Sonia Sotogovernor, and we want to add her name to this view, let's try it:

```
INSERT INTO EMP_PHONE_BOOK (LAST_NAME, FIRST_NAME, PRIMARY_PHONE)
     VALUES ('Sotogovernor', 'Sonia', '212-555-1212');

Error starting at line 1 in command:

INSERT INTO EMP_PHONE_BOOK (LAST_NAME, FIRST_NAME, PRIMARY_PHONE)
     VALUES ('Sotogovernor', 'Sonia', '212-555-1212')

Error report:
SQL Error: ORA-01400: cannot insert NULL into ("EFCODD"."EMPLOYEES"."EMPLOYEE_ID")
01400. 00000 -  "cannot insert NULL into (%s)"
```

Whoops. What's wrong here? See the error message? Remember that our underlying table is the EMPLOYEES table, and it contains a PRIMARY KEY of EMPLOYEE_ID, as we see in Figure 10-1. But our view doesn't include that column. As a result—there is no way for us to INSERT a value through the EMP_PHONE_BOOK view so that it will provide a value for the required column of EMPLOYEE_ID. We cannot execute an INSERT statement on this view.

However, we can execute an UPDATE statement on the view. For example:

```
UPDATE EMP_PHONE_BOOK
   SET PRIMARY_PHONE = '202-555-1212'
WHERE  LAST_NAME  = 'Hoddlestein'
   AND  FIRST_NAME = 'Howard';
```

This statement works perfectly fine on the view. The reason: the changes we're making with this UPDATE statement do not violate any underlying constraints.

If there are any constraints on the underlying table that you cannot possibly honor when attempting to issue an INSERT, UPDATE, or DELETE on a VIEW, then the statement won't work. The VIEW object must provide access to any of the underlying table's columns in such a way that the constraints can be honored in order to satisfy those constraints and execute the statement successfully. Otherwise, the INSERT, UPDATE, or DELETE statement will fail.

In addition, a view that is based on aggregate rows will not be updatable.

You will be prevented from using INSERT, UPDATE, or DELETE if you create a view based on a SELECT statement that includes any of the following:

- Omission of any required columns in that underlying table
- GROUP BY or any other aggregation, such as set operators (which we discuss in Chapter 12) or hierarchical queries (discussed in Chapter 16)
- DISTINCT
- A FROM clause that references more than one table—that is, subqueries in the SELECT, or most joins

Regarding that last item—it is technically possible to execute DML changes on joins where all updatable columns belong to a key-preserved table. The details go beyond the scope of this book. For the most part, you will not be able to issue DML changes to a VIEW object based on a join.

As we've already seen, a view's SELECT statement may include expressions as part of the columns in its formation, such as

```
CREATE OR REPLACE VIEW EMP_PHONE_BOOK
      AS SELECT EMPLOYEE_ID,
                FIRST_NAME || ', ' || LAST_NAME EMP_NAME,
                PRIMARY_PHONE
         FROM EMPLOYEES;
```

Note that the preceding query concatenates the FIRST_NAME and LAST_NAME columns into one expression. As a result, the individual columns cannot be modified with an INSERT or UPDATE statement—there is no way to singularly refer to the individual columns, unless they are added as individual items in the select list. However, EMPLOYEE_ID, the required column, is included as an individual column, so this would be a satisfactory statement:

```
INSERT INTO EMP_PHONE_BOOK (EMPLOYEE_ID, PRIMARY_PHONE)
             VALUES
             (102, '800-555-1212');
```

That statement will successfully execute on our EMP_PHONE_BOOK view and add a new row to the underlying table—assuming the primary key value for EMPLOYEE_ID is accepted as a new unique entry. But we're not able to INSERT a row through the VIEW using an INSERT statement that references the EMP_NAME column alias, nor its component columns FIRST_NAME and LAST_NAME. We simply have to omit any references to those columns in our DML statements for our DML to execute successfully.

We may DELETE a row in this view. For example:

```
DELETE FROM EMP_PHONE_BOOK WHERE EMPLOYEE_ID = 102;
```

This statement will successfully delete the entire row for EMPLOYEE_ID of 102. If we issued a similar DELETE statement for any other existing value we can access—such as PRIMARY_PHONE or EMPLOYEE_ID—and the row were found, then the row—the entire row of the underlying table—would be deleted. That includes data in columns we can't even see with the view. The whole row will delete.

With regard to the general question of using INSERT, UPDATE, and/or DELETE on any given view, the general answer is really very simple: if the view provides row-level (not aggregated) access to one—and only one—table and includes the ability to access the required columns in that table, then you can use INSERT, UPDATE, and/or DELETE on the view to effect changes to the underlying table, in accordance with the restrictions we listed earlier. Otherwise, you may not be able to successfully execute a change to the view's data.

 on the **Job** *Note that the INSTEAD OF trigger in PL/SQL can be used to cause a non-updatable view to behave as though it were updatable. But PL/SQL features are not addressed on the exam.*

Inline Views

An *inline view* is a subquery that is contained within a larger SELECT statement in such a way that it replaces the FROM clause of a SQL statement.

Here's an example (line numbers added):

```
01  SELECT *
02  FROM (SELECT * FROM DUAL);
```

In this example, the inline view is included in the parentheses at the end of line 2.

There is no limit to the number of inline views you can nest within inline views:

```
SELECT * FROM (SELECT * FROM (SELECT * FROM (SELECT * FROM DUAL)));
```

This "unlimited nesting" is different than the limit for typical subqueries, where the limit is 255 nested subqueries.

Inline views can be combined with various complex queries, such as those that use JOIN and GROUP BY clauses and more. For example:

```
01   SELECT A.SHIP_ID, A.COUNT_CABINS, B.COUNT_CRUISES
02   FROM (SELECT    SHIP_ID, COUNT(SHIP_CABIN_ID) COUNT_CABINS
03         FROM      SHIP_CABINS
04         GROUP BY  SHIP_ID) A
05         JOIN
06        (SELECT   SHIP_ID, COUNT(CRUISE_ORDER_ID) COUNT_CRUISES
07         FROM      CRUISE_ORDERS
08         GROUP BY SHIP_ID) B
09   ON    A.SHIP_ID = B.SHIP_ID;
```

This statement is a single SELECT that pulls data from two inline views, one on lines 2 through 4, and the second on lines 6 through 8.

Inline views can be any valid SELECT statement, placed into a SQL statement where the FROM clause would normally go.

One great usage of an inline view is to address an issue involving the pseudocolumn ROWNUM. ROWNUM automatically assigns row numbers to each row in a table. The challenge with ROWNUM is that it assigns numbers before the ORDER BY clause is processed. As a result, you cannot sort rows and then use ROWNUM to number them—the results will be mixed up, since the ROWNUM is computed before the ORDER BY is processed. But you can move the ORDER BY clause into an inline view and then use the ROWNUM pseudocolumn on the outer query to display row numbers correctly. For example:

```
SELECT ROWNUM, INVOICE_ID, ACCOUNT_NUMBER
FROM  (SELECT INVOICE_ID, ACCOUNT_NUMBER
        FROM INVOICES ORDER BY INVOICE_DATE)
WHERE ROWNUM <= 3;
```

ROWNUM	INVOICE_ID	ACCOUNT_NUMBER
1	2	cre-kit-A1233-V01
2	3	ae-TRR
3	4	INV-PR-0101

In this example, we use the ORDER BY in the inline view to sort our rows by INVOICE_DATE, and then we use ROWNUM in the outer query to limit our output to just the first three rows of data. We also include ROWNUM in our select list so that it appears in the output. Without the inline view, odds are that our ROWNUM values would be in an apparently random order, instead of sequential.

on the
Job

So why would you want to use an inline view? There are many reasons. As I've already demonstrated, inline views may be used to create complex joins built on aggregated queries. Another benefit has to do with the nature of dynamic SQL as it's used with third-generation languages. Many popular web sites are built on web pages that are dynamically formed from a combination of Java, PL/SQL, or C++ code that pulls data from the database and merges the output with the languages used to form web pages. A full example of such a scenario is beyond the scope of this book, but it's worth noting that such systems rely heavily on routines that create SQL code dynamically, during execution, in response to queries from end users. Such dynamic scenarios can benefit greatly from the ability to, for example, create a standard outer query in which the inline view can be substituted by dynamic code. An end user may perform a search that might draw data from any number of various sources, yet present the output through a fixed series of data elements. The inline view can support such a situation.

Retrieving Data

Retrieving data from a view is the same as retrieving data from a table. Views behave just like tables, and as such, they can be described, queried, joined, subqueried—in short, for all practical purposes, there is no difference between querying from a view versus querying from a table.

ALTER VIEW

The ALTER VIEW statement is used to accomplish any of the following tasks:

- Create, modify, or drop constraints on a view.
- Recompile an invalid view.

The subject of constraints on a view is not something that is covered on the exam. Oracle does not enforce view constraints without special configuration (see DISABLE NOVALIDATE in Oracle's documentation).

Recompiling a view is a step you may wish to take if you've created a view and then later performed some sort of modification on the underlying table or tables upon which the view is created. Depending on the change you make to the view's source table, the view may be rendered invalid as a result. In Chapter 14 we'll see how you can determine if a view is invalid or not, by querying the data dictionary. An invalid view cannot be used. If a view is invalid, it will require recompilation.

Here is an example of a statement that recompiles a view:

```
ALTER VIEW VW_EMPLOYEES COMPILE;
```

You cannot change a view's SELECT statement with the ALTER VIEW statement. Instead, you must drop and recreate the view.

Once completed successfully, the view is back in working condition. If it does not compile, you know that the change to the underlying table may have fundamentally changed the nature of the VIEW's structure. For example, if a view queries a particular named column from an underlying table, and that column is renamed or dropped, then the recompilation will not work and you may need to recreate the view and reassess your code.

CERTIFICATION OBJECTIVE 10.02

Create, Maintain, and Use Sequences

A *sequence* is an object that is predominantly used for one purpose: to generate data for primary key columns in tables. While that is the primary purpose of a sequence, there's nothing inherent in the structure of a sequence to limit you to such a purpose. You can use a sequence to generate numeric sequences for any reason. But all a sequence does is issue sequentially increasing (or decreasing) numbers, according to the rules you define when you create the sequence.

Creating Sequences

Here's a sample of the SQL statement to create a sequence:

```
CREATE SEQUENCE SEQ_ORDER_ID;
```

This example is a complete statement and represents the simplest form of a CREATE SEQUENCE statement. The syntax is as follows:

- The required CREATE SEQUENCE keywords
- The required name of the sequence that you specify, according to the rules of naming database objects

Note that nothing in the code ties it to a particular table or other database object—nothing, that is, other than perhaps the choice of the name, which is a naming convention we use but is not required.

Here's the complete syntax for a sequence:

```
CREATE SEQUENCE sequence_name sequence_options;
```

There are several *sequence_options* that can each be specified, separated by spaces, as desired. Sequences can be set to start at any number and increment—or decrement—by any number. They can sequentially generate without ceasing or be given a range within which they continuously generate new numbers. They can be given a fixed series of numbers to generate, after which they cease generating numbers.

The sequence options include the following:

- **INCREMENT BY** *integer*　Each new sequence number requested will increment by this number. A negative number indicates the sequence will descend. If omitted, the increment defaults to 1.
- **START WITH** *integer*　Specifies the first number that will start the sequence. If omitted, START WITH defaults to MINVALUE (which we discuss in a bit) for ascending sequences, or MAXVALUE for descending sequences, unless NOMINVALUE or NOMAXVALUE are specified either explicitly or implicitly (by default), in which case START WITH defaults to 1.
- **MAXVALUE** *integer*　Specifies the maximum number for the sequence. If omitted, then NOMAXVALUE is assumed.
- **NOMAXVALUE**　Specifies that there is no MAXVALUE specified.
- **MINVALUE** *integer*　Specifies the minimum number for the sequence. If omitted, NOMINVALUE is assumed, unless a MINVALUE is required by the presence of CYCLE, in which case the default is 1.
- **NOMINVALUE**　Specifies that there is no MINVALUE specified.
- **CYCLE**　When the sequence generator reaches one end of its range, restart at the other end. In other words, in an ascending sequence, once the generated value reaches the MAXVALUE, the next number generated will be the MINVALUE. In a descending sequence, once the generated value reaches the MINVALUE, the number generated will be the MAXVALUE.

■ **NOCYCLE**   When the sequence generator reaches the end of its range, stop generating numbers. NOCYCLE is the default. If no range is specified, NOCYCLE has no effect.

Here's another example of the CREATE SEQUENCE statement:

```
CREATE SEQUENCE SEQ_ORDER_ID START WITH 1 INCREMENT BY 1;
```

This SQL statement performs the same task as the earlier CREATE SEQUENCE statement you saw. This example explicitly specifies the default features. You can adjust those defaults if you wish, like this:

```
CREATE SEQUENCE SEQ_ORDER_ID START WITH 10 INCREMENT BY 5;
```

This statement will start with the number 10 and increment each successive number by 5.

Using Sequences

Now that we've created a sequence, what do we do with it? Here's an example:

```
INSERT INTO ORDERS (ORDER_ID, ORDER_DATE, CUSTOMER_ID)
VALUES (SEQ_ORDER_ID.NEXTVAL, SYSDATE, 28);
```

In this sample INSERT statement, we insert a row into the ORDERS table that consists of three values. The first value is SEQ_ORDER_ID.NEXTVAL. This reference is to the sequence generator SEQ_ORDER_ID along with its pseudocolumn NEXTVAL, which performs the following two tasks:

■ Advances the sequence generator to the next available number.

■ Returns that value.

If the sequence generator SEQ_ORDER_ID had just been created, and if it was created with the default values for the START WITH and INCREMENT BY, then the initial call to NEXTVAL will obtain the starting value of 1. If the next call to the sequence generator is also a call to the NEXTVAL pseudocolumn, then it will be advanced again by 1, to a value of 2.

All sequence generators have two pseudocolumns:

■ **NEXTVAL**   This increments the sequence to the next number, according to the sequence's original CREATE SEQUENCE directives. It also returns the newly incremented number.

■ **CURRVAL**   This displays the current number that the sequence is
holding. However, this call is only valid from within a session in which
the NEXTVAL pseudocolumn has already been invoked. You cannot use
CURRVAL in your initial call to any given sequence generator within a
session.

The advantage to CURRVAL becomes apparent when working with a set of
tables that involve PRIMARY KEY and FOREIGN KEY relationships. Consider the
entity-relationship diagram (ERD) in Figure 10-2.

Let's create a couple of sequence generators for use with these tables:

```
CREATE SEQUENCE SEQ_CRUISE_CUSTOMER_ID;
CREATE SEQUENCE SEQ_CRUISE_ORDER_ID;
```

Now—let's insert some new rows into these tables (line numbers added):

```
01    INSERT INTO CRUISE_CUSTOMERS
02      (CRUISE_CUSTOMER_ID, FIRST_NAME, LAST_NAME)
03      VALUES
04      (SEQ_CRUISE_CUSTOMER_ID.NEXTVAL, 'Joe', 'Schmoe');
05
06    INSERT INTO CRUISE_ORDERS
07      (CRUISE_ORDER_ID, ORDER_DATE, CRUISE_CUSTOMER_ID)
08      VALUES
09      (SEQ_CRUISE_ORDER_ID.NEXTVAL, SYSDATE, SEQ_CRUISE_CUSTOMER_ID.CURRVAL);
```

FIGURE 10-2

ERD diagram
for the CRUISE_
CUSTOMERS
and CRUISE_
ORDERS tables

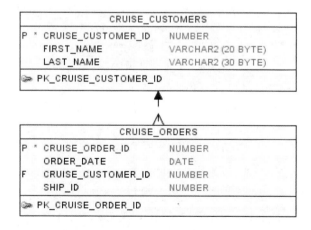

There are three calls to our sequence generators in the preceding code:

- In line 4 we call SEQ_CRUISE_CUSTOMER_ID.NEXTVAL to generate a new primary key.
- At the end of line 9 we call the same sequence generator with the CURRVAL pseudocolumn. This directs the sequence generator to use the same value that was just assigned in the line 4 call—ensuring that our PRIMARY KEY–FOREIGN KEY relationship between these two tables will be respected.
- At the beginning of line 9, we call SEQ_CRUISE_ORDER_ID.NEXTVAL to generate a new primary key for the CRUISE_ORDERS table.

The result of these INSERT statements and uses of the sequence generators helps to ensure that we can join our tables to produce valid and meaningful output. A few important points to keep in mind about sequences:

- You cannot invoke CURRVAL in your first reference to a sequence within a given session. NEXTVAL must be the first reference.
- If you attempt to execute a statement, such as an INSERT, that includes the sequence reference NEXTVAL, the sequence generator will advance to the next number even if the INSERT statement fails.
- You cannot invoke CURRVAL or NEXTVAL in the DEFAULT clause of a CREATE TABLE or ALTER TABLE statement.
- You cannot invoke CURRVAL or NEXTVAL in the subquery of a CREATE VIEW statement, nor of a SELECT, UPDATE, or DELETE statement.
- In a SELECT statement, you cannot combine CURRVAL or NEXTVAL with a DISTINCT operator.
- You cannot invoke CURRVAL or NEXTVAL in the WHERE clause of a SELECT statement.
- You cannot use CURRVAL or NEXTVAL in a CHECK constraint.
- You cannot combine CURRVAL or NEXTVAL with the set operators UNION, INTERSECT, or MINUS.
- You can call a sequence pseudocolumn from anywhere within a SQL statement that you can use any expression.

That last point is important—a reference to a sequence must include its pseudocolumn, and such a reference is considered to be a valid expression, or a component of an expression. So assuming you're working with a table PROJECTS that has a column PROJECT_COST, you could invoke a sequence SEQ_PROJ_COST like this:

```
SELECT PROJECT_COST / (3 * SEQ_PROJ_COST.NEXTVAL) FROM PROJECTS;
```

That is valid syntax. Whether it's useful or not is up to your business rules. But SQL recognizes this syntax and will execute it successfully.

The bottom line: references to the pseudocolumns of sequences are valid expressions.

Any SQL statement that is executed with a call to a sequence's *NEXTVAL pseudocolumn will advance the sequence, even if the SQL statement fails.*

CERTIFICATION OBJECTIVE 10.03

Create and Maintain Indexes

An INDEX is an object you can create in the database that supports faster queries on tables. For a given table, the INDEX stores a set of presorted data from one or more columns that you designate. Also stored in the INDEX is the address of data from the source table. SQL can use the INDEX object to speed up querying of WHERE and ORDER BY clauses. For example, if a WHERE clause references any indexed column (or columns), then SQL will automatically consider the index as it determines the optimal query strategy for the SQL statement. The result: queries may be significantly faster, depending on the amount of data involved, and also depending on the number of indexes that may be applied to a table.

You cannot create an index on columns of LOB or RAW datatypes. Given that, you can create as many indexes as you wish on any given table. However, as you add additional indexes, you'll eventually reach a point of diminishing returns—each index added to a table can potentially increase the workload on future INSERT, UPDATE, and DELETE statements. But let's hold off on that discussion for a bit. For now, we just want to say that the SQL system will let you create as many indexes as you wish.

Remember that the WHERE clause can appear in a SELECT, UPDATE, or DELETE statement. Also note that a SELECT statement, in the form of a subquery, may appear within an INSERT statement or a variety of statements that CREATE objects such as the TABLE or VIEW. An INDEX object can potentially benefit any of these situations.

Implicit Index Creation

If you create a constraint on a table that is of type PRIMARY KEY or UNIQUE, then as part of the creation of the constraint, SQL will automatically create an index to support that constraint on the column or columns, if such an index does not already exist.

For example, consider the following SQL statement:

```
CREATE TABLE SEMINARS
(SEMINAR_ID      NUMBER(11)    PRIMARY KEY,
 SEMINAR_NAME    VARCHAR2(30)  UNIQUE);
```

This statement will create the table SEMINARS, two CONSTRAINTs, and two INDEX objects. These INDEX objects will be named automatically by the SQL system. Later in this section, you'll see how to manually create these indexes. Also later, in Chapter 14, you'll see how you can query the data dictionary to see these implicitly created indexes, but for now, here's a query on the data dictionary that can confirm their creation:

```
SELECT TABLE_NAME, INDEX_NAME
FROM   USER_INDEXES
WHERE  TABLE_NAME = 'SEMINARS';

TABLE_NAME                           INDEX_NAME
------------------------------------ ------------------------------
SEMINARS                             SYS_C009932
SEMINARS                             SYS_C009931
```

In the output of this example, you can see that the system assigned the names SYS_C009932 and SYS_C009931 to the indexes.

As an alternative, you can query elsewhere in the data dictionary to see the columns that are involved in the indexes:

```
SELECT INDEX_NAME, COLUMN_NAME
FROM    USER_IND_COLUMNS
WHERE   TABLE_NAME = 'SEMINARS';


INDEX_NAME                         COLUMN_NAME
------------------------------     -------------------------------
SYS_C009931                        SEMINAR_ID
SYS_C009932                        SEMINAR_NAME
```

In these examples, we applied each constraint to a single column. Had we created a composite PRIMARY KEY, or a composite UNIQUE constraint, then all columns involved in the constraint would have also been indexed as a composite index, and the column names would be listed in the output of this second query on the data dictionary.

Single Column

Here is an example of a SQL statement that creates a single column index:

```
CREATE INDEX IX_INV_INVOICE_DATE ON INVOICES(INVOICE_DATE);
```

This SQL statement creates a simple index called IX_INV_INVOICE_DATE, on the column INVOICE_DATE in the table INVOICES. This will result in an object that sorts values in the INVOICE_DATE column of the INVOICES table. Once such an index exists, queries that reference INVOICE_DATE in the WHERE clause may return results significantly faster:

```
SELECT * FROM INVOICES WHERE INVOICE_DATE = SYSDATE;
```

This query may search the table by first searching in the index. The reason we say "may" is because of something called the "optimizer".

Optimizer

All SQL statements use the Oracle Database *optimizer*. The optimizer processes all SQL statements to determine the best course of action in determining the result. For any SQL statement that needs to scan data in a table—such as a query with a WHERE clause or an ORDER BY clause—the optimizer will consider whether or not an available index on the queried table will contribute toward faster performance. The existence of an index does not guarantee its use.

For example, let's consider the SELECT statement against the INVOICES table that we just reviewed. Whether or not an index is used for that query depends on the nature of the data found in the INVOICE_DATE column that is specified in the WHERE clause. If, for example, all of the rows in the INVOICES table have the same value for INVOICE_DATE, the index may not be used. On the other hand, if each row happens to have a unique INVOICE_DATE value, then the index most likely will be used. The difference has to do with the concept of *selectivity*. If a column tends to include data that is less repetitive and more unique, it is said to have a higher degree of selectivity, and an index on such a column would be attractive to the optimizer. But if data in a given column is relatively repetitive, it is said to have a lower degree of selectivity and will be less likely to be included in an index.

In the sample SELECT you just looked at, if the SQL optimizer determines to use the index, and if evidence is found in the index that a row of INVOICES matches the desired result, the index points the query directly to the row(s) in the table, and the result is achieved—much faster than otherwise would have occurred.

Usage

The Oracle Database optimizer will consider the use of an index in any query that specifies an indexed column in the WHERE clause or ORDER BY clause, depending on how the index column is specified. There are some guidelines for structuring your SQL statement so that the optimizer will be more likely to apply the index. The guidelines are as follows:

- For best results, the indexed column should be specified in a comparison of equality.
- A "greater than" or some other comparison may work.
- A "not equals" will not invoke an index.
- The LIKE comparison may invoke an index as long as the wildcard character is not in the leading position—in other words, the expression LIKE '%SMITH' will not invoke an index, but LIKE 'SMITH%' may invoke an index.
- A function on a column will prevent the use of an index—unless the index is a function-based index, which we'll discuss in detail in Chapter 11.

Furthermore, certain types of automated datatype conversions will eliminate the index.

The design of an indexing scheme is something that falls under the general category of *performance tuning*. There is no single comprehensive approach to index design for a given database application. The approach you take depends upon a variety of factors, including the amount and selectivity of data expected, and the anticipated frequency and types of the various SQL statements you intend to execute on the database. A system that will not be queried much but will be heavily populated with INSERT statements would not benefit much from indexes, since each INSERT will be slower as it updates the tables and all associated INDEX objects. On such a database, infrequent queries may not justify the creation of INDEX objects and their associated performance trade-off. On the other hand, an application that involves a great deal of updating via UPDATE statements will benefit with thoughtfully designed indexes.

exam

ⓦatch

The optimizer will do everything it can to use an index for a given query if at all possible, and if the index is beneficial. It only avoids an index if its use would be detrimental, such as in the case of a table with a large number of rows with an indexed column that has low selectivity.

There's an old rule of thumb that recommends no more than five indexes on the average table in a transaction-based application. But that—again—depends on intended usage. I've implemented applications in which some tables have had as many as nine indexes applied, and the result was positive. That was a situation where queries on the table were not using primary keys so much but instead used a variety of text-based lookups.

Performance tuning is the subject of many books and is a topic that goes far beyond this book—and the exam. For the exam, it's important to understand the syntax of creating indexes—both single column and composites—and their intended purpose and general usage.

Maintenance

Indexes are automatically maintained in the background by SQL and require no effort on your part to keep their lookup data consistent with the table. However, note that this means each future INSERT, UPDATE, and DELETE statement you issue will have to work harder. Each DML statement that modifies data in a table that is indexed will also perform index maintenance as required. In other words, each index you add to a table puts more workload on each DML statement that affects indexed data.

Build the indexes that contribute to your application's overall performance, and don't build indexes unless they are necessary. And plan to periodically review your index structures to determine which indexes may no longer be needed—an existing application burdened with unnecessary indexes may benefit from the removal of indexes.

on the **Job**

There are a number of performance tuning tools and techniques to assist with designing indexes. One is the EXPLAIN PLAN feature, which reveals the internal workings of a given SQL statement and provides insight into how SQL will optimize a given statement, including the use of indexes for a given SQL statement. It's a great tool. And it's not in the list of certification objectives for the exam, so we won't get into it here. You may wish to explore one of the other books in the Oracle Press line to learn more about it.

Composite

A *composite* index is an index that is built on two or more columns of a table, like this:

```
CREATE INDEX IX_INV_INVOICE_VENDOR_ID ON INVOICES(VENDOR_ID, INVOICE_DATE);
```

In this example, the result is one single index that combines both columns. A composite index copies and sorts data from both columns into the composite index object. Its data is sorted first by the first position column, second by the second position column, and so on, for all of the columns that form the composite index.

A WHERE clause that references all of the columns in a composite index will cause the SQL optimizer to consider using the composite index for processing the query. For example, this query would encourage the optimizer to use the composite index IX_INV_INVOICE_VENDOR_ID to maximum advantage:

```
SELECT * FROM INVOICES WHERE VENDOR_ID = 10 AND INVOICE_DATE = SYSDATE;
```

Note that the WHERE clause in the preceding example references the columns that make up the composite INDEX object. Next, consider this query:

```
SELECT * FROM INVOICES WHERE VENDOR_ID = 10;
```

This query, which references the first column in the composite index, also invokes the index. The reason: the composite index internally sorts data by the first column first, and the second column second. Given that, the internally copied and sorted data from the indexed table is comparable in structure to a single-column index based on—in this example—the VENDOR_ID column.

But now consider this query:

```
SELECT * FROM INVOICES WHERE INVOICE_DATE = SYSDATE;
```

This query references the second column in the composite query, but not the first. The composite index structure is primarily sorted on the first column of its structure, which in the example we're working with, is VENDOR_ID. But this query does not reference VENDOR_ID. Nevertheless, the SQL optimizer may still consider applying the index due to a feature known as "skip scanning".

Skip Scanning

Thanks to *skip scanning,* a WHERE clause that references any columns within a composite index may invoke the index in its processing. However, the performance benefit is not identical. In skip scanning, SQL treats a composite index as a combination of several indexes. How many? That depends on the level of selectivity that results in the indexing of the first—or *leading*—column of the INDEX object. If the first column contains only a few unique values within a large number of rows, the index—if used—may be applied a relatively few number of times. On the other hand, if the leading column contains data that is relatively unique across the rows, then the index—if used—may be reviewed frequently. In other words, a skip scan will do an index scan once for each unique value in the first column. This isn't quite as beneficial as a simple one-column index, and its benefit varies, depending on the uniqueness of values in the first column. But the WHERE clause gains some benefit anyway.

The point is that a WHERE clause that references some, but not all, of the columns in a composite index may invoke the index, even if the leading column is not referenced in the WHERE clause. However, including the leading column may result in a more efficient application of the composite index and, therefore, a faster result to the query.

Unique

A *unique* index is one that helps ensure that a column in a table will contain unique information. The syntax for creating a unique index is as follows:

```
CREATE UNIQUE INDEX IX_EMP_SSN ON EMPLOYEES(SSN);
```

This SQL statement creates an index that will ensure that data entered into the SSN column of the table EMPLOYEES is unique.

This is different from the UNIQUE constraint that you can apply to a column on a table. However, note that if you create a PRIMARY KEY or UNIQUE constraint on a table, a unique index will automatically be created along with the constraint. Note that the UNIQUE constraint is more self-documenting within the database. That being said, Oracle Corporation formally recommends the creation of unique indexes to enforce uniqueness in a column, for better results in query performance.

Dropping

You can *drop* an index with the DROP INDEX statement. For example, let's drop our IX_INV_INVOICE_DATE index:

```
DROP INDEX IX_INV_INVOICE_DATE;
```

Note that if you drop a table upon which an index is based, the index is automatically dropped. If you re-create the table, you need to re-create the index.

CERTIFICATION OBJECTIVE 10.04

Create Private and Public Synonyms

The SYNONYM object is a relatively simple object with a surprisingly important purpose. A SYNONYM consists of nothing more than an alternative name—an alias—for another object in the database that may—or may not—already exist. In other words, it's an alternative name for some other database object. At first glance, the SYNONYM might not seem like a terribly useful feature, but it's a critical component of a professional database application implementation, for reasons you're about to see.

You can create synonyms for tables, views, sequences, and other synonyms, as well as a number of other database objects that are included on the exam.

When you create a synonym for another object, that object does not necessarily have to exist already. If it does exist, you are not required to have privileges on the object in order to successfully create a synonym for it. Obviously, however, for the synonym to eventually work, the object must eventually be created, and privileges must eventually be granted—but that can come after the synonym's creation.

First, there are two types of synonyms: *private synonyms* and *public synonyms*. In terms of SQL syntax, there really isn't any such thing as a private synonym. There is instead a SYNONYM and a PUBLIC SYNONYM. You'll look at both in detail next.

Private

The SYNONYM (without the keyword PUBLIC) is often referred to as a *private* synonym. But there is no PRIVATE keyword that's applicable in this context.

Here's an example of a SQL statement that creates a private synonym:

```
CREATE OR REPLACE SYNONYM CO FOR CRUISE_ORDERS;
```

This code creates an alternative name CO for an existing database object name CRUISE_ORDERS. The syntax is as follows:

- The keyword CREATE is required.
- The keywords OR REPLACE are optional—if included, then any preexisting synonym object with the same name will be dropped and re-created according to this statement's directive.
- The keyword SYNONYM is required.
- Next comes the name you specify, according to the rules for naming database objects.
- The keyword FOR is required.
- Finally, include the name of the existing database object for which you wish to create an alias, optionally preceded by its schema name (which isn't included in this example, but we'll look at schema name prefixes in a bit).

If the CRUISE_ORDERS object is a table, then you could now execute the following SQL statement:

```
SELECT * FROM CO;
```

In other words, once you've created a synonym for an object, you can reference that object with the synonym instead of its real name. In addition, the original name of the object is still good and available.

A private synonym is owned by the user account that creates it, and by default is only visible within the user account, just as any other object owned by the user. As with any object owned by the user, the user must take steps to grant privileges on owned objects for other user accounts to get access to that object. In other words, a user may choose to make their private synonym visible to other users, but that requires an explicit effort on the user's part to make that happen, as is true for tables, views, and many other objects—but not all objects. As you'll see in the next section, the PUBLIC SYNONYM is automatically visible to all users. Let's see how that works.

Public

A public synonym is owned by a special system user account called PUBLIC. Every object owned by the PUBLIC account is automatically made visible to all users in the database. A public synonym, once created, is available to everyone in the database.

Users who have been granted the appropriate system privilege may create a public synonym. We'll discuss system privileges in Chapter 18, but for now, note that the system privilege required is the CREATE PUBLIC SYNONYM system privilege.

Here's an example of the statement that creates a public synonym:

```
CREATE PUBLIC SYNONYM WH FOR WORK_HISTORY;
```

It's virtually identical to the syntax for creating a private synonym, with the only difference being the addition of the keyword PUBLIC.

Once it is created, any user in the database can see the public synonym and reference it. However, that doesn't necessarily guarantee that the user can get access to whatever object the synonym represents. In the preceding example, the public synonym WH is another name for the table WORK_HISTORY. Once created, any user can see the public synonym, but that doesn't mean any user can access the WORK_HISTORY table—that requires privileges on the table itself, in addition to the creation of the public synonym.

Object Privileges

One of the most important usages of the public synonym is as an alias for a database object that has been made available by its owner to other users. Consider the table PORTS. Let's say that PORTS is owned by a user called CODD, and that CODD wants other users to see this table. CODD decides to authorize another user account for this purpose; let's call the other user account LARRY. CODD is going to let LARRY read data from the PORTS table. Later, in Chapter 18, we'll look at the issues of user access, roles, and privileges. For now, know that this is the SQL statement that CODD can use to accomplish this. The statement will be this:

```
GRANT SELECT ON PORTS TO LARRY;
```

This statement, executed by CODD, gives user LARRY the ability to query the PORTS table owned by CODD. Once that's been done, user LARRY will be able to query the PORTS table with a query like this:

```
SELECT * FROM CODD.PORTS;
```

Notice that for LARRY to access the table PORTS that is owned by CODD, the user LARRY will have to prefix the table name with the user account name of CODD. This will be true for all queries issued by LARRY on the table PORTS.

But what if CODD decides to turn over maintenance of the PORTS table to someone else? That means CODD will probably move the PORTS table to a different user account. That also means that somebody has to remember to let user LARRY know that he's going to have to change his code in all his queries of the PORTS table, and edit out the CODD prefix, and put in something else.

That's really annoying, not to mention a maintenance headache that's error-prone. But the public synonym can be used here to make life a lot easier. Here's how:

```
CREATE PUBLIC SYNONYM PORTS FOR CODD.PORTS;
```

Now, assuming the SELECT privilege is still in force for user LARRY, any queries user LARRY makes on the PORTS table don't need the schema prefix before the name of the database object PORTS. The following SELECT statement will work from user LARRY's account:

```
SELECT * FROM PORTS;
```

This statement will be interpreted to be the same thing as

```
SELECT * FROM CODD.PORTS;
```

. . . thanks to the PUBLIC SYNONYM.

Now, if user CODD moves the PORTS table to a different user account, all CODD must do is redefine the public synonym object, perhaps like this:

```
CREATE OR REPLACE PUBLIC SYNONYM PORTS FOR NEWOWNER.PORTS;
```

If you have a synonym for a database object, and the database object is dropped, the synonym is not dropped—it exists independently of the object it renames.

CODD doesn't even need to notify user LARRY about the changed location of the PORTS table.

Most commercial database applications make heavy use of public synonyms for every table and view and other referenced object that goes into the database application. A combination of the appropriate GRANT and CREATE public synonym statements set up an application that can easily be relocated later to a different user account without having to tell anyone or change any code. All that is required to move the application is a revised set of SQL statements to drop and recreate the appropriate public synonym objects.

Name Priority

We discussed namespaces in Chapter 2. As you might recall, objects created in the database are placed within different namespaces. You saw this in detail in Figure 2-2, where you saw which objects are assigned to which namespace. Objects within a given namespace cannot share the same name.

A local user account contains a single namespace for the tables, views, sequences, and private synonyms it owns. This means that you cannot create a private synonym that has the same name as a table or view or sequence that already exists and already has that same name. You can, however, create a private synonym with a unique name to represent an existing object of a different name.

But Figure 2-2 also showed us that public synonyms are kept in their own namespace, separate from the user account namespace. This means that you can create a public synonym with the same name as an existing user account synonym.

This raises an interesting issue. Assume you have two valid tables in your user account, one called LAB_RESULTS and another called CABINETS. Consider the following code:

```
CREATE        SYNONYM ACCT_01 FOR LAB_RESULTS;
CREATE PUBLIC SYNONYM ACCT_01 FOR CABINETS;
SELECT * FROM ACCT_01;
```

Question: are we selecting from LAB_RESULTS or CABINETS? We've already seen that it is perfectly valid to create private and public synonyms of the same name. But what happens when you try to use them?

The answer is indicated in Figure 10-3. The priority of referencing objects goes first to local objects. When you are logged in to a given user account and attempt to access a particular object, SQL will first look to the local namespace for that object. If it does not find it, it will then look to the PUBLIC objects.

Now we can answer the earlier question. The SELECT statement was looking for the local object—which was the private synonym ACCT_01, as opposed to the public synonym of the same name. That private synonym is pointing to LAB_RESULTS. So we were querying LAB_RESULTS.

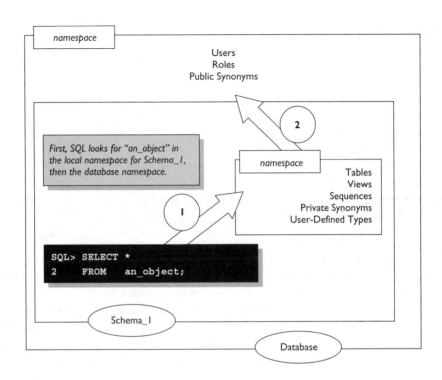

FIGURE 10-3

Named objects conflicts and namespace priority

Replacing

There is no statement that combines ALTER with SYNONYM; not for private synonyms, nor for public synonyms. Instead you can use the OR REPLACE option with CREATE SYNONYM, like this:

```
CREATE OR REPLACE SYNONYM CO FOR CODD.CRUISE_ORDERS;
```

Or, for public synonyms:

```
CREATE OR REPLACE PUBLIC SYNONYM CO FOR CODD.CRUISE_ORDERS;
```

That's the approach to "altering" a synonym.

on the
job

Note the preceding two CREATE statements. One does a "CREATE OR REPLACE" to build a private synonym; the other executes a "CREATE OR REPLACE" to build a public synonym. Question: at the end of these two statements, do you have two synonyms, or one? The answer is two—a synonym is different from a public synonym. A synonym is "private" unless specified otherwise.

Dropping

To remove the synonym CO from the database, you can use this statement:

```
DROP SYNONYM CO;
```

Or for a public synonym CO, you can use this:

```
DROP PUBLIC SYNONYM CO;
```

That's it.

CERTIFICATION SUMMARY

Views are objects that name a query and store the query in the database. Views do not store data. They look and act like tables. Views may be built with simple or complex SELECT statements. GROUP BY, HAVING, join queries, and more are all possible in a VIEW object's SELECT statement.

A SELECT statement can be used to query a view just as it would be used to query a table. But INSERT, UPDATE, and DELETE statements will only work with certain views, not all of them—it depends on whether the view's structure allows appropriate access to the table or tables upon which the view is based. Any DML statement will work with a view based on a single table, provided that the required columns are all included in the select list of the SELECT statement used to create the view, and that the rows of the view are not aggregate rows, and that all of the table's constraints are honored. A view is not necessarily required to include columns that are required by the view's underlying table, but if the view omits such columns, then an INSERT statement cannot add—to the view—a value that is required by the underlying table, and the constraints on the underlying table will reject the INSERT and it won't work for that view.

Any SELECT statement used to create a view must have clearly defined column names. Complex expressions must be assigned a column alias; this will become the name of the column in the resulting view object.

An inline view is a variation on a subquery, in which the SELECT statement replaces a table reference in a FROM clause of any DML statement. An inline view must be enclosed in its own set of parentheses. Once incorporated in a DML statement, the inline view behaves just like a view object would behave.

If the underlying table is modified, the view may require recompilation using the ALTER VIEW . . . COMPILE statement.

Sequence objects are counters. They dispense numbers according to the parameters established when the sequence is first created.

SQL automatically defines pseudocolumns for each sequence. The NEXTVAL pseudocolumn increments the sequence to the next available number as defined in the sequence's parameters defined at the time the sequence is created. The CURRVAL pseudocolumn refers back to whatever the last NEXTVAL reference produced in a given session. In any session with a sequence, the NEXTVAL pseudocolumn must be referenced before the CURRVAL pseudocolumn may be referenced. A reference to a sequence pseudocolumn is a valid expression and can be invoked in many places where expressions are allowed, with certain restrictions.

Indexes are objects that copy a subset of presorted information from a table, and may be referenced automatically by SQL to speed up the processing of a given SQL statement, depending on how that SQL statement is structured and what the Oracle Database optimizer chooses to do. An index can be built on one or more columns in a table. Once created, if a WHERE or ORDER BY clause references the indexed column, SQL may use the index to speed up the process of obtaining a result. An index that is built on multiple columns is known as a "composite" index. A UNIQUE INDEX can be used to enforce a unique rule on a column.

There are two types of synonyms: private and public. Private synonyms exist within a user account. Public synonyms are owned by the system account PUBLIC and are automatically available for everyone's use. Since private and public synonyms exist in different namespaces, it's possible for one user account to create one of each with the same name. In such an event, SQL will look for any reference to the name by first searching in the local namespace (i.e., the user account) and then looking in the public namespace (the PUBLIC account).

TWO-MINUTE DRILL

Create and Use Simple and Complex Views

❑ A VIEW is a SELECT statement that is stored in the database and assigned a name.

❑ The columns and expressions of the SELECT statement used to create a view become the columns of the VIEW.

❑ You can use SELECT statements on views just as you would a table.

❑ You can use INSERT, UPDATE, and/or DELETE statements on some views, depending on the constraints of the view's underlying table or tables, as well as other issues such as whether the view's SELECT statement includes aggregate functions or not.

❑ An "inline view" is a subquery that replaces a table reference in a FROM clause of a DML statement.

❑ The VIEW can be treated like a table, with some limitations.

❑ A VIEW based on a table that is subsequently altered may require recompilation with the ALTER VIEW . . . COMPILE statement.

Create, Maintain, and Use Sequences

❑ A SEQUENCE is an object that dispenses numbers according to the rules established by the sequence.

❑ A SEQUENCE specifies the starting number, the increment (which can be positive or negative), and an optional range of values within which the sequence can generate values.

❑ The starting point can be within the range or at one end of the range.

❑ SEQUENCES are ideal for populating primary key values.

❑ The NEXTVAL pseudocolumn of a sequence returns the next available number in the sequence and must be the first reference to the sequence in any given login session.

❑ The CURRVAL pseudocolumn can return the existing value as already defined by NEXTVAL; it can only be referenced in a session after the NEXTVAL reference has occurred.

❑ A pseudocolumn reference to a sequence is a valid expression and can be referenced anywhere that a valid expression is allowed.

❑ If a valid sequence reference to NEXTVAL occurs within a DML statement that fails, the sequence still advances.

Create and Maintain Indexes

❑ An INDEX object is based on one or more columns in a table.

❑ The INDEX copies data from its table's columns on which it is built, and presorts that data in order to speed future queries.

❑ When the DML statements INSERT, UPDATE, or DELETE are executed on an indexed table so that the indexed data is changed, the index is automatically updated by SQL, thus adding to the workload of the DML statements.

❑ INDEX objects can be built on one or more columns. Multiple-column indexes are "composite" indexes.

Create Private and Public Synonyms

❑ SYNONYM objects are aliases for other objects in the database.

❑ A SYNONYM can be created for objects that do not yet exist in the database.

❑ A private SYNONYM is created with the CREATE SYNONYM statement and is owned by a user account.

❑ A PUBLIC SYNONYM is created with the CREATE PUBLIC SYNONYM statement and is owned by the PUBLIC user account.

❑ PUBLIC SYNONYMs are automatically accessible to all users; however, before user accounts can access the aliased object, the user must have the appropriate privileges for the object for which the PUBLIC SYNONYM is an alias.

SELF TEST

The following questions will help you measure your understanding of the material presented in this chapter. Choose one correct answer for each question unless otherwise directed.

Create and Use Simple and Complex Views

1. Which of the following SQL statements can be executed on any VIEW object? (Choose all that apply.)
   - Ⓐ SELECT
   - B. INSERT
   - C. DELETE
   - D. UPDATE

2. Review the following illustration:

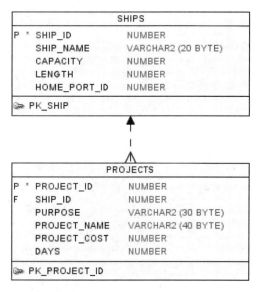

Now review the following SQL code (line numbers added):

```
01   CREATE OR REPLACE VIEW SHIP_CAP_PROJ AS
02   SELECT    SHIP_ID,
03             TO_CHAR(CAPACITY,'999,999'),
04             PROJECT_COST
```

```
05   FROM      SHIPS JOIN PROJECTS
06   USING     (SHIP_ID)
07   WHERE     (PROJECT_COST * 2) < 100000;
```

What will result from an attempt to execute this SQL code?

  A. The statement will fail because of an error in line 3.

  B. The statement will fail because of an error in line 6.

  C. The statement will fail because of an error in line 7.

  D. The statement will execute and the view will be successfully created.

3. Review the illustration from question 2, and the following SQL code:

```
CREATE OR REPLACE VIEW PROJECTS_ROLLUP AS
     SELECT SHIP_NAME, CAPACITY,
            COUNT(PROJECT_ID) NUM_PROJECTS, ROUND(SUM(DAYS)) TOTAL_DAYS
     FROM   SHIPS A JOIN PROJECTS B
     ON     A.SHIP_ID = B.SHIP_ID
     GROUP BY SHIP_NAME, CAPACITY;
```

What can be said of this code?

  A. After the view is created, a valid SELECT statement will work on the PROJECTS_ROLLUP view, but an INSERT will not.

  B. After the view is created, a valid SELECT and valid INSERT statement will work on the PROJECTS_ROLLUP view.

  C. The attempt to create the view will fail because you cannot create a VIEW with a SELECT statement that uses a GROUP BY clause.

  D. The attempt to create the view will fail because you cannot create a VIEW with a SELECT statement that is a join.

4. Review the illustration from question 2, and the following SQL code (line numbers added):

```
01   CREATE OR REPLACE VIEW MAJOR_PROJECTS AS
02     SELECT PROJECT_ID, SHIP_ID, PROJECT_NAME, PROJECT_COST
03     FROM   PROJECTS
04     WHERE  PROJECT_COST > 10000;
05
06   INSERT INTO MAJOR_PROJECTS
07    (PROJECT_ID, SHIP_ID, PROJECT_NAME, PROJECT_COST)
08    VALUES
09    ((SELECT MAX(PROJECT_ID)+1 FROM PROJECTS),
10     (SELECT MAX(SHIP_ID) FROM SHIPS),
11     'Small Project',
12     500);
```

What will result from an attempt to execute these two SQL statements?

A. The CREATE statement will fail because it omits the PURPOSE column from the PROJECTS table.

B. The INSERT statement will fail because of an error on lines 9 and 10.

C. The INSERT statement will fail because the PROJECT_COST value being inserted is not consistent with the WHERE clause on line 4.

D. The CREATE and INSERT statements will successfully execute.

5. You have created a view MED_BENEFITS on a table BENEFITS. After you created the view, the BENEFITS table was altered. Which of the following SQL statements will ensure the view is still valid—or determine if the view requires more substantial modification?

A. COMPILE VIEW MED_BENEFITS;

B. RECOMPILE VIEW MED_BENEFITS;

C. ALTER VIEW MED_BENEFITS COMPILE;

D. ALTER VIEW MED_BENEFITS RECOMPILE;

Create, Maintain, and Use Sequences

6. Which of the following keywords *cannot* be used with the CREATE SEQUENCE statement?

A. CYCLE

B. MAXVALUE

C. INCREMENT

D. JOIN

7. Review this code:

```
DROP    TABLE SHIPS CASCADE CONSTRAINTS;
DROP    SEQUENCE PROJ_ID_SEQ#;
CREATE TABLE SHIPS (SHIP_ID NUMBER PRIMARY KEY,
                    LENGTH  NUMBER);
CREATE SEQUENCE PROJ_ID_SEQ# START WITH 1 INCREMENT BY 4;
INSERT INTO SHIPS (SHIP_ID, LENGTH) VALUES (PROJ_ID_SEQ#.NEXTVAL, 'NOT A NUMBER');
INSERT INTO SHIPS (SHIP_ID, LENGTH) VALUES (PROJ_ID_SEQ#.NEXTVAL, 750);
COMMIT;
```

Note that the first INSERT statement is attempting to enter a string literal 'NOT A NUMBER' into a column declared with a numeric datatype. Given that, what will be the result of this SQL statements?

A. One row added to the SHIPS table, with a SHIP_ID value of 1.

B. One row added to the SHIPS table, with a SHIP_ID value of 5.

C. Two rows added to the SHIPS table. The first SHIP_ID is 1; the second is 5.

D. Two rows added to the SHIPS table. The first SHIP_ID is NULL; the second is 5.

8. Review this code:

```
DROP SEQUENCE PROJ_ID_SEQ#;
CREATE SEQUENCE PROJ_ID_SEQ# START WITH 1 INCREMENT BY 2;
SELECT PROJ_ID_SEQ#.CURRVAL FROM DUAL;
```

What will result from these SQL statements?

A. The SELECT statement will fail because the sequence can only be referenced in an INSERT statement.

B. The SELECT statement will fail because you cannot reference the CURRVAL pseudo-column of a sequence until after you have referenced NEXTVAL for the sequence in a session.

C. The SELECT statement will display a value of 1.

D. The SELECT statement will display a value of 3.

Create and Maintain Indexes

9. An index:

A. Copies all of the data from all of the columns in any given table into a separate object and sorts the data for faster lookups.

B. May improve the performance of an UPDATE statement that uses a WHERE clause, if the WHERE clause performs an equality comparison on an indexed column in a table.

C. Requires a separate INSERT statement each time you add data to a table—one time to add a new row to the table, another time to add the corresponding and necessary data required by the index.

D. Only works with a SELECT statement if you display data that is indexed.

10. Review the following series of SQL statements:

```
CREATE TABLE SUPPLIES_01
(  SUPPLY_ID NUMBER(7),
   SUPPLIER  VARCHAR2(30),
   ACCT_NO   VARCHAR2(50));
CREATE INDEX IX_SU_01 ON SUPPLIES_01(ACCT_NO);
DROP TABLE SUPPLIES_01;
CREATE TABLE SUPPLIES_02
(  SUPPLY_ID NUMBER(7),
   SUPPLIER  VARCHAR2(30),
   ACCT_NO   VARCHAR2(50));
CREATE INDEX IX_SU_02 ON SUPPLIES_02(ACCT_NO,SUPPLIER);
```

Assuming there are no objects already in existence named SUPPLIES_01 or SUPPLIES_02 prior to the execution of the preceding statements, what database objects will result from these statements?

A. A table called SUPPLIES_02, and nothing else

B. A table called SUPPLIES_02, and an index called IX_SU_02

C. A table called SUPPLIES_02, and two indexes called IX_SU_01 and IX_SU_02

D. None of the above

11. An index that is based on more than one column is:

A. Not possible

B. A correlated index

C. A combined index

D. A composite index

12. Review this code:

```
CREATE TABLE SPARES
(  SPARE_ID  NUMBER(8),
   PART_NO   VARCHAR2(30),
   PART_NAME VARCHAR2(80));
```

Assume that no table called SPARES exists at the start of this series of statements. Which of the following will successfully create an index on the SPARES table?

A. CREATE INDEX IX_01 ON SPARES PART_NO,PART_NAME;

B. CREATE INDEX IX_01 ON SPARES COMPOSITE PART_NO,PART_NAME;

C. CREATE INDEX IX_01 ON SPARES (PART_NO,PART_NAME);

D. None of the above

Create Private and Public Synonyms

13. A private synonym:

    A. Can be seen by any user in the database who has privileges on it and has privileges on the synonym's underlying object.

    B. Can only be seen by the user who creates it, and cannot ever be seen by any other user in the database under any circumstances.

    C. Is created with the CREATE PRIVATE SYNONYM statement.

    D. Is also called a "column alias" in a SELECT statement.

14. Review these SQL statements:

```
CREATE TABLE BOXES (BOX_ID NUMBER(7));
CREATE TABLE TRUNKS (TRUNK_ID NUMBER(8));
INSERT INTO TRUNKS VALUES (1);
CREATE OR REPLACE SYNONYM CONTAINERS FOR BOXES;
CREATE OR REPLACE PUBLIC SYNONYM CONTAINERS FOR TRUNKS;
SELECT COUNT(*) FROM CONTAINERS;
```

What will be the result of this SQL code?

    A. At least one of the statements will fail with a error.

    B. The SELECT statement will return a value of 0.

    C. The SELECT statement will return a value of 1.

    D. None of the above.

15. Looking again at the code in the preceding question, how many synonyms—either public or private—will result from that code?

    A. 0

    B. 1

    C. 2

    D. Not enough information is available to make a determination

SELF TEST ANSWERS

Create and Use Simple and Complex Views

1. ☑ **A.** The SELECT statement can be used against any view.
   ☒ **B, C,** and **D** are incorrect. There are many reasons why any given VIEW may reject attempts to execute the INSERT, UPDATE, or DELETE statements. For example, if the VIEW object does not contain sufficient access to its underlying tables, then it might not provide all the column access required to satisfy the underlying constraint restrictions that may exist for any INSERT, UPDATE, or DELETE statement. While many views allow all of these SQL statements to work, it's entirely possible to create a VIEW that does not.

2. ☑ **A.** The error on line 3 is the failure to give the expression a column alias. The VIEW does not assign a name to the second column, so the attempt to create the view fails.
   ☒ **B, C,** and **D** are incorrect. These are not errors. Line 6 is fine; the use of USING works well here. Line 7 is fine; the expression that calculates the result of PROJECT_COST times 2 is fine; expressions in WHERE clauses have no restrictions in a CREATE VIEW statement.

3. ☑ **A.** The syntax for creating the view is correct, and any view can—at a minimum—work with a SELECT statement. But an INSERT will not work with this view since it consists of aggregate rows, as defined by the GROUP BY clause in the view's SELECT statement.
   ☒ **B, C,** and **D** are incorrect. The view will not work with an INSERT because of the GROUP BY. In other words, there is no way to add single-row values through the view, since the view's access to the tables is, by definition, at the aggregate level. Also, the GROUP BY and JOIN conditions for the SELECT are fine; you can most certainly create views with those clauses in the SELECT statement—they just have the effect of limiting the capabilities of the resulting view, as we've seen—it won't accept INSERT statements.

4. ☑ **D.** The statements will successfully execute.
   ☒ **A, B,** and **C** are incorrect. The PURPOSE column is not required in order to create the view—the subquery in line 2 through line 4 is a valid SELECT statement. The code on lines 9 and 10 specifies scalar subqueries and is correct. The lower PROJECT_COST value will not prevent the INSERT from working; however, it will prevent the row from ever being seen through the MAJOR_PROJECTS view. A SELECT statement that attempts to display this row in the future could do so by querying the original table PROJECTS, but not the view MAJOR_PROJECTS, which only sees rows with a PROJECT_COST greater than 10000 but certainly allows them to be inserted through the view into the underlying table.

5. ☑ **C.** ALTER VIEW . . . COMPILE is the correct syntax. The statement will either succeed, in which case the view will be valid once again, or it will fail, indicating that the query upon which the view is based requires further assessment.

☒ **A, B,** and **D** are incorrect. There is no COMPILE VIEW statement. Nor is there a RECOMPILE keyword.

Create, Maintain, and Use Sequences

6. ☑ **D.** JOIN is used in a SELECT statement that connects two or more tables. But it is not used in a CREATE SEQUENCE statement, even thought its ultimate purpose may be to support the integrity of joins.

☒ **A, B,** and **C** are incorrect. CYCLE specifies if the sequence will repeat a range once it reaches the end of the range. MAXVALUE specifies one end of the range. INCREMENT specifies the number by which the sequence will increment.

7. ☑ **B.** There will be one row in the table. The reason: the first INSERT will fail because of the attempt to enter a character string into a numeric column. In the first failed INSERT statement, the PROJ_ID_SEQ# sequence generator will be invoked, and the NEXTVAL reference will use up the first number in the sequence, which will be 1. The second INSERT will succeed and grab the second number in the sequence, which will be 5.

☒ **A, C,** and **D** are incorrect.

8. ☑ **B.** Since the sequence was just created, NEXTVAL must be referenced before CURRVAL. This is also true if you were to log off and end the session, and then log back in to restart the session—the first reference for existing sequences must be NEXTVAL.

☒ **A, C,** and **D** are incorrect. You are allowed to reference sequence generators in any SQL statement where expressions are allowed. If CURRVAL were replaced with NEXTVAL, the correct answer to this question would have been answer C, meaning that the SELECT statement would have displayed a value of 1.

Create and Maintain Indexes

9. ☑ **B.** An index can potentially speed up the WHERE clause of any DML statement, including the UPDATE statement. Comparisons of equality are ideal.

☒ **A, C,** and **D** are incorrect. An index does not copy all of the data from all of the rows of an indexed table but instead copies only that data that is contained within the indexed column or columns. It does not require a separate INSERT statement; instead, any future INSERTs will perform automatic index maintenance as required without any extra effort from you. The SELECT statement does not need to display indexed information for the index to be used.

10. ☑ **B.** While all of the statements will execute successfully, the first DROP statement will drop the table SUPPLIES_01, which will cause the index IX_SU_01 to be dropped as well. In other words, the DROP TABLE SUPPLIES_01 statement has the effect of dropping the table SUPPLIES_01 as well as the index IX_SU_01. The table SUPPLIES_02 and IX_SU_02 will remain at the end.
    ☒ **A, C,** and **D** are incorrect.

11. ☑ **D.** A composite index is built on two or more columns.
    ☒ **A, B,** and **C** are incorrect. Combining columns is definitely possible. But it's not a "correlated index" or "combined index"; those are not terms that are used.

12. ☑ **C.** The correct syntax includes a set of parentheses enclosing the list of columns on which the index is based.
    ☒ **A, B,** and **D** are incorrect. In answer A, the parentheses are missing. In answer B, the word COMPOSITE is used but not appropriate—there is no keyword COMPOSITE that has any relevance in this context. The correct answer C happens to create a composite index, but there's no COMPOSITE keyword.

Create Private and Public Synonyms

13. ☑ **A.** A private synonym is not automatically available to any user in the database, but the owner of the private synonym reserves the right to grant privileges on that synonym to anyone in the database. Contrast this with a public synonym, which is automatically available to every user in the database at the moment it is created.
    ☒ **B, C,** and **D** are incorrect. There is no PRIVATE keyword. The synonym object is not a column alias—the synonym is an object in the database, whereas a column alias is a feature within a SELECT statement that has no scope beyond the immediate execution of the SELECT statement.

14. ☑ **B.** The SELECT will identify the private synonym, which points to BOXES, because local objects are given preference over public objects.
    ☒ **A, C,** and **D** are incorrect. None of the statements has a problem with regard to syntax or execution. The SELECT won't return one row, because the PUBLIC SYNONYM name CONTAINERS is subordinate to the private synonym CONTAINERS. Locally defined objects override other objects with regard to identity and reference.

15. ☑ **C.** The two statements will create two synonyms—one private, the other public.
    ☒ **A, B,** and **D** are incorrect.

11

Managing Schema Objects

T his chapter looks at a variety of tasks, features, and SQL statements, all designed to support the management of database objects and the data contained within them using constraints and indexes in new ways, in new statements and new clauses and in new combinations. This chapter also introduces new features like FLASHBACK and external tables.

Add and Modify Columns

You can add columns to an existing table in the database. The SQL statement used to add or modify a column in a table is the ALTER TABLE statement. ALTER TABLE is a powerful statement with several clauses and options. The general syntax for the ALTER TABLE statement is as follows:

```
ALTER TABLE table_name clause;
```

Here, the *table_name* is the name of an existing table in the database that you wish to change in some fashion—and by "change", I'm not talking about changing the data it contains, but changing the table's structure—for example, its columns, the column datatypes, or the table's constraints.

In addition, "clause" can be many different things. ALTER TABLE has many different optional uses. For this section, we'll be looking at two ALTER TABLE clauses: ADD and MODIFY.

Adding Columns

Let's create a simple table and then, after it's created, add a column to it. First, let's create a table, CRUISE_ORDERS, using the following CREATE TABLE statement:

```
CREATE TABLE CRUISE_ORDERS
(CRUISE_ORDER_ID NUMBER,
 SALES_REP_ID    NUMBER);
```

The following ALTER TABLE statement adds a new column called ORDER_ DATE with a datatype of VARCHAR2(20):

```
ALTER TABLE CRUISE_ORDERS ADD (ORDER_DATE VARCHAR2(20));
```

Notice the structure of this statement:

- The required keywords ALTER TABLE
- The name of the table we wish to alter
- The required keyword ADD
- The name of a new column, and its column specification, enclosed in parentheses

The newly added column will be appended to the end of the current table's list of columns.

For each column, the clause specifies one or more of the following three elements:

- Datatype and datatype specification—required
- DEFAULT and default value—optional
- CONSTRAINT definition—optional

The datatype is required for each column specification. None of the other elements is required. However, if more than one is included, they must be included in the order listed here. In other words, if we want to add a column WEATHER_ CODE to the table CRUISE_ORDERS, and give it a default value of zero and a datatype of NUMBER(2), then this is syntactically wrong:

```
ALTER TABLE CRUISE_ORDERS
    ADD (WEATHER_CODE DEFAULT 0 NUMBER(2));
```

But this is syntactically correct:

```
ALTER TABLE CRUISE_ORDERS
    ADD (WEATHER_CODE NUMBER(2) DEFAULT 0);
```

In other words—the syntax for the column definition is the same as it is for the CREATE TABLE statement.

The syntax for adding multiple columns in a single statement is to use the keyword ADD one time, followed by a required pair of parentheses, inside of which is the series of column specifications, each of which is separated from the other by a comma. For example:

```
ALTER TABLE CRUISE_ORDERS
    ADD (WEATHER_CODE  NUMBER(2) DEFAULT 0,
        TRAVEL_AGENCY VARCHAR2(27) NOT NULL);
```

In this example, we're adding two columns to the CRUISE_ORDERS table: WEATHER_CODE and TRAVEL_AGENCY. Each has its datatype specification included, and the first has a default value of zero, while the second is a NOT NULL column.

Adding NOT NULL Columns

If you are adding a column to a table, and the table already contains data, there are some restrictions you need to keep in mind. For example, if there are already rows in a given table, then you cannot alter that table by adding a new column with the NOT NULL constraint. For example:

```
01   ALTER TABLE CRUISE_ORDERS
02        ADD   FIRST_TIME_CUSTOMER VARCHAR2(5)
03              NOT NULL;
```

This statement might fail: if the CRUISE_ORDERS table already has rows, adding the FIRST_TIME_CUSTOMER column would have the effect of creating one column per row. But those columns would be empty. However, we're trying to add the column with the NOT NULL constraint. The result: the preceding statement will fail if the CRUISE_ORDERS table already contains data.

However, if we add a column with a DEFAULT value, the statement will succeed:

```
01   ALTER TABLE CRUISE_ORDERS
02        ADD   FIRST_TIME_CUSTOMER VARCHAR2(5)
03              DEFAULT 'YES'
04              NOT NULL;
```

This statement is syntactically valid and will execute successfully. Each row already in the CRUISE_ORDERS table will be given a column value of 'YES' for the FIRST_TIME_CUSTOMER column.

(Note: We're assuming, of course, that there is not already a FIRST_TIME_CUSTOMER column in the CRUISE_ORDERS table. If there were, then either of these SQL statements would fail.)

If the statement were executed without the portion on line 3, and no FIRST_TIME_CUSTOMER column were already present, then the statement would parse successfully yet fail in execution if any rows already existed in the CRUISE_ORDERS table. That makes sense if you think about it—when you add a NOT NULL column to existing rows, you are attempting to create an instantly impossible situation—empty columns that are not allowed to be empty. SQL won't let you do it. By providing the DEFAULT value in line 3, you are instructing the table how to handle NULL columns. If there are no rows in the table at the time you create a NOT NULL column, the DEFAULT clause isn't necessary. But if rows exist, and you create a column that must have values in it, then you must also assign those values as you create the column—via the DEFAULT clause. Either that, or you'll experience an execution error and the ALTER TABLE statement will fail.

Modifying Columns

Once we've created a table and its columns, we can modify any of those columns using the ALTER TABLE statement. This is true for any columns—including those created with the CREATE TABLE statement, or added later with the ALTER TABLE . . . ADD statement.

Let's look at the current structure of our CRUISE_ORDERS table:

```
Name                  Null?    Type
----------------      ------   -------
CRUISE_ORDER_ID                NUMBER
SALES_REP_ID                   NUMBER
ORDER_DATE                     VARCHAR2(20)
```

We could try to change the datatype of the ORDER_DATE column with this statement:

```
ALTER TABLE CRUISE_ORDERS MODIFY (ORDER_DATE DATE);
```

If the CRUISE_ORDERS table's ORDER_DATE column is empty, this statement will execute successfully. (We'll soon discuss what happens if it isn't empty.) The statement follows the standard syntax of the ALTER TABLE statement's MODIFY clause:

- The required keywords ALTER TABLE, followed by the name of the table we wish to alter
- The keyword MODIFY
- An opening parenthesis, to begin the enclosure of the column specification
- The name of an existing column in the table
- The datatype of the column
- A closing parenthesis, to end the enclosure of the column specification

Note that parentheses, while part of the formal syntax for column specification in ALTER TABLE statements, are not required unless you are specifying more than one column in a single ALTER TABLE statement.

The syntax rules for the MODIFY clause are similar to—but not identical to—the ADD clause. Specifically:

- You can modify the datatype, DEFAULT status, or constraint.
- Only one such element is required in any MODIFY clause.
- You can include multiple elements in any one MODIFY clause provided you define them in the proper order: datatype, then DEFAULT, then constraint— recognizing that you don't have to specify them all.

Note: The ADD clause differs in that each column specification of the ADD clause requires a datatype.

You cannot use MODIFY to change the column's name. There's a separate RENAME COLUMN clause for that, which we'll look at in a bit.

The column definition syntax that can be included in the MODIFY clause of the ALTER TABLE statement is the same syntax you would use in the ADD clause of ALTER TABLE, which is also the same column definition syntax you use with CREATE TABLE.

Modifying NOT NULL

To add a NOT NULL constraint to a column, we could use this statement:

```
ALTER TABLE CRUISE_ORDERS MODIFY (ORDER_DATE DATE NOT NULL);
```

If you wish to reverse the effects of the NOT NULL constraint, you can't drop the constraint. Instead, you modify the column by changing its NOT NULL constraint to NULL:

```
ALTER TABLE CRUISE_ORDERS MODIFY (ORDER_DATE DATE NULL);
```

The preceding two statements have the effect of adding and removing an unnamed NOT NULL constraint on a column.

Modifying Populated Columns

When we discussed the ADD clause, we had to consider what might happen if we tried to add a column to a table that already had rows in it. With MODIFY, you need to consider if a table has rows, and if it does, if those rows have any data in the column you wish to modify.

Depending on the situation, you may or may not be able to modify a particular column in a table. The rules for what you can modify under what circumstances are spelled out in Table 11-1.

TABLE 11-1   Permissible Changes with the ALTER TABLE ... MODIFY Clause

Type of Change	When the Table Has No Rows	When the Table Has Rows and ...		
		...When the Column is NULL	...When the Column Contains Data and Some NULL Values	...When the Column Contains Data in All Rows
Datatypes	Yes	No. Automatic datatype conversion not supported here.		
Precision and Scale	Yes	Yes, if no existing values lose significant digits or value; otherwise no.		
NOT NULL	Yes	No, unless DEFAULT is specified simultaneously.		Yes
PRIMARY KEY	Yes	No		Yes, if existing values are unique; otherwise no.
UNIQUE	Yes	Only if existing values are unique.		
FOREIGN KEY	Yes	Yes, provided that values match with referenced table's values; otherwise no.		
CHECK	Yes	Yes, if existing values don't violate the CHECK constraint, then no.		
DEFAULT	Yes			

The bottom line: you cannot modify a column to take on properties that conflict with any existing data that is already present in the column. For example:

- You cannot modify a column to make it a NUMBER column if it already contains character strings as data.
- You cannot modify a column to make it a PRIMARY KEY if it already contains duplicate values.

So just use common sense here; understand the functionality of all of the datatypes and constraints, and you'll understand what you can and cannot do.

Let's look at some examples. In our earlier section, the CRUISE_ORDERS table had an ORDER_DATE column with a datatype of VARCHAR2(20). We changed the datatype to DATE. That would be accepted if—and only if—the CRUISE_ORDERS table's ORDER_DATE column was empty at the time of the

ALTER TABLE statement. Otherwise, that ALTER TABLE statement would have been rejected. However, had the CRUISE_ORDERS table contained no data, this statement would have been accepted:

```
ALTER TABLE CRUISE_ORDERS MODIFY ORDER_DATE VARCHAR2(35);
```

In this particular ALTER TABLE statement, we're only changing the precision of the VARCHAR2 datatype from 20 to 35. That is accepted in a table that contains data.

In addition, you could have changed the column's datatype if the column itself had been NULL, despite how many rows might exist in the table.

Let's modify an existing column by adding a new constraint to it. We'll append an in-line constraint specification to the end of the clause, like this:

```
ALTER TABLE CRUISE_ORDERS MODIFY ORDER_DATE NOT NULL;
```

As an alternative, we could've done this:

```
ALTER TABLE CRUISE_ORDERS MODIFY ORDER_DATE CONSTRAINT NN_ORDER_DATE NOT NULL;
```

Here are several modifications to one column in one statement:

```
ALTER TABLE CRUISE_ORDERS
      MODIFY ORDER_DATE DATE
                       DEFAULT SYSDATE
                       CONSTRAINT NN_ORDER_DATE NOT NULL;
```

This statement is valid syntactically and will execute successfully if there are no rows in the table at the time it is executed.

e x a m

ⓦatch   *Remember that an ALTER TABLE statement is a DDL statement, and*   *that when any DDL statement executes, it causes an implied commit event to occur.*

Renaming Columns

You can rename columns using the ALTER TABLE statement with the RENAME COLUMN clause. Here is an example:

```
ALTER TABLE CRUISE_ORDERS RENAME COLUMN SALES_REP_ID TO SALES_AGENT_ID;
```

The syntax is as follows:

- The required keywords ALTER TABLE, followed by the name of the table we wish to alter
- The keywords RENAME COLUMN
- The name of the column we wish to change
- The keyword TO, followed by the new name of the column

All of these elements are required. Note that RENAME uses the keyword COLUMN. The ADD and MODIFY clauses do not include this keyword, but RENAME does.

CERTIFICATION OBJECTIVE 11.02

Drop Columns and Set Column UNUSED

This section looks at what you can do when you find that you have columns you no longer wish to keep in a table. You can choose to drop a column from the database, or as an alternative, you may render it UNUSED. This section looks at how to do either of these tasks.

Dropping Columns

Altering a table to drop columns that are no longer used can free up storage space and potentially improve performance of the table. Any constraints or indices on the column will also be dropped when you drop the column.

Here are two examples—one without parentheses around the column name, another with the parentheses:

```
ALTER TABLE ORDER_RETURNS DROP COLUMN CRUISE_ORDER_DATE;
ALTER TABLE ORDER_RETURNS DROP (CRUISE_ORDER_DATE);
```

Both are valid statements to drop the CRUISE_ORDER_DATE column. Note that the keyword COLUMN is required in the first variation, where the DROP clause syntax omits the parentheses. In the second variation, the keyword COLUMN is omitted, and the parentheses are used.

The first variation is limited to dropping one column per SQL statement. Using the second variation, however, you can drop multiple columns by using the keyword

DROP one time, omitting the keyword COLUMN, and then including a pair of parentheses, followed by a list of the column names you wish to drop. For example:

```
ALTER TABLE ORDER_RETURNS
            DROP (CRUISE_ORDER_DATE, FORM_TYPE, NAME_SUFFIX);
```

You cannot drop all of the columns in a table. A table must have at least one column.

Restrictions

If a column is referenced by a foreign key constraint in another table, then the preceding syntax will trigger a warning message and the attempt to drop the column will fail.

For example, consider this code:

```
CREATE TABLE CRUISE_ORDERS
   (CRUISE_ORDER_ID    NUMBER,
    ORDER_DATE         DATE,
    CONSTRAINT PK_CO PRIMARY KEY (CRUISE_ORDER_ID, ORDER_DATE));
CREATE TABLE ORDER_RETURNS
   (ORDER_RETURN_ID    NUMBER,
    CRUISE_ORDER_ID    NUMBER,
    CRUISE_ORDER_DATE  DATE,
    CONSTRAINT PK_OR PRIMARY KEY (ORDER_RETURN_ID),
    CONSTRAINT FK_OR_CO FOREIGN KEY
            (CRUISE_ORDER_ID, CRUISE_ORDER_DATE)
         REFERENCES CRUISE_ORDERS (CRUISE_ORDER_ID, ORDER_DATE));
```

These SQL statements will create two tables with a FOREIGN KEY relationship connecting them together—see Figure 11-1 for the data model representing the relationship. (Incidentally, this example is a great demonstration of a composite PRIMARY KEY and FOREIGN KEY constraint.)

In the CRUISE_ORDERS table that we just created, we cannot drop the CRUISE_ORDER_ID column, or the ORDER_DATE column, for two different reasons:

- They form part of the PRIMARY KEY constraint, and constrained columns cannot be dropped unless the constraint is first dropped;
- They form part of the referred key in the FOREIGN KEY of another table. They cannot be dropped as long as a FOREIGN KEY constraint refers to them.

Similarly, we cannot drop the column in the ORDER_RETURNS table that is subject to the PRIMARY KEY constraint (ORDER_RETURN_ID), nor the

FIGURE 11-1

Data model
for CRUISE_
ORDERS and
ORDER_
RETURNS

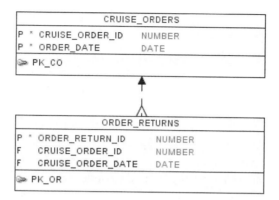

columns that are subject to the FOREIGN KEY constraint (CRUISE_ORDER_ID and ORDER_DATE). The reasons are similar:

- ORDER_RETURN_ID is the PRIMARY KEY of this table.
- CRUISE_ORDER_ID and ORDER_DATE are the FOREIGN KEY for this table.

See Figure 11-2 for an example of the error messages that you'll encounter when trying to drop these constrained columns.

There is a solution here. We need to add the keywords CASCADE CONSTRAINTS to our SQL statements. For example:

```
ALTER TABLE ORDER_RETURNS
            DROP COLUMN CRUISE_ORDER_DATE CASCADE CONSTRAINTS;
```

This statement will successfully drop the CRUISE_ORDER_DATE column in ORDER_RETURNS. It will also drop the associated FOREIGN KEY constraint.

FIGURE 11-2

Attempting to
drop a column
referenced in a
FOREIGN KEY
constraint

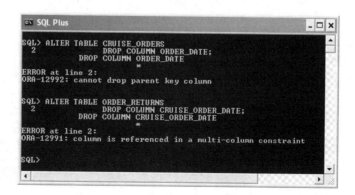

See Figure 11-3 for an example of the results. We could use this same approach to drop all of the columns we just reviewed, but as we stated, the effect of the CASCADE CONSTRAINT keywords with the DROP COLUMN clause is not only to drop the column but also to drop the associated constraints on the column that might prevent the column from being dropped.

UNUSED

Instead of dropping a table column you are no longer using, you may elect to declare it *unused* and leave it in place. Once you set a column as UNUSED, it is never again available; it is as though it has been dropped. As with dropped columns, any constraints or indices on the column will also be dropped. You will never be able to recover a column that is set to UNUSED. A ROLLBACK statement will have no effect—an UNUSED column will not be recovered in a ROLLBACK operation. Once a column is set to UNUSED, you can add new columns that have the same name as any unused columns for the table.

So why wouldn't you just DROP a column instead of setting it to UNUSED? One reason is the performance for the DROP statement versus the SET UNUSED approach. If you're working with a very large table or set of tables, and you need to drop some columns, you may find that the system performance for executing the DROP is temporarily unacceptable, particularly for a system that is in heavy production. If this is an issue, and you need to achieve the look-and-feel of a dropped column immediately, then the SET UNUSED alternative is a welcome option. The performance is speedy, the results are—for all practical purposes—the same, and you can always schedule a

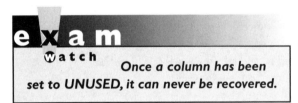

e x a m

ⓦatch *Once a column has been set to UNUSED, it can never be recovered.*

FIGURE 11-3

DROP COLUMN
with CASCADE
CONSTRAINTS

```
SQL Plus                                                    _ □ ×

SQL> ALTER TABLE ORDER_RETURNS
  2             DROP COLUMN CRUISE_ORDER_DATE;
            DROP COLUMN CRUISE_ORDER_DATE
                                  *
ERROR at line 2:
ORA-12991: column is referenced in a multi-column constraint

SQL> ALTER TABLE ORDER_RETURNS
  2             DROP COLUMN CRUISE_ORDER_DATE CASCADE CONSTRAINTS;

Table altered.

SQL>
```

time later to come back and drop the column during a period of low activity in the database.

One thing to keep in mind: there's a limit to the total number of columns any given table can have. That limit is 1,000—you cannot create more than a thousand columns in any one table. If you set a column to be UNUSED, that column will still count as part of the thousand columns toward your limit, until you eventually DROP the column—which you can do; we'll discuss how to drop an unused column in a bit.

The syntax for SET UNUSED is virtually identical to the ALTER TABLE . . . DROP syntax. Simply replace DROP with the keywords SET UNUSED, and the rest is the same. For example:

```
ALTER TABLE ORDER_RETURNS
        SET UNUSED COLUMN CRUISE_ORDER_DATE;
```

As with DROP, the syntax for changing multiple columns to the UNUSED state requires parentheses and eliminates the COLUMN reserved word, like so:

```
ALTER TABLE ORDER_RETURNS
        SET UNUSED (CRUISE_ORDER_DATE, FORM_TYPE, NAME_SUFFIX);
```

You can set as many columns to UNUSED as you wish. The only requirement is that you must, as you might guess, satisfy all constraints and other requirements of a table and its structure—for example, the table still must have at least one valid column at any time—so you cannot set all of its columns to UNUSED.

Tables that have any columns that are set to UNUSED can be found in the data dictionary view USER_UNUSED_COL_TABS. However, this view doesn't reveal any column names that are unused; it simply gives you the names of any and all tables that contain unused columns, and a numeric count of how many unused columns each one contains. You cannot recover the unused columns, nor can you even identify them. But you can drop them. To drop those unused columns, use this statement:

```
ALTER TABLE table_name DROP UNUSED COLUMNS;
```

For example:

```
ALTER TABLE ORDER_RETURNS DROP UNUSED COLUMNS;
```

This statement will drop all unused columns that are associated with the table ORDER_RETURNS.

CERTIFICATION OBJECTIVE 11.03

Add Constraints

In Chapter 2, you created integrity constraints as part of the CREATE TABLE statement. This section discusses how you can use the ALTER TABLE statement to add a constraint to an existing table, how to modify an existing constraint, how to disable a constraint, and how to remove a constraint. If you're looking for a section on using the CREATE CONSTRAINT statement—there isn't one. You don't create integrity constraints directly, but instead create them as part of the CREATE TABLE statement—which you've seen in Chapter 2—or with the ALTER TABLE statement, which is the subject of this section. Note that the term "integrity constraint" and "constraint" are used interchangeably.

Using ALTER TABLE to Add Constraints

When you looked at the CREATE TABLE statement, you saw that there were two major categories of syntax for creating constraints as part of the table:

- In-line, where the syntax for the constraint is included as part of the column definition
- Out-of-line, where the syntax for the constraint is defined on its own, separate from any particular column definition

The same is true when using the ALTER TABLE statement. You can create a constraint in-line or out-of-line.

For example, let's start with the following CREATE TABLE statement:

```
CREATE TABLE CRUISE_ORDERS
(CRUISE_ORDER_ID    NUMBER,
 SALES_AGENT_ID     NUMBER,
 ORDER_DATE         DATE,
 CONFIRMATION_DATE DATE);
```

Now let's look at three different ways to use the ALTER TABLE to add a PRIMARY KEY constraint to this table. First we'll use the in-line syntax:

```
ALTER TABLE CRUISE_ORDERS
    MODIFY CRUISE_ORDER_ID PRIMARY KEY;
```

That's perfectly acceptable. This is in-line because this form of the ALTER TABLE statement is modifying the column, and specifying the constraint as part of the column definition. In this example, the only modification of the column is the addition of the constraint.

Similarly, we could use this second form of in-line, where we do basically the same thing, although we name the constraint with a name of our choosing, as follows:

```
ALTER TABLE CRUISE_ORDERS
    MODIFY CRUISE_ORDER_ID CONSTRAINT PK_NEW_CONSTRAINT PRIMARY KEY;
```

Again, in this example, we've used the in-line approach, where the focus of the ALTER TABLE statement is the column, and as part of the column definition, we've named the constraint PK_NEW_CONSTRAINT.

Here is an example of the out-of-line syntax for adding a constraint to an existing table:

```
ALTER TABLE CRUISE_ORDERS
    ADD CONSTRAINT PK_NEW_CONSTRAINT PRIMARY KEY (CRUISE_ORDER_ID);
```

Notice that in this example, we are not modifying a column. We are using a new clause here, the ALTER TABLE clause ADD CONSTRAINT. The focus of this form of ALTER TABLE is not a column, but the constraint itself.

See Figure 11-4 for an example of what happens when we create this table and then execute the out-of-line form to add a constraint, along with the Oracle SQL messages that result.

The out-of-line syntax is required for constraints that are applied to two or more columns, such as a composite primary key constraint. Such a constraint cannot be created in-line, since it is based on more than one column. For example, let's go back to our primary key on the CRUISE_ORDERS table and create a composite primary key instead:

```
ALTER TABLE CRUISE_ORDERS
    ADD CONSTRAINT PK_NEW_CONSTRAINT
        PRIMARY KEY (CRUISE_ORDER_ID, SALES_AGENT_ID);
```

FIGURE 11-4

CREATE TABLE and ALTER TABLE ADD CONSTRAINT results

```
SQL> CREATE TABLE CRUISE_ORDERS
  2   (CRUISE_ORDER_ID  NUMBER,
  3    SALES_AGENT_ID   NUMBER,
  4    ORDER_DATE       DATE);

Table created.

SQL> ALTER TABLE CRUISE_ORDERS
  2          ADD CONSTRAINT PK_NEW_CONSTRAINT PRIMARY KEY (CRUISE_ORDER_ID);

Table altered.

SQL>
```

This statement creates a primary key based on two columns of the CRUISE_ ORDERS table. We could not accomplish this with the in-line syntax. The out-of-line syntax is the only way for creating composite constraints.

Adding a NOT NULL Constraint

The syntax for working with the NOT NULL constraint has the same limitation with the ALTER TABLE statement that we already observed it has with the CREATE TABLE statement. That is to say: you cannot declare a NOT NULL constraint with the out-of-line syntax; it can only be created with the in-line syntax. In other words, this works:

```
ALTER TABLE CRUISE_ORDERS
      MODIFY CRUISE_ORDER_ID NOT NULL;
```

So does this:

```
ALTER TABLE CRUISE_ORDERS
    MODIFY CRUISE_ORDER_ID CONSTRAINT NN_CRUISE_ORDER_ID NOT NULL;
```

But this does not:

```
ALTER TABLE CRUISE_ORDERS
    ADD CONSTRAINT NN_THIS_IS_WRONG NOT NULL (CRUISE_ORDER_ID);
```

This last sample code will fail. You cannot use the out-of-line syntax to create a NOT NULL constraint—you must use the in-line form.

Know it and act accordingly.

Syntax Notes

The syntax rules for constraints and the ALTER TABLE out-of-line syntax are the same as those with the CREATE TABLE statement's out-of-line syntax. In other words, they are as follows:

- The keywords ALTER TABLE, followed by the name of the table
- The keyword ADD
- The optional keyword CONSTRAINT, and, if included, the name of the constraint you make up, according to the rules for naming database objects (Note: Our example chose to place a PK_ prefix at the start of the PRIMARY KEY constraint to indicate the constraint type, but this style is not required.)
- The type of constraint: either UNIQUE, PRIMARY KEY, FOREIGN KEY, or CHECK (not the NOT NULL constraint, however)
- Finally, the constraint's specification appropriate to the type of constraint you chose, enclosed in a pair of parentheses

If you're creating a UNIQUE or PRIMARY KEY constraint, the specification will include a list of one or more column names from the table, each separated from the other by a comma. If only one column is specified, no comma is required.

If you're creating a NOT NULL constraint, no additional specification is required.

If you're creating a CHECK constraint, then the specification includes an expression to filter incoming column data for each row added to the table. For example:

```
ALTER TABLE CRUISE_ORDERS
    ADD CONSTRAINT CK_ORDER_DATE CHECK (ORDER_DATE <= CONFIRMATION_DATE);
```

The preceding example shows:

- The required keywords ALTER TABLE, followed by the table name
- The required keyword ADD
- The optional keyword CONSTRAINT, which—if used—is followed by the constraint name
- The required keyword indicating the type of constraint, which in this example is CHECK (other types are PRIMARY KEY, UNIQUE, FOREIGN KEY—but not the NOT NULL option, since this is the out-of-line syntax)
- The constraint's expression, which in this case is an expression that compares the value of the incoming ORDER_DATE value and ensures that it is less than or equal to the incoming CONFIRMATION_DATE value

In this example, once the constraint is created on the table, rows won't be accepted by the CRUISE_ORDERS table if the ORDER_DATE is later than the CONFIRMATION_DATE.

In the case of a FOREIGN KEY constraint, the syntax is more involved than the other constraint types, which you've seen before. Here is an example of the FOREIGN KEY constraint added with the ALTER TABLE statement using the out-of-line syntax:

```
ALTER TABLE CRUISE_ORDERS
    ADD CONSTRAINT FK_CRUISE_ORDERS_SALES_AGENTS
        FOREIGN KEY (SALES_AGENT_ID)
        REFERENCES SALES_AGENTS(SALES_AGENT_ID);
```

The preceding FOREIGN KEY constraint has the following syntax:

- The reserved words ALTER TABLE, followed by the table name
- The reserved words ADD CONSTRAINT, followed by the constraint name you make up
- The reserved words FOREIGN KEY, followed by the name of the column in this table to which you are applying the constraint, enclosed in parentheses

■ The reserved word REFERENCES, followed by the name of a different table in the database to which you wish to link this table as a foreign key, followed by the column list in that table to which you wish to relate this table, enclosed in parentheses

The referenced table (in this example, it's SALES_AGENTS) must already exist. The columns in that table are not required to have the same names, but the datatypes must match. In other words, you cannot create a FOREIGN KEY constraint on, for example, a DATE column in one table and then REFERENCE it to, say, a NUMBER column in another table.

As you can see, all of these ALTER TABLE . . . ADD CONSTRAINT statements follow the out-of-line syntax style that you saw with CREATE TABLE earlier.

Modifying Constraints

You can use the ALTER TABLE statement to make a limited number of modifications to a constraint. If your goal is to change the definition of a particular constraint, you'll probably need to drop and recreate it. Examples of situations in which you need to drop and recreate a constraint include

■ Adding or removing columns to the column list of a PRIMARY KEY, FOREIGN KEY, or UNIQUE constraint

■ Changing the logic of a CHECK constraint

■ Changing the table that a FOREIGN KEY constraint references

In such situations as these, you can't modify the constraint, but instead you must drop it and then create it with whatever changes you wish for it to have.

The ALTER TABLE . . . MODIFY statement is limited to changing the state of a constraint. We'll examine how this works when we discuss how to enable and disable constraints in an upcoming section.

Removing Constraints

To remove a constraint, you use the ALTER TABLE statement with the DROP clause option. There are three forms.

DROP PRIMARY KEY

To drop a PRIMARY KEY constraint, you don't need the name of the constraint, since a given table can have one—and only one—PRIMARY KEY. The syntax is as follows:

```
ALTER TABLE table_name DROP PRIMARY KEY options;
```

The options include the following:

- **CASCADE**   This drops any dependent constraints as well. In other words, a FOREIGN KEY may refer to this PRIMARY KEY constraint. Using CASCADE here will drop any and all FOREIGN KEY constraints that reference this PRIMARY KEY constraint. CASCADE is optional; the default is to not cascade.
- **KEEP INDEX or DROP INDEX**   The PRIMARY KEY must have an associated index—this option indicates whether you wish to drop the index as well, or not. The clause is optional. The default is DROP INDEX.

If used, CASCADE must precede KEEP INDEX or DROP INDEX.

DROP UNIQUE

To drop a UNIQUE constraint, you don't need the name of the constraint, just the list of columns that are included in the constraint:

```
ALTER TABLE table_name DROP UNIQUE (column1, column2, . . . ) options;
```

The options for UNIQUE are the same as they are for PRIMARY KEY.

If you drop a PRIMARY KEY constraint with the ALTER TABLE . . . DROP statement, then by default	**you are also dropping the associated INDEX. The same is true for the UNIQUE constraint.**

DROP CONSTRAINT

To drop other constraints, you need the constraint name:

```
ALTER TABLE table_name DROP CONSTRAINT constraint_name options;
```

The only option is CASCADE, which directs whether you wish for dependent constraints to be dropped as well.

Dropping NOT NULL Constraints

You can't really drop a NOT NULL constraint, but you can get the job done using this statement:

```
ALTER TABLE table_name MODIFY column_name NULL;
```

Remember: NOT NULL doesn't work with out-of-line syntax, which is what this section is reviewing for modifying constraints. So you can't use the out-of-line form to get rid of a NOT NULL restriction on a table. Instead, we "add" the keyword NULL, as the above syntax indicates.

Disabling and Enabling Constraints

Sometimes you find yourself in a situation where you wish to make changes to the database that an existing constraint is preventing you from changing. You won't necessarily want to drop the constraint altogether, just render it ineffective for a limited time and purpose. There are many situations in which you would benefit from disabling a constraint. For example, perhaps you need to temporarily import data from a branch office or other source, data that perhaps isn't consistent with your constraint rules, but data that you could easily clean up with some simple UPDATE statements once the data is in your database system.

Even if the incoming data is compliant with the constraints, you may still prefer to temporarily disable the constraints for performance reasons if the data you are importing is large. Performance can be significantly slower when loading data into a table with constraints—one row is validated at a time. Such a process can be significantly slower than simply loading the data without the constraints and then enabling the constraints once the data is in the table, which is a significantly faster alternative.

Another typical scenario in which the ability to disable a constraint is helpful involves the requirement to edit rows that are subject to PRIMARY KEY and FOREIGN KEY constraints. When a parent table has one or more PRIMARY KEY columns that are referenced by the child table's FOREIGN KEY constraint, the parent table is not allowed to remove a PRIMARY KEY value upon which a child row depends. The mechanism that disallows this is the FOREIGN KEY constraint in the child table. However, you can disable that FOREIGN KEY and perform the task.

You'll look at a specific example involving FOREIGN KEY constraints in the next section.

DISABLE

For an example of disabling constraints, let's look at a simplified version of the tables PORTS and SHIPS. See Figure 11-5.

FIGURE 11-5

Diagram of the
PORTS and SHIPS
tables

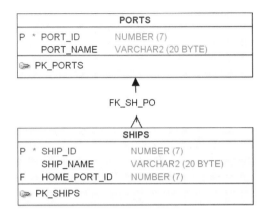

In our example, PORTS is the parent table, with a column PORT_ID, on which is a PRIMARY KEY constraint. SHIPS is the child table to PORTS. SHIPS has a HOME_PORT_ID column and a FOREIGN KEY constraint upon that column that references the PORTS table's PORT_ID column. As you know, the FOREIGN KEY in the SHIPS table means that if any row added to the SHIPS table includes a value for HOME_PORT_ID, that value must already be present in the PORTS table's PORT_ID column.

Here's the SQL code that creates our tables and adds a few rows of data (line numbers added):

```
01   CREATE TABLE PORTS
02    (PORT_ID    NUMBER(7),
03     PORT_NAME  VARCHAR2(20),
04     CONSTRAINT PK_PORTS PRIMARY KEY (PORT_ID));
05   CREATE TABLE SHIPS
06    (SHIP_ID     NUMBER(7),
07     SHIP_NAME    VARCHAR2(20),
08     HOME_PORT_ID NUMBER(7),
09     CONSTRAINT PK_SHIPS PRIMARY KEY (SHIP_ID),
10     CONSTRAINT FK_SH_PO FOREIGN KEY (HOME_PORT_ID) REFERENCES PORTS (PORT_ID));
11   INSERT INTO PORTS VALUES (50, 'Jacksonville');
12   INSERT INTO PORTS VALUES (51, 'New Orleans');
13   INSERT INTO SHIPS VALUES (10, 'Codd Royale', 50);
```

After these statements successfully execute, we cannot delete a row in the PORTS table that is referenced by a SHIPS row:

```
DELETE FROM PORTS WHERE PORT_ID = 50;

Error starting at line 1 in command:
DELETE FROM PORTS WHERE PORT_ID = 50
Error report:
SQL Error: ORA-02292: integrity constraint (EFCODD.FK_SH_PO) violated - child
record found
02292. 00000 - "integrity constraint (%s.%s) violated - child record found"
*Cause:    attempted to delete a parent key value that had a foreign
           dependency.
*Action:   delete dependencies first then parent or disable constraint.
```

The conflict is with a row in the SHIPS table. It contains a HOME_PORT_ID value of 50, and since there's a foreign key constraint that ties HOME_PORT_ID values with the PORTS table's PORT_ID column, then the row with a value of 50 cannot be deleted as long as the child row exists. This restriction was created with the foreign key constraint named FK_SH_PO, as the error message indicates. We created that constraint in line 10 of our SQL code earlier.

With the foreign key constraint in place, any row in the SHIPS table is dependent on the row in the PORTS table that shares the same PORT_ID value. In other words, the SHIPS table contains child rows that are dependent on the parent rows in PORTS.

Note: In this example, the SHIPS table does not require all rows to have a value for HOME_PORT_ID. The HOME_PORT_ID column does not have the NOT NULL constraint. Therefore, it's possible to add rows in SHIPS without a HOME_PORT_ID, and therefore without creating a dependency. Furthermore, the PORTS table is capable of containing rows for which no children exist in SHIPS—not all PORT rows necessarily have a SHIP row sharing the same PORT_ID value in its HOME_PORT_ID column. This all means that, in this example, there may be independent rows in either table. Rows in PORTS that have no child rows in SHIPS can be deleted successfully:

```
DELETE FROM PORTS WHERE PORT_ID = 51;

1 rows deleted
```

(Note how Oracle points out that "1 rows" have been deleted.)

Also, any child row can be deleted in SHIPS, regardless of the foreign key constraint. Child rows can always be deleted without regard for the existence of parent rows. Foreign key constraints never restrict the deletion of child rows. But in any situation involving a foreign key constraint, parent rows cannot be deleted if corresponding child rows exist.

This is why you may wish to disable the foreign key constraint in SHIPS in order to delete the parent rows in PORTS. The statement to disable the constraint in this example is

```
ALTER TABLE SHIPS DISABLE CONSTRAINT FK_SH_PO;
```

In this example, we disable the foreign key constraint by specifying its name. The result: the definition of the constraint remains in the database, but it is rendered ineffective for the time being.

The preceding example of disabling a constraint adheres to the following syntax:

```
ALTER TABLE table_name DISABLE validate_expression constraint_expression;
```

- The required keywords ALTER TABLE
- The name of the table
- The keyword DISABLE
- One of two optional keywords: VALIDATE or NOVALIDATE. Default is VALIDATE
- One of three types of constraint expressions:
  - PRIMARY KEY
  - UNIQUE (*column1*, *column2*, . . .)
  - CONSTRAINT *constraint_name*

In our earlier example, we used the third form of the constraint expression.

To disable any constraint, the syntax you use depends on which type of constraint you wish to disable:

- PRIMARY KEY constraints require that you merely identify the constraint as the PRIMARY KEY for the table.
- UNIQUE constraints require you to identify the columns that are constrained.
- All other constraints require that you name them specifically.

These options are detailed in Table 11-2. If you aren't sure what the names are of the constraints for a given table, you can query the data dictionary. Oracle's data dictionary is a subject we discuss in detail in Chapter 14. For now, this query on the data dictionary will get you a list of the names of all the constraints for a given table, and the type of constraint each one represents:

```
SELECT  CONSTRAINT_NAME, CONSTRAINT_TYPE
FROM    USER_CONSTRAINTS
WHERE   TABLE_NAME = 'SHIPS';


CONSTRAINT_NAME                 CONSTRAINT_TYPE
------------------------------  ---------------
PK_SHIPS                        P
FK_SH_PO                        R
```

The values for CONSTRAINT_TYPE are explained in Chapter 14. For now, note that 'R' is a referential constraint, which is to say it's a foreign key constraint, which refers to another table, which in this case is PORTS.

Returning to our earlier example, once we've disabled the foreign key constraint FK_SH_PO, we can delete any parent rows in the PORTS table as we wish. But doing so will leave child rows in the SHIPS table that are assigned to the PORT row we delete in the PORTS table.

TABLE 11-2 Disabling Constraints—Syntax Alternatives	**To DISABLE a Constraint of Type:**	**Use One of These Syntax Forms:**
	PRIMARY KEY	ALTER TABLE table DISABLE PRIMARY KEY; ALTER TABLE table MODIFY PRIMARY KEY DISABLE;
	UNIQUE	ALTER TABLE table DISABLE UNIQUE (column_list); ALTER TABLE table MODIFY UNIQUE (column_list) DISABLE;
	CHECK FOREIGN KEY	ALTER TABLE table DISABLE CONSTRAINT constraint_name; ALTER TABLE table MODIFY CONSTRAINT constraint_name DISABLE;

ENABLE

Once a constraint has been disabled, it can be enabled once again by executing a variation on the statement we examined earlier to disable it—replacing the word DISABLE with the word ENABLE. For example:

```
ALTER TABLE SHIPS ENABLE CONSTRAINT FK_SH_PO;
```

However, if the data contained in the table no longer supports the constraint, the statement will not execute successfully, and the constraint will not be enabled. Following our example, with the foreign key constraint FK_SH_PO disabled, if a parent row in the PORTS table were deleted, then an attempt to restore the FK_SH_PO constraint on the SHIPS table would result in child rows in SHIPS that have no parents in PORTS. These rows are known as *orphans*. SQL won't allow the constraint to be enabled when orphan rows are present; there must be valid parent rows in the referenced table of the foreign key constraint, which is the PORTS table in this example.

However, if you wish to enable a constraint, and the existing data subject to the constraint honors the requirements of the constraint, then you can enable it successfully.

CASCADE

If you wish to disable a constraint that has referential integrity constraints applied to it, you need the CASCADE keyword. For example, the foreign key constraint on the SHIPS table references the PORT_ID column of the PORTS table, which is the primary key in the PORTS table. You cannot disable the primary key constraint on the PORTS table with this statement:

```
ALTER TABLE PORTS DISABLE PRIMARY KEY;

Error report:
SQL Error: ORA-02297: cannot disable constraint (EFCODD.PK_PORTS) - dependencies
exist
02297. 00000 - "cannot disable constraint (%s.%s) - dependencies exist"
*Cause:    an alter table disable constraint failed becuase the table has
           foriegn keys that are dpendent on this constraint.
*Action:   Either disable the foreign key constraints or use disable cascade
```

(Note: the misspellings of "becuase", "foriegn", and "dpendent" in the preceding error statement are from Oracle's own system, and not this book.)

The problem here is that the PORTS PRIMARY KEY is an integral part of the SHIPS table's FOREIGN KEY. To disable both at the same time, you could use this statement:

```
ALTER TABLE PORTS DISABLE PRIMARY KEY CASCADE;
```

The result: both constraints will be disabled. However, you cannot "cascade" the ENABLE statement. You must enable each constraint individually. For example:

```
ALTER TABLE PORTS ENABLE PRIMARY KEY;
```

This statement will enable the primary key. You'll have to issue additional statements to enable any foreign key constraints that were disabled as a result of the CASCADE clause.

VALIDATE / INVALIDATE

Earlier we saw the optional keywords VALIDATE and INVALIDATE that can be used when enabling a constraint.

These keywords may also be used when disabling a constraint. For example, we could have issued this statement earlier:

```
ALTER TABLE SHIPS ENABLE VALIDATE CONSTRAINT FK_SH_PO;
```

- The keyword VALIDATE is the default.
- The keyword ENABLE may be replaced with DISABLE.
- The keyword VALIDATE may be replaced with NOVALIDATE.

The combinations are described in Table 11-3.

TABLE 11-3	Keyword Combination	Description
Description of Constraint Keywords	ENABLE VALIDATE	Enables the constraint and applies it to existing rows in the table. VALIDATE is the default—therefore, ENABLE VALIDATE has the same effect as ENABLE.
	ENABLE NOVALIDATE	Enables the constraint but does not apply it to existing rows. In other words, it allows existing rows in the table to violate the constraint. Ensures that incoming rows honor the constraint.
	DISABLE VALIDATE	Disables the constraint. If the constraint has an associated index, the index is dropped. Can be used to temporarily speed up massive data imports using EXCHANGE PARTITION, which is beyond the scope of the exam and this book.
	DISABLE NOVALIDATE	The same as DISABLE.

The benefit to NOVALIDATE is that it can support your efforts during development, or during a time in which you are moving and integrating large amounts of data. The use of ENABLE NOVALIDATE will allow you to create a constraint on a table but not yet apply it to the table's data.

The VALIDATE or NOVALIDATE keyword is optional and may be omitted from the ALTER TABLE ENABLE and ALTER TABLE DISABLE statements.

on the **Job**

Oracle formally recommends the following series of steps in performing a large data load into a table (or tables) in which constraints apply:

- *DISABLE the constraints. Take the default value of NOVALIDATE.*

- *Move the data into the table.*

- *ENABLE NOVALIDATE the constraints on the table.*

- *ENABLE VALIDATE the constraints on the table.*

The preceding series of steps is intended to achieve optimal performance in working with large amounts of data.

DROP TABLE and CASCADE CONSTRAINTS

The DROP TABLE statement drops tables. For example:

```
DROP TABLE SHIP_HISTORY;
```

The previous statement will drop the SHIP_HISTORY table and any constraints and index objects on the table. However, if the table has any referential integrity constraints—that is, any FOREIGN KEY constraints in other tables that are dependent on a PRIMARY KEY or UNIQUE constraint in the SHIP_HISTORY table, then the DROP TABLE statement shown above will fail. But this will work:

```
DROP TABLE SHIP_HISTORY CASCADE CONSTRAINTS;
```

The previous statement drops the SHIP_HISTORY table, its integrity constraints and indices, and any referential integrity constraints—that is, any FOREIGN KEY constraints of other tables—that depend on a PRIMARY KEY or UNIQUE constraint of SHIP_HISTORY.

If any FOREIGN KEY constraint is disabled, DROP TABLE on the PRIMARY KEY table will still fail if the constraints exist, unless CASCADE CONSTRAINTS is included in the DROP TABLE statement.

DELETE and ON DELETE

Remember that you cannot DELETE a row in a table if dependent child rows exist. The reason is the FOREIGN KEY constraint on the child table, which is dependent on the PRIMARY KEY in the parent table. As we saw earlier, one alternative approach is to DISABLE the FOREIGN KEY constraint in SHIPS. Once disabled, you may delete the parent rows in PORTS.

Another alternative is create the FOREIGN KEY with the ON DELETE CASCADE clause. To do that, we'll first need to drop the old constraint, and for that, we'll need the name of the constraint. You can obtain that information from the data dictionary with the following query:

```
SELECT TABLE_NAME, CONSTRAINT_NAME, CONSTRAINT_TYPE FROM USER_CONSTRAINTS
WHERE R_CONSTRAINT_NAME IN (SELECT CONSTRAINT_NAME FROM USER_CONSTRAINTS
                WHERE TABLE_NAME = 'PORTS' AND CONSTRAINT_TYPE = 'P')
```

The previous query finds the name of the PRIMARY KEY constraint for PORTS, then returns the names of any tables and their referential integrity constraints that refer to the PORTS table's PRIMARY KEY constraint. For example:

```
TABLE_NAME                       CONSTRAINT_NAME                   C
-------------------------------  -------------------------------   -
SHIPS                            FK_SHIPS_PORTS                    R
```

Once you have the name of the referential integrity constraint, you can drop it, then recreate it with the ON DELETE CASCADE clause:

```
ALTER TABLE SHIPS DROP CONSTRAINT FK_SHIPS_PORTS;
ALTER TABLE SHIPS ADD CONSTRAINT FK_SHIPS_PORTS FOREIGN KEY (HOME_PORT_ID)
        REFERENCES PORTS (PORT_ID) ON DELETE CASCADE;
```

Now, any attempt to delete a row in PORTS should be successful. It will also try to delete any and all rows in the SHIPS table with a value in the HOME_PORT_ID column that matches the PORT table's PORT_ID value (or values) that are being deleted. Note, however, that it still might not work—if other tables have FOREIGN KEY constraints that are dependent on the PORTS or SHIPS table, the DELETE statement will fail for the same reasons. If it fails for any of these reasons, none of the rows are deleted—not in SHIPS, nor in PORTS.

As an alternative, you can create the FOREIGN KEY with the ON DELETE SET NULL clause instead. The syntax is similar to ON DELETE CASCADE:

```
ALTER TABLE SHIPS DROP CONSTRAINT FK_SHIPS_PORTS;
ALTER TABLE SHIPS ADD CONSTRAINT FK_SHIPS_PORTS FOREIGN KEY (HOME_PORT_ID)
        REFERENCES PORTS (PORT_ID) ON DELETE SET NULL;
```

Now any attempts to delete rows in the PORTS table will cause any rows in SHIPS that match (SHIPS.HOME_PORT_ID = PORTS.PORT_ID) to set their HOME_PORT_ID values to NULL. The SHIPS rows will otherwise remain in the SHIPS table, but they will now be "orphan" rows. Any referential integrity constraints that might refer to the SHIPS table will be unaffected, since no rows in the SHIPS table are deleted when a PORTS table row is deleted.

DEFERRABLE and DEFERRED

You can temporarily set a constraint to DEFERRED so that a large set of data might be processed without any constraint checking until after the transaction is completed. To do this, create the constraint with the DEFERRABLE clause, as follows:

```
ALTER TABLE SHIPS DROP CONSTRAINT FK_SHIPS_PORTS;
ALTER TABLE SHIPS ADD CONSTRAINT FK_SHIPS_PORTS FOREIGN KEY (HOME_PORT_ID)
        REFERENCES PORTS (PORT_ID) DEFERRABLE;
```

The default setting for constraints is NOT DEFERRABLE.

Once the constraint has been created as DEFERRABLE, you may issue this statement during a session:

```
SET CONSTRAINT FK_SHIPS_PORTS DEFERRED;
```

Alternatively, you can set all constraints to DEFERRED:

```
SET CONSTRAINT ALL DEFERRED;
```

Once the SET CONSTRAINT command establishes a given constraint—or all constraints—as DEFERRED, the current transaction will temporarily ignore the deferred constraints, and accept rows of data that might violate those constraints. However, once a commit event occurs, the constraint automatically changes state from DEFERRED to IMMEDIATE, and the constraints will be applied. If any are violated, the commit will fail and all data is rolled back.

At any time, you can restore the default behavior of constraints with this command:

```
SET CONSTRAINT FK_SHIPS_PORTS IMMEDIATE;
```

Alternatively, you can set all constraints to IMMEDIATE:

```
SET CONSTRAINT ALL IMMEDIATE;
```

Once set to IMMEDIATE, constraints go back to their default behavior, and are checked after each DML statement is executed.

This approach is somewhat similar to disabling commands, only it's a more temporary state.

Renaming Constraints

You can rename an existing constraint on a table using the RENAME CONSTRAINT clause of the ALTER TABLE statement. Here's an example:

```
ALTER TABLE CRUISE_ORDERS
       RENAME CONSTRAINT SYS_C0015489 TO PK_CRUISE_ORDER_ID;
```

The syntax is as follows:

- The reserved words ALTER TABLE, followed by the table name
- The reserved words RENAME CONSTRAINT
- The existing name of the constraint you are renaming
- The reserved word TO
- The new name of the constraint you are renaming

Any constraint may be renamed. This can be particularly useful in situations where you may have created a constraint using the in-line syntax of the CREATE TABLE statement, which creates a constraint but allows the system to automatically assign a name.

See Table 11-4 for a summary of SQL statement syntax for creating and modifying constraints.

TABLE 11-4   Constraint Syntax Summary

	CREATE TABLE	ALTER TABLE

In-line unnamed	CREATE TABLE *table_name* (
	  column_name datatype
	    inline_constraint,
	    . . .
	  ) ;
		ALTER TABLE *table_name*
		  ADD|MODIFY (*column_name* . . .
		    inline_constraint,
		    . . .
		  ) ;

In-line named	CREATE TABLE *table_name* (
	  column_name datatype
	    CONSTRAINT *constraint_name*
	    inline_constraint,
	    . . .
	  ) ;
		ALTER TABLE *table_name*
		  ADD|MODIFY (*column_name* . . .
		    CONSTRAINT *constraint_name*
		    inline_constraint,
		    . . .
		  ) ;

TABLE 11-4   Constraint Syntax Summary (*Continued*)

	CREATE TABLE	ALTER TABLE

Out-of-line	CREATE TABLE *table_name* (
	  column_name datatype,
	  ...,
	  CONSTRAINT *constraint_name*
	   outOfLine_constraint,
	  ...
	  );
		ALTER TABLE *table_name*
		
		ADD|MODIFY (
		  CONSTRAINT *constraint_name*
		   outOfLine_constraint,
		  ...
		  );

Type	*inline_constraint*	*outOfLine_constraint*
PRIMARY KEY	PRIMARY KEY	PRIMARY KEY (*column_list*)
FOREIGN KEY	REFERENCES *table_name* (*column_list*)	FOREIGN KEY (*column_list*) REFERENCES *table_name* (*column_list*)
UNIQUE	UNIQUE	UNIQUE (*column_list*)
CHECK	CHECK (*expression*)	CHECK (*expression*)
NOT NULL	NOT NULL	(*** Not Applicable ***)

Examples—assuming a table PORTS with a PRIMARY KEY of PORT_ID:

FOREIGN KEY, in-line, unnamed (anonymous)

```
CREATE TABLE SHIPS
   (SHIP_ID NUMBER, HOME_PORT_ID NUMBER REFERENCES PORTS (PORT_ID));
```

FOREIGN KEY, in-line, named:

```
CREATE TABLE SHIPS
   (SHIP_ID NUMBER, HOME_PORT_ID NUMBER CONSTRAINT FK_SHIPS_PORTS
                                  REFERENCES PORTS (PORT_ID));
```

FOREIGN KEY, out-of-line:

```
CREATE TABLE SHIPS
   (SHIP_ID  NUMBER, HOME_PORT_ID NUMBER,
    CONSTRAINT FK_SHIPS_PORTS FOREIGN KEY (HOME_PORT_ID)
                       REFERENCES PORTS (PORT_ID));
```

CERTIFICATION OBJECTIVE 11.04

Create Indexes Using the CREATE TABLE Statement

At the time a table is initially created, one or more indexes may be created along with the table. This section looks at this issue and what the options are for index creation as part of the CREATE TABLE statement.

Automatic Index Creation

Whenever you create a table with a constraint of type PRIMARY KEY or UNIQUE, an index is automatically created for you by default. You can choose to override this behavior and tell SQL to not create an index if you wish.

For example, this statement will create an index:

```
CREATE TABLE INVOICES (INVOICE_ID    NUMBER(11) PRIMARY KEY,
                       INVOICE_DATE DATE);
```

The preceding CREATE TABLE statement includes two columns, and a single constraint of type PRIMARY KEY. The result will be the creation of

- One table
- One constraint
- One index

The index will be assigned a system-generated name, which can be found with the following query:

```
SELECT  INDEX_NAME
FROM    USER_INDEXES
WHERE   TABLE_NAME = 'INVOICES';

INDEX_NAME
--------------------------------
SYS_C0013186
```

In our example, we've queried the data dictionary view USER_INDEXES and discovered that we now have an index associated with our new table INVOICES, and the index is called SYS_C0013186.

(Note: The data dictionary will be discussed in Chapter 14.)

USING INDEX

You can specify an index's creation as part of the CREATE TABLE statement. The USING INDEX clause only works for PRIMARY KEY and UNIQUE constraints. It can be appended to any PRIMARY KEY or UNIQUE constraint specification, including the in-line anonymous, in-line named, and out-of-line syntax.

Let's revisit our INVOICES table example. We could have used this syntax (line numbers added):

```
01   CREATE TABLE INVOICES
02     (INVOICE_ID    NUMBER(11) PRIMARY KEY
03                               USING INDEX (CREATE INDEX IX_INVOICES
04                                                 ON INVOICES(INVOICE_ID)),
05      INVOICE_DATE DATE
06     );
```

Note the syntax here:

- The PRIMARY KEY column is created at the end of line 2 as before.
- The USING INDEX keywords are next.
- Within parentheses, we include a complete CREATE INDEX statement.

The preceding example will successfully create the table, along with the index, giving the index a name we specify. There will be no system-assigned names given to automatically generated indexes with this CREATE TABLE statement; we have control over the index's naming and form.

In this next example, we modify the CREATE TABLE slightly so as to name the constraint as well as the index:

```
01   CREATE TABLE INVOICES
02     (INVOICE_ID    NUMBER(11) CONSTRAINT PK_INVOICE_ID PRIMARY KEY
03                               USING INDEX (CREATE INDEX IX_INVOICES
04                                                 ON INVOICES(INVOICE_ID)),
05      INVOICE_DATE DATE
06     );
```

Notice line 2, where we include the keyword CONSTRAINT followed by the constraint name. Everything else in the statement is identical to the previous example.

In the two examples we've just examined, the USING INDEX clause was appended to an in-line constraint. We could have done the same thing with an out-of-line constraint, like this:

```
01    CREATE TABLE INVOICES
02      (INVOICE_ID    NUMBER(11),
03       INVOICE_DATE DATE,
04       CONSTRAINT    CK_INVOICES_INVOICE_ID PRIMARY KEY (INVOICE_ID)
05                     USING INDEX (CREATE INDEX IX_INVOICES
06                                            ON INVOICES(INVOICE_ID))
07      );
```

This example creates the same table and the same index, but with the out-of-line constraint syntax. Remember that the out-of-line syntax allows us the option of creating constraints on two or more columns.

In the rare instance when you create a composite index along with multiple constraints that call on the same index, a special syntax is required. For example, if we decide to create a composite index on both of our columns in the INVOICES table, we can use this syntax:

```
01    CREATE TABLE INVOICES
02    (INVOICE_ID    NUMBER(11),
03     INVOICE_DATE DATE,
04     CONSTRAINT    UN_INVOICES_INVOICE_ID UNIQUE (INVOICE_ID, INVOICE_DATE)
05                   USING INDEX (CREATE INDEX IX_INVOICES
06                                          ON INVOICES(INVOICE_ID, INVOICE_DATE)),
07     CONSTRAINT    UN_INVOICES_INVOICE_DATE UNIQUE (INVOICE_DATE, INVOICE_ID)
08                   USING INDEX IX_INVOICES
09    );
```

In this example, we create two constraints and one index, referencing the newly created index IX_INVOICES in line 8 by specifying the same name of the index we create in line 5.

exam

ⓦatch
The USING INDEX clause for creating indices can be used to specify an existing index by appending a constraint specification with "USING INDEX index_name" and nothing else.

Create Function-Based Indexes

A *function-based* index is an index that is created on one or more columns that are used as one or more input parameters to a function. The advantage is that if you find yourself frequently querying a table using that function, then you can incorporate the function into the index and increase the likelihood that the Oracle Database optimizer will use the index in queries.

For example, consider the following table:

```
CREATE TABLE CUSTOMERS
  (CUSTOMER_ID    NUMBER(11) PRIMARY KEY,
   LAST_NAME      VARCHAR2(30));
CREATE INDEX IX_CUSTOMERS_LAST_NAME ON CUSTOMERS (UPPER(LAST_NAME));
```

This example shows how we can create the index so that data in the LAST_NAME column is indexed as though the column were already converted to uppercase letters with the function UPPER.

Now we can run the following query:

```
SELECT * FROM CUSTOMERS WHERE UPPER(LAST_NAME) = 'SMITH';
```

Had we created a typical (non-function-based) index on the LAST_NAME column, this query would not benefit from the index. But now, with the function-based index implemented, we improve the odds that the optimizer will invoke the index for queries that use the same function as we coded into the function-based index.

Function-based indexes do not necessarily need to be based on a SQL function per se. Any expression will be accepted. For example:

```
CREATE TABLE GAS_TANKS (GAS_TANK_ID NUMBER(7), TANK_GALLONS NUMBER(9), MILEAGE
NUMBER(9));
CREATE INDEX IX_GAS_TANKS_001 ON GAS_TANKS (TANK_GALLONS * MILEAGE);
```

In the preceding example, there is no particular SQL function. Instead there is an equation, and this is valid for creating a function-based index. Any future queries on the GAS_TANKS table that use this expression will leverage the power of the index. Note that SQL is smart enough to recognize whether you've changed the position of the values within an expression without modifying the end results of the expression. In other words, the query

```
SELECT * FROM GAS_TANKS WHERE MILEAGE*TANK_GALLONS > 750;
```

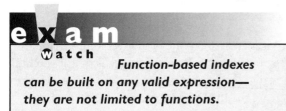

may use the index, even though the expression reverses the position of MILEAGE and TANK_GALLONS. The computed values are the same, and the SQL index recognizes that fact.

Function-based indexes can be built on any valid expression— they are not limited to functions.

CERTIFICATION OBJECTIVE 11.06

Perform FLASHBACK Operations

The topic of Oracle's FLASHBACK operations is quite involved. To develop a complete understanding of all of what Oracle offers with FLASHBACK operations requires more study than what is necessarily required to pass the exam. I'll provide some background information to give you an idea of what we are talking about, and then I'll discuss the specific FLASHBACK operations that are relevant to the exam and to this chapter's focus, which is the overall subject of managing schema objects. This won't be the last word on the subject of FLASHBACK operations that you need to understand for the exam; we'll revisit the topic of FLASHBACK again in Chapter 15, when we look at how to manipulate large amounts of data over time. This book will present what you need to know for the exam, but you may wish to continue your study of FLASHBACK operations beyond what is required for the exam.

Overview

Oracle's FLASHBACK operations include a variety of statements you can use to recover objects and/or the data contained with them, as well as dependent objects and data. The sort of tasks you can accomplish with FLASHBACK operations include

- Recovering complete tables you may have inadvertently dropped
- Recovering data changes within one or more tables resulting from a series of DML statements
- Performing data analysis on data that's been changed over periods of time
- Comparing data that existed at one point in time with data that existed at another point in time
- Performing queries as of a prior time period

FLASHBACK operations can support multiple user sessions gaining access to historical data dynamically, on any table—including the same tables—at the same time, with each user session potentially accessing different points in the history of the table simultaneously, all while the database is up and running in full operational mode.

Some FLASHBACK operations require various configuration steps; some of those configurations can be involved and might require intervention by the database administrator. The configuration steps involved can affect system parameters, table clauses, and a feature of the database known as the undo segments, which have a purpose that goes beyond FLASHBACK.

Recover Dropped Tables

In this chapter, we're only focusing on managing schema objects. Within the set of available FLASHBACK operations, the feature that affects schema objects as a whole is the FLASHBACK TABLE statement. This statement can recover a previously dropped table you specify from an historical point-in-time that you specify. However, there are limitations—for example, you cannot flash back to a point prior to when the table's structure may have been altered.

You can identify a point in time in a variety of ways:

- Immediately prior to when a table was dropped
- A specific time identified by a value of datatype TIMESTAMP
- A specific transaction identified by the system change number (SCN)
- A predetermined event identified by a database object known as the RESTORE POINT

When used to restore a table, FLASHBACK TABLE restores the dropped table with either its original name or a new name you provide with the statement. It also recovers any indexes on the table, other than bitmap join indexes. All constraints are recovered, except for referential integrity constraints that reference other tables—in other words, foreign key constraints. Granted privileges are also recovered.

The beginning syntax of a FLASHBACK TABLE statement is as follows:

- The required keywords FLASHBACK TABLE
- One or more table names, separated by commas
- The required keyword TO

In other words:

```
FLASHBACK TABLE table_name TO ...
```

More than one table can be included in the list. Additional table names must be separated by commas:

```
FLASHBACK TABLE table1, table2, table3 TO ...
```

That's the beginning. There are several ways to complete this statement. Here is how you complete it if you wish to recover a dropped table:

- The required keywords BEFORE DROP
- The optional keywords RENAME TO, followed by a new name for the table, if you wish to recover the dropped table into an object with a different name

Here is an example of a SQL session where we create a table, drop it, and then use FLASHBACK TABLE to restore the dropped table (line numbers added):

```
01    CREATE TABLE HOUDINI (VOILA VARCHAR2(30));
02    INSERT INTO HOUDINI  (VOILA) VALUES ('Now you see it.');
03    COMMIT;
04    DROP   TABLE HOUDINI;
05    FLASHBACK TABLE HOUDINI TO BEFORE DROP;
06    SELECT * FROM HOUDINI;
```

Note the FLASHBACK TABLE statement on line 5. It combines the beginning:

```
FLASHBACK TABLE HOUDINI TO
```

with

```
BEFORE DROP
```

It omits the optional RENAME TO and the new name.

The Recycle Bin

The Flashback Drop feature recovers complete tables that are still retained in the "recycle bin", and it can do so in spite of the fact that such a change results from the DROP TABLE statement, which, by definition, is DDL and therefore involves an implied COMMIT. In spite of this, we can recover the table if it is still in the recycle bin.

Tables are put into the recycle bin automatically by SQL whenever a DROP TABLE statement is issued. A table's dependent objects, such as indexes, are also placed into the recycle bin, along with the table's constraints.

The recycle bin is not counted as space that is used by a given user account.

A user account's dropped objects are retained in a separate recycle bin for each user. You may inspect the contents of your own recycle bin with the following query:

```
SELECT * FROM USER_RECYCLEBIN;
```

That query is identical to this one:

```
SELECT * FROM RECYCLEBIN;
```

RECYCLEBIN is a synonym for USER_RECYCLEBIN. In other words, the preceding two queries are identical.

There is a DBA_RECYCLEBIN, which allows user accounts with database administrator (DBA) privileges to see all dropped objects in the database.

If your user account has privileges on an object, then your user account will be able to see the object in the recycle bin in the event it is dropped.

You don't need to inspect the recycle bin before issuing a FLASHBACK statement. But you might find it helpful.

The recycle bin is affected by the "recyclebin" initialization parameter and can be turned on or off accordingly with the following ALTER SESSION statements:

```
ALTER SESSION SET recyclebin = ON;
ALTER SESSION SET recyclebin = OFF;
```

Either of these statements takes effect immediately. The initial state of the recycle bin is dependent on the setting for recyclebin in the initialization parameter file, which is controlled by the DBA.

Dependent Objects

When a table is recovered, any associated dependent objects are also recovered, including the following:

- Indexes, except for bitmap join indexes
- Constraints, but with limitations—for example, restoring dropped tables does not recover referential constraints, meaning FOREIGN KEY constraints
- Other objects that I don't discuss in this book and are not a subject of the exam, such as triggers

Objects that have the same name that are dropped can all be retrieved with FLASHBACK operations. For example, if a table VENDORS was dropped, then recreated and dropped, then there will be two VENDORS tables in the recycle bin. The last one dropped will be the first one retrieved.

Objects such as indexes will be recovered with system-assigned names—not the names they were originally given. You can rename each retrieved object with the RENAME TO clause of the FLASHBACK TABLE statement as it is retrieved. As of this writing, renaming retrieved objects is beyond the scope of the exam.

Statement Execution

The FLASHBACK TABLE statement operates as a single statement. If it fails, nothing in the statement succeeds. In other words, if there's an attempt to restore three tables in a single statement and the third attempt is erroneous for whatever reason, none of the tables will be restored.

PURGE

The PURGE statement permanently removes a given item from the recycle bin—for example, to permanently remove the HOUDINI table from the recycle bin so that it cannot be recovered:

```
PURGE TABLE HOUDINI;
```

After executing this statement, the table HOUDINI cannot be recovered with the FLASHBACK TABLE statement we used earlier.

Note that the table must have first been dropped in order for PURGE to execute successfully.

Purging may be performed automatically by the Oracle database's own automatic space reclamation operations. If that happens, the table is not in the recycle bin and cannot be recovered with FLASHBACK operations.

Recovering Tables in Time

This section discusses some additional ways to complete the FLASHBACK TABLE statement.

In addition to performing a flashback operation to restore a dropped table, you can flash back an existing table to a specific point in time, showing its state prior to any committed changes that may have been transacted since the point in time of interest.

The syntax can take any of these three forms.

```
FLASHBACK TABLE HOUDINI TO SCN scn_expression;
FLASHBACK TABLE HOUDINI TO TIMESTAMP timestamp_expression;
FLASHBACK TABLE HOUDINI TO RESTORE POINT restore_point_expression;
```

The recommended form of these three is the first: the SCN, which is the system change number. This is the mechanism that is recommended by Oracle for identifying points in time in the database. For example, let's revisit our table HOUDINI:

```
01    CREATE TABLE HOUDINI (VOILA VARCHAR2(30));
02    INSERT INTO HOUDINI  (VOILA) VALUES ('Now you see it.');
03    COMMIT;
04    EXECUTE DBMS_LOCK.SLEEP(15);
05    DELETE FROM HOUDINI;
06    COMMIT;
07    EXECUTE DBMS_LOCK.SLEEP(15);
08    FLASHBACK TABLE HOUDINI TO TIMESTAMP
09                   SYSTIMESTAMP - INTERVAL '0 00:00:20' DAY TO SECOND;
```

Let's review the preceding code:

- Line 3: We commit our change to the table.
- Line 4: This is a statement that suspends processing for 15 seconds. The choice of 15 seconds is arbitrary; the intent here is to allow some time to pass.
- Line 6: We commit the deletion of the one row.

■ Line 8 and line 9: This statement attempts to restore the table back to where it was 20 seconds earlier. Note that line 9 contains nothing more than an expression of the TIMESTAMP datatype, which in this case is a call to the SYSTIMESTAMP function minus a 20-second interval. The SYSTIMESTAMP function returns the current time as defined by the Oracle database server's operating system. Following the call to the function is the symbol for subtraction—the "minus" sign—followed by a literal value representing a time interval of 20 seconds.

So—what is the result of this series of statements? Here it is:

```
Error report:
SQL Error: ORA-08189: cannot flashback the table because row movement is not
enabled
08189. 00000 -  "cannot flashback the table because row movement is not enabled"
*Cause:    An attempt was made to perform Flashback Table operation on a table
           for which row movement has not been enabled. Because the Flashback
           Table does not preserve the rowids, it is necessary that row
           movement be enabled on the table.
*Action:   Enable row movement on the table
```

What is wrong here? The problem is that the capability to perform FLASHBACK operations to restore an existing table to an older state—is not a capability that exists by default. It only works on tables where the ROW MOVEMENT feature has been enabled. Here's how to create the table with ROW MOVEMENT enabled:

```
CREATE TABLE HOUDINI (VOILA VARCHAR2(30))
        ENABLE ROW MOVEMENT;
```

To enable ROW MOVEMENT on a table that's already been created:

```
ALTER TABLE HOUDINI ENABLE ROW MOVEMENT;
```

If we were to go back and redo our earlier series of statements with ROW MOVEMENT enabled on the table, our FLASHBACK TABLE statement would work perfectly, and we'd restore our table to its original state. Once restored, we could query the table and see all the data in that table as it existed at the time we specified in our FLASHBACK TABLE statement.

Data restoration is "permanent". It invokes an implicit COMMIT so that the restored data is committed.

Limitations

You cannot use the FLASHBACK TABLE statement to restore older data to an existing table if the table has been structurally altered with the ALTER TABLE statement in such a way that it can't accept the full definition of older data. For example, if a column has been dropped or a column's datatype changed, the FLASHBACK TABLE statement won't successfully restore the older data.

Marking Time

There are several ways to identify the point at which you wish to restore data in the database. You saw three in the previous section, and I'll discuss them a bit more here.

SCN

The system change number, or SCN, is a numeric stamp that the database automatically increments for every committed transaction that occurs in the database. This includes both explicit and implicit commits, for all external or internal transactions. The SCN is automatically managed by the database in real time. Every committed transaction is assigned an SCN.

If you wish to determine the current SCN at any given moment in the database, use the function DBMS_FLASHBACK.GET_SYSTEM_CHANGE_NUMBER. For example (line numbers added):

```
01    SELECT DBMS_FLASHBACK.GET_SYSTEM_CHANGE_NUMBER FROM DUAL;
02
03    GET_SYSTEM_CHANGE_NUMBER
04    -----------------------
05    5896167
```

This example shows the request and the answer. In this case, the SCN is 5896167. If you were to hesitate a few seconds and run the same statement in line 1 again, you might get a different value returned for SCN.

on the
Job

The SCN can also be found with the query SELECT CURRENT_SCN FROM V$DATABASE, which is a query of the data dictionary. We'll discuss the data dictionary later in Chapter 14, but for now, note that Oracle officially recommends that if your goal is to obtain an SCN from within an application or any comparable code, then you should use the DBMS_FLASHBACK .GET_SYSTEM_CHANGE_NUMBER function that we demonstrated earlier. This recommendation implies that you should steer away from tapping the V$DATABASE view for the SCN number. The DBMS_FLASHBACK.GET_ SYSTEM_CHANGE_NUMBER function is a function written in the PL/SQL language, and it is part of the DBMS_FLASHBACK package. See Oracle's reference manual on PL/SQL packages if you wish to learn more—but you don't need to do that for the exam.

Each time a transaction is committed in the database, the SCN is incremented and stored with each row in each table.

The SCN for a given row can be found in the pseudocolumn ORA_ROWSCN. As is the case with any pseudocolumn, it can be included as an expression in any SELECT statement. For example,

```
SELECT ORA_ROWSCN, VOILA
FROM   HOUDINI;
```

returns each row in the table HOUDINI, along with the values in the VOILA column as well as the assigned SCN number for each row.

Timestamp

A TIMESTAMP value specifies a point in time. You'll recall that the TIMESTAMP datatype stores the year, month, day, hour, minute, second, and fractional seconds, and that a literal value may be converted to the TIMESTAMP datatype with the TO_TIMESTAMP function, like this:

```
SELECT TO_TIMESTAMP('2009-08-25 13:15:08.232349',
                    'RRRR-MM-DD HH24:MI:SS:FF')
FROM   DUAL;
```

This example shows the TO_TIMESTAMP function, a literal value, and a format mask that defines the location within the literal value of each component that forms a valid TIMESTAMP value. Note the use of fractional seconds, where more than two digits are accepted. Also recall that MI is the format mask for minutes—not MM, which is the format mask for months.

The FLASHBACK_TABLE function can use a TIMESTAMP value to specify a point in time in the database to within three seconds of accuracy.

If a specific point in the database is needed, don't use TIMESTAMP—use SCN instead.

If you attempt to flash back to a point in time at which the database did not exist, you'll get an error indicating "invalid timestamp specified".

If the time you're referencing closely aligns with a time at which the object or data didn't exist, and the SCN/Timestamp correlation misses your target and overshoots into a time frame in which the object or data didn't exist, you may get an Oracle error.

You can use a combination of one or more conversion functions to address this discrepancy, as we discuss in the next section.

Conversion Functions

SCN numbers can be converted into their equivalent TIMESTAMP values, and vice versa. The conversions are not exact, however, because the SCN and TIMESTAMP do not represent moments in time that are precisely identical.

The conversion functions are

- **SCN_TO_TIMESTAMP(s1)**   Takes an SCN expression as input, returns a TIMESTAMP value roughly corresponding to when the SCN was set.
- **TIMESTAMP_TO_SCN(t)**   Takes a TIMESTAMP expression representing a valid past or present timestamp as input, returns an SCN value roughly corresponding to when the TIMESTAMP occurred.

For example, let's perform two separate conversions of timestamp values to SCN values (line numbers added):

```
01    SELECT TIMESTAMP_TO_SCN(SYSTIMESTAMP) NOW,
02           TIMESTAMP_TO_SCN(TO_TIMESTAMP('01-AUG-09 09:12:23',
03                                          'DD-MON-RR HH:MI:SS')) NOT_NOW
04    FROM    DUAL;
05
06    NOW                      NOT_NOW
07    --------------------- ---------------------
08    5911139                  5639192
```

In this example, we convert the current timestamp value, as defined by SYSTIMESTAMP, to its SCN equivalent. We also convert a date in the past to its SCN equivalent. The first column's alias is NOW; the second column's alias is NOT_NOW.

Note: Any time referenced must be within a range that is relevant to the database—i.e., the function recognizes times that apply to whenever the database installation has been in existence.

There is not a direct one-to-one relationship between timestamps and SCN values. For example, suppose you take a valid SCN value and convert:

```
SELECT TIMESTAMP_TO_SCN(SCN_TO_TIMESTAMP(5895585))
FROM DUAL;

TIMESTAMP_TO_SCN(SCN_TO_TIMESTAMP(5895585))
-------------------------------------------
5895573
```

Note what happens here: one SCN goes in, and a slightly different SCN is ultimately returned.

For any work effort in which you require precision in specifying timing, Oracle recommends using SCN numbers, and obtaining them with the DBMS_ FLASHBACK packaged function GET_SYSTEM_CHANGE_NUMBER, which we reviewed earlier. Also note: It is important that if you wish to use FLASHBACK to restore to a specific point, you obtain that point precisely. One way to do that is the RESTORE POINT, which we discuss next.

RESTORE POINT

A RESTORE POINT is an object in the database you create to represent a given moment in the database. That moment can be identified by a TIMESTAMP value or an SCN.

Here's an example of the CREATE RESTORE POINT statement:

```
CREATE RESTORE POINT balance_acct_01;
```

Once executed, you can use this as a restore point representing the moment at which the CREATE RESTORE POINT statement was executed. You can refer to the restore point later in the current session, or in a later session:

```
FLASHBACK TABLE HOUDINI TO RESTORE POINT balance_acct_01;
```

This statement restores the HOUDINI table to the point in time that correlates to the "balance_acct_01" restore point.

When you no longer need the RESTORE POINT, you can drop it:

```
DROP RESTORE POINT balance_acct_01;
```

You can find existing restore points with the data dictionary view V$RESTORE_ POINT. Note that users do not "own" RESTORE POINT objects; their scope is the entire database. They exist until they are dropped, or age out of the control file.

CERTIFICATION OBJECTIVE 11.07

Create and Use External Tables

An external table is a read-only table that is defined within the database but exists outside of the database. In more technical terms, the external table's metadata is stored inside the database, and the data it contains is outside of the database.

External tables have a number of restrictions on them. You can query them with the SELECT statement, but you cannot use any other DML statements on them. You can't create an INDEX on them, and they won't accept constraints.

Benefits

So why would you create an external table? Their primary benefit is to create an easy-to-use bridge between SQL tables and non-database data sources. If you've ever used the Oracle tool SQL*Loader, or Data Pump, then you'll be pleased to discover that the external table feature was designed to incorporate the functionality found in those tools into a SQL context.

A great example is when you have some non-SQL data source that regularly produces information needed in the database, such as a flat file transfer, a web site reference, a spreadsheet application, a legacy 3GL application, or something comparable. If that data source is capable of providing some sort of formatted flat file, then it can be structured in such a way that it can be copied directly into a file that the SQL external table will instantly recognize and be able to query. In other words, it will create the sort of one-way data transfer into the SQL database, but using SQL SELECT statements instead of utilities such as SQL*Loader.

Creating External Tables

To create an external table, you can declare its columns and their datatypes. You can also populate the external table with a subquery at the time you create it.

But that's about all you can do with external tables. They are restricted in a number of ways:

- You cannot create a column with a LOB datatype—no CLOB, BLOB, NCLOB, etc.
- You cannot add a constraint to an external table.
- You cannot change the column of an external table to UNUSED. If you try, SQL will process the statement but will actually drop the column.

Essentially, all you do with an external table is declare its structure and define the parameters by which the SQL database communicates with the external table. In order to establish that communication, you must first understand two subjects:

- DIRECTORY objects
- The Oracle utilities SQL*Loader and Oracle Data Pump

We'll look at those next, and then we'll create an external table.

DIRECTORY Objects

To create an external table, we'll need to identify the location in the operating system where the external file containing the table will reside. For this, we need to look at the CREATE DIRECTORY statement.

The CREATE DIRECTORY statement creates an object in the database that represents the name of a directory on the server's file system. Here's an example:

```
CREATE OR REPLACE DIRECTORY directory_name AS directory_reference;
```

where *directory_name* is a name you specify, just as you would any other database object, and *directory_reference* is a string literal, surrounded by single quotation marks, that identifies a location within your Oracle server's file system, into which you wish for external tables to be stored. For example:

```
CREATE OR REPLACE DIRECTORY BANK_FILES AS 'F:\bnk_files\trnsfr';
```

The result of this statement is that we've just created an object in the database named BANK_FILES that looks to the operating system where the Oracle server resides and assumes that the directory reference in the string literal is consistent with the syntax required for that particular operating system. In this case, we're pointing to a Windows drive 'F:' and its root level directory "bnk_files", within which is the subdirectory "trnsfr"—that subdirectory is our target.

The DIRECTORY object will not parse this reference but instead will just store it as is. If it's incorrect, you won't find out until later when you try to use the DIRECTORY object.

Also, the DIRECTORY object will not create the subdirectory; the assumption here is that the subdirectory already exists. If it does not, you won't get an error message until you use the DIRECTORY object later.

The keywords OR REPLACE are optional.

In our example, the name BANK_FILES is a name we specify. This name is the name assigned to the object, and this name is how we will reference the DIRECTORY object in the future.

Once a directory has been created, the owner must grant READ and/or WRITE access to any user who may use it:

```
GRANT READ ON DIRECTORY directory_name TO username;
```

That includes users who may wish to use external tables that are built with the directory objects.

Oracle Utilities

The Oracle database provides a number of utilities that accompany their database product. Those utilities that are important to external tables include

- SQL*Loader
- Oracle Data Pump Export
- Oracle Data Pump Import

Each is documented in the Oracle Corporation reference manual titled "Oracle Utilities". Together, the utilities provide capabilities that allow external data sources to communicate with SQL objects within the database.

A complete review of their capabilities is beyond the scope of the exam and therefore this book. But it's important for the exam to recognize that a large component of the definitions associated with the declaration of an external table come from these utilities.

Creating an External Table

Let's walk through an example. Let's say we have an external text file containing the following data about invoices:

```
ID   INV_DATE      ACCT_NO
---  ------------  --------------
701  03/15/09      CODDA009
702  03/17/09      CODDA010
703  03/18/09      CODDA011
```

We want to create an external table for this data; let's call it INVOICE_DATA.TXT.

First, we go to the file system on which the Oracle database resides, locate the same drive, and we create a subdirectory off of the root level. We'll call it "LOAD_INVOICES". Then we create the associated DIRECTORY object:

```
CREATE DIRECTORY INVOICE_FILES AS '\LOAD_INVOICES';
```

By this point, we won't necessarily have to have created the LOAD_INVOICES directory, nor to have put the INVOICE_DATA.TXT file in that directory. But for the sake of our example, now we do so, before continuing.

Next, we execute a CREATE TABLE statement that references the directory, along with the necessary clauses to tell Oracle SQL to load the external file, and how to load it (line numbers added):

```
01   CREATE TABLE INVOICES_EXTERNAL
02   ( INVOICE_ID      CHAR(3),
03     INVOICE_DATE    CHAR(9),
04     ACCOUNT_NUMBER CHAR(13)
05   )
06   ORGANIZATION EXTERNAL
07     (TYPE ORACLE_LOADER
08      DEFAULT DIRECTORY INVOICE_FILES
09      ACCESS PARAMETERS
10        (RECORDS DELIMITED BY NEWLINE
11         SKIP 2
12         FIELDS (INVOICE_ID      CHAR(3),
13                 INVOICE_DATE    CHAR(9),
14                 ACCOUNT_NUMBER CHAR(13))
15        )
16      LOCATION ('INVOICE_DATA.TXT')
17      );
```

Once this statement executes, we end up with an external table in the database called INVOICES_EXTERNAL.

- Note lines 2 through 4 where we declared our table using the datatypes CHAR. You'll recall these are fixed-length datatypes. We did this to accommodate the transfer of rows in from the text file in lines 12 through 14. Each column's datatype is set to CHAR, the fixed-length alphanumeric datatype, and the counts for each datatype correspond to the counts of the columns in the text file 'INVOICE_DATA.TXT', which is identified in line 16 and is in the directory stored in the directory object INVOICE_FILES, named in line 8.

- Lines 1 through 5 form a complete CREATE TABLE statement by themselves, without the external table clause. But starting on line 6 are the keywords and clauses used to declare the external table, and together, lines 1 through 17 form the complete CREATE TABLE statement for our example.

- Line 6 includes the keywords ORGANIZATION EXTERNAL, which are required.

- Line 7 is where we specify that we are using ORACLE_LOADER, aka the SQL*Loader features. An alternative TYPE value here would be ORACLE_DATAPUMP.

- Line 9 begins the set of values for ACCESS PARAMETERS, which are enclosed within the parentheses that open on line 10 and close on line 15.

- Three ACCESS PARAMETERS are used here: RECORDS, SKIP, and FIELDS.

- Line 10—RECORDS DELIMITED BY NEWLINE—means that each new line starts a new row of data for the INVOICES_EXTERNAL table.

- Line 11—SKIP 2—tells ORACLE_LOADER that the first two lines of the INVOICE_DATA.TXT file are to be skipped—they just contain header information.

- Line 12—FIELDS—starts the specifications for each column, where each column's length is carefully specified to match the length in the INVOICES_DATA.TXT file.

Many more ACCESS PARAMETERS exist that are not invoked here. I could probably write a separate book just on all the options and features that exist with the various clauses for the types ORACLE_LOADER and ORACLE_DATAPUMP. But I won't, and you shouldn't need that for the exam.

Using an External Table

Once we've created an external table, we can SELECT from it just like any other table—for example:

```
SELECT * FROM INVOICES_EXTERNAL;

INVOICE_ID INVOICE_DATE ACCOUNT_NUMBER
---------- ------------ --------------
701        03/15/09      CODDA009
702        03/17/09      CODDA010
703        03/18/09      CODDA011
```

Many external tables will start with source data that is rough and unformatted. However, the first step is just to get it in the database. Once that is accomplished, you can use the various conversion functions and other features of SQL to clean up and reformat the data:

```
SELECT  TO_NUMBER(INVOICE_ID),
        TO_DATE(INVOICE_DATE,'MM/DD/RR') INVOICE_DATE,
        LTRIM(ACCOUNT_NUMBER,' ') ACCOUNT_NUMBER
FROM    INVOICES_EXTERNAL;


INVOICE_ID                INVOICE_DATE               ACCOUNT_NUMBER
--------------------      ------------------------   --------------
701                       15-MAR-09                  CODDA009
702                       17-MAR-09                  CODDA010
703                       18-MAR-09                  CODDA011
```

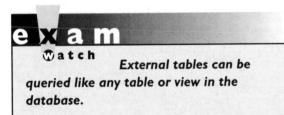

External tables can be queried like any table or view in the database.

Note the output—the numbers are reformatted, the date values are converted, and the account numbers have been trimmed up and everything looks terrific.

Remember that you cannot use INSERT, UPDATE, or DELETE statements on external tables.

CERTIFICATION SUMMARY

The ALTER TABLE statement can be used with the ADD clause to add columns to a table that's already been created, and with the MODIFY clause to modify the existing columns of the table. Changes to a column can include changes to datatype, and to scale and precision, but you cannot change a table in such a way that existing data would be in conflict with the change, or that would cause loss of detail in data.

The RENAME clause of the ALTER TABLE statement can be used to rename columns in a table.

Columns can be dropped from a table. Columns that are part of a referential constraint—in other words, a FOREIGN KEY constraint—may be dropped with the CASCADE CONSTRAINTS keywords added so that the constraints are dropped as well. Columns may be set to UNUSED to render them virtually dropped, but sparing the processing overhead required to drop a column. An UNUSED column is no longer available, and it can be dropped later.

The ALTER TABLE statement can be used to add or modify constraints. The NOT NULL constraint has limited syntax requirements, but other constraints can be added using in-line or out-of-line syntax. A constraint can be disabled and enabled with the ALTER TABLE statement. You can also change a constraint's name.

Index objects support application performance tuning. Indexes can be built on one or more columns of a table; multicolumn index objects are known as composite indexes. When a query references indexed columns in its WHERE clause, SQL will consider using the index as part of its processing strategy and the results may be returned more quickly.

An index can be created explicitly with the CREATE INDEX statement, or created as part of the CREATE TABLE statement, either implicitly, such as when you create a PRIMARY KEY constraint, or explicitly, such as with the USING INDEX keywords.

Function-based indexes are built on an expression. The result is an index that may be automatically invoked by any query that uses the same expression.

Flashback operations can restore data to a previous point in time, with some limitations. The point to which you restore data can be identified using values of datatype TIMESTAMP, or SCN, or RESTORE POINT. Tables that have been dropped but that are still in the recycle bin can be recovered. Any table that's been purged from the recycle bin is gone for good. Data that's been changed in existing tables can be restored to some previous point in time, provided that the table's structure hasn't been changed in such a way that the table is no longer able to receive the restored data—such as perhaps having had a column dropped.

External tables exist outside of the database. The process that supports them has its roots and syntax in the SQL*Loader tool, but the result is a table that can be described just like any other. External tables can be queried but cannot receive data input via INSERT, UPDATE, or DELETE.

TWO-MINUTE DRILL

Add and Modify Columns

- ❑ The ALTER TABLE statement can be used to add or modify columns.
- ❑ The ADD clause of ALTER TABLE can be used to add a column to a table.
- ❑ A column is added by specifying the column name and datatype; optionally, you can add a constraint and a default value.
- ❑ The MODIFY clause can be used to modify existing columns in a table.
- ❑ A column's datatype and other characteristics can be modified, but only insofar as the change does not conflict with any existing data in the table.
- ❑ You cannot change a column's datatype if the column contains data already.

Drop Columns and Set Column UNUSED

- ❑ The DROP clause of ALTER TABLE can be used to remove a column from a table.
- ❑ Once a column is removed with DROP, the data is lost.
- ❑ Dropping a column can consume significant processing time if the table involved contains a lot of data.
- ❑ If you drop a column with a constraint, the constraint is also dropped. The same is true for any index objects on the column; they are also dropped.
- ❑ SET UNUSED renders a column permanently unavailable; it cannot be recovered.
- ❑ The SET UNUSED clause can benefit a large table in heavy production that cannot afford the overhead processing power of a DROP.
- ❑ After a table has columns that are set to UNUSED, they can be dropped with the DROP UNUSED COLUMNS clause of ALTER TABLE.

Add Constraints

- ❑ The ALTER TABLE statement can be used to add constraints to a table with the ADD clause.
- ❑ The DROP clause can be used to drop constraints.
- ❑ A disabled constraint can be enabled again later, provided that the data contained with the column satisfies the constraint.

Create Indexes Using the CREATE TABLE Statement

❑ When a PRIMARY KEY or UNIQUE constraint is created as part of a CREATE TABLE statement, and if no existing index supports the constraint, then an index is automatically created as part of the constraint.

❑ The USING INDEX clause can be invoked to explicitly define the index.

Create Function-Based Indexes

❑ A function-based index can be based on an expression; it does not necessarily need to include a SQL function, and can simply be based on an expression of any kind.

❑ Queries that use the same function or expression may benefit from the index.

Perform FLASHBACK Operations

❑ FLASHBACK TABLE can be used to restore a table that has been dropped.

❑ If a table has been dropped, it goes into the recycle bin.

❑ You can investigate the contents of the recycle bin to determine what objects are available for use by FLASHBACK operations.

❑ Once an object has been dropped, if it is also purged with the PURGE statement, it is no longer able to be recovered with FLASHBACK TABLE.

❑ In addition to restoring a dropped table, the FLASHBACK TABLE statement can also be used to restore data within the table as of a particular time in the database.

❑ Time in the database is marked by either a system change number (SCN), a RESTORE POINT, or a timestamp.

Create and Use External Tables

❑ An external table is a read-only table within the database that stores data outside of the database.

❑ The communication between the external table's data storage file and database objects is based on the logic of SQL*Loader or Oracle Data Pump.

❑ You use a database object known as the DIRECTORY object as part of the definition of an external table.

SELF TEST

The following questions will help you measure your understanding of the material presented in this chapter. Choose one correct answer for each question unless otherwise directed.

Add and Modify Columns

1. Assume a table INVOICES exists in the database, it contains no rows, and it has a column called DISCOUNT. Which of the following statements will *not* execute? (Choose two.)

   A. ALTER TABLE INVOICES ADD COLUMN DEPOT_ID NUMBER;
   B. ALTER TABLE INVOICES ADD DEPOT_ID DEFAULT 0 NUMBER;
   C. ALTER TABLE INVOICES DROP COLUMN DISCOUNT;
   D. ALTER TABLE INVOICES RENAME COLUMN DISCOUNT TO DISC;

2. Review the following SQL statements:

   ```
   CREATE TABLE INVOICES (INVOICE_ID NUMBER, DISCOUNT NUMBER(3));
   INSERT INTO INVOICES VALUES (7,5);
   INSERT INTO INVOICES VALUES (3,12);
   ```

   After executing these SQL statements, which of the following SQL statements will fail to execute? (Choose two.)

   A. ALTER TABLE INVOICES MODIFY DISCOUNT PRIMARY KEY;
   B. ALTER TABLE INVOICES MODIFY DISCOUNT VARCHAR2(3);
   C. ALTER TABLE INVOICES MODIFY DISCOUNT DEFAULT 'Zero';
   D. ALTER TABLE INVOICES MODIFY INVOICE_ID PRIMARY KEY;

3. You have a table called CUSTOMERS, and you want to change the name of a column in the CUSTOMERS table from NAME to LAST_NAME. Which of the following statements could you use?

   A. RENAME NAME TO LASTNAME;
   B. ALTER TABLE CUSTOMERS RENAME COLUMN NAME TO LASTNAME;
   C. ALTER TABLE CUSTOMERS RENAME NAME LASTNAME;
   D. It can't be done.

Drop Columns and Set Column UNUSED

4. The difference between dropping a column from a table with DROP and setting a column to be UNUSED is:

A. An UNUSED column can be recovered.

B. The UNUSED column and its data are retained within the table's storage allocation and counts against the total limit on the number of columns the table is allowed to have.

C. A column that is dropped with DROP no longer appears within the table's description as shown with the DESC or DESCRIBE statement, whereas a column that is set to UNUSED still appears in the table's structure as shown in the output of the DESC statement.

D. Nothing.

5. Review the following SQL statement:

```
CREATE TABLE LETTERS (LETTER_ID NUMBER(7), POSTAGE NUMBER(7));
```

Which of the following will change POSTAGE to be an UNUSED column?

A. ALTER TABLE LETTERS MODIFY POSTAGE SET UNUSED;

B. ALTER TABLE LETTERS MODIFY COLUMN POSTAGE SET UNUSED;

C. ALTER TABLE LETTERS SET UNUSED COLUMN POSTAGE;

D. ALTER TABLE LETTERS SET COLUMN POSTAGE UNUSED;

Add Constraints

6. Review the following illustration:

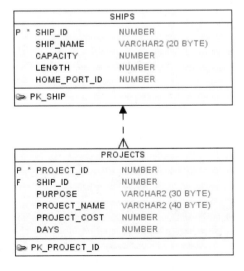

You are tasked with adding a constraint so that the PROJECTS table will not accept any rows with a value for the DAYS column of more than 90. You are aware that there are already rows in the PROJECTS table with a value for DAYS of 120. What will happen when you attempt to apply a constraint on the table? Assume the constraint is applied with the defaults of ENABLE VALIDATE.

A. It will succeed, and the existing values for DAYS will remain unchanged, but no new rows will be accepted unless the DAYS value is less than 90.

B. It will succeed, and the existing values for DAYS will be changed automatically by the system to NULL.

C. It will succeed, but the rows in which DAYS is greater than 90 will be assigned a status of INVALID.

D. It will fail and the constraint will not be created.

7. Review the illustration from question 6. You are tasked with adding a constraint so that the PROJECTS table will not accept any rows with a value for the DAYS column of more than 90. Which of the following statements will accomplish the task?

A. ALTER TABLE PROJECTS ADD CK_DAYS CHECK (DAYS <= 90);

B. ALTER TABLE PROJECTS ADD (DAYS) CHECK (DAYS <= 90);

C. ALTER TABLE PROJECTS MODIFY DAYS CONSTRAINT CK_DAYS CHECK (DAYS <= 90);

D. ALTER TABLE PROJECTS MODIFY DAYS ADD CONSTRAINT CK_DAYS CHECK (DAYS <= 90);

Create Indexes Using the **CREATE TABLE** Statement

8. Review the following illustration:

```
                    SHIP_CABINS
P *  SHIP_CABIN_ID    NUMBER
     SHIP_ID          NUMBER (7)
     ROOM_NUMBER      VARCHAR2 (5 BYTE)
     ROOM_STYLE       VARCHAR2 (10 BYTE)
     ROOM_TYPE        VARCHAR2 (20 BYTE)
     WINDOW           VARCHAR2 (10 BYTE)
     GUESTS           NUMBER (3)
     SQ_FT            NUMBER (6)
     BALCONY_SQ_FT    NUMBER (6)

  PK_SHIP_CABIN_ID
```

Now review this SQL statement:

```
CREATE INDEX RN_SC FOR TABLE SHIP_CABINS (ROOM_NUMBER);
```

Which of the following statements is true for this SQL statement?

A. It will fail due to a syntax error because of an error with the index name.

B. It will fail due to a syntax error because of the FOR TABLE keywords.

C. It will successfully execute but create an index that is INVALID.

D. It will successfully execute and create an index as intended.

9. Review the illustration from question 8, and these SQL statements:

```
CREATE INDEX RT_INDEX ON SHIP_CABINS (ROOM_TYPE, ROOM_STYLE);
SELECT * FROM SHIP_CABINS WHERE ROOM_STYLE = 'SUITE';
```

Which of the following assertions about these SQL statements is true?

A. The SQL optimizer will not consider the RT_INDEX index because the WHERE clause does not reference the ROOM_TYPE column.

B. The SQL optimizer will consider the RT_INDEX index in exactly the same fashion that it would if the WHERE clause referenced ROOM_TYPE instead of ROOM_STYLE.

C. The SQL optimizer will consider the RT_INDEX index once for each unique value in the ROOM_TYPE column, until it finds all the values that satisfy the WHERE clause.

D. The SQL optimizer will consider the RT_INDEX index once for each unique value in the ROOM_STYLE column, until it finds all the values that satisfy the WHERE clause.

10. Review these SQL statements (line numbers added):

```
01    CREATE TABLE ITEMS
02      (ITEM_NUM  NUMBER(7) PRIMARY KEY,
03       ITEM_NAME VARCHAR2(30));
04    CREATE TABLE REPAIR_HISTORY
05     ( REPAIR_HISTORY_ID    NUMBER(11) PRIMARY KEY,
06       REPAIR_DATE          DATE,
07       ITEM_NUM             NUMBER(11) REFERENCES ITEMS(ITEM_NUM),
08       REPAIR_TRACKING      VARCHAR2(11) UNIQUE,
09       REPAIR_AGENT         VARCHAR2(30) USING INDEX
10                            (CREATE INDEX IX_RA ON
11                                    REPAIR_HISTORY (REPAIR_AGENT) ),
12    NOTES                   VARCHAR2(200));
```

How many indexes on the REPAIR_HISTORY table will be created as a result of these statements?

A. None, because the CREATE TABLE statement in line 4 will fail due to a syntax error in line 9 through line 11

B. One

C. Two

D. Three

11. Review this code and note the placeholder for *option* in italics:

```
01   CREATE TABLE REPAIR_HISTORY
02   ( REPAIR_HISTORY_ID    NUMBER(11) PRIMARY KEY option,
03     REPAIR_DATE          DATE);
```

To create an INDEX within this CREATE TABLE statement, what can be substituted for *option*?

A. USING INDEX (CREATE INDEX IND_PK)

B. USING INDEX (CREATE INDEX IND_PK ON REPAIR_HISTORY)

C. USING INDEX (CREATE INDEX IND_PK ON REPAIR_HISTORY(REPAIR_HISTORY_ID))

D. USING INDEX IND_PK (REPAIR_HISTORY_ID)

Create Function-Based Indexes

12. Review the following SQL statement:

```
CREATE INDEX IND_004 ON SHIP_CABINS ((SQ_FT + BALCONY_SQ_FT)/GUESTS);
```

Which of the following statements will cause the optimizer to consider this index?

A. SELECT * FROM SHIP_CABINS WHERE SQ_FT + BALCONY_SQ_FT < 500;

B. SELECT * FROM SHIP_CABINS WHERE ((BALCONY_SQ_FT + SQ_FT)/GUESTS) < 500;

C. SELECT * FROM SHIP_CABINS WHERE (SQ_FT/GUESTS) < 500;

D. SELECT * FROM SHIP_CABINS WHERE (GUESTS/(SQ_FT + BALCONY_SQ_FT)) < 500;

Perform FLASHBACK Operations

13. Review the following SQL code (line numbers added):

```
01   DROP    TABLE PO_BOXES;
02   CREATE TABLE PO_BOXES (PO_BOX_ID NUMBER(3), PO_BOX_NUMBER VARCHAR2(10))
03                 ENABLE ROW MOVEMENT;
04   INSERT INTO PO_BOXES VALUES (1, 'A100');
05   INSERT INTO PO_BOXES VALUES (2, 'B100');
06   COMMIT;
07   EXECUTE DBMS_LOCK.SLEEP(30);
08   DELETE FROM PO_BOXES;
09   COMMIT;
10   EXECUTE DBMS_LOCK.SLEEP(30);
```

Which of the following statements could be added as line 11, and recover the deleted rows from the PO_BOXES table?

A. FLASHBACK TABLE PO_BOXES TO TIMESTAMP SYSTIMESTAMP—INTERVAL '0 00:00:45' DAY TO SECOND;

B. FLASHBACK TABLE PO_BOXES TO SYSTIMESTAMP—INTERVAL '0 00:00:45' DAY TO SECOND;

C. FLASHBACK TABLE PO_BOXES INTERVAL '0 00:00:45' DAY TO SECOND;

D. FLASHBACK TABLE PO_BOXES TO TIMESTAMP INTERVAL '0 00:00:45' DAY TO SECOND;

14. Review the following SQL code (line numbers added):

```
01    CREATE TABLE PO_BOXES (PO_BOX_ID NUMBER(3), PO_BOX_NUMBER VARCHAR2(10))
02                ENABLE ROW MOVEMENT;
03    INSERT INTO PO_BOXES VALUES (1, 'A100');
04    INSERT INTO PO_BOXES VALUES (2, 'B100');
05    COMMIT;
06    DROP TABLE PO_BOXES;
07    COMMIT;
08    PURGE TABLE PO_BOXES;
09    COMMIT;
```

What statement will recover the PO_BOXES table after these statements are executed?

A. FLASHBACK TABLE PO_BOXES TO BEFORE DROP;

B. FLASHBACK TABLE PO_BOXES TO TIMESTAMP SYSTIMESTAMP—INTERVAL '0 00:00:03' DAY TO SECOND;

C. FLASHBACK TABLE PO_BOXES TO BEFORE COMMIT;

D. None of the above

Create and Use External Tables

15. The purpose of the CREATE DIRECTORY statement is to create a named object in the database:

A. That lists names of user accounts that have external privileges

B. That contains lookup reference material for queries

C. That identifies the root directory of the Oracle server installation

D. That points to a directory you choose somewhere within the Oracle server's file system

SELF TEST ANSWERS

Add and Modify Columns

1. ☑ **A and B.** These answers are correct, meaning that the SQL statements shown will not execute and will fail. The reasons: You cannot include the COLUMN keyword in the ADD or MODIFY clause of ALTER TABLE. If you include the DEFAULT keyword, then it must follow any datatype specification, not precede it.

   ☒ **C and D** are incorrect. These statements are syntactically correct. Even though you cannot include the COLUMN keyword in the ADD or MODIFY clauses of the ALTER TABLE statement, the COLUMN keyword is a part of the DROP clause and the RENAME clause.

2. ☑ **B and C.** These answers are correct, meaning that the SQL statements here will fail to execute. You cannot change a populated column from one datatype to another—in this case, you cannot change a populated NUMBER to VARCHAR2. Even though SQL could theoretically do an automatic datatype conversion in this particular scenario, it won't. Also, you cannot set the DEFAULT value for a column to something that conflicts with its datatype.

   ☒ **A and D** are incorrect. These are fine. Either column could be made into the primary key.

3. ☑ **B.** This is the correct syntax.

   ☒ **A, C,** and **D** are incorrect. You can change the name of a column in a table. The RENAME COLUMN clause is part of the ALTER TABLE statement and requires use of the keyword TO, as shown in answer B.

Drop Columns and Set Column UNUSED

4. ☑ **B.** The UNUSED column is still stored as part of the table. There's no storage benefit to the table—no space is reclaimed from an unused column.

   ☒ **A, C,** and **D** are incorrect. Neither a column dropped with DROP nor an UNUSED column can be seen in the table's structure. A column, once set to UNUSED, can never be recovered. It can only be dropped.

5. ☑ **C.** The SET UNUSED keywords follow the table name and precede the keyword COLUMN, followed by the name of the column to be set to UNUSED.

   ☒ **A, B,** and **D** are incorrect. The syntax doesn't use the MODIFY option, but rather the SET UNUSED option, along with the keyword COLUMN and the column name.

Add Constraints

6. ☑ **D.** The attempt to add the constraint to the table will fail. All existing rows in the table must satisfy the constraint at the time it is added.

☒ **A, B,** and **C** are incorrect. All wrong. The addition of the constraint will not change existing values in any way. No rows will be marked as invalid.

7. ☑ **C.** This is the correct syntax. When the MODIFY clause is used to modify a column, the in-line syntax for a constraint is what you must use.

☒ **A, B,** and **D** are incorrect. While it's possible to add the constraint using the ADD clause of ALTER TABLE, these particular examples are not valid. For one thing, the CONSTRAINT keyword is required after ADD when adding a CHECK constraint. Were that included in Answer A, the syntax there would work fine. But Answer B is another story—note the reference to the DAYS column in parentheses. CHECK constraints do not require a column reference, not even in the out-of-line syntax; the column reference should be included within the expression, which in this instance—it is. As for the remaining incorrect answer, whenever the MODIFY clause is used to modify a column, the ADD keyword is not used.

Create Indexes Using the **CREATE TABLE** Statement

8. ☑ **B.** The FOR TABLE keywords are not valid in this context. They should be replaced simply with the word ON and nothing more.

☒ **A, C,** and **D** are incorrect.

9. ☑ **C.** The INDEX is a composite, which means that it includes more than one column. Given that, and the fact that the query's WHERE clause specifies a column other than the leading column in the index, the query optimizer considers performing a "skip scan" to search the index once for each unique value in the ROOM_TYPE column.

☒ **A, B,** and **D** are incorrect. The INDEX may be considered, but it will probably not be used in the same way it would were the first column referenced instead of the second column.

10. ☑ **A.** You cannot use the USING INDEX clause in a CREATE TABLE statement unless you are using it as part of a PRIMARY KEY or UNIQUE constraint, and neither is involved with line 9.

☒ **B, C,** and **D** are incorrect. Were it not for the improper use of USING INDEX in line 9, the table would create two indexes automatically—one as a result of the PRIMARY KEY constraint in line 5, and one as a result of the UNIQUE constraint.

11. ☑ **C.** The correct syntax restates the table name and column name, as well as the name of the index.

☒ **A, B,** and **D** are incorrect.

Create Function-Based Indexes

12. ☑ **B.** The fact that the columns SQ_FT and BALCONY_SQ_FT are reversed in the expression is not an issue—the index will still be used.

☒ **A, C,** and **D** are incorrect. None of the other options represents an expression that is recognizable to the function-based index. Answer D is the closest in the sense that it includes all of the components, but by reversing the positions of the values with regard to the division operator, the result is a fundamentally different equation.

Perform FLASHBACK Operations

13. ☑ **A.** This is the correct syntax—the TO TIMESTAMP clause with the expression that starts with the current date and time and subtracts an interval of 45 seconds.

☒ **B, C,** and **D** are incorrect. Answer B is missing the keyword TIMESTAMP. Answer C is missing the keywords TO TIMESTAMP, and includes an incomplete expression that only represents a time interval of 45 seconds. Answer D has the keyword TIMESTAMP but also has the incomplete expression that only includes the interval value and nothing more.

14. ☑ **D.** None of the above. The PURGE statement on line 8 prevents any recovery from being possible. PURGE cleans out the recycle bin of the objects specified in the PURGE statement, from which FLASHBACK TABLE recovers objects.

☒ **A, B,** and **C** are incorrect. Were it not for the PURGE, answer A would be correct. Answer B is syntactically correct, but again, only were it not for the PURGE statement in the code sample. There is no BEFORE COMMIT option for FLASHBACK TABLE.

Create and Use External Tables

15. ☑ **D.** CREATE DIRECTORY lets you create a database object name for a directory you choose. Later you can use this object for creating an external table.

☒ **A, B,** and **C** are incorrect.

12

Using the Set Operators

T his chapter describes the set operators in SQL. Set operators work with sets of output data from two or more SELECT statements. They combine standalone SELECT statements in ways that cannot be done with joins or other conventional methods in SQL.

Set operators are ideal for a variety of situations where a SELECT statement's output can be combined with other data that isn't necessarily related through a structured key relationship but can still be combined into one complete output data set. A series of SELECT statements combined with set operators may include a single ORDER BY clause at the end of the series of SELECT statements. Set operators should not be confused with the reserved word SET that is used with SQL statements like UPDATE. The set operators have nothing to do with the keyword SET and don't use it.

CERTIFICATION OBJECTIVE 12.01

Describe Set Operators

There are four set operators: UNION, UNION ALL, INTERSECT, and MINUS. Set operators combine two or more separate SELECT statements so that their output is merged in some manner. Each set operator merges the data in a different way. The set operators are described in Table 12-1 and summarized in Figure 12-1.

The UNION operator merges the resulting row sets of one SELECT statement with the resulting row sets of another, so that all of the records from both SELECT statements are included in the final output. UNION also eliminates any duplicate records that might result in the combined output.

TABLE 12-1	Set Operator	Description
The Set Operators	UNION	Combines row sets. Eliminates duplicate row sets.
	UNION ALL	Combines row sets. Does not eliminate duplicate row sets.
	INTERSECT	Includes all row sets that are present in both queries.
	MINUS	Subtracts the rows in the second row set from the rows in the first row set.

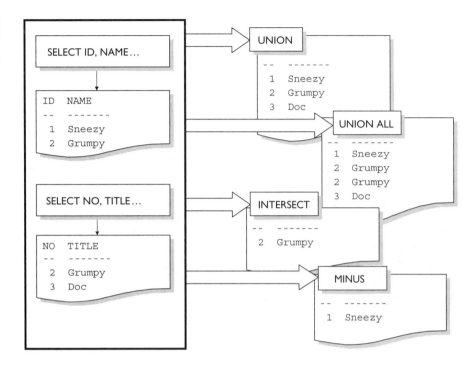

FIGURE 12-1

The set operators in action

UNION ALL does the same thing as UNION, except that it does not eliminate duplicate rows.

INTERSECT combines both sets of rows so that only those rows that were present in both SELECT statements appear in the final result.

MINUS starts with the first set of rows and then uses the second SELECT statement's row set to see if any duplicates occur. If they do, those duplicates are completely removed altogether, leaving only those rows that uniquely exist in the first SELECT statement's row set.

The only rules for ensuring that the SELECT statements will combine successfully with any of the set operators are as follows:

■ The number of expressions selected in the select lists must be identical in each SELECT statement.

■ The datatypes of each expression must match, so that each SELECT statement's first expression shares the same datatype group with the other first expressions, and each second expression shares the same datatype group with the other second expressions, etc. By datatype group, we mean datatypes that are either identical or can be made to be identical by SQL through automatic datatype conversion.

■ Large datatypes such as BLOB and CLOB cannot be used.

■ The ORDER BY clause cannot be included in the SELECT statements—except for the final SELECT statement.

The SELECT statements are not required to have any sort of PRIMARY KEY / FOREIGN KEY relationships. Their tables and columns don't have to be identical in any other way—they don't have to be named with the same names—none of that applies. Each individual SELECT statement can be a complete, standalone statement (but without an ORDER BY clause), with all the complexities of any SELECT statement, including GROUP BY clauses, subqueries, and everything that forms a complete SELECT statement. As long as the numbers of columns are identical, and the respective datatype groups match up, the set operators will perform as intended—subject to the restrictions we just identified.

ⓦatch *You can combine complex SELECT statements with the set operators. Examples include SELECT statements that involve multi-table joins, subqueries, aggregate functions, and/or GROUP BY clauses.*

CERTIFICATION OBJECTIVE 12.02

Use a Set Operator to Combine Multiple Queries into a Single Query

Let's look at the syntax for the set operators. Each is very simple—they each connect two SELECT statements, causing them to behave as one.

UNION

To demonstrate the use of UNION, we'll look at an exercise in which we are trying to combine e-mail addresses from different tables. First, we'll look at one of the two tables shown in Figure 12-2, the CONTACT_EMAILS table.

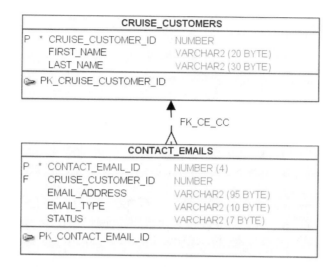

FIGURE 12-2

Diagram of
the CRUISE_
CUSTOMERS
and CONTACT_
EMAILS tables

Notice the column EMAIL_ADDRESS in the CONTACT_EMAILS table. Let's
get a data listing:

```
SELECT  CONTACT_EMAIL_ID, STATUS, EMAIL_ADDRESS
FROM    CONTACT_EMAILS;


CONTACT_EMAIL_ID           STATUS   EMAIL_ADDRESS
----------------------     -------  -------------------
1                          Opt Out  bubblegum@tlivecar.com
2                          Valid    nora@astann.com
3                          Valid    watcher@foursigma.org
```

Next, let's look at another table called ONLINE_SUBSCRIBERS, shown in
Figure 12-3. You can see that it has a column called simply EMAIL. Let's get a data
listing for that table as well:

```
SELECT  ONLINE_SUBSCRIBER_ID, EMAIL
FROM    ONLINE_SUBSCRIBERS;


ONLINE_SUBSCRIBER_ID       EMAIL
----------------------     -------------------------------
1                          pendicott77@kasteelinc.com
2                          watcher@foursigma.org
3                          hardingpal@ckofca.com
```

FIGURE 12-3

Diagram of
the ONLINE_
SUBSCRIBERS
table

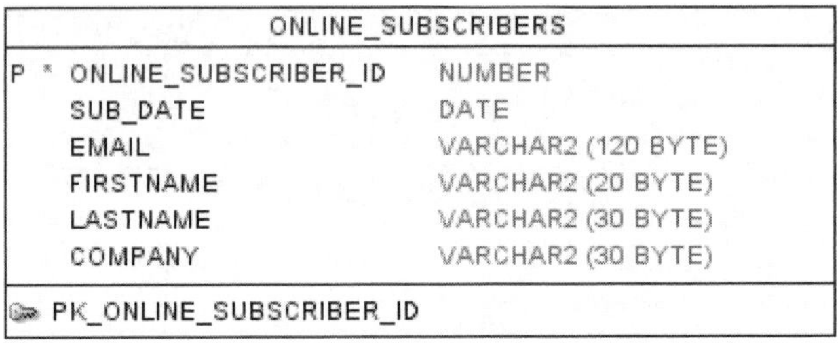

ONLINE_SUBSCRIBERS	
P * ONLINE_SUBSCRIBER_ID	NUMBER
SUB_DATE	DATE
EMAIL	VARCHAR2 (120 BYTE)
FIRSTNAME	VARCHAR2 (20 BYTE)
LASTNAME	VARCHAR2 (30 BYTE)
COMPANY	VARCHAR2 (30 BYTE)
☞ PK_ONLINE_SUBSCRIBER_ID	

In order to demonstrate the set operator UNION, we'll create two SELECT statements with similar select lists—but by similar, we mean only that the select lists are identical in the number of expressions in the list, and their respective datatype groups. The first SELECT will include a WHERE clause to limit our rows to 'Valid' data. Let's give it a try (line numbers added):

```
01   SELECT CONTACT_EMAIL_ID, EMAIL_ADDRESS
02   FROM   CONTACT_EMAILS
03   WHERE  STATUS = 'Valid'
04   UNION
05   SELECT ONLINE_SUBSCRIBER_ID, EMAIL
06   FROM   ONLINE_SUBSCRIBERS;
```

Notice how we've structured this UNION query:

■ Both SELECT statements have two expressions in their select lists (line 1 and line 5).

■ The datatypes of each list's first expression are the same—in this case, they are both numeric—CONTACT_EMAIL_ID (line 1) and ONLINE_SUBSCRIBER_ID (line 5).

■ The datatypes of each list's second expression are the same—in this case, they are both character: EMAIL_ADDRESS (line 1) and EMAIL (line 5).

Here's the output from our UNION:

```
CONTACT_EMAIL_ID          EMAIL_ADDRESS
----------------------    -----------------------------
1                         pendicott77@kasteelinc.com
2                         nora@astann.com
2                         watcher@foursigma.org
3                         hardingpal@ckofca.com
3                         watcher@foursigma.org
```

Notice the first column of output under the heading CONTACT_EMAIL_ID. The output shown includes data from both SELECT statements, which means you're seeing values from the column CONTACT_EMAIL_ID of the first SELECT, and the column ONLINE_SUBSCRIBER_ID of the second SELECT statement.

Logically, though, there's a problem: the values for CONTACT_EMAIL_ID and ONLINE_SUBSCRIBER_ID don't really represent the same information. Both are primary key values, but for different tables, and they don't really belong in the same column—they represent totally different values. The evidence of this problem is present in the list of email addresses—we only wanted a single list of unique values, but instead we have a duplication of at least one email address. The reason is that UNION looks at the entire row of output from each SELECT, and shows unique occurrences of the combined set of columns in the row. The first occurrence of the email address "watcher@foursigma.org" has a first column value of 2, and the second has a first column value of 3, so as far as the UNION is concerned, these are unique rows of data.

Let's remove the illogical references to the first column in this example, and produce something that makes more sense (line numbers added):

```
01    SELECT EMAIL_ADDRESS
02    FROM   CONTACT_EMAILS
03    WHERE  STATUS = 'Valid'
04    UNION
05    SELECT EMAIL
06    FROM   ONLINE_SUBSCRIBERS;
```

The result:

```
EMAIL_ADDRESS
---------------------------
hardingpal@ckofca.com
nora@astann.com
pendicott77@kasteelinc.com
watcher@foursigma.org
```

The result of UNION (line 4) is a combination of the original rows, with any duplicate values removed. In this case, there were two rows for the email address "watcher@foursigma.org", but only one is shown in our final result.

Notice that the output columns have headings from the first SELECT statement's expressions (line 1). We'll have more to say about that when we discuss ORDER BY and column references. For now, let's move on to the UNION ALL set operator.

UNION ALL

The only difference between UNION and UNION ALL is that duplicate values aren't removed from UNION ALL. If we were to execute the same SQL statement from the last example with the UNION ALL set operator, it would look like this:

```
01    SELECT  EMAIL_ADDRESS
02    FROM    CONTACT_EMAILS
03    WHERE   STATUS = 'Valid'
04    UNION ALL
05    SELECT  EMAIL
06    FROM    ONLINE_SUBSCRIBERS;
```

The results:

```
EMAIL_ADDRESS
---------------------------
nora@astann.com
watcher@foursigma.org
pendicott77@kasteelinc.com
watcher@foursigma.org
hardingpal@ckofca.com
```

Notice that the duplicate entry is included. The value for 'watcher@foursigma.org' appears in both tables, so it appears twice in the output of our UNION ALL use of the SELECT statement.

Notice also that the ordering of the rows is totally different—remember that without an explicit ORDER BY clause, you can never guarantee the ordering of rows in any SELECT statement. We'll look at how to use ORDER BY later in this chapter. First—let's look at another set operator.

INTERSECT

The set operator INTERSECT looks for common values among the rows of the SELECT statement. Let's change our example to use INTERSECT:

```
01    SELECT  EMAIL_ADDRESS
02    FROM    CONTACT_EMAILS
03    WHERE   STATUS = 'Valid'
04    INTERSECT
05    SELECT  EMAIL
06    FROM    ONLINE_SUBSCRIBERS;
```

And the results:

```
EMAIL_ADDRESS
------------------------------
watcher@foursigma.org
```

Just one row was common between the two SELECT statements.

INTERSECT will eliminate duplicate rows. If one or both SELECT statement row sets contains duplicates within its own set of rows, the resulting output from INTERSECT will eliminate those duplicates.

MINUS

The final set operator is MINUS. Up to now, the results of the set operators would be the same regardless of which SELECT statement was placed first before the set operator. That's not the case with MINUS, however. MINUS will start with the first SELECT statement and remove any rows from that SELECT's output that might happen to appear in the second SELECT's output. The results may differ, depending on which SELECT is placed first, and which is placed second.

Using our same example, here is the SELECT from CONTACT_EMAILS first:

```
01    SELECT  EMAIL_ADDRESS
02    FROM    CONTACT_EMAILS
03    WHERE   STATUS = 'Valid'
04    MINUS
05    SELECT  EMAIL
06    FROM    ONLINE_SUBSCRIBERS;
```

The results:

```
EMAIL_ADDRESS
--------------------
nora@astann.com
```

But now let's reverse the placement of the SELECT statements:

```
01    SELECT  EMAIL
02    FROM    ONLINE_SUBSCRIBERS
03    MINUS
04    SELECT  EMAIL_ADDRESS
05    FROM    CONTACT_EMAILS
06    WHERE   STATUS = 'Valid';
```

The results:

```
EMAIL
--------------------
hardingpal@ckofca.com
pendicott77@kasteelinc.com
```

Notice that the results are completely different. Notice also that the column heading is different—the column has taken the heading of the first SELECT statement, as it always does, but now the first SELECT statement is different, and along with it (in this example), so is the heading.

Combinations

The set operators may be used in multiple combinations, such as

```
SELECT...
UNION
SELECT...
INTERSECT
SELECT...
```

Such combinations can be continued indefinitely.

Set operators have equal precedence among themselves, meaning that they will all execute from start to finish, in the order that they appear in the SELECT statement. To change the order of execution, use parentheses, like this:

```
SELECT...
UNION
(SELECT...
INTERSECT
SELECT...)
INTERSECT
SELECT...
```

Just be sure to use the parentheses so that:

- The code enclosed is a standalone query and does not include an ORDER BY clause.
- The enclosed code is placed into the outer query as though it were a single, standalone SELECT statement, without the ORDER BY clause.
- If an ORDER BY is desired, it must be the final clause in the entire series of statements.

Follow those rules, and you can connect as many SELECT statements together as required.

on the
Ôob

The set operators are useful for requirements to combine the data of two tables into one output listing when the two tables have no primary key— foreign key relationship with each other.

CERTIFICATION OBJECTIVE 12.03

Control the Order of Rows Returned

As with any SELECT statement, the ORDER BY clause is the only way to determine the ordering of rows that appear in output. As we already know, the ORDER BY clause determines how to sort rows by identifying a series of one or more expressions that have something to do with the table—or tables—that are involved with the SELECT statement. Often the expression is simply a column within each row, but ORDER BY also accepts complex expressions. These expressions may involve one or more columns and perform some sort of transformation on the data.

However, when set operators are involved, there's a bit of an issue—how do you identify data in the rows when there are multiple rows from multiple tables that aren't necessarily consistent with each other in terms of names or structures?

The answer is that the ORDER BY clause is a bit restricted in this situation. The clause is restricted to identifying common expression items in the select list, and nothing more. There are two ways to identify them, and we've seen these earlier—by reference and by position. The following sections show examples of these approaches with the set operators.

ORDER BY—By Position

One way to sort rows of output that result from a series of SELECT statements combined with set operators is to use the "by position" approach. For example:

```
01    SELECT 'Individual',
02           LAST_NAME || ', ' || FIRST_NAME
03    FROM   CRUISE_CUSTOMERS
04    UNION
```

```
05   SELECT CATEGORY,
06          VENDOR_NAME
07   FROM   VENDORS;
```

The preceding example combines rows from two tables. The first query has two expressions:

- A string literal, 'Individual'
- A concatenation of two columns, LAST_NAME and FIRST_NAME, separated by a comma and a space

The second SELECT statement has two expressions:

- The column CATEGORY
- The column VENDOR_NAME

Here are the results:

```
'INDIVIDUAL' LAST_NAME||','||FIRST_NAME
------------ -----------------------------------------------------
Individual   Bryant, William
Individual   Gilbert, Nada
Individual   MacCaulay, Nora
Partner      Acme Steaks
Supplier     Acme Poker Chips
```

We can sort the rows with an ORDER BY that identifies the position within the select list of the expression we wish to sort by, like this:

```
01   SELECT 'Individual',
02          LAST_NAME || ', ' || FIRST_NAME
03   FROM   CRUISE_CUSTOMERS
04   UNION
05   SELECT CATEGORY,
06          VENDOR_NAME
07   FROM   VENDORS
08   ORDER BY 2;
```

The result:

```
'INDIVIDUAL' LAST_NAME||','||FIRST_NAME
------------ -----------------------------------------------------
Supplier     Acme Poker Chips
Partner      Acme Steaks
Individual   Bryant, William
Individual   Gilbert, Nada
Individual   MacCaulay, Nora
```

Remember: When using ORDER BY with a series of SELECT statements connected with set operators, you can only use ORDER BY once, at the end.

ORDER BY—By Reference

There is another way to use ORDER BY with set operators. ORDER BY reference is when you name one of the columns in the SELECT statement's expression list. When using set operators, the column names used in the first SELECT statement are in force. Using our earlier example, let's add column aliases to our first SELECT statement, and we'll be able to use ORDER BY:

```
01   SELECT   'Individual' CONTACT_CATEGORY,
02            LAST_NAME || ', ' || FIRST_NAME POINT_OF_CONTACT
03   FROM     CRUISE_CUSTOMERS
04   UNION
05   SELECT   CATEGORY,
06            VENDOR_NAME
07   FROM     VENDORS
08   ORDER BY POINT_OF_CONTACT;
```

Note the column alias POINT_OF_CONTACT that is specified at the end of line 2, and used in the ORDER BY in line 8. The results:

```
CONTACT_CATEGORY POINT_OF_CONTACT
---------------- ----------------------------------------------------
-----
Supplier         Acme Poker Chips
Partner          Acme Steaks
Individual       Bryant, William
Individual       Gilbert, Nada
Individual       MacCaulay, Nora
```

So—either the "by position" or "by reference" approach works with ORDER BY—just be sure that you make it the last clause of the entire series of SELECT statements.

If you combine a series of three or more SELECT statements with set operators, your ORDER BY clause must be the final clause, and can only specify columns by name if it uses the column names from the very first SELECT statement, regardless of how many SELECT statements might be connected with set operators.

CERTIFICATION SUMMARY

The set operators combine the rows from several independent SELECT statements in various combinations. Set operators allow you to combine rows without a join, by merging entire sets of rows based solely on ensuring that the number of expressions and datatypes involved match up.

The set operators include UNION, UNION ALL, INTERSECT, and MINUS.

UNION combines rows and eliminates duplicates that might appear as a result of the combination. UNION ALL combines rows but does not eliminate any duplicates. INTERSECT looks only for duplicates, and only the duplicates become the output from the SELECT statement. MINUS takes the set of rows from the first SELECT and removes any for which duplicates exist in the second set.

You can combine several SELECT statements with as many set operators as you wish. They will execute one after the other, unless you choose to override that behavior using parentheses.

Each SELECT statement can be a complex query, with multiple joins, subqueries, and GROUP BY clauses. However, only one ORDER BY clause is allowed, and it must be at the end of the series of SELECT statements and set operators.

ORDER BY with set operators can sort rows by position or reference. If by reference, the first SELECT statement's expression names are in effect for the entire series of SELECT statements. You can use column aliases in the first (or any) SELECT statement if you wish, but it is not required.

TWO-MINUTE DRILL

Describe Set Operators

❑ UNION combines the output of two SELECT statements, eliminating any duplicate rows that might exist.

❑ INTERSECT combines the output of two SELECT statements, showing only the unique occurrences of data present in both rowsets, and ignoring anything that doesn't appear in both sets.

❑ MINUS takes the first SELECT statement's output and subtracts any occurrences of identical rows that might exist within the second SELECT statement's output.

❑ UNION ALL does the same thing as UNION but does not eliminate duplicate rows.

Use a Set Operator to Combine Multiple Queries into a Single Query

❑ The set operators are placed between two SELECT statements.

❑ The two SELECT statements can be simple or complex and can include their own GROUP BY clauses, WHERE clauses, subqueries, and more.

❑ The ORDER BY clause, if used, must be the final clause of the combined SELECT statements.

❑ You can connect multiple SELECT statements with multiple set operators.

❑ The set operators have equal precedence.

❑ You can use parentheses to override set operator precedence.

Control the Order of Rows Returned

❑ If an ORDER BY clause is used, it must be placed at the very end of the SQL statements.

❑ Multiple SELECTs that are connected with set operators may be sorted by position or reference.

❑ When using ORDER BY reference, the column name in force is whatever column name exists in the first SELECT statement.

SELF TEST

The following questions will help you measure your understanding of the material presented in this chapter. Choose one correct answer for each question unless otherwise directed.

Describe Set Operators

1. The set operators do *not* include which one of the following keywords:
   A. ALL
   B. SET
   C. MINUS
   D. UNION

2. You are tasked with cleaning up a database application. There are two tables in the database: ORDERS contains completed ORDERS, and ORDER_RETURNS contains duplicate information for all ORDERS that were later returned. Your goal is to find out if any rows in ORDER_RETURNS exist that were never in the ORDERS table to begin with. Which of the following set operators should you use?
   A. ALL
   B. SET
   C. MINUS
   D. UNION

3. Review the following illustrations:

```
SELECT * FROM FURNISHING:

CAT#    ITEM_NAME    ADDED       SECTION
-----   ---------    ------      -------
1       Side table   23-DEC-09   LR
2       Desk         12-SEP-09   BR
3       Towel        10-OCT-09   BA
```

```
SELECT * FROM STORE_INVENTORY:

NUM     AISLE        PRODUCT     LAST_ORDER
----    -----        -------     ----------
77      F02          Jacket      2009-09-09
78      B11          Towel       2009-11-11
79      SP01         Lava lamp   2009-12-21
```

```
                    FURNISHINGS
 P *  CAT#           NUMBER
      ITEM_NAME      VARCHAR2 (15 BYTE)
      ADDED          DATE
      SECTION        VARCHAR2 (10 BYTE)
 ⊙ PK_CAT#
```

```
                  STORE_INVENTORY
 P *  NUM            NUMBER
      AISLE          VARCHAR2 (7 BYTE)
      PRODUCT        VARCHAR2 (15 BYTE)
      LAST_ORDER     DATE
 ⊙ PK_NUM
```

Next, review the following SQL code (line numbers added):

```
01    SELECT    TO_CHAR(A.LAST_ORDER,'RRRR-MM-DD')
02    FROM      STORE_INVENTORY A
03    ORDER BY 1
04    UNION
05    SELECT    ADDED
06    FROM FURNISHINGS;
```

What will result from an attempt to execute this SQL statement?

A. It will fail with a syntax error because of the TO_CHAR conversion function on line 1.

B. It will fail because of the table alias in lines 1 and 2, which cannot be used in this context.

C. It will fail with a syntax error on line 3, because you cannot use an ORDER BY in this context.

D. It will execute successfully.

4. When combining two SELECT statements, which of the following set operators will produce a different result, depending on which SELECT statement precedes or follows the operator?

A. MINUS

B. UNION ALL

C. INTERSECT

D. UNION

5. Which of the following statements about set operators is true?

    A. If you add the reserved word ALL to the end of any set operator, it will change the behavior of the set operator by removing duplicate rows.

    B. Set operators can be used to combine INSERT statements.

    C. You can connect two SELECT statements together with one set operator.

    D. The UNION set operator has precedence over the others.

Use a Set Operator to Combine Multiple Queries into a Single Query

6. Review the first two illustrations from question 3, then review this SQL code:

```
SELECT NUM, PRODUCT FROM STORE_INVENTORY
INTERSECT
SELECT CAT#, ITEM_NAME   FROM FURNISHINGS;
```

How many rows will result from this query?

    A. 0

    B. 1

    C. 3

    D. 6

7. Review the first two illustrations from question 3, and then review this SQL code:

```
01    SELECT '--', SECTION
02    FROM   FURNISHINGS
03    WHERE  CAT# NOT IN (1,2)
04    UNION ALL
05    SELECT TO_CHAR(LAST_ORDER,'Month'), AISLE
06    FROM   STORE_INVENTORY;
```

How many rows will result from this query?

    A. 0

    B. 4

    C. 6

    D. It will not execute because it will fail with a syntax error.

8. Review the first two illustrations from question 3, and then review this SQL code:

```
(  SELECT PRODUCT  FROM STORE_INVENTORY
   UNION ALL
```

```
      SELECT ITEM_NAME FROM FURNISHINGS
)
INTERSECT
(  SELECT ITEM_NAME FROM FURNISHINGS WHERE ITEM_NAME = 'Towel'
   UNION ALL
   SELECT ITEM_NAME FROM FURNISHINGS WHERE ITEM_NAME = 'Towel'
);
```

How many rows will result from this code?

A. 1

B. 2

C. 4

D. 6

9. Review the first two illustrations from question 3, as well as the ONLINE_SUBSCRIBERS table in Figure 12-3, and then review this SQL code:

```
01    SELECT COUNT(*)
02    FROM   ONLINE_SUBSCRIBERS
03    WHERE  SUB_DATE IN
04              (SELECT LAST_ORDER FROM STORE_INVENTORY
05               UNION
06               SELECT ADDED      FROM FURNISHINGS);
```

What will happen when this SQL statement is executed?

A. It will fail with a syntax error because you cannot use an aggregate function like COUNT(*) in line 1 in this context.

B. It will fail with a syntax error starting at line 4.

C. It will execute, but it will not perform as intended, because the second SELECT statement within the subquery on line 6 will not execute; only the first SELECT in the subquery on line 4 will execute.

D. It will execute successfully.

10. Review the first two illustrations from question 3, as well as the ONLINE_SUBSCRIBERS table in Figure 12-3, and then review this SQL code:

```
01    SELECT    (SELECT LAST_ORDER FROM STORE_INVENTORY
02               UNION
03               SELECT ADDED "Date Added" FROM FURNISHINGS)
04    FROM      ONLINE_SUBSCRIBERS
05    ORDER BY 1;
```

What will happen when this SQL statement is executed?

A. It will fail with an execution error on line 1.

B. It will execute, but the UNION will not work as expected.

C. It will execute and display one column under the heading "Date Added".

D. It will execute and display one column under the heading LAST_ORDER.

11. Review the first two illustrations from question 3, as well as the ONLINE_SUBSCRIBERS table in Figure 12-3, and then review this SQL code:

```
01   SELECT   (SELECT PRODUCT FROM STORE_INVENTORY
02                INTERSECT
03                SELECT ITEM_NAME FROM FURNISHINGS)
04   FROM     ONLINE_SUBSCRIBERS;
```

What will happen when this SQL statement is executed?

A. It will fail with a general syntax error.

B. It will fail with an execution error.

C. It will execute, but the INTERSECT will not work correctly.

D. It will execute and repeat the value 'Towel' for each row of the ONLINE_SUBSCRIBERS table.

12. Review the first two illustrations from question 3, as well as the ONLINE_SUBSCRIBERS table in Figure 12-3, and then review this SQL code:

```
01   SELECT   A.SUB_DATE, COUNT(*)
02   FROM     ONLINE_SUBSCRIBERS A JOIN
03                (SELECT LAST_ORDER, PRODUCT FROM STORE_INVENTORY
04                 UNION
05                 SELECT ADDED, ITEM_NAME FROM FURNISHINGS) B
06   ON       A.SUB_DATE = B.LAST_ORDER
07   GROUP BY A.SUB_DATE;
```

Which of the following are true about this SQL statement? (Choose two.)

A. The GROUP BY clause on line 7 is not allowed here.

B. The B.LAST_ORDER reference at the end of line 6 refers to data included in the ADDED column referred to in line 5.

C. The JOIN at the end of line 2 is not allowed in this context.

D. The statement is syntactically correct and will execute successfully.

Control the Order of Rows Returned

13. Review the first two illustrations from question 3, as well as the ONLINE_SUBSCRIBERS table in Figure 12-3, and then review this SQL code:

```
01    SELECT   A.SUB_DATE, COUNT(*)
02    FROM     ONLINE_SUBSCRIBERS A JOIN
03                  (SELECT LAST_ORDER, PRODUCT FROM STORE_INVENTORY
04                   UNION
05                   SELECT ADDED, ITEM_NAME FROM FURNISHINGS) B
06    ON       A.SUB_DATE = B.LAST_ORDER
07    GROUP BY A.SUB_DATE;
```

Where can you add an ORDER BY to this code? (Choose two.)

- **A.** At the end of line 5 before the parentheses
- **B.** Between lines 5 and 6
- **C.** After line 7
- **D.** Nowhere

14. The ORDER BY clause can be included in a SELECT with set operators if:

- **A.** It follows the first SELECT statement.
- **B.** It follows the final SELECT statement.
- **C.** It is used in each SELECT statement and its ORDER BY expressions match in datatype.
- **D.** The ORDER BY clause cannot be used in a SELECT with set operators.

15. Review the first two illustrations from question 3, and then review this SQL code:

```
01    SELECT '--' "Order Date", SECTION
02    FROM   FURNISHINGS
03    WHERE  CAT# NOT IN (1,2)
04    UNION ALL
05    SELECT TO_CHAR(LAST_ORDER,'Month') "Last Order", AISLE
06    FROM   STORE_INVENTORY;
```

Which of the following are valid ORDER BY clauses for this query? (Choose two.)

- **A.** ORDER BY AISLE
- **B.** ORDER BY "Last Order"
- **C.** ORDER BY SECTION
- **D.** ORDER BY 1

SELF TEST ANSWERS

Describe Set Operators

1. ☑ **B.** The keyword SET is not used with the set operators.
   ☒ **A, C,** and **D** are incorrect. ALL is part of the UNION ALL clause. MINUS and UNION are both set operators.

2. ☑ **C.** MINUS is what you would use. That is the set operator with which you can remove rows from one table that are also present in the second table, resulting in output that shows rows from the first table that are not present in the second.
   ☒ **A, B,** and **D** are incorrect. ALL is not a full set operator; it works with UNION ALL but is not a set operator on its own. SET is not a set operator. UNION would combine records from both tables, which is not what is desired here.

3. ☑ **C.** The ORDER BY of the first SELECT statement in line 3 is incorrect and causes the statement to fail.
   ☒ **A, B,** and **D** are incorrect. The TO_CHAR conversion function in line 1 is correct syntax. It ensures that the datatypes for LAST_ORDER and ADDED correspond to each other. The table alias on lines 1 and 2 is fine. But the entire statement will not execute for the reason explained above for answer C.

4. ☑ **A.** The only set operator that changes its end result based on which SELECT statement precedes or follows the set operator is MINUS.
   ☒ **B, C,** and **D** are incorrect.

5. ☑ **C.** You can connect two SELECT statements together with one set operator.
   ☒ **A, B,** and **D** are incorrect. The reserved word ALL only works with UNION. Set operators can only combine SELECT statements, not other SQL statements. All set operators have equal precedence; only parentheses can be used to override set operator precedence.

Use a Set Operator to Combine Multiple Queries into a Single Query

6. ☑ **A.** No rows will result. The reason: we're trying to intersect rows, which means to show only those rows that are common between the two rowsets. While both tables share a value of 'Towel', the SELECT statements are including the NUM and CAT# columns from the two tables. The result: neither row that includes 'Towel' is a complete match.
   ☒ **B, C,** and **D** are incorrect.

7. ☑ **B.** The first select will produce one row. The second will produce three rows. The UNION ALL set operator will combined the results and return four rows.

   ☒ **A, C,** and **D** are incorrect. The syntax is fine and the statement will execute.

8. ☑ **A.** Only one row will result, as explained below.

   ☒ **B, C,** and **D** are incorrect. It might be tempting to have chosen answer B, since the first and second SELECT statement combinations with the UNION ALL will produce two rows containing the value for 'Towels', and so will the second UNION ALL. But the INTERSECT will eliminate duplicate rows and return one row for 'Towel'.

9. ☑ **D.** It will execute successfully. Set operators are perfectly acceptable in a subquery.

   ☒ **A, B,** and **C** are incorrect.

10. ☑ **A.** Since we know from the data listings that the results of the SELECT statements with the set operator UNION will produce multiple rows, the statement will fail, since a scalar subquery is what is expected here by the outer query.

    ☒ **B, C,** and **D** are incorrect. UNION is fine, but the end result caused a problem for reasons unrelated to the UNION. The column heading issues don't apply, but if the subquery had not produced the execution error, answers C and D would still be incorrect—the heading would be a concatenated version of the entire string of characters forming the subquery.

11. ☑ **D.** We can tell from the data listing that the subquery will return one value representing the INTERSECT of both queries. That, and the fact that the subquery will return just one column in that one row, makes this a scalar subquery, albeit a risky one, since there's no guarantee that it will always execute as a scalar subquery. But it will work given the data listings, and the subquery will perform as though it were a literal value within the outer SELECT, returning the same result for each row of the ONLINE_SUBSCRIBERS table.

    ☒ **A, B,** and **C** are incorrect. There is nothing wrong syntactically with the SQL statement, and as we discuss in describing the correct choice, because of the data listings we are provided with, we can tell that there will be no execution errors either. The INTERSECT will perform just fine.

12. ☑ **B** and **D.** This is a valid SQL statement that will execute successfully. The subquery on lines 3 through 5 is the complete UNION and is treated as an inline view in this context. As such, it behaves like any other inline view and is perfectly fine in this context. At the end of line 5 is a table alias B that is given to the inline view, and that table alias is used in line 6 to identify the column of the inline view called LAST_ORDER, which represents the first column of the combined SELECT statements, including the ADDED column.

    ☒ **A** and **C** are incorrect. GROUP BY is allowed, as is the JOIN, for reasons explained under the correct choice.

Control the Order of Rows Returned

13. ☑ **A and C.** The ORDER BY can go at the end of the inline view, or at the end of the entire SQL statement.

    ☒ **B and D** are incorrect.

14. ☑ **B.** The ORDER BY is optional, but if used, it must be the last clause in the entire series of SELECT statements.

    ☒ **A, C, and D** are incorrect. ORDER BY cannot be used in any SELECT statements within a series of SELECT statements connected by set operators. It can only be placed at the end, following the final SELECT statement.

15. ☑ **C and D.** Any ORDER BY that uses the "by reference" technique must reference column names of the first SELECT statement. So ORDER BY SECTION is valid. Also, the "by position" is accepted, so ORDER BY 1 is good.

    ☒ **A and B** are incorrect. The AISLE column name isn't recognized, since it isn't a column in the first SELECT statement. The same is true for the "Last Order" column alias.

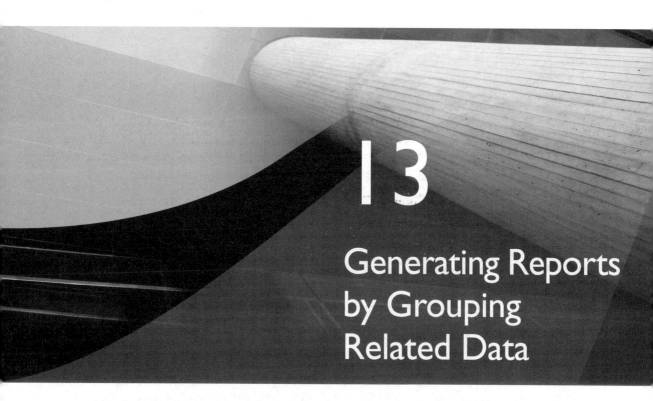

13
Generating Reports by Grouping Related Data

CERTIFICATION OBJECTIVES

Too his chapter is about a number of extensions to the capabilities of the GROUP BY clause of the SELECT statement, CUBE, ROLLUP, and GROUPING SETS. We'll also examine a function named GROUPING that supports the GROUP BY operations discussed in this chapter. Each is addressed separately in the pages that follow, starting with ROLLUP.

CERTIFICATION OBJECTIVE 13.01

Use the ROLLUP Operation to Produce Subtotal Values

The ROLLUP operation is a subclause of GROUP BY that aggregates the aggregate data in the SELECT statement's output. The aggregated aggregate rows are known as *superaggregate* rows. ROLLUP is of primary benefit with the aggregate function SUM, but it works with other aggregates as well. ROLLUP returns a single summary row for each grouped set of records within a SELECT statement that uses the GROUP BY clause. ROLLUP is part of GROUP BY and as such is parsed as part of the GROUP BY clause within the overall execution of the SELECT statement.

For example, consider the following data listing from the table SHIP_CABINS:

```
SHIP_CABIN_ID         ROOM_STYLE ROOM_TYPE            SQ_FT
--------------------- ---------- -------------------- ----------------------
1                     Suite      Standard             533
2                     Stateroom  Standard             160
3                     Suite      Standard             533
4                     Stateroom  Standard             205
5                     Suite      Standard             586
6                     Suite      Royal                1524
7                     Stateroom  Large                211
8                     Stateroom  Standard             180
9                     Stateroom  Large                225
10                    Suite      Presidential         1142
11                    Suite      Royal                1745
12                    Suite      Skyloft              722
```

We can write a SELECT statement that will group these rows according to the values in the ROOM_STYLE and ROOM_TYPE columns and add up the total amount of square feet in each group. Here's the SQL statement:

```
SELECT    ROOM_STYLE, ROOM_TYPE, ROUND(SUM(SQ_FT),0) SUM_SQ_FT
FROM      SHIP_CABINS
WHERE     SHIP_ID = 1
GROUP BY ROOM_STYLE, ROOM_TYPE
ORDER BY ROOM_STYLE, ROOM_TYPE;
```

The output of this GROUP BY follows:

```
ROOM_STYLE ROOM_TYPE              SUM_SQ_FT
---------- -------------------- ----------------------
Stateroom  Large                  436
Stateroom  Standard               545
Suite      Presidential           1142
Suite      Royal                  3269
Suite      Skyloft                722
Suite      Standard               1652
```

Here is where the ROLLUP operation comes in. We can use ROLLUP to add up subtotals and totals within the SQL statement's output for each grouped category. Let's use ROLLUP on the combination of ROOM_STYLE and ROOM_TYPE:

```
SELECT    ROOM_STYLE, ROOM_TYPE, ROUND(SUM(SQ_FT),2) SUM_SQ_FT
FROM      SHIP_CABINS
WHERE     SHIP_ID = 1
GROUP BY ROLLUP (ROOM_STYLE, ROOM_TYPE)
ORDER BY ROOM_STYLE, ROOM_TYPE;
```

Here's the output (line numbers added):

```
01    ROOM_STYLE ROOM_TYPE              SUM_SQ_FT
02    ---------- -------------------- ----------------------
03    Stateroom  Large                  436
04    Stateroom  Standard               545
05    Stateroom                         981
06    Suite      Presidential           1142
07    Suite      Royal                  3269
08    Suite      Skyloft                722
09    Suite      Standard               1652
10    Suite                             6785
11                                      7766
```

This listing shows these effects of ROLLUP:

- Lines 5 and 10 show the subtotals for each ROOM_STYLE group—notice the NULL value displayed in the ROOM_TYPE column to indicate the presence of a subtotal line.
- Line 11 shows a grand total for the entire set of output.

The syntax rules for ROLLUP include the following:

- The keyword ROLLUP is used after the keywords GROUP BY, and is part of the GROUP BY clause.
- The keyword ROLLUP is followed by a grouping expression list enclosed in parentheses.
- ROLLUP can be repeated for each grouping in the GROUP BY clause you wish to roll up.

You can include as many GROUP BY groups as you would in a typical GROUP BY clause. ROLLUP can be used to compute a subtotal for each group.

You can use any aggregate function with ROLLUP. For example, AVG will compute averages for each group.

The ROLLUP operation can be used as part of a series of GROUP BY expressions. For example, we can take our example SQL statement and add the column WINDOW as a grouped value, retaining our ROLLUP operation we were already performing. The result looks like this (line numbers added):

```
01    SELECT   WINDOW, ROOM_STYLE, ROOM_TYPE, ROUND(SUM(SQ_FT),2) SUM_SQ_FT
02    FROM     SHIP_CABINS
03    WHERE    SHIP_ID = 1
04    GROUP BY WINDOW, ROLLUP (ROOM_STYLE, ROOM_TYPE)
05    ORDER BY WINDOW, ROOM_STYLE, ROOM_TYPE;
06
07    WINDOW     ROOM_STYLE ROOM_TYPE              SUM_SQ_FT
08    ---------- ---------- -------------------- ----------------------
09    Balcony    Suite      Presidential         1142
10    Balcony    Suite      Royal                3269
11    Balcony    Suite      Skyloft              722
12    Balcony    Suite      Standard             1652
13    Balcony    Suite                           6785
14    Balcony                                    6785
15    None       Stateroom  Large                211
16    None       Stateroom                       211
```

17	None			211
18	Ocean	Stateroom	Large	225
19	Ocean	Stateroom	Standard	545
20	Ocean	Stateroom		770
21	Ocean			770

By incorporating a standard GROUP BY expression as well as the ROLLUP operation, we prevent a grand total value from being displayed but obtain subtotal values for each WINDOW value. ROLLUP computes and displays subtotals and totals for the expressions contained with the set of parentheses that follow the ROLLUP keyword.

For every n groups, ROLLUP produces n+1 groupings.

The rows that are displayed as a result of the GROUP BY clause are known as regular rows. The other rows—the aggregated aggregate rows—are known as superaggregate rows.

watch The GROUP BY clause is processed by SQL before the select list. Therefore it doesn't recognize column aliases created in the select list—this applies to ROLLUP and CUBE as well.

CERTIFICATION OBJECTIVE 13.02

Use the CUBE Operation to Produce Crosstabulation Values

The CUBE operation is something of a three-dimensional version of ROLLUP. CUBE goes beyond the functionality of ROLLUP by calculating subtotals for every possible grouping within the columns selected and grouped. The CUBE is part of the GROUP BY and as such is parsed as part of the GROUP BY clause within the overall execution of the SELECT statement.

watch CUBE can potentially produce the greatest amount of output of all the GROUP BY features examined in this chapter.

Let's take our ROLLUP example from before and make one simple change: we'll replace the keyword ROLLUP with the keyword CUBE:

```
SELECT    ROOM_STYLE, ROOM_TYPE, ROUND(SUM(SQ_FT),2) SUM_SQ_FT
FROM      SHIP_CABINS
WHERE     SHIP_ID = 1
GROUP BY CUBE (ROOM_STYLE, ROOM_TYPE)
ORDER BY ROOM_STYLE, ROOM_TYPE;
```

Here's the output (line numbers added):

```
01   ROOM_STYLE ROOM_TYPE            SUM_SQ_FT
02   ---------- -------------------- --------------------
03   Stateroom  Large                436
04   Stateroom  Standard             545
05   Stateroom                       981
06   Suite      Presidential         1142
07   Suite      Royal                3269
08   Suite      Skyloft              722
09   Suite      Standard             1652
10   Suite                           6785
11              Large                436
12              Presidential         1142
13              Royal                3269
14              Skyloft              722
15              Standard             2197
16                                   7766
```

Notice that these results include three lines that we had with ROLLUP:

- Lines 5 and 10 show the subtotals for each ROOM_STYLE group—notice the NULL value displayed in the ROOM_TYPE column to indicate the presence of a subtotal line.
- Line 16 shows a grand total for the entire set of output.
- Lines 11 through 15 show subtotals for each ROOM_TYPE value.

For n expressions, CUBE returns 2 to the nth power groupings.

The syntax rules for CUBE are the same as for ROLLUP. The grouping expression list can include multiple GROUP BY groups specified within the GROUP BY clause, each separated within the required parentheses by a comma.

on the Job *Both ROLLUP and CUBE are an efficient ways to execute a single SQL statement to calculate totals and subtotals for different levels of aggregated data.*

Use the GROUPING Function to Identify the Row Values Created by ROLLUP or CUBE

The GROUPING function identifies superaggregate or aggregate rows produced by a ROLLUP or CUBE operation in a SELECT . . . GROUP BY statement. It returns a value of the NUMBER datatype, and its value is either a one (1) or a zero (0).

The GROUPING function is only valid in a SELECT statement that uses a GROUP BY clause. While GROUPING may be used in a GROUP BY that doesn't include the ROLLUP or CUBE operation, it doesn't produce anything meaningful without those operators—it will always return a zero if ROLLUP and CUBE are absent from the statement.

For example, let's add the GROUPING function to the same ROLLUP operation we looked at a few pages ago (line numbers added):

```
01    SELECT    GROUPING(ROOM_TYPE), ROOM_STYLE,
02              ROOM_TYPE, ROUND(SUM(SQ_FT),2) SUM_SQ_FT
03    FROM      SHIP_CABINS
04    WHERE     SHIP_ID = 1
05    GROUP BY ROLLUP (ROOM_STYLE, ROOM_TYPE)
06    ORDER BY ROOM_STYLE, ROOM_TYPE;
```

The function is on line 1. Notice that we've passed one parameter to the GROUPING function—the name of a grouped item specified in the GROUP BY clause from line 5.

Here's the output:

GROUPING(ROOM_TYPE)	ROOM_STYLE	ROOM_TYPE	SUM_SQ_FT
0	Stateroom	Large	436
0	Stateroom	Standard	545
1	Stateroom		981
0	Suite	Presidential	1142
0	Suite	Royal	3269
0	Suite	Skyloft	722
0	Suite	Standard	1652
1	Suite		6785
1			7766

Notice that the GROUPING function assigned a "1" to each superaggregate row—meaning a row that shows a subtotal or total of the expression specified in GROUPING—in this case, ROOM_TYPE—as a result of the ROLLUP function.

This is what the GROUPING function does—it differentiates between superaggregate rows and regular rows in the output of a ROLLUP or CUBE operation.

Once you programmatically differentiate between regular and superaggregate rows, you can bring other functions into play to customize output or perform some other conditional action. For example, the following SQL statement uses NVL and DECODE to display different information for superaggregate rows (line numbers added):

```
01    SELECT    NVL(
02                   DECODE(GROUPING(ROOM_TYPE),1,UPPER(ROOM_STYLE),
03                       INITCAP(ROOM_STYLE)),
04                   'GRAND TOTAL') ROOM_STYLE_FORMATTED,
05             ROOM_TYPE,
06             ROUND(SUM(SQ_FT),2) SUM_SQ_FT
07    FROM      SHIP_CABINS
08    WHERE     SHIP_ID = 1
09    GROUP BY ROLLUP (ROOM_STYLE, ROOM_TYPE)
10    ORDER BY ROOM_STYLE, ROOM_TYPE;
```

Here's the output—notice that the superaggregate rows show the ROOM_STYLE in all caps for subtotals, and the words 'GRAND TOTAL' for the final row.

```
01    ROOM_STYLE_FORMATTED ROOM_TYPE                SUM_SQ_FT
02    ------------------- --------------------     ------------
03    Stateroom            Large                    436
04    Stateroom            Standard                 545
05    STATEROOM                                     981
06    Suite                Presidential             1142
07    Suite                Royal                    3269
08    Suite                Skyloft                  722
09    Suite                Standard                 1652
10    SUITE                                         6785
11    GRAND TOTAL                                   7766
```

The GROUPING function is the key to providing customized behavior to the results of a ROLLUP or CUBE statement that highlights or in some other fashion changes its behavior for superaggregate rows of data.

e**x**am

ⓦatch **GROUPING is ideal when** **function, to process and/or format output**
used in combination with DECODE or **that differentiates between aggregate and**
string concatenation, or some other SQL **superaggregate data.**

Use **GROUPING SETS** to Produce a Single Result Set

The GROUPING SETS operation is another subclause of GROUP BY. It provides a finer level of detail in specifying which groups you wish to display, with optional subtotals and an optional grand total. With GROUPING SETS, you can be more selective with the results of a GROUP BY clause, and specify particular groups you wish to include in your output, omitting the rest—potentially reducing processing time accordingly.

To demonstrate GROUPING SETS, let's first revisit the CUBE operation and expand our SELECT statement to look at more data than what we saw earlier in this chapter (line numbers added):

```
01    SELECT    WINDOW, ROOM_STYLE, ROOM_TYPE, ROUND(SUM(SQ_FT),2) SUM_SQ_FT
02    FROM      SHIP_CABINS
03    WHERE     SHIP_ID = 1
04    GROUP BY CUBE(WINDOW, ROOM_STYLE, ROOM_TYPE)
05    ORDER BY WINDOW, ROOM_STYLE, ROOM_TYPE;
```

Here is the output (line numbers added):

```
01    WINDOW ROOM_STYLE ROOM_TYPE           SUM_SQ_FT
02    ------ ---------- ------------------- --------------------
03    None   Stateroom  Large               436
04    None   Stateroom  Standard            180
05    None   Stateroom                      616
06    None   Suite      Presidential        1142
07    None   Suite      Standard            1119
08    None   Suite                          2261
09    None              Large               436
10    None              Presidential        1142
11    None              Standard            1299
12    None                                  2877
13    Ocean  Stateroom  Standard            365
14    Ocean  Stateroom                      365
15    Ocean  Suite      Royal               3269
16    Ocean  Suite      Skyloft             722
17    Ocean  Suite      Standard            533
18    Ocean  Suite                          4524
19    Ocean             Royal               3269
```

```
20   Ocean              Skyloft          722
21   Ocean              Standard         898
22   Ocean                               4889
23          Stateroom   Large            436
24          Stateroom   Standard         545
25          Stateroom                    981
26          Suite       Presidential     1142
27          Suite       Royal            3269
28          Suite       Skyloft          722
29          Suite       Standard         1652
30          Suite                        6785
31                      Large            436
32                      Presidential     1142
33                      Royal            3269
34                      Skyloft          722
35                      Standard         2197
36                                       7766
```

This output listing is obviously rather lengthy. We can use GROUPING SETS to selectively choose particular groups of data, ignoring any unwanted groups in the output. The GROUPING SETS syntax is somewhat similar to ROLLUP and CUBE:

- The reserved words GROUPING SETS must follow GROUP BY.
- A pair of parentheses follows GROUPING SETS.
- Enclosed in the parentheses are a series of lists, each of which specifies one or more groups. These lists are each separated by commas, and all enclosed in parentheses.
- Each set specifies separate GROUP BY clause groups.

In other words, each list constitutes a separate set of one or more valid GROUP BY expressions. It's as if you were running several GROUP BY statements at once, combining the results together.

Let's revise line 4 of our sample query to replace the CUBE clause with an example of GROUPING SETS:

```
01   SELECT    WINDOW, ROOM_STYLE, ROOM_TYPE, ROUND(SUM(SQ_FT),2) SUM_SQ_FT
02   FROM      SHIP_CABINS
03   WHERE     SHIP_ID = 1
04   GROUP BY GROUPING SETS((WINDOW, ROOM_STYLE),(ROOM_TYPE),NULL)
05   ORDER BY WINDOW, ROOM_STYLE, ROOM_TYPE;
```

This example uses GROUPING SETS to specify three groups:

- The first group, WINDOW and ROOM_STYLE, is equivalent to executing a SELECT statement with a GROUP BY WINDOW, ROOM_STYLE.

- The second group is ROOM_TYPE by itself, which is the equivalent to executing a SEELCT statement with a GROUP BY ROOM_TYPE.
- The third group is NULL, which is the equivalent (in GROUPING SETS syntax) of asking for a single grand total.

Here's the output (line numbers added):

```
01    WINDOW ROOM_STYLE ROOM_TYPE               SUM_SQ_FT
02    ------ ---------- --------------------    ----------
03    None   Stateroom                          616
04    None   Suite                              2261
05    Ocean  Stateroom                          365
06    Ocean  Suite                              4524
07                      Large                   436
08                      Presidential            1142
09                      Royal                   3269
10                      Skyloft                 722
11                      Standard                2197
12                                              7766
```

Note that we target the specific groups we wish to see and exclude the rest. Instead of 36 rows of output, we get only 12.

- The output of the first grouping set—WINDOW and ROOM_STYLE—is included in lines 3 through 6.
- The output of the second grouping set—ROOM_TYPE—is included in lines 7 through 11.
- The output of the final grouping set—the grand total—is included in line 12.

ⓌＡＴＣＨ **To understand GROUPING SETS, you must first have a solid understanding of the GROUP BY clause. Remember that NULL is used in GROUPING SETS to cause a grand total to be calculated and displayed.**

The GROUPING SETS clause identifies one or more GROUP BY lists and processes each individually. In other words, if you were to execute two or three different GROUP BY clauses on the same table or set of tables, you could alternatively use a single SELECT statement with the GROUPING SETS operation and combine the various groups from each GROUP BY clause into one. The GROUPING SETS operation combines the resulting row sets with a UNION ALL operation.

The GROUPING SETS keywords are a useful and efficient midpoint between a GROUP BY clause, and a GROUP BY clause with ROLLUP or CUBE.

CERTIFICATION SUMMARY

There are a number of operations you can perform with GROUP BY to generate subtotals and totals at various group levels, and selectively process individual groups of rows in unique combinations that a single SQL statement could not otherwise do.

The ROLLUP operation identifies expressions specified in the GROUP BY clause. ROLLUP defines levels for superaggregation, so that subtotals and totals will be computed and displayed in the context of the GROUP BY statement's output.

The CUBE operation calculates and displays subtotals and totals for all combinations of GROUP BY clause expressions.

The GROUPING function returns a number one or zero to each row of output, to identify each row as either a regular row or a superaggregate row. The result empowers other functions within your SELECT statement to be able to customize output and customize processing at the grouped level.

The GROUPING SETS operation specifies sets of GROUP BY clause expressions in various combinations, providing a finer level of access to directing GROUP BY to perform aggregation selectively. The use of GROUPING SETS can potentially reduce unnecessary processing and speed up results.

TWO-MINUTE DRILL

Use the ROLLUP Operation to Produce Subtotal Values

❑ The ROLLUP operation is only allowed with the GROUP BY clause.

❑ ROLLUP calculates subtotals and total values for the grouped sets of records.

❑ The keyword ROLLUP follows GROUP BY.

❑ Following the keyword ROLLUP is a set of parentheses that identifies the GROUP BY items that are to be aggregated with ROLLUP.

❑ ROLLUP may be included with other GROUP BY expressions; each must be separated by commas.

Use the CUBE Operation to Produce Crosstabulation Values

❑ The CUBE operation is only allowed with the GROUP BY clause.

❑ CUBE tallies subtotals and totals for all combinations of the grouped expressions.

❑ The keyword CUBE appears after GROUP BY and is followed by the CUBE list, enclosed in parentheses, citing the GROUP BY expressions to be CUBEd.

Use the GROUPING Function to Identify the Row Values Created by ROLLUP or CUBE

❑ The GROUPING function identifies a grouped row set as either a regular row or a superaggregate row.

❑ A regular row is a non-ROLLUP or non-CUBE row of typical GROUP BY output.

❑ A superaggregate row is a GROUP BY row that represents a subtotal or total as directed by ROLLUP or CUBE.

❑ The GROUPING function returns a value of 1 for superaggregate rows or 0 for regular rows.

❑ You can combine GROUPING with other functions to customize output format and behavior for superaggregate rows versus regular rows.

Use **GROUPING SETS** to Produce a Single Result Set

❑ The GROUPING SETS operator is ideal for GROUP BY queries that work with multiple groups and relatively large amounts of data.

❑ The GROUPING SETS operator allows you to specify one or more GROUP BY combinations in a single query.

❑ The use of GROUPING SETS offers advantages over ROLLUP or CUBE when only some of the subtotaled rows are desired.

SELF TEST

The following questions will help you measure your understanding of the material presented in this chapter. Choose one correct answer for each question unless otherwise directed.

Use the ROLLUP Operation to Produce Subtotal Values

1. The ROLLUP operation can be used with:
   A. Only SUM
   B. Only SUM and AVG
   C. All aggregate functions other than COUNT
   D. Any aggregate function

2. Review the following illustration:

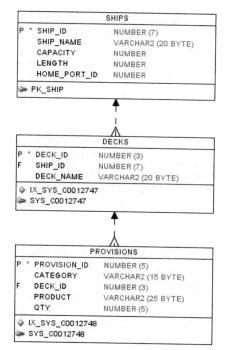

Now review this SQL code (line numbers added):

```
01   SELECT   D.DECK_NAME, P.CATEGORY, P.PRODUCT, SUM(P.QTY) QTY
02   FROM     DECKS D JOIN PROVISIONS P
03   ON       D.DECK_ID = P.DECK_ID
04   GROUP BY ROLLUP(D.DECK_NAME, P.CATEGORY, P.PRODUCT);
```

What can be said of this SELECT statement?

A. It will fail due to an error on line 1.

B. It will fail due to an error on line 4.

C. It will execute and produce a subtotal for each grouped expression but no grand total value.

D. It will execute and produce a subtotal for each grouped expression as well as a grand total.

3. Review the illustration in question 2, and then review this SQL code (line numbers added):

```
01    SELECT   CAPACITY, AVG(LENGTH)
02    FROM     SHIPS
03    GROUP BY ROLLUP CAPACITY;
```

What can be said of this SELECT statement?

A. It will fail due to an error on line 1.

B. It will fail due to an error on line 3.

C. It will execute, but the output will be meaningless because the AVG function doesn't work correctly with ROLLUP.

D. It will execute and produce output as desired.

4. Review the illustration in question 2, and then review this SQL code (line numbers added):

```
SELECT   PRODUCT, MIN(QTY)
FROM     PROVISIONS
GROUP BY ROLLUP (PRODUCT);
```

How many superaggregate rows will be displayed by this statement?

A. One

B. Two

C. One for each distinct value for PRODUCT

D. One for each distinct value for PRODUCT, plus one more

Use the CUBE Operation to Produce Crosstabulation Values

5. The CUBE operation can only be performed with:

A. INSERT statements

B. ROLLUP

C. GROUP BY

D. None of the above

6. The CUBE operation used with the SUM function often results in: (Choose two.)
   A. More rows than ROLLUP
   B. Fewer rows than ROLLUP
   C. A grand total
   D. No grand total

7. The CUBE operator:
   A. Requires the ORDER BY clause.
   B. Requires at least three grouped items.
   C. Displays regular rows and superaggregate rows.
   D. Will not work with joins.

8. Review the illustration in question 2, and then review this SQL code (line numbers added):

```
01    SELECT   SHIP_ID, ROUND(LENGTH,-2) LGTH, SUM(CAPACITY)
02    FROM     SHIPS
03    GROUP BY CUBE (LGTH, SHIP_ID)
04    ORDER BY SHIP_ID;
```

   What can be said of this SELECT statement?
   A. It will fail due to a syntax error because you cannot use the ROUND function in line 1.
   B. It will fail due to a syntax error because the column alias LGTH in line 1 won't be recognized by the GROUP BY in line 3.
   C. It will successfully execute but the use of ROUND will produce meaningless output.
   D. It will successfully execute and produce output as desired.

Use the GROUPING Function to Identify the Row Values Created by ROLLUP or CUBE

9. The purpose of the GROUPING function is to: (Choose the best answer.)
   A. Group rows dynamically according to common information.
   B. Compute the aggregate value as it applies to each group of rows.
   C. Differentiate between regular rows and superaggregate rows.
   D. Automatically identify commonly named columns for possible GROUP BY aggregation.

10. The GROUPING function can only work:
    A. With an aggregate function such as SUM or AVG
    B. With the GROUP BY clause
    C. With the ROLLUP or CUBE operations
    D. With data that contains NULL values

11. Review the illustration in question 2, and then review this SQL code (line numbers added):

```
01    SELECT    GROUPING(HOME_PORT_ID) A
02    FROM      SHIPS
03    GROUP BY HOME_PORT_ID;
```

What can be said of this SQL statement?

A. The value for the column represented by a column alias of "A" will always be zero.

B. The value for the column represented by a column alias of "A" will always be one.

C. The statement will fail due to a syntax error.

D. None of the above.

Use GROUPING SETS to Produce a Single Result Set

12. The GROUPING SETS operation combines the equivalent of several GROUP BY clauses with the functionality of which of the following? (Choose the best answer.)

A. UNION

B. UNION ALL

C. INTERSECT

D. MINUS

13. Review the illustration in question 2, and then review this SQL code (line numbers added):

```
01    SELECT    D.SHIP_ID, D.DECK_NAME, P.CATEGORY, SUM(P.QTY)
02    FROM      DECKS D JOIN PROVISIONS P
03    ON        D.DECK_ID = P.DECK_ID
04    GROUP BY GROUPING SETS ((D.SHIP_ID), (D.DECK_NAME, P.CATEGORY));
```

You are tasked with editing the preceding SQL statement to include a superaggregate row in the output that shows the grand total summing up all of P.QTY for all rows. How should line 4 be changed in order to accomplish this task?

A. GROUP BY GROUPING SETS (NULL, (D.SHIP_ID), (D.DECK_NAME, P.CATEGORY));

B. GROUP BY GROUPING SETS (SUM(P.QTY), (D.SHIP_ID), (D.DECK_NAME, P.CATEGORY));

C. No change to line is required; it will already perform as required

D. No change to line 4 can accomplish the task

14. Review the illustration in question 2, and then review this SQL code (line numbers added):

```
01    SELECT    P.CATEGORY,
02              P.PRODUCT,
03              P.DECK_ID,
04              SUM(P.QTY) SUM_QTY
05    FROM      PROVISIONS P JOIN DECKS D
06    ON        P.DECK_ID = D.DECK_ID
07    GROUP BY GROUPING SETS ((P.CATEGORY, P.PRODUCT),(P.DECK_ID))
08    ORDER BY P.CATEGORY, P.PRODUCT, P.DECK_ID;
```

In the preceding SQL statement, the output column SUM_QTY will include calculated values for each row. What will some of those rows—but not all—include as values in the SUM_QTY column? (Choose the single best answer.)

A. One sum for each group of rows that have the same value for P.CATEGORY

B. One sum for each group of rows that have the same value for P.PRODUCT

C. One sum for each group of rows that have the same value for P.DECK_ID

D. A single grand total for all rows in the PROVISIONS and DECKS tables that satisfy the join condition

15. Which of the following GROUP BY operations is most likely to produce the greatest number of rows of output, all other things being equal? (Choose the single best answer.)

A. CUBE

B. ROLLUP

C. GROUPING SETS

D. Impossible to say

SELF TEST ANSWERS

Use the ROLLUP Operation to Produce Subtotal Values

1. ☑ **D.** You can use ROLLUP with any aggregate function.
   ☒ **A, B,** and **C** are incorrect. ROLLUP tends to be most useful with SUM, but you can use it with any aggregate function.

2. ☑ **D.** The statement is syntactically correct and will produce subtotals for all grouped items as well as a grand total.
   ☒ **A, B,** and **C** are incorrect. No errors exist in the code.

3. ☑ **B.** The ROLLUP operator must be followed by the grouped items enclosed in parentheses. The lack of parentheses around CAPACITY will trigger a syntax error, and the statement will not successfully execute.
   ☒ **A, C,** and **D** are incorrect. There is no error on line 1. If there were parentheses around CAPACITY on line 3 this statement would execute and produce valid output. The use of AVG is fine here, as long as you recognize what is being computed, which is the average value for each grouped item, which in this case is rows with the same value for CAPACITY.

4. ☑ **A.** There will be one superaggregate row. The output will include one aggregate row for each product value, plus one superaggregate row showing the grand total summing up the aggregate rows.
   ☒ **B, C,** and **D** are incorrect.

Use the CUBE Operation to Produce Crosstabulation Values

5. ☑ **C.** GROUP BY. You cannot use CUBE without it.
   ☒ **A, B,** and **D** are incorrect.

6. ☑ **A** and **C.** The ROLLUP operator performs a limited number of subtotal calculations. CUBE performs every possible combination, including the grand total.
   ☒ **B** and **D** are incorrect.

7. ☑ **C.** CUBE displays regular rows and superaggregate rows.
   ☒ **A, B,** and **D** are incorrect. ORDER BY is fine and helpful but not required. Joins are allowed. The number of grouped items is not required to be a minimum of three; any amount will do.

8. ☑ **B.** The CUBE operation is parsed like a typical GROUP BY, which means that line 3 is parsed before the SELECT statement's select list (line 1), so the column alias won't be recognized. The solution is to reference the full expression in the GROUP BY.
☒ **A, C,** and **D** are incorrect. The rest of the statement is syntactically correct, and it will execute fine once the column alias issue is addressed.

Use the GROUPING Function to Identify the Row Values Created by ROLLUP or CUBE

9. ☑ **C.** The GROUPING function identifies the rows that would normally be returned by GROUP BY—i.e., regular rows—from those that are the result of aggregate calculations determined as a result of the ROLLUP or CUBE group operations.
☒ **A, B,** and **D** are incorrect.

10. ☑ **B.** The GROUP BY clause is required for GROUPING to be invoked; otherwise, a syntax error will result.
☒ **A, C,** and **D** are incorrect. GROUPING does not require other aggregate functions, although it will work well with them. It does not technically require the ROLLUP or CUBE operation to be present, although it doesn't produce anything meaningful without them. NULL values have no bearing on the performance of GROUPING.

11. ☑ **A.** Since neither ROLLUP or CUBE is included, the GROUPING result will always be zero—there cannot be any superaggregate rows without ROLLUP or CUBE, so there cannot be any returned values of 1.
☒ **B, C,** and **D** are incorrect. There is no syntax error in the statement; it will function, albeit without much in the way of meaningful output, since there is no ROLLUP or CUBE operator included in the GROUP BY clause.

Use GROUPING SETS to Produce a Single Result Set

12. ☑ **B.** UNION ALL is the correct answer.
☒ **A, C,** and **D** are incorrect.

13. ☑ **A.** If a value of NULL is included as one of the GROUPING SET lists, its presence will cause GROUPING SETS to include the grand total in the output as a superaggregate row.
☒ **B, C,** and **D** are incorrect.

14. ☑ **C.** The answer lies in line 7. There is one sum for each group of rows that have the same value for P.DECK_ID as defined by the GROUPING SET operation. That's because there is one 'column list' in the GROUPING SET that consists solely of P.DECK_ID. The other grouping set value is a two-column set, not one.

    ☒ **A, B,** and **D** are incorrect. The answer cannot be P.CATEGORY because there is not one GROUPING SET list that consists solely of P.CATEGORY, but rather there is one that consists of both P.CATEGORY and P.PRODUCT combined, so the grouped rows will be aggregated according to unique values found in the combination of those two columns, not in the columns individually. Also, there is no provision for a grand total in this implementation of GROUPING SET; for that to have been included, a NULL set would need to be included somewhere in the GROUPING SET list of values.

15. ☑ **A.** CUBE tends to produce the largest number of rows, as it produces every possible combination of aggregations from among the rows.

    ☒ **B, C,** and **D** are incorrect.

14

Managing Objects
with Data
Dictionary Views

This chapter describes a valuable tool that all Oracle professionals should understand. The data dictionary is Oracle's built-in real-time reference source for all information about the applications that you build in your database. Armed with the full capabilities of the data dictionary, you can obtain information on the database objects that have been created within your database, who created them, when, and much more.

Use the Data Dictionary Views to Research Data on Your Objects

The *data dictionary* is a collection of database tables and views. It is automatically built and populated by the Oracle database. The information stored in the data dictionary includes the full description of all the database objects you create as part of your application: tables, views, indexes, constraints, synonyms, sequences, and more. In other words, the result of each DDL statement you've studied in this book is recorded in the dictionary, and the information is automatically maintained by the Oracle system in real time as you change database objects and their structures.

The information stored in the data dictionary includes (but is not limited to)

- The names of database objects, their owners, and when they were created
- The names of each table's columns, along with datatypes, precision, and scale
- Any constraints
- Views, indexes, synonyms, sequences
- Much more

This chapter will explore how the data dictionary is structured, and what sort of information is contained within it. We'll go through some examples of how to extract valuable information and use the data dictionary to assist you as you build your applications.

The data dictionary is often referred to as "metadata". The term *metadata* means "data about data", and that is what the data dictionary is—it's a comprehensive detailed database that tracks everything there is to know about the database applications you create within the Oracle system. Every time you create a database object, the Oracle system works in the background to record that object's name and structure, and make that information available to you by way of the data dictionary. Every object created by every user is documented within the data dictionary.

Structure

The data dictionary consists of tables and views that are owned by the user account SYS. As owner, SYS has full privileges over these tables and views. No user should ever alter data owned by SYS, or else the integrity of the database may be compromised.

on the Job

The SYS account is one of a few powerful accounts that comes with every implementation of the Oracle database. The SYS account is something of a "super user" account, with master privileges to virtually everything in the database. Generally, no developer uses the SYS account for anything other than database system maintenance, and often it's the database administrator (DBA) who possesses exclusive access to the SYS account.

All data dictionary information is stored in tables, but much of that data is presented to users through views. In other words, users don't get direct access to the tables of the data dictionary; they instead get access to the views, which provide somewhat limited access in order to protect the integrity of the data dictionary.

In addition, many data dictionary objects are renamed via public synonyms, and those are the names by which you know the data. In other words, there are multiple levels of abstraction that separate users from the underlying data. No matter—the ability to read the information in the data dictionary is a great asset to all SQL professionals.

Every DDL statement that is issued throughout the database causes an automatic update to the data dictionary. That update is handled by the Oracle system and applied to the base tables that form the foundation of the data dictionary. Users do not explicitly update any information in the dictionary.

(Note: there is one exception to this. Users may optionally choose to add comments, which you'll explore later in this chapter.)

As of this writing, there are over 2,000 views in the data dictionary. One in particular is a good starting point: DICTIONARY. This view contains information about the views that compose the data dictionary. It includes the name of each view, along with a brief explanation of each view. You'll look at it a bit later.

The USER_TABLES view contains information about the tables owned by the current user account. In other words, no matter which account you log in to, you can query the USER_TABLES view and get detailed information about the tables owned by whatever account you are logged in with.

A full description of the USER_TABLES view would show that it consists of 50 columns. Some of the columns include

- **TABLE_NAME**   The name of the table.
- **STATUS**   Indicates whether or not the table is currently valid and therefore available for use.
- **ROW_MOVEMENT**   Indicates whether ROW MOVEMENT has been enabled for the table. (See our discussion in Chapter 11 about the FLASHBACK TABLE statement for more information about enabling and disabling ROW_MOVEMENT.)
- **AVG_ROW_LEN**   The average length of the rows currently stored in the table.

These are just some of the several dozen columns that are in the USER_TABLES view.

But what if you wish to see information about tables other than your own? Well it just so happens there are two other views in the data dictionary that have almost the identical set of columns as USER_TABLES:

- **ALL_TABLES**   Shows all the same table information, but for tables to which the current user has privileges, regardless of owner.
- **DBA_TABLES**   Shows all the same table information, but for all the tables in the entire database, regardless of owner or table privileges.

These other two views also have an additional column:

- **OWNER**   The owner of the table in question.

And that makes sense—there is no need for OWNER in the USER_TABLES view, since that view only shows information about one owner—the current owner.

This naming pattern of using one of these three prefixes—USER_, ALL_, DBA_—is a pattern that is used throughout the data dictionary. Many of the data dictionary views that store information about objects in the database have names that start with one of these three prefixes. Some examples are listed in Table 14-1.

TABLE 14-1	Prefix	# of Views[1]	Description
Prefixes of some of the Data Dictionary Views	USER_	359	Objects owned by the current user accessing the view.
	ALL_	334	Objects owned by any user in the database to which the current user has privileges.
	DBA_	670	All objects in the database.
	V_$ (for views) V$ (for public synonyms)	488	Dynamic performance views, each of which has a public synonym counterpart. Stores information about the local database instance.
	GV_$ (for views) GV$ (for public synonyms)	450	Global dynamic performance views.
	Other SM$, AUDIT_, CHANGE_, TABLE_ CLIENT_, COLUMN_, DICT_, DATABASE_, DBMS_, GLOBAL_, INDEX_, LOGSTDBY_, NLS_, RESOURCE_, ROLE_, SESSION_, CLIENT_RESULT_CACHE_STATS$, or no prefix, etc.	40	The remaining views of the data dictionary have a variety of prefixes and unique individual names.

[1] View counts were determined using Oracle 11.1.0.7.0. Other versions may vary.

As you can see from Table 14-1, the vast majority of data dictionary views have a prefix of USER_, ALL_, or DBA_. A set of three views that have the USER_, ALL_, and DBA_ prefix and share the same suffix, such as TABLES, draw their data from a single data dictionary table. For example, USER_CONSTRAINTS, ALL_CONSTRAINTS, and DBA_CONSTRAINTS share the same data dictionary table.

Note that public synonyms are not listed in the USER_SYNONYMS view, which only shows private synonyms. Even if you're logged in to a user account that created a particular public synonym object, you'll still not find it listed in the USER_SYNONYMS view. Instead you'll find it in ALL_SYNONYMS and DBA_SYNONYMS.

TABLE 14-2	Suffix	Description
Selected Data Dictionary Views Showing Objects Owned by the Current User	USER_CATALOG	All tables, views, synonyms, and sequences owned by USER
	USER_COL_PRIVS	Grants on columns of tables owned by USER
	USER_CONSTRAINTS	Constraints on tables owned by USER
	USER_CONS_COLUMNS	Accessible columns in constraint definitions for tables owned by USER
	USER_DEPENDENCIES	Dependencies to and from a user's objects
	USER_ERRORS	Current errors on stored objects owned by USER
	USER_INDEXES	Indexes owned by USER
	USER_IND_COLUMNS	Columns in user tables used in indexes owned by USER
	USER_OBJECTS	Objects owned by USER
	USER_SEQUENCES	Sequences owned by USER
	USER_SYNONYMS	Private synonyms owned by USER (Public synonyms are displayed in ALL_SYNONYMS and DBA_SYNONYMS.)
	USER_TABLES	Tables owned by USER
	USER_TAB_COLUMNS	Columns in USER's own tables and views
	USER_TAB_PRIVS	Grants on objects owned by USER
	USER_VIEWS	Views owned by USER

Dynamic Performance Views

Table 14-1 includes references to a set of views that begin with the prefixes V_$ and GV_$. These are defined as the dynamic performance views and the global dynamic performance views.

Dynamic performance views display information about current database activity in real time. They receive data dynamically from the database through mechanisms that go beyond the scope of this book. For our purposes, it's important to know that they are maintained automatically by the system and are available for querying—with some limitations.

The dynamic performance views start with the prefix V_$. There are public synonyms created for each of the views, and they have similar names but begin with the prefix V$.

Simple queries on dynamic performance views are accepted, but complex queries, with or without joins, require some special attention. Oracle formally recommends that the dynamic nature of these views does not guarantee read consistency for anything other than the simplest of single-view queries, so it's advised that you perform complex joins and/or queries by

- Creating a set of temporary tables to mirror the views
- Copying the data out of the views and into a set of temporary tables
- Performing the join on the temporary tables

This way, you'll avoid getting bad results caused by a lack of read consistency.

Some of the dynamic performance synonyms (that point to views that point to tables) include the following:

- **V$DATABASE**   Includes information about the database itself, including the database name, the date created, the current operating system platform, and much more.
- **V$INSTANCE**   Includes the instance name, the host name, the startup time, and much more.
- **V$PARAMETER**   The current settings for system parameters, such as NLS_LANGUAGE, NLS_DATE_LANGUAGE, NLS_CURRENCY, NLS_TIME_FORMAT, NLS_TIME_TZ_FORMAT, NLS_TIMESTAMP_ TZ_FORMAT, SQL_VERSION, and much more.
- **V$SESSION**   Many current settings for each individual user session, showing active connections, login times, machine names that users are logged in to, the current state of transactions, and much more.

Remember, only simple queries are recommended when querying the V$ (v-dollar) views directly.

- **V$RESERVED_WORDS**   Current list of reserved words, including information indicating if the keyword is always reserved or not, and if not, under what circumstances it is reserved.
- **V$OBJECT_USAGE**   Useful for monitoring the usage of INDEX objects.
- **V$TIMEZONE_NAMES**   Includes two columns: TZNAME, which is time zone region, and TZABBREV, which is the time zone abbreviation.

Reading Comments

The data dictionary is rich with comments that help describe the intent of the various views of the data dictionary, and the columns within them. In addition to the comments that are provided in the DICTIONARY view for each of the individual data dictionary views, you can also view comments about the columns within those views, or for any object stored anywhere in the database:

- **ALL_TAB_COMMENTS** Displays comments for all objects in the database.

- **ALL_COL_COMMENTS** Displays comments for all columns of all tables and views in the database.

Say you're looking at a data dictionary view like USER_SEQUENCES, and you wish to learn more about its columns. Here's a query that will help you:

```
SELECT '*TABLE: ' || TABLE_NAME, COMMENTS
FROM   ALL_TAB_COMMENTS
WHERE  OWNER = 'SYS'
  AND  TABLE_NAME = 'USER_SYNONYMS'
UNION
SELECT 'COL: ' || COLUMN_NAME, COMMENTS
FROM   ALL_COL_COMMENTS
WHERE  OWNER = 'SYS'
  AND  TABLE_NAME = 'USER_SYNONYMS' ;
```

That's the query; here are the results:

```
'*TABLE:'||TABLE_NAME      COMMENTS
----------------------     -----------------------------------------------
*TABLE: USER_SYNONYMS      The user's private synonyms
COL: DB_LINK               Database link referenced in a remote synonym
COL: SYNONYM_NAME          Name of the synonym
COL: TABLE_NAME            Name of the object referenced by the synonym
COL: TABLE_OWNER           Owner of the object referenced by the synonym
```

As you can see, we're using the data dictionary to study the data dictionary. The right-side listing under COMMENTS is helpful in describing the contents of the view in the data dictionary. You can use this technique to inspect all of the contents of the data dictionary.

Adding Comments

You can add your own comments to the data dictionary to add notes and descriptions about the tables and columns you create. The COMMENT statement is what we use to add comments to the data dictionary for a particular database object. Its syntax is as follows:

```
COMMENT ON objectType fullObjectName IS c1;
```

where:

- *objectType* is one of the keywords TABLE, COLUMN, or some other objects that are not subjects of the certification exam, such as INDEXTYPE, OPERATOR, MATERIALIZED VIEW, and others.
- *fullObjectName* is the name of the object for which you wish to add a comment. If it's a TABLE, name the table. But if it's a column, use the TABLE.COLUMN syntax.
- *c1* is the full text of the comment you wish to add.

When you add a comment to the table, the comment will be displayed in the data dictionary views USER_TAB_COMMENTS, ALL_TAB_COMMENTS, and DBA_TAB_COMMENTS.

When you add a comment to a column in a table, the comment will be displayed in the data dictionary views USER_COL_COMMENTS, ALL_COL_COMMENTS, and DBA_COL_COMMENTS.

For example, let's say we wish to add a comment to the data dictionary about the PORTS table. Here's an example:

```
COMMENT ON TABLE PORTS
          IS 'Listing of all ports of departure and arrival.';
```

To see the results, you could use this query:

```
SELECT COMMENTS
FROM   USER_TAB_COMMENTS
WHERE  TABLE_NAME = 'PORTS';

COMMENTS
--------------------------
Listing of all ports of departure and arrival.
```

Here's an example of adding a comment to a table's column:

```
COMMENT ON COLUMN PORTS.CAPACITY
            IS 'Maximum number of passengers (exclusive of crew).';
```

You can't really drop a comment from the data dictionary. Instead, you change it to a blank, like this:

```
COMMENT ON TABLE PORTS IS '';
```

CERTIFICATION OBJECTIVE 14.02

Query Various Data Dictionary Views

Let's take a look at some useful examples of the data dictionary in action.

DICTIONARY

The DICTIONARY view is a great starting point for any investigation of the data dictionary. If we DESCRIBE the view, we get the following:

```
DESC DICTIONARY;

Name                                Null      Type
--------------------------------    --------  ------------------------
TABLE_NAME                                    VARCHAR2(30)
COMMENTS                                      VARCHAR2(4000)
```

There are just two columns in the DICTIONARY view, but note that the second column can potentially hold a great deal of information.

In my current installation of the Oracle database, I'm showing 2,340 entries in this view. You can run a simple query to list all of its contents in your own user account:

```
SELECT   TABLE_NAME, COMMENTS
FROM     DICTIONARY
ORDER BY TABLE_NAME;
```

The output is too much to list here, and it's generally the same here as it will be on your own Oracle database implementation, depending on which version you're using. You might want to run this query in your own user account and review its output. If you're looking for something specific, such as anything that addresses index objects, you might try a query like this:

```
SELECT    TABLE_NAME, COMMENTS
FROM      DICTIONARY
WHERE     UPPER(COMMENTS) LIKE '%INDEX%'
ORDER BY TABLE_NAME;
```

That query will locate anything in the DICTIONARY table that mentions "index" in the comments. The result will include the name of the data dictionary view that lists all of the indexes, the one that lists all of the columns upon which an index is based, etc.

Then, if you locate a particular entry in the dictionary you want to know more about—for example, USER_DEPENDENCIES—you can run the following query to get comments on that particular view and its columns:

```
SELECT COLUMN_NAME, COMMENTS
FROM   ALL_COL_COMMENTS
WHERE  OWNER = 'SYS'
  AND  TABLE_NAME = 'USER_DEPENDENCIES';
```

Those queries should help to zero in on helpful information in the data dictionary.

Identifying a User's Owned Objects

There are a variety of data dictionary views from which you might gather data about your own user account's objects. Two views in particular are a good starting point: USER_CATALOG and USER_OBJECTS.

USER_CATALOG

The USER_CATALOG view displays a summary listing of tables, views, synonyms, and sequences owned by the user. See Figure 14-1 for a diagram of the view.

FIGURE 14-1

Diagram of the USER_CATALOG data dictionary view

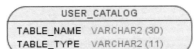

Here's a sample query to get a quick overview of what a particular user account may own:

```
SELECT TABLE_TYPE, COUNT(*)
FROM   USER_CATALOG
GROUP BY TABLE_TYPE;

TABLE_TYPE   COUNT(*)
-----------  ----------------------
SEQUENCE     21
TABLE        35
VIEW         2
SYNONYM      1
```

Be sure you have at least a basic working knowledge of each of the data dictionary views that track the basic objects in the database—tables, views, sequences, synonyms, sequences, constraints—and the difference for each with regard to the USER_, DBA_, and ALL_ prefixes.

There are only two columns in USER_CATALOG: TABLE_TYPE and TABLE_NAME, where TABLE_NAME is actually the name of the table, view, sequence, or synonym object.

A synonym for USER_CATALOG is CAT.

USER_OBJECTS

The USER_OBJECTS view contains information about all objects owned by the user. A synonym for USER_OBJECTS is OBJ. See Figure 14-2 for a diagram.

FIGURE 14-2

Diagram of the USER_OBJECTS data dictionary view

USER_OBJECTS	
OBJECT_NAME	VARCHAR2 (128)
SUBOBJECT_NAME	VARCHAR2 (30)
OBJECT_ID	NUMBER
DATA_OBJECT_ID	NUMBER
OBJECT_TYPE	VARCHAR2 (19)
CREATED	DATE (7)
LAST_DDL_TIME	DATE (7)
TIMESTAMP	VARCHAR2 (19)
STATUS	VARCHAR2 (7)
TEMPORARY	VARCHAR2 (1)
GENERATED	VARCHAR2 (1)
SECONDARY	VARCHAR2 (1)
NAMESPACE	NUMBER
EDITION_NAME	VARCHAR2 (30)

Inspecting Tables and Columns

The USER_TABLES table (synonym TABS) is helpful for inspecting table metadata, as is its companion USER_TAB_COLUMNS (synonym COLS). This section will look at USER_TAB_COLUMNS in particular.

Here's a query that will display some of the most basic information about a table and its columns. Let's get column information for the table shown in Figure 14-3.

Here is a SELECT statement that will pull information from the data dictionary about the columns of this table:

```
SELECT
  COLUMN_NAME,
  DECODE(
    DATA_TYPE,
    'DATE'    , DATA_TYPE ,
    'NUMBER'  , DATA_TYPE || DECODE(DATA_SCALE,
                NULL,
                NULL,
                '(' || DATA_PRECISION || ',' || DATA_SCALE || ')'),
    'VARCHAR2', DATA_TYPE || '(' || DATA_LENGTH || ')', NULL)
    DATA_TYPE
FROM    USER_TAB_COLUMNS
WHERE   TABLE_NAME = 'INVOICES';
```

Here's the output:

```
COLUMN_NAME                        DATA_TYPE
--------------------------------   --------------------
INVOICE_ID                         NUMBER
INVOICE_DATE                       DATE
ACCOUNT_NUMBER                     VARCHAR2(80)
TERMS_OF_DISCOUNT                  VARCHAR2(20)
VENDOR_ID                          NUMBER
TOTAL_PRICE                        NUMBER(8,2)
SHIPPING_DATE                      DATE
```

FIGURE 14-3

Diagram of the
INVOICES table

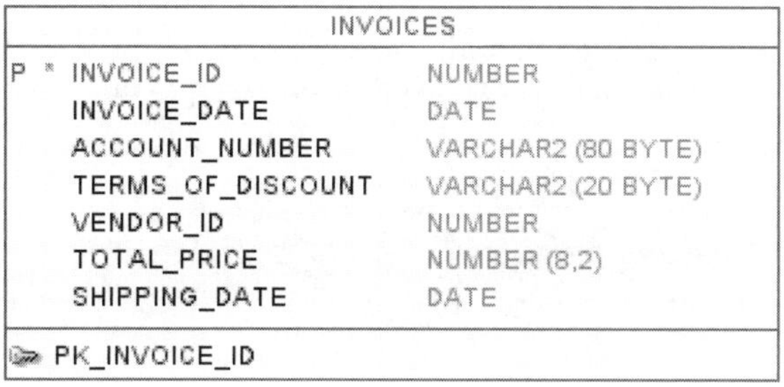

INVOICES	
P * INVOICE_ID	NUMBER
INVOICE_DATE	DATE
ACCOUNT_NUMBER	VARCHAR2 (80 BYTE)
TERMS_OF_DISCOUNT	VARCHAR2 (20 BYTE)
VENDOR_ID	NUMBER
TOTAL_PRICE	NUMBER (8,2)
SHIPPING_DATE	DATE
⊳ PK_INVOICE_ID	

Note: For the record—the preceding SELECT statement isn't totally perfect. It only addresses datatypes of DATE, NUMBER, and VARCHAR2, and in the event a NUMBER datatype has a precision but no scale, the formatting won't come out looking quite right. That being said, the point here is to illustrate the sort of query you might want to do in order to extract data dictionary information out of the database.

Compiling Views

One of the many useful tasks you can accomplish with the data dictionary is to check for the status of a view that you've created. Remember from Chapter 10 that a view is a named query based on a table, and that after the view has been created, if the table is altered for any reason, you may have to recompile the view. For example, if a table's structure is altered, such as by a change to a column's datatype, or perhaps if a column is dropped from the table altogether—a column that is used by the view—then it may change the status of the view to 'INVALID'.

You can check the data dictionary's USER_OBJECTS view to determine the status of any of your views, like this:

```
SELECT    STATUS, OBJECT_TYPE, OBJECT_NAME
FROM      USER_OBJECTS
WHERE     STATUS = 'INVALID'
ORDER BY OBJECT_NAME;
```

In our case, the output is:

```
STATUS    OBJECT_TYPE          OBJECT_NAME
-------   ------------------   ----------------
INVALID VIEW                   EMP_PHONE_BOOK
INVALID VIEW                   VW_EMPLOYEES
```

So now we know we need to recompile these views. See Chapter 10 for details about how to recompile a view.

The data dictionary contains a lot of information about views, including the query upon which the view is based, which can be found in the USER_VIEWS view and its TEXT column. Here's a query on the data dictionary that asks for the query that was used to create the view VW_EMPLOYEES:

```
SELECT TEXT
FROM   USER_VIEWS
WHERE  VIEW_NAME = 'VW_EMPLOYEES';
```

Here is the output:

```
TEXT
----------------------------------------------------------
SELECT EMPLOYEE_ID,
            LAST_NAME || ', ' || FIRST_NAME EMP_NAME,
            PRIMARY_PHONE
      FROM    EMPLOYEES
```

In summary, all of the metadata for your database is stored in the data dictionary, and available for display and inspection.

Checking Privileges

Privileges are discussed at length in Chapter 18, when we discuss user access. For now, note that privileges can be inspected using the following views:

- **USER_SYS_PRIVS**   System privileges granted to the current user
- **USER_TAB_PRIVS**   Granted privileges on objects for which the user is the owner, grantor, or grantee
- **USER_ROLE_PRIVS**   Roles granted to the current user
- **DBA_SYS_PRIVS**   System privileges granted to users and roles
- **DBA_TAB_PRIVS**   All grants on objects in the database
- **DBA_ROLE_PRIVS**   Roles granted to users and roles
- **ROLE_SYS_PRIVS**   System privileges granted to roles
- **ROLE_TAB_PRIVS**   Table privileges granted to roles
- **SESSION_PRIVS**   Session privileges which the user currently has set

Each can be inspected by the user to determine the current state of privileges and roles. See Chapter 18 for a full discussion of user access, privileges, and roles, including sample queries of these data dictionary views.

Inspecting Constraints

The USER_CONSTRAINTS view is one of the more useful views. Here's a query you might run to check the current state of constraints on a table CRUISES:

```
SELECT CONSTRAINT_NAME, CONSTRAINT_TYPE, R_CONSTRAINT_NAME, STATUS
FROM    USER_CONSTRAINTS
WHERE   TABLE_NAME = 'CRUISES';
```

Here is an example of the output:

```
CONSTRAINT_NAME            CONSTRAINT_TYPE R_CONSTRAINT_NAME   STATUS
------------------------   --------------- ------------------ --------
PK_CRUISE                  P                                  ENABLED
FK_CRUISES_CRUISE_TYPES    R               PK_CRUISE_TYPE_ID   ENABLED
FK_CRUISES_SHIPS           R               PK_SHIP             ENABLED
FK_CRUISES_EMPLOYEES       R               PK_EMPLOYEES        ENABLED
```

The output lists all of the constraints on the CRUISES table. We're seeing four: one primary key and three foreign keys.

How do you know which constraint is a PRIMARY KEY, and which is a FOREIGN KEY? The answer is by the CONSTRAINT_TYPE column. The possible entries in the CONSTRAINT_TYPE column are

- P = PRIMARY KEY
- R = FOREIGN KEY. The R is for "referential integrity".
- U = UNIQUE
- C = CHECK or NOT NULL constraint

The DELETE_RULE column shows if a foreign key constraint was created with ON DELETE CASCADE or ON DELETE SET NULL.

The SEARCH_CONDITION column is particularly useful for inspecting CHECK constraint criteria. For example:

```
SELECT  SEARCH_CONDITION
FROM    USER_CONSTRAINTS
WHERE   CONSTRAINT_NAME = 'CK_PROJECT_COST'
  AND   CONSTRAINT_TYPE = 'C';


SEARCH_CONDITION
------------------------
PROJECT_COST < 1000000
```

Take note of the constraints with unexpected values for CONSTRAINT_TYPE: R for FOREIGN KEY, and C for NOT NULL, as well as for CHECK.

The data dictionary provides additional information about constraints in the USER_CONS_COLUMN data dictionary view. That view contains all the information about which columns in CRUISES are constrained, and what the names are of the referenced tables and columns that make up the FOREIGN KEY constraints.

Finding Columns

One query I find useful is this:

```
SELECT  TABLE_NAME
FROM    USER_TAB_COLUMNS
WHERE   COLUMN_NAME = 'EMPLOYEE_ID';
```

That's a query that looks for all tables in the current user account that happen to have a column named EMPLOYEE_ID. Seems simple enough, but I find that a rather helpful query from time to time.

on the job

There are many helpful software tools available that will extract data dictionary information—such as comments—and provide a nice point-and-click interface to make it easy to navigate. That's all very helpful. But sometimes you'll find yourself in a situation where you simply don't have access to those tools. And you might even realize that a particular application you're developing could benefit by programmatically accessing data dictionary information by way of SQL statements to draw data into your application for some project requirement. The point is that the data dictionary is a certification exam objective for a good reason—a comfortable understanding of its information and an ability to navigate it easily is important for any serious SQL professional.

CERTIFICATION SUMMARY

The data dictionary is a powerful tool. It consists of a series of tables and views that are automatically maintained by the Oracle system to document the state of every object in the database. Whenever a DDL statement is executed, the data dictionary is updated in some fashion.

The data dictionary is often referred to as "metadata", a term which means "data about data". The data dictionary contains information about the database objects you create—their structures, names, status, and more.

The SYS account owns the data dictionary's underlying base tables, which cannot be changed directly by users. Instead, all of the tables have views and—in some cases—public synonyms that have been created, and it is these the user accesses in a read-only mode.

Many of the data dictionary views follow a prefix pattern that indicates the contents of the view. Views with a prefix of USER_ show data about objects owned by the user accessing the view. ALL_ is the prefix for objects that exist anywhere in the database to which the current user has access. DBA_ is the prefix for views that show data about all objects in the database, regardless of who owns them, or what privileges may be granted to them.

Information in the data dictionary includes the names of tables and their columns, including each column's datatype, along with its precision, scale, and/or length where applicable. All of the database objects are listed in the data dictionary: all tables, views, indexes, sequences, constraints, synonyms, and more.

Views that have a prefix of V$ or some variation are dynamic performance views and show real-time database performance information. Oracle cannot guarantee the read consistency of these views, so it's recommended that for dynamic performance views you limit your access to single table queries. If more complex queries and/or joins are required, you are advised to first copy data out of the views into your own temporary tables and then query those tables, for better results and data integrity.

You can add comments to the entries in the data dictionary for your own tables and columns using the COMMENT statement. You cannot delete comments, but instead update comments with a blank string.

The data dictionary can be used to perform a variety of useful tasks, such as obtaining information about time zones, determining if a view requires recompilation, identifying any privileges that are currently granted, and much more.

TWO-MINUTE DRILL

Use the Data Dictionary Views to Research Data on Your Objects

❑ The data dictionary is made of tables that store data about the database.

❑ The data dictionary contains the metadata for your database.

❑ It contains information about tables, views, constraints, indexes, sequences, synonyms, roles, privileges, and any and all other objects you might create in the database.

❑ It keeps track of all the users in the database, and which user account owns which objects, who has privileges on which object, the status of each object, and more.

❑ Oracle automatically updates and maintains the data dictionary views with each DDL statement executed throughout the database.

❑ The data dictionary views that begin with the prefix USER_ contain information about objects owned by the user accessing the view.

❑ The ALL_ prefix indicates a data dictionary view that contains information about objects that might be owned by any user in the database, but to which the accessing user has privileges.

❑ The DBA_ prefix is affixed to all views that contain data about all objects in the database.

❑ The V$ or GV$ prefix identifies views that are part of the set of dynamic performance tables and views, which show real-time performance data about the database.

❑ Most (but not all) of the data dictionary views are stored with comments that provide brief descriptions about each view and what it contains; many of the columns of the views also have comments.

❑ You can add comments of your own alongside the data dictionary record for your own objects that you've created.

❑ The COMMENT statement is how you store a comment in the data dictionary for any table you own, and also for its associated columns.

Query Various Data Dictionary Views

❑ The DICTIONARY view is a great starting point for finding what you might be looking for in the data dictionary.

❑ The USER_CATALOG view contains a summary of information about some of the major objects owned by your user account.

❑ The USER_OBJECTS view is similar but with much more information.

❑ You can get a full listing from the data dictionary for your tables; their columns; and associated datatypes, lengths, precision, and scale.

❑ The status of objects is also stored—for example, the data dictionary flags views that are invalid and might need recompilation.

❑ All roles and privileges of all users on all objects are stored somewhere in the data dictionary.

❑ If you have the name of a column and aren't sure which table it might be part of, the data dictionary can assist.

SELF TEST

The following questions will help you measure your understanding of the material presented in this chapter. Choose one correct answer for each question unless otherwise directed.

Use the Data Dictionary Views to Research Data on Your Objects

1. One place to get a master list of all the views that form the data dictionary:
   A. DICTIONARY
   B. DATA_DICTIONARY
   C. CATALOG
   D. USER_CATALOG

2. You are tasked with querying the data dictionary view that lists only those sequences to which you currently have privileges, but don't necessarily own. To do this, you log in to your own user account and query the data dictionary view called:
   A. ALL_SEQUENCES
   B. DBA_SEQUENCES
   C. USER_SEQUENCES
   D. USER_PRIV_SEQUENCES

3. Which of the following actions will *not* cause the contents of the data dictionary to be changed in some way?
   A. Create a new table.
   B. Modify the datatype of an existing column.
   C. Execute a valid COMMENT statement.
   D. None of the above.

4. The data dictionary is owned by:
   A. PUBLIC
   B. SYS
   C. SYSTEM
   D. Each individual user

5. You can add your own comments to the data dictionary with the COMMENT statement using which of the following? (Choose two.)
   A. INDEX
   B. COLUMN
   C. SYNONYM
   D. TABLE

6. You need to get information about columns in a table you do not own, nor do you have privileges to it. Which view can you query to get this information?
   - A. DBA_TAB_COLUMNS
   - B. ALL_TAB_COLUMNS
   - C. ALL_COLUMNS
   - D. It can't be done

7. Which among the following is considered an acceptable query with V$DATAFILE?
   - A. A join with two other objects in the data dictionary
   - B. A complex GROUP BY with multiple levels of aggregation
   - C. A query that displays rows from the table with no joins
   - D. All of the above

8. You are tasked with the job of adding a comment to the data dictionary to accompany the column PIER in the table MARINA. Which of the following will execute successfully?
   - A. COMMENT ON COLUMN (MARINA.PIER) IS 'Number of piers';
   - B. COMMENT ON COLUMN MARINA.PIER IS 'Number of piers';
   - C. COMMENT ON COLUMN MARINA(PIER) IS 'Number of piers';
   - D. COMMENT ON TABLE COLUMN MARINA.PIER IS 'Number of piers';

9. Now you have changed the purpose of the PIER column in the MARINA table and wish to remove the comment you just created in the last question. Which of the following statements will remove the comment?
   - A. COMMENT ON COLUMN MARINA.PIER DROP;
   - B. COMMENT ON COLUMN MARINA.PIER IS NULL;
   - C. COMMENT ON COLUMN MARINA.PIER SET UNUSED;
   - D. COMMENT ON COLUMN MARINA.PIER IS '';

Query Various Data Dictionary Views

10. When you're looking for a particular bit of data and you're not sure where in the data dictionary it might be, a good starting point is: (Choose the best answer.)
    - A. SELECT * FROM V$DATABASE;
    - B. SELECT * FROM GV_$START_HERE;
    - C. SELECT * FROM DICTIONARY;
    - D. SELECT * FROM V$RESERVED_WORDS;

11. The USER_CONSTRAINTS view in the data dictionary lists FOREIGN KEY constraints in the CONSTRAINT_TYPE column with which of the following single-letter abbreviations?

    A. K

    B. R

    C. F

    D. G

12. You are tasked to work with a view. The view's underlying table has been altered. What information can the data dictionary provide at this point? (Choose all answers that are correct.)

    A. The status of the view so that you can determine if the view requires recompilation.

    B. The current state of the table.

    C. The query that was used to create the view.

    D. The names of columns in the underlying table.

13. The term "metadata" means:

    A. Data about data

    B. Global data that is accessible throughout the database

    C. Data that is automatically updated and maintained by the database system

    D. Distributed data

14. Which of the following data dictionary views does not have an OWNER column?

    A. USER_TABLES

    B. ALL_INDEXES

    C. DBA_CONS_COLUMNS

    D. All of the above

15. If an ALTER TABLE . . . DROP COLUMN statement is executed against an underlying table upon which a view is based, the status of that view in the data dictionary changes to

    A. COMPILE

    B. INVALID

    C. ALTERED

    D. FLAG

SELF TEST ANSWERS

Use the Data Dictionary Views to Research Data on Your Objects

1. ☑ **A.** DICTIONARY. You can run a DESC DICTIONARY statement to see the two columns that form DICTIONARY, and then query it for additional information.
   ☒ **B, C,** and **D** are incorrect. There is no system view called DATA_DICTIONARY. CATALOG is also incorrect. There is a view in the data dictionary called USER_CATALOG; it's a useful resource for finding information about tables, views, and other database objects the current user owns.

2. ☑ **A.** ALL_SEQUENCES will list any sequences in the database, regardless of owner, to which your account has been granted access.
   ☒ **B, C,** and **D** are incorrect. DBA_SEQUENCES will list all sequences in the database, regardless of who owns them, and regardless of who has privileges on them. USER_SEQUENCES will list only those sequences that your user account currently owns. There is no view called USER_PRIV_SEQUENCES.

3. ☑ **D.** None of the above.
   ☒ **A, B,** and **C** are incorrect. All of these will enact some sort of change to the information in the data dictionary. Any DDL that creates or modifies objects will update the object listings in the data dictionary. The COMMENT statement adds to the data dictionary a comment about a particular object.

4. ☑ **B.** SYS is the owner of the data dictionary.
   ☒ **A, C,** and **D** are incorrect. Neither PUBLIC nor SYSTEM owns the data dictionary, although both are valid users in the system.

5. ☑ **B** and **D.** TABLE and COLUMN objects are supported by the COMMENT statement.
   ☒ **A** and **C** are incorrect. You cannot add comments of your own to the data dictionary for an INDEX or SYNONYM object.

6. ☑ **A.** DBA_TAB_COLUMNS is the view that contains information about columns in tables, and because of the DBA_ prefix, you know it contains information about tables and columns that exist anywhere in the database, regardless of owner or privileges granted.
   ☒ **A, C,** and **D** are incorrect. ALL_TAB_COLUMNS would be correct if you were limiting your search to tables and columns to which you've been granted privileges, for that is what the ALL_ prefix indicates. There is no ALL_COLUMNS view in the data dictionary.

7. ☑ **C.** The V$ prefix indicates that V$DATAFILE is a public synonym for a dynamic performance view, for which Oracle Corporation does not guarantee read consistency. Therefore you are recommended to limit your direct access of V$ objects to simple queries.

☒ **A, B,** and **D** are incorrect. Oracle Corporation officially advises against using any of the V$ objects in complex queries and/or joins.

8. ☑ **B.** The correct syntax is to use the keywords COMMENT ON COLUMN, followed by the table name and column name, separated by a period, and the keyword IS, followed by the string.
☒ **A, C,** and **D** are incorrect. Parentheses are not a part of the COMMENT statement. The keyword TABLE is only used when adding a comment to a table.

9. ☑ **D.** There really isn't a statement to explicitly drop a comment or delete it. The practice is to overwrite the old comment with a blank space.
☒ **A, B,** and **C** are incorrect. None of these options are valid statements. They contain bits and pieces of valid reserved words from other statements but do not apply to COMMENT.

Query Various Data Dictionary Views

10. ☑ **C.** The DICTIONARY view summarizes the names of tables and views in the data dictionary, along with detailed comments about each one.
☒ **A, B,** and **D** are incorrect. The V$DATABASE and V$RESERVED_WORDS objects are valid public synonyms for data dictionary views, but these are part of the set of dynamic performance tables and not good for getting an overview of the dictionary as a starting point. There is no such object in the Oracle data dictionary called GV_$START_HERE.

11. ☑ **B.** R is the answer. R stands for "referential integrity", and indicates the presence of a FOREIGN KEY constraint in the CONSTRAINT_TYPE column of the USER_CONSTRAINTS data dictionary view.
☒ **A, C,** and **D** are incorrect. It's not K or G. And you'd think it would be F, but it's not. Alas. R makes sense, though, when you think about it.

12. ☑ **A, B, C,** and **D.** The data dictionary can assist with all of the answers listed.
☒ **None** are incorrect.

13. ☑ **A.** Metadata is "data about data".
☒ **B, C** and **D** are incorrect.

14. ☑ **A.** USER_TABLES does not have nor need an OWNER column, since the view only presents a set of tables owned by the user accessing them.
☒ **B, C,** and **D** are incorrect. Even if you haven't looked in detail at these views, you can rely on the fact that views that start with ALL_ and DBA_ have a column showing OWNER information, since they contain, by definition, objects owned by—potentially—more than one user.

15. ☑ **B.** It changes to INVALID. Recompiling the view could restore the status of the view to VALID.
☒ **A, C,** and **D** are incorrect.

15

Manipulating Large Data Sets

This chapter looks at a variety of features and operations that are useful for working with large groups of data. Many of these features combine SQL statements we've already reviewed, but in this chapter we look at new combinations of these features, and new keywords and clauses to broaden capabilities and combine tasks into a single SQL statement. The result is more flexibility and power, as well as more efficient performance in your production code. The operations we'll review here include additional features to the INSERT statement, so that you can use one INSERT statement to add multiple rows of data to a given table, or to several tables, with and without conditional logic. We'll look at the SQL statement MERGE. We'll see how to create a table without specifying column names or datatypes, and how to create a table that will be instantly populated upon successful completion of the CREATE TABLE statement. All this and more await you in this chapter. We'll start by looking at a familiar topic in a new and more expansive way: subqueries.

CERTIFICATION OBJECTIVE 15.01

Manipulate Data Using Subqueries

We've already seen how subqueries can be incorporated into SELECT statements to make the combined SQL statement more powerful and more flexible. We're going to continue that discussion here by looking at new ways to use the subquery. The SQL statements we'll look at here include CREATE TABLE, INSERT, and UPDATE.

CREATE TABLE and Subqueries

The CREATE TABLE statement can include a subquery to speed up the process of creating and populating a table. The prerequisite with this form of SQL statement is that there be some sort of data already available in the database that we wish to use to build new database objects. If that's not the case, this syntax is not helpful. But if there is already any sort of data that can be displayed using a SELECT statement—including SELECTing from external tables, for example—then this syntax is a powerful way to quickly create tables in the database that are immediately populated with data.

The syntax for this form of CREATE TABLE requires the AS SELECT clause. For this reason, this particular form of CREATE TABLE is often referred to as CTAS: "Create Table As Select".

Let's look at the syntax. First, consider the table shown in Figure 15-1.

FIGURE 15-1

Diagram of the
INVOICES table

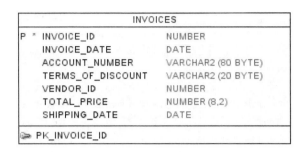

The INVOICES table includes a column for SHIPPING_DATE. Let's say that
we decide to archive rows out of the INVOICES table a year after shipping. Let's
write a new CREATE TABLE statement in the CTAS form based on the table in
Figure 15-1 (line numbers added):

```
01    CREATE TABLE INVOICES_ARCHIVED AS
02        SELECT *
03        FROM   INVOICES
04        WHERE  SHIPPING_DATE < (ADD_MONTHS(SYSDATE,-12));
```

In this example, we select rows from the INVOICES table and use them as the
basis for the new table called INVOICES_ARCHIVED. As soon as we've done this,
we can issue the following DESCRIBE command:

```
DESC INVOICES_ARCHIVED

Name                              Null      Type
------------------------------    --------  ----------------------
INVOICE_ID                                  NUMBER
INVOICE_DATE                                DATE
ACCOUNT_NUMBER                              VARCHAR2(80)
TERMS_OF_DISCOUNT                           VARCHAR2(20)
VENDOR_ID                                   NUMBER
TOTAL_PRICE                                 NUMBER(8,2)
SHIPPING_DATE                               DATE
```

The new table INVOICES_ARCHIVED was created without any columns explicitly
defined in the CREATE TABLE statement. The CTAS statement interpreted the
subquery and used the entire set of column definitions from the query on INVOICES to
build the new table INVOICES_ARCHIVED. In this example, we used the asterisk
format as the SELECT statement's select list. We've seen before that this is an alternative
to listing each column in the table by name. The result is that each column name and
datatype from INVOICES was used to create the new table INVOICES_ARCHIVED.
Furthermore, any rows returned by the subquery in the preceding example (lines 2
through 4) are automatically inserted into the newly created table.

However—any CONSTRAINT or INDEX objects, or any other supporting objects that might exist for the source table or tables, are not replicated but need to be created individually if desired for the new table, with one exception: any explicitly created NOT NULL constraints on the queried table are copied into the new table, are assigned a system-generated name, and form part of the new table's definition. NOT NULL constraints that were created implicitly—for example, as part of a PRIMARY KEY constraint—are not included.

The CTAS syntax will accept any valid subquery, including those that use joins, set operators, the GROUP BY clause, and complex expressions in the select list. For example, here's a CTAS statement that joins two tables (line numbers added):

```
01  CREATE TABLE ROOM_SUMMARY AS
02     SELECT   A.SHIP_ID,
03              A.SHIP_NAME,
04              B.ROOM_NUMBER,
05              B.SQ_FT + NVL(B.BALCONY_SQ_FT,0) TOT_SQ_FT
06     FROM     SHIPS A JOIN SHIP_CABINS B
07     ON       A.SHIP_ID = B.SHIP_ID;
```

This example is a valid CREATE TABLE statement. Note the column alias at the end of line 5. You cannot create a table unless you provide a name for each column. If you use CTAS to create a table based on a subquery that is lacking column names, you can include a column alias within the subquery to ensure that each column is created with a name.

There's an alternative syntax in which you can provide column names as part of the CREATE TABLE clause of the CREATE TABLE statement, like this:

```
01  CREATE TABLE ROOM_SUMMARY (SHIP_ID, SHIP_NAME, ROOM_NUMBER, TOT_SQ_FT)
02     AS
03     SELECT   A.SHIP_ID,
04              A.SHIP_NAME,
05              B.ROOM_NUMBER,
06              B.SQ_FT + NVL(B.BALCONY_SQ_FT,0)
07     FROM     SHIPS A JOIN SHIP_CABINS B
08     ON       A.SHIP_ID = B.SHIP_ID;
```

The statement above defines each column's name in line 1. Any valid database name may be provided—they are not required to match the subquery's column names. Note the fourth column of the subquery, which is specified in line 6, and is given the name TOT_SQ_FT in line 1 of the CREATE TABLE statement.

If you omit a column name, then the CREATE TABLE using the CTAS syntax statement will fail.

The table that results from our preceding example looks like this:

```
DESC ROOM_SUMMARY
Name                                Null      Type
--------------------------------    --------  -------------------------|
SHIP_ID                                       NUMBER(7)
SHIP_NAME                                     VARCHAR2(20)
ROOM_NUMBER                                   VARCHAR2(5)
TOT_SQ_FT                                     NUMBER
```

Note: Tables created with the CTAS syntax in this way do not maintain any connection with the source tables. Any changes made to the data or structure of the source tables do not have any impact in our newly created tables. The subqueries exist to create the initial data structure and data population and nothing more. Once the CTAS statement has been executed and the subquery has created the initial data population, there is no connection between the newly created table and whatever source table or tables were used.

INSERT and Subqueries

We've already seen how to use a scalar subquery within an INSERT statement to include a value within an overall INSERT. This section describes something that goes far beyond that—how to use the INSERT statement and leverage the subquery syntax to populate multiple rows of data in a single statement.

To illustrate this concept, let's work with two existing tables—CRUISE_CUSTOMERS and EMPLOYEES, as shown in Figure 15-2.

FIGURE 15-2

Diagrams of the CRUISE_CUSTOMERS and EMPLOYEES tables

CRUISE_CUSTOMERS	
P * CRUISE_CUSTOMER_ID	NUMBER
FIRST_NAME	VARCHAR2 (20 BYTE)
LAST_NAME	VARCHAR2 (30 BYTE)
PK_CRUISE_CUSTOMER_ID	

EMPLOYEES	
P * EMPLOYEE_ID	NUMBER (7)
SHIP_ID	NUMBER (7)
FIRST_NAME	VARCHAR2 (20 BYTE)
LAST_NAME	VARCHAR2 (30 BYTE)
POSITION_ID	NUMBER
SSN	VARCHAR2 (11 BYTE)
DOB	DATE
PRIMARY_PHONE	VARCHAR2 (20 BYTE)
PK_EMPLOYEES	
IX_EMPLOYEES	

We'll pull data out of EMPLOYEES to add new rows to the CRUISE_CUSTOMERS table, using the INSERT statement with a subquery. Here's the example (line numbers added):

```
01  INSERT INTO CRUISE_CUSTOMERS
02    (CRUISE_CUSTOMER_ID, FIRST_NAME, LAST_NAME)
03    SELECT SEQ_CRUISE_CUSTOMER_ID.NEXTVAL,
04           EMP.FIRST_NAME,
05           EMP.LAST_NAME
06    FROM   EMPLOYEES EMP;
```

In this SQL statement, we use a subquery that selects rows from the EMPLOYEES table. Notice that SEQ_CRUISE_CUSTOMER_ID.NEXTVAL is the first expression in the SELECT statement's list; note that it is not a column in the EMPLOYEES table at all but is a reference to the sequence generator for the CRUISE_CUSTOMERS table. The remaining two columns are from EMPLOYEES, and all three values are inserted into the CRUISE_CUSTOMERS table in the three columns identified in line 2. In this form of INSERT, the output of the subquery becomes the set of input values for the INSERT. Note that the datatypes for the expressions in the SELECT statement subquery must match the datatypes in the target table of the INSERT statement.

All of the rows returned by the subquery (lines 3 through 6) are inserted into the CRUISE_CUSTOMERS table as specified in line 1.

If any one row fails the INSERT due to a constraint violation or datatype conflict, the entire INSERT fails and no rows are inserted.

Any valid subquery may be used within the INSERT statement.

on the **Job**

CTAS and INSERT statements with subqueries are very useful in testing environments for creating test tables filled with test data.

UPDATE and Correlated Subqueries

The UPDATE statement is capable of updating many rows within a single execution. This is true for virtually any of the various forms of UPDATE. Also, in Chapter 9 we saw how we can optionally use single-row and multiple-row subqueries in a WHERE clause, which, when incorporated in an UPDATE statement, can empower that UPDATE to modify potentially many rows in the target table based on what might be many rows within the subquery. We've also looked at how to use a scalar subquery within the SET clause of an UPDATE statement.

This section looks at something that goes a bit beyond those capabilities. This section describes how to use UPDATE and a correlated subquery to update multiple rows in something of an integrated fashion. The important word here is "correlated"—this technique ties the UPDATE statement's target rows with the subquery's rows in a correlated fashion. Correlated subqueries in an UPDATE can potentially modify each row in a given table with different values for each row—something that the previous forms of UPDATE we've reviewed up to now are not capable of doing.

For an example, we'll work with a variation of the PORTS table—see Figure 15-3. Notice that we have two numeric columns at the end of the table's structure—one called TOT_SHIPS_ASSIGNED, and one called TOT_SHIPS_ASGN_CAP.

These represent aggregate values that we're going to calculate by way of a GROUP BY query on the SHIPS table. The GROUP BY will aggregate rows for all ships assigned to a given home port, defined by HOME_PORT_ID. We can create a SELECT statement to get the data we're looking for like this (line numbers added):

```
01    SELECT    HOME_PORT_ID,
02              COUNT(SHIP_ID)  TOTAL_SHIPS,
03              SUM(CAPACITY)   TOTAL_SHIP_CAPACITY
04    FROM      SHIPS
05    GROUP BY HOME_PORT_ID
06    ORDER BY HOME_PORT_ID;
```

The output of our SELECT is as follows:

```
HOME_PORT_ID              TOTAL_SHIPS           TOTAL_SHIP_CAPACITY
----------------------    --------------------  -------------------
1                         1                     2052
2                         4                     6895
3                         2                     5948
                          1                     2974
```

FIGURE 15-3

Diagram of the
PORTS table

```
                          PORTS
P *  PORT_ID                  NUMBER
     PORT_NAME                VARCHAR2 (20 BYTE)
     COUNTRY                  VARCHAR2 (40 BYTE)
     CAPACITY                 NUMBER
     TOT_SHIPS_ASSIGNED       NUMBER (7)
     TOT_SHIPS_ASGN_CAP       NUMBER (7)

  PK_PORT
```

Note that the values of HOME_PORT_ID correspond back to the PORTS table. Also, we apparently have a ship that isn't assigned a home port.

To use this information and update the PORTS table in a single UPDATE statement, we use the preceding SELECT statement and transform it into a correlated subquery within the UPDATE statement. That means we need to

- Create table aliases and reference all appropriate columns with their corresponding table alias.

- Connect the subquery with the outer UPDATE statement using a WHERE clause.

Here's the UPDATE statement (line numbers added):

```
01    UPDATE PORTS PT
02      SET (TOT_SHIPS_ASSIGNED, TOT_SHIPS_ASGN_CAP) =
03        (SELECT   COUNT(S.SHIP_ID)  TOTAL_SHIPS,
04                  SUM(S.CAPACITY)   TOTAL_SHIP_CAPACITY
05          FROM    SHIPS S
06          WHERE   S.HOME_PORT_ID = PT.PORT_ID
07          GROUP BY S.HOME_PORT_ID);
```

Notice that we've done the following:

- Line 2: listed all of the columns we are updating in the UPDATE table, enclosed in parentheses.

- Line 2: added the assignment operator of the "equal" sign at the end of the line.

- Lines 3 through 7: enclosed the subquery in parentheses.

- Line 3: removed the reference to HOME_PORT_ID in the subquery's select list, since we have no need to assign that value to the PORTS table.

- Lines 3 and 4: specified a column alias for each expression in the subquery's select list—which is not required here, but looks good nonetheless.

- Line 6: added a WHERE clause to connect the UPDATE statement with the subquery—this is where the correlation is specified.

So the correlation occurs on line 6. We also added a table alias for each table, and referenced each column name with the appropriate table alias prefix. That really isn't required in this particular example, since there are no columns of the same

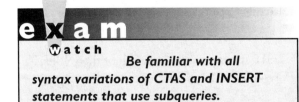

Be familiar with all syntax variations of CTAS and INSERT statements that use subqueries.

name in both tables, so there are no reference conflicts in this example. But it's still good design to alias every column so the source of each column is clear.

This UPDATE statement will update multiple columns and multiple rows—all from a single UPDATE statement.

CERTIFICATION OBJECTIVE 15.02

Describe the Features of Multitable INSERTs

The multitable INSERT statement is a variation on the INSERT statement syntax we've already seen. A multitable INSERT statement repeats the INTO clause of the INSERT statement to insert data into more than one table. Each INTO clause applies to just one table, but by repeating the INTO clause, you can add data to multiple tables. The multitable INSERT must have a subquery to select rows for inserting.

Multitable INSERT statements can accomplish a variety of tasks, including the following:

- Query data from one table, and insert the data into multiple tables with conditional logic, such as transforming data into a series of archive tables.

- Exchange data between two similar systems of different requirements— perhaps between a transaction-based application and a data warehouse optimized for analysis.

- Support logical archiving at any level of detail with logical decision points embedded in the INSERT statements.

- Integrate complex queries with GROUP BY, HAVING, set operators, and more, all while moving any number of rows dynamically, distributing output into multiple data targets, and programming logical decision points to control data distribution.

- Transform data that is stored in rows and levels into a cross-tabulation output, the type you would typically see in a spreadsheet application.

There are two general types of multitable INSERT statements: unconditional and conditional.

- Unconditional multitable INSERT statements process each of the INSERT statement's one or more INTO clauses without condition, for all rows returned by the subquery.

- Conditional multitable INSERT statements use WHEN conditions before INTO clauses to determine if the given INTO clause (or clauses) will execute for a given row returned by the subquery. In other words, for each row returned by the INSERT statement's subquery, each WHEN condition's expression is considered and evaluates to either a true or false condition. If true, the associated INTO clause(s) will execute. If false, it will not. Finally, an optional ELSE clause can include an alternative INTO clause that can be executed if none of the WHEN conditions are found to be true.

Let's look at the overall syntax for the multitable INSERT statement. First, we'll examine an unconditional multitable INSERT statement. The syntax repeats the INTO statement from one to many times as required:

```
INSERT ALL
  INTO tab1 VALUES (col_list1)
  INTO tab2 VALUES (col_list2)
  INTO tab3 VALUES (col_list3)
  ...
subquery;
```

The unconditional multitable INSERT statement syntax just shown assumes the following:

- The keyword ALL is required in an unconditional multitable INSERT. Note, however, that while the presence of the keyword ALL is indicative of a multitable INSERT, it doesn't necessarily indicate the unconditional multitable INSERT, as you'll see in the next section.

- Following the keyword ALL, there must be at least one INTO clause.

- You can include multiple INTO clauses.

- Each INTO may have its own VALUES clause.

- Each VALUES list is optional; if omitted, the select list from the subquery will be used.

- The *subquery* is a subquery.

The conditional multitable INSERT statement syntax is similar but adds the WHEN condition, like this:

```
INSERT option
  WHEN expression THEN
     INTO tab1 VALUES (col_list1)
  WHEN expression THEN
     INTO tab2 VALUES (col_list2)
  . . .
  ELSE
     INTO tab3 VALUES (col_list3)
subquery;
```

For each row returned by the subquery, each WHEN condition is evaluated and determined to either be true or false. If true, then the WHEN condition's associated set of one or more INTO clauses is executed; otherwise, processing skips over the INTO clauses to the next WHEN condition. If none of the WHEN conditions evaluate to true, the ELSE clause is processed and its associated set of one or more INTO clauses is executed.

The conditional multitable INSERT statement syntax just shown is used as follows:

- The *option* is one of two keywords: ALL or FIRST.
- ALL is the default and may be omitted.
- FIRST is the alternative keyword; it indicates that the only set of INTO clauses that will execute are those that follow the first WHEN clause that evaluates to true.
- You can include multiple WHEN conditions.
- Each WHEN condition is followed by one or more INTO clauses.
- Each INTO may have its own VALUES clause; if omitted, the subquery's select list must match the number and datatypes of the INTO table's columns.
- Each *expression* evaluates to true or false and should involve one or more columns from the subquery.
- The *tab* and *col_list* are the components of the INSERT statement that will execute if the WHEN expression evaluates to true.
- The optional ELSE . . . INTO clause, if included, must be last.
- The *subquery* is required, and must be a valid subquery.

A conditional multitable INSERT statement will process each row returned by the subquery.

The multitable INSERT statement always uses a subquery. As we know, a subquery may return anywhere from zero to many rows. For each individual row returned by a subquery, processing does a pass through the set of WHILE ... INTO clauses. But the way it processes the WHILE ... INTO clauses differs based on whether the keyword ALL or FIRST is used.

If the keyword ALL is specified, then all of the WHEN conditions will be evaluated for each row returned by the subquery. For each WHEN condition that evaluates to true, the corresponding INTO clause—or clauses—that follow the WHEN will be executed. For each WHEN condition that evaluates to false, the corresponding INTO clause—or clauses—will not be executed. All of the WHEN conditions are evaluated if the keyword ALL is specified at the beginning of the multitable INSERT statement.

On the other hand, if the keyword FIRST is used, then for each row returned by the subquery, WHEN conditions are evaluated until the first true condition is encountered. As soon as a WHEN condition is determined to be true, the corresponding set of one or more INTO clauses that follows the WHEN will be executed. Processing will then skip over the remaining WHEN conditions for that row of the subquery.

In either situation—INSERT FIRST or INSERT ALL—if no WHEN condition was found to be true, and if the optional ELSE clause is present, then the ELSE clauses' INTO clause will be executed for the row. Then processing moves on to the next row returned by the subquery.

Note that for the conditional multitable INSERT statement—which is to say any multitable INSERT with a WHEN condition—ALL is the default keyword. If no WHEN condition is used, then the multitable INSERT is unconditional, and the ALL keyword must be present.

In other words, you may not omit the keyword in an unconditional multitable INSERT like this:

```
INSERT
  INTO ... VALUES ...
  INTO ... VALUES ...
  subquery;
```

The preceding statement shows incorrect syntax, since it omits the ALL option and yet has no WHEN condition—therefore it is syntactically incorrect. However, you may do something like this:

```
INSERT ALL
  INTO ... VALUES ...
  INTO ... VALUES ...
  subquery;
```

The preceding unconditional multitable INSERT correctly shows the ALL keyword.

The conditional multitable INSERT allows you to omit the keyword, like this:

```
INSERT
  WHEN ... THEN
    INTO ... VALUES ...
  WHEN ... THEN
    INTO ... VALUES ...
  subquery;
```

The default keyword is ALL. In all forms of the multitable INSERT, the subquery is required; it is not optional. And as is always the case with any INSERT that uses a subquery, the INSERT statement will execute once for each row returned by the subquery.

Note: If any one INTO clause fails with an execution error for any one row returned by the subquery, then the entire statement fails for all rows of the subquery, and no data change results.

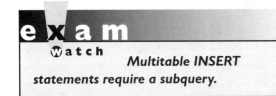

exam

⊕atch   *Multitable INSERT statements require a subquery.*

CERTIFICATION OBJECTIVE 15.03

Use the Following Types of Multitable **INSERTS**: Unconditional, Conditional, and Pivot

In this section, we'll continue our discussion of multitable INSERT statements. We'll look at some examples of its various forms, and how they can be used to process large amounts of data, using conditional logic and affecting multiple tables, all from within a single SQL statement.

Unconditional

Let's look at an example of an unconditional multitable INSERT statement. For our example, we'll work with the CRUISE_ORDERS table—see Figure 15-4.

FIGURE 15-4

Diagram for
the CRUISE_
ORDERS table

```
                        CRUISE_ORDERS
P *  CRUISE_ORDER_ID       NUMBER
     ORDER_DATE            DATE
     CRUISE_CUSTOMER_ID    NUMBER
     SHIP_ID               NUMBER (7)

 PK_CRUISE_ORDER_ID
```

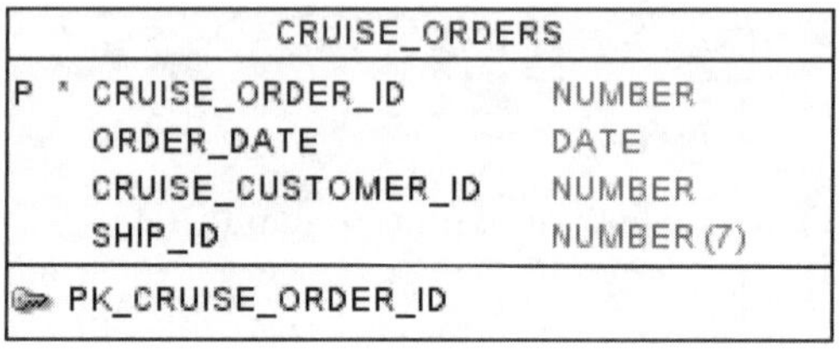

We also have three identically structured tables named CO_2008, CO_ELCARO, and CO_ARCHIVED, each with the same columns as the table CRUISE_ORDERS. The three identically structured tables are used for archiving and analyzing the CRUISE_ORDERS table data.

Here is an example of a valid SQL statement that queries the CRUISE_ORDERS table and inserts the output into each of our three archive tables (line numbers added):

```
01   INSERT ALL
02       INTO CO_2008      (CRUISE_ORDER_ID, ORDER_DATE,
03                             CRUISE_CUSTOMER_ID, SHIP_ID)
04       VALUES            (CRUISE_ORDER_ID, ORDER_DATE,
05                             CRUISE_CUSTOMER_ID, SHIP_ID)
06       INTO CO_ELCARO    (CRUISE_ORDER_ID, ORDER_DATE,
07                             CRUISE_CUSTOMER_ID, SHIP_ID)
08       VALUES            (CRUISE_ORDER_ID, ORDER_DATE,
09                             CRUISE_CUSTOMER_ID, SHIP_ID)
10       INTO CO_ARCHIVED  (CRUISE_ORDER_ID, ORDER_DATE,
11                             CRUISE_CUSTOMER_ID, SHIP_ID)
12       VALUES            (CRUISE_ORDER_ID, ORDER_DATE,
13                             CRUISE_CUSTOMER_ID, SHIP_ID)
14       SELECT CRUISE_ORDER_ID, ORDER_DATE, CRUISE_CUSTOMER_ID, SHIP_ID
15       FROM   CRUISE_ORDERS;
```

Note that we have three INTO clauses here. If the subquery returns, for example, three rows, then the end result of this INSERT statement will be to insert nine rows: three into the CO_2008 table (line 2), three into the CO_ELCARO table (line 6), and three into the CO_ARCHIVED table (line 10).

As we see in the preceding example, the unconditional INSERT statement uses the keyword ALL (line 1), followed by one or more INTO clauses (lines 2, 6, and 10), each of which specifies a table and the columns into which we are inserting data, followed by the VALUES list.

The VALUES list can specify expressions found in the subquery's select list. In our example, in line 4 we specify CRUISE_ORDER_ID as the first expression in the VALUES list to be inserted into the CO_2008 table. This corresponds to the

CRUISE_ORDER_ID column in the subquery select list in line 14. The other VALUES lists that refer to CRUISE_ORDER_ID (line 8 and line 12) are specifying that same column. Each VALUES list in a multitable INSERT can specify any column names or expressions that are in the subquery select list.

On the other hand, the column references within each INTO list (each starting at lines 2, 6, and 10) specify the columns of the tables named for the INTO clause. In our example, line 2 names the CO_2008 table, and the INTO list that follows on line 2 and line 3 specifies columns in the CO_2008 table.

You'll recall that in a standard INSERT statement, the list of values in the VALUES expression list must match in number and in datatype (or be able to be automatically converted to a matching datatype) with the columns specified in the INTO clause. The same is true here for each pair of INTO and VALUES lists.

Each VALUES expression list may use any complex expression in specifying the value to be inserted into its corresponding table and column. For example:

```
01   INSERT ALL
02        INTO CO_2008      (CRUISE_ORDER_ID, ORDER_DATE,
03                           CRUISE_CUSTOMER_ID, SHIP_ID)
04        VALUES            (CRUISE_ORDER_ID, SYSDATE, 14, 1)
05        INTO CO_ELCARO    (CRUISE_ORDER_ID, ORDER_DATE,
06                           CRUISE_CUSTOMER_ID, SHIP_ID)
07        VALUES            (CRUISE_ORDER_ID, ORDER_DATE+30, 15, 1)
08        INTO CO_ARCHIVED  (CRUISE_ORDER_ID, ORDER_DATE,
09                           CRUISE_CUSTOMER_ID, SHIP_ID)
10        VALUES            (CRUISE_ORDER_ID, ORDER_DATE,
11                           CRUISE_CUSTOMER_ID, SHIP_ID)
12    SELECT CRUISE_ORDER_ID, ORDER_DATE, CRUISE_CUSTOMER_ID, SHIP_ID
13    FROM   CRUISE_ORDERS;
```

In this example, we are choosing to insert some values that are different than the subquery is returning. For the CO_2008 table, in lines 2 through 4, we are defining the ORDER_DATE for all rows to be SYSDATE, and the CRUISE_ CUSTOMER_ID to be the literal value of 14, and the SHIP_ID to be a literal value of 1. For the CO_ELCARO table, in lines 5 through 7, we are giving each row an ORDER_DATE that is 30 days beyond the incoming value in the subquery, and we're assigning the number 15 to each CRUISE_CUSTOMER_ID, and 1 to each SHIP_ID. For the CO_ARCHIVED table, in lines 8 through 11, we are choosing to pass through values from the subquery unchanged.

As the example shows, the VALUES list can specify column names and expressions from the subquery's select list but may also define any valid SQL expression. The INTO column list must specify columns in the table into which the INTO statement is inserting data.

If the VALUES list is omitted, the columns of the subquery become the de facto VALUES list and therefore must match the columns of the corresponding INTO clause. By "match", we mean that they must match in number, and in datatype, or be of such datatypes that an automatic datatype conversion may be performed.

If there is no column list in the INTO clause, the subquery's select list must match the columns in the table of the INTO clause.

Conditional

Conditional multitable INSERT statements use conditional logic to determine which INTO clause or clauses to process. Each row that is returned by the subquery is processed through a series of one or more WHEN conditions. Each WHEN condition is followed by a set of one or more INTO clauses.

For each row returned by the subquery, each WHEN condition is evaluated to be either true or false. If true, the following set of one or more INTO clauses are executed. If false, the set of one or more INTO clauses are skipped over, and the next WHEN condition is evaluated.

An ELSE clause may optionally be included in the conditional multitable INSERT statement. If present, it must define its own set of one or more INTO clauses, and the ELSE/INTO clauses must follow all WHEN conditions/INTO clause combinations. If all WHEN conditions are skipped for any given row, then the ELSE clause's INTO will be processed. Otherwise, it will be skipped for that row.

Each row returned by the subquery is processed according to these rules we have just reviewed.

Let's look again at our table INVOICES, and the archive table INVOICES_ARCHIVED, in which we stored invoice records that are over a year old. See Figure 15-1 for the INVOICES table, and Figure 15-5 for the INVOICES_ARCHIVED table.

Let's say our organization is engaged in a merger and we are tasked with the job of integrating data from another application. The newly acquired company has provided us with the table WO_INV, as shown in Figure 15-6.

FIGURE 15-5

Diagram for the INVOICES_ARCHIVED table

INVOICES_ARCHIVED	
INVOICE_ID	NUMBER
INVOICE_DATE	DATE
ACCOUNT_NUMBER	VARCHAR2 (80 BYTE)
TERMS_OF_DISCOUNT	VARCHAR2 (20 BYTE)
VENDOR_ID	NUMBER
TOTAL_PRICE	NUMBER (8,2)
SHIPPING_DATE	DATE

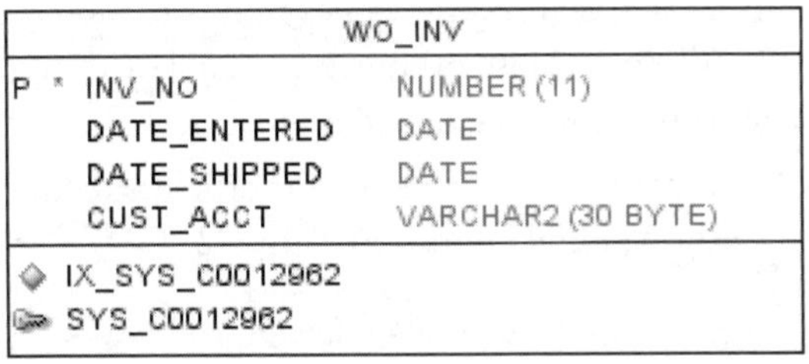

FIGURE 15-6

Diagram for the
WO_INV table

WO_INV	
P * INV_NO	NUMBER (11)
DATE_ENTERED	DATE
DATE_SHIPPED	DATE
CUST_ACCT	VARCHAR2 (30 BYTE)
◇ IX_SYS_C0012962	
⊶ SYS_C0012962	

We need to create an INSERT statement that will

■ Pull data from the WO_INV table.

■ Insert WO_INV's invoice information from within the past year into our
INVOICES table.

■ Insert WO_INV's invoice information that is over a year old into our
INVOICES_ARCHIVED table.

It's a perfect task for a conditional multitable INSERT statement, as follows
(line numbers added):

```
01    INSERT FIRST
02      WHEN (DATE_SHIPPED < (ADD_MONTHS(SYSDATE,-12))) THEN
03        INTO INVOICES_ARCHIVED (INVOICE_ID, INVOICE_DATE,
04                                SHIPPING_DATE, ACCOUNT_NUMBER)
05        VALUES (INV_NO, DATE_ENTERED, DATE_SHIPPED, CUST_ACCT)
06      ELSE
07        INTO INVOICES (INVOICE_ID, INVOICE_DATE,
08                                SHIPPING_DATE, ACCOUNT_NUMBER)
09        VALUES (INV_NO, DATE_ENTERED, DATE_SHIPPED, CUST_ACCT)
10      SELECT INV_NO, DATE_ENTERED, DATE_SHIPPED, CUST_ACCT
11      FROM   WO_INV;
```

In this statement, we see the following:

■ A subquery on lines 10 through 11. Note the subquery includes a column
DATE_SHIPPED.

■ Line 2 compares the DATE_SHIPPED value in a WHEN condition.

■ If line 2 evaluates to true for a given row from the subquery, the INSERT
statement will take that row's data and insert it into the INVOICES_
ARCHIVED table, as specified on line 3. The columns in the INVOICES_
ARCHIVED table are specified in lines 3 and 4.

- Line 5 defines the values from the subquery that will be inserted if the WHEN clause on line 2 is true. For example, the subquery's column INV_NO (line 5) will be inserted into the target table's column INVOICE_ID (line 3).

- Line 6 is an ELSE clause that will execute for each row that does not satisfy the WHEN condition in line 2.

In the example we just reviewed, there was one WHEN condition and one ELSE condition. Let's look at an example with multiple WHEN conditions. Let's say you had three archive tables, named INVOICES_THRU_2009, INVOICES_THRU_2008, and INVOICES_THRU_2007, and wished to insert rows from the incoming table into each archived table based on the year of the DATE_SHIPPED value. Note that each table is not mutually exclusive; for example, the INVOICES_THRU_2009 table will contain invoices from 2009, 2008, and 2007, as well as earlier. One row returned by the subquery might be inserted into all three tables.

To accomplish this task, you could use the following INSERT statement (line numbers added):

```
01   INSERT
02     WHEN (TO_CHAR(DATE_SHIPPED,'RRRR') <= '2009') THEN
03       INTO INVOICES_THRU_2009 (INVOICE_ID, INVOICE_DATE,
04                                SHIPPING_DATE, ACCOUNT_NUMBER)
05       VALUES (INV_NO, DATE_ENTERED, DATE_SHIPPED, CUST_ACCT)
06     WHEN (TO_CHAR(DATE_SHIPPED,'RRRR') <= '2008') THEN
07       INTO INVOICES_THRU_2008 (INVOICE_ID, INVOICE_DATE,
08                                SHIPPING_DATE, ACCOUNT_NUMBER)
09       VALUES (INV_NO, DATE_ENTERED, DATE_SHIPPED, CUST_ACCT)
10     WHEN (TO_CHAR(DATE_SHIPPED,'RRRR') <= '2007') THEN
11       INTO INVOICES_THRU_2007 (INVOICE_ID, INVOICE_DATE,
12                                SHIPPING_DATE, ACCOUNT_NUMBER)
13       VALUES (INV_NO, DATE_ENTERED, DATE_SHIPPED, CUST_ACCT)
14     SELECT INV_NO, DATE_ENTERED, DATE_SHIPPED, CUST_ACCT
15     FROM   WO_INV;
```

Notice that there is no keyword FIRST or ALL in this example. Therefore the statement will default to ALL. Since there are three WHEN conditions, each with an associated INTO clause, then each and every WHEN condition that evaluates to true will execute. Also, this example omits the ELSE clause, so if any row from the subquery does not satisfy a WHEN condition, then no action will be taken for that particular row returned by the subquery.

After any WHEN condition, you may include more than one INTO clause. For example, let's say we have a table INVOICES_CLOSED that takes any invoice rows that shipped prior to 2008. We might modify our example like this (line numbers added):

```
01   INSERT
02     WHEN (TO_CHAR(DATE_SHIPPED,'RRRR') <= '2009') THEN
03       INTO INVOICES_THRU_2009 (INVOICE_ID, INVOICE_DATE,
04                                 SHIPPING_DATE, ACCOUNT_NUMBER)
05       VALUES (INV_NO, DATE_ENTERED, DATE_SHIPPED, CUST_ACCT)
06     WHEN (TO_CHAR(DATE_SHIPPED,'RRRR') <= '2008') THEN
07       INTO INVOICES_THRU_2008 (INVOICE_ID, INVOICE_DATE,
08                                 SHIPPING_DATE, ACCOUNT_NUMBER)
09       VALUES (INV_NO, DATE_ENTERED, DATE_SHIPPED, CUST_ACCT)
10       INTO INVOICES_CLOSED   (INVOICE_ID, INVOICE_DATE,
11                                 SHIPPING_DATE, ACCOUNT_NUMBER)
12       VALUES (INV_NO, DATE_ENTERED, DATE_SHIPPED, CUST_ACCT)
13     WHEN (TO_CHAR(DATE_SHIPPED,'RRRR') <= '2007') THEN
14       INTO INVOICES_THRU_2007 (INVOICE_ID, INVOICE_DATE,
15                                 SHIPPING_DATE, ACCOUNT_NUMBER)
16       VALUES (INV_NO, DATE_ENTERED, DATE_SHIPPED, CUST_ACCT)
17     SELECT INV_NO, DATE_ENTERED, DATE_SHIPPED, CUST_ACCT
18     FROM   WO_INV;
```

Note the new INTO clause, lines 10 through 12. This INTO is subject to the WHEN condition in line 6. In other words, if DATE_SHIPPED is in the year 2008 or before, the INSERT statement will add the candidate row to both the INVOICES_THRU_2008 table and the INVOICES_CLOSED table. One WHEN condition is the gateway to both INTO clauses.

What this example shows us is that any WHEN condition can have multiple INTO clauses that follow it. If the WHEN condition evaluates to true, all of its INTO clauses will execute. If the WHEN condition evaluates to false, execution will skip over the INTO clauses and move on directly to either the next WHEN condition, an ELSE if it is present, or the next row in the subquery.

The INSERT ALL will evaluate each and every WHEN condition, and process all INTO clauses for all WHEN conditions that evaluate to true. Therefore the INSERT ALL may result in a single row being added to more than one table.

The INSERT FIRST will evaluate every WHEN condition until one of them evaluates to true. It will then process that WHEN condition's INTO, and skip the remaining WHEN conditions. The INSERT FIRST will only process zero or one WHEN condition; however, it may also result in a single row being added to more than one table, but only if the first true WHEN condition has more than one INTO clause.

Table aliases in the subquery of a multitable INSERT are not recognized outside in the rest of the INSERT—for example, you can't reference them from within a WHEN condition or INTO statement. If a subquery's column reference depends on a table alias, be sure to use a column alias for the column, and then reference the column alias.

For example, see Figure 15-7.

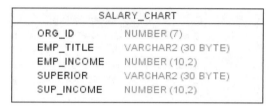

FIGURE 15-7

Diagram of the
POSITIONS and
SALARY_CHART
tables

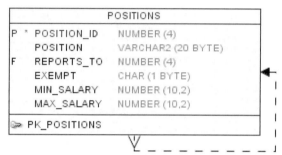

In a query that queries rows from the POSITIONS table and conditionally inserts them into the SALARY_CHART table, we cannot use this query (line numbers added):

```
01    INSERT
02      WHEN (B.MAX_SALARY-A.MAX_SALARY < 10000) THEN
03      INTO SALARY_CHART (EMP_TITLE, SUPERIOR,
04                                EMP_INCOME, SUP_INCOME)
05      VALUES            (A.POSITION, B.POSITION,
06                                A.MAX_SALARY, B.MAX_SALARY)
07    SELECT A.POSITION,
08           B.POSITION,
09           A.MAX_SALARY,
10           B.MAX_SALARY
11    FROM   POSITIONS A JOIN POSITIONS B
12      ON   A.REPORTS_TO = B.POSITION_ID
13    WHERE  A.MAX_SALARY > 100000;
```

This statement will not work. Here is the result:

```
Error at Command Line:6 Column:35
Error report:
SQL Error: ORA-00904: "B"."MAX_SALARY": invalid identifier
00904. 00000 -  "%s: invalid identifier"
```

Notice how the subquery is a self-join and uses table aliases to identify each table and column reference. These table aliases are perfectly fine in the subquery but are not recognized beyond the subquery. In other words, the attempts to reference each table alias from within the WHEN condition or VALUES clause are invalid.

So what do we do? The solution is to specify a column alias to any column names within the subquery that use a table alias, then reference the column alias from the rest of the conditional INSERT statement, like we do below in lines 5 and 6 (line numbers added):

```
01    INSERT
02      WHEN (BOSS_SALARY-EMPLOYEE_SALARY < 10000) THEN
03      INTO SALARY_CHART (EMP_TITLE, SUPERIOR, EMP_INCOME,     SUP_INCOME)
04      VALUES            (EMPLOYEE,  BOSS,     EMPLOYEE_SALARY, BOSS_SALARY)
05    SELECT A.POSITION    EMPLOYEE,
06           B.POSITION    BOSS,
07           A.MAX_SALARY EMPLOYEE_SALARY,
08           B.MAX_SALARY BOSS_SALARY
09    FROM    POSITIONS A JOIN POSITIONS B
10      ON    A.REPORTS_TO = B.POSITION_ID
11    WHERE   A.MAX_SALARY > 100000;
```

Note that this version has done more than is required, and applies column aliases to each column in the subquery, then references those column aliases from the WHEN and VALUES clauses. We only needed column aliases on A.POSITION and B.POSITION in lines 5 and 6, so we can reference the column aliases in line 4. Either way, this version of the conditional INSERT is syntactically correct.

You cannot execute a multitable INSERT on a view; it can only be used with a table.

Sequence generators do not behave consistently in a multitable INSERT statement. If you try to use a sequence generator within the subquery, you'll get a syntax error. If you try to include one within the expression list of the INTO statement, you may or may not get the functionality you wish—the NEXTVAL function will not advance as you might expect it to. The reason: a multitable insert is treated as a single SQL statement. Therefore, if you reference NEXTVAL with a sequence generator, Oracle's documentation warns that NEXTVAL will be incremented once in accordance with the sequence generator's parameters and stay that way for the duration of a pass through the multitable insert. In other words, a conditional INSERT with a single INTO, one that invokes a single sequence generator once with a NEXTVAL, will increment the sequence once for each row returned by the subquery—regardless of whether or not the WHEN condition is true. For example, consider this example:

```
01    INSERT
02      WHEN (TO_CHAR(DATE_ENTERED,'RRRR') <= '2009') THEN
03        INTO INVOICES_ARCHIVED (INVOICE_ID, INVOICE_DATE)
04        VALUES (SEQ_INV_NUM.NEXTVAL, DATE_ENTERED)
05      SELECT INV_NO, DATE_ENTERED FROM  WO_INV;
```

The sequence generator in line 4 will increment for each row returned by the subquery, regardless of whether the WHEN condition is true or not. For this example, assume the sequence generator has just been created and has never been used, and that it has the default settings of an initial value of 1 and an increment of 1. Given that, then if the subquery returns ten rows, and if, for instance, the final row alone causes the WHEN condition in line 2 to be true, then the one row inserted into the INVOICES_ARCHIVED table will be assigned a value of 10 for the INVOICE_ID column.

Remember: a table alias defined in a subquery of a multitable INSERT is not recognized throughout the rest of the INSERT statement. Also, if a multitable INSERT statement fails for any reason, the entire statement is rolled back and no rows are inserted in any of the tables.

If this statement contained additional calls to the same sequence generator, in additional INTO clauses, they would not cause the sequence generator to increment. The sequence generator increments with each row of the subquery returned, no more, no less, regardless of additional calls to NEXTVAL.

Oracle's documentation warns that "you cannot specify a sequence in any part of a multitable insert statement". The only place you'll get the syntax error is in the subquery, but know that attempts to invoke a sequence generator from the WHEN or INTO clauses of the INSERT may produce undesirable results.

Pivot

You can use a conditional multitable INSERT statement to transform data from a spreadsheet structure to a rows-and-columns structure. This section describes the technique.

First, let's start with the following data listing:

```
ROOM_TYPE            OCEAN             BALCONY           NO_WINDOW
-------------------  ----------------  ----------------  ---------
ROYAL                1745              1635
SKYLOFT              722               722
PRESIDENTIAL         1142              1142              1142
LARGE                225                                 211
STANDARD             217               554               586
```

This is the sort of data that you might find in a typical spreadsheet display. Let's say that this spreadsheet has been stored in an external table. The table's structure is shown in Figure 15-8.

FIGURE 15-8

Diagram of the
SHIP_CABIN_
GRID table

SHIP_CABIN_GRID	
ROOM_TYPE	VARCHAR2 (20 BYTE)
OCEAN	NUMBER
BALCONY	NUMBER
NO_WINDOW	NUMBER

FIGURE 15-8

Diagram of the
SHIP_CABIN_
GRID table

Next, you're given the task of moving this data into the table shown in Figure 15-9. This isn't a straightforward row-for-row insert with a subquery. This data must be transformed so that each column from the spreadsheet is transformed into an individual row in the new table.

The following query will accomplish the task (line numbers added):

```
01   INSERT ALL
02     WHEN OCEAN IS NOT NULL THEN
03       INTO SHIP_CABIN_STATISTICS (ROOM_TYPE, WINDOW_TYPE, SQ_FT)
04       VALUES (ROOM_TYPE, 'OCEAN', OCEAN)
05     WHEN BALCONY IS NOT NULL THEN
06       INTO SHIP_CABIN_STATISTICS (ROOM_TYPE, WINDOW_TYPE, SQ_FT)
07       VALUES (ROOM_TYPE, 'BALCONY', BALCONY)
08     WHEN NO_WINDOW IS NOT NULL THEN
09       INTO SHIP_CABIN_STATISTICS (ROOM_TYPE, WINDOW_TYPE, SQ_FT)
10       VALUES (ROOM_TYPE, 'NO WINDOW', NO_WINDOW)
11   SELECT ROWNUM RN, ROOM_TYPE, OCEAN, BALCONY, NO_WINDOW
12     FROM SHIP_CABIN_GRID;
```

Note how each row of the subquery is considered three times. For a given row returned by the subquery, each of three columns of the row is individually considered. If any one of the three columns OCEAN, BALCONY, or NO_ WINDOW is not NULL, then a row is inserted into the target table. It's possible that some individual rows returned by the subquery will result in three new rows being added to the target table SHIP_CABIN_STATISTICS.

FIGURE 15-9

Diagram of the
SHIP_CABIN_
STATISTICS table

SHIP_CABIN_STATISTICS	
SC_ID	NUMBER (7)
ROOM_TYPE	VARCHAR2 (20 BYTE)
WINDOW_TYPE	VARCHAR2 (10 BYTE)
SQ_FT	NUMBER (8)

Let's take a look at the results:

```
SELECT    ROOM_TYPE, WINDOW_TYPE, SQ_FT
FROM      SHIP_CABIN_STATISTICS
ORDER BY  ROOM_TYPE, WINDOW_TYPE;

ROOM_TYPE                WINDOW_TYPE SQ_FT
-------------------      ----------- ------------------------------
LARGE                    NO WINDOW   211
LARGE                    OCEAN       225
PRESIDENTIAL             BALCONY     1142
PRESIDENTIAL             NO WINDOW   1142
PRESIDENTIAL             OCEAN       1142
ROYAL                    BALCONY     1635
ROYAL                    OCEAN       1745
SKYLOFT                  BALCONY     722
SKYLOFT                  OCEAN       722
STANDARD                 BALCONY     554
STANDARD                 NO WINDOW   586
STANDARD                 OCEAN       217
```

In this example, the conditional multitable INSERT transformed incoming data from a spreadsheet summary style into a row-by-row structure, all within a single SQL statement. In this way, the conditional multitable INSERT statement "pivots" the data by changing columns into rows.

on the job

Note that this "pivot" technique is different from SQL operations that use the keyword PIVOT or UNPIVOT. What we've described here is a technique that uses the conditional multitable INSERT to pivot data. The keyword PIVOT, while somewhat similar in function, is a separate feature and not discussed here, nor is it listed in the exam certification objectives.

CERTIFICATION OBJECTIVE 15.04

Merge Rows in a Table

The MERGE statement is a SQL DML statement that combines the functionality of INSERT, UPDATE, and DELETE, all into a single SQL statement. There isn't anything you can do with MERGE that you cannot already do with some combination of those three DML statements. However, if it's possible to use MERGE as an alternative to executing two or more DML statements, then MERGE is preferable, since it combines multiple DML actions into a single SQL statement, resulting in a single pass through the database. In other words, it will perform more efficiently.

The syntax of MERGE follows (line numbers added):

```
01    MERGE INTO table
02    USING table | subquery
03    ON condition
04    WHEN MATCHED THEN UPDATE SET col = expression | DEFAULT
05         where_clause
06         DELETE where_clause
07    WHEN NOT MATCHED THEN INSERT (col, col2)
08         VALUES (expr1, expr2 | DEFAULT)
09         where_clause
10    WHERE condition;
```

Note the following:

■ Line 1: INTO specifies the target into which you are either inserting or updating rows; it can be a table or an updatable view.

■ Line 2: USING identifies the source of the data, which can be a table, view, or subquery.

■ Line 3: The ON condition for MERGE behaves essentially like a WHERE clause. It determines how to compare each row in the USING data source with each row in the MERGE INTO data target. The ON condition can use Boolean operators and expressions to form complex comparisons. In practice it is often limited to comparing primary key values, but this is not required.

■ Lines 4 through 6 are considered the *update clause* and identify the logic by which the MERGE will update target rows; it cannot update a column in the ON condition.

■ Lines 7 through 9 are considered the *insert clause* and identify the logic by which the MERGE will insert rows into the target table.

■ Lines 1 through 3 are required; all other lines are optional.

As you can see, it's an involved statement. Let's look at an example in action— let's say you are responsible for an application that uses the WWA_INVOICES table (see Figure 15-10), and you have been tasked to bring in data from an outside table, ONTARIO_ORDERS (see Figure 15-11).

FIGURE 15-10

Diagram of
the WWA_
INVOICES table

FIGURE 15-10

Diagram of
the WWA_
INVOICES table

FIGURE 15-11

Diagram of the
ONTARIO_
ORDERS table

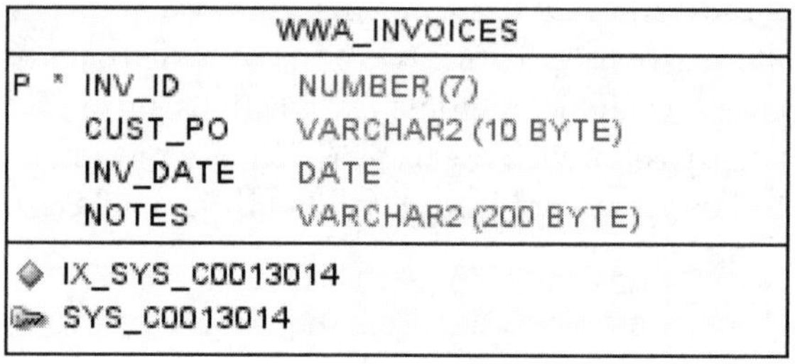

FIGURE 15-11

Diagram of the
ONTARIO_
ORDERS table

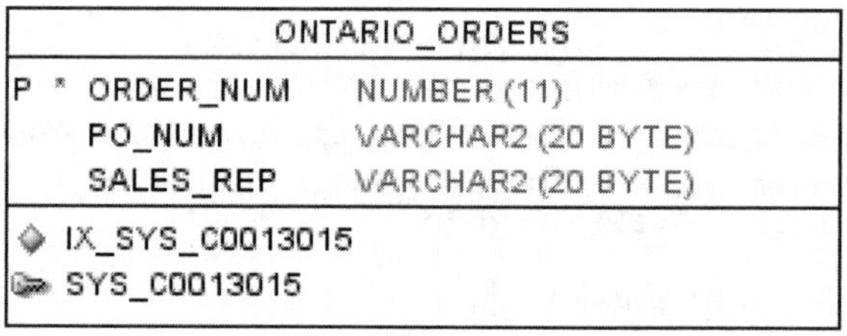

The data listing for the WWA_INVOICES table follows:

```
INV_ID                    CUST_PO    INV_DATE              NOTES
--------------------      ---------- -------------------   -----
10                        WWA-200    17-DEC-09
20                        WWA-001    23-DEC-09
```

For the ONTARIO_ORDERS table:

```
ORDER_NUM                 PO_NUM              SALES_REP
--------------------      ------------------- --------------------
882                       WWA-001             C. Nelson
883                       WWA-017             J. Metelsky
884                       NBC-201             D. Knight
```

Let's use MERGE to bring the data from ONTARIO_ORDERS into the
WWA_INVOICES table (line numbers added):

```
01   MERGE INTO WWA_INVOICES WWA
02     USING ONTARIO_ORDERS ONT
03     ON   (WWA.CUST_PO = ONT.PO_NUM)
04     WHEN  MATCHED THEN UPDATE SET
05           WWA.NOTES = ONT.SALES_REP
06     WHEN  NOT MATCHED THEN INSERT
07           (WWA.INV_ID, WWA.CUST_PO, WWA.INV_DATE, WWA.NOTES)
08           VALUES
```

```
09                   (SEQ_INV_ID.NEXTVAL,
10                              ONT.PO_NUM, SYSDATE, ONT.SALES_REP)
11    WHERE SUBSTR(ONT.PO_NUM,1,3) <> 'NBC';
```

The preceding MERGE statement includes the following features:

- Line 1: we specify that we are going to merge rows into the table WWA_INVOICES.
- Line 1: we assign a table alias WWA to the table WWA_INVOICES.
- Line 2: we specify the ONTARIO_ORDERS table as the data source and give that table an alias of ONT.
- Line 3: we define the ON condition, indicating that the columns CUST_PO and PO_NUM are where the common information exists that will "join" the rows logically in order to associate them with each other for the merge.
- Lines 4 through 5 are the "update clause".
- Lines 6 through 10 are the "insert clause".
- Line 11 is the WHERE clause for the MERGE, filtering out rows from the USING data source—in this case, ONTARIO_ORDERS.

The result of our MERGE is to merge rows from ONTARIO_ORDERS into WWA_INVOICES. If we query the WWA_INVOICES table, here are the results, after the MERGE:

```
SELECT * FROM WWA_INVOICES;

INV_ID                   CUST_PO    INV_DATE           NOTES
----------------------   ---------- ----------------   ---------
10                       WWA-200    17-DEC-09
20                       WWA-001    23-DEC-09          C. Nelson
40                       WWA-017    30-JUL-09          J. Metelsky
```

Notice the following:

- We merged the row where CUST_PO equals "WWA-001".
- We added the row where CUST_PO equals "WWA_017".
- Our MERGE statement's WHERE clause correctly omitted the row where the PO_NUM was NBC-201.

MERGE is a useful and efficient process. In this example, we saw how we performed an INSERT and UPDATE statement in a single MERGE statement.

Our example did not make use of the DELETE feature of the "update clause" within MERGE. But we could have included one, like this:

```
01   MERGE INTO WWA_INVOICES WWA
02     USING ONTARIO_ORDERS ONT
03     ON    (WWA.CUST_PO = ONT.PO_NUM)
04     WHEN  MATCHED THEN UPDATE SET
05           WWA.NOTES = ONT.SALES_REP
06           DELETE WHERE WWA.INV_DATE < TO_DATE('01-SEP-09')
07     WHEN  NOT MATCHED THEN INSERT
08           (WWA.INV_ID, WWA.CUST_PO, WWA.INV_DATE, WWA.NOTES)
09           VALUES
10           (SEQ_INV_ID.NEXTVAL,
11                     ONT.PO_NUM, SYSDATE, ONT.SALES_REP)
12     WHERE SUBSTR(ONT.PO_NUM,1,3) <> 'NBC';
```

In this example, we've added line 6, which contains the "delete clause" for the MERGE. But take note:

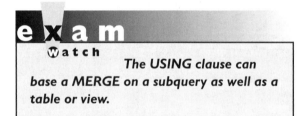

The USING clause can base a MERGE on a subquery as well as a table or view.

■ The "delete clause" only affects rows that are a result of the completed "update clause" and remain in the target table—which in this instance is WWA_INVOICES.

■ Rows added as a result of the "insert clause" are unaffected by the "delete clause".

So MERGE represents a combination of the UPDATE and INSERT DML statements, and to a lesser and somewhat limited extent, the DELETE statement.

CERTIFICATION OBJECTIVE 15.05

Track the Changes to Data over a Period of Time

This section reviews a number of features that support the ability to investigate older versions of rows in the database that have been changed and committed. In other words—if you have already issued any number of INSERT, UPDATE, or DELETE statements and subsequently committed those changes any number of times, you have the ability to go back prior to those committed changes and query the older versions of the data, prior to when the changes were committed. You can display different versions of the rows that have existed at prior times. You can query historic data and combine such a query with queries from other times, or of current data. There are a few restrictions—for example, you won't be able to query data changes prior to any DDL statements that altered the structure of the table or tables you are querying. The oldest data you can query is limited to data within a particular time period that is dependent on the configuration of the database. Database configuration is under the control of the database administrator (DBA) and is determined by factors outside the control of your application code. As a result, flashback operations, while technically capable of being integrated within production code of your application, may not be ideal for such a situation. However, these operations are potentially useful when performing ad hoc analysis, system development, system testing, and other comparable scenarios.

Flashback operations include just some of the many options for managing historic data and managing data changes. Table 15-1 shows flashback operations and compares them with other major options for performing data recovery.

Note that the certification exam addresses TCL and flashback operations. It does not address the underlying architecture of either, nor does it deal with the import and export utilities mentioned in Table 15-1.

TABLE 15-1	Option	Examples	Data Recovery Timeframe	Recommended Use
Data Recovery Options and Comparisons	Transaction Control Language (TCL)	COMMIT, ROLLBACK, SAVEPOINT statements	Current session	Application design; production code
	Flashback Operations	FLASHBACK TABLE, SELECT . . . AS OF, SELECT . . . VERSIONS BETWEEN, etc.	Recent sessions (minutes/hours, depending on configuration)	Application development support; recovering recent data changes; performing analysis comparing current data with recently changed data; analysis of recent transactions
	Backup Recovery	Import/Export Utilities	Long term (days/ weeks/months/ longer, depending on configuration)	Recovering older data

We've already looked at transaction control language (TCL), including the SQL statements COMMIT, ROLLBACK, and SAVEPOINT. Those statements are used to control transactions in production systems. TCL supports transactions within a given login session.

Flashback operations serves as an alternative to backup and recovery operations. Flashback can recover data programmatically—in other words, using SQL statements. Oracle Corporation's documentation stresses that the various flashback operations support programmatic access to historic data. However, the underlying support structures upon which flashback operations depend are outside the boundaries of a typical application and may require a unique configuration to accommodate the specifics of any given application. Furthermore, depending on hardware limitations, the time frame within which flashback operations can apply may vary from one database implementation to another. Any application that incorporates flashback operations must take the potential for these environmental variations into account.

In Chapter 11 we examined the FLASHBACK TABLE statement. This section looks at Flashback Query operations and related features. Specifically, we'll look at the following:

- **Flashback Query (FQ)** For querying a table as it existed in the past
- **Flashback Version Query (FVQ)** For querying multiple past points at once and comparing rows as they existed at various points in history
- **Flashback Transaction Query (FTQ)** For querying the data dictionary and obtaining a variety of metadata about historical rows in the database—including information about the transaction that caused the most recent changes

Note that flashback operations are limited; you cannot recover any data from any time in the past but are limited to recovering data changed within the amount of time defined by the undo retention period. We'll discuss that after we've looked at Flashback Query.

Flashback Query

Oracle's Flashback Query (FQ) feature enables you to query data as it existed in the database at a previous moment in time. The query will produce results as it would have done during that moment in time, regardless of changes to the data that may have already been committed.

The FQ feature is a clause of the SELECT statement involving the keywords AS OF. To demonstrate the AS OF feature in Oracle SQL, let's look at a simple example with a table we'll call CHAT:

```
CREATE TABLE CHAT
(CHAT_ID    NUMBER(11) PRIMARY KEY,
 CHAT_USER VARCHAR2(9),
 YACKING    VARCHAR2(40));

CREATE SEQUENCE SEQ_CHAT_ID;
```

There's our table and a sequence generator; let's put some data into the CHAT table:

```
INSERT INTO CHAT VALUES (SEQ_CHAT_ID.NEXTVAL, USER, 'Hi there.');
INSERT INTO CHAT VALUES (SEQ_CHAT_ID.NEXTVAL, USER, 'Welcome to our chat room.');
INSERT INTO CHAT VALUES (SEQ_CHAT_ID.NEXTVAL, USER, 'Online order form is up.');
INSERT INTO CHAT VALUES (SEQ_CHAT_ID.NEXTVAL, USER, 'Over and out.');
COMMIT;
```

Next, let's see what we did—we'll examine data from the primary key column CHAT_ID, and also a pseudocolumn we haven't yet examined called ORA_ROWSCN:

```
SELECT CHAT_ID, ORA_ROWSCN, SCN_TO_TIMESTAMP(ORA_ROWSCN)
FROM CHAT;
```

CHAT_ID	ORA_ROWSCN	SCN_TO_TIMESTAMP(ORA_ROWSCN)
1	5576336	30-JUL-09 10.43.37.000000000 PM
2	5576336	30-JUL-09 10.43.37.000000000 PM
3	5576336	30-JUL-09 10.43.37.000000000 PM
4	5576336	30-JUL-09 10.43.37.000000000 PM

The ORA_ROWSCN pseudocolumn displays the SCN value for the row. We examined the SCN in Chapter 11—remember that the SCN is the system change number, which is assigned by the database and is incremented and assigned automatically by the database for every committed transaction that occurs in the database, for all internal and external transactions, and all explicit and implicit commits. What we see in this example is the primary key and SCN information associated with our inserted rows. Our four INSERT statements specified the use of the sequence generator SEQ_CHAT_ID to assign values to the primary key

CHAT_ID of 1, 2, 3, and 4. The INSERT statements were committed, and the SQL database stored the associated SCN for the commit transaction with each row. This is the value we see in the pseudocolumn ORA_ROWSCN.

In the preceding query, we used the conversion function SCN_TO_TIMESTAMP to see the timestamp that corresponds to the SCN values in ORA_ROWSCN.

Now we'll wait a minute or two.

on the
ⓘ o b

If you ever need to build a timed delay into a script, you can use the command EXECUTE DBMS_LOCK.SLEEP(s), executed on a line by itself, complete with semicolon termination character at the end. The parameter s is the number of seconds you wish to delay a process. You can learn more about that command and a great deal more in Oracle's documentation about PL/SQL packages. PL/SQL is not part of the exam.

After a couple of minutes, we'll delete all of the rows we just added to the database:

```
EXECUTE DBMS_LOCK.SLEEP(120);
DELETE FROM CHAT;
COMMIT;
```

We've just deleted our four rows. Furthermore, we've committed the changes. Let's confirm that the data is gone:

```
SELECT * FROM CHAT;
CHAT_ID                  CHAT_USER YACKING
--------------------     --------- -------------------------------
0 rows selected
```

Seems like it's all gone, doesn't it? BUT WAIT . . . here comes FQ to the rescue—let's look at what the CHAT table looked like 90 seconds ago:

```
SELECT *
FROM CHAT
AS OF TIMESTAMP SYSTIMESTAMP - INTERVAL '0 0:01:30' DAY TO SECOND;

CHAT_ID                  CHAT_USER YACKING
--------------------     --------- -------------------------------
1                        TESTIT    Hi there.
2                        TESTIT    Welcome to our chat room.
3                        TESTIT    Online order form is up.
4                        TESTIT    Over and out.
```

Note what we are doing here—in the SELECT statement we are using the AS OF clause, in which we query for data in the table as of a moment in time equal to the current time minus a time interval of 0 days, 0 hours, 1 minute, and 30 seconds, specified by the literal value as follows:

```
INTERVAL '0 0:01:30' DAY TO SECOND
```

And suddenly—there's our data. Yet this data is not currently present in the table—we already eliminated it with a DELETE, and we even used COMMIT to make the changes "permanent". So where did it come from? The FQ feature retrieves older versions of rows from within Oracle's rollback segments, the same feature of the database that supports TCL execution. Rollback segments—also known as undo segments—contain older versions of data for as long as the undo retention period allows.

The result: We can investigate changes performed to a table over time, within limitations.

Those limitations are defined by the undo retention period.

Undo Retention Period

Flashback Query operations can obtain historic data that existed during the time frame specified by the database system's undo retention period. The duration of the undo retention period depends upon the configuration of your database and its undo management, which is under the control of the database administrator (DBA). In practice, the time frame within which you can recover data using Flashback Query is generally in the range of several minutes to several hours, possibly a day or longer, but generally not much more. You can get some insight into the undo retention period within your database with this query:

```
SELECT NAME, VALUE
FROM   V$SYSTEM_PARAMETER
WHERE  NAME LIKE ('undo%');

NAME                             VALUE
------------------------         -------------
undo_management                  AUTO
undo_tablespace                  UNDOTBS1
undo_retention                   900
```

This query on the data dictionary view V$SYSTEM_PARAMETER reveals the values of three important initialization parameters. These initialization parameter values are set as follows:

- UNDO_MANAGEMENT set to AUTO indicates that the Automatic Undo Management feature is turned on; this is correct to support Flashback Query operations.
- The UNDO_TABLESPACE identifies an undo tablespace, which is beyond the scope of the exam and this book—but anyone working with Flashback Operations would benefit from a study of this feature—see one of the Oracle Press books about Oracle database architecture.
- The UNDO_RETENTION is specified in seconds—the preceding example shows an undo retention of 900 seconds, which equates to 15 minutes. Note, however, this does not necessarily represent the undo retention period, which depends on this value, but also on available space and other factors beyond the scope of the exam—and this book.

The best answer here is: check with your database administrator. As for the undo retention period: there is no absolute time frame that is easily established for flashback support; it is dependent on a series of issues, all of which are under the control of the DBA.

FQ Syntax

There are two formats for performing an FQ:

```
SELECT  *
FROM    tablename
AS OF   TIMESTAMP timestamp_expression;
```

and

```
SELECT  *
FROM    tablename
AS OF   SCN scn_expression;
```

The *timestamp_expression* or *scn_expression* cannot be a subquery.

One tremendous advantage to accessing historical data in this fashion is that it can be done without changing the table by restoring exported data, and thus overwriting existing data. This means we can query data from multiple timeframes simultaneously, including the present time. For example (line numbers added):

```
01    SELECT CHAT_ID, CHAT_USER, YACKING
02    FROM CHAT
03    AS OF TIMESTAMP SYSTIMESTAMP - INTERVAL '0 0:01:30' DAY TO SECOND
04    MINUS
05    SELECT CHAT_ID, CHAT_USER, YACKING
06    FROM  CHAT;
```

Note our use of the set operator MINUS in line 4. The first SELECT on lines 1 through 3 will return any rows that were in the table at the time specified in line 3, which is 90 seconds prior to the current time. The second SELECT returns all rows in the CHAT table at the current time. By using the set operator MINUS with these two SELECT statements, we are asking to display the difference between their results—in other words, only those rows that have been removed since the timestamp specified in line 3.

Let's look a little more closely at the syntax in line 3 specifically. First are the reserved words AS OF TIMESTAMP. The portion that follows is an expression that evaluates to a datatype of TIMESTAMP:

```
SYSTIMESTAMP - INTERVAL '0 0:01:30' DAY TO SECOND
```

First, the function SYSTIMESTAMP specifies the current date and time according to the Oracle database server's operating system. From that value, we subtract a time interval, which we specify with this literal value:

```
INTERVAL '0 0:01:30' DAY TO SECOND
```

This literal value specifies a time interval of one minute, thirty seconds. In other words, 90 seconds.

The result is that the entire expression evaluates to a timestamp value representing a moment in time that was 90 seconds prior to the current time.

If you use Oracle's FQ using AS OF TIMESTAMP, Oracle will internally translate the timestamp value to the nearest corresponding SCN value and then perform the query using the SCN. Remember that SCN values are assigned systematically within a three-second degree of granularity, and that there is not an exact one-to-one correspondence between timestamp values and SCN values.

SELECT statements that use the AS OF clause can be joined to other queries. They can be used to create VIEW objects. They can be used in any way that any other SELECT statement can be utilized.

on the Job *You can create a view with a SELECT ... AS OF statement to more easily investigate older data in a given table. For example, a query to create a view that will display the previous day's version of the CHAT table is: CREATE VIEW YESTERDAYS_CHAT AS SELECT * FROM CHAT AS OF TIMESTAMP (SYSTIMESTAMP-1);*

Flashback Version Query

Oracle's Flashback Version Query (FVQ) takes the FQ feature a step further. With FVQ, you can display rows from multiple committed versions of the database over a range of time. You can perform analysis, do comparisons, and execute virtually any DML statement against any time range of the database.

Each row displayed as the result of an FVQ is a committed version of the row that was in the database at some point in the past. FVQ will not show rows that were not committed. If a row was added with the INSERT command and then later removed with a DELETE statement, but never committed during that time with an implicit or explicit commit event, then FVQ will not display the row at all in any form. Only historically committed changes are returned by the FVQ operation, within the range of time specified, and within the range allowed and supported by flashback operations.

VERSIONS BETWEEN TIMESTAMP

The syntax for FVQ using TIMESTAMP is as follows (line numbers added):

```
01    SELECT * FROM tablename
02    VERSIONS BETWEEN TIMESTAMP timestamp_expression1
03                        AND timestamp_expression2;
```

A query using this syntax will show any given row once for each of its versions, however many there were, as they each existed in the table within the range identified by the VERSIONS clause.

The preceding syntax has the following rules and guidelines:

- The required keywords VERSIONS BETWEEN follow the FROM clause.
- If the WHERE clause is included, it follows the VERSIONS BETWEEN clause.
- The keyword TIMESTAMP in line 2 is required for the TIMESTAMP variant of VERSIONS BETWEEN.
- The values for *timestamp_expression1* can be a valid expression with the datatype of TIMESTAMP, or it can be the reserved word MINVALUE, where MINVALUE represents the earliest TIMESTAMP available for the data retained for the table.
- The keyword AND in line 3 is required.
- The value for *timestamp_expression2* can be a valid expression with the datatype of TIMESTAMP, or it can be the reserved word MAXVALUE, where MAXVALUE represents the latest TIMESTAMP available for the data retained for the table.

These rules apply to FVQ with VERSIONS BETWEEN TIMESTAMP. You can also use FVQ with SCN, which we discuss next.

VERSIONS BETWEEN SCN

You can use FVQ with SCN instead of TIMESTAMP:

```
01    SELECT * FROM tablename
02    VERSIONS BETWEEN SCN scn_expression1
03                    AND scn_expression2;
```

Other than the use of SCN, the same syntax rules of VERSIONS BETWEEN TIMESTAMP apply to this variation, including MINVALUE and MAXVALUE.

Whenever you use a value of datatype TIMESTAMP to identify a past time in the database, SQL will internally translate that value to the closest SCN that was established at the given time, and use the SCN value to process the statement.

Rules of FVQ

Note that you cannot use the VERSIONS clause when querying a view. But you can use SELECT with a VERSIONS clause to create a view, meaning that VERSIONS can be included in the subquery of a CREATE VIEW statement.

The FVQ feature includes a set of pseudocolumns that provide information about each version of the row, to help identify how each row came to exist, and when. The pseudocolumns are identified in Table 15-2. These pseudocolumns help to clarify the rows that are returned from the FVQ query by differentiating each row from the other. For example:

```
SELECT    CHAT_ID, VERSIONS_STARTSCN, VERSIONS_ENDSCN, VERSIONS_OPERATION
FROM      CHAT
VERSIONS BETWEEN TIMESTAMP MINVALUE
                 AND MAXVALUE
ORDER BY  CHAT_ID, VERSIONS_OPERATION DESC;
```

CHAT_ID	VERSIONS_STARTSCN	VERSIONS_ENDSCN	VERSIONS_OPERATION
1		6311693	
1	6311693		D
2		6311693	
2	6311693		D
3		6311693	
3	6311693		D
4		6311693	
4	6311693		D

TABLE 15-2	Pseudocolumn	Explanation
Flashback Version Query (FVQ) Pseudocolumns	VERSIONS_STARTTIME VERSIONS_STARTSCN	Starting time or SCN for when the version of the row was created. If NULL, then the row version was created before the lower time boundary returned by the BETWEEN clause.
	VERSIONS_ENDTIME VERSIONS_ENDSCN	Expiration time or SCN for the version of the row. If NULL, then the row version is still current, or the row version resulted from a DELETE (see VERSIONS_OPERATION).
	VERSIONS_XID	Identifies the transaction that created the row. (Useful for Flashback Transaction Query.)
	VERSIONS_OPERATION	Identifies the operation that performed whatever change created the row version: either I for INSERT, U for UPDATE, or D for DELETE.

Note that the output shows two versions of rows for each CHAT_ID value. The second row for each CHAT_ID value shows a value of D in the pseudocolumn VERSIONS_OPERATION, indicating that the version represented was deleted with a DELETE statement.

A row version is valid on and past its VERSIONS_STARTTIME, and up to but not including its VERSIONS_ENDTIME. In other words, the row version is considered to have been valid at and after the time of its VERSIONS_STARTTIME, but only valid before the time of its VERSIONS_ENDTIME, not at the same time as the VERSIONS_ENDTIME.

The same truths apply to the VERSIONS_STARTSCN and VERSIONS_ENDSCN.

You can combine the AS OF clause and the VERSIONS BETWEEN clause in a single SELECT statement. For example:

```
SELECT   CHAT_ID, VERSIONS_STARTSCN, VERSIONS_ENDSCN, VERSIONS_OPERATION
FROM     CHAT
VERSIONS BETWEEN TIMESTAMP MINVALUE
                 AND MAXVALUE
AS OF    TIMESTAMP SYSTIMESTAMP - INTERVAL '0 00:15:00' DAY TO SECOND
ORDER BY CHAT_ID, VERSIONS_OPERATION DESC;
```

Note that the VERSIONS BETWEEN clause precedes the AS OF clause; this is required. When combined, the VERSIONS BETWEEN values are determined AS OF the time specified by the AS OF clause. In other words, the VERSIONS

BETWEEN parameters are defined from the perspective of the AS OF query. Rows that existed later than the AS OF data will return a NULL value. The same is true for rows that precede the first value of the BETWEEN clause.

exam

watch
Note that the AS OF and VERSIONS clauses of the SELECT statement are considered flashback operations, even though they do not use the FLASHBACK reserved word in their syntax.

Flashback Transaction Query

Oracle's Flashback Transaction Query (FTQ) feature is a query on the data dictionary view FLASHBACK_TRANSACTION_QUERY. The view looks like this:

```
DESC FLASHBACK_TRANSACTION_QUERY;
Name                                    Null      Type
--------------------------------------- --------  -----------------------
XID                                               RAW(8)
START_SCN                                         NUMBER
START_TIMESTAMP                                   DATE
COMMIT_SCN                                        NUMBER
COMMIT_TIMESTAMP                                  DATE
LOGON_USER                                        VARCHAR2(30)
UNDO_CHANGE#                                      NUMBER
OPERATION                                         VARCHAR2(32)
TABLE_NAME                                        VARCHAR2(256)
TABLE_OWNER                                       VARCHAR2(32)
ROW_ID                                            VARCHAR2(19)
UNDO_SQL                                          VARCHAR2(4000)
```

Note the first column in the view: XID. This is the global transaction identifier. Each transaction that is executed within the database is tracked and assigned a global transaction identifier, which is essentially a transaction identification number. The XID value is of the RAW datatype, which is a binary value, and is not interpreted by the Oracle database. But it can be converted into readable form using the RAWTOHEX function, which converts RAW data into character data that represents the hexadecimal equivalent of the RAW data, which is binary. The function HEXTORAW converts character data containing hexadecimal notation back into the RAW datatype.

on the Job

Hexadecimal refers to a base-16 numeric scale. Decimal, of course, is base-10, and binary is base-2. Because there is a direct exponential relation between base-2 and base-16, hexadecimal notation, or hex, is a great way to present base-2 data in a relatively succinct fashion. If any of this is confusing to you, don't worry—you don't need to understand it all for the exam—but do be aware of the RAW datatype and the ability to convert to character output in hexadecimal notation.

The XID column in the data dictionary view FLASHBACK_TRANSACTION_ QUERY corresponds to the FVQ VERSIONS_XID pseudocolumn we saw in Table 15-2. We can use that pseudocolumn in an FVQ to locate a specific transaction that caused a change to a table, and then use the FLASHBACK_TRANSACTION_ QUERY data dictionary view to identify the specific SQL statement and its associated UNDO_SQL value—which is the SQL that can undo the transaction.

For example, let's look at our CHAT table again, but this time let's use the RAWTOHEX conversion function to display the contents of the VERSIONS_XID pseudocolumn, which would be otherwise unreadable:

```
SELECT    CHAT_ID, VERSIONS_OPERATION, RAWTOHEX(VERSIONS_XID)
FROM      CHAT
VERSIONS BETWEEN TIMESTAMP MINVALUE AND MAXVALUE
WHERE     CHAT_ID = 1
ORDER BY VERSIONS_OPERATION DESC;
```

This query shows all versions of the row in the CHAT table for which the primary key of CHAT_ID is equal to 1. Note the WHERE clause follows the VERSIONS BETWEEN clause.

Here is the output from our table:

```
CHAT_ID                   VERSIONS_OPERATION RAWTOHEX(VERSIONS_XID)
---------------------- ------------------ ----------------------
1
1                         D                  04002000C10E0000
```

That's our output. We don't need to display this output in order to get the UNDO_ SQL value for this transaction though; we can use a subquery, like this:

```
SELECT UNDO_SQL
FROM    FLASHBACK_TRANSACTION_QUERY
WHERE   XID = (SELECT    VERSIONS_XID
               FROM      CHAT
               VERSIONS BETWEEN TIMESTAMP MINVALUE
                         AND MAXVALUE
               WHERE     CHAT_ID = 1
               AND       VERSIONS_OPERATION = 'D');
```

The preceding query is asking the data dictionary view FLASHBACK_ TRANSACTION_QUERY for the value in the UNDO_SQL column that corresponds to our CHAT table row in which the CHAT_ID is equal to 1, in the version that was deleted. Here is the answer—and please note—the output is too wide to be displayed in the book, so we've allowed it to line-wrap, and displayed the line numbers to let you know where each row begins:

```
01    UNDO_SQL
02    ------------------------------------------------------------------------
03    insert into "EFCODD"."CHAT"("CHAT_ID","CHAT_USER","YACKING") values
      ('4','EFCODD','Over and out.');
04    insert into "EFCODD"."CHAT"("CHAT_ID","CHAT_USER","YACKING") values
      ('3','EFCODD','Online order form is up.');
05    insert into "EFCODD"."CHAT"("CHAT_ID","CHAT_USER","YACKING") values
      ('2','EFCODD','Welcome to our chat room.');
06    insert into "EFCODD"."CHAT"("CHAT_ID","CHAT_USER","YACKING") values
      ('1','EFCODD','Hi there.');
```

Note that our UNDO_SQL value for just the one row where CHAT_ID = 1 shows four INSERT statements. Why? Because the transaction that caused the CHAT_ID = 1 row to be deleted was a single DELETE statement that didn't just delete the one row, but all the rows that existed in the table at that time—in other words, all four of these rows. Therefore, the UNDO_SQL statement that is required to undo that DELETE statement will quite correctly restore all four rows. That is what this UNDO_SQL column shows—the necessary SQL code that will undo the transaction.

If you were to execute these SQL statements, you would effectively "undo" the DELETE that removed the CHAT_ID row of 1—and all the other rows as well.

In this example, we only reviewed the contents of the UNDO_SQL column, but as you can see from the description of the FLASHBACK_TRANSACTION_QUERY view that we displayed earlier, there is much more information available—such as the SCN at the time of the COMMIT that saved the changes, and more.

exam

☻atch   *Note that a "transaction" in SQL is not necessarily just one SQL statement. Technically speaking, a single "transaction" consists of all the SQL statements that are executed from one commit event to another commit event. Keep in mind that a ROLLBACK statement can interrupt a transaction and resets the starting point of the next transaction. SCN values are assigned to transactions. UNDO_SQL shows the code to undo the effects of a single SQL statement, which may be less than a single transaction as defined in this paragraph.*

Note that the UNDO_SQL code cannot necessarily perform a complete restoration of all the data throughout the database as it existed before—depending on the situation. For example, the ROWID values won't be the same. And depending on the sequence of changes that have occurred, you may need to step through a series of undo statements, and you won't be able to just jump quickly to a previous state of the table using this technique.

CERTIFICATION SUMMARY

Subqueries can be used in SQL statements to process large numbers of database rows from within a single SQL statement.

The CREATE TABLE statement can use a subquery to populate a table and assign its column names and datatypes all at the same time. The UPDATE statement can use a correlated subquery to update multiple columns and multiple rows using varying values and varying comparison conditions.

The INSERT statement can be augmented with a number of clauses to introduce conditional logic into its execution, and to add data to more than one table from within a single INSERT statement. Conditional logic can be added with a WHEN condition and optionally the ELSE keyword. The INSERT ALL form will test incoming data against each WHEN condition, and the INSERT FIRST form will stop at the first WHEN condition that evaluates to true. In either situation, the optional ELSE clause can define an insert that will execute if all previous WHEN conditions failed. Conditional INSERT statements may be used to "pivot" data from columns into rows and back again.

The MERGE statement does not do anything you cannot otherwise do with a series of other DML statements, but its advantage is its powerful ability to perform multiple operations from within a single SQL statement, and therefore a single execution and single pass through the database.

Oracle's flashback operations analyze data over time. The AS OF clause of the SELECT statement can query a table at a particular moment in time, as far back as the undo retention period supports. The VERSIONS BETWEEN clause compares rows of data in all its different versions over time. The data dictionary view FLASHBACK_TRANSACTION_QUERY supports many forms of analysis, including the ability to identify the UNDO_SQL code that can logically reverse the effects of a given DML statement.

TWO-MINUTE DRILL

Manipulate Data Using Subqueries

❑ The CREATE TABLE AS SELECT statement, also known as CTAS, uses a subquery to populate the new table's rows.

❑ CTAS can also be used to name each column in the new table.

❑ CTAS can also define the datatype of each new column.

❑ Subqueries in CTAS must provide a name for each column; complex expressions should be named with a column alias.

❑ The UPDATE statement can use a correlated subquery to set values to one or more columns from one or more rows within a data source at one time.

❑ In the UPDATE statement with correlated subquery, the table alias for the UPDATE table can be referenced within the subquery.

❑ The INSERT statement can be used with a subquery to insert more than one row at a time.

Describe the Features of Multitable INSERTs

❑ Multitable inserts are useful for applying conditional logic to the data being considered for insertion.

❑ Conditional logic can evaluate incoming rows of data in a series of steps, using several evaluation conditions, and offer alternative strategies for adding data to the database, all in a single SQL statement.

❑ Multitable INSERT statements offer flexibility and performance efficiency over the alternative approaches of using multiple SQL statements.

Use the Following Types of Multitable INSERTs: Unconditional, Conditional, and Pivot

❑ Multitable INSERT statements may use conditional operations such as the WHEN condition and the ELSE clause.

❑ A WHEN condition can be used to evaluate incoming data and determine if it should be inserted into the database, and if yes, which table and which columns are to be inserted.

❏ The ELSE clause is a last alternative choice that will execute if no WHEN condition evaluated to true.

❏ Both WHEN and ELSE are associated with their own unique INSERT statement directives; depending on which conditions apply, the appropriate INSERT statement directives will execute.

❏ Each condition can INSERT data in different ways into different tables.

❏ The INSERT FIRST statement tests each WHEN condition and executes the associated INSERT statement directives with the first WHEN condition that evaluates to true.

❏ The INSERT ALL statement executes all of the WHEN conditions that evaluate to true.

❏ The ELSE clause executes for either the INSERT FIRST or INSERT ALL statement when none of the WHEN conditions have executed.

❏ The subquery of a multitable INSERT determines the data that will be considered in the insert logic; it can be a complex query, and can include joins, GROUP BY clauses, set operators, and other complex logic.

Merge Rows in a Table

❏ The MERGE statement is one of the SQL DML statements, alongside SELECT, INSERT, UPDATE, and DELETE.

❏ MERGE replicates some of the functionality found in INSERT, UPDATE, and DELETE and combines it all into a single statement that executes with a single pass through the database.

❏ MERGE doesn't do anything new that you cannot already do with existing DML statements, but it does them more efficiently in combination.

❏ The MERGE statement includes an "update clause" and an "insert clause".

❏ The WHEN MATCHED THEN UPDATE keywords form the "update clause".

❏ The WHEN NOT MATCHED THEN INSERT keywords form the "insert clause".

❏ The DELETE clause of the MERGE statement only deletes rows that were first updated with the "update clause" and remain after a successful update; they must also meet the WHERE condition of the "delete clause".

Track the Changes to Data over a Period of Time

❑ The AS OF clause of SELECT can query data in the table as it existed AS OF a particular time in the past, as defined by a TIMESTAMP value or SCN, and within the limitations of the undo retention period.

❑ The AS OF clause comes after the FROM and before any WHERE clause that might be used within the SELECT statement.

❑ The VERSIONS BETWEEN clause can display rows as they existed in their various states of changes within a range of time.

❑ The VERSIONS BETWEEN clause marks time ranges in terms of SCN or timestamp values.

❑ The VERSIONS BETWEEN clause activates a number of pseudocolumns to identify the time range and other data associated with the historic data returned by the VERSIONS BETWEEN clause.

❑ The data dictionary view FLASHBACK_TRANSACTION_QUERY can be used with the VERSIONS BETWEEN clause to identify metadata associated with a particular transaction that caused the changes to a particular version of the row returned by the VERSIONS BETWEEN clause.

SELF TEST

The following questions will help you measure your understanding of the material presented in this chapter. Choose one correct answer for each question unless otherwise directed.

Manipulate Data Using Subqueries

1. A CREATE TABLE statement can include a subquery as long as the subquery satisfies which of the following requirements?

    A. It cannot use any joins.

    B. It must have column names for each column specified.

    C. It must return data.

    D. None of the above.

2. Review the diagrams of the tables PORT_INVENTORY, STORE_INVENTORY, and SHIP_INVENTORY, shown below:

```
                STORE_INVENTORY
P * NUM              NUMBER
    AISLE            VARCHAR2 (7 BYTE)
    PRODUCT          VARCHAR2 (15 BYTE)
    LAST_ORDER       DATE
⊛ PK_NUM
```

```
                SHIP_INVENTORY
P * NUM              NUMBER
    AISLE            VARCHAR2 (7 BYTE)
    PRODUCT          VARCHAR2 (15 BYTE)
    LAST_ORDER       DATE
⊛ PK_SHIP_INV_NUM
```

```
                PORT_INVENTORY
P * NUM              NUMBER
    AISLE            VARCHAR2 (7 BYTE)
    PRODUCT          VARCHAR2 (15 BYTE)
    LAST_ORDER       DATE
⊛ PK_PORT_INV_NUM
```

Now consider the following SQL statement:

```
INSERT INTO STORE_INVENTORY (NUM, PRODUCT)
{keyword} SELECT SEQ_SHIP_NUM.NEXTVAL, PRODUCT FROM PORT_INVENTORY;
```

Which of the following replaces the {keyword} reference in this INSERT statement in order to form a valid INSERT statement?

A. VALUES

B. AS

C. IN

D. Nothing

Describe the Features of Multitable INSERTs

3. An INSERT statement can: (Choose two.)

A. Add rows into more than one table.

B. Add data into more than one column in a table.

C. Delete rows by overwriting them.

D. Join tables together.

4. A multitable INSERT statement:

A. Can accomplish tasks that cannot otherwise be done in any combination of SQL statements.

B. Will create any tables in which it attempts to INSERT but that do not yet exist.

C. Can use conditional logic.

D. Is capable of inserting rows into non-updatable views.

Use the Following Types of Multitable INSERTs: Unconditional, Conditional, and Pivot

5. Review the diagrams of the SPARES table below:

SPARES	
SPARE_ID	NUMBER (8)
PART_NO	VARCHAR2 (30 BYTE)
PART_NAME	VARCHAR2 (80 BYTE)
◆ IX_01	

Also examine the diagrams in question 2, and consider the following SQL statement (line numbers added):

```
01   INSERT ALL
02     WHEN (SUBSTR(PART_NAME,1,4) = 'MED-') THEN
03       INTO STORE_INVENTORY (NUM, AISLE, PRODUCT, LAST_ORDER)
```

```
04          VALUES (SPARE_ID, 'Back', PART_NAME, SYSDATE)
05        INTO SHIP_INVENTORY (NUM, AISLE, PRODUCT, LAST_ORDER)
06          VALUES (SPARE_ID, 'Back', PART_NAME, SYSDATE)
07      WHEN (SUBSTR(PART_NAME,1,4) = 'ARR-') THEN
08        INTO PORT_INVENTORY (NUM, AISLE, PRODUCT, LAST_ORDER)
09          VALUES (SPARE_ID, 'Back', PART_NAME, SYSDATE)
10    SELECT SPARE_ID, PART_NO, PART_NAME
11    FROM    SPARES;
```

Regarding this SQL statement, which of the following statements is true?

A. The statement will fail because there is no ELSE clause.

B. The statement will fail because it is missing a WHEN condition.

C. The statement will add a row returned from the SPARES table to the SHIP_INVENTORY table only if the WHEN condition on line 2 evaluates to true.

D. The statement will add every row returned from the SPARES table to the SHIP_INVENTORY table.

6. Review the SQL statement in the preceding question. If one of the INTO clauses executed on a table and resulted in a constraint violation on that table, what would result?

A. The row would not be inserted and the INSERT statement would skip to the next row returned by the subquery, and perform another pass through the WHEN conditions.

B. The row would not be inserted and the INSERT statement would stop. No additional rows would be returned by the subquery or processed, but rows that have already been processed are unaffected.

C. The row would not be inserted, the INSERT statement would stop, and all rows affected by the INSERT statement would be rolled back, as if the INSERT statement had never been executed.

D. None of the above.

7. Review the diagrams in question 2 and question 5, and consider the following SQL statement (line numbers added):

```
01    INSERT FIRST
02      WHEN (SUBSTR(PART_NAME,5,3) = 'OPS') THEN
03       INTO STORE_INVENTORY (NUM, AISLE, PRODUCT, LAST_ORDER)
04          VALUES (SEQ_NUM.NEXTVAL, 'Back', PART_NAME, SYSDATE)
05      WHEN (SUBSTR(PART_NAME,1,4) = 'PAN-') THEN
06        INTO SHIP_INVENTORY (NUM, AISLE, PRODUCT, LAST_ORDER)
07          VALUES (SEQ_SHIP_NUM.NEXTVAL, 'Back', PART_NAME, SYSDATE)
08      ELSE
09        INTO PORT_INVENTORY (NUM, AISLE, PRODUCT, LAST_ORDER)
```

```
10       VALUES (SEQ_PORT_NUM.NEXTVAL, 'Back', PART_NAME, SYSDATE)
11     SELECT SPARE_ID, PART_NO, PART_NAME
12     FROM    SPARES
13     WHERE   LENGTH(PART_NO) > 2;
```

Which one of the following answers correctly identifies data that, if present in the SPARES table, will be inserted by this conditional INSERT statement into the table—or tables— identified by the answer?

A. PART_NO = 123; PART_NAME = 'BAH-OPS,' in both STORE_INVENTORY and PORT_INVENTORY

B. PART_NO = 401; PART_NAME = 'PAN-OPS,' in both SHIP_INVENTORY and PORT_INVENTORY

C. PART_NO = 170; PART_NAME = 'TRA-OPS,' in STORE_INVENTORY

D. PART_NO = 4; PART_NAME = 'PAN-OPS,' in both STORE_INVENTORY and SHIP_INVENTORY

8. Review the diagrams in question 2 and question 5, and examine the following statement (line numbers added):

```
01    INSERT
02      WHEN (PART_NO < 500) THEN
03       INTO STORE_INVENTORY (NUM, PRODUCT)
04        VALUES (SPARE_ID, PART_NAME)
05       INTO PORT_INVENTORY (NUM, PRODUCT)
06        VALUES (SPARE_ID, PART_NAME)
07      WHEN (PART_NO >= 500) THEN
08       INTO SHIP_INVENTORY (NUM, PRODUCT)
09        VALUES (SPARE_ID, PART_NAME)
10     SELECT SPARE_ID, PART_NO, PART_NAME
11     FROM    SPARES;
```

Which of the following statements are true for this SQL statement?

A. If the first WHEN condition in line 2 is true, the INTO clause in line 3 through line 4 will be executed, after which processing will skip to the next row returned by the subquery.

B. If the first WHEN condition in line 2 is true, the WHEN condition in line 7 will not be evaluated.

C. No matter which WHEN condition is true, the INTO clause in line 5 will be executed regardless.

D. Regardless of whether the first WHEN condition is true or not, the second WHEN condition will be evaluated.

9. Let's modify the SQL statement from the last exercise and add a sequence generator to the subquery (line numbers added):

```
01    INSERT
02      WHEN (PART_NO < 500) THEN
03       INTO STORE_INVENTORY (NUM, PRODUCT)
04        VALUES (SPARE_ID, PART_NAME)
05       INTO PORT_INVENTORY (NUM, PRODUCT)
06        VALUES (SPARE_ID, PART_NAME)
07      WHEN (PART_NO >= 500) THEN
08       INTO SHIP_INVENTORY (NUM, PRODUCT)
09        VALUES (SPARE_ID, PART_NAME)
10      SELECT SEQ_SPARES_ID.NEXTVAL SPARE_ID, PART_NO, PART_NAME
11      FROM    SPARES;
```

Which one of the following statements is true?

A. The statement will fail with a syntax error.

B. The statement will execute but only NULL values will be inserted for numbers into the target tables identified in the INTO clauses.

C. The statement will execute but the same number will be generated for all the rows inserted.

D. The statement will execute and perform successfully.

Merge Rows in a Table

10. The MERGE statement includes a USING clause. Which of the following statements is NOT true of the USING clause?

A. It can be used to specify a subquery.

B. The data it identifies remains unchanged after the MERGE statement executes.

C. The USING clause is optional.

D. It can be used to specify an inline view.

11. See the diagrams in question 2. You want to merge rows from the PORT_INVENTORY table into the SHIP_INVENTORY table. You start with the following SQL statement:

```
01    MERGE INTO SHIP_INVENTORY A
02    USING PORT_INVENTORY B
03    ON (A.NUM = B.NUM)
04    WHEN NOT MATCHED THEN INSERT
05      (A.NUM, A.AISLE, A.PRODUCT, A.LAST_ORDER)
06      VALUES
07      (B.NUM, B.AISLE, B.PRODUCT, B.LAST_ORDER)
08    WHERE TO_CHAR(A.LAST_ORDER,'RRRR') = '2009';
```

What will this SQL statement do?

A. It will fail with a syntax error because you must have an ELSE clause.

B. It will fail with a syntax error because you cannot reference the target table (SHIP_INVENTORY) in the WHERE clause in line 8.

C. It will add rows from PORT_INVENTORY to SHIP_INVENTORY that do not already exist in SHIP_INVENTORY, limited to LAST_ORDER values from the year 2009.

D. It will add rows from PORT_INVENTORY to SHIP_INVENTORY that do not already exist in SHIP_INVENTORY, regardless of the value for LAST_ORDER.

12. Examine the SQL syntax in the last statement. Which of the following two alternatives for line 3 are syntactically correct?

```
OPTION 1:   ON (A.NUM = B.NUM AND A.AISLE = B.AISLE)
OPTION 2:   ON (A.LAST_ORDER < B.LAST_ORDER)
```

A. Only option 1

B. Only option 2

C. Both option 1 and option 2

D. Neither option 1 nor option 2

Track the Changes to Data over a Period of Time

13. Which one of the following is a valid SQL statement?

A.
```
SELECT *
FROM SHIPS
AS OF TIMESTAMP SYSTIMESTAMP - INTERVAL '0 00:30:00' DAY TO SECOND;
```

B.
```
SELECT *
FROM SHIPS
WHERE VERSIONS BETWEEN IN (MINVALUE AND MAXVALUE);
```

C.
```
SELECT *
FROM SHIPS
AS OF SCN (SELECT ORA_ROWSCN-50
           FROM SHIPS
           WHERE ROWNUM < 2);
```

D.
```
SELECT *
FROM SHIPS
AS OF DATE SYSDATE - INTERVAL '0 00:30:00' DAY TO SECOND;
```

14. How does a table change as the result of the execution of a valid flashback operation using the AS OF clause?

   A. The table is restored to its state at the beginning of the undo retention period.

   B. The table is enhanced with additional historic data it did not contain before.

   C. It's impossible to know what happens to the table.

   D. No change occurs to the table.

15. Examine this SQL code (line numbers added):

```
01   CREATE TABLE PROMOTIONS
02      (PROMOTION_ID NUMBER(7),
03       PROMOTER     VARCHAR2(30));
04   INSERT INTO PROMOTIONS VALUES (1,'Barnum');
05   COMMIT;
06   EXECUTE DBMS_LOCK.SLEEP('120');
07   UPDATE PROMOTIONS SET PROMOTER = 'P.T. Barnum.'
08        WHERE PROMOTION_ID = 1;
09   INSERT INTO PROMOTIONS VALUES (2,'D. King');
10   EXECUTE DBMS_LOCK.SLEEP('240');
11   DELETE FROM PROMOTIONS;
12   COMMIT;
13   SELECT     PROMOTION_ID, PROMOTER, VERSIONS_OPERATION,
14              RAWTOHEX(VERSIONS_XID) VERSIONS_XID
15      FROM    PROMOTIONS
16      VERSIONS BETWEEN TIMESTAMP MINVALUE AND MAXVALUE;
```

The SELECT statement on line 13 will return data that includes values for VERSIONS_XID. Which SQL statements will be represented in the output of this SELECT statement? Choose all that apply.

   A. Line 4—INSERT

   B. Line 7—UPDATE

   C. Line 9—INSERT

   D. Line 11—DELETE

SELF TEST ANSWERS

Manipulate Data Using Subqueries

1. ☑ **D.** None of the items listed is a restriction on the subquery of a CTAS.
   ☒ **A, B,** and **C** are incorrect. Joins are allowed. The subquery is not required to have column names for each column specified if the CTAS provides names in the CREATE TABLE clause. Returned data is not required.

2. ☑ **D.** There is no keyword for this form of INSERT statement. The subquery itself is sufficient and correct.
   ☒ **A, B,** and **C** are incorrect. Any attempt to use the keywords VALUES, AS, or IN in this context will result in a syntax error.

Describe the Features of Multitable INSERTs

3. ☑ **A** and **B.** INSERT statements can add rows to more than one table using conditional and unconditional logic. INSERT statements can also add data to more than one column in any given table.
   ☒ **C** and **D** are incorrect. INSERT cannot overwrite data; it adds new rows to a table. INSERT does not perform joins.

4. ☑ **C.** Multitable INSERT statements can use conditional logic, with statements such as WHEN and ELSE.
   ☒ **A, B,** and **D** are incorrect. Multitable INSERTS do not do anything you couldn't otherwise do with one or more SQL statements. Their advantage is that they can accomplish complex SQL tasks in a single pass that might otherwise require multiple passes through the database, thus yielding performance advantages. And nothing can add rows into a non-updatable view—if it's not updatable, it's not updatable.

Use the Following Types of Multitable INSERTs: Unconditional, Conditional, and Pivot

5. ☑ **C.** The WHEN condition in line 2 determines whether the INTO clauses in lines 3, 4, 5, and 6 will execute.
   ☒ **A, B,** and **D** are incorrect. The ELSE clause is not required. No particular WHEN condition is required. The INTO clause for SHIP_INVENTORY is subject to the WHEN condition in line 2.

6. ☑ **C.** The entire statement fails, and all inserted rows are rolled back. It is as if the statement had never been executed. Had this statement included any calls to a sequence generator and its NEXTVAL pseudocolumn would have advanced the count in the generator, that effect would remain unchanged. However, this example does not include any sequence generators, so that particular exception does not apply.

   ☒ **A, B,** and **D** are incorrect.

7. ☑ **C.** The PART_NO of 170 has a length of 3, and that is longer than 2, so the WHERE clause in line 13 is found to be true, and the row will be evaluated by the rest of the INSERT FIRST statement. Next, the PART_NAME of PAN-OPS will cause the first WHEN condition to be true, and since this is an INSERT FIRST statement, no other WHEN condition will be considered.

   ☒ **A, B,** and **D** are incorrect. These answers result from various interpretations of the WHEN conditions and ELSE. In an INSERT FIRST statement, the first WHEN condition that evaluates to true is the only condition that is executed. All others are ignored. If no WHEN is found to be true, then the optional ELSE clause will be processed.

8. ☑ **D.** Both WHEN conditions will be evaluated because the conditional INSERT is an INSERT ALL statement.

   ☒ **A, B,** and **C** are incorrect. If the first WHEN condition is true, both INTO clauses that follow it will be executed—that includes the INTO on line 5 through line 6. Whether the first WHEN condition is true or false, the second will also be evaluated, since this is an INSERT ALL statement. The INTO in line 5 through line 6 will only be evaluated if the first WHEN condition is true.

9. ☑ **A.** The statement will yield a syntax error and not execute. No sequence generator is allowed in the subquery.

   ☒ **B, C,** and **D** are incorrect. Oracle Corporation formally advises against using a sequence generator in a multitable INSERT statement. While it will be rejected in the subquery, a sequence generator may be included in the VALUES clause of the INTO statement but with potentially unpredictable or undesirable results.

Merge Rows in a Table

10. ☑ **C.** The USING clause is not optional; it is required in the MERGE statement.

    ☒ **A, B,** and **D** are incorrect. USING can identify a table, view, or subquery. An inline view is also acceptable. It identifies the source of data to be merged; the source data remains unchanged after the MERGE statement is executed.

11. ☑ **B.** It will fail because the WHERE clause references something that is not in the source table. The WHERE clause is an extension of USING, which specifies the target table. The A table alias reference is meaningless and will fail.

☒ **A, C,** and **D** are incorrect. There is no ELSE clause in MERGE, so it is not only not required, it is not accepted.

12. ☑ **C.** Both options are acceptable. The ON condition can be any comparison of expressions, and it can include Boolean operators.

☒ **A, B,** and **D** are incorrect individually.

Track the Changes to Data over a Period of Time

13. ☑ **A.** The statement SELECT with AS OF TIMESTAMP is syntactically correct.

☒ **B, C,** and **D** are incorrect. You do not put VERSIONS BETWEEN after the WHERE clause, much less as a part of the WHERE clause. VERSIONS BETWEEN, if used, precedes the WHERE clause, if used. Also, VERSIONS BETWEEN does not use the IN keyword. The AS OF SCN clause cannot take a subquery as an argument. The AS OF clause only works with SCN and TIMESTAMP, not DATE values, so the SYSDATE option won't be accepted, nor will the DATE keyword.

14. ☑ **D.** No change occurs to the table. Flashback operations leverage data that is already in the undo segments, but cause no changes to occur to the table.

☒ **A, B,** and **C** are incorrect.

15. ☑ **A** and **D.** The INSERT on line 4 was committed, and the row it created was removed with the DELETE statement in line 11, which was also committed. The other statements were not explicitly committed, so therefore are not included.

☒ **B** and **C** are incorrect. The UPDATE in line 7 was not committed, nor was the INSERT in line 9; both were removed with the DELETE before a COMMIT event occurred, therefore they were omitted. The curious thing about this DELETE statement is that it removed the committed row from line 4, and the uncommitted changes from lines 7 and 9. Only the committed events are identified in the VERSIONS BETWEEN feature, so some of the DELETE statement's effects are tracked, but others are not.

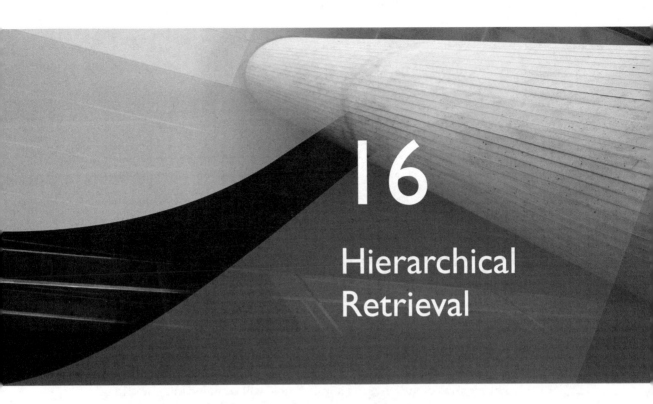

16

Hierarchical Retrieval

T his chapter discusses the *hierarchical query* which is based on data structured in a self-join table or view. The hierarchical query uses clauses in the SELECT statement to create a dynamic, tree-structured report appropriate for corporate organization charts, a distribution chain, family genealogy research, or any situation that requires a multilevel data structure.

Interpret the Concept of a Hierarchical Query

The hierarchical query extends the typical parent-child relationship into a multigenerational construct. In the typical parent-child relationship, one table will contain parent rows, and another table will contain child rows. In other words, only two generations are represented. For example, we've already seen our PORTS table, which contains data about ports, and where each port can be home to one or more ships in the SHIPS table. In this situation, each PORT row may be a parent to any SHIP row. In other words, we have the parent row's generation, and the child row's generation, and no more generations beyond these two.

Hierarchical data is structured differently to allow for the possibility of multiple generations. Instead of two separate tables with one parent table and one child table, all data is contained within a single table or comparable structure (such as a view), and the multiple generations are defined based on the data within each row. The result is that we might have parent–child–grandchild–great-grandchild, and so on. The hierarchical structure allows for a theoretically endless number of generations.

The classic example of a hierarchy is an organization chart, in which a CEO is the top level, or the root node, and everyone in the organization who reports directly to the CEO is a *child* record at the second level. Furthermore, each employee who reports to the second level is a *grandchild* of the root node and exists at the third level relative to the root node, and so on (see Figure 16-1). The first level shows the CEO, which serves as the *root node* of this hierarchy. The second level consists of *nodes* that report to the root node. Each of these represents a *branch* in the *tree*, where the CFO ends its particular branch, making it a *leaf node*. But the other two nodes continue to Level 3, and so on.

Nodes that extend to two or more additional nodes at the next level are considered *forks*. Nodes that do not fork are just nodes. For example—see

FIGURE 16-1

Architecture of a
hierarchical join

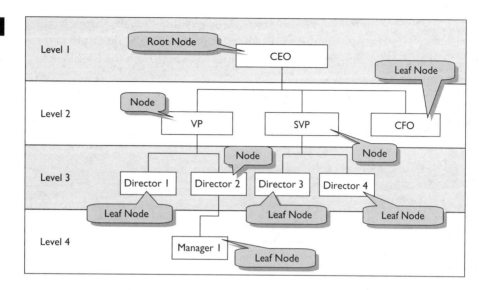

"Director 2" in Level 3. The organization branches from that node to Level 4, but only to one node of "Manager 1", so the "Director 2" node would not be considered a fork. But the nodes for the VP and SVP would be considered forks.

In SQL, the structure that would hold all of the information for these nodes and their relationships may consist of just one table with a self-join. Let's look at an example.

First, let's create a table that will support a hierarchical structure:

```
CREATE TABLE EMPLOYEE_CHART
(  EMPLOYEE_ID  NUMBER(7) PRIMARY KEY,
   TITLE        VARCHAR2(20),
   REPORTS_TO   NUMBER(7));
```

The EMPLOYEE_CHART table will store data from our organizational chart in Figure 16-1. For the table, we created a PRIMARY KEY constraint. We also included a column for TITLE, showing the titles from Figure 16-1. We also added a column called REPORTS_TO that will contain the EMPLOYEE_ID of the superior in the organization. In order to apply a constraint to this column, let's add a foreign key for it:

```
ALTER TABLE EMPLOYEE_CHART
  ADD CONSTRAINT FK_EM_EM
     FOREIGN KEY (REPORTS_TO)
     REFERENCES EMPLOYEE_CHART (EMPLOYEE_ID);
```

This foreign key isn't necessarily required to make the hierarchical query perform correctly. But it's good design; it documents the intention of the REPORTS_TO column, showing that its values will come from the EMPLOYEE_ID column of the same table.

Next we'll add the following data so that the table's contents appear as follows:

```
EMPLOYEE_ID            TITLE                   REPORTS_TO
--------------------   -------------------     ----------------------
1                      CEO
2                      VP                      1
3                      SVP                     1
4                      CFO                     1
5                      Director 1              2
6                      Director 2              2
7                      Director 3              3
8                      Director 4              3
9                      Manager 1               6
```

Note the structure, where each row contains a primary key value for EMPLOYEE_ID, and also a foreign key in the REPORTS_TO column. The value for REPORTS_TO is the EMPLOYEE_ID value of another row. For example, "Manager 1" reports to "Director 2" as evidenced by the REPORTS_TO column's value of 6, which matches the EMPLOYEE_ID for "Director 2".

This is the type of data structure that supports a hierarchical query. This relationship is a "self-join" and is fully extensible—the levels in the hierarchy can easily be extended beyond the four levels represented here.

To create a hierarchical query on this data structure, we'll need to look at some new features of the SELECT statement, which we address in the next section.

CERTIFICATION OBJECTIVE 16.02

Create and Format Hierarchical Data

In our last section, we built a data structure to support a hierarchical query. The diagram for that structure is represented in Figure 16-2.

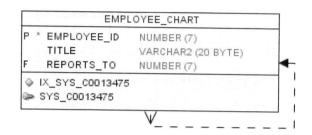

FIGURE 16-2

Diagram for the
EMPLOYEE_
CHART table

To create a hierarchical query, we use the SELECT statement clauses START
WITH and CONNECT BY, as follows (line numbers added):

```
01    SELECT      LEVEL, EMPLOYEE_ID, TITLE
02    FROM        EMPLOYEE_CHART
03    START WITH  EMPLOYEE_ID = 1
04    CONNECT BY REPORTS_TO = PRIOR EMPLOYEE_ID;
```

In the preceding SQL statement, we do the following:

- Line 3: The START WITH clause identifies the root node of our query. In
  this case, we're choosing to start with the row containing information about
  the CEO, which we specify by identifying a START WITH EMPLOYEE_ID
  = 1, which is pointing to the primary key of the CEO. It is good design to use
  the primary key here, but it's not syntactically necessary—any expression that
  uniquely identifies a row in the table will accomplish the task.

- Line 4: We establish the self-join hierarchical relationship using CONNECT
  BY and PRIOR. By specifying that we wish to connect each row by relating
  the REPORTS_TO column to the EMPLOYEE_ID column, we're identifying
  the values to use when comparing one row to another. But the placement
  of the keyword PRIOR is critical—it must be placed before one of the two
  column references. The choice determines if the hierarchy will traverse up
  the tree or down the tree from the START WITH row. In this example,
  PRIOR is placed before the EMPLOYEE_ID reference. This indicates that for
  each row in the EMPLOYEE_CHART table, SQL will go find the next row
  in the hierarchy by locating a row with a REPORTS_TO value that is equal
  to the PRIOR row's EMPLOYEE_ID value.

- Line 1: We've chosen to add a reference to the LEVEL pseudocolumn, which
  is available to any hierarchical query that uses the START WITH and
  CONNECT BY clause. Once the keywords START WITH and CONNECT

BY are included, LEVEL is automatically defined to show the hierarchical level of the row relative to the root node of the hierarchical query, as defined in the START WITH clause. Its use isn't required.

The output of this query looks like this:

```
LEVEL                  EMPLOYEE_ID            TITLE
----------------       ----------------       -------------------
1                      1                      CEO
2                      2                      VP
3                      5                      Director 1
3                      6                      Director 2
4                      9                      Manager 1
2                      3                      SVP
3                      7                      Director 3
3                      8                      Director 4
2                      4                      CFO
```

Notice that the LEVEL value corresponds to the diagram we looked at originally in Figure 16-1. That happens to be true in this situation because we chose to START WITH the CEO node and work our way down the tree. However, note that the value for LEVEL is calculated relative to the root node of the query, and we could have chosen a different root node within this same data. More on that in a bit.

Oracle formally stipulates that the CONNECT BY clause must have one occurrence of the keyword PRIOR included within it. This is documented but as of this writing isn't built into the system—you will not receive a syntax error if you omit the PRIOR clause. But note that you are required to include it in order to satisfy the documented requirements of the CONNECT BY clause.

The START WITH and CONNECT BY clauses are both required to create a hierarchical query. The order of clauses is not important—either clause can precede the other. However, the SELECT statement's WHERE clause, if used, must precede both START WITH and CONNECT BY. Furthermore, the ORDER BY clause, if used, follows both START WITH and CONNECT BY. And beware, the ORDER BY clause, when used with hierarchical queries, requires special consideration, which we'll get in to a bit later.

Create a Tree-Structured Report

One common technique for using LEVEL is to incorporate it into some formatting functions to produce more readable output. For example, the LPAD function can be used to add spaces and indent the TITLE values based on the level each value represents. Here's an example:

```
SELECT      LEVEL, EMPLOYEE_ID, LPAD(' ', LEVEL*2) || TITLE TITLE
FROM        EMPLOYEE_CHART
START WITH EMPLOYEE_ID = 1
CONNECT BY REPORTS_TO = PRIOR EMPLOYEE_ID;
```

This query concatenates spaces in front of the TITLE data to indent the start of whatever value is included in each row. In this example, LPAD will add more spaces for greater levels; for each LEVEL, two spaces are indented. The results are as follows:

LEVEL	EMPLOYEE_ID	TITLE
1	1	CEO
2	2	VP
3	5	Director 1
3	6	Director 2
4	9	Manager 1
2	3	SVP
3	7	Director 3
3	8	Director 4
2	4	CFO

The result is output that is easier to read—as you glance down the column of values for TITLE, you can see more easily where TITLE values of the same level are lined up.

This sort of technique is one common way to display hierarchical data from a self-join.

Choosing Direction

In a hierarchical query, the choice of where to place the keyword PRIOR is instrumental in determining the direction of the query. Our example started with the CEO row and moved down through the chain of command:

```
CONNECT BY REPORTS_TO = PRIOR EMPLOYEE_ID
```

To move in the opposite direction, move the PRIOR keyword to the opposite side of the equal sign, like this:

```
CONNECT BY PRIOR REPORTS_TO = EMPLOYEE_ID
```

However, if your query is starting at one end of the hierarchy already, then to move in the opposite direction won't get you more than one row—you're already at one end of the query. A reverse hierarchical query is more helpful when starting at another location in the hierarchy, such as one of the leaf nodes of the overall organization chart, like this:

```
SELECT      LEVEL, EMPLOYEE_ID, LPAD(' ', LEVEL*2) || TITLE TITLE
FROM        EMPLOYEE_CHART
START WITH EMPLOYEE_ID = 9
CONNECT BY PRIOR REPORTS_TO = EMPLOYEE_ID;
```

Here we are beginning our hierarchy with EMPLOYEE_ID = 9, which is the "Manager 1" title, and moving up the org chart toward the CEO, as is indicated by reversing the position of the keyword PRIOR. The results are as follows:

LEVEL	EMPLOYEE_ID	TITLE
1	9	Manager 1
2	6	Director 2
3	2	VP
4	1	CEO

Notice that this results in a more limited number of rows. By starting from the position of the "Manager 1" row and working our way up, we are only connecting to those rows in the hierarchy that have a directly upward relationship to the starting point.

Note that the LEVEL value shows the level relative to the root node of the query—not necessarily the root node of the overall hierarchy within the table. In other words, in our example, "Manager 1" is at LEVEL 1, and the CEO is at LEVEL 4.

We are not limited to starting our hierarchical query from the root node or a leaf node; we could initiate from somewhere within the query at any node and work in either direction.

Remember, to reverse direction in a hierarchical query, move PRIOR to the other side of the equal sign. Also, if you prefix a column name with PRIOR in the select list (SELECT PRIOR EMPLOYEE_ID, ...), you specify the "prior" row's value.

ORDER SIBLINGS BY

You have to be careful when trying to order the rows of output in a hierarchical query. By default, if you omit the ORDER BY clause altogether, the query attempts to sort rows in an order that's reflective of the hierarchy. Display will start first with a LEVEL 1 row. If that row is superior to any LEVEL 2 rows, those rows will display next before another LEVEL 1 row displays. The same approach is taken at LEVEL 2, so that rows will display down to leaf node levels before the next rows show at the higher levels. The result is a display that is meaningful to the hierarchy. But if you try to order these rows with the ORDER BY clause, you'll create a syntactically correct statement that probably doesn't help you much, such as this:

```
SELECT      LEVEL, EMPLOYEE_ID, LPAD(' ', LEVEL*2) || TITLE TITLE_FORMATTED
FROM        EMPLOYEE_CHART
START WITH EMPLOYEE_ID = 1
CONNECT BY REPORTS_TO = PRIOR EMPLOYEE_ID
ORDER BY TITLE;
```

In this example, we've changed the alias for the reformatted TITLE column to TITLE_FORMATTED. This way, we can reference the original unformatted version of the TITLE column in our ORDER BY clause. Another way would have been to use ORDER BY 3, but in this case we've chosen to stick with the column name. Either way, the results come out somewhat meaningless, like this—here is the output of our sample query:

```
LEVEL             EMPLOYEE_ID        TITLE_FORMATTED
----------------- ------------------ -----------------------
1                 1                  CEO
2                 4                    CFO
3                 5                      Director 1
3                 6                      Director 2
3                 7                      Director 3
3                 8                      Director 4
4                 9                        Manager 1
2                 3                    SVP
2                 2                    VP
```

Look carefully at this output. It is not what you might think it is. For example, the four "Director" titles all appear to report to the CFO. But as we've seen earlier—they really don't. All we have here is an alphabetical listing of TITLE values, but their row ordering is not consistent with their position in the hierarchy. They are each indented correctly, but not necessarily underneath their direct report.

This is where we might use the ORDER SIBLINGS BY clause instead. Let's do the same query with this one change, and we'll see very different results:

```
SELECT      LEVEL, EMPLOYEE_ID, LPAD(' ', LEVEL*2) || TITLE TITLE_FORMATTED
FROM        EMPLOYEE_CHART
START WITH EMPLOYEE_ID = 1
CONNECT BY REPORTS_TO = PRIOR EMPLOYEE_ID
ORDER SIBLINGS BY TITLE;
```

LEVEL	EMPLOYEE_ID	TITLE_FORMATTED
1	1	CEO
2	4	CFO
2	3	SVP
3	7	Director 3
3	8	Director 4
2	2	VP
3	5	Director 1
3	6	Director 2
4	9	Manager 1

Notice that our TITLE values are now alphabetized for a given level, but not across all levels. The rows are sorted within their hierarchical structure. That's because ORDER SIBLINGS sorts rows within each given level, not across levels, thus retaining the hierarchical relationship across rows of output.

Note that our earlier use of ORDER BY did not create an error message, just misleading output. So be careful here—ORDER SIBLINGS BY is what you want to use if you are trying to sort rows in a hierarchical query.

SYS_CONNECT_BY_PATH

The SYS_CONNECT_BY_PATH function is a useful feature for formatting hierarchical data output. It takes two arguments: a column you wish to include as data, and an expression used to separate each level represented within the output. It takes two parameters:

- The first parameter is the value to be displayed within the path.
- The second parameter is a separating character.

Here's an example:

```
SELECT      LEVEL, EMPLOYEE_ID, SYS_CONNECT_BY_PATH(TITLE,'/') TITLE
FROM        EMPLOYEE_CHART
START WITH EMPLOYEE_ID = 1
CONNECT BY REPORTS_TO = PRIOR EMPLOYEE_ID;
```

LEVEL	EMPLOYEE_ID	TITLE
1	1	/CEO
2	2	/CEO/VP
3	5	/CEO/VP/Director 1
3	6	/CEO/VP/Director 2
4	9	/CEO/VP/Director 2/Manager 1
2	3	/CEO/SVP
3	7	/CEO/SVP/Director 3
3	8	/CEO/SVP/Director 4
2	4	/CEO/CFO

This output shows the full path from the root node in each row. The character separating each level within the string comes from the second argument of the SYS_CONNECT_BY_PATH function.

CONNECT_BY_ROOT

The CONNECT_BY_ROOT operator will display any data from the root node row of a given row. Like the PRIOR operator, it is only valid in hierarchical queries. In other words, no matter which row of output prints in the hierarchical query's output, that row is capable of accessing data from the same root node row with the CONNECT_BY_ROOT operator. It takes one parameter—an expression that will be processed against the root node's row to determine the response. Generally, a column of the root node row is included in the parameter. For example:

```
SELECT      LEVEL, EMPLOYEE_ID, TITLE, CONNECT_BY_ROOT TITLE AS ANCESTOR
FROM        EMPLOYEE_CHART
START WITH EMPLOYEE_ID = 3
CONNECT BY REPORTS_TO = PRIOR EMPLOYEE_ID;
```

This example starts with a root node of EMPLOYEE_ID of 3, which is the SVP title. Therefore, any row's attempt to use the CONNECT_BY_ROOT operator will reference that same root node row, no matter the requesting row. In this example, for each row, our reference to CONNECT_BY_ROOT is showing the TITLE column from the root node row, which is the SVP row, and giving the output the column alias of ANCESTOR:

LEVEL	EMPLOYEE_ID	TITLE	ANCESTOR
1	3	SVP	SVP
2	7	Director 3	SVP
2	8	Director 4	SVP

The CONNECT_BY_ROOT operator empowers any row in the hierarchical query's output to directly reference any data from within the root node row.

CERTIFICATION OBJECTIVE 16.03

Exclude Branches from the Tree Structure

You can use the WHERE clause in a hierarchical query to filter out specific rows from your output, just as you would with any other query. But with a hierarchical query, you can go further: you can selectively restrict entire branches of the tree of your output. This is done from within the CONNECT BY clause.

For example, if we go back to our original query that starts with the CEO and shows all of our organization, we can choose to exclude, say, the branch starting with the SVP position and every subordinate row. Here's the query:

```
SELECT      LEVEL, EMPLOYEE_ID, LPAD(' ', LEVEL*2) || TITLE TITLE
FROM        EMPLOYEE_CHART
START WITH EMPLOYEE_ID = 1
CONNECT BY REPORTS_TO = PRIOR EMPLOYEE_ID
   AND      EMPLOYEE_ID <> 3;
```

The query will exclude the EMPLOYEE_ID of 3, which is the TITLE value of 'SVP'. Now—the hierarchical query is generated by traversing the tree and moving from the root node to the leaf nodes logically from row to row. By excluding the EMPLOYEE_ID value of 3 in the CONNECT BY clause, you essentially tell the query to ignore that entire branch. The result:

LEVEL	EMPLOYEE_ID	TITLE
1	1	CEO
2	2	VP
3	5	Director 1

```
       3                         6                          Director 2
       4                         9                           Manager 1
       2                         4                         CFO
```

Notice that the SVP and all subordinate rows are gone.

In this particular example, we could have achieved the same result with this query:

```
SELECT     LEVEL, EMPLOYEE_ID, LPAD(' ', LEVEL*2) || TITLE TITLE
FROM       EMPLOYEE_CHART
START WITH EMPLOYEE_ID = 1
CONNECT BY REPORTS_TO = PRIOR EMPLOYEE_ID
    AND    TITLE <> 'SVP';
```

In other words, all you're doing in the CONNECT BY is identifying rows by finding some sort of data that can identify the row. There's no particular requirement to use the primary key column—although it can be good design, depending on the situation.

As we have seen in this example, the CONNECT BY can use Boolean operators such as AND and OR in its syntax. Also, functions can be used to formulate expressions in much the same way that a WHERE clause would do.

Note: if you wish to include a WHERE clause, it is placed before the START WITH clause. For example, assuming we have a table FORMER_EMPLOYEES with a primary key column called ID, we could do something like this:

```
SELECT     LEVEL, EMPLOYEE_ID, LPAD(' ', LEVEL*2) || TITLE TITLE
FROM       EMPLOYEE_CHART
WHERE      EMPLOYEE_ID NOT IN (SELECT ID FROM FORMER_EMPLOYEES)
START WITH EMPLOYEE_ID = 1
CONNECT BY REPORTS_TO = PRIOR EMPLOYEE_ID
    AND    TITLE <> 'SVP';
```

This query shows how a WHERE clause can be included, provided it precedes the START WITH clause.

exam **watch**

It's theoretically possible to use the WHERE clause to omit rows that will collectively represent an entire branch. But that's not the same thing as identifying a branch and excluding it as a branch. CONNECT BY is the clause that can identify a branch and exclude it in its entirety.

CERTIFICATION SUMMARY

The hierarchical query is a feature in SQL that can create tree-structured output from row-based table data. It requires a particular structure that involves a table—or view—that is structured as a self-join, with hierarchical relationships defined within the primary key and foreign key relationship of the self-join. Typical examples are organization charts of employees or divisions, family trees, or any other data structure in which multiple generations of parent-child-grandchild-etc. relationships may exist.

Any row of data within the hierarchy is considered a "node". The starting point, or trunk, is the "root node". A node that has two more children is considered a "fork". A node that has no children is a "leaf node".

The syntax for the hierarchical query uses the START WITH clause to define the root node of the hierarchy. The CONNECT BY clause defines the self-join as well as the direction in which the query will traverse the tree, or hierarchy. The keyword PRIOR is used within the CONNECT BY clause to determine the direction of the query. CONNECT BY may also be used to exclude any node, in which case all associated child records will be excluded as well; the effect is to exclude the entire branch represented by the excluded node.

The pseudocolumn LEVEL is automatically calculated to display the value corresponding to the level within the hierarchy, where LEVEL 1 is the root node, LEVEL 2 is the child level relative to the root, and so on. The LEVEL pseudocolumn is helpful in formatting output to create indentation of data and thus highlight the nature of the hierarchy in displayed output.

START WITH and CONNECT BY may appear in any order within the SELECT statement. However, the WHERE clause, if used in the SELECT statement, must precede the CONNECT BY and START WITH clauses. The ORDER BY clause may be used, but it must follow the CONNECT BY and START WITH clauses. The ORDER BY clause is tricky, however, in that it sorts rows without respect to the hierarchical ordering of data. The better choice for sorting rows is probably ORDER SIBLINGS BY, depending on the desired result.

The function SYS_CONNECT_BY_PATH can show the complete path from root node to current node for any given node. The CONNECT_BY_ROOT operator can be called from within any node's row to reference data from the root node row.

TWO-MINUTE DRILL

Interpret the Concept of a Hierarchical Query

❑ A hierarchical query extends the parent-child relationship into a structure that can be multigenerational, in which multiple levels of relationships may be added to a given table so that each row may form a relationship at a new generational level beyond the typical parent-child-grandchild-etc. relationship.

❑ Hierarchical queries are based on a self-join table.

❑ All rows in a hierarchical query represent a node.

❑ The starting point of the hierarchical query is the root node.

❑ Any node that branches into two or more children is a fork.

❑ Any node that ends with no children is a leaf node.

Create and Format Hierarchical Data

❑ The SELECT statement clauses START WITH and CONNECT BY are used to form a hierarchical query.

❑ The START WITH clause identifies the root node.

❑ The CONNECT BY clause defines the self-join relationships.

❑ There must be at least one use of the PRIOR keyword in the CONNECT BY, according to Oracle's documentation.

❑ The PRIOR row determines the direction of the hierarchical query.

❑ The pseudocolumn LEVEL identifies the generational level from the root node.

❑ The ORDER SIBLINGS BY clause sorts rows within a generational level without compromising the default hierarchical ordering of output rows.

❑ The SYS_CONNECT_BY_PATH function can show the complete path to any given node from the root node within a single data element.

❑ The CONNECT_BY_ROOT operator can reference a root node row from any row of a hierarchical query.

❑ The order of clauses, if used, in a SELECT statement is SELECT, FROM, WHERE, START WITH, CONNECT BY, and ORDER BY, where the START WITH and CONNECT BY can be interchanged.

Exclude Branches from the Tree Structure

❑ The CONNECT BY clause can be used to exclude complete branches from the tree.

❑ The WHERE clause can exclude individual rows but will not exclude complete branches automatically.

SELF TEST

The following questions will help you measure your understanding of the material presented in this chapter. Choose one correct answer for each question unless otherwise directed.

Interpret the Concept of a Hierarchical Query

1. The earliest ancestor in a hierarchy is known as the: (Choose the best answer.)

A. Fork

B. Leaf node

C. Root node

D. Grandchild

2. Which of the following join conditions is generally associated with a hierarchical query? (Choose the best answer.)

A. Self-join

B. Natural join

C. Nonequijoin

D. None in particular

3. Examine the data model and data listing for the DISTRIBUTORS table shown below.

DISTRIBUTORS		
P * ID	NUMBER (3)	
LOCATION	VARCHAR2 (20 BYTE)	
LOC_TYPE	VARCHAR2 (10 BYTE)	
F UPLINE	NUMBER (3)	
◇ IX_SYS_C0013505		
⊶ SYS_C0013505		

ID	LOCATION	LOC_TYPE	UPLINE
1	New York	HQ	
2	Memphis	REGIONAL	1
3	Minneapolis	REGIONAL	1
4	Salt Lake	REGIONAL	1
5	Atlanta	LOCAL	2
6	Wichita	LOCAL	2
7	Sacramento	LOCAL	4
8	El Paso	LOCAL	4

Which of the rows of output is a potential root node for a hierarchical query? (Choose all that apply.)

A. ID = 1

B. Any row with a LOC_TYPE of 'REGIONAL'

C. Any row with a LOC_TYPE of 'LOCAL'

D. ID = 7

Create and Format Hierarchical Data

4. To identify a root node, you must:

    A. Use the START WITH clause to identify a row, but only if you use the primary key.

    B. Use the START WITH clause to identify a row.

    C. Use the CONNECT BY clause to identify a row, but only if you use the primary key.

    D. Use the CONNECT BY clause to identify a row.

5. Examine the diagram and the data listing shown in question 3, then consider the following SQL statement (line numbers added):

```
01    SELECT LEVEL, LOC_TYPE, LOCATION, CONNECT_BY_ROOT(LOC_TYPE)
02    FROM    DISTRIBUTORS
03    START WITH ID = 7
04    CONNECT BY PRIOR UPLINE = ID;
```

What will be the value for LEVEL for the row with a LOCATION value of 'Sacramento'?

    A. 1

    B. 2

    C. 3

    D. 4

6. Examine the diagram and the data listing shown in question 3, and consider the SQL statement shown in question 5. How many total rows will result from the query?

    A. 0

    B. 1

    C. 3

    D. 8

7. Examine the diagram and the data listing shown in question 3, along with the SQL statement shown in question 5. For this example, which of the following could replace line 3 to establish the root node as New York?

    A. START WITH LOCATION = 'New York'

    B. START WITH PRIOR ID

C. START WITH ROOT NODE

D. None of the above

8. Examine the diagram and the data listing shown in question 3, along with the SQL statement shown in question 5. Which of the following statements will be true of the values displayed in the fourth column of output, as indicated by the fourth expression in the SELECT list, specified at the end of line 1? (Choose two.)

A. The value will be the same for each row of output.

B. The value will be NULL for the first row of output.

C. At least one row will display the value 'LOCAL' for the fourth column.

D. At least one row will display the value 'HQ' for the fourth column.

9. Examine the diagram and the data listing shown in question 3, along with the SQL statement in question 5. How could you edit the SQL statement to reverse the direction of the hierarchical output?

A. Change line 3 to START WITH to ID = 1.

B. Change line 4 to CONNECT BY UPLINE = PRIOR ID.

C. Add as line 5 ORDER BY LOCATION DESC.

D. It can't be done.

10. According to Oracle's documentation, how many occurrences of the keyword PRIOR must exist in a CONNECT BY clause?

A. 0

B. 1

C. 2

D. There is no rule

11. Which of the following options is a list of SELECT statement clauses in the proper order in which they can appear in a syntactically correct SELECT statement?

A. SELECT, FROM, START WITH, CONNECT BY, WHERE

B. SELECT, FROM, WHERE, CONNECT BY, START WITH

C. SELECT, FROM, START WITH, WHERE, CONNECT BY

D. None of the above

12. Examine the diagram and the data listing shown in question 3, and the following hierarchical query SQL statement (line numbers added):

```
01   SELECT LEVEL, LOC_TYPE, LOCATION
02   FROM   DISTRIBUTORS
03   START WITH LOC_TYPE = 'HQ'
04   CONNECT BY UPLINE = PRIOR ID
05   ORDER BY LOCATION;
```

What will be true of the output from this SQL statement?

A.   There will only be one row of output.

B.   The statement will fail because of a syntax error in line 3.

C.   The statement will execute and produce output as intended.

D.   The rows will not be sorted hierarchically.

13.   Which of the following functions can list, for a given node, the complete hierarchical path to that node from the root node?

A.   SYS_CONNECT_BY_PATH

B.   CONNECT_BY_ROOT

C.   START_WITH

D.   CONNECT_BY

Exclude Branches from the Tree Structure

14.   Which clause of the SELECT statement is used to exclude entire branches from the output of a hierarchical query?

A.   START WITH

B.   CONNECT BY

C.   WHERE

D.   HAVING

15.   Examine the diagram and the data listing shown in question 3, along with the following hierarchical query SQL statement (line numbers added):

```
01    SELECT LEVEL, LOC_TYPE, LOCATION
02    FROM   DISTRIBUTORS
03    WHERE  LOCATION <> 'El Paso'
04    START WITH LOC_TYPE = 'HQ'
05    CONNECT BY PRIOR ID = UPLINE
06                  AND ID <> 4;
```

What will be true of the output from this SQL statement?

A.   The row with a LOCATION of 'New York' will be omitted from output.

B.   The row with a LOCATION of 'Sacramento' will be omitted from output.

C.   All three rows with a LOC_TYPE of 'REGIONAL' will be displayed.

D.   None of the above.

SELF TEST ANSWERS

Interpret the Concept of a Hierarchical Query

1. ☑ **C.** The "root node" is the best answer.
   ☒ **A, B,** and **D** are incorrect. A leaf node is the far end of any branch from the root node. A fork is any node that has two or more children. A grandchild is a third-level node below any given node.

2. ☑ **A.** Typically a self-join is associated with a hierarchical query.
   ☒ **B, C,** and **D** are incorrect. While these joins are theoretically possible as part of a structure that supports a hierarchical query, the self-join is more likely and the best answer.

3. ☑ **A, B, C,** and **D.** Any row is a potential candidate root node to be identified by the START WITH clause.
   ☒ **None** are incorrect.

Create and Format Hierarchical Data

4. ☑ **B.** The START WITH clause identifies the root node. And while the primary key is an ideal way to identify a row, it is not required by the START WITH clause.
   ☒ **A, C,** and **D** are incorrect.

5. ☑ **A.** The correct answer is 1, because 'Sacramento' has an ID of 7, and the START WITH clause defines that row as the root node for the query. The LEVEL pseudocolumn will assign a value of 1 to the root node of the hierarchical query.
   ☒ **B, C,** and **D** are incorrect.

6. ☑ **C.** The results will include three rows. The reason: the START WITH points to the row with an ID of 7, which is the LOCATION of 'Sacramento'. By specifying CONNECT BY PRIOR UPLINE = ID, the query is stipulating that it wishes to find the next row by finding a value of ID that matches the 'Sacramento' row value of UPLINE, since 'Sacramento' will be the "prior" row to the next row.
   ☒ **A, B,** and **D** are incorrect.

7. ☑ **A.** By specifying LOCATION = 'New York', the START WITH identifies the row for 'New York' and will start with that row. You could also have used START WITH ID = 1, which is ideal, since that's the primary key—but either works fine in this example.
   ☒ **B, C,** and **D** are incorrect. The keyword PRIOR doesn't apply here. The keywords ROOT NODE don't exist.

8. ☑ **A** and **C**. The values will be 'LOCAL' for every row of output. The reason: the CONNECT_BY_ROOT operator shows data for the root node, accessible by each row of output from the hierarchical query.

   ☒ **B** and **D** are incorrect. No value in this example will be NULL, since the root node of ID = 7 contains the value 'LOCAL' for the LOC_TYPE column.

9. ☑ **B**. By moving PRIOR to the other side of the equal sign in the CONNECT BY clause, you reverse the direction in which SQL will traverse the hierarchical tree.

   ☒ **A, C,** and **D** are incorrect. Changing START WITH will specify a different root node, but it will not reverse direction. Adding an ORDER BY clause will sort the output rows but not affect the hierarchical processing, which will include the assignment of values to the pseudocolumn LEVEL.

10. ☑ **B**. While you can get away syntactically with omitting the PRIOR keyword as of the writing of this book, Oracle's formally published position is that the CONNECT BY clause must have one proper usage of the PRIOR keyword in order to be correct.

    ☒ **A, C,** and **D** are incorrect.

11. ☑ **B**. The WHERE clause, if used, must precede the START WITH and CONNECT BY clauses. The START WITH and CONNECT BY clauses can appear in any order with respect to each other.

    ☒ **A, C,** and **D** are incorrect. Answer A is wrong because WHERE cannot follow CONNECT BY and/or START WITH. Answer C is wrong because START WITH cannot precede WHERE.

12. ☑ **D**. The ORDER BY clause will cause the rows to sort alphabetically by LOCATION, which will alter the hierarchical sorting of output. The better choice here would be ORDER SIBLINGS BY LOCATION.

    ☒ **A, B,** and **C** are incorrect. The output will display all of the eight rows of the table in this example. There is no syntax error in line 3; the reference to LOC_TYPE of 'HQ' will identify the row with an ID of 1 as the root node. But it's incorrect to say that the output will be produced as intended, since the ORDER BY clause is not what is typically used with a hierarchical query, but rather the ORDER SIBLINGS BY is the better choice, as is explained for the correct answer.

13. ☑ **A**. The SYS_CONNECT_BY_PATH is the correct function.

    ☒ **B, C,** and **D** are incorrect. CONNECT_BY_ROOT does not show the full list; it merely shows information from the root node row. There is no START_WITH function, nor a CONNECT_BY function; those are clauses of the SELECT statement—but without the underscores, as in START WITH and CONNECT BY.

Exclude Branches from the Tree Structure

14. ☑ **B.** CONNECT BY establishes the self-join and the direction of the hierarchy, and can also be used to exclude a hierarchical branch from the output listing.

☒ **A, C,** and **D** are incorrect. START WITH does not exclude branches, it establishes the root node. WHERE can exclude individual rows but not branches directly. HAVING can exclude groups identified in a GROUP BY clause, but it does not explicitly filter out branches from a hierarchical query.

15. ☑ **B.** The row with a LOCATION of 'Sacramento' will be omitted. The reason: because of the CONNECT BY including the expression ID <> 4, the hierarchical query will omit the row where ID = 4, which is 'Salt Lake'. The rest of the CONNECT BY specifies that the hierarchical processing will be traversing from the root node of LOC_TYPE = 'HQ', which in this case is LOCATION 'New York', and move to the next row by finding an UPLINE value that matches the prior row's ID value. So from ID = 1, we move to the next rows with an UPLINE of 1, but one of those is 'Salt Lake', which we are omitting via the ID <> 4 clause. Had we included 'Salt Lake', we would've traversed the hierarchy to the child rows of 'Salt Lake', which include 'Sacramento'. But by omitting 'Salt Lake', we never get 'Sacramento'. Hence, it is excluded from output.

☒ **A, C,** and **D** are incorrect. 'New York' is included—it's the root node identified in the START WITH clause—and nothing in the rest of the SQL statement omits the row. We won't get all rows with a LOC_TYPE of 'REGIONAL', since we are omitting 'Salt Lake'.

17
Regular Expression Support

This chapter explores the use of *regular expressions* in Oracle SQL. The term "regular expressions" refers to a specific language for working with text. You can use regular expressions to specify some complex character patterns and perform complex searches in a succinct and efficient manner.

Regular expressions have an identity that goes beyond SQL and Oracle. They are used in Unix, C, and elsewhere. This chapter will look at the functionality of regular expressions and Oracle SQL's capabilities for working with them.

CERTIFICATION OBJECTIVE 17.01

Using Metacharacters

The heart of regular expressions is the set of metacharacter operators. (Note: "meta character" is how it's spelled in the exam objectives list, but it's spelled "metacharacters" elsewhere in Oracle's documentation. We'll use "metacharacters", but don't be thrown if you see it spelled as two words elsewhere.) Metacharacter operators are special symbols and codes you use when defining patterns for searches using regular expressions. See Table 17-1 for a listing of the metacharacter operators, also known as regular expression operators. If you've worked with regular expressions before, this section will be a great refresher. If you've never worked with regular expressions before, it might not make much sense until we get to some examples— which we'll examine in the next section when we discuss how to use regular expressions with functions.

TABLE 17-1	#	Operator	Description
Regular Expression Operators	1	( )	Treats the enclosed expression or set of literals as a subexpression.
	2	[. . .]	A bracket expression, consisting of a pair of brackets enclosing a list of one or more expressions: collating elements, collating symbols, equivalence classes, character classes, or range expressions. The closing bracket symbol may have other meanings—it may appear within the expression as a part of one of the enclosed expressions; if not then it closes the bracket expression. The bracket expression forms a *matched list* when it opens with something other than the sequence "[.", "[:", or "[=", as detailed in entries 4, 5, and 6.

	#	Operator	Description
TABLE 17-1 Regular Expression Operators *(Continued)*	3	[^...]	A "not equals" bracket expression. The caret indicates that the enclosed expressions are not to be matched.
	4	[. . . . .]	Specifies a collation element in accordance with the current locale. Useful in situations where two or more characters are needed to specify a single collating element, such as in Czech, Welsh, and others, where 'ch' represents a single collating element. For example, to establish a range of letters from 'a' to 'ch', you would use [a..[.ch.]].
	5	[: . . . :]	Specifies a character class—see Table 17-2 and Table 17-3.
	6	[= . . . =]	Specifies an equivalence class. For example [=e=] represents e, é, è, ë, etc.
	7	.	Match any character in the database character set.
	8	?	Match zero or one occurrence of the preceding subexpression.
	9	*	Match zero or more occurrences of the preceding subexpression.
	10	+	Match one or more occurrences of the preceding subexpression.
	11	{n1}	Match precisely *n1* occurrences of the preceding subexpression.
	12	{n1,}	Match *n1* or more occurrences of the preceding subexpression.
	13	{n1,n2}	Match between *n1* to *n2* occurrences of the preceding subexpression, inclusive.
	14	\	Depending on the context, the backslash could be just a backslash. If it's followed by another regular expression operator, the backslash transforms that operator into a literal value. For example, \+ is a literal plus sign instead of the symbol to match one or more occurrences of the preceding subexpression, as is explained elsewhere in this table.
	15	\n1	Backreference. Repeats the '*n1*th' subexpression within the previous expression.
	16	|	Logical OR. Used to separate two expressions; one of the expressions is matched.
	17	^	Beginning of line anchor.
	18	$	End of line anchor.

Notice the fifth item listed in Table 17-1—it's the entry for character classes, and its description refers to Table 17-2 and Table 17-3. The character classes described in Table 17-2 are references to POSIX character classes, which are independent of character sets. On the other hand, the examples of character ranges shown in Table 17-3 are specific to character sets.

TABLE 17-2	Character Class	All Characters of Type
POSIX Character Classes	[:alnum:]	Alphanumeric characters. Includes letters and numbers. Omits punctuation marks.
	[:alpha:]	Alphabetic characters. Includes letters only.
	[:blank:]	Blank space characters.
	[:cntrl:]	Control (non-printing) characters.
	[:digit:]	Numeric characters.
	[:graph:]	All [:punct:], [:upper:], [:lower:], [:digit:] character classes combined.
	[:lower:]	Lowercase alphabetic characters.
	[:print:]	Printable characters.
	[:punct:]	Punctuation characters.
	[:space:]	Space (non-printing) characters.
	[:upper:]	Uppercase alphabetic characters.
	[:xdigit:]	Valid hexadecimal characters.

TABLE 17-3	Range	All Characters of Type
Examples of Character Ranges	[A–Z]	All uppercase alphabetic characters.
	[a–z]	All lowercase alphabetic characters.
	[0–9]	All numeric digits.
	[1–9]	All numeric digits excluding zero.

There's a school of thought out there that advocates the use of POSIX character classes where possible, so that multilingual applications can automatically leverage benefit from configuration changes to the underlying POSIX character classes in globalized application deployment. This is a good idea. But—having said that—note that you need to understand both approaches for the certification exam—both the character classes described in Table 17-2 and the character-specific range examples demonstrated in Table 17-3.

Note that the character classes shown in Table 17-2 are specified in lowercase letters. This is required—if you include them in a regular expression pattern using uppercase letters, such as [:ALPHA:], you'll get a syntax error.

You can use regular expressions in a specific set of Oracle SQL functions and conditions that we address in the next sections of this chapter.

We'll look at examples next.

CERTIFICATION OBJECTIVE 17.02

Regular Expression Functions

Oracle SQL includes several functions that extend the capabilities of some of the existing string functions such as SUBSTR and INSTR. These extensions consist of functions that support regular expressions. See Table 17-4 for a list and an accompanying description of them.

TABLE 17-4 Regular Expression Functions

Regular Expression Function	Parameters	Description
REGEXP_SUBSTR	(s1, pattern1, p1, n1, m1) s1—a character string. Required. pattern1—a regular expression. Required. p1—numeric. Optional. Defaults to 1. n1—numeric. Optional. Defaults to 1. m1—one or more of the match parameter text literals, see Table 17-5. Optional.	Searches within s1 for any string that matches the pattern defined in pattern1. Starts looking at position p1 in the string. Looks for the n1'th occurrence of the pattern. Performs the match in accordance with the instructions specified by m1. Output: Character string representing the matched pattern found within s1 that matched pattern1.
REGEXP_INSTR	(s1, pattern1, p1, n1, opt1, m1) s1—a character string. Required. pattern1—a regular expression. Required. p1—numeric. Optional. Defaults to 1. n1—numeric. Optional. Defaults to 1. opt1—numeric, limited to either 0 or 1. Optional. Defaults to 0. m1—one or more of the match parameter text literals, see Table 17-5. Optional.	Searches within s1 for any substring that matches the pattern defined in pattern1. Starts looking at position p1 in the string. Looks for the n1'th occurrence of the pattern. Performs the match in accordance with the instructions specified by m1. Output: Numeric value representing the location of the pattern within the source string. If opt1 = 1, then it returns the location of the first position after the pattern.

(Continued)

TABLE 17-4	Regular Expression Functions (*Continued*)

Regular Expression Function	Parameters	Description
REGEXP_REPLACE	(*s1, pattern1, rep1, p1, o1, m1*) *s1*—a character string. Required. *pattern1*—a regular expression. Required. *repl*—string. Optional. Defaults to NULL. *p1*—a numeric value, optional. Defaults to 1. *o1*—numeric value, optional. Defaults to 0. *m1*—one or more of the match parameter text literals, see Table 17-5. Optional.	Replaces *o1* occurrences of *pattern1* within *s1* with *rep1*, starting at position *p1* within *s1*. Performs the match in accordance with the instructions specified by *m1*.

TABLE 17-5	Match Parameter Value	Description
Match Parameter Text Literals	'c'	Case-sensitive matching.
	'i'	Case-insensitive matching.
	'n'	Enables the '.' (period) character (which is the "match-any-character" character) to match the newline character. Otherwise, '.' matches any character but does not treat the newline character as a character.
	'm'	Treat the source character string as multiple lines. Any occurrences of the anchor characters (^ and $) are assumed to be the start and end of lines within the string. Without it, the source character string is assumed to be one line of text.
	'x'	Ignores whitespace characters.

TABLE 17-6	Regular Expression Condition	Parameters	Description
Regular Expression Condition REGEXP_LIKE	REGEXP_LIKE	(*s1*, *pattern1*, *m1*) *s1*—a character string. Required. *pattern1*—a regular expression. Required. *m1*—one or more of the match parameter text literals, see Table 17-5. Optional.	Compares the pattern represented in *pattern1* with the string in *s1* and determines if there is a match. Performs the match in accordance with the instructions specified by *m1*. Output: Boolean. True if the pattern finds a match, false if it does not. (Note: Does not use the wildcard operators that LIKE uses.)

In addition to the regular expression functions, there is also one regular expression condition, listed in Table 17-6.

Note that if the match parameter text literals (Table 17-5) are used in a conflicting combination, such as 'ic', the last value will take precedence and any prior conflicting values will be ignored.

In the parameter lists described in Table 17-4 and Table 17-6, the REGEXP functions and the REGEXP condition take regular expression patterns as input parameters. A regular expression pattern uses regular expression operators, which we can draw from Tables 17-1, 17-2, and 17-3.

Let's consider the following string:

```
'123 Maple Avenue'
```

Let's take a look at the following SQL statement:

```
SELECT REGEXP_SUBSTR('123 Maple Avenue', '[a-z]') ADDRESS
FROM   DUAL;

ADDRESS
-------
a
```

Notice the output. The value returned is a letter "a", taken from the second letter within "Maple". The reason: our regular expression pattern, which we passed into the function as the second parameter, identifies a bracketed set of values. The bracketed set is explained in Table 17-1, item 2, and represents a list of characters that form our pattern. In essence, we are looking for any one occurrence of the characters specified in this list; the first character that matches is good, and in this case it was the letter "a". Remember: text is case sensitive by default, so if we wanted to capture that capital letter "M", we would need to do something to indicate our desire to include capital letters in our search. One way is this:

```
SELECT REGEXP_SUBSTR('123 Maple Avenue', '[A-Za-z]') ADDRESS
FROM   DUAL;


ADDRESS
-------
M
```

By expanding our list of possible character matches, we have included upper- and lowercase letters. But we are only retrieving the first letter and no more. That's because our bracketed list, by default, only retrieves the first character that represents one occurrence of any of the characters within the bracketed list. Let's add the plus sign operator to the end of our pattern, indicating that we want to return one or more consecutive characters that match our pattern:

```
SELECT REGEXP_SUBSTR('123 Maple Avenue', '[A-Za-z]+') ADDRESS
FROM   DUAL;


ADDRESS
-------
Maple
```

The plus sign operator is explained in Table 17-1, item number ten. This SQL statement starts its search in the first position of the target string and looks for the first occurrence of the pattern, which is specified to be any number of consecutive occurrences of the letters "A" through "Z" in either upper- or lowercase. In our example, we did not include a blank space in our set of bracketed characters to match, so as soon as a blank space was encountered, the returned value ended—with the "e" in "Maple".

We've been using character ranges of "a" through "z". As an alternative, we can use a reference to the full set of alphabetic characters, like this:

```
SELECT REGEXP_SUBSTR('123 Maple Avenue', '[[:alpha:]]+') ADDRESS
FROM   DUAL;


ADDRESS
-------
Maple
```

Note that the character class reference is enclosed in brackets, even though the reference itself already contains brackets. This is necessary. And beware! Don't forget that the brackets around the character class are an integral part of that class. Omitting them will be accepted syntactically, but it's logically erroneous:

```
SELECT REGEXP_SUBSTR('123 Maple Avenue', '[:alpha:]+') ADDRESS
FROM    DUAL;

ADDRESS
-------
apl
```

This example does not define the alphabetic character class. Instead, it defines a set of individual characters, including a colon character and the letters "a", "l", "p", and "h", followed by a repetition of the letter "a" and the "colon" character. The result is that the returned value represents the first complete continuous pattern that matches that particular set of characters we specified—"apl". It's syntactically accurate, but on a practical level it's probably worthless. So beware—this is yet another example of how SQL will let you do something erroneous and never complain.

on the job *Character classes such as [:alpha:] are preferable to letter ranges such as [a–z] in multilingual environments for consistency and flexibility in your applications.*

Remember that there are more than two parameters for this function. The third and fourth parameters default to 1. The third parameter defines where in the target string you will begin your search, and the fourth parameter defines which occurrence that matches your pattern you wish to return. In these examples, we've taken the default values for both the third and fourth parameters. But let's change that—we'll restore our correct character class reference, and we'll look for the second occurrence of our pattern:

```
SELECT REGEXP_SUBSTR('123 Maple Avenue', '[[:alpha:]]+', 1, 2) ADDRESS
FROM    DUAL;

ADDRESS
-------
Avenue
```

Now let's go back to the first occurrence of a pattern match and try a different character class reference:

```
SELECT REGEXP_SUBSTR('123 Maple Avenue', '[[:alnum:]]+') ADDRESS
FROM   DUAL;

ADDRESS
-------
123
```

In this example, we returned the first string that matched the alphanumeric character class. That class allows for numeric characters, and now we've retrieved the first numeric string from the target string.

Let's try a different character class. This time we'll query the ORDER_ADDRESSES table and show both the original column and the transformed column value in the same output:

```
SELECT ADDRESS2, REGEXP_SUBSTR(ADDRESS2,'[[:digit:]]+') ZIP_CODE
FROM   ORDER_ADDRESSES;

ADDRESS2                                          ZIP_CODE
------------------------------------------------- -----------
Tulsa, OK 74103                                   74103
Bugscuffle, TN 37183                              37183
Issaquah, WA 98027                                98027
Santa Barbara, CA 93109                           93109
Havre De Grace, MD 21078                          21078
Ronks, PA 17572                                   17572
Weeki Wachee, FL 34607                            34607
Kalamazoo, MI 49001                               49001
Little Egg Harbor Township, NJ 08087              08087
Pumpkin Center, OK 74451                          74451
Woonsocket, RI 02895                              02895
```

This example looks for the first occurrence of a continuous pattern of digits.

If you wish to look for a fixed literal value, that's simple—just leave out the brackets, like this:

```
SELECT REGEXP_SUBSTR('123 Maple Avenue', 'Maple') ADDRESS
FROM   DUAL;

ADDRESS
-------
Maple
```

You can mix and match literals and operators:

```
SELECT REGEXP_SUBSTR('she sells sea shells down by the seashore',
                     's[eashor]+e' ) THE_RESULT
FROM    DUAL;


THE_RESULT
----------
she
```

The example above looks for a pattern that starts with the letter "s", followed by any one or more consecutive occurrences of the letters "e", "a", "s", "h", "o", or "r", and finally ending in the letter "e". While the final word "seashore" matches this pattern, the first word "she" is what is found first. If the first word "she" in the source string were capitalized, as in "She", then that word would not be found by our pattern, since patterns are case sensitive and our pattern is specifically looking for a lowercase "s". Instead, the first three letters of "shell" would be returned.

To look for a particular string, you can use parentheses:

```
SELECT REGEXP_SUBSTR('she sells sea shells down by the seashore',
                     's(eashor)e' ) THE_RESULT
FROM    DUAL;

THE_RESULT
----------
seashore
```

By using parentheses, you are no longer looking for the first one or more consecutive occurrences of the letters included within but instead are now looking for the letter "s", followed by the string "eashor", followed by the letter "e". It's the same thing as this:

```
SELECT REGEXP_SUBSTR('she sells sea shells down by the seashore',
                     'seashore' ) THE_RESULT
FROM    DUAL;
```

However, parentheses give you the opportunity to mix strings with other metacharacter operators:

```
SELECT REGEXP_SUBSTR('she sells sea shells down by the seashore',
                     '[[:alpha:]]+(shore)' ) THE_RESULT
FROM    DUAL;

THE_RESULT
----------
seashore
```

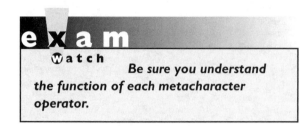

This example looks for any occurrences of a complete word that ends with the string "shore". The character class [:alpha:] is enclosed in brackets to specify that the matched list being sought consists of any one occurrence of an alphabetic character, and the plus sign operator after the bracketed list transforms the pattern to become one "or more consecutive" occurrences of an alphabetic character.

To look for any one example of a set of multicharacter options, you can enclose the list in parentheses to declare it as a single grouped expression, and then separate each entry with the logical OR operator:

```
SELECT ADDRESS2, REGEXP_SUBSTR(ADDRESS2,'(TN|MD|OK)') STATE
FROM    ORDER_ADDRESSES;

ADDRESS2                                        STATE
----------------------------------------------  ------------------------
Tulsa, OK 74103                                 OK
Bugscuffle, TN 37183                            TN
Issaquah, WA 98027
Santa Barbara, CA 93109
Havre De Grace, MD 21078                        MD
Ronks, PA 17572
Weeki Wachee, FL 34607
Kalamazoo, MI 49001
Little Egg Harbor Township, NJ 08087
Pumpkin Center, OK 74451                        OK
Woonsocket, RI 02895
```

Note that the parentheses are a key part of one of the regular expression operators. If you need to specify any of the operators as a literal value instead of an operator, you must precede it with a backslash. For example, this search will interpret the parentheses in the pattern as the grouping expression operator:

```
SELECT REGEXP_SUBSTR('Help desk: (212) 555-1212', '([[:digit:]]+)') AREA_CODE
FROM    DUAL;

AREA_CODE
---------
212
```

This variation will interpret the parentheses as literal values and include them in the targeted substring:

```
SELECT REGEXP_SUBSTR('Help desk: (212) 555-1212', '\([[:digit:]]+\)') AREA_CODE
FROM    DUAL;


AREA_CODE
---------
(212)
```

In this particular set of two examples, we get output in both situations. But if you need to locate a literal character in a place where a pattern might be expecting an operator that requires the same character, you need to use the backslash in front of the character to specify that you intend for the character—in this case the opening and closing parentheses—to be a literal character instead of the regular expression operator.

As we have seen, the bracketed expression can represent any number of characters within a larger pattern definition. For example:

```
SELECT ADDRESS2, REGEXP_SUBSTR(ADDRESS2,'[TBH][[:alpha:]]+') NAME
FROM    ORDER_ADDRESSES;

ADDRESS2                                       NAME
---------------------------------------------- --------------
Tulsa, OK 74103                                Tulsa
Bugscuffle, TN 37183                           Bugscuffle
Issaquah, WA 98027
Santa Barbara, CA 93109                        Barbara
Havre De Grace, MD 21078                       Havre
Ronks, PA 17572
Weeki Wachee, FL 34607
Kalamazoo, MI 49001
Little Egg Harbor Township, NJ 08087           Harbor
Pumpkin Center, OK 74451
Woonsocket, RI 02895
```

This query looks for any strings that match a pattern in which the first letter is either a "T", a "B", or an "H", followed by any number of alphabetic characters. Notice that we are only looking for the first such occurrence within any string—the string that produces "Harbor" also has a substring for "Township", but our function only asks for the first occurrence.

Here's an example that uses the "not equal" sign—the caret—to indicate that we want the second occurrence of a string that doesn't have a semicolon included:

```
SELECT REGEXP_SUBSTR('BMW-Oracle;Trimaran;February 2010', '[^;]+', 1, 2)
       AMERICAS_CUP
FROM   DUAL;


AMERICAS_CUP
------------
Trimaran
```

In this example, we have no spaces in the source string, only punctuation marks. We could try going with the [[:alpha:]] pattern instead, but had we done that in this example, we'd return a value of "Oracle" instead of "Trimaran", since "Oracle" is the first string separated by non-alphabetic characters—the dash between "BMW" and "Oracle" separates those strings. But we included the bracketed expression "[^;]+", which specifies multiple characters that are "not equal to the semicolon character", which is to say that we are stipulating that we only want the semicolon to serve as the substring separation character. And also note—we are specifying the fourth parameter of the REGEXP_SUBSTR function to have a value of 2, so we're looking for the second occurrence of our pattern of a string that does not include the semicolon.

Here's an example of the metacharacter operator "$" that specifies the end-of-line position:

```
SELECT ADDRESS2, REGEXP_SUBSTR(ADDRESS2,'[37]$') LAST_DIGIT
FROM   ORDER_ADDRESSES;


ADDRESS2                                    LAST_DIGIT
----------------------------------------    -------------
Tulsa, OK 74103                             3
Bugscuffle, TN 37183                        3
Issaquah, WA 98027                          7
Santa Barbara, CA 93109
Havre De Grace, MD 21078
Ronks, PA 17572
Weeki Wachee, FL 34607                      7
Kalamazoo, MI 49001
Little Egg Harbor Township, NJ 08087        7
Pumpkin Center, OK 74451
Woonsocket, RI 02895
```

In this case, we're looking for the first occurrences of either a '3' or a '7' that is followed immediately by the end-of-line anchor. In other words, we're looking for strings that end in either a '3' or a '7'. If we were looking for occurrences of strings that ended with '37' together, we could omit the square brackets, like this:

```
SELECT ADDRESS2, REGEXP_SUBSTR(ADDRESS2,'37$') LAST_DIGIT
FROM    ORDER_ADDRESSES;
```

And if we wanted to search for strings that ended in '83', '78', or either a '1' or a '2', we could use this:

```
SELECT ADDRESS2, REGEXP_SUBSTR(ADDRESS2,'(83|78|1|2)$') LAST_DIGIT
FROM    ORDER_ADDRESSES;

ADDRESS2                                 LAST_DIGIT
---------------------------------------- ----------------------------------------
--- Tulsa, OK 74103
Bugscuffle, TN 37183                     83
Issaquah, WA 98027
Santa Barbara, CA 93109
Havre De Grace, MD 21078                 78
Ronks, PA 17572                          2
Weeki Wachee, FL 34607
Kalamazoo, MI 49001                      1
Little Egg Harbor Township, NJ 08087
Pumpkin Center, OK 74451                 1
Woonsocket, RI 02895
```

The next section will expand our discussion and look at methods for editing text through pattern matching and replacement.

The regular expression functions are just like any other function— *and may be used in any SQL statement and clause that accepts any valid SQL function.*

CERTIFICATION OBJECTIVE 17.03

Replacing Patterns

The function REGEXP_REPLACE uses regular expressions to identify patterns and replace them with something else.

For example, consider this pattern:

```
[.]+
```

This pattern encloses a period in a pair of square brackets, which is to say any single occurrence of a literal period character. But it's followed by the plus sign operator, which repeats the previous reference one or more consecutive times. The result: we are specifying any number of one or more consecutive occurrences of the literal period character. This example uses the function REGEXP_REPLACE to replace the pattern with a single hyphen:

```
SELECT REGEXP_REPLACE('Chapter 1 ....................... I Am Born',
                      '[.]+','-') TOC
FROM    DUAL;


TOC
---------------------
Chapter 1 - I Am Born
```

In the next example, we look for any occurrence of the following list of characters:

!@#$%^&*()

To specify that we are looking for any single occurrence of these characters, we enclose them in square brackets. Once again, let's replace any single occurrence of the characters in our list with a single dash:

```
SELECT REGEXP_REPLACE('And then he said *&% so I replied with $@($*@',
                '[!@#$%^&*()]','-') PRIME_TIME
FROM    DUAL;


PRIME_TIME
-----------------------------------------------
And then he said --- so I replied with ------
```

In the preceding example, we could have replaced any consecutive string of those characters in our list with a single occurrence of a dash by adding the plus sign operator after our bracketed list, like this:

```
SELECT REGEXP_REPLACE('And then he said *&% so I replied with $@($*@',
                '[!@#$%^&*()]+','-') PRIME_TIME
FROM    DUAL;


PRIME_TIME
---------------------------------------
And then he said - so I replied with -
```

By adding the single plus sign operator after the square brackets, we specify any number of repetitions of the characters within our list.

A classic use of the REGEXP_REPLACE function is to clean up unnecessary blank spaces from within a string. Here's one approach:

```
SELECT REGEXP_REPLACE('and      in      conclusion,  2/3rds  of  our      revenue ',
                      '( ){2,}', ' ') TEXT_LINE
FROM    DUAL;

TEXT_LINE
------------------------------------------
and in conclusion, 2/3rds of our revenue
```

This example uses a regular expression that opens with a set of parentheses enclosing a single blank space. The number two that follows is enclosed in curly braces with a comma, which is to say that it defines the pattern to be the preceding character—a single blank space—in two or more successive occurrences. In other words, we're looking for any occurrences of two or more continuous blank spaces. If we find one, the third argument to the function says to replace it with a single blank space. The cleaned-up text appears below the query.

One advantage to an approach like this lies in the ability to easily identify the number of repetitions of a given character you wish to replace. While this example only shows two spaces, how many times have you found yourself dealing with text files that contained multiple blank spaces you wished to retain, combined with dozens and perhaps many hundreds of generated blank spaces fattening up a text file unnecessarily, blank spaces you wish to eliminate? Using this sort of technique, you could eliminate all repetitions of blank spaces that number, say, 20, which could help dramatically reduce your unused file space while simultaneously preserving any correctly formatted text with some more modest usage of blank space elsewhere in the file.

Let's build a more complex example. We'll start with something simple—let's replace a city name with the string constant 'CITY'. To start, we'll replace the first occurrence of a text string in the ADDRESS2 column and limit our output to the first five rows for our example:

```
SELECT ADDRESS2,
       REGEXP_REPLACE(ADDRESS2, '(^[[:alpha:]]+)', 'CITY') THE_STRING
FROM   ORDER_ADDRESSES
WHERE  ROWNUM <= 5;

ADDRESS2                                 THE_STRING
---------------------------------------- -------------------------------
Tulsa, OK 74103                          CITY, OK 74103
Bugscuffle, TN 37183                     CITY, TN 37183
Issaquah, WA 98027                       CITY, WA 98027
Santa Barbara, CA 93109                  CITY Barbara, CA 93109
Havre De Grace, MD 21078                 CITY De Grace, MD 21078
```

Notice that our last two rows of output didn't quite work as we might have wished. Some of our city names contain spaces, so the word search didn't replace the complete names of 'Santa Barbara' or 'Havre De Grace'. We can resolve this by including a space as one of the acceptable characters for our target substring to be replaced. Within the set of square brackets is the bracketed character class for alphabetic characters, meaning that the operator

```
[:alpha:]
```

simply represents all alphabetic characters within the set of acceptable characters, which in turn is enclosed in square brackets, like this:

```
[[:alpha:]]
```

All we need to do is slip in a single blank space in the list of acceptable characters:

```
[[:alpha:] ]
```

Let's keep our plus sign operator, which indicates that we're looking for any continuous string of these characters, in any order:

```
[[:alpha:] ]+
```

Now let's put it all together, keeping the ^ operator at the front, which—in this context—is the anchor to the first position in the search string:

```
SELECT ADDRESS2,
       REGEXP_REPLACE(ADDRESS2, '(^[[:alpha:] ]+)', 'CITY') THE_STRING
FROM   ORDER_ADDRESSES
WHERE  ROWNUM <= 5;

ADDRESS2                                    THE_STRING
------------------------------------------- --------------------
Tulsa, OK 74103                             CITY, OK 74103
Bugscuffle, TN 37183                        CITY, TN 37183
Issaquah, WA 98027                          CITY, WA 98027
Santa Barbara, CA 93109                     CITY, CA 93109
Havre De Grace, MD 21078                    CITY, MD 21078
```

The first character that did not match our pattern is the comma. Our pattern specified alphabetic characters and a space, but not a comma. The result is shown in the right column in the preceding example.

Now let's expand this a bit. Let's define three consecutive patterns. We already have the first pattern, which is anchored to the start of the search string and looks for a consecutive series of alphabetic characters and/or a space, until something else is encountered, all enclosed in a pair of parentheses:

```
(^[[:alpha:] ]+)
```

Next, let's allow for a comma literal followed by a space literal:

```
,
```

(There's a blank space following that comma that will become apparent in a bit.)

Next, let's create a second pattern, enclosed in parentheses to group it together as a single pattern. We'll look for any two alphabetic characters:

```
([[:alpha:]]{2})
```

The square-bracketed set of characters—which is the character class [:alpha:] with its own set of square brackets—defines the list of possible characters, and the curly braces following it specify a fixed number of occurrences of these characters. The number *2* indicates that we're only looking for two alphabetic characters. This is our state abbreviation that we're looking for.

Finally, let's create a third pattern, which we'll use to define a five-digit ZIP code:

```
([[:digit:]]{5})
```

Putting it all together into one overall pattern looks like this:

```
'(^[[:alpha:] ]+), ([[:alpha:]]{2}) ([[:digit:]]{5})'
```

NOW—let's do something different with our replacement pattern. Let's use the backreference expression to take out three subexpressions from our search, and reposition each subexpression as follows:

```
'\3 \2 \1'
```

This pattern says to replace the search string with the third subexpression, the second subexpression, and then finally the first subexpression, in order.

Putting it all together, we get this:

```
SELECT ADDRESS2,
       REGEXP_REPLACE(ADDRESS2,
                  '(^[[:alpha:] ]+), ([[:alpha:]]{2}) ([[:digit:]]{5})',
                  '\3 \2 \1') THE_STRING
FROM   ORDER_ADDRESSES
WHERE  ROWNUM <= 5;
```

```
ADDRESS2                                      THE_STRING
------------------------------------          ------------------------
Tulsa, OK 74103                               74103 OK Tulsa
Bugscuffle, TN 37183                          37183 TN Bugscuffle
Issaquah, WA 98027                            98027 WA Issaquah
Santa Barbara, CA 93109                       93109 CA Santa Barbara
Havre De Grace, MD 21078                      21078 MD Havre De Grace
```

Notice that the comma that is present after each city name in our source string has been omitted from the result in our output string. This is because the backslash specifies subexpressions, which are enclosed in parentheses. The comma is identified in our original pattern, but not within any set of parentheses, so it is not included in our three subexpression references. We can choose to include it in a subexpression, like this:

```
SELECT ADDRESS2,
       REGEXP_REPLACE(ADDRESS2,
              '(^[[:alpha:] ,]+) ([[:alpha:]]{2}) ([[:digit:]]{5})',
              '\3 \2 \1') THE_STRING
FROM   ORDER_ADDRESSES
WHERE  ROWNUM <= 5;
```

We could also choose instead to include the comma within our set of subexpression references. For that matter, we can add any punctuation with our subexpression references. For example, let's add a dash between subexpressions 2 and 1, and put double-quotation marks around subexpression 1 like this:

```
SELECT ADDRESS2,
       REGEXP_REPLACE(ADDRESS2,
              '(^[[:alpha:] ]+), ([[:alpha:]]{2}) ([[:digit:]]{5})',
              '\3 \2-"\1"') THE_STRING
FROM   ORDER_ADDRESSES
WHERE  ROWNUM <= 5;
```

```
ADDRESS2                                      THE_STRING
------------------------------------          ------------------------
Tulsa, OK 74103                               74103 OK-"Tulsa"
Bugscuffle, TN 37183                          37183 TN-"Bugscuffle"
Issaquah, WA 98027                            98027 WA-"Issaquah"
Santa Barbara, CA 93109                       93109 CA-"Santa Barbara"
Havre De Grace, MD 21078                      21078 MD-"Havre De Grace"
```

These are just a few examples of the sort of replacements you can achieve using the REGEXP_REPLACE function and regular expressions.

Be sure you are comfortable with mixing and matching different metacharacter operators to form patterns.

CERTIFICATION OBJECTIVE 17.04

Regular Expressions and CHECK Constraints

You can incorporate regular expressions into CHECK constraints. By defining a pattern within the CHECK constraint using a regular expression, you can establish something of a template for incoming data, establishing a requirement that all incoming data match, for example, a particular format.

As an example, consider the following pattern that defines an e-mail address:

```
CREATE TABLE EMAIL_LIST
(  EMAIL_LIST_ID    NUMBER(7)  PRIMARY KEY,
   EMAIL1           VARCHAR2(120),
   CONSTRAINT CK_EL_EMAIL1
     CHECK (
       REGEXP_LIKE (EMAIL1,
               '^([[:alnum:]]+)@[[:alnum:]]+.(com|net|org|edu|gov|mil)$'
                 )
                 )
);
```

The CHECK constraint here uses the REGEXP_LIKE function to establish input restrictions on the EMAIL1 column. Any incoming data is required to match the pattern specified in the second parameter of the REGEXP_LIKE function. A complete explanation of this pattern is provided in Table 17-7.

	#	Regular Expression Operator	Explanation
TABLE 17-7 Explanation for the sample CHECK Constraint's Regular Expression	1	^	Anchors the first pattern at the beginning of the string.
	2	(	Opens a grouped expression (a subexpression) that is closed with # 7 (see below).
	3	[	Opens a bracketed expression containing a matched list of values.
	4	[:alnum:]	Specifies the character class of alphanumeric characters.
	5	]	Closes the bracketed expression that was opened in # 3 (see below).
	6	+	Specifies that any of the values in the bracketed expression contained within # 3 through # 5 repeat continuously. Any characters encountered that are not in the bracketed expression will end this part of the pattern.
	7	)	Closes the grouped expression that was opened with # 2.
	8	@	The literal value @.
	9	[	Opens a bracketed expression containing a matched list of values.
	10	[:alnum:]	Specifies the character class of alphanumeric characters.
	11	]	Closes the bracketed expression that was opened in # 9.
	12	+	Specifies that the any of the values in the bracketed expression contained within # 9 through # 11 repeat continuously. Any characters encountered that are not in the bracketed expression will end this part of the pattern.
	13	.	The literal value of a period (.).
	14	(	Opens a grouped expression.
	15	com | net | org | edu | gov | mil	Identifies a set of expressions separated by the logical OR operator, which means that whatever occurs at this point in the pattern must be one of the options listed in the set of OR values.

TABLE 17-7	#	Regular Expression Operator	Explanation
Explanation for the CHECK Constraint's Regular Expression *(Continued)*	16	)	Closes the grouped expression that was opened in # 14.
	17	$	Anchors the final pattern to the end of the string—in other words, no extraneous characters after the completion of the pattern are allowed.

Once we've created our table with its CHECK constraint, we can try to use it:

```
INSERT INTO EMAIL_LIST VALUES (1, 'someone@corbinian.com');

1 rows inserted

INSERT INTO EMAIL_LIST VALUES (2, 'lellison@oracle.omc');

Error starting at line 1 in command:
INSERT INTO EMAIL_LIST VALUES (2, 'lellison@oracle.omc')
Error report:
SQL Error: ORA-02290: check constraint (EFCODD.CK_EL_EMAIL1)
violated
02290. 00000 -  "check constraint (%s.%s) violated"
*Cause:    The values being inserted do not satisfy the named
check

*Action:   do not insert values that violate the constraint.
```

The CHECK constraint will accept valid input and reject invalid e-mail addresses that are not in the correct format.

As we have seen, CHECK constraints may include regular expression functions and operators.

---

exam ⓦatch

Remember that CHECK constraints on a table perform as a gateway for incoming data on the constraint column or columns. If the incoming data violates the constraint, the table will not accept the incoming data.

CERTIFICATION SUMMARY

The language of regular expressions is found throughout the world of software development. Support for regular expressions is found in Unix, C, and many other languages and operating systems. Regular expression operators offer powerful flexibility in defining patterns for performing text searches, text replacement, and related tasks. Oracle SQL offers support for regular expression operators, along with functions that extend the capabilities of SQL to incorporate regular expression patterns into SQL.

Regular expression operators include a number of special characters to perform tasks such as anchoring a pattern to the beginning or end of a string; defining a series of a particular set of character literals, defining a range of values, defining a character class, defining equivalent characters that involve accents and other special symbols, and much more. The backslash can be used to precede any operator that you wish to treat as a character literal.

Regular expression functions such as REGEXP_SUBSTR extend the capability of SQL functions such as SUBSTR so that regular expression operators may be used to define patterns in performing text searches.

The function REGEXP_REPLACE can replace patterns found within a target string. The backreference operator can be used to reference defined patterns within the replacement string, to reorder or otherwise restructure data in a variety of ways.

CHECK constraints may be defined with regular expression functions and patterns to apply more flexibility to filtering input data. The REGEXP_LIKE condition is useful in this context, as are any of the regular expression operators.

TWO-MINUTE DRILL

Using Metacharacters

❑ Metacharacter operators form the foundation of regular expressions.

❑ Regular expression patterns are built with metacharacter operators.

❑ Depending on the context, certain character literals may be regular expression operators with special capabilities, or they may be character literals.

❑ Regular expressions can include character literals.

❑ Literals enclosed in square brackets represent a set of possible values, or matched list.

❑ Parentheses enclose a grouped expression, or subexpression.

❑ An expression followed by a plus sign, question mark, or asterisk will be interpreted as a pattern that can repeat based on each operator's rules.

❑ You can specify character ranges.

❑ Character classes can serve as an alternative to ranges and provide better support for multilingual applications.

Regular Expression Functions

❑ There are SQL functions that provide support for regular expressions.

❑ REGEXP_SUBSTR, REGEXP_INSTR, REGEXP_LIKE, and REGEXP_REPLACE have counterparts in SQL and extend the capabilities of those counterparts to provide regular expression support.

Replacing Patterns

❑ The REGEXP_REPLACE function can replace substrings within a target string using regular expressions.

❑ The use of regular expressions with a task like string replacement is a much more powerful alternative to the use of a function such as REPLACE, which doesn't support regular expressions.

❑ The regular expression backreference operator can be used as the third parameter to replace a pattern, and to specify grouped expressions within the pattern as part of the replacement.

Regular Expressions and CHECK Constraints

❑ You can create CHECK constraints that use regular expressions.

❑ CHECK constraints can use regular expression patterns to define restrictions and requirements on incoming data for a given table.

❑ The REGEXP_LIKE condition is useful in applying the CHECK constraint to a given table.

SELF TEST

The following questions will help you measure your understanding of the material presented in this chapter. Choose one correct answer for each question unless otherwise directed.

Using Metacharacters

1. You can use regular expression functions: (Choose the best answer.)
   A. Only in the WHERE clause of SELECT statements
   B. Only in WHERE clauses and CHECK constraints
   C. Only in a SELECT statement or a CHECK constraint
   D. Anywhere you can use a SQL function of a comparable datatype

2. The operator to anchor a pattern to the beginning of a string is:
   A. ^
   B. =
   C. $
   D. *

3. You need to define a regular expression pattern that accepts any one of the string literal values of DC, VA, or MD. Which of the following patterns will do this?
   A. '(DC, VA, MD)'
   B. '(DC ? VA ? MD)'
   C. '(DC * VA * MD)'
   D. '(DC|VA|MD)'

4. You need to define a regular expression pattern that specifies a string of one or more alphabetic characters. Which of the following patterns will do this?
   A. '[:alpha:+]'
   B. '[:alpha:]+'
   C. '[[:alpha:]+]'
   D. '[[:alpha:]]+'

5. Which of the following character classes defines only uppercase letters?
   A. [:upper:]
   B. [:UPPER:]
   C. [:ALPHA:]
   D. None of the above

Regular Expression Functions

6. You are tasked to identify the position of a given pattern within a larger string. Which of the following functions will you be sure to use? (Choose the best answer.)
   A. REGEXP
   B. REGEXP_INSTR
   C. REGEXP_SUBSTR
   D. REGEXP_REPLACE

7. Which of the following may *not* be used within a parameter of the REGEXP_LIKE function?
   A. '[:alpha:]'
   B. '%' as a wildcard operator
   C. '*' as a regular expression operator
   D. '%' as a literal value

8. Examine the following SQL statement:

```
SELECT REGEXP_SUBSTR(
        'Dickens, Charles.  "Our Mutual Friend."  Riverside Press, 1879.',
        '[[:alnum:]]+', 1, 5) THE_ANSWER
FROM    DUAL;
```

What will be the answer?
   A. Friend
   B. Friend.
   C. Friend."
   D. None of the above

9. You are tasked to extract the first occurrence of any characters within a character-based column PRESS_RELEASE in a table PR that are enclosed within parentheses. For example:

```
' when the company Codd Cruise Lines (CCLX, 24.74) was '
```

Your task is toextract the substring enclosed in parentheses, inclusive, which in this example is '(CCLX, 24.74)'. Which of the following SQL statements will you use?
   A. SELECT REGEXP_SUBSTR(PRESS_RELEASE,
                           '\([^)]+\)') PRESS_RELEASE
      FROM PR;
   B. SELECT REGEXP_SUBSTR(PRESS_RELEASE,
                           '([[:alnum:]])') PRESS_RELEASE
      FROM PR;

C. ```
SELECT REGEXP_SUBSTR(PRESS_RELEASE,
                     '\([[:alpha:]]+\)') PRESS_RELEASE
FROM PR;
```

D. ```
SELECT REGEXP_SUBSTR(PRESS_RELEASE,
                     '\(([^)]+)') PRESS_RELEASE
FROM PR;
```

Replacing Patterns

10. The third parameter of the REGEXP_REPLACE function specifies the replacement for whatever matches the pattern, which is specified in the second parameter. What will replace the pattern if the third parameter is omitted?

A. NULL.

B. Nothing—the statement will fail.

C. The pattern is left in place and the original string remains unchanged.

D. None of the above.

11. Examine the following SQL statement and its output:

```
SELECT TEXT_STREAMING FROM ENTRIES WHERE ENTRY_ID = 12;

TEXT_STREAMING
----------------------------------------------------------------
times     sun      chronicle      circulation      examiner
```

Which of the following queries will strip out the extra blank spaces from the text above? (Choose two.)

A. ```
SELECT REGEXP_REPLACE(TEXT_STREAMING,
                      '( ){2,},' ' ') THE_ANSWER
FROM ENTRIES
WHERE ENTRY_ID = 12;
```

B. ```
SELECT REGEXP_REPLACE(TEXT_STREAMING,
                      '( )*,' ' ') THE_ANSWER
FROM ENTRIES
WHERE ENTRY_ID = 12;
```

C. ```
SELECT REGEXP_REPLACE(TEXT_STREAMING,
                      '[[:blank:]]*,' ' ') THE_ANSWER
FROM ENTRIES
WHERE ENTRY_ID = 12;
```
```

D.
```
SELECT REGEXP_REPLACE(TEXT_STREAMING,
                       '[[:blank:]]+,' ' ') THE_ANSWER
FROM ENTRIES
WHERE ENTRY_ID = 12;
```

12. Examine the following SQL statement:

```
SELECT REGEXP_REPLACE('Charles Dickens','([[:alpha:]]+) ([[:alpha:]]+)',
'\2')
FROM    DUAL;
```

What will this SQL statement return when executed?

A. h

B. Dickens

C. Charles Dickens

D. None of the above

Regular Expressions and CHECK Constraints

13. You are tasked to create a CHECK constraint on a column to ensure that any incoming data for phone numbers is entered in a format like this:

```
(101)202-3330
```

Which of the following regular expression patterns will work in the CHECK constraint? (Choose the *best* answer.)

A. `'\([[:digit:]]{3}\)[[:digit:]]{3}-[[:digit:]]{4}'`

B. `'[[:digit:]-()]{13}'`

C. `'\([1-9]{3}\)[1-9]{3}-[1-9]{4}'`

D. `'\([1-9]+\)[1-9]+-[1-9]+'`

14. Which of the following patterns, if used in a CHECK constraint, will ensure that incoming data to a column will be accepted if it starts with the word "buy" or starts with the word "sell", and that anything else will be rejected?

A. `'^(buy|sell)'`

B. `'(^buy|sell)'`

C. `'^[[:buysell:]]'`

D. `'([buysell])'`

15. Examine the following SQL code:

```
CREATE TABLE CUSTOMER_COMMENTS
(CUSTOMER_COMMENTS_ID NUMBER(7) PRIMARY KEY,
 INCOMING_REQUEST VARCHAR2(80),
 CONSTRAINT CK_IR CHECK (REGEXP_LIKE(INCOMING_REQUEST,'([please])$'))
);
```

Which of the following string values will be accepted as input to the INCOMING_REQUEST column by the CHECK constraint? (Choose all that apply.)

A. 'please submit my order'

B. 'I would like to place an order please'

C. 'sorry but I fell asleep'

D. 'be careful with that last one'

SELF TEST ANSWERS

Using Metacharacters

1. ☑ **D.** You can use regular expression functions anywhere that SQL functions of a comparable datatype can be used.
   ☒ **A, B,** and **C** are incorrect. Answer D is the best answer.

2. ☑ **A.** The caret is the beginning-of-line anchor.
   ☒ **B, C,** and **D** are incorrect. The equal sign is part of the equivalence class. The $ operator is the end-of-line anchor. The * operator is intended to repeat the preceding subexpression zero or more times.

3. ☑ **D.** The parentheses form a grouping, or subexpression, within which the desired values need to be separated by the logical OR operator, which is the pipe literal value of " | ".
   ☒ **A, B,** and **C** are incorrect.

4. ☑ **D.** The plus sign operator must follow the bracketed expression, which in turn encloses a character class with its own brackets.
   ☒ **A, B,** and **C** are incorrect. Answer A specifies a series of individual characters ':, a, l, p, h, a, :, +'. In other words, the attempt to specify the character class [:alpha:] and the plus sign operator all fail because the outer brackets are recognized as a bracketed expression, which encloses a list of individual characters; that is how its contents are recognized. Answer B is the same, but the plus sign operator is in the correct place. Still, the character class is not correctly specified. In Answer C, the character class is correctly specified, but by including the plus sign operator within the bracketed expression, it is not interpreted as the regular expression operator but instead is recognized as a literal plus sign.

5. ☑ **A.**
   ☒ **B, C,** and **D** are incorrect. Character classes must be specified in lowercase letters.

Regular Expression Functions

6. ☑ **B.** The REGEXP_INSTR function returns a number indicating the position within a string of a given pattern.
   ☒ **A, C,** and **D** are incorrect. There is no REGEXP function. As for the others, while you may find some need to use one or the other of these functions as part of your overall approach, REGEXP_INSTR is the best answer.

7. ☑ **B.** The REGEXP_LIKE function does not use the same wildcard operators as LIKE. (Note: the % and * characters are accepted as string literals.)
   ☒ **A, C,** and **D** are incorrect.

8. ☑ **A.** The answer will be the word "Friend" alone.

☒ **B, C,** and **D** are incorrect. The pattern identifies alphanumeric values alone. That excludes punctuation marks.

9. ☑ **A.** Answer A has the correct pattern for the following reasons: characters one and two specify an open parenthesis as a literal, with a preceding backslash to specify the parenthesis as an opening parenthesis rather than as a grouping expression. Character three is an opening square bracket of a bracketed expression, followed by a caret and closing parenthesis, and the closing bracket to the bracketed expression, and the plus sign operator. These characters (three through seven) specify a set of characters which is just one character really, which is "not the closing parenthesis". It does not require the backslash here because it's not possible to place a grouping expression within the square brackets, so there's no confusing this literal closing parenthesis with a grouping expression. The caret indicates that this bracketed expression defines the set of values that shouldn't be found—as opposed to the list that should be found. In other words, this bracketed expression specifies that we will look for characters that match the list—which is everything other than the closing parentheses. You could call this "not the closing parenthesis"—and since the plus sign operator is present, we will look for one or more characters through the rest of the string until we find a closing parenthesis. When we do, we stop. Finally, we specify a literal parenthesis which, if found, will become part of the returned result of this function.

☒ **B, C,** and **D** are incorrect. Answer B is wrong because the parentheses are treated as operators instead of literal values. You should start by looking for the first occurrence of an open parenthesis, but the inclusion at the beginning of the pattern uses an open parenthesis without the backslash preceding it, so it's treated as the first part of a grouping expression operator. Answer C is wrong because, among other things, it uses the alpha character class within the parentheses, yet our example shows that the parentheses should accept any characters, including numerics and commas. Answer D is close but wrong—its last closing parenthesis is treated as an operator instead of a literal.

Replacing Patterns

10. ☑ **A.** NULL replaces the pattern within the target string if the third parameter is omitted.

☒ **B, C,** and **D** are incorrect.

11. ☑ **A and D.** In answer A, the placement of {2,} specifies that the preceding pattern—a single blank space—may repeat two or more times. In answer D, the + operator specifies that the preceding pattern—a single blank space—may repeat multiple times.

☒ **B and C** are incorrect. The use of * in this context is erroneous—the asterisk specifies that any occurrence of the previous pattern, which is the single blank space, be replaced for each occurrence of it that appears zero or more times. The replacement is a blank space. The result: each character is replaced with a blank space.

12. ☑ **B.** The \2 operator identifies the second group in the expression. The group is defined by the grouping operators, which are the parentheses. The second grouped expression is what \2 will return, and in this case, that represents the second full word in the string.
☒ **A, C,** and **D** are incorrect.

Regular Expressions and CHECK Constraints

13. ☑ **A.** This is the best answer, as it best preserves the integrity of the format in retaining a pair of literal parentheses enclosing three digits, followed by three digits, followed by a dash, followed by exactly four digits.
☒ **B, C,** and **D** are incorrect. Answer B will not exclude numbers that have too many numbers in the area code, or too few numbers in the exchange—it will accept any string of 13 characters in any combination of numbers, parentheses literals, and dashes, including those that do not resemble the stated phone number format at all. Answers C and D omit the number zero.

14. ☑ **A.** The caret specifies that the expression that follows it is anchored to the start of the string. The parentheses pair ensures that the caret anchors everything contained within to the beginning of the string. The group is defined with a logical OR to be either the literal string "buy" or "sell".
☒ **B, C,** and **D** are incorrect. Answer B is close—it will accept incoming values that start with the word "buy", and incoming values that use the word "sell" in any position—but it will not require that the word "sell" be in the first position. Answer D is not anchored to the start of the string. Answer C is anchored but references a non-existent character class.

15. ☑ **B, C,** and **D.** The CHECK constraint defines a grouping expression, within which is a bracketed list. Inside the bracketed list is a set of letters 'please', and within the bracketed list, those letters are considered individually. Finally, the $ operator anchors the entire group to the end of the string. Therefore, the constraint requires any one of the letters 'p', 'l', 'e', 'a', 's', or 'e' to be present at the end of the string.
☒ **A** is incorrect.

18
Controlling User Access

This chapter explores the subject of user access and the privileges associated with performing actions in the database. Every action performed by any user account requires a corresponding privilege or set of privileges to perform that action. There are two categories of privileges—*system* privileges are required to perform a task in the database; *object* privileges are required to use those system privileges on any given database object in particular. Privileges may be granted to a user account, or to another database object called a *role*. A role, in turn, can be granted to a user account, which effectively grants the set of privileges collected within the role. Once granted, privileges and roles may later be revoked. Together, privileges and roles are the mechanism for managing and controlling access to the database by user accounts. This chapter looks at how to create and manage privileges and roles.

A word of warning about the sample code contained in this chapter: Some of it has the ability to change your database permanently with results that may be undesirable. Some of our code samples will look at SQL code that uses the SYSTEM user account, a very important account that should be controlled by experienced database administrators in any production database. You should always check with your DBA before trying any code samples from any book, but this chapter in particular includes code that you should not execute in a professional installation without first checking with your DBA.

CERTIFICATION OBJECTIVE 18.01

Differentiate System Privileges from Object Privileges

Throughout this book, we've looked at how a user account can use SQL statements to create and use a variety of database objects. However, before any user account can execute a SQL statement, it must be granted the privilege to execute that SQL statement. Furthermore, once a database object has been created, any user account that uses the database object must be granted privileges to do so.

There are three general categories of privileges, as described in Table 18-1.

We'll review each of the items listed in Table 18-1 in this chapter.

TABLE 18-1	Type of Privilege	Description
Types of Privileges	System privilege	The ability to perform a particular task in the database
	Object privilege	The ability to perform a particular task on a particular database object
	Role	A collection of one or more system privileges and/or object privileges, and/or other roles

System Privileges

System privileges are the right to perform some task in the database. For example, to log in to the database, a user account is granted the system privilege CREATE SESSION. To create a table, a user account must be granted the system privilege CREATE TABLE.

There are over 100 different system privileges. Table 18-2 lists some of the system privileges that are required to perform the tasks we've discussed in this book.

System privileges differ from object privileges in that system privileges are what a user account must have to create database objects, among other things. Then, once created, object privileges on a particular database object can be granted to other users.

TABLE 18-2	System Privilege	Description
Some System Privileges	CREATE SESSION	Connect to the database.
	CREATE TABLE	Create a table in your user account. Includes ability to ALTER and DROP TABLE. Also includes ability to CREATE, ALTER, and DROP INDEX objects.
	CREATE VIEW	Create a view in your user account. Includes ALTER and DROP.
	CREATE SEQUENCE	Create a sequence in your user account. Includes ALTER and DROP.
	CREATE SYNONYM	Create a synonym in your user account. Includes ALTER and DROP. Does not include PUBLIC synonyms—see CREATE PUBLIC SYNONYM.
	CREATE ROLE	Create a role. Includes ALTER and DROP.
	CREATE PUBLIC SYNONYM	Create a synonym in the PUBLIC account. Does not include DROP, which is separate.

(Continued)

TABLE 18-2

Some System
Privileges
(*Continued*)

System Privilege	Description
DROP PUBLIC SYNONYM	Drop a synonym from the PUBLIC account.
CREATE ANY TABLE	Create a table within any user account.
ALTER ANY TABLE	Alter a table within any user account.
DELETE ANY TABLE	Delete from any table within any user account.
DROP ANY TABLE	Drop any table within any user account.
INSERT ANY TABLE	Insert into any table within any user account.
SELECT ANY TABLE	Select from any table within any user account.
UPDATE ANY TABLE	Update any table within any user account.
CREATE ANY VIEW	Create a view in any user account.
DROP ANY VIEW	Drop a view from any user account.
CREATE ANY INDEX	Create an index in any user account.
ALTER ANY INDEX	Alter an index in any user account.
DROP ANY INDEX	Drop an index from any user account.
CREATE ANY SEQUENCE	Create a sequence in any user account.
ALTER ANY SEQUENCE	Alter a sequence in any user account.
DROP ANY SEQUENCE	Drop a sequence from any user account.
SELECT ANY SEQUENCE	Select from a sequence in any user account.
CREATE ANY SYNONYM	Create a synonym in any user account.
DROP ANY SYNONYM	Drop a synonym from any user account.
CREATE ANY DIRECTORY	Create a directory in any user account.
DROP ANY DIRECTORY	Drop a directory from any user account.
ALTER ANY ROLE	Alter a role in the database.
DROP ANY ROLE	Drop any role in the database.
GRANT ANY ROLE	Grant any role in the database.
FLASHBACK ANY TABLE	Perform flashback operations on any table in the database.
CREATE USER	Create a user account.
ALTER USER	Alter a user account.
DROP USER	Drop a user account.
GRANT ANY PRIVILEGE	Grant any system privilege to any user account in the database.
GRANT ANY OBJECT PRIVILEGE	Grant, to any user account in the database, any object privilege that the object's owner is also able to grant.

For example, the right to execute the SQL statement CREATE TABLE and create a new database table—is a system privilege. But the ability to change rows of data in, for example, a table called BENEFITS owned by a user account named EUNICE—is an object privilege. In other words, an object privilege is the right to do something to a particular object.

As an analogy, consider the concept of a driver's license. A driver's license is sort of like a system privilege—it's the right to drive a car in a general sense. Once you have a driver's license, if you get a car, you can drive it. But you don't have the right to drive anyone's car in particular unless the owner specifically authorizes you to do so.

The driver's license is like a system privilege. The right to drive someone else's car is like an object privilege. You need both in order to drive a car and be in full compliance with the law. The same is true in the database—you need system privileges to perform particular tasks, and object privileges to perform those tasks on an object in particular.

Let's look at some of the syntax for granting privileges. And note: for some of the upcoming examples, we'll use the SQL*Plus tool and some SQL*Plus commands. These SQL*Plus commands do not require the semicolon termination character that is required in SQL statements.

We'll use the SQL*Plus command CONNECT to log in to another user account. You can also use the SQL*Plus command SHOW USER to confirm which account is currently active in the session. SQL*Plus commands are useful to know and helpful to use in your SQL sessions. But they are not on the exam.

Prerequisites

Before we get started with GRANT and REVOKE statements, let's review some supporting statements that aren't specifically included in the exam objectives but are useful for demonstrating system privileges, object privileges, roles, and their capabilities.

CREATE, ALTER, and DROP USER

Let's look at how to create a user account to begin with. Any SQL user with the CREATE USER system privilege may execute the CREATE USER statement, whose syntax looks like this:

```
CREATE USER username IDENTIFIED BY password;
```

In this statement, *username* is a name you specify according to the rules for naming database objects. The *password* follows the same rules. (Note: passwords are case sensitive by default starting with Oracle 11g.)

For example, this statement will create a user name JOAN with a password OFARC:

```
CREATE USER JOAN IDENTIFIED BY OFARC;
```

You can use the ALTER USER statement to change the password, like this:

```
ALTER USER JOAN IDENTIFIED BY HAWAII;
```

Finally, you can remove a user from the database using the DROP USER statement, like this:

```
DROP USER username;
```

If a user account owns any database objects, the preceding statement won't work, and you'll need to use this:

```
DROP USER username CASCADE;
```

The CASCADE option directs SQL to drop the user account and all of the objects it owns.

Once a user object has been created, it can be granted privileges, as we'll see in an upcoming section.

CONNECT

The CONNECT statement is not a SQL statement but a SQL*Plus enhancement you can use within the Oracle SQL*Plus tool. Once you've started SQL*Plus, you can use CONNECT to log in or switch login sessions from one user account to another. If, for example, you are using the SQL*Plus tool and have logged in to the EFCODD account and created the user account JOAN, you can log in to the JOAN account directly from EFCODD with this statement:

```
CONNECT JOAN/HAWAII
```

That assumes that the user account JOAN is still using the password HAWAII. It also assumes that JOAN has been granted the minimum system privileges to log in—such as CREATE SESSION.

Also note—a semicolon termination character is not required in SQL*Plus statements. It is accepted but not required. The semicolon termination character is required in SQL statements, but is optional in SQL*Plus statements.

Tablespaces

In the course of setting up a new user account, the topic of tablespaces must be addressed. However, the topic of tablespaces goes beyond our scope and is not included in the exam objectives, so we're going to go with a simple way to address the tablespace requirement, namely:

```
GRANT UNLIMITED TABLESPACE TO username;
```

This would probably not be something that your typical production DBA would do. Tablespaces are controlled by database administrators. A typical DBA generally creates uniquely named tablespaces and carefully allocates space quotas to them. We, however, aren't concerned with any of that for this book or for the exam. So for us, the preceding statement is what we'll include. If you wish to learn more, we heartily encourage you to check out any of the outstanding books from Oracle Press on the topic of database administration. In the meantime, if you're working on your own test system on your own personal machine—this particular statement that grants UNLIMITED TABLESPACE is more than adequate for our purposes going forward. If you're trying these at work—check with your DBA before trying any of the code samples in this chapter.

GRANT and REVOKE

Now let's get down to business. System privileges are granted with the GRANT statement. Here's an example of a SQL session that logs in to the Oracle SYSTEM account, creates a new user, and grants the new user account some initial system privileges using three GRANT statements (line numbers added):

```
01    CONNECT SYSTEM/MANAGER
02    CREATE USER HAROLD IDENTIFIED BY LLOYD;
03    GRANT CREATE SESSION TO HAROLD;
04    GRANT UNLIMITED TABLESPACE TO HAROLD;
05    GRANT CREATE TABLE TO HAROLD;
```

In these statements, here is what we are doing:

- Line 1: Establish a user session with the user account SYSTEM, with a password of MANAGER. The SYSTEM account is installed with every Oracle database, and its initial password at installation defaults to MANAGER. (WARNING: DO NOT TRY THIS on a production system. No self-respecting production system should have a SYSTEM account password still set to the default value of MANAGER anyway, but the point is that if you have installed your own version of the Oracle database on your own local machine, and it is not used for production work, then you can try this, but if you're trying things out within a system at your workplace or somewhere comparable—then be sure to check with your database administrator before trying this.)

- Line 2: We create a brand new user account called HAROLD, with the password LLOYD.

- Line 3: We use the SQL statement GRANT to give the CREATE SESSION privilege to user HAROLD. This is a minimum requirement in order for us to be able to log in to the database with the HAROLD user account; without this GRANT statement, we couldn't successfully log in with the user account HAROLD.

- Line 4: This is one way to ensure that HAROLD can create objects. See our earlier discussion about tablespaces in the previous section.

- Line 5: We GRANT the system privilege CREATE TABLE to user account HAROLD.

See Figure 18-1 for the results of these statements in the SQL*Plus window. Now—let's log in to HAROLD and try out what we've done. For that, we'll try the following SQL statements:

```
CONNECT HAROLD/LLOYD
CREATE TABLE CLOCKTOWER (CLOCK_ID NUMBER(11));
CREATE SEQUENCE SEQ_CLOCK_ID;
```

See Figure 18-2 for the results. Note that we aren't able to create the sequence because we haven't been granted sufficient privileges to do so. For that, we'll need to log back in to the SYSTEM account and grant the system privilege CREATE SEQUENCE to HAROLD. Once that has been accomplished, we can log back in to HAROLD and create the sequence (see Figure 18-3).

FIGURE 18-1	
SQL*Plus session: GRANT statements	

```
SQL> CONNECT SYSTEM/MANAGER
Connected.
SQL> CREATE USER HAROLD IDENTIFIED BY LLOYD;

User created.

SQL> GRANT CREATE SESSION TO HAROLD;

Grant succeeded.

SQL> GRANT UNLIMITED TABLESPACE TO HAROLD;

Grant succeeded.

SQL> GRANT CREATE TABLE TO HAROLD;

Grant succeeded.

SQL>
```

FIGURE 18-2

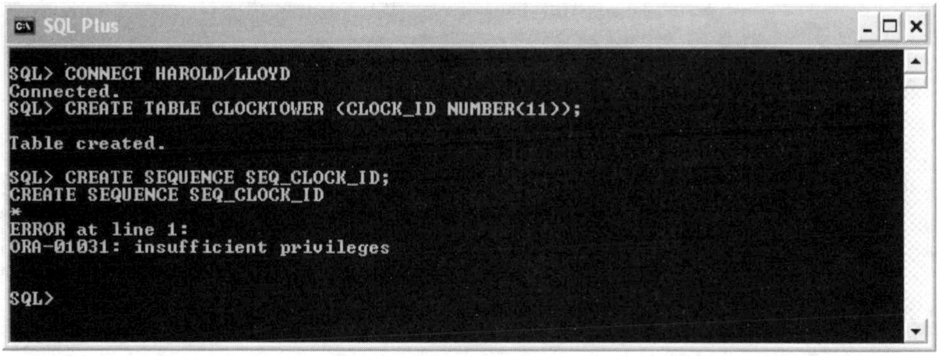

SQL*Plus session: testing system privileges

FIGURE 18-3

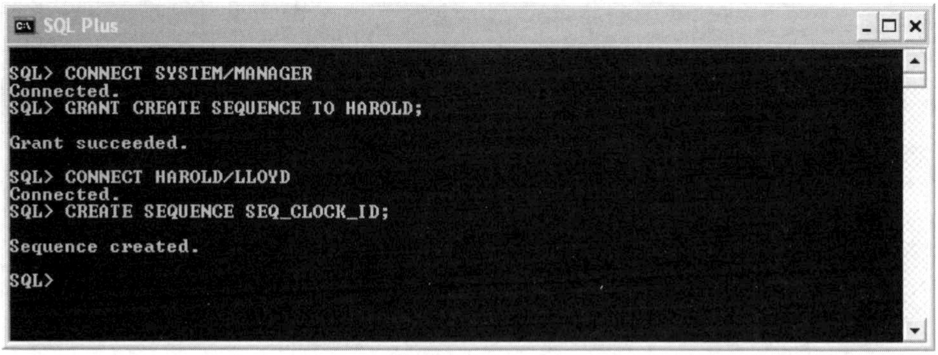

SQL*Plus session: creating the sequence

In these examples, we have been using the SYSTEM account to grant these privileges, but any qualified database administrator (DBA) account will do and is preferable in any serious installation with multiple Oracle users. In such a situation, the less time a developer or DBA spends in the SYSTEM account—or the other restricted default DBA accounts in the Oracle database such as SYS—the less likely a mistake will accidentally cause some serious damage to the database.

The basic syntax for the GRANT statement is simple:

```
GRANT privilege TO user option;
```

where *privilege* is one of the several dozens of system privileges that are already defined in the database—see the *Oracle Database SQL Language Reference Manual* for a complete list. Multiple privileges can be granted at once by separating each additional privilege by a comma, as in GRANT *privilege, privilege, . . .* We'll discuss *option* in an upcoming section.

The basic syntax for REVOKE is comparable:

```
REVOKE privilege FROM user;
```

Note that you grant "TO" and you revoke "FROM".

Once a system privilege is revoked from a user, the effect is immediate. However, any actions taken prior to the revocation stand. In other words, if a user account has been granted the system privilege CREATE TABLE, and then creates some tables, but then has the CREATE TABLE system privilege revoked—the created tables already in existence remain in place. They do not disappear. But the owning user may not create additional tables while the CREATE TABLE system privilege is revoked.

We've looked at a few system privileges, and we've said that they are somewhat like a driver's license. Now let's extend the analogy a little bit—imagine what would happen if you could get a universal driver's license that carried with it the ability to drive anyone's car legally without the car's owner express permission. Such a concept exists within the Oracle database, and it's embodied in the keyword ANY. Let's look at that next.

ANY

Some system privileges include the keyword ANY in the title. For example, there is a system privilege CREATE ANY TABLE, which is the ability to create a table in any user account anywhere in the database. Let's look at a sample session that involves this privilege:

```
CONNECT SYSTEM/MANAGER

CREATE USER LAUREL IDENTIFIED BY POKE;
GRANT CREATE SESSION TO LAUREL;
GRANT UNLIMITED TABLESPACE TO LAUREL;
GRANT CREATE TABLE TO LAUREL;

CREATE USER HARDY  IDENTIFIED BY CLOBBER;
GRANT CREATE SESSION TO HARDY;
GRANT UNLIMITED TABLESPACE TO HARDY;
GRANT CREATE ANY TABLE TO HARDY;

CONNECT LAUREL / POKE
CREATE TABLE MOVIES (MOVIE_ID NUMBER(7));

CONNECT HARDY / CLOBBER
CREATE TABLE LAUREL.TVSHOWS (TVSHOW_ID NUMBER(7));
```

The result of the preceding SQL statements: two user accounts will be created; also, two tables will be created, one table called MOVIES and another table called TVSHOWS. Both tables will exist in the user account LAUREL—the first table was created by LAUREL, but the second table TVSHOWS was created by user account HARDY and created as a table that is owned by LAUREL. The user account HARDY will contain no tables. The official "owner" of both tables is LAUREL, as the data dictionary confirms:

```
SELECT OWNER, TABLE_NAME
FROM   DBA_TABLES
WHERE  OWNER IN ('HARDY','LAUREL');

OWNER                              TABLE_NAME
------------------------------     ------------------------------
LAUREL                             MOVIES
LAUREL                             TVSHOWS
```

When a system privilege includes the keyword ANY in its title, it means that the privilege will authorize a user to perform the task as though they were any user account. In this example, user HARDY was able to create a table and place it in the LAUREL account, a task typically reserved only for user LAUREL. However, since user HARDY has the system privilege CREATE ANY TABLE, then HARDY can create any table in any user account.

ADMIN OPTION

In a previous section we said we would look at the *option* in the GRANT statement's syntax we examined. Here it is: the *option* is an additional clause that may be included with the GRANT statement, as follows:

```
GRANT privilege TO user WITH ADMIN OPTION;
```

When any system privilege is granted with the WITH ADMIN OPTION option, then the recipient receives the system privilege itself, along with the right to grant the system privilege to another user (see Figure 18-4).

The REVOKE statement does not use the WITH ADMIN OPTION clause. Whenever a system privilege is revoked, the entire system privilege is revoked.

If a user—let's call it the first user—grants a system privilege to a second user WITH ADMIN OPTION, and the second user uses the admin option to grant that same system privilege to a third user, then the third user retains the privilege until it is explicitly revoked from the third user. In other words, once the second user has

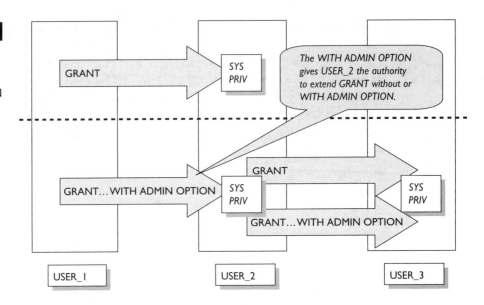

FIGURE 18-4

GRANT versus
GRANT WITH
ADMIN OPTION

granted the third user with the system privilege, it stays with the first user, even if
the first user—or any other qualified user—revokes the system privilege from the
second user. If that happens, the third user still has the system privilege. The only
way the third user will lose the system privilege is if any qualified user revokes the
system privilege explicitly from the third user with a REVOKE statement. In other
words—the REVOKE statement for system privileges does not "cascade". It only
applies to the user to whom the revocation is applied.

ALL PRIVILEGES

As an alternative to granting specific system privileges, a qualified user account,
such as SYSTEM or some other DBA qualified account, can issue the following
statement:

```
GRANT ALL PRIVILEGES TO user;
```

This statement has the effect of granting all system privileges to the user. The WITH
ADMIN OPTION clause may be used with this as well.

Needless to say, this should only be done with great caution, if at all. It is not
easily reversible—in other words, this is not an exact counterpart:

```
REVOKE ALL PRIVILEGES FROM user;
```

This statement will reverse all system privileges granted to the user, assuming that all system privileges have been granted to the user. If not, an error message will result.

PUBLIC

The PUBLIC account is a built-in user account in the Oracle database that represents all users. Any objects owned by PUBLIC are treated as though they are owned by all the users in the database, present and future.

The GRANT statement will work with the keyword PUBLIC in the place of a user account name. For example:

```
GRANT CREATE ANY TABLE TO PUBLIC;
```

This statement grants the CREATE ANY TABLE privilege to every user in the database. The CREATE ANY TABLE privilege gives every user the ability to create any table in any other user account. In other words—mass hysteria. Or something like it. Mind you, we're not recommending you do this—but it's syntactically possible, and you need to be aware of it. While this sort of an example is unlikely, granting to PUBLIC may be useful with a selected number of object privileges, which we'll discuss a bit later.

Note that if you come to your senses and decide to revoke a system privilege from PUBLIC, you can do so without revoking any other system privileges. In other words, consider this statement:

```
REVOKE CREATE ANY TABLE FROM PUBLIC;
```

This statement will reverse the GRANT . . . TO PUBLIC that we issued a few paragraphs earlier, and thankfully will not revoke any individually granted CREATE ANY TABLE system privileges held by any user accounts. It will only revoke the GRANT to PUBLIC.

And if you're even thinking about GRANT ALL PRIVILEGES TO PUBLIC WITH ADMIN OPTION, you can put that thought out of your mind right this second.

Grant Privileges on Tables

Any user with the system privilege CREATE TABLE can create a table. The table, once created, is owned by the user who created it. The owner does not require any explicitly granted privileges on the table. The table owner can use DML to add rows, change data in the table, query the data in the table, and remove rows from the table. But other users do not have that privilege automatically. Other users must have explicitly granted priviliges on the object—which, in this case, is a table.

(Note: The exception, of course, is those users who have the system privileges that allow them to run any DML statements on any table in the database, regardless of who owns it—those system privileges, as we saw in the last section, include SELECT ANY TABLE, INSERT ANY TABLE, UPDATE ANY TABLE, and DELETE ANY TABLE.)

Any user who owns a table—or any other database object—may grant object privileges on their database object to other users in the database.

Object privileges exist for all DML statements—SELECT, INSERT, UPDATE, and DELETE—as well as any DDL statement that is relevant to an existing object: ALTER, for example. Note: there is no separate set of object privileges for the MERGE statement.

Object privileges on a table include all of the DML statements that can be executed against a table. For example, if a user account LISA has the system privilege CREATE TABLE, then LISA can create a table. If LISA takes advantage of this system privilege and creates a table WEBINARS, then LISA can access the new table, but other users are not automatically able to see the table (unless, as we stated earlier, those users possess one of the "ANY" system privileges, such as SELECT ANY TABLE). In order to ensure that other user accounts can execute SQL statements on the table, user account LISA will have to grant object privileges on WEBINARS to other users.

See Figure 18-5 for a SQL*Plus session in which we connect to the SYSTEM account, where we create two user accounts, LISA and HENRY. We give LISA sufficient privileges to connect (CREATE SESSION) and create tables. Note how we combined multiple system privileges in a single GRANT statement. Also, we give HENRY sufficient privileges to create a session—but nothing more.

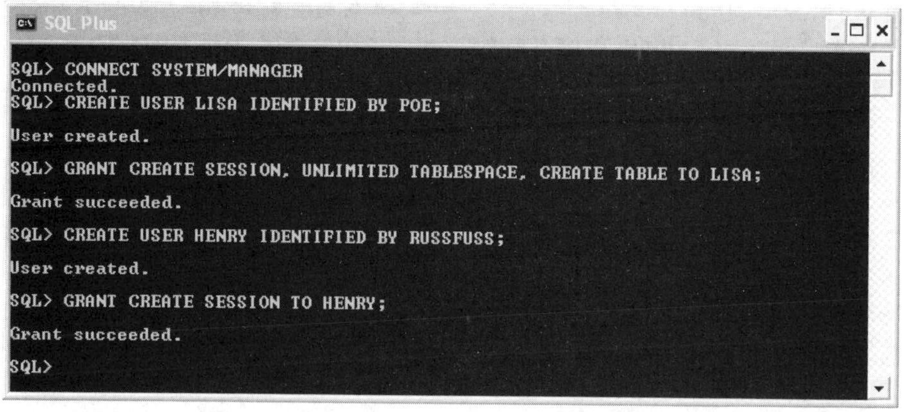

FIGURE 18-5

Creating, granting, and testing object privileges—part 1

```
SQL> CONNECT SYSTEM/MANAGER
Connected.
SQL> CREATE USER LISA IDENTIFIED BY POE;

User created.

SQL> GRANT CREATE SESSION, UNLIMITED TABLESPACE, CREATE TABLE TO LISA;

Grant succeeded.

SQL> CREATE USER HENRY IDENTIFIED BY RUSSFUSS;

User created.

SQL> GRANT CREATE SESSION TO HENRY;

Grant succeeded.

SQL>
```

We continue in Figure 18-6, where we connect to the LISA account and create a table, add data to it, and then grant privileges on the table to HENRY. Then we connect to HENRY, where we can issue SELECT and UPDATE statements, but not INSERT—that particular privilege wasn't granted to HENRY.

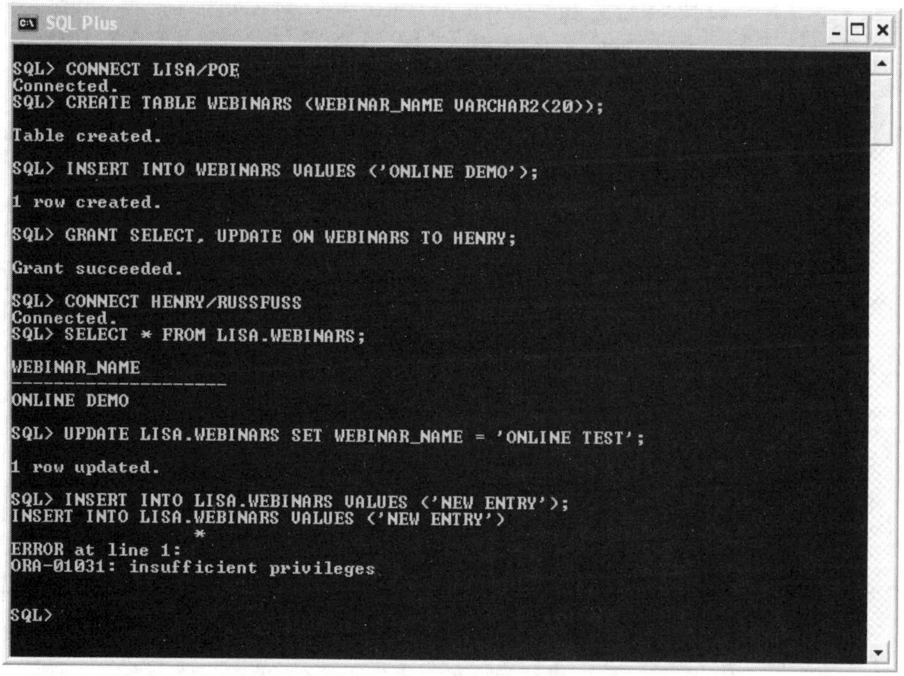

FIGURE 18-6

Creating, granting, and testing object privileges—part 2

```
SQL> CONNECT LISA/POE
Connected.
SQL> CREATE TABLE WEBINARS (WEBINAR_NAME VARCHAR2(20));

Table created.

SQL> INSERT INTO WEBINARS VALUES ('ONLINE DEMO');

1 row created.

SQL> GRANT SELECT, UPDATE ON WEBINARS TO HENRY;

Grant succeeded.

SQL> CONNECT HENRY/RUSSFUSS
Connected.
SQL> SELECT * FROM LISA.WEBINARS;

WEBINAR_NAME
--------------------
ONLINE DEMO

SQL> UPDATE LISA.WEBINARS SET WEBINAR_NAME = 'ONLINE TEST';

1 row updated.

SQL> INSERT INTO LISA.WEBINARS VALUES ('NEW ENTRY');
INSERT INTO LISA.WEBINARS VALUES ('NEW ENTRY')
            *
ERROR at line 1:
ORA-01031: insufficient privileges


SQL>
```

on the **!** job

Take another look at Figure 18-6, and note the moment that the GRANT statement is issued. Remember that any DDL statement carries with it an implicit commit event. In other words, the GRANT statement has the effect of making the results of the INSERT statement permanent in the database. Once that GRANT has executed, the option to ROLLBACK the INSERT statement is no longer available.

Schema Prefixes

Note in Figure 18-6 that when HENRY references a table owned by LISA, HENRY must use the schema prefix to make the reference. In other words, HENRY could not issue a SELECT statement like this:

```
SELECT * FROM WEBINARS;
```

Instead, HENRY uses this sort of reference:

```
SELECT * FROM LISA.WEBINARS;
```

However, you might recall our discussion several chapters ago about the PUBLIC SYNONYM object. Remember that a SYNONYM is an alternative name for a database object. A PUBLIC SYNONYM is a SYNONYM that is owned by the PUBLIC user account, which is an automatically created user account that is maintained by the Oracle database. The PUBLIC user isn't intended to be an account into which you log in to get access—instead, PUBLIC is a mechanism by which you can create globally owned objects. Specifically, anything that is owned by PUBLIC is automatically owned by all users in the database. The same is true for PUBLIC SYNONYMS.

In our earlier example, the user SYSTEM could have given user LISA the system privilege to create public synonyms by issuing the following statement:

```
GRANT CREATE PUBLIC SYNONYM TO LISA;
```

Then, later, the user LISA could have used that system privilege to create a PUBLIC SYNONYM like this:

```
CREATE PUBLIC SYNONYM WEBINARS FOR LISA.WEBINARS;
```

Finally, once user HENRY got around to issuing DML statements on the WEBINARS table, HENRY could have omitted the schema prefix and instead simply executed this statement:

```
SELECT * FROM WEBINARS;
```

In this instance, HENRY would be specifying the WEBINARS object PUBLIC SYNONYM, which in turn points to the object LISA.WEBINARS. Note that no object privilege had to be granted on the PUBLIC SYNONYM object to HENRY. All objects owned by PUBLIC are automatically available and accessible to all users in the database, present and future. However, privileges must be granted to whatever object for which the PUBLIC SYNONYM serves as an alias. It's one thing to have privileges on a PUBLIC SYNONYM that references a table, but it's another thing to have privileges on the table it references. All users have privileges automatically on any object owned by PUBLIC; they do not have automatically granted privileges on anything a PUBLIC SYNONYM references—such privileges must be granted explicitly.

This sort of usage is the most common purpose of the PUBLIC SYNONYM object.

Note that in order to create PUBLIC SYNONYM objects, a user account must have the CREATE PUBLIC SYNONYM system privilege.

Name Priority, Revisited

You may recall our discussion in Chapter 10 about a concept called *name priority*. When a user makes a reference to an object by name, SQL will use that name to search for that object as follows:

- First, SQL looks in the local namespace, which contains objects owned by the user account: tables, views, sequences, private synonyms, and something called user-defined types—which are beyond the scope of the exam.
- Next, SQL looks in the database namespace, which contains users, roles, and public synonyms.

This concept was demonstrated graphically in Figure 10-3.

WITH GRANT OPTION

If you wish to grant another user a particular object privilege, and include the ability for the user to grant that same object privilege to yet another user, then include the WITH GRANT OPTION clause in the GRANT statement. For example:

```
CONNECT LISA/POE
GRANT SELECT, UPDATE ON WEBINARS TO HENRY WITH GRANT OPTION;
```

This grant gives user HENRY the ability to issue SELECT and UPDATE statements on table WEBINARS, along with the ability to grant those privileges to other users. HENRY is not obligated to grant the set of privileges together, HENRY can choose to be selective:

```
CONNECT HENRY/RUSSFUSS
GRANT SELECT ON LISA.WEBINARS TO HAROLD WITH GRANT OPTION;
```

Now user HAROLD has the ability to issue SELECT statements on LISA.WEBINARS, as well as the ability to grant that privilege to others. But HENRY did not pass along the UPDATE privilege.

REVOKE

User LISA may choose to revoke privileges from HENRY, like this:

```
REVOKE SELECT, UPDATE ON WEBINARS FROM HENRY;
```

If user LISA does this, then HENRY and HAROLD lose all privileges, as does anyone to whom they extended privileges with their WITH GRANT OPTION option.

In other words, revoking object privileges "cascades".

Note that the REVOKE statement does not require the WITH GRANT OPTION clause. REVOKE doesn't care whether that option had been included or not, it just revokes all specified privileges and cascades the change throughout all user accounts as required.

ALL PRIVILEGES

The ALL PRIVILEGES option works with granting and revoking object privileges in much the same way it does with system privileges, with some differences. For example:

```
GRANT ALL PRIVILEGES ON WEBINARS TO HENRY;
```

This statements gives all privileges on the object WEBINARS to HENRY, except for the ability to grant privileges. To grant the ability to grant, use this:

```
GRANT ALL PRIVILEGES ON WEBINARS TO HENRY WITH GRANT OPTION;
```

The keyword PRIVILEGES is not required when granting object privileges:

```
GRANT ALL ON WEBINARS TO HENRY;
```

The same is true with REVOKE when used with object privileges:

```
REVOKE ALL PRIVILEGES ON WEBINARS FROM HENRY;
```

This is also good:

```
REVOKE ALL ON WEBINARS FROM HENRY;
```

This shorthand way of revoking object privileges spares the effort of identifying all the individual object privileges that may have already been granted to HENRY on the WEBINARS table, and revokes them all at once.

Note that the keyword PRIVILEGES is optional when working with object privileges, but not when working with system privileges.

If you use REVOKE ALL to revoke object privileges from a user, and no object privileges exist on the object for that user, then no error message results, and the statement executes successfully with no practical effect.

Dependent Privileges

If user A owns a view, which is based on a table that user A also owns, and user A grants privileges on the view to user B, then user B can access the view without privileges to the underlying table.

If user A creates a table and a public synonym, then user B has immediate visibility of the public synonym, because the synonym is owned by PUBLIC and all users have visibility of all objects owned by PUBLIC. However, user B still requires privileges on the table for which the public synonym is an alias. If the public synonym references a view that user A owns, then user B must have object privileges on the view, but is not required to have access to its underlying table.

e x a m
watch

If you grant privileges on a table, then drop the table, the privileges are dropped with the table. If you later recreate the table, you must also grant the privileges again. However, if you restore *a dropped table with the FLASHBACK TABLE . . . BEFORE DROP statement, you will recover the table, its associated indices, and the table's granted privileges, and you will not need to grant the privileges again.*

CERTIFICATION OBJECTIVE 18.03

View Privileges in the Data Dictionary

We've already looked at the data dictionary, and seen how it provides information about the state of objects in the database, as well as providing some historic information as well.

There are many views in the data dictionary that present information about system privileges and object privileges. See Table 18-3 for a listing of some of these views.

For example, to see what system privileges are granted to your current user account, you can query the data dictionary view USER_SYS_PRIVS. Here's what the results might look like from user account LISA:

```
SELECT    PRIVILEGE, ADMIN_OPTION
FROM      USER_SYS_PRIVS
ORDER BY PRIVILEGE;

PRIVILEGE                                   ADMIN_OPTION
----------------------------------------- ------------
CREATE PUBLIC SYNONYM                       NO
CREATE SESSION                              NO
CREATE TABLE                                NO
UNLIMITED TABLESPACE                        NO
```

The equivalent data dictionary view DBA_SYS_PRIVS allows you to see the same information for other users.

TABLE 18-3	Data Dictionary View	Explanation
Data about Privileges in the Data Dictionary	USER_SYS_PRIVS	System privileges granted to current user
	DBA_SYS_PRIVS	System privileges granted to users and roles
	USER_TAB_PRIVS	Grants on objects for which the user is the grantor, grantee, or owner
	ALL_TAB_PRIVS	Grants on objects for which the user is the grantor, owner, or an enabled role or PUBLIC is the grantee
	DBA_TAB_PRIVS	Grants on all objects in the database
	ALL_TAB_PRIVS_RECD	Grants on objects for which the user, PUBLIC, or enabled role is the grantee
	SESSION_PRIVS	Privileges that are enabled to the user

To see all of the object privileges that your current user account may have granted to others, or may have been granted by others, you can use the following query. This is what the results might look like within the user account LISA:

```
SELECT    GRANTOR, OWNER, GRANTEE, TABLE_NAME, PRIVILEGE, GRANTABLE
FROM      USER_TAB_PRIVS
ORDER BY  GRANTOR, OWNER, GRANTEE, TABLE_NAME, PRIVILEGE;
```

GRANTOR	OWNER	GRANTEE	TABLE_NAME	PRIVILEGE	GRANTABLE
EFCODD	EFCODD	LISA	PORTS	DELETE	NO
EFCODD	EFCODD	LISA	PORTS	INSERT	NO
EFCODD	EFCODD	LISA	PORTS	SELECT	NO
EFCODD	EFCODD	LISA	PORTS	UPDATE	NO
EFCODD	EFCODD	LISA	SHIPS	ALTER	NO
EFCODD	EFCODD	LISA	SHIPS	DELETE	NO
EFCODD	EFCODD	LISA	SHIPS	INSERT	NO
EFCODD	EFCODD	LISA	SHIPS	SELECT	NO
EFCODD	EFCODD	LISA	SHIPS	UPDATE	NO
LISA	LISA	HENRY	WEBINARS	SELECT	NO
LISA	LISA	HENRY	WEBINARS	UPDATE	NO

Note that the first several rows show object privileges granted by EFCODD to LISA. The final two rows show object privileges granted by LISA to HENRY.

These are just a few examples of the sort of information the data dictionary provides about system privileges and object privileges that have been granted to and from user accounts within the database.

on the **job** *When inspecting data dictionary views like DBA_TAB_PRIVS or DBA_SYS_ PRIVS to see what privileges have been granted to a particular user account, you can check the GRANTEE column for the appropriate USER name. However, don't forget to also check for rows where GRANTEE = 'PUBLIC'; these privileges are also available to your user account.*

CERTIFICATION OBJECTIVE 18.04

Grant Roles

A ROLE is a database object that you can create, and to which you can assign system privileges and/or object privileges. You can also assign other roles to a given role. Once it is created, you can grant a ROLE to a user just as you can grant privileges to a user. The user is then automatically granted any privileges contained within the ROLE. A ROLE is an excellent way to manage the various privileges required for performing different tasks in the database, and to organize the process of granting and revoking privileges.

You may grant the ROLE to as many user accounts as you wish.

If any privilege is subsequently revoked from the ROLE, it is also revoked from any users to whom the role has been granted. In other words, changes to roles cascade to the users to whom the role is granted.

Three roles in particular have historically been associated with standard Oracle databases, but they are being phased out. On a practical level, though, it's good to know about them, if you don't already. The three roles are CONNECT, RESOURCE, and DBA. The CONNECT role consists of the CREATE SESSION system privilege, intended for the typical generic end user. RESOURCE is a collection of system privileges intended for the typical application developer. DBA is intended for the typical database administrator. Each can be seen in detail in the data dictionary view DBA_SYS_PRIVS (see Table 18-4 for details). All three roles are still included in each implementation of the Oracle database as of this writing, but Oracle has stated formally that the use of these roles is now officially discouraged, and their inclusion in future database implementations is not guaranteed. Oracle Corporation's official position is that you should create your own set of roles as required.

You can refer to the data in Table 18-4 to get an idea of the kind of system privileges you may wish to include in your role objects.

In order to create a ROLE, a user account needs the CREATE ROLE system privilege.

For example, the user account EFCODD owns several tables and wishes to grant privileges on these tables to some users in the database. Some of these users will be performing queries on the tables and nothing more. Others will be responsible for performing changes to the data. Therefore, we wish to create two different roles and grant them the necessary privileges:

```
CONNECT EFCODD/FOUNDER

CREATE ROLE CRUISE_ANALYST;
GRANT SELECT ON SHIPS     TO CRUISE_ANALYST;
GRANT SELECT ON PORTS     TO CRUISE_ANALYST;
GRANT SELECT ON EMPLOYEES TO CRUISE_ANALYST;

CREATE ROLE CRUISE_OPERATOR;

GRANT SELECT, UPDATE, INSERT, DELETE ON SHIPS     TO CRUISE_OPERATOR;
GRANT SELECT, UPDATE, INSERT, DELETE ON PORTS     TO CRUISE_OPERATOR;
GRANT SELECT, UPDATE                 ON EMPLOYEES TO CRUISE_OPERATOR;
```

TABLE 18-4	Role	Privilege
The Classic Roles CONNECT, RESOURCE, and DBA	CONNECT	CREATE SESSION
	RESOURCE	CREATE TRIGGER CREATE SEQUENCE CREATE TYPE CREATE PROCEDURE CREATE CLUSTER CREATE OPERATOR CREATE INDEXTYPE CREATE TABLE
	DBA	Over 100 system privileges, including: CREATE ANY TABLE CREATE PUBLIC SYNONYM CREATE ROLE CREATE SYNONYM CREATE SEQUENCE CREATE USER CREATE VIEW GRANT ANY PRIVILEGE Etc.

In the preceding code, we create two role objects: one called CRUISE_ANALYST, to which we grant some SELECT privileges on tables, and another called CRUISE_OPERATOR, to which we grant some other privileges. Once they are created, we can grant these roles to user accounts in the database:

```
GRANT CRUISE_OPERATOR TO LISA;
GRANT CRUISE_ANALYST  TO HENRY;
```

Once a role is granted, a user has access to all of the privileges within it.

A role can be granted to another role.

A role can be granted WITH ADMIN OPTION to empower the recipient to grant the role to yet another user. For example:

```
GRANT CRUISE_OPERATOR TO LISA WITH ADMIN OPTION;
```

If a user grants a role to another user and uses the WITH ADMIN OPTION, the second user may further grant the same role to a third user. If the first user revokes the role from the second user, the third user retains the role until it is explicitly revoked from the third user by a qualified user.

Table 18-5 lists some of the data dictionary views that provide information about existing roles in the database.

TABLE 18-5	Data Dictionary View	Explanation
Data Dictionary Views with Information about ROLE Objects	DBA_ROLES	All roles that exist in the database
	DBA_ROLE_PRIVS	Roles granted to users and roles
	DBA_SYS_PRIVS	System privileges granted to users and roles
	DBA_TAB_PRIVS	All grants on objects to users and roles
	ROLE_ROLE_PRIVS	Roles that are granted to roles
	ROLE_SYS_PRIVS	System privileges granted to roles
	ROLE_TAB_PRIVS	Table privileges granted to roles
	SESSION_ROLES	Roles that are enabled to the user

Roles exist in a namespace that resides outside of any user account. Therefore, you can create roles with names that are the same as objects within a user account, such as tables and views. That's not necessarily a good idea, but it's allowed in the database.

A user account may be granted multiple roles at once.

CERTIFICATION OBJECTIVE 18.05

Distinguish Between Privileges and Roles

A role object does not represent privileges in and of itself. It is merely a collection of privileges. That being said, a role exists independently of the privileges it may—or may not—contain. Furthermore, the relationship a user account has to a granted role is separate from any privileges that may have been granted directly to the user account. In other words, if a user account already has any object privileges granted directly to it as a result of earlier GRANT statements and then later is granted a role that duplicates any of those privileges, then the role exists separately from those originally granted privileges, which exist independently of the role. If the role is later revoked, that revocation does not adversely affect any separately granted privileges given directly to the user account.

If user HENRY were already granted a privilege that happens to be duplicated within the role CRUISE_ANALYST, and then subsequently the role is granted— but then later the role is revoked, like this:

```
REVOKE CRUISE_ANALYST FROM HENRY;
```

then any object privileges granted directly to HENRY still exist.

For example, examine the following code (line numbers added):

```
01    GRANT SELECT ON INVOICES TO HENRY;
02    CREATE ROLE CRUISE_ACCOUNTANT;
03    GRANT SELECT ON INVOICES TO CRUISE_ACCOUNTANT;
04    GRANT CRUISE_ACCOUNTANT TO HENRY;
05    REVOKE CRUISE_ACCOUNTANT FROM HENRY;
```

User HENRY still has SELECT on INVOICES because of line 1, in spite of lines 2 through 5.

Similarly, if the role is restored but the direct object privilege is revoked, HENRY still has access through the role. In other words (line numbers added):

```
01    GRANT SELECT ON INVOICES TO HENRY;
02    CREATE ROLE CRUISE_ACCOUNTANT;
03    GRANT SELECT ON INVOICES TO CRUISE_ACCOUNTANT;
04    GRANT CRUISE_ACCOUNTANT TO HENRY;
05    REVOKE SELECT ON INVOICES FROM HENRY;
```

HENRY still has privileges on INVOICES in spite of line 5. The reason: the CRUISE_ACCOUNTANT role, from lines 2 through 4.

However, if the object privilege revoked from HENRY in line 5 were also to be revoked from the CRUISE_ACCOUNTANT role, then the object privilege would be removed from HENRY altogether.

CERTIFICATION SUMMARY

A system privilege is the right to perform a task in the database, using a DDL or DML statement on objects in general. The right to perform those tasks on a particular object in the database is an object privilege. Finally, a role combines privileges into a single object, so that a combination of privileges can be managed as a group.

The SQL statements GRANT and REVOKE are used to issue system privileges and object privileges, and also to take them away. Privileges are given to—or taken away from—user accounts. Any user in the database must have privileges to perform any task. The act of logging in requires the CREATE SESSION system privilege. Other privileges include the privilege to CREATE PUBLIC SYNONYM or CREATE TABLE.

The ANY keyword in a system privilege indicates the ability to work with objects that are owned by any user account.

A user account, by default, has object privileges on the objects it owns. Object privileges are required for a user to be able to interact with objects it does not own.

Instead of granting privileges to a user, you may create a role, then grant privileges to a role, and then grant the role to one or more users. The advantage is that if you have multiple users, a role is much easier to change, since you can grant or revoke privileges as desired after the role has been assigned to any number of users, and all of the users will automatically have the new privileges granted or revoked automatically.

The data dictionary provides information about system privileges, object privileges, and roles, from the perspective of both the grantor and the grantee.

TWO-MINUTE DRILL

Differentiate System Privileges from Object Privileges

❑ The right to use any given SQL statement and/or to generally perform a task in the database is a system privilege.

❑ The right to use a system privilege to perform some task on a specific existing object in the database is an object privilege.

❑ Both system and object privileges are granted to and revoked from users in the database.

❑ System privileges may be granted WITH ADMIN OPTION, which provides the ability for the recipient to grant the same privilege to yet another user.

❑ When a system privilege is revoked, the revocation does not cascade—meaning that it is only revoked from the user from whom it is being revoked, not from other users to whom the revoked user may have extended the privilege.

❑ The ALL PRIVILEGES keywords can be used to grant or revoke all privileges to or from a user.

Grant Privileges on Tables

❑ Object privileges correspond to DML statements, and to DDL statements that are relevant to existing objects.

❑ Object privileges may be granted WITH GRANT OPTION, which provides the ability for the recipient to grant the same privilege to yet another user.

❑ When an object privilege is revoked, the revocation cascades—meaning that it is revoked from the user from whom it is being revoked, as well as from other users to whom the revoked user may have extended the privilege.

❑ When a user has been granted access to an object, the object name will require a schema name prefix to be correctly identified.

❑ A PUBLIC SYNONYM can provide an alternative name for the schema-prefixed version of the granted object.

❑ The ALL PRIVILEGES keywords can be used to grant or revoke all privileges to or from a user.

View Privileges in the Data Dictionary

❑ A variety of data dictionary views provide information about system and object privileges.

❑ Users may see privileges granted to them, or granted by them to others, by querying the data dictionary.

Grant Roles

❑ A role is created with the CREATE ROLE statement.

❑ Roles may be granted WITH ADMIN OPTION, which provides the ability for the recipient to grant the same role to yet another user.

❑ Roles exist in a namespace outside of an individual user account.

❑ A role is a collection of privileges and other roles.

❑ A role may be granted to another role.

Distinguish Between Privileges and Roles

❑ A privilege granted directly to a user exists independently from a privilege granted to a role.

❑ If you revoke a privilege directly from a user who also has been granted a role containing the same privilege, the role remains unchanged and the user still has privileges by way of the role.

❑ The same situation is true with regard to revoking privileges directly from roles; if you revoke a privilege from a role that a user already has through a direct grant, the direct grant stays in force.

SELF TEST

The following questions will help you measure your understanding of the material presented in this chapter. Choose one answer for each question, unless otherwise directed.

Differentiate System Privileges from Object Privileges

1. Which of the following SQL statements will authorize the user account JESSE to create tables in each and every user account in the database?
   A. GRANT CREATE ALL TABLE TO JESSE;
   B. GRANT CREATE PUBLIC TABLE TO JESSE;
   C. GRANT CREATE ANY TABLE TO JESSE;
   D. GRANT CREATE TABLE TO JESSE WITH PUBLIC OPTION;

2. You are logged in to user account FRED and have been tasked with granting privileges to the user account ETHEL. You execute the following SQL statements:

   ```
   GRANT CREATE ANY TABLE TO ETHEL WITH ADMIN OPTION;
   REVOKE CREATE ANY TABLE FROM ETHEL;
   ```

   Assuming both statements execute successfully, what is the result?
   A. ETHEL does not have the system privilege CREATE ANY TABLE, nor the right to grant the CREATE ANY TABLE system privilege to any other user.
   B. ETHEL has the system privilege CREATE ANY TABLE because the WITH ADMIN OPTION clause wasn't included in the REVOKE statement.
   C. ETHEL no longer has the system privilege CREATE ANY TABLE but still has the right to grant the CREATE ANY TABLE system privilege to any other user, since the WITH ADMIN OPTION clause was omitted from the REVOKE statement. However, ETHEL may not grant the CREATE ANY TABLE privilege back to itself.
   D. ETHEL no longer has the system privilege CREATE ANY TABLE but still has the right to grant the CREATE ANY TABLE system privilege to any other user, since the WITH ADMIN OPTION clause was omitted. Furthermore, ETHEL may grant the CREATE ANY TABLE privilege back to itself because of the WITH ADMIN OPTION clause.

3. Which of the following is the system privilege that is required as a minimum to allow a user account to log in to the database?
   A. CREATE ANY LOGIN
   B. CREATE ANY SESSION
   C. CREATE SESSION
   D. CREATE TABLE

4. Which of the following is the system privilege that empowers the grantee to create an index in his or her own user account—but not in the accounts of others?

   A. CREATE TABLE

   B. CREATE ANY TABLE

   C. CREATE INDEX

   D. CREATE ANY INDEX

Grant Privileges on Tables

5. Your user account owns a table BACK_ORDERS, and you wish to grant privileges on the table to a user account named CARUSO, which already has the system privileges CREATE SESSION and UNLIMITED TABLESPACE. Examine the following SQL statement:

```
GRANT SELECT ON BACK_ORDERS TO CARUSO;
```

Once this statement has been executed, which of the following statements will be true for user CARUSO?

   A. CARUSO will have SELECT privileges on BACK_ORDERS, but not the ability to give other users SELECT privileges on BACK_ORDERS.

   B. CARUSO will have SELECT privileges on BACK_ORDERS, as well as the ability to give other users SELECT privileges on BACK_ORDERS.

   C. CARUSO will have SELECT, INSERT, UPDATE, and DELETE privileges on BACK_ORDERS, but not the ability to give other users those same privileges on BACK_ORDERS.

   D. CARUSO will have SELECT and ALTER TABLE privileges on BACK_ORDERS, but not the ability to give other users those same privileges on BACK_ORDERS.

6. Your user account owns an updatable view, BACKLOG, which is based on a table, PROJECTS. You are tasked to give SELECT and UPDATE capabilities to another user account named MARINO. Currently, MARINO has no privileges on either the table or the view. You wish for MARINO to have the ability to grant SELECT on the view to other users as well. Examine the following SQL code:

```
GRANT SELECT ON BACKLOG TO MARINO WITH GRANT OPTION;
GRANT UPDATE ON BACKLOG TO MARINO;
```

Which of the following statements is true?

   A. The statements will fail and MARINO will not be able to use the view.

   B. The statements will execute successfully but MARINO will not be able to SELECT from the view because the PROJECTS table has not been granted to MARINO.

C. The statements will execute successfully and MARINO will be able to SELECT from the view, but not UPDATE the view.

D. The statements will execute successfully and perform as intended.

7. User account MUSKIE owns a table CBAY. Which of the following statements can be executed by MUSKIE and enable user ONEILL to execute UPDATE statements on the CBAY table? (Choose three.)

A. GRANT ALL ON CBAY TO ONEILL;

B. GRANT ALL PRIVILEGES TO ONEILL;

C. GRANT ALL TO ONEILL;

D. GRANT INSERT, UPDATE ON CBAY TO ONEILL;

View Privileges in the Data Dictionary

8. Examine the following two claims:

[1] The DBA_TAB_PRIVS data dictionary view allows a user account to see object privileges it has granted to other user accounts.

[2] The DBA_TAB_PRIVS data dictionary view allows a user account to see object privileges granted by other user accounts to itself.

Which of these claims is true?

A. Only [1]

B. Only [2]

C. Both [1] and [2]

D. Neither [1] nor [2]

9. Which of the following data dictionary views contains information about grants on tables that have been made by other users to your user account, as well as grants on tables that have been made by your user account to other user accounts?

A. USER_TAB_COLUMNS

B. USER_TAB_PRIVS

C. USER_TABLES

D. ALL_TAB_PRIVS_RECD

Grant Roles

10. What can be granted to a role? (Choose all that apply.)
    - (A.) System privileges
    - (B.) Object privileges
    - (C.) Roles
    - D. None of the above

11. Which of the following statements will grant the role OMBUDSMAN to user JOSHUA in such a way that JOSHUA may grant the role to another user?
    - (A) GRANT OMBUDSMAN TO JOSHUA WITH ADMIN OPTION;
    - B. GRANT OMBUDSMAN TO JOSHUA WITH GRANT OPTION;
    - C. GRANT OMBUDSMAN TO JOSHUA WITH ROLE OPTION;
    - D. GRANT OMBUDSMAN TO JOSHUA CASCADE;

12. User HARDING owns a table TEAPOT. User HARDING then executes the following SQL statements to give access to the table to user ALBERT:

    ```
    CREATE PUBLIC SYNONYM TEAPOT FOR HARDING.TEAPOT;
    CREATE ROLE DOME;
    GRANT DOME TO ALBERT;
    GRANT SELECT ON TEAPOT TO DOME;
    ```

    Which of the following statements can user ALBERT now execute on the TEAPOT table?
    - A. SELECT * FROM DOME.HARDING.TEAPOT;
    - B. SELECT * FROM HARDING.DOME.TEAPOT;
    - (C.) SELECT * FROM HARDING.TEAPOT;
    - D. None of the above.

Distinguish Between Privileges and Roles

13. A role:
    - A. Takes the place of privileges automatically, so that any privilege granted to a role supersedes any grants that have already been granted directly to a user.
    - B. Cannot be given the same name as a table.
    - C. Can be granted to a user, who can only be granted one role at a time.
    - (D.) Can be created by a user only if that user has the CREATE ROLE system privilege.

14. You have a table FURNISHINGS and are told to grant DELETE privileges on the table to user HEARST. Examine the following SQL statements:

```
GRANT DELETE ON FURNISHINGS TO HEARST;
CREATE ROLE MGR;
GRANT DELETE ON FURNISHINGS TO MGR;
GRANT MGR TO HEARST;
```

Now you are told to change the privileges given to HEARST so that HEARST can no longer execute DELETE statements on the FURNISHINGS table. Which of the following will accomplish the goal? (Choose the best answer.)

A. REVOKE DELETE ON FURNISHINGS FROM HEARST;

B. REVOKE DELETE ON FURNISHINGS FROM MGR;

C. REVOKE DELETE ON FURNISHINGS FROM HEARST, MGR;

D. None of the above

15. Assume a database with three valid users: NEIL, BUZZ, and MICHAEL. Assume all users have the appropriate privileges they require to perform the tasks shown below. Assume NEIL owns a table PROVISIONS. Examine the following code (line numbers added, and assume all password references are valid):

```
01    CONNECT NEIL/neilPassword
02    GRANT SELECT ON PROVISIONS TO BUZZ, MICHAEL;
03
04    CONNECT BUZZ/buzzPassword
05    CREATE VIEW PROVISIONS AS SELECT * FROM NEIL.PROVISIONS;
06    GRANT SELECT ON PROVISIONS TO MICHAEL;
07    CREATE PUBLIC SYNONYM PROVISIONS FOR BUZZ.PROVISIONS;
08
09    CONNECT MICHAEL/michaelPassword
10    CREATE SYNONYM PROVISIONS FOR NEIL.PROVISIONS;
11    SELECT * FROM PROVISIONS;
```

What object is identified in line 11 by the name PROVISIONS?

A. The public synonym created in line 7

B. The synonym created in line 10

C. Nothing, because user NEIL did not include WITH GRANT OPTIONS in the GRANT SELECT ON PROVISIONS TO BUZZ statement.

D. Something else not listed above

SELF TEST ANSWERS

Differentiate System Privileges from Object Privileges

1. ☑ **C.** The system privilege CREATE ANY TABLE is the system privilege that you're looking for in this question. The keyword ANY is found in many system privileges, to indicate that the user authorized with the system privilege may perform the task as though it were any user account in the database.
☒ **A, B,** and **D** are incorrect. There is no ALL keyword in this context, nor does PUBLIC apply here. There is no system privilege with the WITH PUBLIC OPTION keywords.

2. ☑ **A.** The WITH ADMIN OPTION clause is not used in the REVOKE statement.
☒ **B, C,** and **D** are incorrect. They are all interesting ideas, but they are all wrong.

3. ☑ **C.** The CREATE SESSION system privilege is the minimum requirement.
☒ **A, B,** and **D** are incorrect. There is no system privilege CREATE ANY LOGIN or CREATE ANY SESSION. CREATE TABLE is not required to establish a user session.

4. ☑ **A.** The CREATE TABLE privilege also includes the ability to create an index. Remember that a CREATE TABLE statement may include the PRIMARY KEY or UNIQUE constraints, which—if created—will automatically cause the creation of an index to support each constraint.
☒ **B, C,** and **D** are incorrect. There isn't a CREATE INDEX system privilege. The ability is included with CREATE TABLE. CREATE ANY TABLE empowers the grantee the ability to create tables in the accounts of others, which potentially may also create indices in those same accounts. CREATE ANY INDEX is a valid system privilege for creating index objects in user accounts other than your own.

Grant Privileges on Tables

5. ☑ **A.** GRANT SELECT ON table TO user—gives the user the ability to SELECT on the table and nothing more.
☒ **B, C,** and **D** are incorrect. To give CARUSO the ability to SELECT on the table as well as to grant other users SELECT, the WITH GRANT OPTION clause would have to have been included with the GRANT statement, as in GRANT SELECT ON BACK_ORDERS TO CARUSO WITH GRANT OPTION. To grant the other DML statements on the table, each would have to have been included, as in GRANT SELECT, INSERT, UPDATE, DELETE ON BACK_ORDERS TO CARUSO. To grant SELECT and ALTER, both would have to have been named, as in GRANT SELECT, ALTER ON BACK_ORDERS TO CARUSO.

6. ☑ **D.** The statements are syntactically correct and will perform as intended.
☒ **A, B,** and **C** are incorrect. The PROJECTS table does not need to be granted to MARINO, since the VIEW has been granted. Since the VIEW is updatable, then the UPDATE privilege will work as well.

7. ☑ **A, B,** and **D.** All three forms result in the UPDATE privilege being granted to user ONEILL for the CBAY table.
☒ **C** is incorrect. This statement is an invalid SQL statement. It either needs for the keyword PRIVILEGES to grant all system privileges to ONEILL, or it needs to name an object for which ALL privileges should be granted. The question is specifically asking about granting privileges on the CBAY table, so the ALL PRIVILEGES form would not work.

View Privileges in the Data Dictionary

8. ☑ **C.** The data dictionary view DBA_TAB_PRIVS allows a user to see privileges that have been granted to itself, or by itself to others.
☒ **A, B,** and **D** are incorrect.

9. ☑ **B.** USER_TAB_PRIVS is the answer.
☒ **A, C,** and **D** are incorrect. USER_TAB_COLUMNS has no information about grants. Neither does USER_TABLES. The ALL_TAB_PRIVS_RECD view contains data about incoming grants only.

Grant Roles

10. ☑ **A, B,** and **C.** Both system and object privileges, as well as other roles, can be granted to any given role.
☒ **D** is incorrect.

11. ☑ **A.** WITH ADMIN OPTION is what is used for roles.
☒ **B, C,** and **D** are incorrect. WITH GRANT OPTION works for object privileges, but not roles. There is no such clause as WITH ROLE OPTION. CASCADE does not apply here.

12. ☑ **C.** The schema name prefix correctly identifies the table. In addition, since the public synonym TEAPOT references the table, then DESC TEAPOT would also have worked—but that was not one of the options listed.
☒ **A, B,** and **D** are incorrect. You cannot use the role as a prefix or any other component of the name of a database object.

Distinguish Between Privileges and Roles

13. ☑ **D.** The CREATE ROLE privilege is required to create a role.

☒ **A, B,** and **C** are incorrect. A role does not replace privileges but instead is granted alongside of them. A role may be used to replace privileges as a management choice, and in fact such an approach is advisable, but it is not done automatically. Roles exist in a different namespace from tables and may duplicate table names. A user may be granted multiple roles at any given time.

14. ☑ **C.** The SQL statement in answer C accomplishes the goal in one statement.

☒ **A, B,** and **D** are incorrect. Answers A and B are helpful but do not completely accomplish the task. D is wrong because Answer C is correct.

15. ☑ **B.** From within the MICHAEL user account, SQL first searches the local namespace, then the database namespace. The local namespace contains the private synonym and that will be found first, before SQL looks in the database namespace.

☒ **A, C,** and **D** are incorrect. The GRANT statement issued by NEIL does not require WITH GRANT OPTION for the synonyms to function.

A

About the CD

The CD-ROM included with this book comes complete with MasterExam and the electronic version of the book. The software is easy to install on any Windows 2000/XP/Vista computer and must be installed to access the MasterExam feature. You may, however, browse the electronic book directly from the CD without installation. To register for a second bonus MasterExam, simply click the Online Training link on the Main Page and follow the directions to the free online registration.

System Requirements

Software requires Windows 2000 or higher and Internet Explorer 6.0 or above and 20MB of hard disk space for full installation. The electronic book requires Adobe Acrobat Reader.

Installing and Running MasterExam

If your computer CD-ROM drive is configured to auto run, the CD-ROM will automatically start up upon inserting the disk. From the opening screen you may install MasterExam by pressing the MasterExam button. This will begin the installation process and create a program group named LearnKey. To run MasterExam use Start | All Programs | LearnKey | MasterExam. If the auto run feature did not launch your CD, browse to the CD and click on the LaunchTraining.exe icon.

MasterExam

MasterExam provides you with a simulation of the actual exam. The number of questions, the type of questions, and the time allowed are intended to be an accurate representation of the exam environment. You have the option to take an open book exam, including hints, references, and answers; a closed book exam; or the timed MasterExam simulation.

When you launch MasterExam, a digital clock display will appear in the bottom right-hand corner of your screen. The clock will continue to count down to zero unless you choose to end the exam before the time expires.

Electronic Book

The entire contents of the Exam Guide are provided in PDF files. Adobe's Acrobat Reader has been included on the CD.

Help

A help file is provided through the Help button on the Main Page in the lower left-hand corner. An individual help feature is also available through MasterExam.

Removing Installation(s)

MasterExam is installed to your hard drive. For best results removing programs, use the Start | All Programs | LearnKey | Uninstall option to remove MasterExam.

Technical Support

For questions regarding the technical content of the electronic book or MasterExam, please visit www.mhprofessional.com or e-mail customer.service@mcgraw-hill.com. For customers outside the 50 United States, e-mail international_cs@mcgraw-hill.com.

LearnKey Technical Support

For technical problems with the software (installation, operation, removing installations), please visit www.learnkey.com, e-mail techsupport@learnkey.com, or call toll free at 1-800-482-8244.

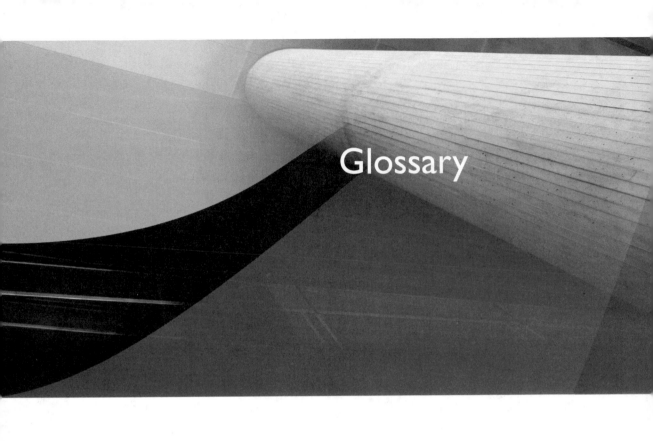

Glossary

1GL First-generation language. The ones and zeros that computers use to communicate. Binary language.

2GL Second-generation language. Assembler language.

3GL Third-generation language. A general category of computer programming languages that tend to support structured or object-oriented programming in a manner that is closer to the spoken word than 2GLs. Common 3GLs: Java, C, FORTRAN, PHP, Perl.

4GL Fourth-generation language. Closer to the spoken word than 3GLs. The most well-known and widely used 4GL is SQL.

administrator *See* database administrator.

aggregate A single value representing any number of other values.

alias An alternative name for something. Example: "Joe" is an alias for "Joseph".

alphabetic Describes the letters of the alphabet.

alphanumeric Describes the letters of the alphabet and numbers.

ALTER A SQL statement that modifies the structure, the name, or some other attribute of an existing object in the database. (Note: There are exceptions to this definition that occur when ALTER is combined with the keywords SESSION or STATEMENT.)

ANSI American National Standards Institute. An organization that oversees a number of voluntary committees that set standards for many industries, including software development and information technology.

attribute A property or characteristic. Examples might include a name, ZIP code, or entry date. Corresponds to a column in a table. *Also see* entity.

BLOB Binary Large Object. A datatype that stores unstructured binary data, up to 128 terabytes. BLOB datatypes can be rolled back or committed. Suitable for storing multimedia data.

Boolean   Refers to the valuation of expressions as either true, false, or unknown, and using the logical operators AND, OR, and NOT. Named after the mathematician George Boole.

built-in   Already present. SQL built-in functions are those that come already installed in a database, as opposed to user-defined functions, that you can create yourself and add to the set of available functions in a database.

Cartesian product   The combination of each row in one table with every row in another table. The result of two or more tables joined together with no specified join criteria. Also known as a cross-join.

case insensitive   Without regard for whether a letter is in uppercase or lowercase form. For example, when performing a case-insensitive comparison of the letter 'A' and the letter 'a', the two are equal.

case sensitive   With regard for whether a letter is in uppercase or lowercase form. For example, when performing a case-sensitive comparison of the letter 'A' and the letter 'a', the two are not equal.

character   The symbols of a writing system.

character class   Also known as POSIX character classes. Shorthand references in regular expressions for specifying a range of characters.

character set   An encoding system for representing characters in bytes.

CHECK constraint   A rule on a table that filters incoming data. Only data that satisfies that rule will be accepted by the table. Also known as a CHECK integrity constraint.

child   A row or record that is one level below another level in a hierarchical data relationship. For example, if one table contains "orders", and another contains the "line items" that each order contains, then a table containing those "line items" would be said to be the "child table". A child table is one that has a foreign key relationship with a parent table, so that rows in the parent table are one level higher in the hierarchy than the rows in the child table. *See also* orphan; parent.

clause   A subset within a larger construct, such as a portion of a statement or command.

CLOB   Character Large Object. A datatype that stores large amounts of character data, up to 128 terabytes. CLOB datatypes can be rolled back or committed.

Codd   The last name of Dr. E.F. Codd, the person credited with forming the original ideas that led to the creation of modern-day relational database programming.

column   A vertical space in a database table. Columns have a name and a datatype.

command   A directive.

COMMENT   A SQL statement to add comments to the data dictionary for database objects you have created.

commit   To cause changes within the current session to be made permanent.

COMMIT   A SQL statement to save data to the database.

condition   A expression that evaluates to a meaningful result to indicate the next course of action. Conditions are used to determine if a statement will take a particular action or not; the decision hinges on whether the condition evaluates to true or false.

conditional   A situation that depends on the evaluation of a condition.

connect   Establish a user session with the database.

constant   *See* literal.

constraint   A rule defining how data is to be processed. A table can have one or more constraints that may restrict it to having certain kinds of data and rejecting others. *See also* referential integrity.

conversion   The act of transforming something from one form to another. Conversion functions in SQL can change data from one datatype to another datatype.

correlated subquery   A subquery that uses, as part of its execution logic, data from an outer query.

CREATE   A reserved word that starts one of many SQL statements, used to create database objects such as tables, views, indexes, sequences, and synonyms.

cross-join   *See* Cartesian product.

data dictionary   A set of tables and views automatically maintained by the Oracle system for documenting the characteristics and status of all objects in the database.

data file   A physical file in the file system for storing data, located in either the operating system file system, or in an Automated Storage Management disk group.

database   An organized collection of information.

database administrator   Often abbreviated DBA. The job of administering the database. The DBA often is tasked with installing the database software and configuring it for use, performing backups and generally making the database system available for use, maintaining at optimal performance, and taking steps to protect against loss of data.

datatype   A set of rules defining a subset of data.

date   A calendar date.

datetime   Any of the set of datatypes DATE, TIMESTAMP, TIMESTAMP WITH TIME ZONE, or TIMESTAMP WITH LOCAL TIME ZONE.

daylight saving time   Time defined as a one-hour offset from standard time to provide more daylight at the end of the working day during seasons in which daylight is limited.

DBA   *See* database administrator.

DBMS   Database management system.

DDL Data Definition Language. A subset of SQL. Refers to the set of SQL statements that is used to create database objects, modify their structure, and remove them from the database.

default When used in association with a parameter, "default" is the value of that parameter when no specific value is assigned. *See* parameter.

DELETE A SQL statement used to remove data from the database.

deprecated Said of a feature that may still exist but is no longer officially supported, and whose use is officially discouraged.

developer An individual engaged in the job of creating applications.

development The act of creating applications.

DML Data Manipulation Language. A subset of SQL. Refers to the set of SQL statements that is used to query existing data in database objects, add data to existing database objects, modify that data, and remove the data from the database.

DROP A reserved word used to start one of many SQL statements, all of which are used to remove certain existing database objects from the database.

Ellison The last name of Larry Ellison, founder of Oracle Corporation, the first company to release a commercial RDBMS product.

entity An organized collection of attributes in a data model. Corresponds to a table. *See also* attribute; ERD.

equijoin A join that uses an equality operator (the equal sign) in the join condition.

ERD Entity-relationship diagram. A diagram that shows entities and how they relate to each other. *See also* entity.

escape character A single character that can take on an alternative purpose separate from its character's standard meaning. For example, a single quotation mark is an escape character when preceding another single quotation mark in a text string delimited by single quotes, so that strings such as 'O"Brian' will be correctly interpreted as *O'Brian* in the database, rather than the truncated string 'O' followed by the characters *Brian'*—which would be meaningless in any SQL statement and would result in a syntax error.

explicit commit   The COMMIT statement.

expression   A combination of literal values, operators, variables, and functions, with the intent of computing a value of a particular datatype.

external table   A SQL table that stores table metadata in the database but stores the table's data outside of the database.

FLASHBACK   A SQL statement used to restore older versions of database objects.

flashback operations   A set of operations that use undo data to support data recovery and the analysis of historical data over time.

foreign key   A referential integrity constraint in a table. A foreign key specifies one or more attributes in one entity that relate to one or more attributes in another entity. Values entered in the foreign key's attributes must already exist in the referenced table's corresponding attributes. *See also* referential integrity, constraint.

function   A set of code that performs a particular task and returns a single result. A SQL function can be used within a SQL expression. A function is one type of subprogram, also known as a program unit. There is another form known as a procedure, which is not included on the exam.

GRANT   A SQL statement used to give system privileges or object privileges to a user account.

hierarchical query   A query that specifies multiple levels of relationship. Typically built on a self-join. Note that a typical join of two tables in a parent-child relationship can be said to be a two-level "hierarchy"; technically that would be accurate. But the term "hierarchical query" in Oracle SQL is generally understood to indicate a particular type of query based on a data model that is capable of supporting more than two levels.

IEEE Institute of Electrical and Electronics Engineers. A non-profit organization with the mission to advance technology as it relates to the use of electricity.

implicit commit A commit event other than the COMMIT statement. The execution of DDL code will result in an implicit commit.

inline view A subquery that performs like a view in support of a single SQL statement.

index A database object that copies a subset of data from a table, presorted, and intended to support faster querying on the indexed table.

inner join A join of two or more tables in which a join condition is specified, and the result consists exclusively of rows in one table that match rows in the other table according to the join condition. If a row in one table has no matching counterpart in the other table, it is not included in the results. *See also* outer join.

INSERT A SQL statement used to store data in a database table.

instance One set of Oracle background processes and memory structures used to access a database.

integrity constraint *See* constraint.

join The act of connecting rows in one table with rows in one or more other tables, based on some criteria that determine how the data in the tables correlates to each other.

key One or more attributes—or columns—used in the definition of an integrity constraint. Keys include primary keys, foreign keys, and unique keys.

keyword A special word used in a SQL command or serving some other special purpose. Keywords are often reserved words, but they are not necessarily reserved.

literal A fixed data value. Also called a constant.

LOB Large Object. Any of a number of datatypes that store large amounts of information. *See also* BLOB; CLOB; NCLOB.

lowercase   The letters of the alphabet in miniscule form, i.e., "a", "b", etc.

MERGE   A SQL statement that performs a combination of INSERT, UPDATE, and/or DELETE statement functionality.

metacharacter operators   Used to define patterns in regular expressions.

metadata   Data about data. For example, is the "account number" at a given organization a numeric value, or is it an alphanumeric value? Or perhaps alphabetic? Metadata describes other data in high-level terms.

multitable insert   A SQL INSERT statement that is able to add rows of data to one or more tables. Multitable inserts can be conditional or unconditional.

namespace   A virtual location within the database in which no database objects may share the same name. All names must be unique within a given namespace.

natural join   A join in which the join criteria are implied based on common names of columns in the tables being joined.

NCLOB   National Character Set Large Object. A datatype that stores large amounts of character data in a national database character set. Stores up to 128 terabytes. NCLOB datatypes can be rolled back or committed.

NLS   National Language Support.

NLS parameters   Variables that customize the behavior of the database in accordance with a given locale. For example, NLS_SORT.

non-equijoin   A join condition that uses operators other than the equality operator to specify the join condition—such as greater-than or less-than operators.

normalization   A specific series of processes intended to support the design of a database to maximize efficiency.

NULL   Unknown. The absence of information.

number   A digit.

numeric   Said of a set of datatypes that accept number data.

object   An item in the database. Objects have properties of structure and security.

object privilege   The right to perform a particular task on a particular object in the database. *See also* system privilege.

operator precedence   The rules defining the order in which operators within an expression are processed.

operators   Symbols that perform tasks on values within an expression.

ORA_ROWSCN   A conservative upper bound of the latest commit time for the transaction that last changed the row. The actual commit SCN of the transaction can be somewhat earlier. *See also* system change number.

Oracle   The leading RDBMS product on the market today.

Oracle Corporation   The first company to produce a commercial RDBMS product.

orphan   A child row in a child table for which there is no corresponding parent row in the corresponding parent table.

outer join   A join of two or more tables in which a join condition is specified, and the result consists of rows in one table that match rows in the other table according to the join condition, as well as rows that do not necessarily match. If a row in one table has no matching counterpart in the other table, it may be included in the results. *See also* inner join.

parameter   A variable that is passed to or from a function or procedure.

parent   A row or record that is one level above another level in a hierarchical data relationship. For example, if one table contains "orders", and another contains the "line items" that each order contains, then a table containing those "orders" would be said to be the "parent table". A parent table is one that is referenced by a foreign key in a child table, so that rows in the parent table are one level higher in the hierarchy than the rows in the child table. *See also* orphan, child.

parse   To analyze code for syntactic accuracy. SQL code that is submitted for execution is parsed first and then executed upon successful completion of the parsing process.

POSIX   Portable Operating System Interface (for Unix). A set of IEEE standards for defining standards and interoperability on a number of issues.

precedence   A logical prioritization of a set of items.

precision   Part of the definition of a numeric datatype. Precision specifies the number of significant digits in the numeric value. *See also* scale.

predicates   These compare one expression to another to produce a true, false, or NULL result. Can be combined with Boolean operators AND, OR, and NOT.

primary key   A unique non-NULL attribute in an entity, or a unique non-NULL column in a table.

private synonym   A synonym that is not a PUBLIC synonym. There is no PRIVATE keyword.

privilege   The right to perform a task in the database. *See also* object privilege; system privilege.

procedure   A set of code that performs a particular task. A procedure may return anywhere from zero to multiple results. Procedures cannot be used within a SQL expression but instead are often invoked in statements by themselves.

production   Professional use. Database applications in "production" are actively storing data for an ongoing organization, as opposed to database applications that are in development or testing.

projection   The concept of querying a subset of columns from a table.

pseudocolumns   Values that are defined automatically by the Oracle system for certain objects in the database, such as tables and sequences. Pseudocolumns can be selected like a column in a table.

PUBLIC   A special database user automatically maintained by the database. PUBLIC represents all users in the database. Granting privileges to PUBLIC has the effect of granting them to all users.

PURGE   A SQL statement to remove objects from the recycle bin.

query   A SELECT statement. A request of the database for some of the data that is contained within it.

RDBMS   Relational database management system.

read consistency   The ability for data in the database to be read and joined in a manner that is accurate. Read consistency represents a view of data that is "frozen" in an instant of time. Read consistency becomes important when joining tables that are being modified in real time, so that as the database queries one table and then another, the combined records reflect what was intended.

record   A set of data elements that are related to each other and represent a meaningful collection of information. One row can be a record; joined rows might also be a record.

recycle bin   The structure in the SQL database into which dropped objects are tracked.

redo logs   A set of operating system files that record all changes made to a database, whether those changes have been committed or not.

referential integrity   A constraint, or rule, on one table's column that requires any value to be stored in that column to be already present in another particular table's column. *See also* foreign key.

regular expression   A language of pattern matching. Not to be confused with expressions. Oracle's support for regular expressions is consistent with the POSIX and Unicode standards.

relational   Having a relation or being related. A database is said to be relational when it is built on data objects that can be joined together based on common criteria within and among the objects.

RENAME   A SQL statement used to change the name of certain objects in the database.

reserved word   Special words set aside for special use and not available for application development. You cannot use reserved words as the names of database objects or variables.

restore point   A marked point in time, to be recorded for possible future reference in support of flashback operations.

REVOKE   A SQL statement to remove system privileges or object privileges that have been granted to a user account.

role   A collection of one or more privileges.

rollback   An action that restores the database to the most recent commit within the current session.

ROLLBACK   A SQL statement used to restore the database to an earlier state. Cancels the effects of a transaction in progress.

row   One set of values for the columns of a table.

savepoint   A marked point in time, to be recorded for possible future rollback.

SAVEPOINT   A SQL statement that marks a point in a session. Future uses of the ROLLBACK statement may choose to restore the database to the point marked by a SAVEPOINT statement.

scalar subquery   A subquery that returns one column in one row as its output—in other words, a single value, as opposed to rows of values, or columns of values.

scale   Part of the definition of a numeric datatype. Scale specifies where rounding will occur in the numeric datatype. *See also* precision.

schema   A collection of tables owned by a user account.

SCN   *See* system change number (SCN).

segment   A level of logical database storage.

SELECT   A SQL statement used to query one or more database tables.

selectivity   The degree of uniqueness of values in a column. If all values in the column are identical, selectivity is said to be low. If the values are all unique, selectivity is said to be high.

selection   The ability to query a subset of rows from a table.

self-join   A join that connects rows in a table with other rows in the same table.

semijoin   A query that returns rows that match an EXISTS subquery.

sequence   A number generator. A database object.

session   A user process in which the user interacts with the database.

set operator   Any of the operators UNION, UNION ALL, INTERSECT, or MINUS.

SQL   *See* Structured Query Language.

standard time   Also known as Winter Time zones. Time as defined by UTC.

statement   A command.

string   A series of characters.

Structured Query Language   A worldwide standard language for interacting with a database.

subquery   A SELECT statement contained within another (outer) SELECT statement, so that the data of the subquery feeds into the processing of the outer query.

superaggregate   An aggregation of aggregate values.

synonym   An alias, or alternative name, for something in the database. A synonym is itself an object in the database.

syntax   The rules for forming a statement, a command, or some other language construct.

SYS   A built-in user account with DBA privileges that comes with all Oracle installations. SYS owns the data dictionary.

SYSTEM   A built-in user account with DBA privileges that comes with all Oracle installations.

system change number (SCN)   A marker that specifies a committed version of the database at a particular point in time. Each committed transaction is assigned an SCN. *See also* transaction.

system privilege   The right to perform a particular task in the database. *See also* object privilege.

table   A storage unit in the database that consists of columns and rows.

tablespace   A mechanism in the database that is home to one or more tables and stores that data in one or more data files.

TCL   Transaction Control Language. A subset of SQL. Refers to the set of SQL statements that is used to control a user's session in which DML statements are used. TCL determines if the results of a DML statement are allowed to be made permanent, or if they are undone from the database.

text   Character-based data.

time zone   A region of the earth that uses uniform standard time as an offset from UTC. There are currently 24 such regions defined in the earth, divided roughly by longitudinal lines. Also known as "time zone region".

time zone name   The name of a time zone region. Examples: "Pacific/Auckland", "America/Indianapolis".

time zone offset   A time difference between the local time and UTC.

timestamp   A value representing the date and time.

transaction   A series of one or more SQL statements that are executed between commit events.

TRUNCATE   A SQL statement used to remove data from a database table.

unconditional   Without restriction.

undo segments   Segments that are maintained automatically by the database to support rollback operations, to assure read consistency, and to otherwise recover from logical corruptions.

Unicode   An industry standard that attempts to create a standardized encoding of every character of every language in existence.

unique   One of a kind.

unique identifier   An unambiguous reference to something, leaving no doubt what is being referenced.

UPDATE   A SQL statement used to modify data in a database table.

uppercase   The letters of the alphabet in majuscule form, also known as capital letters, i.e., "A", "B", etc.

user account   A process that provides password-protected access to and ownership of a set of database objects and privileges.

UTC   Coordinated Universal Time. The new name for Greenwich Mean Time. The universal standard for measuring time internationally. UTC measures time as it exists at the Royal Observatory of Greenwich, London.

variable   A small unit of storage, represented by a name and a datatype, for holding values that can be changed.

view   A named query that is stored in the database.

Winter Time zone   *See* standard time.

INDEX

D

H

I

V

W

GET YOUR FREE SUBSCRIPTION
TO *ORACLE MAGAZINE*

Oracle Magazine is essential gear for today's information technology professionals. Stay informed and increase your productivity with every issue of *Oracle Magazine*. Inside each free bimonthly issue you'll get:

- Up-to-date information on Oracle Database, Oracle Application Server, Web development, enterprise grid computing, database technology, and business trends
- Third-party news and announcements
- Technical articles on Oracle and partner products, technologies, and operating environments
- Development and administration tips
- Real-world customer stories

If there are other Oracle users at your location who would like to receive their own subscription to *Oracle Magazine*, please photocopy this form and pass it along.

Three easy ways to subscribe:

① Web
Visit our Web site at **oracle.com/oraclemagazine**
You'll find a subscription form there, plus much more

② Fax
Complete the questionnaire on the back of this card
and fax the questionnaire side only to **+1.847.763.9638**

③ Mail
Complete the questionnaire on the back of this card
and mail it to **P.O. Box 1263, Skokie, IL 60076-8263**

Want your own FREE subscription?

To receive a free subscription to *Oracle Magazine*, you must fill out the entire card, sign it, and date it (incomplete cards cannot be processed or acknowledged). You can also fax your application to **+1.847.763.9638. Or subscribe at our Web site at oracle.com/oraclemagazine**

○ **Yes, please send me a FREE subscription *Oracle Magazine*.**   ○ No.

○ From time to time, Oracle Publishing allows our partners exclusive access to our e-mail addresses for special promotions and announcements. To be included in this program, please check this circle. If you do not wish to be included, you will only receive notices about your subscription via e-mail.

○ Oracle Publishing allows sharing of our postal mailing list with selected third parties. If you prefer your mailing address not to be included in this program, please check this circle.

If at any time you would like to be removed from either mailing list, please contact Customer Service at +1.847.763.9635 or send an e-mail to oracle@halldata.com. If you opt in to the sharing of information, Oracle may also provide you with e-mail related to Oracle products, services, and events. If you want to completely unsubscribe from any e-mail communication from Oracle, please send an e-mail to: unsubscribe@oracle-mail.com with the following in the subject line: REMOVE [your e-mail address]. For complete information on Oracle Publishing's privacy practices, please visit oracle.com/html/privacy/html

X _____

signature (required)   date

name   title

company   e-mail address

street/p.o. box

city/state/zip or postal code   telephone

country   fax

Would you like to receive your free subscription in digital format instead of print if it becomes available? ○ Yes ○ No

---

YOU MUST ANSWER ALL 10 QUESTIONS BELOW.

① WHAT IS THE PRIMARY BUSINESS ACTIVITY OF YOUR FIRM AT THIS LOCATION? (check one only)

- ☐ 01 Aerospace and Defense Manufacturing
- ☐ 02 Application Service Provider
- ☐ 03 Automotive Manufacturing
- ☐ 04 Chemicals
- ☐ 05 Media and Entertainment
- ☐ 06 Construction/Engineering
- ☐ 07 Consumer Sector/Consumer Packaged Goods
- ☐ 08 Education
- ☐ 09 Financial Services/Insurance
- ☐ 10 Health Care
- ☐ 11 High Technology Manufacturing, OEM
- ☐ 12 Industrial Manufacturing
- ☐ 13 Independent Software Vendor
- ☐ 14 Life Sciences (biotech, pharmaceuticals)
- ☐ 15 Natural Resources
- ☐ 16 Oil and Gas
- ☐ 17 Professional Services
- ☐ 18 Public Sector (government)
- ☐ 19 Research
- ☐ 20 Retail/Wholesale/Distribution
- ☐ 21 Systems Integrator, VAR/VAD
- ☐ 22 Telecommunications
- ☐ 23 Travel and Transportation
- ☐ 24 Utilities (electric, gas, sanitation, water)
- ☐ 98 Other Business and Services _____

② WHICH OF THE FOLLOWING BEST DESCRIBES YOUR PRIMARY JOB FUNCTION? (check one only)

CORPORATE MANAGEMENT/STAFF
- ☐ 01 Executive Management (President, Chair, CEO, CFO, Owner, Partner, Principal)
- ☐ 02 Finance/Administrative Management (VP/Director/ Manager/Controller, Purchasing, Administration)
- ☐ 03 Sales/Marketing Management (VP/Director/Manager)
- ☐ 04 Computer Systems/Operations Management (CIO/VP/Director/Manager MIS/IS/IT, Ops)

IS/IT STAFF
- ☐ 05 Application Development/Programming Management
- ☐ 06 Application Development/Programming Staff
- ☐ 07 Consulting
- ☐ 08 DBA/Systems Administrator
- ☐ 09 Education/Training
- ☐ 10 Technical Support Director/Manager
- ☐ 11 Other Technical Management/Staff
- ☐ 98 Other

③ WHAT IS YOUR CURRENT PRIMARY OPERATING PLATFORM (check all that apply)

- ☐ 01 Digital Equipment Corp UNIX/VAX/VMS
- ☐ 02 HP UNIX
- ☐ 03 IBM AIX
- ☐ 04 IBM UNIX
- ☐ 05 Linux (Red Hat)
- ☐ 06 Linux (SUSE)
- ☐ 07 Linux (Oracle Enterprise)
- ☐ 08 Linux (other)
- ☐ 09 Macintosh
- ☐ 10 MVS
- ☐ 11 Netware
- ☐ 12 Network Computing
- ☐ 13 SCO UNIX
- ☐ 14 Sun Solaris/SunOS
- ☐ 15 Windows
- ☐ 16 Other UNIX
- ☐ 98 Other
- ☐ 99 None of the Above

④ DO YOU EVALUATE, SPECIFY, RECOMMEND, OR AUTHORIZE THE PURCHASE OF ANY OF THE FOLLOWING? (check all that apply)

- ☐ 01 Hardware
- ☐ 02 Business Applications (ERP, CRM, etc.)
- ☐ 03 Application Development Tools
- ☐ 04 Database Products
- ☐ 05 Internet or Intranet Products
- ☐ 06 Other Software
- ☐ 07 Middleware Products
- ☐ 99 None of the Above

⑤ IN YOUR JOB, DO YOU USE OR PLAN TO PURCHASE ANY OF THE FOLLOWING PRODUCTS? (check all that apply)

SOFTWARE
- ☐ 01 CAD/CAE/CAM
- ☐ 02 Collaboration Software
- ☐ 03 Communications
- ☐ 04 Database Management
- ☐ 05 File Management
- ☐ 06 Finance
- ☐ 07 Java
- ☐ 08 Multimedia Authoring
- ☐ 09 Networking
- ☐ 10 Programming
- ☐ 11 Project Management
- ☐ 12 Scientific and Engineering
- ☐ 13 Systems Management
- ☐ 14 Workflow

HARDWARE
- ☐ 15 Macintosh
- ☐ 16 Mainframe
- ☐ 17 Massively Parallel Processing
- ☐ 18 Minicomputer
- ☐ 19 Intel x86(32)
- ☐ 20 Intel x86(64)
- ☐ 21 Network Computer
- ☐ 22 Symmetric Multiprocessing
- ☐ 23 Workstation Services

SERVICES
- ☐ 24 Consulting
- ☐ 25 Education/Training
- ☐ 26 Maintenance
- ☐ 27 Online Database
- ☐ 28 Support
- ☐ 29 Technology-Based Training
- ☐ 30 Other
- ☐ 99 None of the Above

⑥ WHAT IS YOUR COMPANY'S SIZE? (check one only)

- ☐ 01 More than 25,000 Employees
- ☐ 02 10,001 to 25,000 Employees
- ☐ 03 5,001 to 10,000 Employees
- ☐ 04 1,001 to 5,000 Employees
- ☐ 05 101 to 1,000 Employees
- ☐ 06 Fewer than 100 Employees

⑦ DURING THE NEXT 12 MONTHS, HOW MUCH DO YOU ANTICIPATE YOUR ORGANIZATION WILL SPEND ON COMPUTER HARDWARE, SOFTWARE, PERIPHERALS, AND SERVICES FOR YOUR LOCATION? (check one only)

- ☐ 01 Less than $10,000
- ☐ 02 $10,000 to $49,999
- ☐ 03 $50,000 to $99,999
- ☐ 04 $100,000 to $499,999
- ☐ 05 $500,000 to $999,999
- ☐ 06 $1,000,000 and Over

⑧ WHAT IS YOUR COMPANY'S YEARLY SALES REVENUE? (check one only)

- ☐ 01 $500, 000, 000 and above
- ☐ 02 $100, 000, 000 to $500, 000, 000
- ☐ 03 $50, 000, 000 to $100, 000, 000
- ☐ 04 $5, 000, 000 to $50, 000, 000
- ☐ 05 $1, 000, 000 to $5, 000, 000

⑨ WHAT LANGUAGES AND FRAMEWORKS DO YOU USE? (check all that apply)

- ☐ 01 Ajax
- ☐ 02 C
- ☐ 03 C++
- ☐ 04 C#
- ☐ 13 Python
- ☐ 14 Ruby/Rails
- ☐ 15 Spring
- ☐ 16 Struts
- ☐ 05 Hibernate
- ☐ 06 J++/J#
- ☐ 07 Java
- ☐ 08 JSP
- ☐ 09 .NET
- ☐ 10 Perl
- ☐ 11 PHP
- ☐ 12 PL/SQL
- ☐ 17 SQL
- ☐ 18 Visual Basic
- ☐ 98 Other

⑩ WHAT ORACLE PRODUCTS ARE IN USE AT YOUR SITE? (check all that apply)

ORACLE DATABASE
- ☐ 01 Oracle Database 11*g*
- ☐ 02 Oracle Database 10*g*
- ☐ 03 Oracle9*i* Database
- ☐ 04 Oracle Embedded Database (Oracle Lite, Times Ten, Berkeley DB)
- ☐ 05 Other Oracle Database Release

ORACLE FUSION MIDDLEWARE
- ☐ 06 Oracle Application Server
- ☐ 07 Oracle Portal
- ☐ 08 Oracle Enterprise Manager
- ☐ 09 Oracle BPEL Process Manager
- ☐ 10 Oracle Identity Management
- ☐ 11 Oracle SOA Suite
- ☐ 12 Oracle Data Hubs

ORACLE DEVELOPMENT TOOLS
- ☐ 13 Oracle JDeveloper
- ☐ 14 Oracle Forms
- ☐ 15 Oracle Reports
- ☐ 16 Oracle Designer
- ☐ 17 Oracle Discoverer
- ☐ 18 Oracle BI Beans
- ☐ 19 Oracle Warehouse Builder
- ☐ 20 Oracle WebCenter
- ☐ 21 Oracle Application Express

ORACLE APPLICATIONS
- ☐ 22 Oracle E-Business Suite
- ☐ 23 PeopleSoft Enterprise
- ☐ 24 JD Edwards EnterpriseOne
- ☐ 25 JD Edwards World
- ☐ 26 Oracle Fusion
- ☐ 27 Hyperion
- ☐ 28 Siebel CRM

ORACLE SERVICES
- ☐ 28 Oracle E-Business Suite On Demand
- ☐ 29 Oracle Technology On Demand
- ☐ 30 Siebel CRM On Demand
- ☐ 31 Oracle Consulting
- ☐ 32 Oracle Education
- ☐ 33 Oracle Support
- ☐ 98 Other
- ☐ 99 None of the Above

08014204